Netscape Power User's Toolkit

Netscape Power User's Toolkit

The Definitive Guide to Advanced Tools, Techniques & Strategies

For Windows 3.1 & Windows 95

Covers Navigator 3
& Navigator Gold 3

An imprint of
Ventana Communications
Group

BARBARA BOUTON

Library of Congress Cataloging-in-Publication Data

Bouton, Barbara Mancuso, 1955-
    Official Netscape power user's toolkit / Barbara Mancuso Bouton.
        p.   cm.
    Includes index.
    ISBN 1-56604-386-7
    1. Netscape. 2. Internet (Computer network)   I. Title.
TK5105.883.N48B68 1996
005.7'1369—dc20   96-19506
                                                      CIP

First Edition 9 8 7 6 5 4 3 2 1

Printed in the United States of America

Published and distributed to the trade by Ventana Communications Group, Inc.
P.O. Box 13964, Research Triangle Park, NC 27709-3964
919/544-9404
FAX 919/544-9472

Limits of Liability and Disclaimer of Warranty

The author and publisher of this book have used their best efforts in preparing the book and the programs contained in it. These efforts include the development, research, and testing of the theories and programs to determine their effectiveness. The author and publisher make no warranty of any kind, expressed or implied, with regard to these programs or the documentation contained in this book.

The author and publisher shall not be liable in the event of incidental or consequential damages in connection with, or arising out of, the furnishing, performance or use of the programs, associated instructions and/or claims of productivity gains.

Trademarks

Trademarked names appear throughout this book, and on the accompanying compact disk. Rather than list the names and entities that own the trademarks or insert a trademark symbol with each mention of the trademarked name, the publisher states that it is using the names only for editorial purposes and to the benefit of the trademark owner with no intention of infringing upon that trademark.

PRESIDENT/CEO
Josef Woodman

VICE PRESIDENT OF CONTENT DEVELOPMENT
Karen A. Bluestein

MANAGING EDITOR
Lois J. Principe

PRODUCTION MANAGER
John Cotterman

TECHNOLOGY OPERATIONS MANAGER
Kerry L. B. Foster

PRODUCT MARKETING MANAGER
Diane Lennox

ART DIRECTOR
Marcia Webb

ACQUISITIONS EDITOR
JJ Hohn

DEVELOPMENTAL EDITOR
Richard Jessup

PROJECT EDITOR
Jennifer R. Huntley

COPY EDITOR
Gary Weinberg

ASSISTANT EDITOR
Paul Cory

TECHNICAL DIRECTOR
Dan Brown
Cheryl Friedman

TECHNICAL REVIEWER
Richard Jessup

DESKTOP PUBLISHER
Scott Hosa

PROOFREADER
Marie Dobson

INDEXER
Ann Norcross

COVER ILLUSTRATOR
Elena Skrinak

ABOUT THE AUTHOR

Barbara Mancuso Bouton is an author and consultant in the fields of publishing and networking. Barbara is also co-partner of Exclamat!ons, who along with her husband Gary "polish rough ideas" and offer visualization solutions in the 1990s, from Web documents and onscreen presentations to traditional printed productions.

Barbara's use of the Internet as both a communications and research medium led to *Official Netscape Power User's Toolkit*, because in her words, "The Internet today doesn't simply supplement traditional media such as magazines, newspapers, and television. The Internet also *provides* content that cannot be easily found, or doesn't exist in a format other than electronic. It's becoming more and more obvious that the Internet is the 'right place' to be when you need to find information or distribute information about any conceivable topic. But the real question is, 'How do I tap into all this information and make it meaningful?'"

Official Netscape Power User's Toolkit is Ms. Bouton's first book for Ventana; she has also written and coauthored several books, including *Inside Adobe Photoshop 3*, and has created online documentation for NetWare and other applications.

Ms. Bouton can be reached on the Internet at bbouton@dreamscape.com or on CompuServe at 74512,230.

ACKNOWLEDGMENTS

The act of "publishing" is a cooperative effort; no known author can honestly attribute their success solely to themselves, or the successful *communication* contained within a book to their own organizational skills. Publishing can deliver the goods to the reading public only through committee, and like all committees, some individuals' contributions aren't as obvious as others.

To try to restore the balance between the authors' visibility throughout this book, and the crowd who often doesn't receive enough thanks for making a book a reality, I'd like to call your attention to the following talented contributors to the *Power User's Toolkit*, who turned the act of typing facts into the art of publishing help. Thanks to:

- JJ Hohn, Acquisitions Editor, assisted in this book's development in many ways. Her insightfulness and enthusiasm made everything go smoothly—from acquiring some of the great shareware and plug-ins on the Companion CD-ROM to managing the final stages of the project.

- Jennifer Huntley and Heather Grattan, Project Editors extraordinaire. Jennifer and Heather had the daunting task of coordinating the flow of chapters through the many steps it takes to create a book—from rough manuscript to a finished page. Thanks to you, we did it.

- Gary Weinberg and Marie Dobson, whose gentle blue marks and plentiful supply of semicolons have made me look good in print.

- Richard J. Jessup, Technical Editor, who kept a sharp eye on me and offered many keen insights. If you find error in this book, it's my fault and not Richard's.

- Paul Cory, Assistant Editor and CD-ROM guru, for making certain that the Companion CD-ROM was in ship-shape and chock full of goodies before it was sent off for mastering.

- The hard-working folks in the Ventana Production Department, for providing a beautiful frame for my words.

- Netscape Communications, whose breakneck schedules and innovative minds kept me on my toes and gave me plenty to write about. Special thanks go to Andrew Sawicki for his help.

- To CoolTalking Phil James for Chapter 10. It takes two to talk—thanks Phil for being my CoolTalk partner.

- Nancy Acosta of H.A. Technical Services for her assistance and fine research. She made writing Chapters 5 and 7 a breeze. If you ever need to know anything about New York or just want to visit one of the finest sites on the Web, check out Nancy's handiwork at http://www.nuwebny.com.

- Scott Brennan at Dreamscape On-line, Inc., my stalwart Internet Service Provider and friend, who came over one day and said, "You gotta see this Internet thing. It's awesome!" How right you were.

- Jack and Eileen Bouton, thank you for the encouragement you gave as well as the suppers you sent over so your writer children wouldn't starve.

- John and Wilma Mancuso, my parents. You've always been my inspiration. Through the months it took to write this book, you've always understood the challenge of the assignment and offered just the right words of encouragement whenever it was needed most. I hope I've made you proud because you're the best.

DEDICATION

This book is dedicated to my husband and spousal editor, Gary David Bouton, for his unswerving belief in me. Gary was always there to lend a hand, even though he was deep into writing his own Netscape Press book. He listened to my ideas and shared his with me. He created artwork for this book, and always smiled when I asked him to order pizza for dinner. Thank you, darling, for being patient in your love, now and forever.

Contents

SECTION II
TAPPING INTO THE POWER OF NAVIGATOR

Chapter 6 Person to Person With Navigator Mail & Netscape News 361

SECTION III
EXTENDING NAVIGATOR THROUGH PLUG-INS, HELPER APPLICATIONS & NEW TECHNOLOGY

Introduction

Suppose that one day you're thirsty, and someone gives you what is purported to be the most delicious beverage on Earth . . . in a can. Not simply *any* can, mind you; it's three times as big as an ordinary can and it has the most galvanizing claims about how nutritious and satisfying it is. But the can doesn't have a pull-tab on the top—this much-wanted drink requires a can opener!

Okay, for those of you who aren't into analogies, *Official Netscape Power User's Toolkit* is a decidedly *non*-fictitious can opener that will open more possibilities for Web exploration with Netscape Navigator than you can imagine. Although Navigator—and Navigator Gold—come with adequate documentation, perhaps you're the type of Web surfer who wants *more* from your Web browser. You want to discover how to cruise the Web in the smartest fashion, visit sites more quickly, bookmark really cool sites, conduct online searches for specific items, download some of the most exciting shareware, stuff that Navigator's default configuration doesn't seem to want to yield. The *Power User's Toolkit* is both your tool and your tool-*making* kit; you'll gain the experience through this book to use these and future tools you'll come by on the Web—custom exploration, trolling, mail, research tools, and more.

AT WHAT LEVEL DOES THE POWER USER'S TOOLKIT BEGIN?

Computer books are typically written at a specific level of proficiency; you'll find "novice" books on many different applications, and you'll also find texts that require years of computing experience to make sense of the book's contents. The *Power User's Toolkit* was written at a level at which most individuals who have been using a PC for a while will feel comfortable. If you have a modicum of computing proficiency that includes the following, you'll have no trouble navigating this book:

- You're fairly accurate with pointing a cursor and clicking a two- or more button mouse or digitizing tablet stylus. The *Power User's Toolkit* documents techniques using a two-button mouse set up for right-handed users; if you're left-handed and have defined your input device to operate differently from MS Windows default, we usually refer to an action that requires clicking the primary mouse button as simply *clicking* without specifying that we mean the primary mouse button. When the use of the secondary mouse button is required, we call it a right-click.

    Navigator is highly graphical in its features, and for this reason if you have problems accurately "hitting" a target area on screen, we recommend that you practice with MineSweep or some other Windows game before continuing with this book's information . . . or cruising the Net with Navigator.

    This advice having been given, I'd also like to point out that keyboard shortcuts are mentioned throughout this book because we believe that you'll find they get you around the Web faster. They are also provided for folks with special computing requirements, or who are inexperienced with the fine art of "mousing."

- We presume that you are fairly comfortable with either the Windows 95 or Windows 3.1x operating platform conventions. These conventions include the ability to launch an application, to locate System files and utilities as they appear in file windows and in directory trees on your hard disk, and the knowledge of how to copy, move, and delete files.

This book is told from a Windows 95 point of view, and most of the screen figures show the Windows 95 interface. We chose this motif for the book because we feel that Windows 95 is where the future of Intel-based computing is heading, and also because configuring a machine for Internet access is more easily accomplished through Windows 95. However, we acknowledge that there are many users who have *not* chosen Windows 95 as their operating system, and *Power User's Toolkit* contains conventions and techniques that apply to Windows version 3.1 and higher. Basically, there is more drag-and-drop support in Windows 95 for icons and URLs (Uniform Resource Locators), but many of the procedures covered in this book are written to address unique conventions for *all* versions of MS Windows.

Windows 3.1x users *will*, however, have to acquire and configure a WinSock before making use of the Navigator browser—this feature is an integrated connection service in Windows 95—and you should check out Chapter 2, "Installing & Customizing Navigator," before getting too deeply into this book to make Windows 3.1x connections work, so you can follow this book's examples.

■   We also make the assumption that you either have (or plan to subscribe to) an Internet access account, and that you can easily access this account from where you're reading this book! In Chapter 2, "Installing & Customizing Navigator," we'll take you through the process of getting an Internet Service Provider (an *ISP*), and show you how to customize Navigator. If you don't have an Internet subscription yet and you purchased this book as part of your personal game strategy to conquer the Web, we recommend that you read this chapter first.

■   We also assume that you've tooled around on the Web enough to have realized first-hand that the Web changes every day. Sites and resources that were here one day vanish the next. All of the URLs listed in this book and in the Totally Hot Bookmarks List were current and were where we said they'd be at the time of this writing. We tried to pick sites and resources that looked like they were here to stay, but don't be alarmed if we refer to a site that comes up missing or changed when you visit it—that's the nature of the Web. With the skills that you already have and the skills you'll learn in this book, you should be able to find other sites that provide similar or even better resources should one fail you.

■ Finally, we hope you're comfortable with computer slang! The Web is a happening place, the Internet is a cyber-banquet, and the author and editors felt that a "dry" documentation of power user techniques would be inappropriate for the subject matter. We give you the technical explanations for how and why things work in Navigator and the Internet, but we also refer to the action of jumping from one HTTP document to another as *surfing*.

If you're *not* familiar with some of the vernacular of the Web now, however, you *will* be by the end of this book!

WHAT'S IN THE POWER USER'S TOOLKIT?

Like the Internet itself, the *Power User's Toolkit* is broad in its dimensions and covers a lot of ground in many areas. To make the best use of the *Power User's Toolkit*, we've organized this book into sections that relate to a specific area of interest. It wouldn't be a bad thing to read the *Power User's Toolkit* from front to back, but this book is structured so that you can also pick up on a topic you're interested in, such as mail services, and find the contextual support to make a new technique easy to master.

This book is divided into three parts, each part containing power techniques that address a different aspect of the Internet and Netscape Navigator 3.

Part I, "Discovering the Power of Navigator," is a compendium of guides and recommendations for making an Internet connection an extended part of your PC's system. Configuring Navigator and organizing URLs can make the Internet another *dimension* of your computer, and in this section we get into the best way to set up a dial-up connection so your computer can access the Internet.

Chapter 1, "The Best Way to Explore the Web," is an exploration of possibilities found when you use Navigator or Navigator Gold as your browser for the Internet. How do you copy a URL to your desktop for future quick access? How do you approach the creation of content-rich e-mail? What's the best way to keep your Internet Shortcuts separate from your application icons? Learn how to make your desktop Internet-ready, and start your "Webucation" from the outside in through examples and utilities on the Companion CD-ROM.

Chapter 2, "Installing & Customizing Navigator," is where you'll gain the experience with both Navigator *and* a computer system to make the necessary connections and specify the browsing preferences that will save you time—and money—when you go online. Learn how to make a Windows 95 connectoid, establish a relationship with the ISP that best suits your needs, troubleshoot a system for protocol errors, store and manage the inevitable scores of megabytes of incoming files and messages, and more.

Part 2, "Tapping Into the Power of Navigator," integrates Navigator's features with the offerings of the Internet, how you can use a hidden Navigator feature to perform searches, how to send and receive mail and news, use bookmarks, and protect your online privacy while on the Web. This part of the book reveals some of the most wanted but least discovered techniques for power sailing on the Internet.

Chapter 3, "Power Navigation," contains travel tips and Navigator interface solutions for getting the most from the Web in record time and without expending a lot of effort. See how to quickly define a URL in Navigator's Location/Go to: field, learn the important components of a URL, how to leverage the use of the shortcut menu, bookmarks, and Navigator's history list to get back and forth from sites you've visited, and what some of the less obvious interface elements in Navigator's browser can be used for.

Chapter 4, "Retracing Your Steps With Bookmarks, Internet Shortcuts & History Lists," provides example-rich documentation of the shortcuts, bookmarks, and history lists you can access in Navigator to make sense out of an incredibly tangled (World Wide) Web! Learn different techniques that make your online time more fun and more productive by collecting and organizing the URLs (addresses) of the places you've found, so that your next Web adventure is a non-stop excursion.

Chapter 5, "Power Search & Retrieval." One of the obstacles to browsing the Web efficiently is *not* that there aren't enough search capabilities, but perhaps that there are *so many* that it becomes difficult to zero in on a specific document you need. Learn how to conduct Boolean searches, how to access Directory and Search Engines, decide which type of search best suits a specific need, and how to crack Internet files that were created on systems *other* than the familiar DOS/Windows platform. You'll also explore two great ways to send files from Navigator, whether they're reports bound for the home office or the contents of your home page.

Chapter 6, "Person to Person With Navigator Mail & Netscape News," provides in-depth coverage of "alternative" uses for Navigator's browser. HTTP and FTP aren't the only services your Internet Service Provider (ISP) and Navigator provide—there are hundreds of newsgroups out there with information you seek, and a much quicker way to get your mail out these days than running outside to that dome-shaped box on a pole! Learn how to manage your incoming e-mail, attach files to your outgoing mail, and how Navigator 3 integrates Mail and News services so you can correspond and still have time left for some surfing during lunch hour.

Chapter 7, "Maintaining Your Privacy on the Internet," provides you with the information, the reassurance, and the proactive measures you can take to insure against cyber-theft and electronic eavesdropping. How safe are electronic transactions? How private is that love letter to a co-worker? (Hint: it's probably not, so don't post it.) Netscape, major financial institutions, and powerful cryptography are all on your side in keeping private Internet transactions private, and in this chapter, we'll take you through not only the methods, but also the mechanisms by which Internet messages and services are becoming as secure as a physical safety deposit box.

Chapter 8, "The Intranet," takes a look at the feasibility and logistics of setting the Intranet protocols for in-house, corporate communications. If you think that your company's network is feature-poor, and security-oriented to the point of locking you out of the system, good news is already in place. Navigator and other Netscape products are quickly replacing traditional corporate networking due to cost-effectiveness and ease of use and configuration. If you're in a deciding position at your company over networking solutions, this chapter is for you. And if you don't have a say in how your office networks computers, here are the facts that might make life easier for you, and tell a very compelling story to the folks who write the checks.

Part 3, "Extending Navigator Through Plug-ins, Helper Applications & New Technology," takes a look at the wave of new functionality you can expect *today* from Navigator and its extended architecture. Navigator, like MS Windows, is an integrating environment, and when a new technology becomes available, you simply plug it into your current configuration. Video, audio, VRML worlds are only the beginning of Navigator support for Web "objects"—platform-independent files and programs that make the Web the hottest property for new computer innovations. See where Navigator takes you in Part 3 when you tap into, and plug into, programs and utilities that make the Web come alive.

Chapter 9, "Taking a Look at Plug-ins," covers more than 20 of the most robust, intriguing, and enabling technologies that you can add to Navigator for fun or for work. Learn where to find a plug-in for portable documents, virus detection and cleanup, online presentations, and even digital movies. Chapter 9 makes recommendations for why you'd want a specific plug-in, when you'd be most likely to need to read a data type the plug-in supports, and what document creation programs are used to generate content that a specific plug-in can decode.

Chapter 10, "CoolTalk." When is a browser not a browser? Answer: when it's a telephone, a real-time chat line, or a whiteboard that can send live annotations written on a screen capture around the world. If you've ever been professionally thwarted by the inability to communicate visually online, CoolTalk is the answer, and Chapter 10 shows you how to use the Internet as a one-on-one communications vehicle. Tired of long-distance telephone charges? CoolTalk may also provide you with an alternative, as well as the means for inexpensive long-distance education and corporate conferencing without investing a dime in additional hardware.

FROM COVER TO COVER . . . TO COMPANION CD-ROM

One of the nicer things about writing books in today's wired society is that whatever cannot be successfully explained through words or pictures can be conveyed electronically. In the back of this book is the *Power User's Toolkit* Companion CD-ROM, which contains many important resources that demonstrate an example in this book . . . and beyond.

You'll find specific files on the Companion CD-ROM that relate to exercises in the book's chapters; in Chapter 1, for example, we'll ask you to load a file from the Companion CD-ROM that is located, interestingly enough, in the CHAP01 folder.

However, the education—and the fun—doesn't end when you reach the end of the *printed* tale you hold before you. The Companion CD-ROM is also packed with shareware utilities, Navigator plug-ins, additional documentation, and an absolutely awesome Totally Hot Bookmarks list, containing over 500 of the "must-see" URLs and FTP sites on the Web, all neatly organized to plug right into Navigator. Additionally, if you see the Web as a place to actively participate, many fine resources can be found in *The Argyle Pages*, a Web-linked document in Acrobat format on the Companion CD-ROM. *The Argyle Pages* list the resources for the top design, desktop publishing, VRML-creation, and other software; where to get it, who to contact, and what a specific software application can provide you, the future Web Author.

Additionally, the BOUTONS folder on the Companion CD-ROM contains some home-baked goods you might want to investigate for some fresh ideas and tools for Web content. The TEXTURES folder contains over 100 custom (as in "you won't find them in software packages or on the Web"), seamless, tiling pattern files that are ideal for use as backgrounds on HTML pages. They're in TIF format, they can be easily converted to GIF interlaced format with the utilities found on the CD, and they can be added to documents using Navigator Gold in about two steps. The BOUTONS folder also contains original TrueType and Type 1 fonts; you might want to peruse WebKnobs, a digital font particularly useful for creating buttons on HTML pages when used in combination with many popular Windows paint programs. See the PUTFONT.PDF document in the BOUTONS folder for an Acrobat preview of the character map for these typefaces.

Sidle up to the Companion CD-ROM feast, and don't forget to read the documentation for installation instructions and license agreements for the applications.

STEP 1: PLUG IN THE TOOLS!

Now that you've got the ingredients, it's time to open the can and get on with the enjoyment and education to follow as you learn how the tools you own, the tools you've yet to use, and the tools of your own curiosity and intuition can lead you to greater power when tooling down the greatest information highway in the universe. Turn the page, and let's take the next step. . . .

Discovering the Power of Navigator

The Best Way to Explore the Web

The title of this book, *Official Netscape Power User's Toolkit*, might be interpreted in two ways. Yes, this book is for power users, folks who are experienced with computer communications, applications, hardware, and operating systems—there's plenty of information in this book as these topics relate to Netscape Navigator 3.

But what if you want to *become* a power user? If you're beginning your adventures with a personal computer and online communications, this book will give you the tools you need to become proficient with the way your computer, communications, and Navigator work together. By understanding the integration of hardware, software, and communications, you become a skilled user, and the "toolkit"—the chapters to follow and the Companion CD-ROM—become a foundation upon which you'll continue to refine your skills.

Your first step in using the Internet is to take a look at the package, see what it will mean to the way you work, and see what Navigator can do to supercharge your Internet connectivity. We hope Chapter 1 opens some creative possibilities to you.

We acknowledge, however, that a good part of the fun (yes, *fun!*) of working with a new application is being able to achieve immediate results. Therefore, this chapter is a compendium of tricks and techniques that you can use to make Navigator as accessible as your PC's on-switch and poses several Windows configurations for making Navigator a part of your everyday desktop. The best way to explore the Web is through Netscape Navigator, and the best way to take a trip is to plan ahead. To make the most from your prime Internet power tool, let's see how this new software fits into the arrangement of your system and your desktop.

Beyond the Browser: The New Graphical Workspace

In the same way that many users migrated to Windows as a graphical metaphor for the mind-numbing commands, switches, and parameters we'd go through to accomplish a simple task, Netscape Navigator offers *high-level control* (gross control over operations with a high degree of abstraction) of Internet media. About five minutes after you've installed a copy of Navigator and connected with your Internet Service Provider, it appears, superficially at least, as though you have a nifty graphical browsing utility for the World Wide Web. However, one of Navigator's more subtle powers is the services *integration* that it provides: Windows, mail, news groups, Web objects, FTP transfer, and many more direct routes to and from your hard disk can all be managed from Navigator's interface.

Not surprisingly, because Navigator and Navigator Gold are bona fide Windows applications, you have already learned many of the necessary techniques for making the most out of Navigator. Drag and drop support in Navigator allows you to treat objects you're viewing on the Web like any object on your hard disk. It's natural, then, to make Navigator an *extension* of the Windows Desktop, so that you work as quickly on the Net as you do within a spreadsheet or word processor, and move information as efficiently on the Net as on a local area network. This section takes a look at several different strategies that you can employ under Windows 3.1x and Windows 95, to make Navigator part of your desktop and bring the world to your office.

THE WINDOWS 3.1X INTERNET PROGRAM GROUP

Because Windows 3.1x doesn't support the placement of programs, files, or other digital object types directly on the desktop, there are a number of workarounds you can create to make the Internet, through Navigator, a quick and accessible place from the moment Program Manager loads. If you have a Winsock and Navigator installed, it's a good idea to keep the program icons in a unique group; we'll add to this group and show you how to make lightning-fast site connections shortly. If you don't have a Winsock or Navigator installed, put a bookmark right here, check out Chapter 2, "Installing & Customizing Navigator," and some great techniques will still be here when you get back!

Because Windows 3.1x actually is a graphical layer that requires MS-DOS to run, many tasks can be performed from a command line. Fortunately, the 16-bit version of Navigator (the version you must use if you're running Win 3.1x) can be launched, *and* a connection executed to a specific site through the use of a single command line entry. Better still is that you have to go through the drudgery of typing a special command line entry only once—an icon can be created for this action, and it, too, should go in a special Program Group.

Let's hypothesize that your work requires you to check the Internet for mail, national news, and the latest stock quotes the first thing in the morning, and you'd like to get these chores done within about 15 minutes. One possible solution would be to create program icons for each place you'd like to go, which would give you the option of starting your day's journey with any of the tasks. In Figure 1-1, you can see that the Connections Program Group is populated with a number of services and locations; each icon represents a unique starting point for an Internet session. Clicking any one of these icons causes a copy of Navigator to load, and the information about a specific location is requested at that time. No fumbling for an address, nothing to type—frequently visited locations can be indexed in a number of ways for Navigator to use. Once online you'll want to use bookmarks (see Chapter 4, "Power Search & Retrieval") and the links you find in pages instead of these group icons to go from site to site.

For a comprehensive start to your own bookmarks collection, check out the Totally Hot Bookmarks List on the Companion CD-ROM. In Chapter 4, you'll see how these addresses can easily be added to your existing bookmarks list.

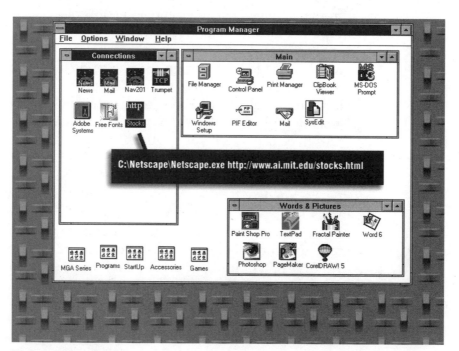

Figure 1-1: *Locations on the Internet and Navigator can all be located in the same program group as icons.*

In the previous figure, the callout to the Stocks icon shows the command line you'd need to type to make MIT's stocks page your first stop of the day. If you have a favorite location you'd like to use in the following example, bring it along. Here's how to make the fastest connection to a site in Windows 3.1x:

1. In this example, Navigator is located in the Netscape directory on drive C. If your location is different, substitute the directory and drive letter throughout this example. From Program Manager, choose File, New.

2. If you don't have a Program Group for your Internet stuff, click the Program Group radio button, and name the group something evocative, like "Connections."

3. Once you have your new program group, choose File, New, then click the Program Item radio button.

4. In the Description field, type Stock Report (or whatever site on the Net you want to go to).

5. Click in the Command Line field, then click Browse, and find the NETSCAPE .EXE file in the Browse dialog box (chances are it's in the NETSCAPE default directory). Click OK to return to the Program Item Properties dialog box, and add the command line to run Navigator.

6. Insert the text cursor in the Command Line field, and drag to the right until you can see the last characters of the command line. Press the space bar once.

7. Type in the full URL of the location on the Net you'd like Navigator to immediately connect with upon startup. See Chapter 3, "Power Navigation," if you're unsure of the syntax of an URL, or know only a partial URL of a site you'd like to turn into a program group icon. For this example, you can type in: http://www.ai.mit.edu/stocks.html.

    By doing so, you can have access to the stock market at your fingertips.

8. Click OK, and you're done. Your program group will have a Navigator icon with the title Stock Report beneath it.

Because Windows 3.1x doesn't natively support a Winsock (as Windows 95 does), you're not a lone double-click away from stock reports in the morning—a shareware Winsock such as Trumpet, featured in the previous figure, still needs to be launched, but you're pretty close to Internet desktop automation now. You'd use the same steps to launch Navigator and directly connect to an FTP site, to compose mail . . . think of the continuing needs you have, and create a unique program icon.

NAVIGATOR'S INTERNAL SWITCHES & CUSTOM ICONS

Navigator offers integrated newsgroup and mail services; you don't have to leave the Web page you're viewing to access either. Additionally, in the Appearance tab under Options, General Preferences in Navigator, you can customize the startup to offer you Mail or News before Navigator goes to the home page of your choice.

But to keep with the scenario described earlier, if you're running Windows 3.1x and want to connect directly upon startup of Navigator to Mail or News, this too, can be assigned to a program icon through a command line.

To create a program icon that automatically launches Navigator Mail services, follow the steps in the preceding example, and type C:\NETSCAPE\NETSCAPE.EXE -Mail in the Command Line. Make sure to leave a space after "EXE" before typing in the Mail switch (the "-mail"). To launch News service with a double-click, type -NEWS after a space after the path to NETSCAPE.EXE.

You can use these steps to create "instant" connections to wherever you like, but eventually, you might find that all the icons to these custom connections look alike—by default, the Navigator icon is assigned to Navigator's executable, even though the command line is followed with a specific and unique URL. Regardless of the version of Windows that you use, unique icons would be nice; users tend to grow more accustomed to clicking an icon or a position onscreen than we do to reading an icon title before we leap. The PUTICONS.DLL file in the CHAP01 directory on the Companion CD-ROM will go a long way to solving the problem of "look-alike" icons. If you copy this file to your Windows directory, you'll find over 100 unique icons created to help you visually sort out your desktop with all the new programs and connections. In Figure 1-2, you can see that a mail icon is being created for a program group. If you click the Change Icon button, and select PUTICONS.DLL from your hard disk, you'll find not one but several mail icons that you can assign to different Navigator connections.

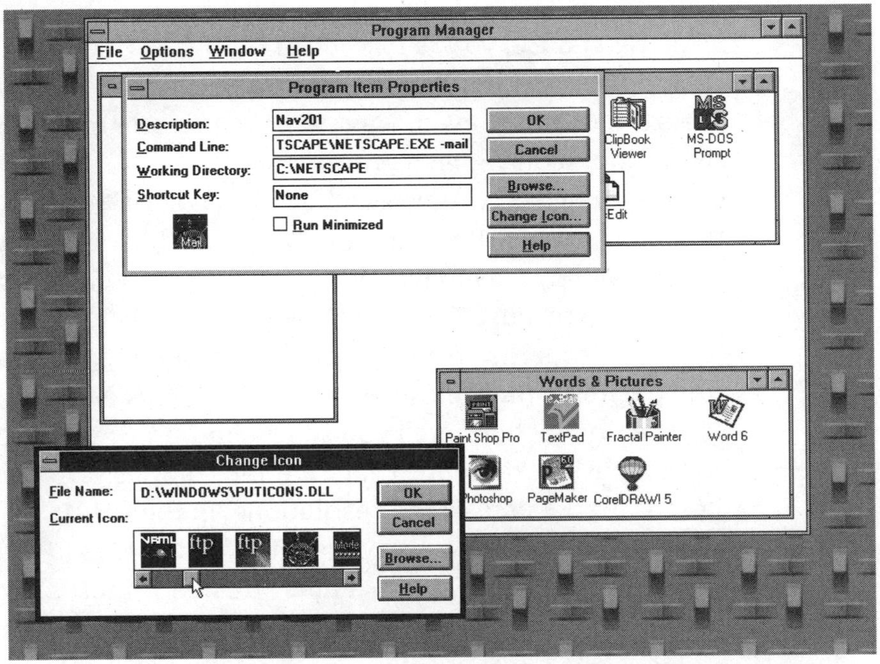

Figure 1-2: *Choose the type of service—mail, a Web site, or other connection— and give it an icon in your program group that's easy to find at a moment's notice.*

Integration of programs and areas outside of your system is a strange concept, but if you think of Navigator's connectivity powers as simply an object-oriented *extension* of Program Manager, you'll see your Program Manager's groups come together as both an online and local resource for getting work done.

NORTON DESKTOP: MAKING THE DESKTOP CONNECTION

Many users of Windows 3.1x bought desktop replacements, such as Norton Desktop and Central Point Software's (now part of Symantec) PC Tools for Windows. Most of the desktop replacements for Program Manager succeeded in getting programs out of groups, placing them in space-saving toolboxes, and generally leaving more room on the desktop for other things such as printers and drive windows.

If, by chance, you're using one of these desktop/Program Manager/File Manager replacements as your Windows shell, creating desktop connections to Navigator is a simple matter of copying a Navigator icon within a group.

In Figure 1-3, you can see that Navigator 3 was added to the Business group. By Shift+dragging the icon to the desktop, you create a copy, command line and all. To then customize the Navigator icon to launch mail or other services, click the duplicate icon, choose Properties from the pop-up menu, then add a space and the desired URL after the command line to Navigator.

The Connections area you see in Figure 1-3 is actually a custom wallpaper background. There are four of these wallpapers, in different motifs and screen resolutions, in the CHAP01 folder of the Companion CD-ROM. Copy the DT____.BMP files to your Windows directory, choose Control Panel, Desktop, then select the wallpaper you want from the Wallpaper|File drop-down list.

Liberate your connections under Windows 3.1x! Get them into a program group or on the desktop where you can easily access them.

If you moved to Windows 95 as an operating system, or plan to move shortly, greater support for connecting to the Internet is available. The following sections cover methods you might want to consider using in Windows 95 for making your desktop the Grand Central Station of communications.

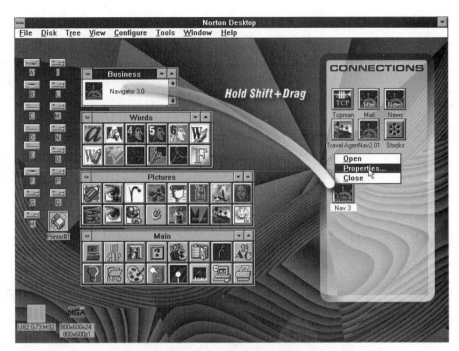

Figure 1-3: *When using Norton Desktop in Windows 3.1x, you can drag a group icon onto the desktop.*

MAKING INTERNET SHORTCUTS IN WINDOWS 95

The way you work in Windows 95 to move and view files is very much like the presentation of graphical objects you'll find on the World Wide Web, which is both a composite of many HTML documents and the graphical portion of the Internet. Like Windows 95, Navigator and Navigator Gold feature full-right button support of shortcut menus. Options for performing routines, such as copying, that appear on shortcut menus are *context-sensitive*; that is, the options that are available to users depend upon the object over which you right-click.

CD-ROM

In Figure 1-4 you can see the beginning of a "Navigator-oriented" desktop in Windows 95. As mentioned in the previous section, the Power User's Toolkit Companion CD-ROM (in the CHAP01 folder) contains different desktop wallpaper designs, all of which feature a "Connections well" to help keep off-system connections separate from local files and programs. Copy any or all of the BMP files to your Window folder (the files for high video resolutions are indicated with "800" in their filename, while low resolution wallpaper is indicated by a "640" in the filename). If you'd like to follow along in the examples below, you can load the custom wallpaper by right-clicking the desktop. Choose Properties from the shortcut menu, then choose an image file from the Wallpaper scrolling list on the Background tab.

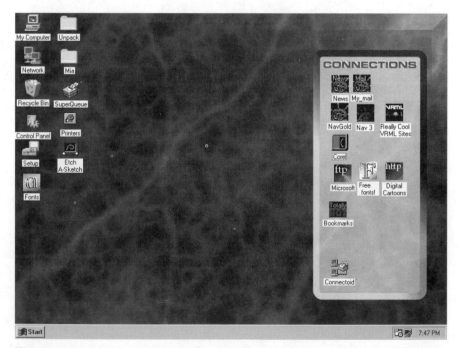

Figure 1-4: *Make the workspace that Windows 95 first displays—the desktop—your personalized work area for accessing files and Internet connections through Navigator.*

Because Windows 95 treats everything—files, programs, even URLs you've copied to the clipboard—as objects that retain their native properties, you can use this capability to create objects on your desktop that are Internet Shortcuts. In the following example, you'll see how to snag an Internet address (URL) off of a home page on the Net, and add this link to your desktop. When you need to quickly visit this location in the future, all you need to do is double-click the icon, and Navigator and Windows 95 handle the negotiations. (If you haven't set up the Windows 95 Dial-Up Networking software and the AutoDial software for automatically making an Internet connection yet, check out Chapter 2, "Installing & Customizing Navigator," for specific instructions). Internet Shortcuts an also be used when you already have an active Internet connection and Navigator open. Clicking a Shortcut then loads the URL in the Navigator's Location field and sends you off to the site without opening another copy of Navigator. To make an Internet Shortcut:

1. Launch Navigator. If the site to which you want to make the shortcut is on the Web, open an active connection to the Internet, type the URL into the Location field, and hit return.

    Alternatively, if you already have a bookmark for the site, you don't need to open an Internet connection. Just launch Navigator, and then press Ctrl+B to open the Bookmarks window. If the Connect To dialog box appears, click the Cancel button. Any of your favorite places will do here; in this example, we've chosen Adobe Systems' Acrobat page.

2. Right-click in an empty area of the Web page to bring up the shortcut menu. Choose Internet Shortcut from the menu. In the Create Internet Shortcut dialog box, edit the entry in the Description if necessary to make it meaningful to you. Click OK, and the Internet Shortcut will appear on your desktop.

    If you are making a shortcut to a link in the Bookmarks window or to a link on any Web page, right-click the link and choose Internet Shortcut from the menu as seen in Figure 1-5. As when making a shortcut to a page, edit the Description in the Create Internet Shortcut dialog box if necessary, then click OK.

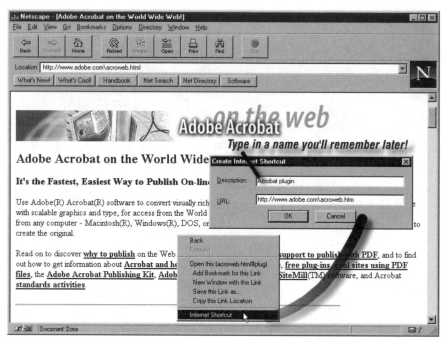

Figure 1-5: *Links in hypertext (HTML) documents can easily be made into Internet shortcuts.*

3. Click the Minimize button in the upper right of Navigator's windowpane, or close Navigator to see the new Internet Shortcut on the desktop.
    You're done!

TIP

If, by chance, you tried the Microsoft Internet Explorer that came with Windows 95 before you switched to Navigator, you can drag any Favorites you created out of Internet Explorer's Favorites window and place them on your desktop. They are simply Internet Shortcuts, just like the one you made in Navigator in the previous example. They'll work just fine with Navigator as long as you installed Navigator after you installed Microsoft's Internet Explorer.

GIVING AN INTERNET SHORTCUT A CUSTOM ICON

CD-ROM

As mentioned earlier in this chapter, PUTICONS.DLL is located in the CHAP01 folder of the Companion CD-ROM. This icon file contains over 100 custom icons specifically designed for Navigator and the Internet Shortcuts you create. By default, Windows 95 uses the same icon for every new shortcut, and can make your desktop shortcuts look both monotonous and hard to pinpoint. Copy the PUTICONS.DLL file to your Windows folder, and the next time you create a desktop shortcut, right-click the icon, choose Properties from the shortcut menu, click the Shortcut tab, then click the Change Icon button. You can then choose from the PUTICONS collection, or from a collection of icons you might already own, to make every desktop connection a highly visible and unique one.

Because both the World Wide Web and Windows 95 are so graphically driven, you might find that the new long filename convention that this 32-bit operating system affords you is great for tracking down a file in a folder, but perhaps not too great when you're trying to conserve desktop space. In Figure 1-6, you can see that the author has created a shortcut to a Really Cool VRML Site. However, the PUTICON.DLL file has a VRML icon, and there's really no purpose for the title beneath the icon for easy identification.

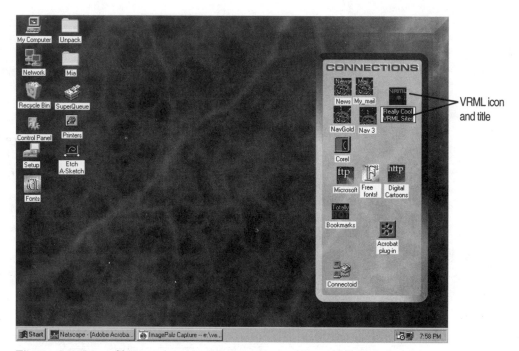

Figure 1-6: Long filenames can run twice or more of the width of their associ-ated icon, making it difficult to arrange desktop icons to minimize wasted space.

Although every shortcut must have a title, you can abbreviate the title to a single character, by clicking the title to select it, then clicking the title a second time to open it for editing. As you can see in Figure 1-7, a capital "I" has been typed in place of the original title, and the VRML site shortcut icon can now be moved closer to neighboring icons without overlapping titles.

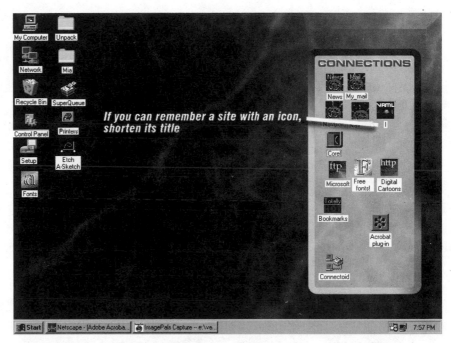

Figure 1-7: *Your Windows 95 desktop will become cluttered with files and shortcuts more quickly than you imagine. Conserve desktop real estate by abbreviating icon titles.*

TIP

If you embrace the idea of making your Windows 95 desktop your connection to the world, there's a freeware suite of utilities that you can download from Microsoft that takes desktop customizing a step beyond.

Power Toys is a collection of utilities that includes Tweak UI, a program that can remove the shortcut arrow from shortcut icons. If you've ever had to stop and ponder what the symbol on an icon means because of this intrusive element, Tweak UI will make a shortcut icon look exactly like a program or file icon (however, take caution not to accidentally delete an actual file or program instead of a shortcut icon!).

Additionally, Tweak UI allows you to remove Windows 95 icons that you might have unsuccessfully attempted to move or delete. The Microsoft Network icon, the Internet Explorer icon, and even the Recycle Bin can all be removed (but not deleted) from your desktop to make way for desktop items of your own. Power Toys comes with absolutely no guarantee—Microsoft doesn't want to hear about any problems you might have with them—but the author has used Tweak UI for over half a year with no problems. You can download Power Toys from http://www.microsoft.com/windows/software/powertoy.htm.

Because Navigator depends upon an operating system to perform, we've spent a little time so far to give you an idea of how each software supports the other. In the following sections, we take a look at other methods you can use in your work—and at your leisure—for making the quickest, most accurate connections to wherever you like in the world.

THE POWER USER'S TOTALLY HOT BOOKMARKS LIST

In addition to power tips, configuration, and advanced surfing techniques found in later chapters, the Totally Hot Bookmarks List, TOTALHOT.HTM in the CHAP01 folder on the Companion CD-ROM, can be your best start to using the Internet the most efficiently. The Totally Hot Bookmarks List is a compendium of resources on the Net for art, sports, Java applets, hardware support from major manufacturers, plug-ins for Navigator, software sites, online versions of Bartlett's Quotations, e-zines (electronic magazines), and much more.

The Totally Hot Bookmarks List was compiled for your use as an HTML document, with every listing linked to the corresponding site. Chapter 4, "Power Search & Retrieval," takes you through the methods for adding, appending, and replacing Navigator Bookmarks, but if you want immediate access to more than 500 of the most important and exciting places on the Net, here's how to get going in six easy steps:

1. From My Computer or File Manager, open the drive window for your CD-ROM.

2. Double-click the CHAP01 folder of the Companion CD-ROM, then click and drag the TOTALHOT.HTM file onto your desktop to copy it to the desktop. If you are using Windows 3.1x, copy the file to a directory on your hard disk.

3. Launch your Internet or Intranet connection.

4. Chances are that you have a Navigator shortcut on your desktop (Navigator, by default, puts a shortcut there, and previous examples show you how to manually do this). Double-click the Navigator shortcut icon to launch Navigator.

5. Click the Restore button (middle, right on Navigator's window frame), then click and drag the title bar, and move the window out of the way so that you can see the Totally Hot Bookmarks icon on your desktop.

6. Click and drag the icon into Navigator's browser window. You now have a selection of over 500 places to go, as seen in Figure 1-8. Find a site you like and click it!

Figure 1-8: *You can drag any HTML document into Navigator's browser window to view; if the document has links, you can access them the same way that you make links to and from documents on the Web.*

Alternatively, you can double-click the TOTALHOT document icon on your desktop to launch Navigator or load the page into Navigator's browser window if Navigator is already open. Although the Totally Hot Bookmarks List was intended to appeal to a broad market, there might be some customizing you'd like to perform on the document to make it more personal, or perhaps you'd like to copy some of the bookmarks to your own Bookmarks list. See Chapter 4, "Retracing Your Steps," for complete instructions on how Navigator Bookmarks work and how to edit them.

NAVIGATOR GOLD & YOUR PERSONAL LAUNCH PAD

Every time you visit Netscape's home page, you have an opportunity to create your Personal Workspace that assembles itself through Java technology. If you haven't already done this, you might care to check it out and see how it fits into your plans (see Chapter 2, "Installing & Customizing Navigator," for details), but right now, you'll see how to create a similar document—an HTML document containing your most frequently accessed sites—through the courtesy of Navigator Gold's Editor feature. The advantage to creating your own "launch pad" is that it is always accessible to you.

The primary difference between Navigator and Navigator Gold is the Editor window. Within it, you can make the Net a two-way, interactive experience, by creating documents exactly like the ones you visit on the Web. Navigator Gold's Editor puts within everyone's reach the capability to create HTML documents, which would otherwise require experience in writing in HTML source code. In Figure 1-9, you can see a launch pad that we've created for our favorite sites; it's a graphical document, and clicking either link text or one of the buttons takes us to a site of our choice. We'll walk you through the steps in Navigator Gold for creating your own launch pad shortly.

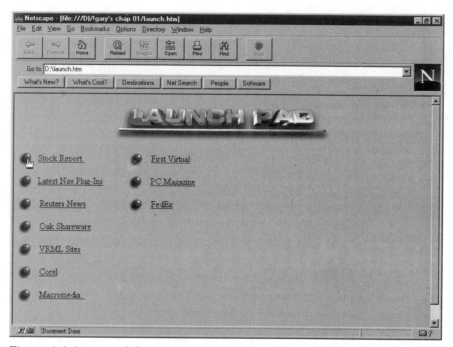

Figure 1-9: *You can define an HTML page of your own creation as the home page whenever you launch Navigator.*

In the previous figure, the LAUNCH.HTM document might have appeared as the picture of simplicity, when in fact, it's composed of text commands that arrange and display text and graphics in a fairly highly structured order. Figure 1-10 is a split screen of the same document, with part of the HTML code displayed. Fortunately, Navigator Gold's Editor is WYSIWYG (what you see is what you get)—completely object-oriented. You don't have to know how to use the HTML tags to create amazing layouts; you simply type, drag, and drop.

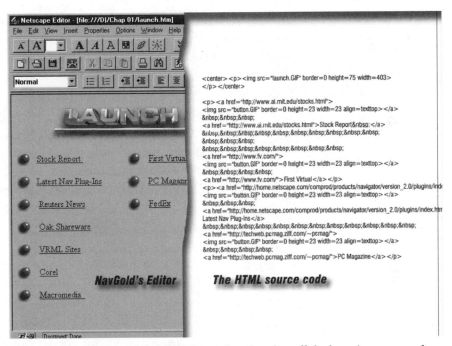

Figure 1-10: *Navigator Gold's Editor takes the edge off the learning curve when you want to compose an HTML document for personal use, or for posting on the Web.*

Let's take the creation of your personal launching pad with modest expectations in the following example. Your assignment is to create a single link in an HTML document; creating several links simply involves the repetition of the steps, and we'll show you how to completely compose the document later in this chapter. Here's how to get the ball rolling:

1. Copy a URL to the Windows 95 clipboard. For this example, it's not really important what the URL is; you can copy any of the links from the Totally Hot Bookmarks List if you like (right-click the link and choose Copy Link Location). Think of a more descriptive name than the URL offers for this link. For example, if you'd like to check out Letraset's site for cool fonts every month, the site is http://www.esselte.com/letraset/productshowcase/. However, the descriptive name, the name you'll use for your launch pad entry, should be something like "Cool Letraset Fonts."

2. Launch Navigator Gold, then choose File, New Document, then choose Blank. Your other two choices, From Template and Wizard, need to be chosen when you have an active Internet connection going because these options are run from Netscape's servers.

3. The Navigator Gold Editor appears onscreen. Choose File, Save from the Editor's menu. Name the file LAUNCH.HTM and save it to the Desktop. The Navigator Editor requires that a document be named before any links or graphics can be placed in the document. Insert your cursor in the window, and type the descriptive name for your link.

4. Highlight the text, then click the Link button on the Editor's toolbar (the one with the chain link on the button). This displays the Properties dialog box. Alternatively, you can right-click the text after you've highlighted it, and choose Paragraph, List Properties from the shortcut menu.

5. Click the Link tab, then place your cursor in the *Link to a page location or file* field, and then press Ctrl+V. This pastes the URL that you copied to the clipboard earlier.

6. Click Apply, then click Close. Congratulations, you've created your first link in an HTML document.

7. Choose File, Save, to save your document with the new link.

8. Many users find it easier to identify and click a graphical element onscreen, such as a button, than text. If you'd like to add a button link to the same location as your first launch pad entry, copy the BUTTON.GIF image from the CHAP01 folder on the Companion CD-ROM to the same location on your hard disk where you saved the LAUNCH.HTM document.

9. Insert your cursor before the link text, then click the Insert Image button on Navigator Gold's toolbar.

CD-ROM

10. In the Properties dialog box, on the Image tab, click the Browse button, then choose BUTTON.GIF from the location on your hard disk.

11. Click the Align Top button, as shown in Figure 1-11. Text in an HTML document always aligns relative to a graphic. In this example, by aligning the text with the top of the button graphic, there will be less space between subsequent links that you can add to this launch pad document. You have no control over the leading (inter-line spacing) of text in an HTML document, but by making small graphics, and aligning text to them with the top, you minimize wasted space between lines of text.

    Also note the callouts in Figure 1-11. Because this HTML document is for your personal use and not for posting on a Web server, you can ignore popular conventions and color the text and make it a relative size that suits your own reading needs.

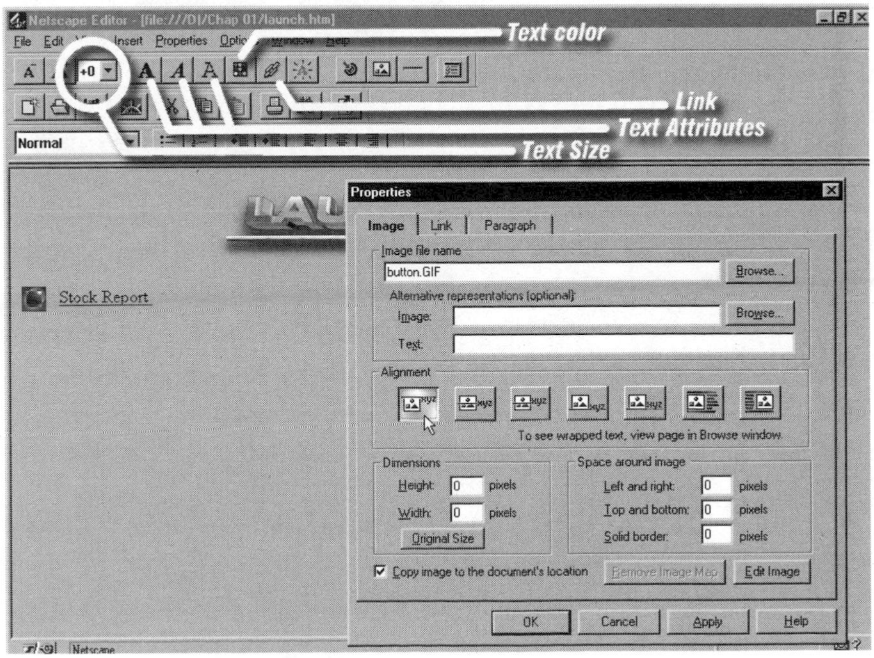

Figure 1-11: *You can make a graphic link as easily as you link text in Navigator Gold's Editor.*

12. Click the Original Size button, then highlight the zero in the *Space around image, Solid border field*, and type 0. Navigator Gold assumes that graphics link are contained in documents to be posted on the Web, and offers a friendly service—that of creating a colored link border—around graphics. However, you probably don't want a visible border around such a small button, and this step removes the default border, and specifies that you want the graphic displayed on the page at its original size.

13. Click the Link tab in the Properties dialog box, insert your cursor in the *Link to a page location or local file* field, then press Ctrl+V to paste a copy of the URL on the clipboard into this field.

14. Click Apply, then click OK. Your launch pad now has text and a button, both of which will take you to the URL you specified the next time you have an open connection to the Internet when Navigator displays this document.

CD-ROM

In addition to the BUTTON.GIF graphic, you'll find a title graphic you can use to embellish your launch pad, in the CHAP01 folder of the Companion CD-ROM. LAUNCH.GIF is a small, interlaced GIF graphic that takes little time for Navigator to read into the HTML document, and you might want a title for this file to make it easier to discern from the other documents you'll create in Navigator Gold's Editor.

To add the LAUNCH.GIF file, follow these steps:

1. In Navigator Gold's Editor, place your cursor in front of the button graphic in the LAUNCH.HTM document.

2. Press Enter three or four times to move the button graphic and link text down by a few lines. Pressing Enter enters the HTML code for breaks <BR> in your document.

3. Copy the LAUNCH.GIF file to the same location on your hard disk as the button image and your LAUNCH.HTM document.

4. Insert your cursor at the top of the page, then click the Insert Image button on Navigator Gold's toolbar.

5. Click the Browse button to the right of the *Image filename* field, choose the LAUNCH.GIF image, click the Original size button, type 0 in the *Space around image, Solid border* field, click Apply, then click OK.

6. Because there is no text surrounding the LAUNCH graphic, it's okay here to choose to align the graphic to the horizontal center of the page. You wouldn't want to do this if a graphic you put on a page had text directly following it, but because you've put breaks between the text and the link button and text, you can align the LAUNCH graphic independently of any following HTML elements. Click the LAUNCH graphic to select it, then click the align center icon (it looks like an align center text icon in a word processor) on the toolbar. Done!

You'll notice as you work with Navigator Gold's Editor that the look and feel is quite similar to Microsoft's Windows 95 WordPad, or other word processor or desktop publishing application. However, behind the scenes, Navigator Gold's Editor is generating HTML text similar to that shown in Figure 1-10, that describes the placement and properties of every element you place within the document. For example, the breaks you were asked to add in the previous example are written to HTML format as
 tags. Tags place text and graphics, and have attributes that describe the precise size, padding, alignment, and other qualities of HTML contents.

The reason why we're spending a little time here to explain the structure of HTML language is that there are many ways you can define the display of text and graphics in an HTML document and achieve an aesthetically pleasing layout. To align multiple items on a page in neat rows or columns, you can use a table, a frameset, or non-breaking space. Of these three choices, the easiest to employ is the non-breaking space; Navigator Gold requires the outside assistance of a text editor to create frames or tables in a document. Let's suppose you want to create a two-column launch pad, with buttons and links arranged so that you have access to all of them without scrolling the document window. If you already have links in mind for the example to follow, copy them to a text editor before launching Navigator Gold's Editor; it'll make copying them to the launch pad HTML document easier. If you don't have any links in mind but would like to follow along, copy the LINKS.TXT file from the CHAP01 folder on the Companion CD-ROM to your hard disk, and open it in a text editor such as NOTEPAD.EXE or TextPad, the shareware utility included on the Companion CD-ROM.

Here's how to create a two-column launch pad:

1. First things first; let's try out the non-breaking space element between the first button you created on your launch pad and the link text. Open the document in Navigator Gold's Editor, put your cursor between the button and the link text (use the Tab key to move between page elements if you have a hard time inserting your cursor), then press Shift+space bar. This puts a non-breaking space between the button and the text.

2. Press Shift+space bar a few more times (four is plenty) until the text has been pushed away from the button so that the text looks indented.

3. You'll notice that an underscore spoils the space between the text and the button because the spaces have the same link property as the text; we haven't changed the properties for the spaces yet. Highlight only the spaces, right-click, and choose Paragraph, List Properties from the shortcut menu.

4. Click the Character tab in the Properties dialog box, then click the Clear All Settings button. Click Apply, then click Close. As you can see in Figure 1-12, this procedure removes the underline from the non-breaking spaces. The space between the button and the text no longer contains a link to the specified URL.

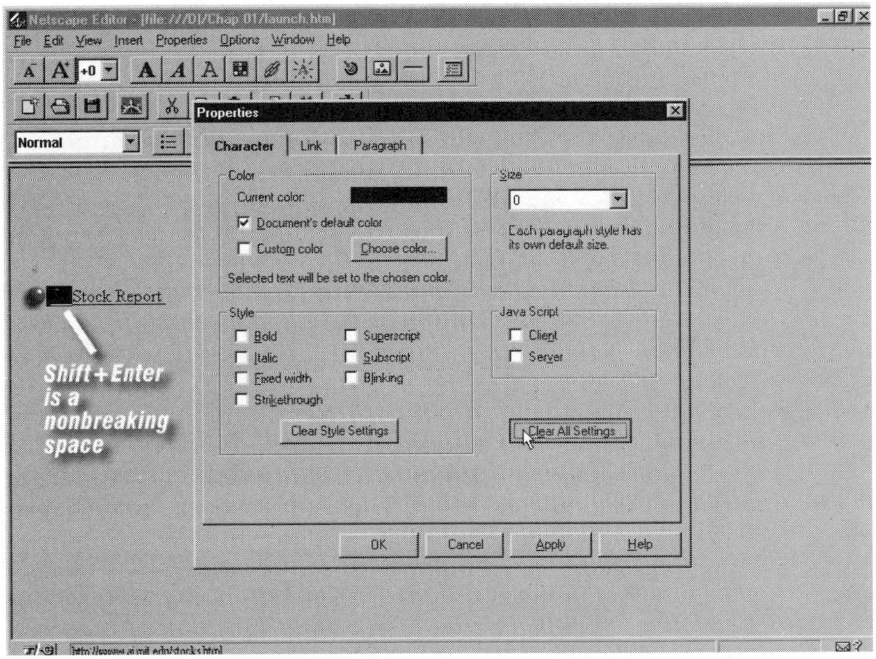

Figure 1-12: *You can remove links from text—or blank spaces—within an HTML document as easily as you create them with the Properties dialog box.*

5. Click the button image, press Ctrl+C, place your cursor at the end of the first text link, press Enter, then press Ctrl+V to paste a copy of the button at the beginning of the second line.

6. Go to your text editor and copy the URL for the second site that you want to link to in your launch pad document.

7. Switch back to Navigator Gold's Editor, right-click the second button image, then choose Image Link Properties from the shortcut menu.

8. Click the Link tab in the Properties dialog box, highlight the text in the *Link to a page location or local file* field, then press Ctrl+V to paste the URL you copied from your text editor. This step is important because when you copy a graphic that already has a link, you copy the link as well. Unless you paste a new URL into the Link field, all your buttons will link to the location attached to the original button!

9. Click OK to confirm your editing and return to the document.

10. Click your cursor to the right of the button, press Shift+space bar four times (or the number of times you did for the spaces between the first button and text link), then type a user-friendly name for your second site. In the LINKS.TXT file, the latest plug-ins and other components for Navigator are at the URL http://home.netscape.com/comprod/mirror/navcomponents_download.html. If you used this URL in step 8, type "Navigator Plug-Ins" now.

11. Place your cursor in front of the first character of your descriptive name (the "N" in Navigator, in this example), then highlight to the right until the entire descriptive name is chosen.

12. Right-click and choose Link Properties from the shortcut menu.

13. Insert your cursor in the *Link to a page location or local file* field, then press Ctrl+V to paste a copy of the URL on the clipboard into this area. Click Apply, then click Close.

14. Repeat these steps with different URLs until you've come to the bottom of the page in the Editor's window. This editing window is of the same dimensions as Navigator's browser window, so you can be assured that if your document doesn't scroll in the editing window, it won't scroll as viewed in Navigator's browser window either.

15. To start your second column of links, insert your cursor after the text link on the top line of your launch pad document, then press Shift+space bar for as many times as it takes to advance the text cursor to the last character of the longest text link in the first column. Then, press Shift+space bar four more times.

16. Click any of the button graphics, press Ctrl+C, then insert your cursor at the end of the top line (the underscores make this easy to locate), and press Ctrl+V.

17. Now that the button rests in its final position, highlight the space underscores that precede it, right-click and choose Paragraph, List Properties, click the Clear All Settings in the Character tab, click Apply, then click Close.

18. Use steps 5 through 9 to link the button to the URL of your choice, and then follow steps 10 through 13 to complete the second column. As shown in Figure 1-13, the launch pad could even go to three columns wide, and depending upon the screen resolution you use for your monitor, you could have more than 20 sites at your fingertips with your personal launch pad.

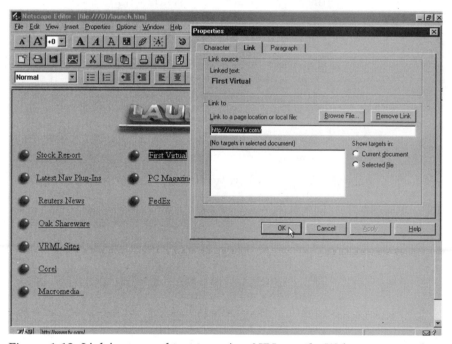

Figure 1-13: *Link images and text to various URLs on the Web, so you can then quickly check out the sites that interest you the most after you connect to the Internet.*

CD-ROM LAUNCH.HTM is located in the CHAP01 folder of the Companion CD-ROM, if you'd like to inspect the author's example of a launch pad for Navigator. If you copy the LAUNCH.GIF, the BUTTON.GIF, and the HTML document to the same folder on your hard disk, you can edit this page to make links of your own in Navigator Gold Editor.

Although the launch pad idea is a good one for storing sites you want to visit frequently, it's a time-consuming process to load this page every time you have a connection open and launch Navigator. Chapter 2, "Installing & Customizing Navigator," discusses various strategies for changing options and customizing Navigator, but there's a very quick way to change the default page that Navigator automatically loads—Netscape's home page—as your startup page.

1. Copy the path on your hard disk that is the location of your launch pad document to a text file. Highlight the text and copy it to the clipboard. For example, if you put your personal launch pad document in c:\stuff, copy c:\stuff\launch.htm to the clipboard.

2. Launch Navigator, then choose Options, General Preferences from the menu.

3. In the Start with field, highlight the Netscape text, then press Ctrl+V to paste a copy of your file's location into this field. You're done.

Because your startup page is now located locally—it refers to a path to your hard disk instead of a URL on the Internet—Navigator will make no attempt to establish connections to the Internet through Windows 95's connectoids. You'll need to establish your connection manually if you choose to load a personal site as your home page.

INTEGRATING NAVIGATOR WITH YOUR WORK

So far in this chapter we've concentrated upon integrating Navigator with your Windows desktop, but we can carry this integration process a step farther and make Navigator an integral part of your everyday *business life*. In businesses across the world, it's "first come, first served" when it comes to closing a business deal or becoming a preferred business supplier. Navigator Gold can assist you in climbing to the top of your profession if you know how to automate basic business practices. Some of the specific steps for office automation are described in detail in future chapters of this book, so don't worry if one or two steps are unfamiliar at this point; this is only a "dry run" to demonstrate some of the possibilities that Navigator holds.

TIP

Note that the example in this section uses Navigator Gold's integrated HTML Editor to create an HTML document. Navigator Gold's graphically based editor insulates you from having to learn how to write HTML source code. If you don't have Navigator Gold, you'll have to create your HTML documents in a text editor or in some other HTML editor, either of which require more than a basic understanding of HTML's tagged markup language.

In the following example, let's suppose you are the sales manager for a technology company. We'll keep this example loosely defined because we're trying to show a routine here that you can employ in your specific work situation. Here's the scenario: you get to work at 8:30 AM and the folks in engineering tell you that their new Model 2501 something-or-other will be ready to ship by the end of the week. One of the engineers tells you that the specs for the product are in the 2501 folder on the network's drive Z, and they're accompanied by a scanned photo file of the piece of machinery. The WHATZIT.TIF image and the m-2501.htm document are in the CHAP01 folder of the Companion CD-ROM if you'd like to follow the next example on your system. Here's how to get the word out on the Model 2501 to as many prospective customers in your database as you can think of and still have time to hit the office's 9:00 AM doughnut trolley.

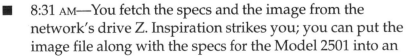

- 8:31 AM—You fetch the specs and the image from the network's drive Z. Inspiration strikes you; you can put the image file along with the specs for the Model 2501 into an

HTML document, attach the HTML document to e-mail to your customers, and they'll be able to see exactly what your company has to offer.

- You stand less than a 50-50 chance that scanned images will be in any of the formats that are accepted as embedded items in an HTML document, so you open the image in your copy of Paint Shop Pro (the shareware version is available on the Companion CD-ROM). Paint Shop Pro has input/ output conversion filters for no less than 17 different file types, so you can be fairly assured that most any type of image someone tosses you can be converted to a type acceptable for the Web.

CD-ROM

- 8:35 AM—Fortunately, the folks in engineering anticipated that you'd want to send copies of this image to clients and kept the file dimensions small—specifically, fewer than 250 pixels on a side. In general, you should keep the dimensions of an image file that you want to send as a stand-alone file or embed in an HTML document down to 30K or less. A GIF format image has 1/3 or less original file information than an original scanned color image (and approximately the same size as a grayscale image), so if a color TIF, Targa, or BMP image someone asks you to e-mail is under 100K, the color reduction and compression process a program performs to create a GIF format image puts the image within the ballpark for e-mailing.

In Paint Shop Pro, you must reduce the color depth of the image to make it ready to be saved in GIF format. Choose Colors, Decrease Color Depth, then choose 256 colors (8-bit) from the menu.

- Because color reduction necessarily eliminates original colors and image quality, the best method for retaining image content is Error Diffusion. In Figure 1-14, you can see that the Error Diffusion radio button has been clicked, and an Optimized color palette has also been chosen. An optimized color palette means that Paint Shop Pro will look for the 256 most frequently appearing colors in your original image, and average the rest of the colors to the best matches within the final 256 colors. The Standard option is generally not preferred with photographic images because this is a fixed palette of Windows system colors; any colors in your image that don't correspond to Windows standard color palette will be given the closest match, and this frequently leads to excessive patterning within the image. Click OK, and Paint Shop Pro makes a copy of your original image (WHATZIT.TIF, in this example).

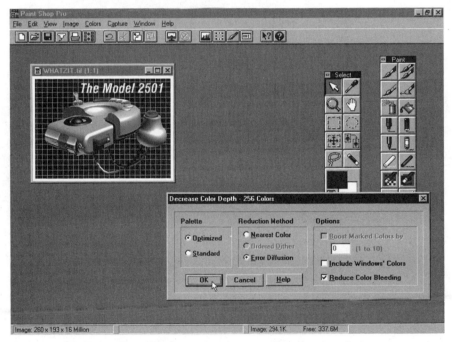

Figure 1-14: *Paint Shop Pro is an easy-to-use paint program that can convert most any type of bitmap graphics to GIF89a or JPEG format for embedding in a document.*

■ 8:36 AM—Choose File, Save and save the copy of the machinery image in the GIF 89a, interlaced format. In Figure 1-15, you can see the Save As dialog box. When you choose the GIF format, there are several sub-formats of the CompuServe standard for images. Make sure you choose Version 89a-Interlaced in Paint Shop Pro's File Sub-Format drop-down list. By doing this, images you put in an HTML document will begin to display immediately on the recipient's machine.

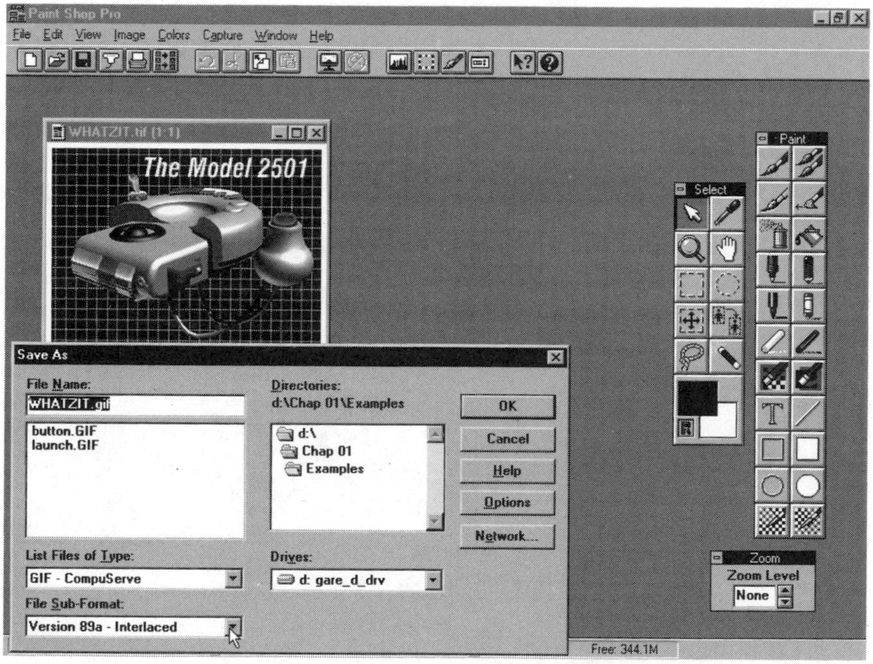

Figure 1-15: *GIF 89a format images will immediately begin to display onscreen; other formats for GIF images require that the entire file downloads before displaying.*

■ 8:40 AM—You've saved the image, closed Paint Shop Pro, and launched Navigator Gold. It's time to compose a spec sheet to e-mail to your clients. Choose File, New Document, Blank, type in a headline ("For Immediate Release" is a good starter), then highlight the headline, choose the +2 font size from the toolbar's drop-down list, and then click the Font color icon and choose a bright headline color from the Colors palette.

CD-ROM

■ If you're following the example here, and are a little stuck for text at this point, WHATZIT.TXT is in the CHAP01 folder on the Companion CD-ROM; open the file in a text editor, copy the contents to the clipboard, then paste the clipboard text into Navigator Gold's Editor. This procedure is also good in *non*-example situations, when you need to compose an HTML document with someone else's text. As a rule, it's usually good to compose your documents in a word processor or a text editor that includes a spell-checker. Alternatively, you can use a plug-in, such as CyberSpell, which will check your e-mail for spelling mistakes before you send it.

■ 8:42 AM—Save the document as M-2501.HTM to your hard disk in the same location as you saved the GIF image.

■ 8:45 AM—Give your audience an opportunity to immediately respond to your message with a return address link. To do this, type your e-mail address at the bottom of the document (ex: frank_popco@servername.com), highlight it, then press Ctrl+C to copy it to the clipboard. Then right-click the highlighted text, and choose Character Properties from the shortcut menu.

■ Click the Link tab in the Properties dialog box, insert your cursor in the *Link to a page location or local file* field, and press Ctrl+V. Place your cursor before your address and type: mailto:

See Figure 1-16. The mailto: scheme is a special type of URL that when accessed by a user, opens their browser's mail window. However, not all Internet users use mail-capable browsers like Navigator, so typing your address within the document gives these customers an easy way to copy your mailing address for a reply. See Chapter 6, "Person to Person With Navigator Mail & Netscape News," for details on Mail and different types of URL schemes you can use as links in Navigator Gold.

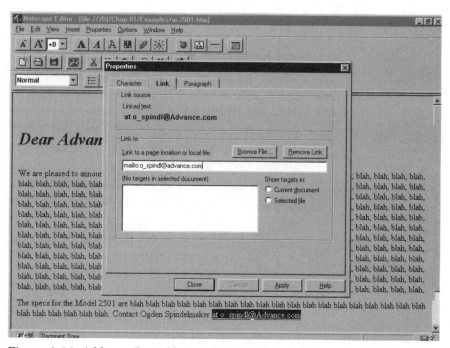

Figure 1-16: *Add a mailto: address to your HTML document to make responding to your message as easy as clicking!*

- 8:50 AM—Save the document again, click the View in browser button to return to Navigator, and open Netscape Mail (Window, Netscape Mail, or click the mail icon in the lower right of Navigator's browser window). Click the Mail To: button on the toolbar to start a new message and fire off a clean, professional cover letter for your sales information in the mail composition window.

  In Chapter 6, "Person to Person With Navigator Mail & Netscape News," you'll see how to create a signature file and what the components of such an automatic attachment to the bottom of a message should be. In this hypothetical example, it's probably a good idea to include your e-mail address—you can never mark your return address on messages too many times. Also, if you have continuing correspondence with customers, it can really speed up the task of distributing press releases by keeping addresses in Navigator's address book. Don't worry about the address book or the signature file right now, though. This is simply a walk-through intended to show you how efficiently you can automate rote procedures, to leave yourself more time for the personal aspects of your profession.

Alternatively, if you've covered the content of your sales message in the HTML document, you might choose to leave the message area in your e-mail blank. There's an advantage to doing this if you're sending more than one attachment; the shorter your message, the more space is left on a single screen of your recipient's mail browser to show the attachments as they come in.

- Fill in the Subject line in the Message Composition window. This line is one of the first that your recipient will read, so make the line an attention-getting one.

- Click the Attach button on the toolbar, then click the Attach File button. Doing this displays the Enter file to attach dialog box, which is a directory of your hard disk(s). Choose the GIF graphic first, then click Open. Mail attachments are sent in the order you specify, and in this example, we'll presume that you want the recipients to see the Model 2501 picture before the spec sheet.

- Click the Attach File button again, then choose the HTML document you saved last, and click Open. You'll notice that you have the option here of sending the attachment As Is, or you might want to choose Convert to Plain Text if you are certain that your customers don't use Navigator. In this example, let's presume that your customers do use Navigator; they'll see the attachment in their Mail window exactly as you composed it in Navigator Gold's Editor. You can add as many attachments to a message as you like; click OK when you've got your attachments queued up. See Figure 1-17.

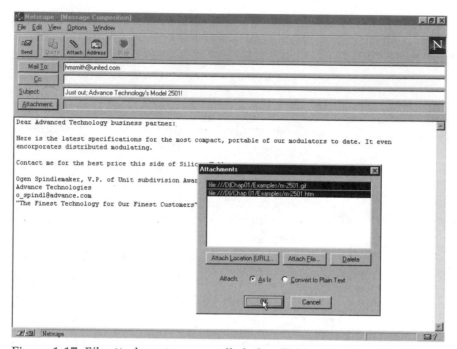

Figure 1-17: *File attachments can usually be handled by a number of mail reader programs, but recipients who use Navigator will see HTML documents and other Web elements within a message exactly as you've designed them.*

■ 8:55 AM—You click the Address button on the toolbar. Again, Navigator's address book is something you'll learn to populate and use later in this book, but if you already have a list of clients stored here, click the name of the primary recipient of this message, then click the To button (see Figure 1-18). Click other names that you want to send copies of the message to, then click either the Cc: button, or if you don't wish to advertise to your Mail To correspondent that they aren't alone in your campaign here, click the Bcc (Blank copy): button after choosing a name.

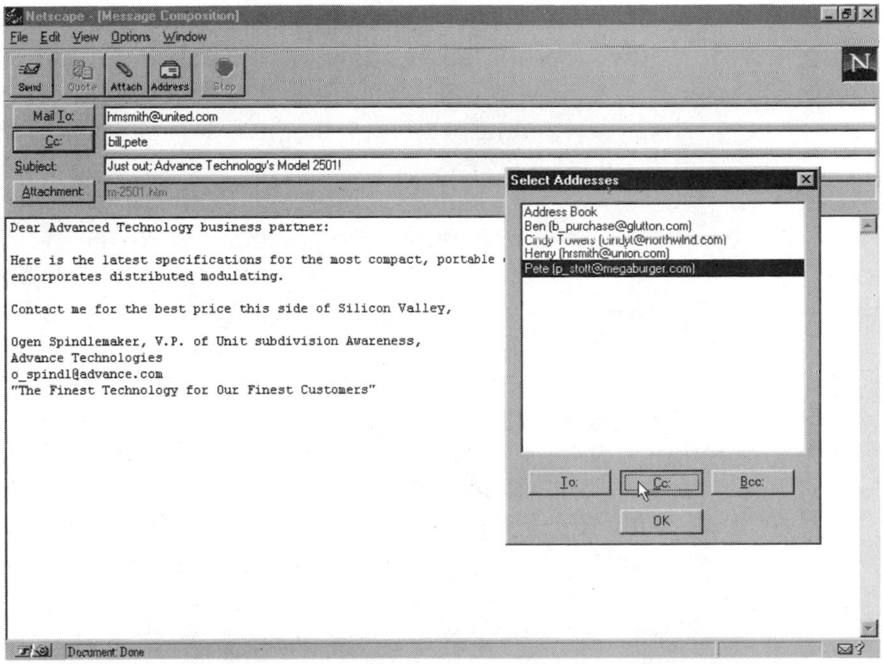

Figure 1-18: *Why send a separate message to every one of your clients? Conserve Internet bandwidth: create once, copy many times.*

■ 8:57 AM—Write a brief cover letter explaining the attached documents, then click Send. Again, the cover letter isn't mandatory—you can leave the message filed blank—but you cannot attach files without creating a message file to at least one recipient.

If you have a connectoid set up in Windows 95, Navigator will do the driving to your project's completion; all you need to do is login your name and password after Navigator displays Windows 95's Connect to dialog box. If you don't have Windows 95's integrated TCP/IP/Winsock/dialin connectoid set up, check out Chapter 2, "Installing & Customizing Navigator," on configuring your connection to your Internet provider. Many corporations provide direct dial-in connections to the Internet; connecting is basically the end of your involvement in spreading the word about the Model 2501 or your own product.

It's 9:00 AM now, and you can smell the coffee coming down the hallway. While most of the working world is pulling into the office, you've already solicited five, or five score of clients, all within a half hour's time. Although the product is fictitious in this example, the sales tool is a very real one, and the scenario suggested can be used to get through to a busy telephone number, get to a customer before the competition, and generally make the most of your computer. And all of this comes to you through an understanding of the power of connectivity and Navigator. In Figure 1-19, you can see the document created in the previous example as it displays on the recipient's monitor. All you've asked of the recipient is to click your name, and they can immediately respond to the message. Depending upon the price of the goods, and how your firm conducts secure transactions, you might be asked through return mail for a follow-up, voice-to-voice type call, or you might return from the doughnut trolley only to find half a dozen purchase requests.

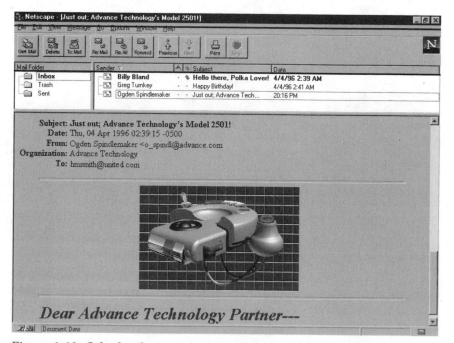

Figure 1-19: *Color brochures and catalogs take days to print, and days to deliver. Send an HTML document as an attachment to your e-mail and get ahead of the competition.*

TIP

The author once had a communications problem with a client who couldn't visualize a product design. Three years ago, the expedient way around this problem was to send a fax. To facilitate communications between your office and a client's today, you might consider recommending Navigator or Navigator Gold, or even buying a copy for your client, as a means to send, and continue sending, content-rich documents.

New to Navigator 3.0 are enhancements and built-in features that required plug-in support in previous versions. You can now play an embedded movie, engage in some pretty cool talk, and experience greater speed with extra Web security in this new version. The following section takes a look at new features you might want to become more familiar with if you're currently using version 2.0, or if you're completely new to Navigator 3.0.

Enhanced Media Support in Version 3.0

When the idea of a World Wide Web of inter-linked documents was first conceived, the possibility of sending graphics, and even text that had some sort of formatting, was thought of as a revolutionary and welcome idea. Flash forward by less than three years, and Netscape is busy making the Web a full-blown multimedia experience. Sound, movies, and interactive communications have been somewhat supported in previous versions of Navigator browser, but the evolution of Navigator has been toward self-support. You'll always find plug-ins to help decode a proprietary Web object such as an ASAP presentation or a handy graphics parser such as Figleaf's, but basic support for animation, sound, and interactivity is in place in version 3, and in this section we'll take a look at what you might be missing.

LiveAudio

Navigator's NAPlayer is gone from version 3; in its place is an inline player for HTML documents that have embedded sounds in any number of common file formats. When an embedded sound is clicked upon in a document, an unobtrusive set of LiveAudio player controls pop up. From this console, you can play, rewind, and adjust the volume of the audio clip.

Although LiveAudio can play AU (Sun native sounds), AIF (Macintosh), MIDI (Musical Instrument Digital Interface), and Windows WAV files without the user's need for a conversion utility, you must have a sound card installed on your system to experience Web documents that include sound. Many Windows users adopted the PC-Speaker for Windows software sound driver that became available with Windows 3.1x programs such as the Energizer Bunny screen saver, and IconHear It animated icons, but this software driver is not supported in Navigator. If you're going to get into the Web action, invest the $100 or so for a Creative Labs Sound Blaster compatible card for your machine.

WHY DOES MIDI SOUND SO MUCH BETTER?

Unlike WAV files, and other digital sound files you might encounter on the Web from Macintosh and UNIX machines, MIDI files are fundamentally different in structure from bitmap-type sound files. WAV, AIF, and AU digital sound files are created by *mapping* the frequencies of music across a timeline to *bits* of information saved in a file format. If it were not for the independent invention of digital sound on different operating platforms, bitmap sound files would probably be easily exchanged because they essentially store and play back sound information in identical fashions. A bitmap sound file such as a WAV file includes all the information about the playback: the types of instruments used, the tempo, and the frequency of each note are stored in much the same way that color information is stored in a bitmap image file such as a TIF image.

MIDI music, on the other hand, contains information about speed, frequency, and instruments used in composing music, but indicates what instrument should be used to playback a song, instead of carrying the musical instrument information within the saved MIDI format. An analogy can be made here: WAV sound files contain a recording of music, while MIDI files contain the *recipe* for playing back the music. It's sort of like comparing a performance to the sheet music used in the performance.

With Navigator 3.0, native support for assigning instruments to MIDI files is included, and you might actually find playback of MIDI files to be faster on your system than a WAV or AU sound file because information about playback is typically smaller—and can travel to your system faster—with the MIDI format.

In addition to its ease of use and capability to read different sound formats, LiveAudio is also designed to take advantage of streaming audio; you do not have to wait for an embedded sound file to completely download to your system to begin hearing the sound. In Figure 1-20, you can see a site that features many different sound clips. The music note graphics are linked to sound files on the server, and clicking the notes pops up the LiveAudio console. You can have more than one session of the LiveAudio player open at the same time, much the same way that you can have multiple sessions of Navigator Browser open. With multiple instances of LiveAudio open, it's easy to compare sound files. As you can also see in Figure 1-20, if the audio console looks a little cryptic, you can right-click the console to bring up Shortcut menu controls.

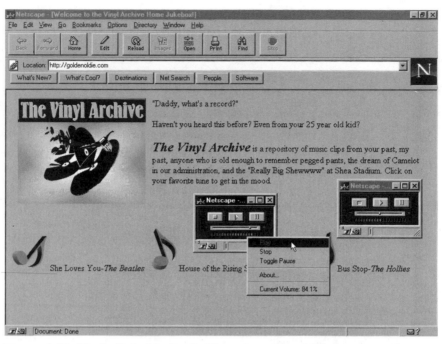

Figure 1-20: *The built-in LiveAudio Player in version 3.0 brings streaming, platform-independent sound to Web pages.*

CRUMMY SOUND? DON'T BLAME YOUR SOUND CARD!

Sound is a relatively new thing to the IBM-PC platform, and if you, by chance, should visit a site whose music sounds less than ideal, don't necessarily place the blame on your sound card or speakers. Sound, like digital images, has a bandwidth when it's saved to a file format. Basically, sounds on the Web can fall into different formats: CD quality, speech quality, and telephone quality, although you might hear other descriptions that all lead to a qualitative analysis of the sampling rate at which a digital sound was encoded. The best quality sound you'll hear on the Web was sampled at 44,000Hz, and it's possible that it's also a stereo recording. On the low end of the digital spectrum is 8,000Hz and below. Files recorded at a low sampling rate often sound tinny, as though they were played through a $15 transistor radio. Additionally, sounds might be digitized at a high sampling rate, but the recording engineer might have not understood the medium, or someone might be "experimenting" with digital sound samples.

In any event, most sound cards and supporting hardware today can play a symphonic recording with high fidelity, and if something sounds awry on the Web, it's probably the fault of the audio content—the recording—and not your audio subsystem.

LiveVideo: Streaming Animation Online

Improvements have been made to the video capabilities of Navigator in version 3.0 to include cross-platform compatibility and to allow digital movies to begin playing the moment they are accessed from a site. Unless you have a compelling reason to play stand-alone QuickTime movies from Apple's Player utility, you can now watch embedded Macintosh and Windows-based movie files from within Navigator's browser. The QuickTime plug-in is part of Navigator 3.0, and was installed when you installed Navigator. But there is a catch; for the QuickTime plug-in to work you must have QuickTime 2.1.1 for Windows or later installed on your computer. QuickTime 2.1.1 for Windows *does not* come with Navigator—you must download it from Apple Computer Corp. at http://quicktime.apple.com/qt/sw/sw.html.

The good news is that you'll most likely begin to see more and more sites using embedded video due to the support of the browser. In Figure 1-21, you can see an online theater which allows the visitor to play one or more of the "feature films" this week. In addition to entertainment possibilities, streaming video files will also open new opportunities to educators and corporate Intranet users; if you can't explain it in words, show a training film!

Figure 1-21: *The inline play of video means that you don't have to leave Navigator to play an AVI or QuickTime file, and there's no intrusive helper window spoiling the view.*

It should be noted here that Navigator's—and indeed much of the online community's—use of the term "video" generally describes a digital animation or a video clip saved to AVI or QuickTime format. Live video feeds will gain popularity on the Web as bandwidth and file compression problems are solved, but for the most part, a "movie" you can access on the Web has either been prepared from videotape as a Video for Windows or QuickTime file, or it's a digital animation creation. VDONet—the firm who licenses VDOLive server and browser software—uses a different file format and a different technology for the display of video content, and this medium does not ever reside on the visitor's hard disk: only a live connection to a VDOLive server will bring such a broadcast to you. The VDOLive plug-in for Navigator is available on the Netscape Power Pack 2.0 or can be downloaded from VDOnet's site at http://www.vdolive.com/.

Similarly, video conferencing is not accomplished using Navigator's new LiveVideo capability. Video conferencing requires massive hardware support, a bandwidth that makes a POTS (plain old telephone system) line look like a human hair in diameter, and special software on both party's systems. However, interactive online communications is alive and well on a more modest scale in the form of CoolTalk, a new feature we'll get to in the next section.

CoolTalk: Meta-Conferencing for Two

CoolTalk is a new technology acquired by Netscape Communications and included with Navigator 3.0 that takes advantage of the cheap, multimedia-orientation of the World Wide Web on a more personal, one-to-one basis. There are essentially three "modes" of CoolTalk:

- The Audio conferencing mode, which offers full duplex, telephone-like conversation. Audio conferencing requires that both parties have a sound card and microphone working on their systems.

- The whiteboard mode, an electronic version of a sketch-pad but which requires no special hardware.

- The chat mode, which can be run simultaneously with the whiteboard mode of communications. In chat mode you can send text-based messages or text files to the person you're talking to.

Although Chapter 10, "CoolTalk," gets into detailed discussions on how to install CoolTalk and operate in the different modes, this chapter is about "possibilities," and this section gets into a little of what CoolTalk is good *for*, besides being an exciting new enabling technology.

"Reaching Out" for Less

CoolTalk's Audio Conferencing capability will surely be of the most appeal to users who have family overseas. The long distance rate for overseas calls depends upon local telephone company structures, but CoolTalk Audio Conferencing's charge is the same as the charge for accessing the Internet. The disadvantage to CoolTalk is that Internet Service Providers in Europe and other countries might charge an hourly fee for access time, so even though your CoolTalk "call" might amount to a pittance, the other party might incur a fee similar to that of an overseas call.

Because CoolTalk is a one-to-one scenario, you must plan in advance, and stick to a mutual agreement between both callers as to the time you will meet on the Net. You're essentially spawning a connection where you, or the other party, become a unique "point" on the Internet; this point disappears after both of you have closed the connection. CoolTalk's Audio conferencing is full-duplex—you and the other party can speak at the same time—and this mode of communication dynamically scales according to the speed of the connection and the quality of the lines. This means that if the other party has a slower connection, *your* connection will not suffer in audio quality. Netscape uses multiple compression formats in CoolTalk communication to ensure the best possible sound for each user.

Like a conventional telephone, Netscape's implementation of CoolTalk allows for the screening of calls, a mute button, and a speed dialer with which you can open a connection to frequently accessed parties. Additionally, Netscape has created a Web-based telephone book, where you can look up other users of CoolTalk. And if you're in an office environment where connections are constantly maintained to the Internet (or if you own a dedicated line that's always open), you can use CoolTalk's "telephone answering machine" feature to pick up calls while you're away. Do *not* mistake this feature as a replacement for your trusty audiocassette-driven telephone answering machine—you still need a way to answer calls placed through Ma Bell—but many of CoolTalk's capabilities do indeed spell an attractive alternative to the type of communications that require a handset pressed against your ear.

Sharing a Whiteboard Across Town

The electronic version of a traditional whiteboard—that Formica-based thing you can erase felt pen strokes from with a sponge—is perhaps one of the most intriguing things in CoolTalk. Netscape CoolTalk and its whiteboard capability only ships with version 3.0 or later of Navigator and Navigator Gold. If you downloaded the minimum install copy of Navigator or Navigator Gold from

Netscape's site, you didn't get CoolTalk or Live 3D. These are important, integral parts of Navigator. CoolTalk and Live 3D can be downloaded as separate files from http://home.netscape.com/comprod/mirror/navcomponents_download.html.

Recently, I was asked to explain a PageMaker layout over the telephone to the publisher of a user group newsletter. Try as I might—even resorting to making gestures the publisher obviously couldn't see—it was a futile attempt to convey a graphical idea across a medium designed to carry sound. If, on the other hand, the publisher and I had agreed upon a time for a CoolTalk whiteboard conference, I'd have been able to draw—on my publisher's monitor—exactly where the second color dropped out of the masthead, and where the Styles palette is located in PageMaker. In Figure 1-22, you can see the whiteboard interface; the tools look more or less like a paint program's, and the Capture utility allows the user to take a snapshot of anything on your monitor: applications, Windows 95's desktop, or a design you're working on in a graphics application.

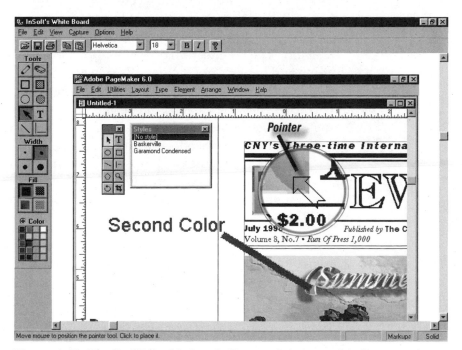

Figure 1-22: *The CoolTalk whiteboard allows real-time, graphical communications between Navigator users.*

Text can be marked on a captured image in whiteboard; callouts can be indicated, and a floating, oversized cursor can be moved in real time to indicate different areas of the screen. Tools can be better explained to other users without the necessity of faxes or a car trip (imagine trying to teach a technique to someone halfway across the world), and annotating map directions is a breeze. Additionally, users can exchange annotating roles—if your "student" has a different opinion of something, you can allow him or her to control the session for a while and make whiteboard notes that appear on *your* monitor.

The whiteboard idea will probably find its best use among educators, consultants, and corporations that have remote offices, but it's also simply fun to use. Large board rooms could easily be outfitted with video cards and monitor-to-video converters to make whiteboard endeavors display on multiple screens or large projection television sets. The whiteboard is the closest, most economical representation of the two-way television—a dream of science-fiction authors for more than half a century.

As you'll see in other chapters in this book, what Navigator doesn't have in native support, it more than makes up for in its *extensibility*. The architecture of Navigator was designed around plug-ins and helper applications. (See Chapter 9, "Taking a Look at Plug-ins.") The benefit of this unique design is two-fold: you'll be able to access new types of media designed for the Web through Navigator plug-ins, and you can also work with existing applications to create content for documents using present technology. The following section provides a glimpse at a communications solution for users who are more comfortable with word processors than online communications and HTML composition. Want to become a part of the action? "PDF" your thoughts!

ADOBE ACROBAT TECHNOLOGY & NAVIGATOR

At the time of this writing, Adobe Systems had released a late public beta version of a new plug-in for Navigator, code name "Acrobat 3.0." For those familiar with Acrobat Reader, this is the next generation of the stand-alone utility; Reader version 3 for Windows will soon be both an offline browser of Acrobat documents and a plug-in for Navigator. What Acrobat 3.0 does is allow Internet users to read a document online with exactly the same appearance it had when created. HTML documents have certain limitations of text formatting and graphics capabilities at present, but an Acrobat document—although usually larger than an equivalent HTML file—offers *document fidelity* right down to your selection of fonts, and formatting is as easy to establish and retain as any document you'd create in a word processor. Acrobat Portable Document Format (PDF)'s ease of composition is due to the fact that you can compose an Acrobat document in almost any program you like. Part of the Acrobat publishing system is a driver, similar to a print or video driver, but the PDF driver creates a unique document from an existing one that's a combination of video and printing technology.

A prerequisite to the successful previewing and reception of an Acrobat document is to have a copy of the Acrobat 3.0 Reader plug-in installed. It can be downloaded from Adobe's site (http://www.adobe.com). This plug-in's install program automatically detects a copy of Navigator on the user's system, and makes the correct MIME type and file extension entries to call the plug-in whenever an Acrobat document is encountered on the Web.

To use the PDF driver to create Acrobat documents, all you need to do is get Acrobat Pro; it's a modest investment on par with most of today's applications, but it also liberates your creative instincts to compose Web-ready content in any number of applications. After Acrobat Pro installs, you'll find two new drivers in your Printers folder: the PDF Writer, which automatically converts documents sent to it to PDF format, and the Acrobat Distiller driver, which offers greater compression options than the PDF Writer, but is generally used to make PDF files from PostScript documents.

CorelDRAW!, Microsoft Word, PageMaker, and other graphically oriented files are as easy to port to Acrobat format as choosing File, Print. Here's how this technology can be used to make documents that can be viewed as you created them, onscreen in Navigator:

1. Open a text or graphics-based application, and create your document. In Figure 1-23, you can see a fictitious sales sheet for a pottery company being created in WinWord. Unlike the HTML format for documents, an Acrobat document can contain vector artwork, TIF, Targa, or BMP bitmap graphics, and other imported file types. If you can get a graphic into a word processor, the Acrobat publishing system can make the document Web-ready.

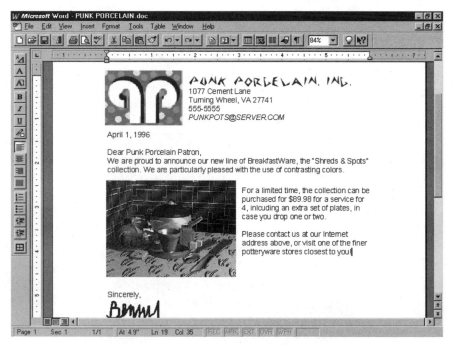

Figure 1-23: Create a document you want to send as an attachment to Netscape Mail, or embed in an HTML document, in your favorite application. If you can print to file from this application, the document can become an Acrobat document.

2. Choose File, Print, then choose the Acrobat PDFWriter from the list of Printers offered in your application.

3. Choose Options for the PDFWriter device driver. In the Options dialog box, you may choose to embed the fonts used in your document, the page size as it will appear onscreen as an Acrobat document, and the type of compression used for any graphics you might have added to the document. The decision to embed fonts ensures that the viewer of this document will see the same fonts as those you used, but take care not to use too many different fonts in your document—the more fonts used, the larger the saved Acrobat document.

4. Click the Print button in your application's Print dialog box; specify where you want the document to be written to on your hard disk, and you're done.

The additional perk to creating Acrobat documents is that Acrobat documents can be viewed across different operating platforms. Windows users, Macintosh users, and OS/2 users can view your document, as you created it, by simply adding the appropriate Amber plug-in to their collection of installed Navigator plug-ins. UNIX users can view your PDF documents by using Acrobat Reader as a helper application. All users can view PDF based files offline with the Amber plug-in or the Acrobat Reader utility, so you can also offer a PDF document for downloading instead of online display. Figure 1-24 shows the document you saw created in Figure 1-23, but it's being viewed in Navigator, courtesy of the Acrobat plug-in.

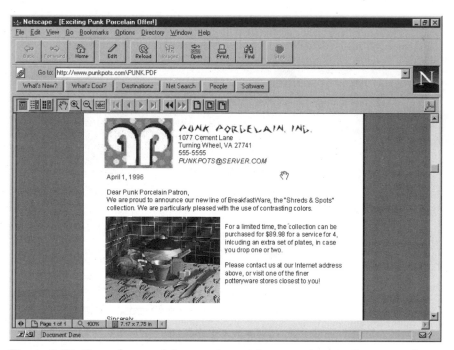

Figure 1-24: *Ease of use and document consistency are two good reasons why you might decide to publish for the Web in Acrobat format.*

Ease of use is the reason why we've singled out Acrobat in this chapter as a format you might want to try as a part of your interactive communications scheme with Navigator. We might similarly point to Macromedia's Extreme 3D for the creation of a VRML virtual world (*.WRL) Web object, or to desktop audio studios such as GoldWave, or even to VDOLive for the authoring of digital video for the Web. If you want to be a participant on the Internet, your route to travel can branch into as many different areas of expression as the applications you're familiar with; this chapter has touched upon but a few. However, if your purpose for purchasing Navigator was to make the Internet your most complete personal resource for business or leisure, this is what the chapters to follow will help you configure, customize, discover, and refine.

Moving On

In order to make the "possibilities" discussed in this chapter into "realities," you'll want to work from the outside of your system inward to make Navigator work at its best for you. In Chapter 2, "Installing & Customizing Navigator," we'll take you through the process of finding the right Internet Service Provider, deciding upon the best connection to the Internet for your needs, and installing and configuring Navigator so that everything you find worthwhile on the Net is within easy reach. Now that we've examined the appearance and possibilities of your new toolkit, it's time to open the lid and tune it.

2

Installing & Customizing Navigator

Unless you work in one solitary application such as a spread-sheet program, you've probably noticed by now that the quality of a program's performance depends on how well the system *outside* the program is optimized. This is particularly true of Navigator because Navigator's power comes to you through the right connections, plug-ins, helper applications, and the optimization of your PC's operating system.

An optimized copy of Navigator depends upon more connections than you might realize. Do you have all the plug-ins you need, so that every enhanced site on the Web appears as the creator intended it to be viewed? Is your appreciation of a Web site dampened slightly because your modem or Internet Service Provider (ISP) connection is too slow?

This chapter provides the information on the "big picture" of connecting to the world. You'll learn how to:

- Choose a competent and inexpensive ISP.

- Achieve independence from an MIS department or ISP when you need to troubleshoot an installation or other communications problem.

- Install and configure the system software you need in order to connect to the Internet.

- Define personal preferences in Navigator.
- Define the right Multipurpose Internet Mail Extensions (MIME) types for plug-ins and helper applications.

In short, this chapter works from the outside of the system inward, to get Navigator up and working according to the way *you* work.

The Internet Service Provider: The Human Part of Your Internet Connection

Before we discuss the hardware and software requirements, configurations, workarounds, and procedures for smooth Internet sailing, the first connection you need to make is a flesh-and-blood one: Unless you *are* an ISP, you'll need the services of one.

Not very long ago, finding a competent and affordable provider was difficult; many areas either had no local access to providers, or the service that *was* available was limited in scope or was costly. Today, unless you live in a very rural or remote part of the country, the hard part isn't finding an ISP, but is instead choosing one. Not only have a plethora of small, local ISPs sprung into business, but it seems that every national and international company even remotely related to communications have rushed into the arena and are *begging* to be your ISP!

Now is a good time to evaluate what you need and want from an ISP and see if your current ISP measures up to your expectations and to the competition. If they do, great—you need look no further. But if your present ISP doesn't meet the criteria listed in this section, you may want to look for another provider.

ISPs are professionals who have invested time and hardware and have made the negotiations to become a physical part of the Internet—to which you link whenever you need to get to a file, a service, your mail, or a newsgroup. You establish your presence on the Net through the dial-up connection (discussed in this chapter) to your ISP's servers. Like your choice of an accountant, an auto mechanic, or other specialist, an ISP should be chosen based on how well the two of you can work together for the long term. It's a pain to re-establish your presence on the Internet if you decide after a few weeks that you don't care for your ISP—or they don't care for you.

Of the many services an ISP can support, the most basic are speedy connections and a wide selection of services. The following is a list of not-so-obvious qualities you might want to look for in a long-term relationship with an ISP:

Flat Rates: If you connect to the Internet with a 14.4 or 28.8 baud modem, there is absolutely *no reason* why you should pay for connect time on an hourly basis. There are many providers who offer unlimited, full-service, 24-hours-a-day, seven-days-a-week, for a flat rate that is currently running from about $20 to $30 a month. If you have or will be getting ISDN (Integrated Services Digital Networks) telephone service, look for an ISP that offers ISDN dial-in connections at a reasonable rate. Most ISPs who currently offer ISDN dial-in service charge by the hour. But as ISDN telephone service becomes more affordable for both you and the ISP, expect to see more ISPs moving to flat-rate service.

Local access: Unless you are in an extremely remote part of the country, you should be able to find an Internet provider who offers local, toll-free numbers for both technical support and for making 14.4K or 28.8K dial-in connections. If you travel a lot or if you expect to move your physical address any time in the foreseeable future, you'll want to find a service provider that has local access numbers ("points of presence") in many different cities and perhaps even different countries.

If you have ISDN telephone service, the phone company usually bills you based on the amount of time you use the connection. When your ISDN service is billed according to the amount of time you use the connection, even a local, non-toll call to your provider's access number will incur a charge. Some phone companies, however, have a rate structure that permits you to use your ISDN connection without incurring time-based billing charges *if* both you and your ISP are served by the same telephone company central office. If this is the case, finding an ISP who uses the same central office that you do becomes an important consideration.

Full Internet Services: The Internet provider you choose should offer *full* Internet service, which should be accessed though a PPP (*Point-to-Point Protocol*) connection. PPP is easier to configure and is a more modern, reliable, and capable connection method than SLIP

Serial Line Internet Protocol (SLIP). A SLIP connection can handle e-mail and is useful for browsing Web pages that don't contain many high-bandwidth multimedia features. A PPP-based connection will enable you to take advantage of Internet conferencing, direct video such as C-Me C-U, and other content that can tax the bandwidth of a connection. You should not have to pay extra for an e-mail account or for access to a wide variety of newsgroups. You should also have full access to the WWW, FTP, Gopher, IRC, Telnet, and Mud Internet services.

Sign-on assistance and kit: At the very least, an ISP should provide complete configuration information and dial-in scripts for their service. See the information in the section "Connection Checklist" later in the chapter for the sign-on information that should be provided.

Software independence: Make sure that the provider allows you to use any Internet browser, mail reader, news reader, or other Internet software you want. Don't accept being locked into using proprietary software. As a customer, you're paying for unrestricted access and should not be locked into using tools that don't meet your needs. Ask about using Navigator 3.0 as a browser before you sign the agreement. If the ISP thinks you're talking about *Norton* Navigator, keep shopping.

General technical support: Any service provider you choose should offer easily accessible technical support. You should be able to reach a human being on the phone at least during normal business hours. Technical support by e-mail should be available and answered within one day.

A low user-to-dial-in-connection ratio: All of the above doesn't mean a thing if you frequently get a busy signal when you try to dial in. Twenty to thirty users to each incoming phone line is recommended; but sometimes even the largest of ISPs can't maintain this ratio because their subscription base is growing faster than they can install extra lines and equipment.

Financial and technical know-how to stay in business and expand: This one is tough to gauge. Local ISPs don't have the deep pockets that large corporations have, but they *do* have a personal investment in the success of their business that large companies typically don't demonstrate. Local ISPs also often have the drive and the desire to provide personal attention to their customers. On the other hand, large corporations can afford to run "loss-leader specials": you subscribe for a very attractive, almost unrealistic price, and the company makes its money from subscriptions by the volume of traffic. This practice is straight out of Economics 101. Internet services are exactly like any other consumer commodity today. However, many large companies have also entered the field of online services, only to close up shop abruptly. Discontinuing Internet services can affect a large firm's quarterly earnings, but it's usually not a big deal in the scheme of corporate affairs. However, discontinued service *would* be a big deal to you if *your* provider leaves the market!

You'll have to go with your instincts on this one: Should you buy from the corner store where you know the people, or from the big chain store?

Home page services: Does your future ISP allocate space on its servers for your personal home page at no extra charge? Some do and some don't. If you want to set up a home page for your business, how much would it cost? If they do provide home page services, are home pages on separate servers and are connections separate to the Internet from those that handle customer Internet-bound traffic? Ideally, home pages and commercial sites that attract a lot of traffic should be on systems separate from those that carry subscriber connections. Just as you are limited by the amount of information that your connection to your provider can carry, your provider is limited in the amount of in- and outbound traffic its connections to the Internet can handle. You don't want your connection to be slow because of incoming traffic, nor would you want your home page to be difficult to reach because of outbound traffic.

TIP

When looking for a provider, check out the Totally Hot Bookmarks list on the Companion CD-ROM. It contains links to comprehensive directories of national, regional, and local Internet providers.

Also look in your newspaper (printed or online) for news announcements from phone companies, cable companies, and other large organizations. Many national and regional telephone companies—such as AT&T, MCI, and Bell Atlantic—as well as the major online services' Internet divisions, have recently joined a densely populated field of Internet providers who offer flat-rate service. More are sure to follow.

System Requirements for Navigator

Connecting to the Internet and running Netscape Navigator requires a combination of the right hardware and software. At a bare minimum, you need:

- an Intel 386sx or better computer

- 4MB of RAM

- Windows 3.1, Windows 3.11, or Windows for Workgroups 3.11

- a 14.4K modem

- a standard telephone line

You'll be happier and much more productive, however, if you use an Intel 486 or better, at least 8MB of RAM, and a 28.8K modem.

These are the bare-bones specifications for Navigator 3, but with Windows 95 and today's applications, you *always* seem to need more RAM than you currently own, and you also need at least a high-end 486 and a 28.8K modem to quickly process Internet media through Navigator. This is especially true if you expect to take advantage of the growing multimedia components of the Web and the growing numbers of plug-ins and helper applications—each of which has its own additional hardware requirements. Ideally, you should have a Pentium-based PC with 32MB or more of RAM, Windows 95 or Windows NT, and a 28.8K modem.

But even with a Pentium processor, if your system lacks sufficient RAM, a bottleneck develops resulting in a lot of disk churning, slow performance, and sometimes a system crash. One can never have too much RAM.

Navigator Gold has higher base hardware requirements than does Netscape Navigator. You must have a 486 with at least 6MB of RAM, and 8MB is recommended. Again, the more RAM you have the better, especially if you're using Navigator Gold.

PLANNING AHEAD: HARD DISK STORAGE NEEDS

The Navigator program files in and of themselves don't take up much hard disk space—2MB for the 16-bit Windows 3.x version and 4.5MB for the 32-bit Windows 95/NT version. But when you consider the amount of space taken by the cache, the temp folder, plug-ins, helper applications, accumulated e-mail, and the files you download, you soon discover you'll need a hard disk beginning at a gigabyte to accommodate the needs of Navigator and the other applications you want to use. Before you install Navigator, you should think about how you will use Navigator. Will you subscribe to lots of mailing lists and keep the messages? Will you download lots of shareware, freeware, and demo files? When you visit multimedia sites, will you want to download lots of movie and sound clips? How much space will you need for these pursuits? Setting aside 100 to 150MB is not unreasonable. Do you remember how quickly Windows 3.x or Windows 95 directories filled up your drive space? Consider the following *very* conservative estimates of hard disk usage:

- Navigator 16-bit version needs: 2MB

- Navigator 32-bit version needs: 4.6MB

- Empty disk space for the temp folder needs: 20MB
  (This is used by Navigator, Navigator plug-ins, and all of your other Windows applications.)

- Your Netscape cache needs: 5MB

- A dozen or more plug-ins need: 50MB

- Most plug-ins require at least 2MB apiece with some using 4 or 5MB. The Netscape electronic edition of the Netscape PowerPack 2.0 [Netscape SmartMarks 2.0, Netscape Chat 2.0, Internet AntiVirus protection from Norton, Inso's CyberSpell] requires over 13MB of hard disk space. You surely will accumulate many more than this, especially after you've taken a look at Chapters 9, "Taking a Look at Plug-ins," and 10, "CoolTalk," and all the wonderful stuff on the Companion CD-ROM.

- A very modest amount of accumulated e-mail needs: 3MB
  (If you've subscribed to a single high-volume mailing list,
  a week's worth [400] of text-only messages adds up to
  1.25MB.)

- Program files you download to uncompress need: 20MB
  These require space for the compressed file, the uncompressed file, and then the installed version of the program.
  Software authors are turning out revisions of their programs
  very quickly these days, so it's easy to accumulate a lot of
  files—some of which are redundant because they will replace older versions in a very short time.

So you see, conservatively, we've already filled *102.6MB* of hard
disk space, and that's only if you promptly delete the file archives
after you install the programs. Moreover, these figures don't take
into account files that are added to the Window's System folder. If
you have more than one hard disk in your computer, you can split
the load between the drives by paying careful attention to where
plug-ins install their support files, where you locate your cache,
mail, and temp space folders, and where files go when you download them. It will be much easier to keep track of what you have,
however, if you install all your Navigator-related programs on one
drive.

If you're already tight on hard drive space, consider purchasing
a new or additional hard drive. The cost of large hard disks has
dropped dramatically (currently a 1.6-gb drive is around $250), and
removable media drives like Iomega's Zip have also become very
affordable and common. *Don't,* however, use removable media for
installed programs, mail storage, temp drive space, and the like;
removable media does not play as fast as a hard disk, and programs occasionally won't run from media that you can take off
your system. (Windows 95's Registry and Windows 3.1's WIN.INI
are a little fussy about relative application paths). Instead, use removable media to store HTML pages you've saved and the archive
files for the software and other files you download.

Defragmenting Your Hard Disk

Once you've determined how much space you will need for Navigator and its many plug-ins and made that space available, you should defragment your hard disk(s). When files are written to hard disk they are not always written in one continuous piece. The system software is designed to start writing a file in the first piece of open space it finds. If that amount of space turns out not to be large enough, it writes the rest of the file in the next bit of free space it finds, and so on. If you save lots of files and delete lots of files, the disk becomes fragmented. A map of the disk showing occupied and unoccupied space would look a bit like a slice of Swiss cheese—some data, a "hole" where a file has been deleted, and then more data. When a drive is fragmented it takes longer to access files because the pieces that make up the file are in different places on the disk.

Defragmenting takes each file and moves it to a place on your hard disk where there is room to write the entire file in one piece. You should also set the defragmentation program to defragment empty space on the disk. By defragmenting the empty space on the disk, all of the empty space is consolidated into one area. This means that when you install Navigator or save files to disk, it is much more likely that they will be written to consecutive sectors.

Windows 3.1 users can use DOS's defrag.exe to defragment their disk. Windows 95 users can the Windows 95 defragmenting tool found by opening the Properties window for the disk, clicking the Tools tab, and then clicking the Defragment Now button. To make sure your defragmentation tool is set to defragment both files and empty space, click the Advanced button in the Advanced Defragmenter window and then choose Full defragmentation (both files and free space).

This process can take anywhere from a few minutes to a few hours depending on the size of the disk, how much free space is available, and how fragmented the drive is. Defragmenting is a job that is usually best for times when you don't need to use your computer, such as during lunch or after hours.

ISDN vs. POTS Lines

The other bottleneck you face in speedy access to the Internet is the kind of telephone connection you have between your computer and that of your ISP. The most common kind of connection used to connect a modem is a standard telephone line, or POTS (Plain Old Telephone Service). A new, high-speed, digital-based service telephone service called ISDN (Integrated Services Digital Networks) is becoming more widely available and more affordable. A connection to the Internet using an ISDN digital phone line and the special ISDN connection device that replaces your modem is four times faster than a 28.8K modem running across a POTS line, and it's ten times faster than a 14.4K modem on a POTS line.

To get ISDN service installed is not easy, foolproof, or without cost. Many local telephone companies have convoluted and time-consuming processes you must wade through to get the service ordered, installed, and working. The service is not available in all areas, and you usually have to be within three miles of the central office that services your phone line. All the phone company provides is the line; it's then up to you to ensure that the ISDN interface device you buy to connect your computer to the line is compatible with your telephone company switching center's ISDN equipment. How much you'll pay for ISDN service depends on your phone company. Rates vary from truly affordable to obscenely expensive.

Before you order an ISDN connection, you also have to consider who you will be "calling" with it. An ISDN line is not a connection to the Internet by itself; you will still need to dial into an ISP. If you plan to use the line to connect to your organization's Intranet from a remote location, the Intranet must be set up to handle dial-in ISDN connections. In either case, who you dial-in to must also have ISDN service from their phone company, or you won't be able to make the connection.

If it sounds like establishing ISDN service is more hassle than it's worth, that's because it *is* a hassle—but for many it is a worthwhile bother. ISDN connections are so much faster than a 28.8K modem connection on a POTS line that the Web won't seem like the same place. Graphically intense pages pop onscreen, and large files transfer in the blink of an eye. If you telecommute by dialing into your organization's Intranet, it will seem like you are at work using the LAN and not sitting home in your den. If the Internet or Intranet is important to your work, or if your time is the one commodity you never have enough of, definitely consider having an ISDN line installed. But before you call your phone company or buy any ISDN-capable equipment, do some research, subscribe to the *comp.dcom.isdn* newsgroup, and visit the many ISDN sites listed in the Totally Hot Bookmarks list on the Companion CD-ROM. You'll be glad you did.

In this book, we assume that you're using a standard phone line and a standard modem because that is currently what most Internet users have and because the issues involved in acquiring and installing ISDN equipment and service vary so widely from place to place.

CONNECTIVITY SOFTWARE

To make your computer ready to connect to the Internet, you need special system software. The purpose of this software is to translate the data generated by your Windows-based applications into the universally understood data format of the Internet, and vice versa. All different kinds of computers connect to and comprise the Internet; therefore, to successfully communicate, a universally agreed way to package, track, and transport non-platform-specific data was established. The TCP/IP (*Transmission Control Protocol/ Internet Protocol*) protocol is the communications standard that the Internet community has agreed to use to accomplish this goal.

TCP/IP

TCP/IP is actually two sets of rules/software that describe how the data from all of these different kinds of computers should be handled. This team of protocols works together somewhat like a real-world shipping department and a courier service. The TCP part of the protocol (the "shipping" department) takes the data stream from your computer and breaks it down into manageable, easily identifiable, and traceable *packets* of data. The packets of data are then handed over to the IP part of the protocol (the "courier" service). The IP protocol software takes the packets from TCP, finds out where they're going, repackages the packets into its own IP format, and delivers each packet to its intended destination. At the destination computer, the TCP part of its TCP/IP software receives the packets from IP, checks to see if all of the packets have arrived, and checks to see that none were damaged. TCP then takes all of the packets and reassembles them into their original data stream format. If it finds that any packets are missing or damaged, the destination TCP software sends a request back through the Internet to your computer's TCP software and requests that the missing or damaged packets be sent again.

On Windows-based computers, the TCP/IP software requires a companion piece of software: the *Winsock*. The Winsock software acts as an application-friendly intermediary (*front end*) between the application and the fairly complex TCP/IP software. Windows Internet applications "talk" to the Winsock software, and the Winsock in turn takes what it "hears" (the data) and sends it to the TCP/IP protocol software.

If you connect to the Internet via your organization's network or TCP/IP-based Intranet, all you need is a Winsock, the TCP/IP software, and the proper network drivers for your LAN. However, if you use a modem to connect to your Internet provider, or if you are dialing into your organization's Intranet as a remote user, you need special dial-in software—PPP or SLIP software—instead of network drivers.

PPP & SLIP

Once the information from your application has been processed by the Winsock and its companion TCP/IP software, it is ready to travel on a TCP/IP network. But if your Internet access is via a dial-in account to a TCP/IP network, then you need additional software to bridge the non-TCP/IP-governed portion of the journey when your data is carried by the phone line. PPP or SLIP software does the job. Either one controls and monitors the modem connection, repackages the TCP/IP information into a suitable format for transport over a phone line without damaging it, and generally supervises this leg of the transmission to and from your modem. When the information from your computer reaches the other end of the modem connection, the other computer's PPP or SLIP software restores the data into the packets of information that the TCP/IP protocol uses, then sends it out to the Internet. When information comes *to* you, the reverse of all of these steps happens. Which protocol you use—PPP or SLIP—depends on what the receiving computer uses. When you sign on with an ISP, they will tell you which kind of service they provide. Likewise, if you are connecting to your organization's Intranet, your network administrator will advise you as to whether you should use PPP or SLIP. If you have a choice, choose the PPP protocol. PPP is a newer, more robust, and more flexible protocol and is more adept at handling existing and emerging Internet services and content.

WHERE DO YOU GET THIS INTERNET SOFTWARE?

Windows 3.1, Windows 3.11, and Windows for Workgroups 3.11 did not ship with any TCP/IP, PPP, SLIP, or Winsock software, but many ISPs include connectivity software in their sign-on packages. If your ISP didn't provide it (and this is a bad sign), your best bet is to get the 16-bit version of Trumpet Winsock by Trumpet Software. Trumpet Winsock is probably the most widely used and reliable software for Windows 3.1x users, and it contains all the components you need—Winsock, TCP/IP, SLIP, PPP, and a dialing program that logs you on to your ISP's computer—all in one package. Trumpet is a shareware program that you can find on most BBSes, on all the major online services, and of course on the Internet. We'll walk you through the installation of this great piece of software in the"Windows 3.1x Connectivity Installation" section later in the chapter.

Unlike previous versions of Windows, Windows 95 ships with a 32-bit Winsock, TCP/IP, SLIP, and PPP software. We recommend that you use the Windows 95 provided software, rather than a third-party solution. The Windows 95 supplied software is what all the software developers test against first, which tends to make it the most widely supported connectivity software. Netscape Navigator has been tested on a wide variety of 32-bit Winsocks and will work with them; but unless you have a compelling reason that leads you elsewhere, it's best to stick with the software provided by Windows 95 itself. Besides, you already own it!

The CD version of Windows 95 comes with a dialing/login utility. If you bought Windows 95 on floppy disk, or if you just find the Windows 95 dialing/login utility hard to use, you can use a wonderful freeware utility called RoboDun that makes automating your login a breeze. Later in this chapter, in the section "Windows 95 Setup," you'll see how to install and configure Windows 95's native connectivity software, RoboDun, and how to automate it all by tapping into the Windows 95-supported AutoDial feature.

WHICH NAVIGATOR TO CHOOSE— 16- OR 32-BIT SOFTWARE

Once you get your connection running, you need to have something to access the Internet *with*—either Netscape Navigator or Netscape Navigator Gold. If your operating system is Windows 3.1, 3.11, or Windows for Workgroups 3.11, you *must* use the 16-bit version of Navigator or Navigator Gold—even if you haveWin32s installed on your computer. Win32s is a collection of system files that enables true 32-bit programs such as Adobe Photoshop to run under the 16-bit, Windows 3.1x operating system. The 32-bit version of Navigator demands a true 32-bit operating system and won't function in the "emulated" 32-bit environment that Win32s provides. Navigator, the 16-bit version, doesn't require that Win32s software be installed on your computer, but if it *is* installed, Win32s needs to be version 1.20 or later. Versions of Win32s prior to version 1.20 replaced some 16-bit system components with ones that are incompatible with the 16-bit version of Navigator. Win32s, version 1.20 or later, can be obtained from Microsoft's CompuServe forum (Go MSL), Microsoft Download Service BBS (206-936-6735), or at ftp://ftp.microsoft.com/softlib/mslfiles/PW1118.EXE. In all cases, the file you need is pw1118.exe.

Windows 95 users can use either the 16- or the 32-bit version of Navigator. We recommend that you use the 32-bit version because it has been optimized for the 32-bit Windows 95 environment. If you choose to use the 16-bit version of Navigator, however, you can't use the 32-bit Windows 95 connectivity software (you'll crash if you try), and you'll need the same kind of 16-bit connectivity software that Windows 3.1 surfers use. In this chapter, it's assumed that you are using the 32-bit Netscape Navigator or Navigator Gold and the 32-bit native Windows 95 connectivity software.

CONNECTION CHECKLIST

The following connection checklist is the information you'll need to have handy to make the installation and configuration of system connectivity and Netscape Navigator go smoothly. Your ISP or network administrator may have already given you this information in a sign-on handout or information sheet. If you received an information sheet, compare it to the connection checklist that follows. If you're missing any piece of information, or if you don't have an information sheet, call your ISP or network administrator before you proceed any further. It will save you a lot of time and frustration if you have all the necessary information at your fingertips. In addition to the information your ISP or network administrator provides, you'll also need to find your modem manual and sift through it to find specific information that relates to the capabilities of your modem.

Information your ISP or network administrator should provide:

What is my dial-up username?

What is my dial-up password?

What is my local access phone number (for your ISP or for your LAN)?

What terminal settings do I use to dial in? 8, N, 1? 7, E, 1?

What kind of connection do I use—PPP, SLIP, or CSLIP (Van Jacobson CSLIP compression)?

Is my IP address automatically assigned? If not, what is the IP Address?What is the Subnet Mask for my IP Address?

What is the Default Gateway IP Address, if any?

What is the Primary DNS (Domain Name Server) or name server IP Address?

What is the Secondary DNS or name server IP Address?

Do I use a WINS name server? If so, what are the Primary and Secondary addresses?

What is the root domain name (domain suffix) of my ISP or organization?

What is the name of the News (NNTP) server?

What is my e-mail address? Is this the same address that the recipients of my mail will see?

What is my e-mail POP user name?

What is my e-mail password?

What is the name or IP Address for the incoming POP mail server?

What is the name or IP Address for the outgoing SMTP mail server?

Can I use IP header compression?

Do I need to use a PAP (Password Authentication Protocol) sign-in? If so, what is my username and password?

Do I need to configure my system to access the Internet through a proxy or firewall? If so, what is the URL of the proxy configuration file? What are the IP addresses and port numbers of the proxy server and the various proxy services (FTP, Gopher, HTTP, Security, WAIS, and SOCKS host)? What are the addresses of the servers that are local to me?What is the IP Address for the Proxy server?

What is my firewall password, if any?

What are the phone number and hours of operation for my ISP or organization's technical support service?

What is the e-mail address of my ISP or organization's technical support service?

Modem information you need to provide (check your modem manual):

What is the brand name and model of my modem?

Is it a 14.4K or a 28.8K modem?

What communications port (SLIP port) does my modem use?

Does my modem support compression?

Does it use a 16550-compatible UART?

What is the default power-on initialization string for my modem?

Does my modem support Hardware (RTS/CTS)-based flow control (hardware handshaking)?

If I'm using Windows 3.x, does my modem support DCD (RLSD) or DSR online status detection?

If the phone line my modem uses has call waiting, what needs to be dialed to temporarily disable call waiting?

When you have all of this information in hand, you're ready to start configuring your system for the Internet.

Getting Your Hands Dirty—Setting Up System Software

If you already have a working connection to the Internet, you can skip over this section. But if you're having problems, or if you need to set up an Internet connection at home or for a friend or co-worker, read on. The steps you need to take depend on which version of Windows you have. The first part of this section is devoted to setting up necessary software in Windows 3.1, and the second part covers setting up the software in Windows 95.

Windows 3.1x Connectivity Installation

Before installing connectivity software, you need to *get* the connectivity software (see "Where Do You Get This Internet Software?" earlier in this chapter). Several shareware and commercial packages are available, but the 16-bit version of Peter Tattam's *Trumpet Winsock* is probably the most widely used and respected connectivity package. If you received an evaluation copy of Trumpet Winsock in your ISP's sign-on package, some of the configuring has most likely already been done for you. If you downloaded a copy or are changing ISPs, you'll need to configure the software. In this section, you'll learn how to install version 2.1 of Trumpet. If you are using an older version, you still should be able to follow the instructions. If you are using a connectivity package other than Trumpet, you should read the documentation carefully—but much of what you'll have to do to install your package will be similar to the steps used to install Trumpet.

> **TIP**
>
> *Trumpet Winsock 2.1 is shareware that you have 30 days to evaluate. After 30 days, the program will stop working. If you want to keep using Trumpet, be sure to register the software and pay the modest registration fee before your 30 days are up, or you won't be able to connect to the Internet.*

If you download a copy of Trumpet, it is usually contained in a Zip archived file. Trumpet doesn't have an installation program; all the files run when copied to a single directory. Use File Manager to create a directory, and name the directory Trumpet (or a similar, easy-to-locate name). Use WinZip, PKZip, or other unarchiving application to extract all the files to the directory you created. Now we're ready to configure Trumpet.

1. The directory to which you extracted the Trumpet files needs to be added to your AUTOEXEC.BAT file's path statement. Use File Manager to make a backup copy of your AUTOEXEC.BAT file (C:\autoexec.bat, where C is where DOS is located), and save the copy to a floppy diskette or to a temporary directory. Then open the AUTOEXEC.BAT file that is in the root of your C drive using NOTEPAD.EXE or other text editor. Scroll down until you find the line that starts with Path= (no space after Path) or Path = (single space after Path). In this example, we use the following path statement (your own path statement will look different but will follow the same general format):

   PATH=C:\;C:\DOS;D:\WINDOWS;C:\BIN;e:\WORD

   Notice that there is no space following the equal symbol in a path statement and that the paths to directories are separated by semicolons. The path statement is not case-sensitive, so it's alright to mix and match upper and lower case. This example path statement is relatively short. If yours is longer, be sure that it doesn't exceed 128 characters—anything after the 128th character is ignored by your system. If it looks like you are running out of character spaces in your path statement, rename the directory to which you extracted Trumpet. Something short, such as T or TW, will do the trick.

2. Go to the end of the line and directly after the last character (don't add a space), enter a semicolon (;) and follow the semicolon with the path to the directory into which you extracted Trumpet. For example, if you extracted Trumpet into D:\trumpet, and your path statement is like the example path, the new path would look like this:

   PATH=C:\;C:\DOS;D:\WINDOWS;C:\BIN;e:\WORD;D:\trumpet

3. Save the file as AUTOEXEC.BAT so that the edited file over-writes the original, then exit NOTEPAD.EXE. Changes made in AUTOEXEC.BAT don't take effect until you restart your computer, so close Windows and reboot the computer. When you're back in Windows, choose File, Run, and enter TCPMAN.EXE. Trumpet Winsock should load, as shown in Figure 2-1. If it doesn't load, you've made a mistake in the path in AUTOEXEC.BAT, and you'll need to correct it with your text editor.

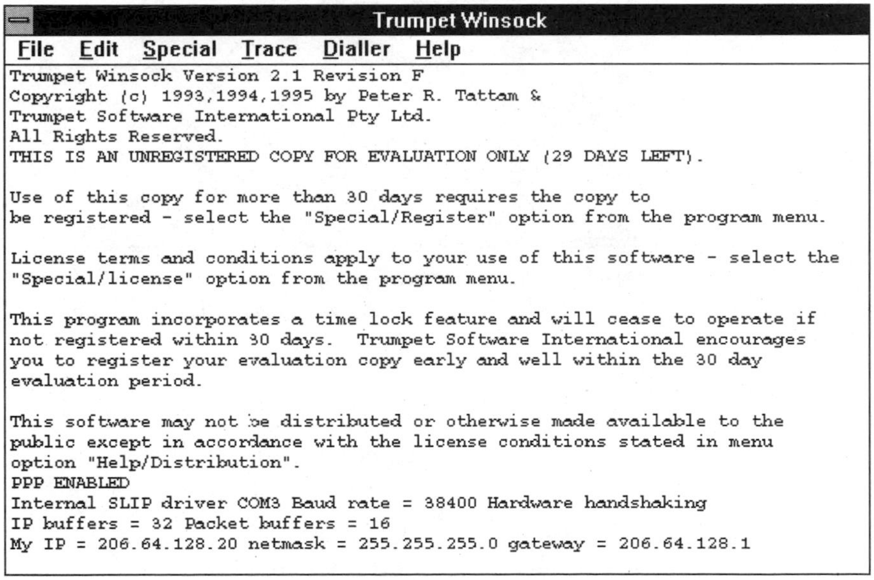

```
┌──────────────────────────── Trumpet Winsock ────────────────────────────┐
│  File   Edit   Special   Trace   Dialler   Help                          │
├──────────────────────────────────────────────────────────────────────────┤
│ Trumpet Winsock Version 2.1 Revision F                                   │
│ Copyright (c) 1993,1994,1995 by Peter R. Tattam &                        │
│ Trumpet Software International Pty Ltd.                                   │
│ All Rights Reserved.                                                     │
│ THIS IS AN UNREGISTERED COPY FOR EVALUATION ONLY (29 DAYS LEFT).         │
│                                                                          │
│ Use of this copy for more than 30 days requires the copy to             │
│ be registered - select the "Special/Register" option from the program menu. │
│                                                                          │
│ License terms and conditions apply to your use of this software - select the │
│ "Special/license" option from the program menu.                          │
│                                                                          │
│ This program incorporates a time lock feature and will cease to operate if │
│ not registered within 30 days.  Trumpet Software International encourages │
│ you to register your evaluation copy early and well within the 30 day    │
│ evaluation period.                                                       │
│                                                                          │
│ This software may not be distributed or otherwise made available to the  │
│ public except in accordance with the license conditions stated in menu   │
│ option "Help/Distribution".                                              │
│ PPP ENABLED                                                              │
│ Internal SLIP driver COM3 Baud rate = 38400 Hardware handshaking         │
│ IP buffers = 32 Packet buffers = 16                                      │
│ My IP = 206.64.128.20 netmask = 255.255.255.0 gateway = 206.64.128.1     │
└──────────────────────────────────────────────────────────────────────────┘
```

Figure 2-1: *A Winsock is a necessary part of your Internet connectivity software. Windows 3.1x users can use the 16-bit, shareware Trumpet Winsock.*

4. From Trumpet's File menu, choose Setup. The setup screen seen in Figure 2-2 appears. Some of the fields may already be filled in if your Internet provider pre-configured the software for you. If not, it'll only take a minute or two to fill out this dialog if you have the information sheet from your ISP handy.

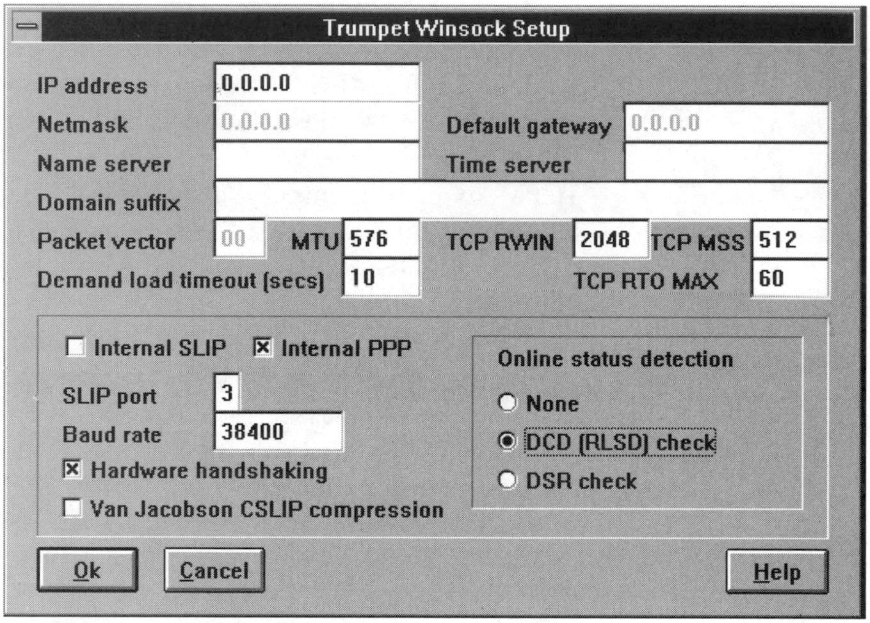

Trumpet Winsock Setup

IP address	0.0.0.0
Netmask	0.0.0.0
Default gateway	0.0.0.0
Name server	
Time server	
Domain suffix	

Packet vector 00   MTU 576   TCP RWIN 2048   TCP MSS 512

Demand load timeout (secs) 10   TCP RTO MAX 60

☐ Internal SLIP   ☒ Internal PPP

SLIP port 3

Baud rate 38400

☒ Hardware handshaking

☐ Van Jacobson CSLIP compression

Online status detection

○ None

◉ DCD (RLSD) check

○ DSR check

[Ok]   [Cancel]   [Help]

Figure 2-2: *If you received Trumpet from your ISP, some of the necessary configuration information may have been filled in for you.*

5. If your ISP told you that you have a SLIP account, make sure that the Internal SLIP checkbox is checked. If you have a PPP account, check the Internal PPP check box. Depending on which checkbox you checked, different configuration options will become available.

6. If your ISP has assigned you a fixed or static IP address, put that number in the IP address field. If your IP address is assigned when you log on, leave this field set to 0.0.0.0. IP addresses consist of four sets of numbers separated by a period. There are no spaces in an IP address. Each set of numbers can contain up to three digits.

7. In the Name Server field, enter the numerical IP address that your ISP gave you for the Name Server or DNS address(es). If your ISP gave you more than one Name Server address, enter the primary or most reliable one first, and then enter the next Name Server address, separating it from the first name with a space. You can enter as many addresses as you have access to.

8. In the Domain suffix field, enter the root domain address of your ISP. This would be something like *myprovider.com* or *myschool.edu*. If you are configuring for accessing communications on an Intranet, ask your network administrator what name you should use here. If you can't find out this information right away, try using part of your e-mail address. For example, if your e-mail address is *jsmith@mailgate.company.com*, try entering *company.com* as the Domain suffix. Depending on how complex your Intranet structure is, this trick may or may not work. ISPs usually only supply one Domain name, but in large educational institutions and companies, your network administrator may give you multiple domain names to use here. If so, you can enter them here. Be sure to separate each name with a space.

   This field is very important because the Name Server is the service that takes readable site addresses and turns them into the numeric addresses that are actually used on the Internet. Domain names are *masks* for numbers that make it easier for humans to remember Internet addresses. For example, Netscape's home page is home.netscape.com, and the *numeric* address is 198.95.249.78.

9. In the SLIP port entry field, enter the serial communications port that your modem uses. Even if you are setting up for PPP, you have to tell Trumpet where your modem can be found. If your modem uses comm 1, put 1 here; if it's comm 2, enter 2 here. . . . If you are uncertain of which serial port your modem uses, try 2 because it's the most common port to use for a modem. After you've configured Trumpet and restarted it, if you guessed wrong, the third line from the bottom in Trumpet Winsock window will read something like this:

   ```
   Unable to open COM2 - Hardware is not available.
   ```

   This is your clue that you entered the wrong comm port number. Try a different number in the SLIP port entry field. Unless you have a special serial board, the correct number will be between 1 and 4 inclusive.

10. In the Baud rate field, enter the speed at which you want your modem to communicate with Trumpet. This is *not* the same, nor is it as straightforward, as specifying 14.4 or 28.8. Accepted values here are 9600, 14400, 19200, 38400, 57600, and 115200. You should use the fastest setting that your modem and your connection can handle. If you have a 14.4K modem, try 19200. If you have problems connecting or staying connected, drop this figure to 14400. If you have a 28.8K modem, try 57600. If you have no problems and you have a new, fast modem, and very "clean" phone lines, try 115200 as the value here. If you have problems at 57600, drop to 38400, or even 19200 under bad phone line conditions.

11. Leave the Hardware handshaking checkbox checked. Almost all PC modems can use hardware handshaking; check your modem documentation to see if yours does. If you have a lot of problems with connections dropping immediately after you've established a connection, check your modem's documentation to see what the default modem string is for your modem to see if it includes support for RTS/CTS (hardware handshaking), and add it if it doesn't. Dropping a connection immediately after establishing one can also be caused by a problem on the computer you are connecting to.

12. If you are using SLIP, check the Van Jacobson CSLIP compression checkbox if your ISP told you to do so. Van Jacobson CSLIP compression is more efficient than plain SLIP, but it will work only if your ISP provides support for it.

13. To use the dialing utility's auto login/logout feature, Trumpet has to have a way of monitoring the connection to see if it is still active. The Online status detection section offers a choice of None, DCD (RLSD) check, or DSR check. If you choose none, you will not be able to access the dialer utility. The choice you make between the remaining two choices depends on the capability of your modem.

    The DCD (RLSD) check is a modem command that checks to see if a carrier signal is present from the modem to which you're connecting. To enable the DCD (RLSD) check, the modem initialization string (or the power-on default setting of your modem) must include support for this feature. This is usually enabled by including an **&C1** in the string.

Another way for Trumpet to check that status of the connection is through DSR (Data Set Ready) checking. This checks to see that the modem is connected to an active telephone line with a carrier signal. DSR checking is usually enabled by placing an **&S1** command in the modem's initialization string or the power-on default setting.

Which method of Online status detection you use depends on which one is supported by your modem. Check your modem documentation for instructions on the proper initialization string to use with your modem.

14. The Packet vector, Demand load timeout, MTU, TCP RWIN, TCP MSS, and TCP RTO MAX entries should be left at their default settings unless your ISP or network administrator has given you other values. All of these settings except Demand load timeout have to do with the size of the data transmission packets and the conditions under which they are transmitted. To optimize these settings, you would have to have detailed information regarding the capability of all the networks that your information passes through, which is practically impossible. Demand load timeout setting specifies the amount of time the Winsock stays active after an application that loaded it has quit. The default setting of 5 seconds is the recommended setting.

FIREWALL & PAP CONFIGURATION

Unless your computer is behind a network firewall, or your ISP or network administrator has told you that your account uses an additional PAP protocol for obtaining Internet access, you can skip over this section. A firewall is a special hardware- and software-based network security system that isolates and protects an Intranet from unwanted intrusion from the Internet. Firewall software is not included in Trumpet, but Trumpet can be configured to work with an existing firewall setup. Do not check the Enable firewall checkbox unless a firewall already exists. If you falsely ask Trumpet to use a firewall where none exists or you fill in the wrong IP numbers, you will not be able to connect to the Internet.

To configure Trumpet for use with a firewall, choose File, Firewall. In the dialog box that appears (see Figure 2-3), check the Enable firewall checkbox. Then fill in the IP address and port number for the firewall server. Enter your special Firewall user ID. Then fill in the IP addresses and network masks of any servers that are on the same side of the firewall as you, and which therefore should be considered local servers. Then click OK. Ask your network administrator for the IP address, port, and mask information; this information does *not* come from telepathy!

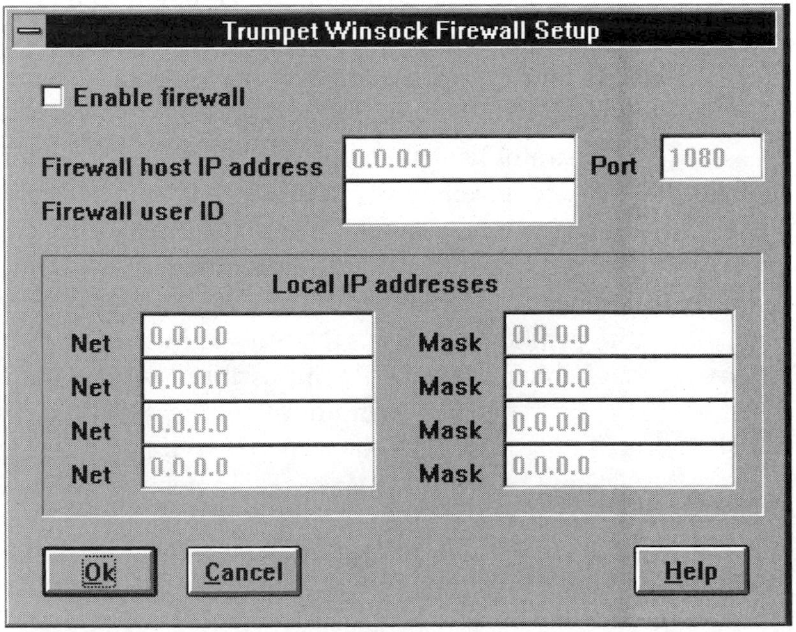

Figure 2-3: *You can configure Trumpet to operate behind a company firewall.*

If you've been instructed to use PAP with your PPP connection, choose File, then PPP Options. In the dialog box that appears, enter your special PAP Username and Password. These will not be the same as your login name and password. Then check the Use Password Authentication Protocol (PAP) checkbox, and click OK.

STARTING UP AN INTERNET CONNECTION

To open up a connection to your ISP using Trumpet, you must run either the Manual login or the Login script from the Dialler menu. The Manual login script makes Trumpet's window act like a communication program's terminal window. When in terminal mode, you issue setup and dialing commands to your modem by typing directly in Trumpet's window. (Consult your modem's manual for other commands you can issue to your modem in a terminal window.) For example, when you choose Manual login from the Dialler menu and type ATDT 555-5555 into Trumpet's window, Trumpet "tells" the modem to use tone dialing to make a call to phone number 555-5555. When the computer at 555-5555 answers, it sends prompts for your username, password, and the kind of service you need. These prompts are displayed in Trumpet's window. You answer the prompts for information by typing in the Trumpet window.

The Login command on the Dialler menu is an automated procedure that sends the dialing commands to the modem, answers the prompts for information, and starts up PPP or SLIP service on your computer. It's a great convenience and a timesaver to configure the login script that the Login command uses, so you don't have to dial and answer the prompts manually every time you want to establish a connection to your ISP.

SETTING UP THE LOGON SCRIPT

Many ISPs provide a custom dialing script for their service. The purpose of a *login dialer script* is to dial the ISPs number and automatically answer any prompts for information such as your username and password. The *bye script* logs you off your ISPs system and closes your connection. If your ISP has provided you with scripts, copy the login.cmd, and bye.cmd files to Trumpet's directory, overwriting the existing scripts. If no scripts were provided, you may be able to use Trumpet's default scripts without modification.

TIP

If you've used your modem to send or receive a fax or have used it with another communications program, reset your modem before starting an Internet session. Most fax software (and some other communications programs) don't reset the modem properly or release the comm port, which makes establishing an Internet connection impossible.

Reset external modems by turning them off and then on. Internal fax/modems can only be reset by completely shutting down your computer and restarting. Ctrl+Alt+Del or pressing the reset button won't reset the modem. Exit all programs, exit Windows, turn the computer off using the power switch, count to five to flush system RAM, and then turn the computer back on and restart Windows.

Many users can set up the login script for Trumpet simply by choosing Login and answering a few questions. If you're experiencing trouble however, the following is a detailed setup routine for getting Trumpet's login script to work for you:

Open Trumpet Winsock if it is not already open. From the Dialler menu, choose Login. If this is the first time you've used this script, you will be prompted by a series of dialog boxes to enter your phone number (see Figure 2-4), your login username, and your login password. When you are prompted to "Enter your phone number," enter the phone number of your ISP, *not* the number you are calling from. The information you give now will be stored in TRUMPET.INI, so you won't be asked for it again. If you need to change any of this information because you mis-entered it or because you are calling a different ISP, run the SETUP.CMD on the Dialler menu. The SETUP.CMD script will prompt you for this information again.

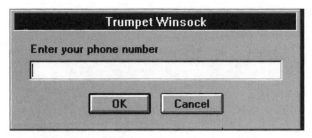

Figure 2-4: *When Trumpet asks for your phone number, enter your ISP's local dial-in access number.*

When you've answered all of the dialog boxes, the login script will run and should connect you to your ISP. Watch the Trumpet window for any error messages. Depending on how your ISP's system is set up, the Trumpet window may start to fill with lines of "garbage "characters. These garbage characters indicate that your ISP has switched from the terminal mode used to collect your login information, to either the SLIP or PPP protocols. If the garbage characters appear, press the ESC key to enable Trumpet to switch into PPP or SLIP mode. If all goes well, you should see text at the bottom of the window that says:

```
Script completed.
PPP Enabled
My IP Address is 111.111.111.1
```

or

```
Script completed.
SLIP Enabled
My IP Address is 111.111.111.1
```

The IP Address 111.111.111.11 in this example is replaced by the IP address that has been assigned to you by your provider. If you are using PPP with a fixed or dynamically assigned IP address or you use SLIP with a fixed IP Address, you're online and ready to launch Navigator. If however, your SLIP account assigns you a different IP Address each time you sign in, you should write down the IP Address on a piece of paper, then without closing Trumpet, go to the File menu and choose Setup. In the IP address field at the top of the dialog box, enter the IP address you copied down, and then click OK. You will have to do this each time you connect unless you have modified the login script to do this for you.

If all did *not* go well, and instead of the text in the window saying Script completed, it says Script aborted, or if you hang somewhere in the process, you need to edit the login script. All scripts can be edited with any text editor, or you can choose Edit Scripts from the Dialler menu. Choosing Edit Scripts displays a list of the .CMD script files; choose one and NOTEPAD.EXE will launch to edit the script. Although Trumpet's Help file offers excellent documentation on the script language and how to edit scripts, it's probably time to call your ISP and ask for assistance. A few common problems you may want to look for before you call your ISP are:

■ The default dialing script assumes your phone line uses tone dialing. If you use pulse dialing instead, choose Edit Scripts from the Dialler menu, choose the LOGIN.CMD script, and click OK. Find the part of the script that reads :

```
output "atdp"$number\13
```

and change it to

```
output "atdt"$number\13
```

■ Your ISP may use text other than that assumed by the default script to prompt you for your username, password, and the kind of service you need: SLIP or PPP. Trumpet looks for *sername, assword, and slip or ppp.* Look in the top of the login script where it reads:

```
$modemsetup = "&c1&k3"
$prompt = ">"
$userprompt = "sername:"
$passprompt = "assword:"
$slipcmd = "slip"
$addrtarg = "our address is"
$pppcmd = "ppp"
$pppready = "PPP."
%attempts = 10
```

If, for example, your ISP prompts for your login name with the text string, *Enter your login name:* and asks for your password with the text string that says *The secret password is:*

Change the lines that read:

```
$userprompt = "sername:"
$passprompt = "assword:"
```

to

```
$userprompt = "login name:"
$passprompl = "password is:"
```

AUTOMATIC CONNECTIONS & OTHER OPTIONS

Trumpet Winsock can be configured to automatically run scripts for you. These settings are made in the Options dialog box, seen in Figure 2-5, that is reached by choosing Dialler and Options from Trumpet's menu.

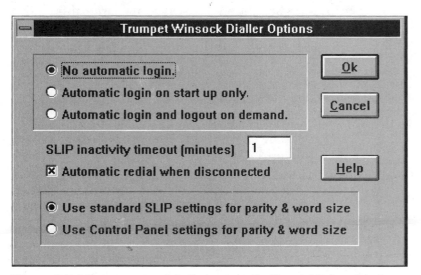

Figure 2-5: *You can run scripts that automatically establish and end your Internet connection.*

The Options dialog offers three login choices: *No automatic login*, *Automatic login on start up only,* and *Automatic login and logout on demand*. The default value is No automatic login, which means that you must start Trumpet and run the scripts from the Dialler menu manually. This is useful if you want to read pages that are stored on your hard disk and therefore don't require an active connection to the Internet.

- Choose *Automatic login on start up only* if you want Trumpet to automatically run the login script whenever you launch Trumpet.

- Choose *Automatic login on start up only* and run the LOGIN.CMD when you start Trumpet by enabling either Automatic login on startup only or Automatic login and logout on demand. Use Automatic login and logout on demand if you want Trumpet to dial your login script as soon as you launch Trumpet and to run the bye script to close the connection when you exit Trumpet.

The SLIP inactivity timeout (minutes) entry field in the Options window is used to set the amount of time Trumpet will stay open after you've closed all Winsock applications such as Navigator. Although the option has SLIP in its name, this setting also applies to PPP connections. Set this to a comfortable value of 1 or 2 minutes if you regularly use other Internet applications in addition to Navigator, such as Netscape Chat. This gives you time to close Navigator and load the other application without having to establish a new connection, yet ensures that if you get distracted you don't unnecessarily tie up your phone and incur online charges with an open, but unused connection. Setting the value to 0 disables the timeout function, which means that Trumpet will never automatically close a connection.

Check the Automatic redial when disconnected checkbox if you want Trumpet to automatically redial every minute whenever Trumpet is running and a connection has not been established. *Use this feature with caution!* When it is enabled, if you automatically or manually run the login script and then change your mind about connecting, it is difficult to keep Trumpet from redialing. If this happens, go to Options and uncheck the Automatic redial disconnected, and then close Trumpet.

The last two options in this dialog box are *Use standard SLIP settings for parity & word size* (the default) and *Use Control Panel settings for parity & word size*. The first refers to a setting of 8, N, and 1, the traditional settings used to connect to hosts in ANSI BBS mode. Most dial-in connections use these terminal mode settings for the portion of the transaction where your username and password are collected. However, if your ISP uses different settings, such as 7, E, and 1, go to Windows 3.1 Control Panel's Port applet and change the Port settings for the communications (serial) port used by the modem. Windows 95 users need to go to the Control Panel's System applet and use the Device Manager to change the port settings for the communications port that the modem uses.

CLOSING YOUR CONNECTION

As enjoyable as it would be to surf the Net all day, there does come a time when you need to hang up and get on with your other activities. To exit Trumpet and break your connection with your ISP, run the BYE.CMD script from the Dialler menu.

WINDOWS 95 SETUP

If you've made the move to Windows 95, system software components for connecting to the Internet came with the operating system. Dial-up software is also included, but isn't installed by default. Try clicking the My Computer icon on the desktop. If there is a Dial-Up Networking folder in the list, you're ahead of the game. If the folder isn't there, it's time to get out your Windows 95 disks or CD and install Dial-Up Networking capability.

From here on in, there are several ways to install Dial-Up if your connection to the Internet is through a PPP-based access account. You can follow the instructions we provide in this section for installing and configuring an Internet connection, or you may have a wizard help you if you've purchased additional software. Netscape's Navigator Personal Edition software bundle comes with a very helpful wizard, and if by chance you bought the MS Windows Plus! Pack (to get the Hover adventure game, of course) you also received an Internet (configuration) wizard. SLIP users, whether you purchased additional software or not, will have to forego the convenience of the wizard because neither Navigator nor Windows 95 will configure a SLIP connection, but we'll show you how to configure one manually in the following sections. If you're traveling the do-it-yourself route, read on.

INSTALLING A MODEM

If you haven't already installed a modem, you should do so now. From the Start menu, choose Settings and then Control Panel. Double click on the Modems icon. In the Modems Properties window, click on the Add button. This launches the Modem Setup wizard, which guides you through the process of telling Windows 95 what kind of modem you have and which comm port it is using. If you allow Windows 95 to autodetect your modem, it will take care of all the details.

After the wizard has finished installing the modem, click on the Diagnostics tab, then select the comm port in the list that the modem uses. Click More Info. Windows 95 will run a communications test on the modem. If Windows 95 reports that it was unable to find the modem (open the port), the modem has not been installed correctly. If it is an external modem, it may not be powered on. To help you figure out what is wrong, run the Hardware Conflict Troubleshooter first, and if this doesn't resolve the problem, run the Modem Troubleshooter. To run either of these troubleshooting wizards, choose Help from the Start Menu. From the Contents tab, click the Troubleshooting book, then choose the wizard you want to run.

If all is working properly, a More Info window will open that displays a lot of technical information about your modem and the port it uses, as seen in Figure 2-6.

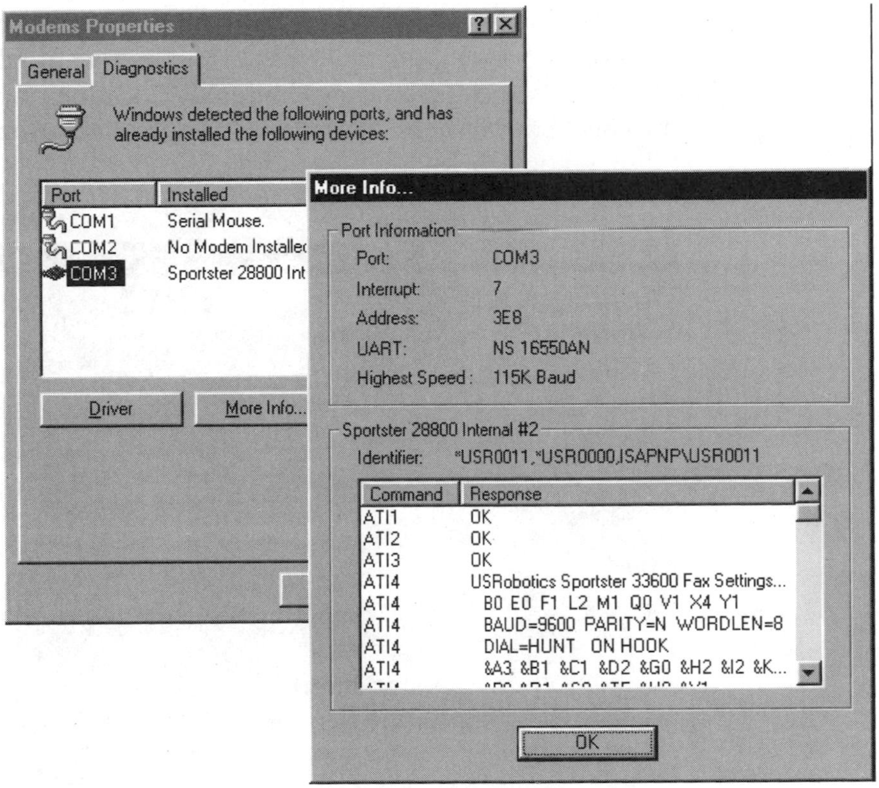

Figure 2-6: *Your modem needs to be acknowledged by Windows 95 before you can make Internet connections. Let Windows 95's wizards guide you through the process.*

The Port Information section displays information about which port, system interrupt, and memory address is used. It also reports what kind of UART chip your serial port uses. Take note of the last two pieces of information: the UART used and the Highest Speed the modem is capable of using. You'll need this information later. Click OK to close the More Info window and then OK again to close the Modem Properties dialog box. Don't bother to customize the Properties of the modem just yet. You'll get a chance to work through Properties step by step shortly. But *do* take a moment to set up the Dialing Properties in the Dialing Preferences field at the bottom of the General tab.

Click the Dialing Properties button. The settings you make in the My Locations tab (seen in Figure 2-7) are fairly straightforward. There are two critical settings in the My Locations tab. The first is the checkbox labeled *This Location has call waiting. To disable it, dial:* followed by a drop-down list of choices.

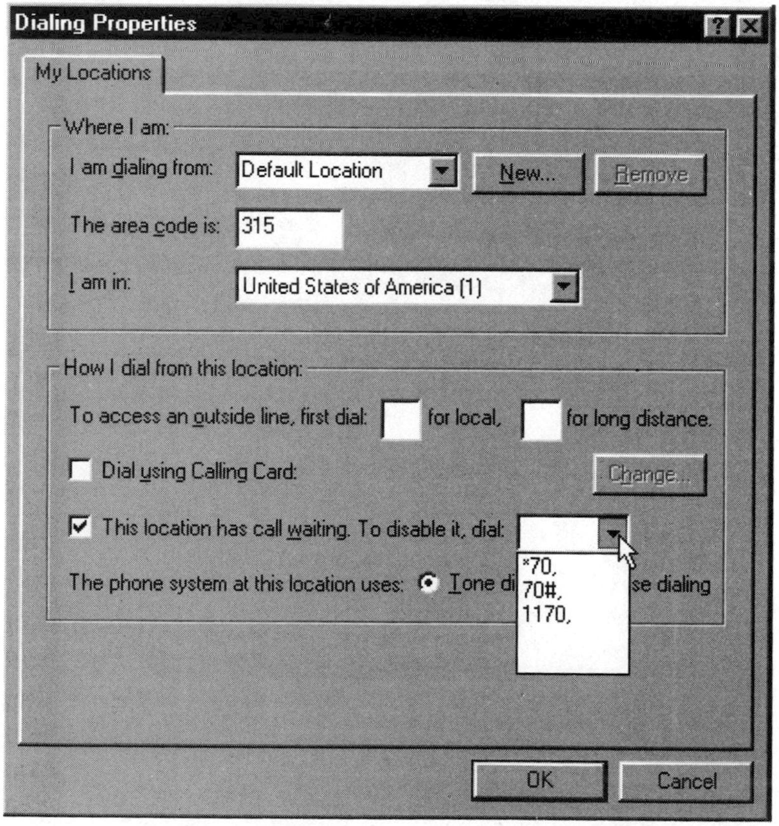

Figure 2-7: *If you have call waiting service, you must configure Windows 95 to temporarily disable call waiting, or an incoming call will break your Internet connection.*

If you subscribe to call waiting and you're unsure of which drop-down list item to choose when the checkbox is checked, call your phone company and ask. It is important to disable call waiting when you are connected to the Internet because an incoming call will break your connection to the Internet. The other important option in the My Locations tab is what kind of dialing you use—Tone dialing (Touch Tone) or Pulse (Rotary) dialing. If the computer you're using is a laptop and you regularly call from different locations, make a Location for each place from which you regularly dial.

INSTALLING WINDOWS 95 DIAL-UP NETWORKING

When you install Dial-Up Networking, you are installing network software that allows your computer to become a node on the vast network that makes up the Internet. Windows 95 will install a Dial-Up Adapter that functions as a virtual network card, in addition to the TCP/IP protocol software and PPP software needed to make the Dial-Up adapter Internet-ready. If you are already connected to a physical LAN (local area network), the Dial-Up Adapter and the TCP/IP protocol software are supplemental to your existing setup, and the components that make up Dial-Up Networking possible are added to your list of installed network components.

To install Windows 95 Dial-Up networking:

1. Open the Start menu, and choose Settings, then Control Panel. When the Control Panel opens, click on the Add/Remove Programs icon, then click on the Windows Setup tab.

2. Click on the Communications checkbox in the Components list. Then click on the Details button and make sure that Dial-Up Networking is checked. (See Figure 2-8.) Choose any other communications components that you want to install.

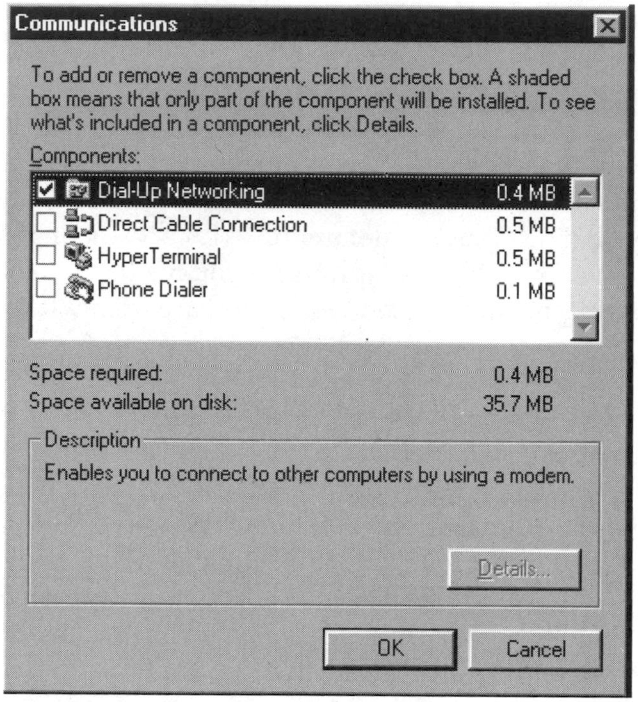

Figure 2-8: *Use Add/Remove Programs to install Dial-Up Networking.*

3. Click OK to close the Communications dialog. Then click OK in the Add/Remove Programs Properties window. Follow the directions that appear onscreen to install the software.

When Dial-Up Networking is installed, support for PPP-based Internet access accounts is automatically installed, but support for SLIP-based access is not. If you need to use SLIP, read the next section on finding and installing the SLIP software. If you don't need SLIP support, move on to the section, "Installing TCP/IP" that follows the SLIP section.

INSTALLING THE WINDOWS 95 SLIP SOFTWARE

If your dial-in account requires SLIP, you'll need to make a second trip to the Windows software to get the SLIP software. Microsoft assumes that everyone uses PPP and doesn't install SLIP when you

install Dial-Up Networking. The SLIP software is on the CD version of Windows 95. If you don't have the CD version of Windows 95, you can get it from Microsoft's BBS, or from one of the major online services. You could also ask a friend to download the administration tools from Microsoft's Internet site at:
http://www.microsoft.com/windows/download/dscrpt.exe.

Or you can download only the SLIP-related files from:
http://www.microsoft.com/ie/download/script.exe.

If you are using a downloaded version of the SLIP software instead of the CD version, follow the directions included with the file. To install the SLIP software from the Windows 95 CD:

1. Open Control Panel and click on the Add/Remove Programs icon.

2. Click on the Windows Setup tab in the Add/Remove Programs Properties box, then click the Have Disk button. Use the Browse button to find the ADMIN\APPTOOLS\ DSCRIPT folder on the Windows 95 CD.

3. Choose the RNAPLUS.INF file and click on OK. Then click on OK in the Install From Disk dialog. In the Have Disk window, put a check mark next to SLIP and Scripting for Dial-Up Networking and then click on the Install button. The software installs, and SLIP will appear as an option for Server Type for Dial-Up Networking. Click on the Close button to close the Add/Remove Programs Properties box.

At the same time that the SLIP software was installed, dial-in scripting software was also added. Scripting is installed in the Start menu's Accessories folder, but you don't need to do anything with scripting software just yet.

INSTALLING TCP/IP

During the installation and configuration of the TCP/IP network components, you may need to restart your computer, so close any running applications before you begin. Also note that when you restart, the restart process takes longer than usual because Windows needs to update your configuration information in the system Registry. Be patient; Windows *will* restart!

1. From the Start menu, open the Control Panel and double-click on the Network icon. Look in the scroll box of the Network Configuration tab seen in Figure 2-9 to see if TCP/IP protocol is installed. If it's not, click on the Add button and choose Protocol from the Select Network Component Type box. Click the Add button in the Select Network Component Type box. If the TCP/IP protocol is in the list, skip the next step and move on to step 3.

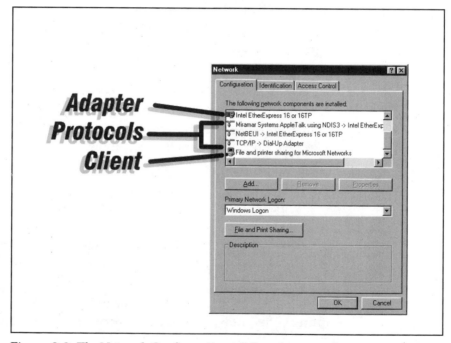

Figure 2-9: *The Network Configuration tab lists the network components that are currently installed on your computer.*

2. In the Select Network Protocol window, click on Microsoft in the Manufacturers list, then select TCP/IP from the Network Protocols list. Then click on OK; you're returned to the Configuration tab.

3. Click on the Dial-Up Adapter icon in the scrolling list, then click on Properties. In the Dial-Up Adapter Properties window, click on the Bindings tab and put a check mark next to TCP/IP->Dial-UP Adapter if a check is not already there. For a dial-up connection to an ISP, TCP/IP should be the only protocol that is bound to the adapter. If you are connecting through your organization's network, you may have to enable other bindings as well. Check with your network administrator on this one.

4. The other tabs in the Dial-Up Adapter Properties are left at their default settings. Click on OK and restart your computer if a dialog box advises you to do so.

CONFIGURING THE TCP/IP DIAL-UP ADAPTER

1. From the Start menu, open the Control Panel and double-click on the Network icon. Look in the scroll box of the Network Configuration tab and click on the TCP/IP->Dial-Up Adapter Protocol to select it, then click on the Properties button.

2. Click on the IP Address tab if it is not on top of the stack of tabs in the TCP/IP Properties window (see Figure 2-10). If you are assigned an IP Address each time you connect, make sure the Obtain an IP Address Automatically box is checked.

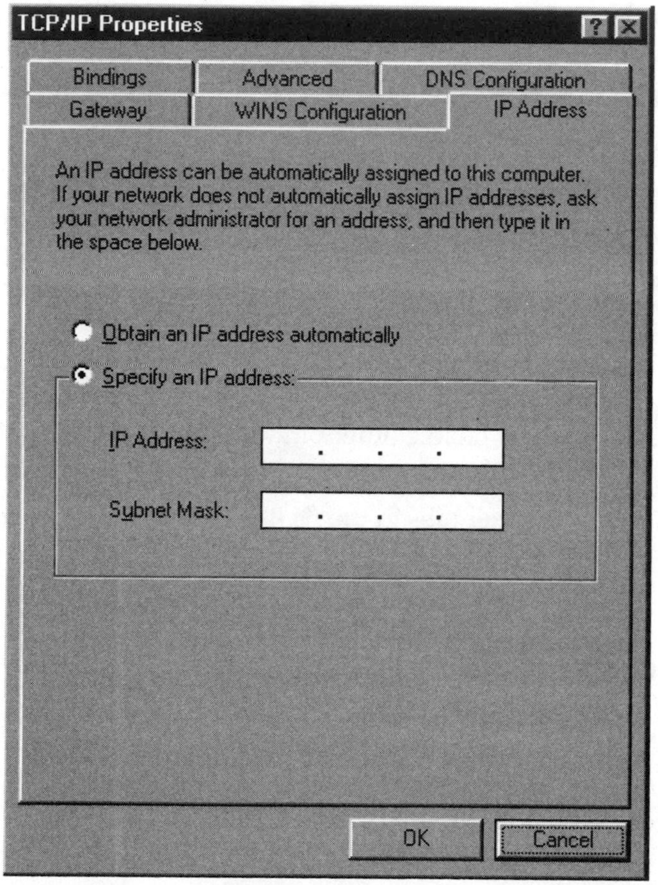

Figure 2-10: *The IP Address is the address that other Internet computers use to send information to you. You may always have the same address from session to session, or you may have a different one each time you connect.*

If you've been assigned a fixed or static IP address by your ISP or network administrator, click the Specify an IP Address radio button. Then enter the IP Address and Subnet Mask you were assigned. This address consists of four sets of up to three digits separated by periods—Windows supplies the periods for the completed IP address. Use the arrow key to move to the next group of digits if you enter fewer than three in each section of the address.

If you have more than one dial-up account, and some have fixed and others have assigned IP addresses, choose Obtain an IP Address Automatically. You will be able to supply the fixed addresses when you make the connectoid for the connection (covered shortly).

3. Click the Bindings tab. Make sure that only the client for your network software is checked. Be sure to *un*check File and printer sharing for Microsoft Networks. This ensures that when you are using this dial-up connection, no one from the Internet can share your files or printers in the same way that you normally share computer resources with others on your Windows 95 or other network. File and printer sharing options are *not* the same as a firewall, however.

For a dial-up connection to an ISP, none of the other tabs in the TCP/IP properties need to contain any information. If you are connecting via your organization's network, consult with your network administrator to determine the proper configuration of these tabs.

CREATING A NEW CONNECTION CONNECTOID

Microsoft calls the icons in the Dial-Up Networking folder *connectoids*. Each connectoid stores the information for a particular dial-up configuration, and when double-clicked, any connectoid starts the dial-up connection. Once Dial-Up networking has been installed (along with SLIP software, if necessary) and the dial-up adapter is configured, it's time to make a connectoid. Click the My Computer icon on the desktop, then open the Dial-Up Networking folder. After it opens . . .

1. Click the Make New Connection icon. In the Make New Connection window, enter a name for the connection, such as *My Internet Provider*, in the *Type a name for the computer you are dialing* field.

2. Select the modem you wish to use from the *Select a modem* drop-down list. Then click on the Configure button.

3. Adjust the *Speaker volume* to your liking. Then from the *Maximum speed* drop-down (see Figure 2-11), choose a speed. The speed you choose here is the speed at which

your computer communicates with your modem, *not* the speed of the modem itself. Use the speed you noted earlier that the Modem Properties More Info window reported as Highest Speed available with your modem. In general, if you have a 14.4K modem, choose 57600. If you have a 28.8K modem, choose 115200. Later, if you find you have trouble maintaining a connection, or you encounter numerous errors in file transfers, come back here and lower the setting to the next one available. Do *not* check the Only connect at this speed checkbox. Doing so will lock you into a fixed speed, which prevents the modem from negotiating a slower speed when line conditions are not quite perfect.

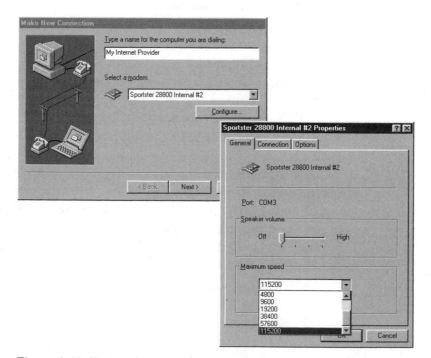

Figure 2-11: *For maximum performance choose the highest speed your modem is capable of handling.*

4. Click the Connection tab. Unless your ISP has told you differently, *Data bits*, *Parity*, and *Stop bits* should be set to 8, None, and 1, respectively, as shown in Figure 2-12.

5. In the Call Preferences field, check *Wait for dial tone before dialing* if you have no plans to dial all of your calls manually to the ISP. Check the Cancel the call if not connected within seconds checkbox, then enter a value that reflects how long it usually takes to make a connection. Sixty seconds is usually adequate.

6. Check the *Disconnect a call if idle for more than __ min* checkbox and then enter a number of minutes in the entry field with which you are comfortable. Enabling this setting automatically disconnects you if Windows 95 detects that no data has been transferred during the time period you specify. Five minutes is enough time for you to get a sandwich and return without getting disconnected, and five minutes also can keep your connect time down if you accidentally leave your computer unattended with a connection open.

7. If you have an internal modem or if the serial port used by your external modem has a 16550-compatible UART, click the Port Settings button. In the Advanced Port Settings window, check the *Use FIFO buffers* check box. *Leave the Receive Buffer* and *Transmit Buffer* settings at their default settings. As the dialog box says, if you have connection problems, come back here and reduce the settings. If you don't have any problems, come back and try higher settings. Higher settings improve performance, but can cause connection problems. Adjust the settings as necessary. If your UART is not 16550-compatible, uncheck the Use FIFO buffers check box if it is checked. Click on OK.

8. Click on the Advanced button. In the Advanced Connection Settings window (seen in Figure 2-12), check the *Use error control* checkbox if your modem supports error correction. Check the *Required to connect* and the *Compress data* checkboxes. The first will make a connection only if error correction can be negotiated with the computer you're connecting to. Almost all ISPs use error-correcting modems. Checking Compress data will increase the transfer rate of uncompressed data such as text, mail, and HTML pages. Files that have been compressed using PKZip or other

compression methods will not compress further, and may actually transfer somewhat slower because your modem will take the time to try to compress them. If you upload and download a lot of zipped files, you may want to leave this option unchecked.

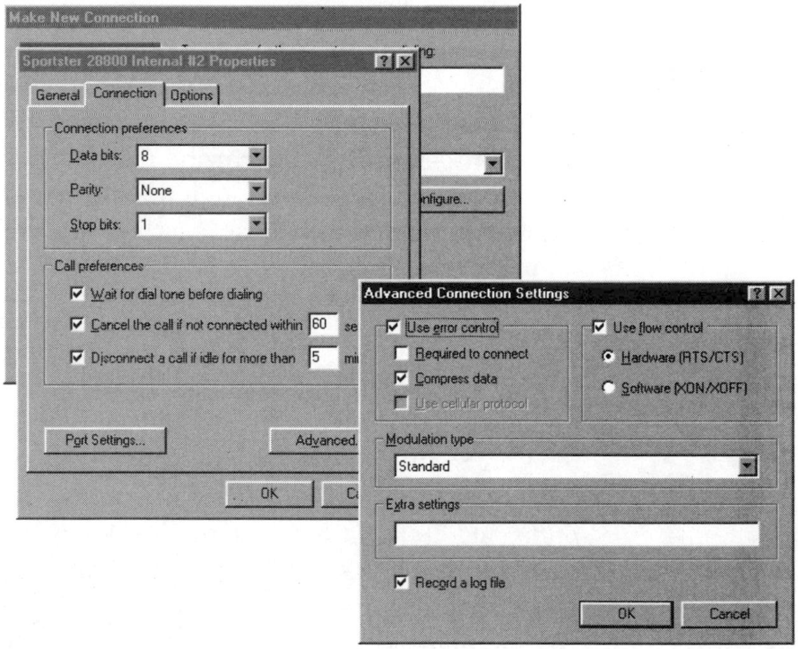

Figure 2-12: *If your modem supports error control, you are more likely to have stable connections.*

9. Check the *Use flow control* checkbox. Select the Hardware (RTS/CTS) radio button. Almost all modems are configured to use Hardware flow control, which is better than the less capable, alternate choice of Software (XON/XOFF) control. Only choose the Software control option if you are certain that your modem *doesn't* support Hardware-based flow control, which is commonly referred to as "Hardware Handshaking."

10. Modulation type is almost always set at *Standard*. If you have a US Robotics HST modem, and are *sure* you are connecting to a US Robotics HST modem, choose this from the drop-down list.

11. The *Extra settings* entry field is used for adding entries to the default initialization string for your modem. Leave this field blank unless you want or need to use a special initialization string for your modem. Check your modem documentation for suggested strings or additions to the default string. Entries made here will override any made in the default initialization string.

12. If you would like to keep a log of the calls you make, check the *Record a log file* checkbox. The log will be written to a file called MODEMLOG.TXT and stored in your Windows folder. This is a useful feature to enable if you suspect that your ISP is overcharging you or if you need to bill a client.

13. Click OK when you have finished making your choices in the Advanced Connection Settings window.

14. Click the Options tab seen in Figure 2-13. In the Connection control field, leave the *Bring up terminal window before dialing* check box *unchecked* unless you want to enter modem commands manually.

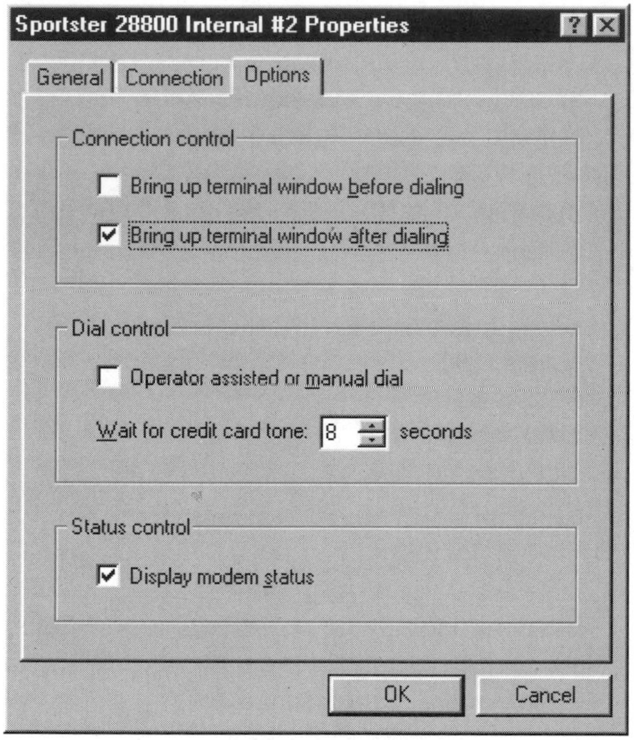

Figure 2-13: *It is important to check the Bring up terminal window after dialing checkbox, or you won't be able to login to your ISP's system.*

15. You must *check* the *Bring up terminal window after dialing* checkbox. This opens a terminal window that enables you to login to your ISP's computers. If left unchecked, neither you nor a dialing utility will be given a chance to enter your username or password.

16. In the Dial control, check the *Operator assisted or manual dial* only if you must dial the number to your ISP yourself. This option is primarily used when you must make a long distance or credit card call from a laptop computer. Increase the setting for the *Wait for credit card tone* to a suitable interval if the place you are calling from takes longer to receive the tone.

17. Check the *Display modem status* checkbox in the Status control field if you want Windows 95 to display a window showing what it is doing—for example, dialing, logging on, and so on.

18. When you've completed making entries in all three tabs—General, Connection, and Options—click on OK to save your settings and return to the Make New Connection Wizard window. Click on the Next button to continue.

19. Enter the area code and phone number of your ISP in the *Area code* and *Telephone number* fields. From the *Country code* drop-down list, choose the country where the ISP is located. Then click on the Next button.

20. If you are satisfied with all your entries, click on the Finish button. If not, click on the Back button and backtrack to the information you want to change. A new connection icon called My Internet Provider (or whatever you named the connection) appears in the Dial-Up Networking folder window.

21. Right-click on the new icon and then choose Properties from the shortcut menu. Leave the *Phone number* fields alone. They contain the information you just entered in the Make New Connection Wizard a few steps ago.

22. In the *Connect using* field, click on the Server Types button.

23. In the Server Types window (see Figure 2-14), click the *Type of Dial-Up Server* drop-down list. If you have a PPP dial-in account, choose *PPP: Windows 95, Windows NT 3.5, Internet* from the drop-down. If your dial-in account uses SLIP, choose *SLIP: UNIX Connection*.

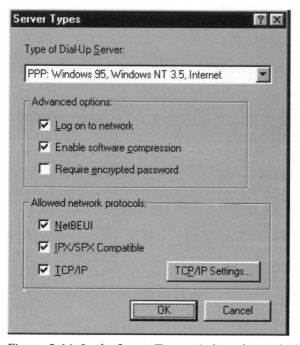

Figure 2-14: *In the Server Types window, choose the kind of dial-up support you need—PPP, SLIP, and the network protocols that will be used.*

If you are connecting via your organization's LAN, choose the appropriate entry for your LAN from the list. For example, if your LAN uses Novell NetWare, choose *NRN NetWare Connect*. If you do not see an appropriate type of server in the list, you will have to go to the Control Panels Network applet and configure the dial-up adapter with the proper software.

24. In the Advanced options section, check *Log on to network* only if the username and password is the same as the one you use to login to your organization's Intranet. If you are dialing into an ISP, leave this box unchecked.

25. Check the *Enable software compression* checkbox only if your modem supports compression. Check your modem documentation to find out if it does.

26. Do *not* check the *Require encrypted password* checkbox unless explicitly told to do so by your ISP or your network administrator.

27. In the *Allowed network protocols* section, check only the protocols you need active for this connection. In almost all cases, the TCP/IP checkbox is the only one that should be checked if you are dialing into an ISP. If you are accessing the Internet through your organization's LAN, check with your network administrator to see if you require other protocols in addition to TCP/IP. Running unnecessary network protocols will degrade the performance of your connection.

28. Click on the TCP/IP button to display the TCP/IP Settings window seen in Figure 2-15.

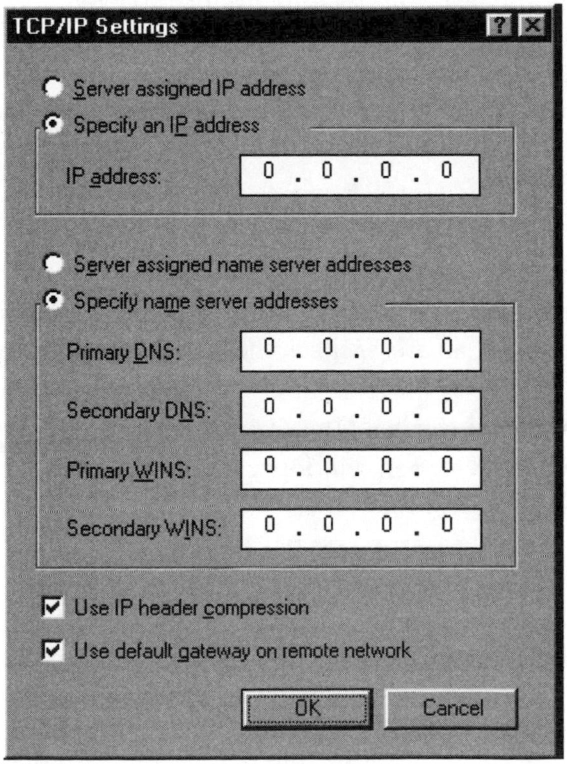

Figure 2-15: *Pay careful attention to the IP addresses entered here; a wrong address will keep you from making a successful connection.*

29. If your ISP assigns you a different IP address each time you dial-in, click the *Server assigned IP address* radio button. If you have been assigned a fixed IP Address, click the *Specify an IP address* radio button and then enter the IP address in the IP address field that becomes available.

30. If your ISP assigns a different name server or DNS address each time you dial in, choose the *Server assigned name server* address. You can also choose this if you only have one dial-in account and you've entered the DNS information in Control Panels Network options for your dial-up adapter.

31. If you were given one or more fixed DNS addresses by your ISP or network supervisor, click the *Specify name server addresses* radio button, then enter the addresses in the Primary and Secondary DNS fields below. The *Primary DNS* address should be the address that is the most reliable of the two addresses. If your Intranet uses WINS addressing (ask your network administrator), enter the *Primary WINS* and *Secondary WINS* addresses in the appropriate fields. You need to get these addresses from your network administrator.

32. Check the *Use IP header compression* checkbox unless your ISP or network administrator advises against it. IP header compression speeds up data transfer.

33. If your ISP or network administrator gave you a default gateway address, check the *Use default gateway on remote network* check box.

34. When you've completed your entries, click OK to close each successive open window until you return to the Dial-Up Networking window.

35. Click the My Internet Provider icon to select it. Choose Connections, then choose Settings from the menu. In the Dial-Up Networking General tab (Figure 2-16), click the *Redial* checkbox. If you get a busy signal or the connection doesn't become established when you dial in to your ISP, Windows 95 will automatically try again. Set the number of times you want it to retry in the times spin box, and the amount of time it should wait between tries, in the two spin boxes below the times spinbox.

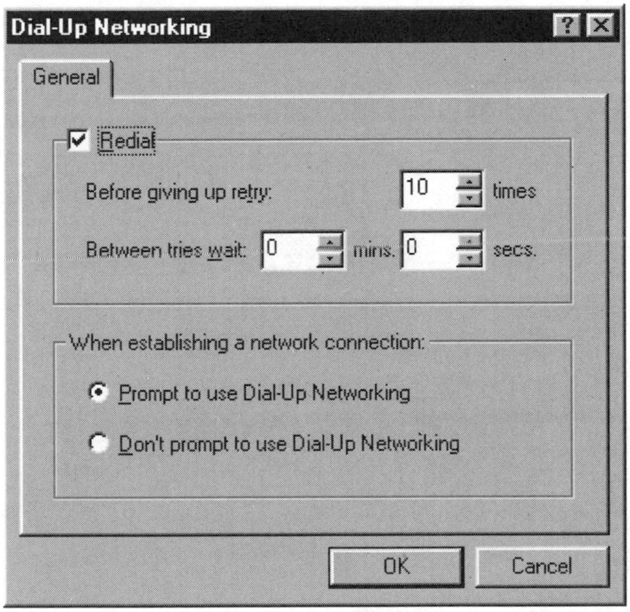

Figure 2-16: *Set the number of times you want to redial your ISP if you get a busy signal the first time.*

36. In the *When establishing a network connection* section, you have two choices, *Prompt to use Dial-Up Networking* and *Don't prompt to use Dial-Up Networking*. Chose the first if you are dialing into your organization's Intranet, or choose the second if you are dialing into an ISP. Click OK when you've finished making your selections.

Congratulations! You've configured for a dial-up connection.

TIP

To make it quick and easy to connect to the Internet, create a shortcut to each Dial-Up connectoid and place the shortcut on your desktop.

ESTABLISHING A CONNECTION TO THE INTERNET

To start an Internet connection, perform the following steps:

1. From My Computer, open the Dial-Up Networking folder. Double-click on the connectoid of the connection you want to use or double-click on a shortcut to the connectoid if you followed the advice in the previous Tip. Windows then displays the Connect To dialog box, seen in Figure 2-17. Click on the Connect button, and Windows dials the number for the connection you've chosen.

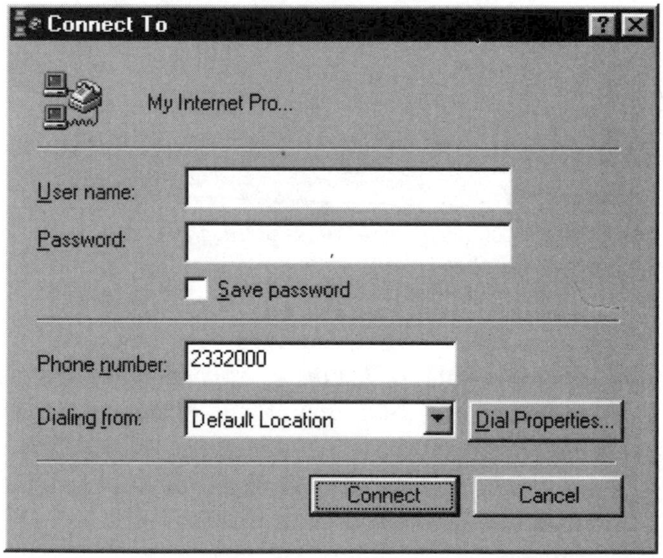

Figure 2-17: *Click on the Connect button to open a dial-up connection to the Internet.*

2. When the other computer answers, the Post-Dial Terminal Screen displays. Answer the prompts for your username and password by typing in the information your ISP gave you. Enter any other information required by your ISP. When a message is displayed that PPP or SLIP service has been established, followed by an IP address that has been assigned to you (or a range of IP addresses) and lines and lines of "garbage" characters (see Figure 2-18), click on Continue (F7).

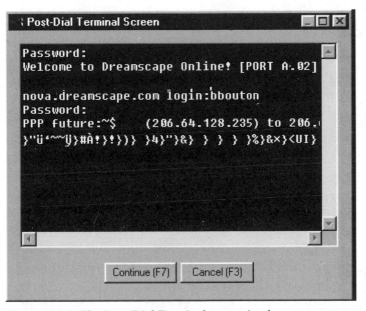

Figure 2-18: *The Post-Dial Terminal screen is where you enter username, password information, and any additional information your ISP has given you to connect to their servers.*

If you are using a SLIP account that assigns a new IP address every time you dial in instead of a static or fixed IP address, you need to write down the IP address that has been assigned to you, then enter it when prompted for it. You need to do this each time you login because the IP address will always be different. If you use RoboDun (an automatic script utility discussed later in this chapter) to automate your login, you can have RoboDun automatically capture the IP address and pass it to the Dial-Up software when it is asked for.

The Post-Dial Terminal Screen closes after the Continue button is clicked. In a moment or two, the status window will change into the Connected to My Internet Pro. . . window (see Figure 2-19), which displays the speed at which you are connected and the time you've been connected. You're connected to the Internet now and can open Netscape Navigator and begin the adventure. Click on the Connect window's Minimize button if you find the window distracting.

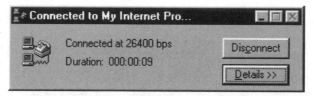

Figure 2-19: *When you see this window you're a part of the Internet!*

When you've had your fill of surfing, close your connection to the Internet by clicking on the Disconnect button on the Connect to window.

Windows 95 & Freeware Dial-in Utilities

The CD version of Windows 95 and the Microsoft Windows Plus! Pack comes with a dial-in scripting utility that can be configured to automatically enter your username, password, and other information required to login to your ISP. If you didn't buy the Plus! Pack or the CD version of Windows 95, you can download the scripting utility from Microsoft's Web site. Your ISP might also have created a Windows 95 dialing script for you to use; ask if one is available. If you have to configure your own script (and Microsoft's utility is *not* a straightforward dial-in solution), you may want to try RoboDun instead.

RoboDun: Freedom From Login Procedures

RoboDun is a great freeware utility by Mark Gamber. You can find RoboDun on the Internet (ftp://ftp.winsite.com/pub/pc/win95/ netutil/rdun61.zip), on most BBSes, and major online services. Many ISPs recommend RoboDun and can provide you with a RoboDun script.

If your ISP doesn't have a RoboDun script available, RoboDun offers good sample scripts you can adapt and clear, easy-to-use instructions and examples of how you can customize your script to meet your needs.

To install RoboDun:

1. Create a folder on your hard disk for RoboDun.

2. Uncompress the archived file you downloaded into the folder.

3. Open Control Panel and double-click the Add/Remove Programs icon. From the Add/Remove Programs window, select the Windows Setup tab and then click on the Have Disk button.

4. Use the Browse feature to locate the ROBODUN.INF file in the folder you created for RoboDun, and click on OK. RoboDun will install itself into your Start Up folder.

To run RoboDun for the first time, open the Start menu's Start Up folder and click the RoboDun icon. When RoboDun is running, it places a small telephone in the Taskbar tray. Double-click the telephone to launch the RoboDun Manager seen in Figure 2-20. Click on the Help button to open the RoboDun Help file. In the Help file, click the RoboDun Scripts link, then click on the link for the kind of connection you need to make—PPP, SLIP, or CompuServe. Select the entire script and copy it to the Windows Clipboard (Ctrl+C). Minimize the Help file.

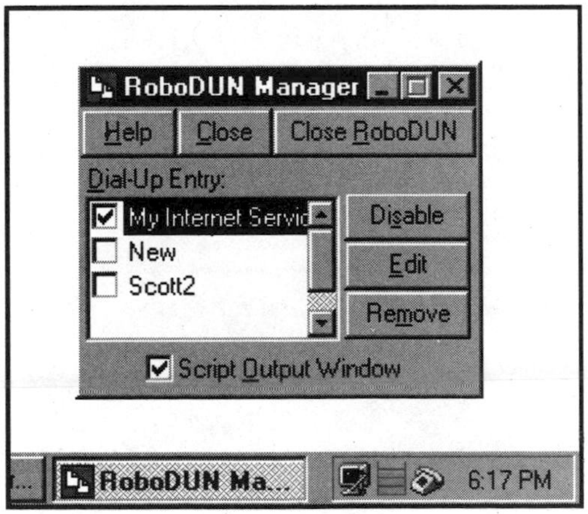

Figure 2-20: *Use the RoboDun Manager to create and manage automated dial-up scripts for each dial-up account you have.*

The RoboDun manager contains a list of all the Dial-Up connections you've made. Select the connection you'd like to create a script for, then click RoboDun Manager's Edit button. In the Edit Script window, paste in the script by pressing Ctrl+V, or clicking the Paste button. In Figure 2-21, the PPP script is being edited.

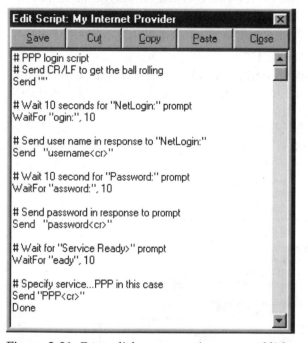

Figure 2-21: *Every dial-up connection you establish can have its own custom script, created by using RoboDun's Edit Script feature.*

The lines of the script that start with a # (pound sign) are not executed. Instead, they are remarks that explain what is happening in the line that follows. At the very least, you will need to edit the lines that begin with Send. Lines that begin with Send transmit data to the Post-Dial Terminal screen exactly as if you manually typed them in. Replace username with the login username your ISP gave you. Be sure to preserve the quote marks and the <cr> that surround the username. Do the same for password, replacing it with your assigned password. In the service section, you may have to change the upper case PPP in the Send line to lowercase if this is the way your ISP expects to receive the command. If your ISP automatically starts PPP (or SLIP) service without a request on your part, delete the Wait for "Service Ready>" prompt and the Specify service sections.

If your ISP provided you with a script, paste the script into the Edit Script window instead of the sample script and replace only the username and the password with your actual login username and password. To test your script, double-click the Dial-Up connectoid for the connection you want to make. When it displays the Post-Terminal Dial screen, RoboDun will appear and run the script you've provided. If there is a problem, RoboDun will stop on the line where it has a problem.

When you've completed editing the script, click Close button to return to the RoboDun Manager. Make sure the Script Output Window is checked. The Script Output Window displays the progress that is being made whenever a script is run. RoboDun puts a checkbox next to connections that have scripts. Scripts are enabled when the checkbox is checked, and manual login is required when the checkbox is unchecked.

Clicking on the Close button closes the RoboDun Manager. Clicking Close RoboDun closes the automatic scripting utility itself. Notice that the telephone icon disappears from the tray. RoboDun will only automatically log you into your provider using the script you created when the scripting utility is running and the telephone icon is displayed in the tray.

Regardless of whether you choose to use Windows 95's solution, or a shareware or freeware dial-in utility, the automated dial-in services get you one step closer to your goal every time you want to use your computer to get connected. There's nothing to mistype, and in seconds you're a part of the Internet.

Adding AutoDial

With a scripting utility like RoboDun automatically logging you
into your ISP, opening an Internet connection is as easy as clicking
a connectoid. But it would be even handier if a connection would
automatically start up whenever you launched Netscape Navigator. This additional level of automation is easy to add by tapping
into the AutoDial feature that came with the Windows Plus! Pack.
If you have an Internet icon in your Control Panel, you already
have AutoDial installed. But there is another way to get AutoDial
capability without purchasing the Plus! Pack. Download
AUTODIAL.ZIP from http://www.creativelement.com/
win95ann/.

AUTODIAL.ZIP is a very small file that contains no instructions
on its use. What it *does* contain, however, is a small
AUTODIAL.REG file that when merged into the Windows 95 system Registry, enables the autodialing feature. It also contains the
file URL.DLL. This DLL is required for AutoDial to work. You may
already have a copy of URL.DLL installed in the Windows\System
folder. If not, copy the file to your Windows\System folder. To
merge (install) the information in AUTODIAL.REG into your system Registry, right-click AUTODIAL.REG and choose Merge from
the shortcut menu.

Once AutoDial is installed, click on the Internet icon in Control
Panel. The Internet Properties window shown in Figure 2-22 appears. In the AutoDial tab, check the Use AutoDial checkbox and
choose the default dial-up connection you want to use every time
you launch Netscape Navigator. The *Auto disconnect* checkbox will
close your connection if no activity is detected for the period of
time that you specify in the *Disconnect if idle* spinbox. The *Perform
system security check before dialing* feature will notify you your Dial-
Up Adapter connection has been setup for file and printer sharing.
Sharing resources while connected to the Internet poses a security
risk.

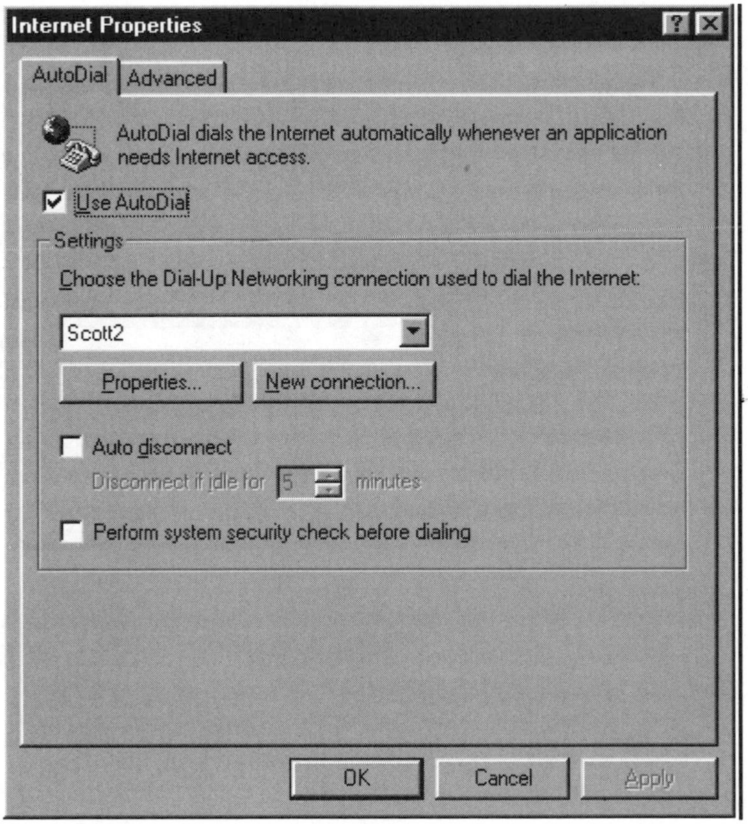

Figure 2-22: *AutoDial can automatically get your Internet connection going every time you want to use Netscape Navigator.*

If you access the Internet through a proxy server, click on the Advanced tab. On the Advanced tab, check the Use Proxy Server check box, and then enter the IP address for your *Proxy Server* in the Settings field. Be sure to enter the IP addresses of any local servers you have access to in the *Bypass proxy on* field (seen in Figure 2-23).

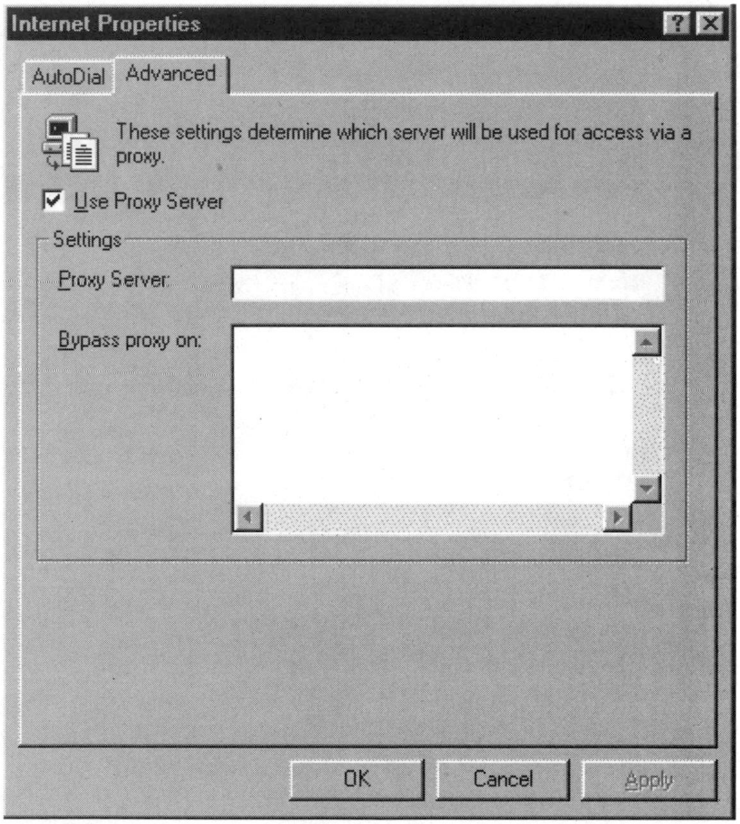

Figure 2-23: *Corporate networks often use a proxy server to connect to the Internet. Make sure you choose Bypass proxy only if you're connecting to a company server, and not the Internet.*

Click OK to close the Internet Properties window, and you're done. Now, every time you click Netscape Navigator icon to launch it, AutoDial will automatically bring up the Connect to window for the connection you've specified. All you do is press the Connect button and before you know it, you're cruising the Internet with Navigator.

TIP

If you want to automate even further, there are a number of shareware and freeware programs that can "push" the Connect button for you (Dunce is the name of one such program) and others that can launch a connection for you at times you specify. When you combine these programs with the site-grabbing software discussed in Chapter 3, "Power Navigation," you end up with a powerful way to automate your online time. The Totally Hot Bookmarks list contains jumps to some of the best automation software.

INSTALLING NAVIGATOR

Now that you have the ISP of your dreams, your hardware is humming, and your system and connectivity software are in place, it's time to take a look at the "orchestra leader"—Navigator itself.

If you already have a copy of Navigator 3 or Navigator Gold installed, you can skip over this section, but do take a look at customizing preferences and the plug-ins sections. Even if you do have a copy, Netscape updates Navigator quite often and, depending on your license agreement, you may want to upgrade your copy. You definitely want to upgrade if you're using any version of Navigator prior to Navigator 3.0. A lot has changed.

Fully registered versions of Navigator are available through a wide variety of retail and mail-order outlets, as well as through the Netscape General Store. Evaluation copies, public betas, and software subscription updates are available from Netscape's FTP sites on the Web. Many ISPs also offer Navigator as part of their sign-on bundle. If you received Navigator on disk or on a CD, follow the installation instructions provided with the package. The installation *procedures* are quite similar regardless of how you get Navigator, however, so you may want to read through the following section.

In this section, it's assumed that you or a friend has downloaded the latest update to Navigator; it's the appropriate version of Navigator for your computer, and you have a working connection to the Internet. See the beginning of this chapter for system requirements.

Running the Setup Program

Downloaded copies of Navigator come in a single, compressed file archive. Files that have 32 in their file names are for use in Windows 95 or Windows NT, and those that have 16 in their names are designed for Windows 3.1x or Windows for Workgroups 3.11. When downloading Navigator or Navigator Gold from Netscape's site you also have your choice of downloading a Minimum or a Standard version. The Minimum version does not contain the Netscape extra components such as Live 3D, a VRML (Virtual Reality Modeling Language) plug-in, or CoolTalk (an Internet conferencing, telephone, and whiteboard program). Netscape considers these extra components to be integral parts of Navigator and strongly suggests that you download the Standard version of Navigator that contains them. If you've downloaded the Minimum version (it's a much smaller and quicker download) we recommend that you download these individual components from the Netscape Component page: http://home.netscape.com/comprod/mirror/navcomponents_download.html.

When you've downloaded the appropriate version of Navigator, create a temporary folder on your hard disk and move the file archive into the directory. Close any running applications, including things that run in the background such as Microsoft Office Manager. Disable any virus-checking software you may have running. Virus detection software and other running applications can interfere with any software installation process. When you've taken care of these housekeeping matters, it's time to install the software.

1. Double-click the file archive. You will be asked if you want to install Navigator. Click Yes. This launches the installation wizard that decompresses the archive, guides you through the installation, and afterward cleans away temp files that the installer created. The installer then displays the welcome screen. Click on the Next button to proceed with the installation.

2. The Choose Destination Location window displays. If you've never had a copy of Navigator installed or if you accept the suggested location, Navigator will put its files in a very deep directory structure, for example

C:\Program Files\Netscape\Navigator\. If you have a previously installed copy of Navigator, Setup will suggest reusing and thereby overwriting the existing copy of Navigator.

In either case, you may not *want* to accept the default location recommendation. You may not want to overwrite your existing version of Navigator until you are certain that the new version is installed correctly. Also some users have had problems with Netscape News keeping the available newsgroup information separate for each news server because of the space used in the Program Files folder name. Some Navigator third-party plug-ins also have problems with folder names that have spaces in them. We recommend that you *do not* accept the default location and that you choose to install Netscape Navigator to a location such as C:\NNav or C:\Netscape\Nav, where C is the drive on which you install the program. Keep the folder names as short as possible and without spaces, and make sure the drive you choose has lots of free space.

TIP

If you take our advice and install into a new folder/directory instead of overwriting a previous installation of Navigator, you'll have some additional work to do. Any plug-ins that you installed in the previous version will have to be reinstalled so that they will work in the new copy of Navigator. If you installed over the old copy of Navigator, however, then you won't have to reinstall the plug-ins.

To change the location where Navigator installs, click the Browse button and either choose an existing directory from the Choose Directory window or enter the path using the folder name(s) you'd like Navigator to create and use. For example, if you want Navigator to install to C:\NNav and you haven't created an empty NNav folder, type C:\NNav into the Path entry field. Navigator will then display a confirmation box asking if you want this folder created. Click Yes. When you have finished specifying the location where you want Navigator to install, click OK.

3. The next question Navigator asks is if you want to install CoolTalk. Click Yes to install CoolTalk or No to skip the CoolTalk installation. The installation of Navigator and its components begins immediately after you click the CoolTalk query box's Yes or No button.

   If you don't install CoolTalk now and after reading Chapter 10, "CoolTalk," you decide you do want CoolTalk, you'll either have to reinstall all of Navigator (answering Yes when you get to this point) or download the stand-alone version of CoolTalk and install it.

When the installation wizard has completed copying the files, making the Registry entries, and creating the program group, if you chose to install CoolTalk you're asked if you'd like to enable the CoolTalk Watchdog. The Watchdog automatically launches CoolTalk when another user places a CoolTalk call to you. Unless you are permanently connected to the Internet you should click No.

CONNECTING TO NETSCAPE'S SITE TO COMPLETE THE SETUP

The last question you're asked is if you want to connect to Netscape's site to continue the setup. In *actuality*, the setup of the software on your computer is complete at this point. This offer at the conclusion of Navigator setup allows you to do the following things:

- Register your new Navigator software.

- Go directly to the Quick Purchase section to investigate your purchasing options.

- Go to VeriSign and obtain a personal Digital Passport security certificate (see Chapter 7, "Maintaining Your Privacy on the Internet," for information on digital ID security certificates.

- Find and download Netscape Navigator components and third-party plug-in applications. If you are installing from the Minimum version downloaded from Netscape's site, you should take this opportunity to download the components that were not included in that package (CoolTalk and Live3D). If you downloaded the Standard version, all of the integral Netscape components were included, but you may want to investigate some of the many plug-ins that are available. The Companion CD-ROM contains many of the most valuable plug-ins so you may want to skip this section of the setup for now until you've had a look around the Companion CD-ROM and tried out a few of the plug-ins.

- Download the latest version of Navigator or Navigator Gold.

- Connect to the Netscape home site and begin your Internet excursions. Don't click Yes to go to the Netscape site unless you have an active Internet connection open (which is not recommended when installing software). Instead, minimize the Setup window and launch your Internet connection. Or if you'd prefer to continue this process later (or bypass it altogether), click the No button. You can visit the setup site at any time in the future by typing the following URL in Navigator's Location field: http://home.netscape.com/misc/registration/setup/.

If you *do* go to the Netscape Navigator Setup page (shown in Figure 2-24), you'll be led step by step through the setup process by a series of linked pages. You can go straight through or skip over any part of the setup process. Unless you get side tracked on one of the third-party plug-in pages, you'll finish up the setup process on the Congratulations page as seen in Figure 2-25. From this page you can click the links and go to Netscape's Destinations pages (a series of links to great places on the Web), to the Netscape General Store (do a little shopping), or you can click the My Page button and start creating your own Netscape Personal Workspace.

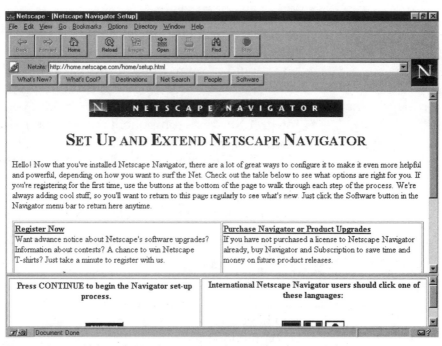

Figure 2-24: *Although Navigator setup is complete, you might want to continue on to Netscape's site to register your software and check out other Netscape programs and get third-party plug-ins.*

Figure 2-25: *From the Congratulations page you can go just about anywhere.*

If none of these places appeal to you, click on the Home button on the toolbar to go to Netscape's home page where you'll find announcements regarding Navigator, Netscape products, and other interesting news. Netscape's home page is a great place to start your Internet travels, but on a day-to-day basis, wouldn't it be nice to have your own launching spot on the Web? Well you can. Click on the My Page button on the Congratulations page or on the My Page link on Netscape's home page (toward the bottom of the page) and you'll soon be on your way to building your own custom starting point for your Web travels.

CREATING YOUR OWN PERSONAL WORKSPACE

Netscape's Personal Workspace is a new Netscape page-building service that creates a custom startup page you can use as your personal Internet home base, just as you would use Netscape's own home page. The page that the Personal Workspace Wizard builds can contain links to your favorite sites, links to top news, search, and reference sites, as well as the latest Netscape news. Your Personal Workspace also behaves like a mini-personal information manager (*PIM*) when you choose to add a notepad to your Workspace. Jot down messages, reminders, and to-do lists in the notepad window, and they will display each time you open your Personal Workspace. Your Personal Workspace is only a click or two away whenever you're online.

Building your own Personal Workspace is as easy as clicking a few buttons and links. If you'd like to try your hand at Workspace building, click on the My Page button on Netscape's home page. If you can't find the My Page button (Netscape's home page is constantly changing), type the URL for the Personal Space Wizard (http://home.netscape.com/custom/index.html) into the browser's Location/Go to: field, then press the Enter key.

It may take a few moments for the wizard to load and become active—Netscape's home page is a very busy one. If it takes too long, click in the Location/Go to: field and then press Enter to reload the page. Reloading establishes a new connection that may find a quicker route through Internet traffic from your computer to Netscape's than the first one did. You're ready to begin when the Create Your Personal Workspace page loads (see Figure 2-26). Click on the Continue button and follow the onscreen directions.

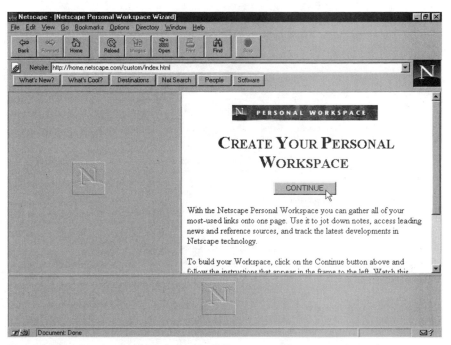

Figure 2-26: *You're ready to begin building yourself a Personal Workspace when you see this screen.*

When you've completed designing your Workspace, click on the Build button. The Wizard will store the information needed to design your Personal Workspace in the COOKIE.TXT file located on your hard disk in the Navigator folder.

The next time that you click on the My Page button or link on Netscape's home page or load the URL: http://home.netscape.com/custom/show_page.html, a JavaScript on Netscape's site will be sent to your computer. When the JavaScript has been received by your computer, it goes to work reading the COOKIE.TXT file and then assembles and displays your Personal Workspace as a viewable, working page as shown in Figure 2-27.

Figure 2-27: *Your Personal Workspace can contain links to favorite sites as well as a notepad where you can store reminders and to-do lists.*

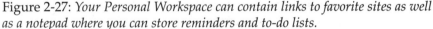

HOW PRIVATE IS YOUR PERSONAL WORKSPACE?

There are many personal reasons, as well as legitimate business reasons, for ensuring that Internet communications are secure and private. Your privacy is assured when you build a Personal Workspace because the choices you make in the wizard—the links and notes you make—are stored on your hard disk in the COOKIE.TXT file and not on the Internet or on Netscape's computers. The JavaScript processing of the COOKIE.TXT file occurs on your computer; no one on the Internet can access your personal information. Additionally, because JavaScript-generated pages will not print, no one who has access to your computer, including you, can print a copy of your home page using Navigator's printing feature. Anyone *can*, however, print your Personal Workspace page as a series of print screen graphics; press the Print Screen key on your keyboard and then paste the graphic into a program that can accept graphics, and print from there. The COOKIE.TXT file can also be printed from a text editor, and notes you make in your Personal Workspace appear in the file as text, such as colorful epithets you might have for your place of employment. So take due precaution to ensure that a curious co-worker doesn't spill the cookies!

Because your Personal Workspace is JavaScript driven, it can only be created or displayed if you've allowed the use of JavaScript in Navigator's Network Preferences. The assembly of the page is dependent on the JavaScript that Netscape sends to your computer and the proper interpretation of your COOKIE.TXT file, so you must have an active Internet connection going and be able to make contact with the Netscape site to make your Personal Workspace appear. If you've created a Personal Workspace and like the feature, you can put the URL: http://home.netscape.com/custom/show_page.html in your Navigator General Preferences options so that it displays each time you open Navigator.

TRAP

Simply because a cookie is a text file that you can read with a text editor, don't ever edit *the file. Editing "breaks" a cookie and makes it unacceptable to the server that issued the cookie. The server will write a new one that will undo any changes you've made. For more information about cookies, check out http://www.netscape.com/newsref/std/cookie_spec.html.*

If you want to know whenever a site is creating and attempting to store a cookie on your computer, enable the Show an Alert Before Accepting a Cookie checkbox in Navigator's Network Preferences.

CUSTOMIZING FOR PERFORMANCE

With a few exceptions, Navigator's default settings will work fine for you as you make your first forays out to the Net. But if you want to tweak Navigator's performance or customize it to work the way *you* want it to, you'll need to spend some time in the various Preferences dialogs. In this section, you'll see how to make

Netscape Navigator into your *personal* edition of Navigator. All of Navigator's and Navigator Gold's Preferences dialogs are found on the Options menu of any version of Navigator's window. Both Navigator and Navigator Gold offer identical preference options, except Navigator Gold has an additional set of options that are used to configure Navigator Gold's Editor. If you're impatient to get going and want to fine tune later, be sure to at least fill in a few necessary facts about you and your Internet connections in the Mail and News Preferences dialog. See Chapter 6, "Person to Person With Navigator Mail & Netscape News," for complete information about these options.

GENERAL PREFERENCES

General Preferences is where you specify how Navigator windows and their contents display, what kind of fonts are used, how color, images, and various Internet file formats are handled, what language is used and most importantly, which helper applications Navigator uses. Let's step through the seven tabs found in the General Preferences dialog.

APPEARANCE TAB

Options on General Preferences' Appearance tab, shown in Figure 2-28, control how the toolbar is displayed, which one of Navigator's services is launched when you start Navigator, what URL is used for your startup home page, and how you want hypertext links to display.

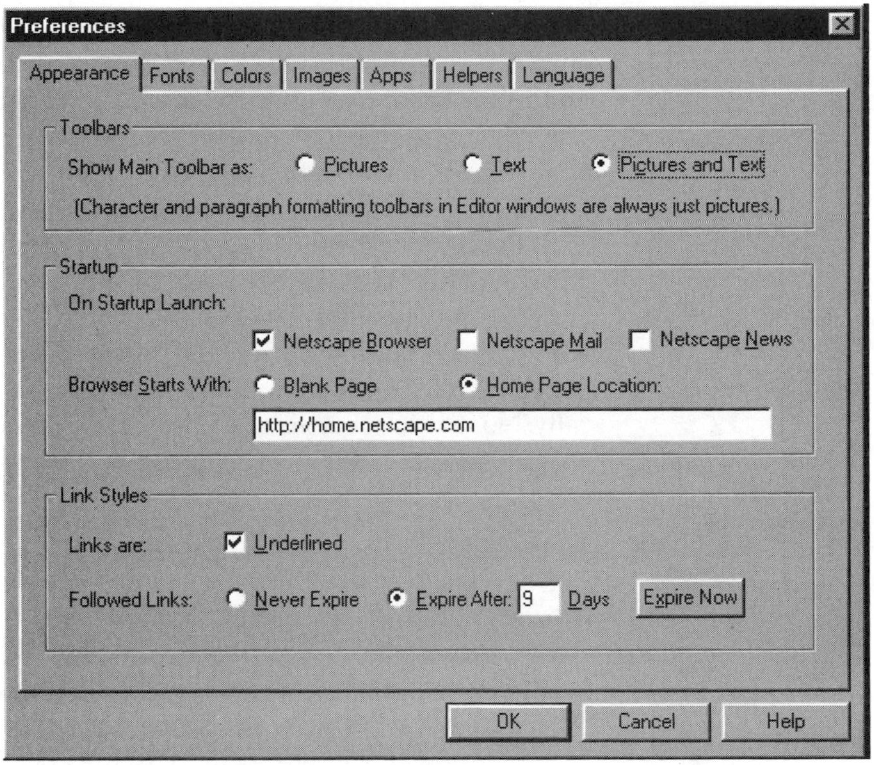

Figure 2-28: *The General Preferences tab.*

■ The *Show Main Toolbar* field has three options: *Pictures*, *Text* and *Pictures, and Text*, that determine the face of the Toolbar buttons. Pictures and Text is the default choice, but it is also the choice that takes up the most room on the screen. To maximize screen real estate, you may want to change this setting to either Pictures or Text. Better yet, see Chapter 3, "Power Navigation," for tips on how use keyboard short-cuts and other strategies for eliminating the need to have the toolbar on the screen all the time.

- The *On Startup Launch* checkboxes: *Netscape Browser* (the default), *Netscape Mail*, and *Netscape News* determine which windows automatically open when you launch Navigator. You can check one, two, or all three boxes, but if you leave all the boxes unchecked, the Netscape Browser checkbox will check itself. If you use Navigator primarily to check for Mail throughout the day, you can save a lot of time by checking only the Netscape Mail checkbox. When you launch Navigator, only the Mail window will open, and you won't be slowed down while the browser loads a home page, nor will you have to open the Mail window automatically. No matter what you decide here, the other Navigator modules are still only a few clicks away on the Windows menu.

- The *Browser Starts With* radio buttons, *Blank Page* and *Home Page Location* (the default), determine if the Navigator Browser will load a page on opening or not. When Blank Page is chosen, the URL that is specified in the text entry field below the Start With radio buttons is loaded into the Browser's Location field, but Navigator will not load the URL unless you place your cursor in the Location Field and then press Enter. If you have enabled the AutoDial feature, it is useful to temporarily enable the Blank Page setting when you will be viewing or if you are writing HTML pages and want to view them locally. AutoDial will not attempt to establish an Internet connection if Blank Page is selected or if the entry in the field below the Start With radio buttons is empty or points to a file on your hard disk.

   If you choose the default Start With option, Home Page Location, enter an URL in the text entry field below the radio buttons. The default entry here is Netscape's home page, but you can use any URL. This URL is used whenever you launch Navigator's Browser and when you click on the Home button on the toolbar. If you've configured your own

Netscape Personal Workspace, you may want to make the URL for it your default home page. To do so, place the URL, http://home.netscape.com/custom/index.html in the entry field and make sure you have clicked on the Home Page Location radio button.

■ The *Links are Underlined* checkbox determines if the colored text in a document that serves as a link is underlined. Underlining of links serves as an important visual clue that you are looking at a link and not simply text that the author of the page added color to. Unless you find the underlining to be very disruptive to your reading, leave this box checked. The underline will disappear when the box is unchecked, but the text will still display in the color associated with the kind of link the text is. Link color is defined in the Colors tab. If you've turned underlining off, you can tell if colored text is a link or not by hovering your cursor over the text. If the cursor takes on the shape of a pointing hand, the colored text is a link.

■ The Followed Links section offers the options of Never Expire, Expire After a user-defined number of days, and the Expire Now feature. These options control when, if ever, a link you've taken is changed back to the unfollowed color. Expire Now is a handy option if you share your copy of Navigator with family or co-workers. If you click on the Expire Now button and answer Yes in the confirmation dialog, at the end of each Navigator session all links are immediately marked as unvisited and where you've been won't distract other users.

THE FONTS TAB

Options on the General Preferences Fonts tab, seen in Figure 2-29, control which font is used to display all text in all of Navigator's module, as well as which character set is used.

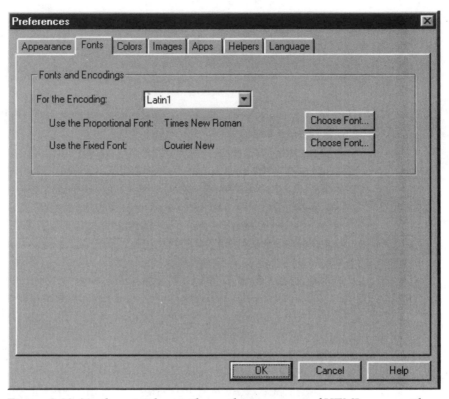

Figure 2-29: *You have total control over the appearance of HTML pages as they display in Navigator. You can choose a font and a character set.*

- The For the Encoding drop-down box offers: Latin1, Japanese, Latin2, Chinese (Big5), Korean, Chinese (GB), Cyrillic, Greek, Turkish, and User Define. You should leave this setting at its default of Latin 1, unless you have a need to view pages in any of the listed languages.

- The *Use the Proportional Font* and the *Use the Fixed Font* areas of the Fonts dialog box report on what fonts you are currently using to display incoming text, as well as the fonts used in the Mail and News message content windows and in the Message Composition windows. The Proportional Font is used in most of the text displayed in the body of HTML documents. The Fixed Font is used in forms, FTP listings, and in areas of HTML documents where the author specified its use. Unlike a proportional font, all of the characters in a fixed font take up the same amount of character width. Fixed fonts resemble the output of a manual typewriter or characters displayed in a text editor while Proportional fonts look more like a typeset page of text. Click the Choose Font button next to each of the fonts to change the font used and its base size. The defaults are Times New Roman 12 pt for the Proportional Font and Courier New 10 pt for the Fixed Font. The base size of the font is the size of the font that is used for body copy. Headlines will be larger than the base size, and subscripts and superscripts will be smaller than the base size.

We recommend that you use the default settings because the authors of Web pages design a page with these font settings in mind. If you change the font or the point size, pages may not be as nicely composed, nor will you see the page as the author hoped you would. However, which font and what size you choose is entirely up to you. If you find that text in HTML documents or in the Message Composition is too small or too large for you to read comfortably, change the Base size of the font here by clicking the Choose Font button. Any change you make in this Options tab affects all text displayed in all of the Navigator windows.

In the Choose Base Font dialog box that displays when you click either of the Choose Font buttons, you'll notice that some fonts listed have two T's next to them and others do not. The two T's mean that the font is a TrueType font. When choosing a font, try to pick a TrueType font. TrueType displays a little better onscreen and is easier on the eyes than Type 1 or other system fonts. A Type 1 font, however, is usually a better choice when printing a page, especially if you have a PostScript printer.

COLORS TAB

The Colors tab seen in Figure 2-30 is where you choose which colors will be used for links and page background color. The Colors tab is also used to select if an image of yours will be used for the background or if you will allow the author of the page you are viewing to determine these matters. We strongly recommend that you use the default settings. If you change these settings, particularly if you check the Always Use My Colors and Overriding Document check box, you will *never* see a page as the author intended it to display. Some graphics will become difficult to see because they will be lost in the either the background color you choose or in the image you've defined as the background. As always, it's up to you to decide how you want things to look, but this set of options is probably one that you *don't* want to exercise.

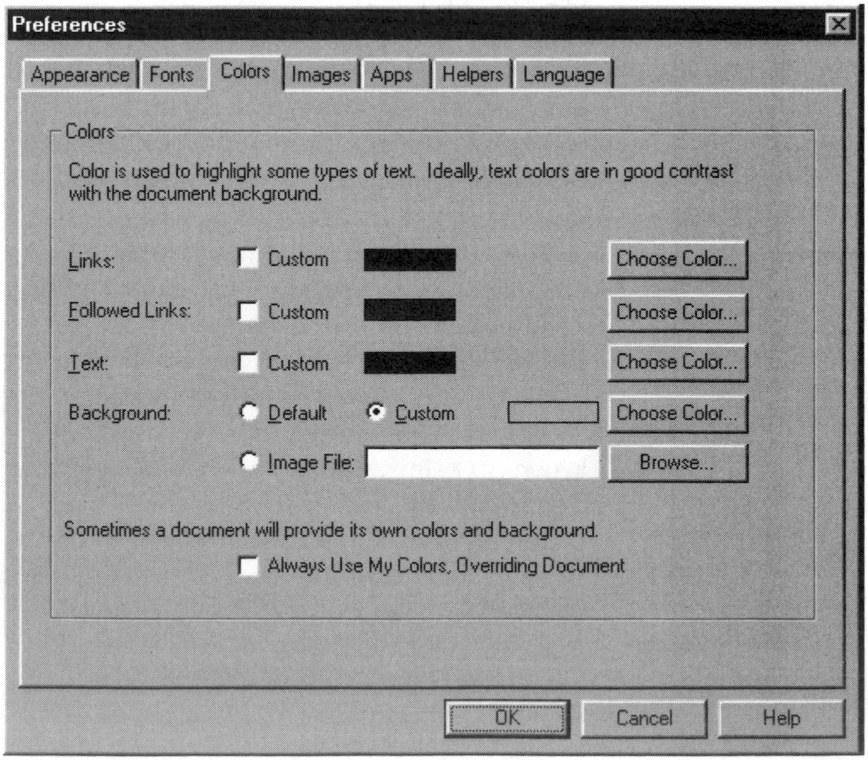

Figure 2-30: *Changing the default settings prevents you from seeing Web pages as they were meant to be seen.*

■ The default color for *Links* that are unfollowed is blue, *Followed Links* are purple, the default Text color is black, the *Background* color is light gray, and no *Image File* is used as wallpaper. Each of these options can be changed by either clicking the checkbox or radio button next to the option, then clicking the related Choose Color or Browse button to select the new color or image. Whenever a Choose Color button is clicked, the Windows color picker appears where you can choose a color for the option. If you click the Browse button, the *Select a backdrop image* drives and folders dialog box appears. Any image file that is in the GIF or JPG file format can chosen as the background image. If you choose to use this feature, choose a small, quick loading image file that will tile to fill the window.

The *Always Use My Colors Overriding Document* option is unchecked by default. If you check this box, which is not recommended, you will undo all the hard and wondrous work Web page authors have gone through to create rich, colorful, and exciting pages for you. If you do, however, reach a site where the colors and the wallpaper used make it painful for you to assimilate the content of the site, open up this tab, check this box, click OK, and then reload the offending page. You will get a plain, vanilla view. Just remember to come back and uncheck this box, or all of the Web will take on an austere, uniform look.

IMAGES TAB

The Images tab, seen in Figure 2-31, is where you specify when and how images will be displayed.

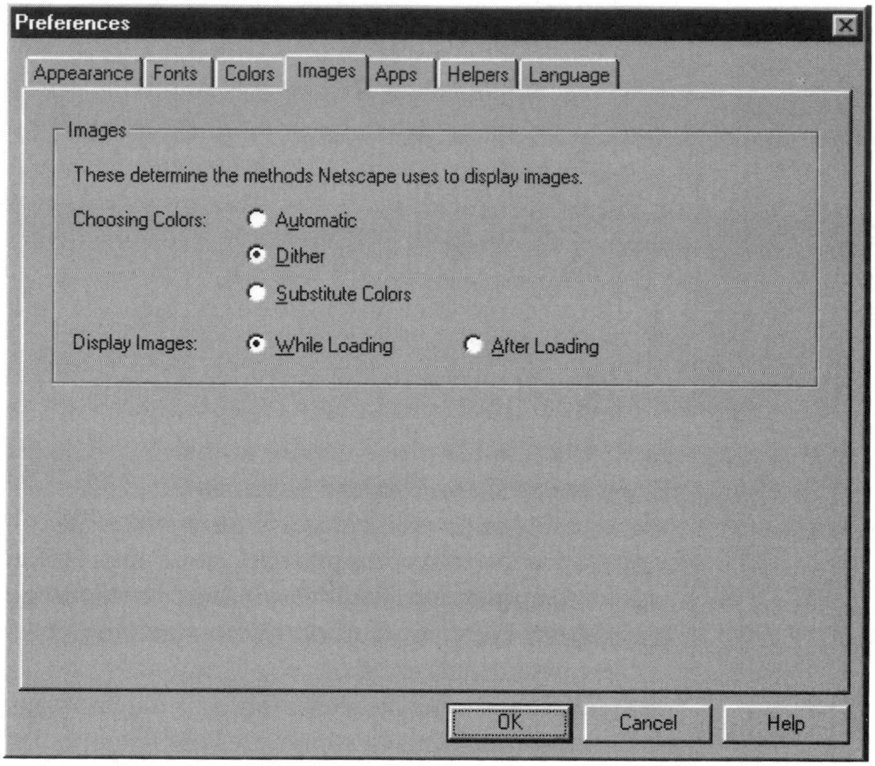

Figure 2-31: *You can choose how background images display on pages you download.*

- The first set of options on the Images tab, *Choosing Colors*, offers the choices of *Automatic*, *Dither*, and *Substitute Colors*. These option settings only affect how the colors in an image are displayed if your computer is set to display 16 or 256 colors. If your computer display is running in 16-bit Hi-Color (32,000 or 64,0000 colors) or 24-bit TrueColor (16.7 million colors), these settings don't change your view of an image. The color depth (the number of colors your computer displays at one time) is dependent on the capability of your monitor, your video card, the amount of RAM on the video card, and the video drivers available for your card.

When your monitor displays 256 or fewer colors, it doesn't have enough colors available to display all the different colors that might be in an image. The Dither and Substitute Colors options are different methods that Netscape uses to approximate the display of colors that are not available on your system. *Dithering* "fakes" a color by representing it as a pattern made out of available colors that when viewed from a distance approximate the original colors. The Substitute Colors option looks at each color in the image and finds the closest match it can, which sometimes looks fine, depending on the content of the image. The default option, Automatic, allows Navigator to decide which method is most appropriate for the image. You will usually get the best overall results if you choose the Automatic setting. Your best option, however, would be to avoid this option altogether and configure your computer display to use Hi-Color or TrueColor. See the following sidebar for information on how to change the color depth capability of your display.

CHANGING THE COLOR DEPTH OF YOUR VIDEO DISPLAY

In Windows 95 these settings are made and changed by right-clicking a blank area of the Desktop, then choosing Properties from the shortcut menu. When the Display Properties dialog box appears, click the Settings tab. The Colors Palette drop-down list will display the choices for color depth that are available on your computer. The options that are available on the Colors Palette drop-down may change if you choose a different desktop size, and you may have to reduce the desktop size before TrueColor or Hi-Color options become available. In general, the larger the Desktop area the fewer choices you will have. If you want to see all images at their best, choose Hi-Color or TrueColor if available. Choose 256 Color or 16 Color (images and photographs look dreadful in 16 colors) if you have system problems or incompatibilities that appear when using higher color modes. On older computers with small amounts of system and video RAM, a lower color depth such as 256 colors will speed up screen redraw and tax your system less.

To change color depth in Windows 3.1x, close any active applications. From Program Manger, find the Windows Setup icon (usually in the Main group) and double-click it to launch the Windows Setup applet. When Windows Setup displays, choose Options and then Change System Settings. Click the down arrow next to the Display drop-down list to display a list of installed and available video drivers. Drivers for your video card usually have the manufacturer's name mentioned in them someplace. Choose a driver that supports the combination of color depth and screen size you want to use. The higher the color depth you choose, the better the images will display. Click OK. Specify that Windows should use the current driver (by clicking the button labeled Use Current Driver in the next dialog box), and then choose Restart Windows. Window will restart using the new color depth and screen resolution.

The last option you can set from the Colors tab is when the images display—*While Loading* (the default) or *After Loading*. While Loading allows images to begin drawing to the screen as soon as the graphics data arrives on your computer. This option is particularly useful because many times you can see enough of a graphic before it is loaded to decide if you want to stick around for it to completely load. After Loading causes images to be drawn to the screen only after the entire page and its components have been received. Pages received from the Internet do *not* load faster if this option is chosen, but Intranet pages may load slightly faster.

TIP

Neither of these options determine if graphics should be allowed to Auto Load. That is accomplished by checking or unchecking Auto Load Images from the Browser's Options menu. Changes made on the Options menu such as disabling Auto Load Images and showing or hiding the toolbar carry over from session to session.

APPS TAB

The Apps tab (Figure 2-32) deals with supporting applications. On this tab, you specify which programs should be used to make Telnet connections, to view the source code of HTML documents you view online, and where to place temporary files.

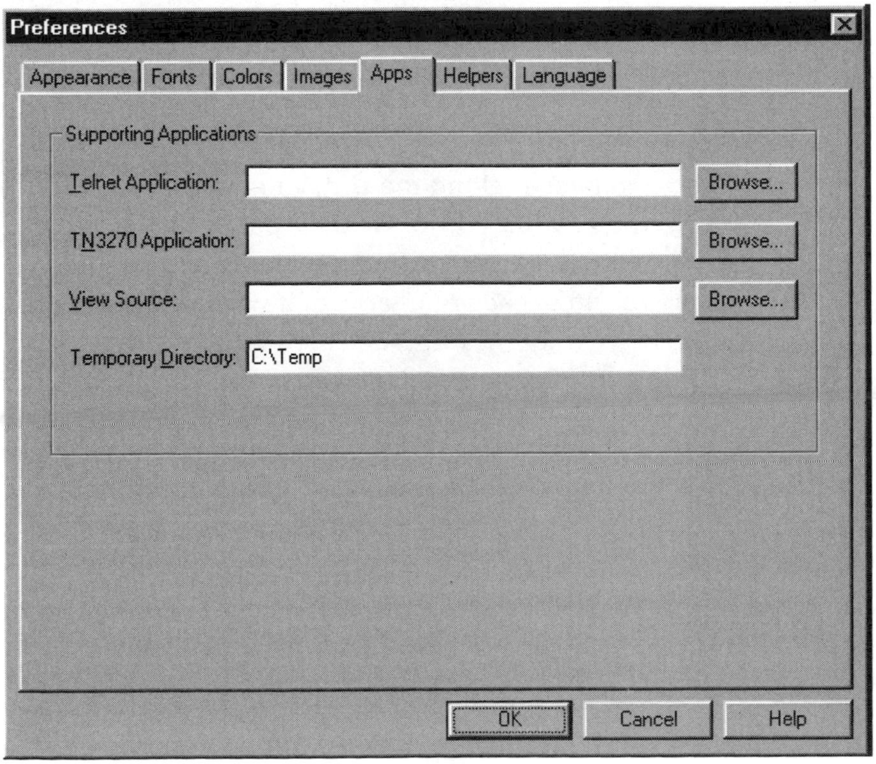

Figure 2-32: *Make sure the Temporary Directory field is set to an existing directory on a drive with a lot of free space on it.*

What is Telnet?

Before Navigator and the meteoric rise of the World Wide Web, one of the primary ways people got around electronically was by using Telnet. Telnet is a text-based Internet scheme that allows you to log into another system remotely. Depending on your access privileges, with Telnet, you can do whatever you could do if you were sitting in front of the server. If you've ever logged on to CompuServe in Terminal mode, or used an Opus-based BBS, you'd feel at home in a Telnet session.

Just as you use Navigator to handle your interaction with HTTP-based Web servers, Telnet applications make the connection for you to servers that offer Telnet services. Telnet was once a very important service, but now fewer and fewer sites offer Telnet because they are moving their content to Web servers. When you enter a Telnet URL into Navigator's Location field or click a link to a Telnet site, Navigator recognizes that a Telnet-capable application is required to make the connection. Netscape in this situation automatically launches whichever Telnet program you specify in this tab and passes along the URL you want to the application.

Windows 95 comes with a basic Telnet application called TELNET.EXE., which is found in the Windows folder. If you need to access Telnet sites regularly, or if you are using Windows 3.x, you probably might want to get a full-featured Telnet application. The Totally Hot Bookmarks list on the Companion CD-ROM has entries for sites where you can download freeware and shareware Telnet applications.

- The Telnet Application and TN3270 Application entry boxes are where you specify the path to the Telnet application of your choice. To use the Telnet application that came with Windows 95, enter TELNET.EXE in this field. TN3270 is a special form of Telnet that the Windows 95 Telnet application doesn't handle, so if you need to connect to a TN3270 Telnet site, you'll have to acquire and specify a different application here.

■ View Source is where you get to choose whether you want to use the default Navigator viewer, or if you'd prefer to use your favorite text editor to view HTML source code and other ASCII text files. If you leave this field blank, the Navigator viewer is used. When you specify a text editor such as NOTEPAD.EXE, you can edit a file you view and then save it to disk from the text editor. The Navigator viewer only displays and allows you to copy text to the Clipboard; no text editing is offered—but it does display document source text faster than a text editor.

■ The Temporary Directory option is a very important option for both Windows 95 and Windows 3.1x users. Navigator, helper applications, plug-ins, and usually all of your other applications use this space to temporarily store data. If there is not enough room to store the data, or if the directory no longer exists, an error will occur in the application attempting to access this location on the hard disk. The temporary directory specified here should be on a drive with a lot of empty space, and it's better if the drive is not compressed by disk compression programs such as DriveSpace, DoubleSpace, or Stacker.

   If you are having problems printing or with plug-in or helper applications, check to be sure that this entry points to a directory that exists and that the drive still has plenty of room on it; 20 to 30MB is a perilously low amount of free drive space. When it installs, Navigator places an entry to C:\Temp in the Temporary Directory field, but if your C drive is crowded, you should make a Temp folder on a drive that has more room and then put the path to that folder in the Temporary Directory entry field. Temporary files are supposed to be automatically deleted when the application that put them there is through with them, or when you close the application. But sometimes this doesn't happen, so it is a good idea to regularly check the contents of your Temp folder and delete anything in it. If you use Windows 3.1x, do this from a DOS prompt when Windows is not running. If you use Windows 95, it will not let you delete any temporary files that are currently being used. If you suspect that the file you want to delete is not in fact being used, exit Windows 95 by choosing Restart in MS-DOS mode from the Exit Windows dialog box, and then try deleting the files from the MS-DOS 7 prompt.

HELPERS TAB

The Helpers tab, shown in Figure 2-33, is the place to go to specify helper programs, if any, that you want Navigator to call upon when Navigator encounters a file of a type it does not natively support or can play through the use of plug-ins. This is also where you edit or create MIME types and associate them with file extensions.

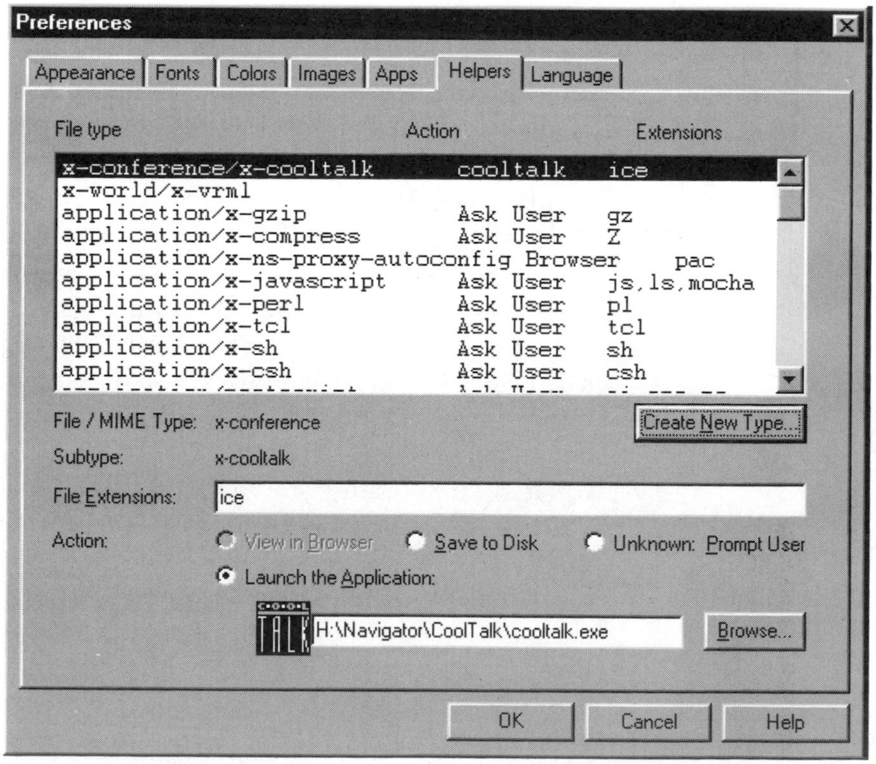

Figure 2-33: *With the right plug-ins, Navigator can display any type of electronic media you find on the Internet. Choose your Helper apps in the Helpers tab.*

LANGUAGE TAB

The Language tab (see Figure 2-34), can be used to notify servers that you connect to and that understand the Language header, that you are willing and able to accept pages that contain foreign language content. The order from top (most important) to bottom (least important) in the list indicates the priority of your language preferences. This does *not* mean that Navigator will display the foreign characters onscreen if they can't be expressed by a supported Font encoding and a font that uses that encoding. To do that, you need to get a copy of Navigator that was made for a specific language (currently available in Japanese, French, and German), or you need to obtain and install viewer helper applications for the desired language.

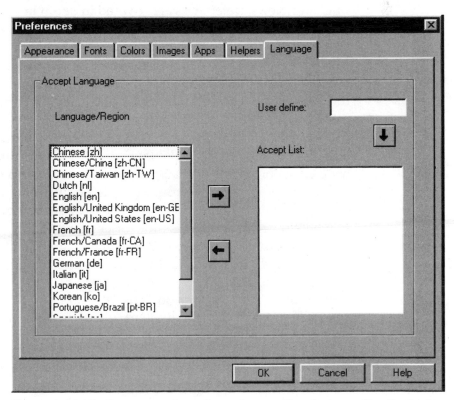

Figure 2-34: *The Language tab can be used to specify a font encoding for foreign languages. However, you still need a font that supports the character encoding.*

For example, if you want to be able to view Chinese characters, you would have to choose the appropriate Font encoding scheme in the Fonts tab, have an appropriate Chinese font installed on your computer, and then configure a MIME type and designate a viewer for Chinese text. You can find links to viewers for Chinese text on the Read Chinese in Net Applications page at http://herb.biol. uregina.ca/liu/pub/win-app.html. To find links to viewers for other languages, check out WWW Foreign Language Resources at http://www.itp.berkeley.edu/~thorne/HumanResources.html.

If your language of choice is always US English, you do not have to make any entries in this tab.

MAIL & NEWS PREFERENCES

Mail and News Preferences are covered in depth in Chapter 6, "Person to Person With Navigator Mail & Netscape News." The Mail and News Preferences consist of five tabs of options. To get Mail and News services going on a basic level in Navigator, you must fill in the options in two of the five tabs, the Servers tab, and the Identity tab. Until you do, you won't be able to send or receive any mail, read newsgroups, or log into most FTP sites. If you had a copy of the previous version of Navigator or any of the beta releases of Navigator installed, Navigator 3 or Navigator Gold 3 may have been able to find and automatically enter your previous Mail and News preferences for you. Check to be sure that they've been entered and that the information is correct. Pay particular attention to where the Mail and News directories point.

An installation of a newer version of Navigator will use your previous directories and files that contain information you've collected. Your mail, your newsgroup records, bookmarks, and address lists *aren't* lost when you reinstall or upgrade. This holds true even when you install to a different folder. If you've installed your new copy of Navigator into a new directory or folder, and you want to tidy up your hard disk, be sure to move the files found in the previous Mail and News directories into the new directory structure. Then move copies of your bookmarks and address lists into the new folder structure and open them using the File Open command in both the Bookmarks window and the Address window. This will "move" the registry/INI entries, so they no longer point to the previous folders. You can then delete the previous directory structure from the hard disk. If you had a plug-ins directory in the previous installation, you can try moving the plug-ins into the new installation's plug-in folder. Some plug-ins will work just fine this way, but others (CyberSpell, for example) may require reinstallation.

NETWORK PREFERENCES

Network Preferences found on the Options menu is where you tell Navigator about how you want to handle caching, how the data stream from servers should be handled, and if you're connected to the Internet through a Proxy Server and if so, how the Proxy is configured. Network Preferences is also where you decide if you want to enable your copy of Navigator to accept Java and JavaScript instructions, if you want to be alerted before Navigator accepts a cookie or submits a form by e-mail. This is also where you can tell Navigator to use your e-mail address as your anonymous FTP password.

CACHE TAB

The Network Preferences' Cache tab, seen in Figure 2-35, determines how much of your system resources are devoted to memory and disk caching, where the cache is located, an option for purging the cache, and how often the cache is consulted. Caching is a method that Navigator uses to temporarily store the most recently accessed pages and their page elements on hard disk and in memory. This speeds things up when you flip back and forth among pages in a single session and when you frequently visit the same sites, because hard disk and memory are so much faster to access than the information coming through the modem. Some multimedia objects that send their data as a stream instead of downloading the entire file, such as VDO movies, are never placed in cache.

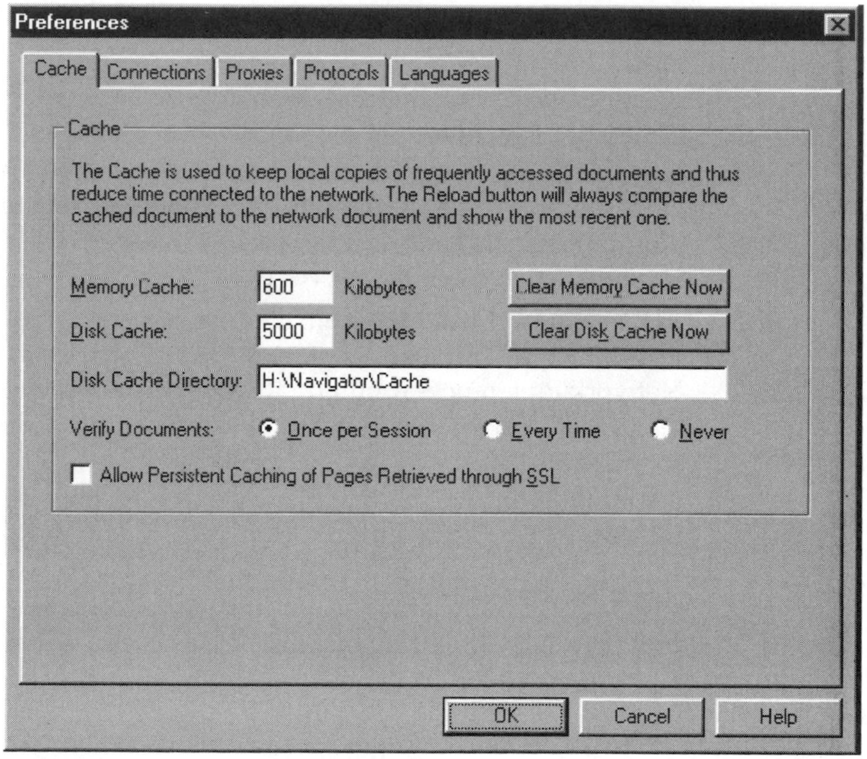

Figure 2-35: *Adjust the amount of system resources used in the Network Preferences tab.*

- *Memory Cache* entry field is where you determine how much of your system RAM should be devoted to caching the most recent pages you've viewed. The default setting for Memory Cache is 600K. If you have 8MB or less on your computer, you should not increase this figure. If you have more, you can increase the figure to about 1024K, and see if you notice a performance boost in Navigator. You might not because the more RAM you specify for Memory Cache, the less that Navigator, Navigator plug-ins and helpers, and any other programs you're running have to work with. When applications run out of RAM, they start swapping to disk and that imposes a significant performance penalty. You can fine-tune Navigator by settling on an amount of Memory Cache that balances page saving and application performance; unless your system has more than, say, 64MB of RAM, it's difficult to have both.

■ The *Disk Cache* entry field is set to 5000K (5MB) by default. If you have a lot of empty hard disk space, you may want to increase this setting. Do not *decrease* the setting, though. Java applications, JavaScript, and other processes tend to be come unstable and cause hangs and crashes when this setting is reduced. This cache is *not* cleared when you exit Navigator. The delay you experience and the hard disk activity you hear is cache maintenance, not an indication that the cache is being deleted. If you devote more space to the Disk Cache so that more data can be stored locally, expect the end of session cache maintenance to take longer.

TIP

Make sure that the Disk Cache is not set to 0K. Some early beta versions of Navigator defaulted to 0K instead of 5000K and this caused problems.

■ The *Clear Memory Cache Now* and *Clear Disk Cache Now* buttons are, not surprisingly, used to delete the current contents of each cache. Navigator automatically clears the Memory cache and frees up the memory for other applications when you close Navigator. The entire contents of Disk Cache is never automatically cleared by Navigator. Instead, when the maximum amount of disk space you've allowed becomes occupied, Navigator replaces the oldest information with new incoming information.

Use the Clear Memory Cache buttons to clear the Memory Cache and the Disk Cache when you come upon a page with very large graphics that have partially loaded, and you want to view the page without graphics. Turning Auto Load graphics off does not stop the display of graphics that are already in cache. Clearing the disk cache is also recommended if you are updating your copy of Navigator and are installing into the same folders. You can also use Windows Explorer or File Manager to delete all the files in the Cache folder.

- The *Disk Cache Directory* field specifies where on your system the Disk Cache is located. By default, Navigator places it in the Navigator directory structure, but it can go anywhere. If you're tight on disk space on the drive where you installed Navigator, delete the contents of the current cache and make a new folder on another drive. Name the folder NavCache or something else that will remind you of its purpose later, and then place the path to that folder in the Disk Cache Directory field. Restart Navigator after you've done this.

- The *Verify Documents* option offers the following choices: Once per Session (the default), Every Time, and Never. This option controls how often Navigator checks the cache to see if the document you've requested from a server is in the cache, and if it is older than the one on the server. If the copy in cache and the copy on the server have the same revision date, the page is loaded from cache. If the revision date of the cached copy is older than the server copy, the page is downloaded from the server. Sometimes, you may find that Navigator can't make contact with the server, but finds that the page you requested is in cache. When this happens, Navigator notifies you that it is displaying the copy that was stored in cache. Making the revision date comparisons takes time, so the choice here is between speed and knowing that the page you see is the newest version of the page.

The default of Once per Session is usually a better choice than Every Time because if you flip back and forth between pages in a single session, the comparison is made only once in that session, and not every time you access a page. Every Time is slower, but useful if you access a lot of sites that are built on the fly and are interactive. If you get the feeling that you're not seeing what you should, click on the Reload button. The Reload button forces Navigator to get a new copy of the page from the server. If you choose Never, you will never know when a previously visited page has changed until enough new sites have been visited to push that page out of the cache.

■ The *Allow Persistent Caching of Pages Retrieved through SSL* checkbox is unchecked by default. This is actually a security option, because when this checkbox is unchecked, pages received from secure servers are not cached. This means that they are never written to the memory or disk cache where they could be retrieved by someone with physical access to your computer. Leaving this checkbox unchecked increases the level of security you enjoy when conducting business with secure servers, but it will slow down your access to these servers because every element and every page you see must be sent every time they are needed and can't be loaded from the disk or memory cache. We recommend you leave this checkbox in its default, unchecked state.

THE CONNECTIONS TAB

The Connections tab seen in Figure 2-36 has two options. One for setting the Number of Connections and another for setting the size of the Network Buffer Size. The first you probably don't have to change at all, and the second one you probably should change, but only on a day when you have time to experiment with this setting. Read on to find out why.

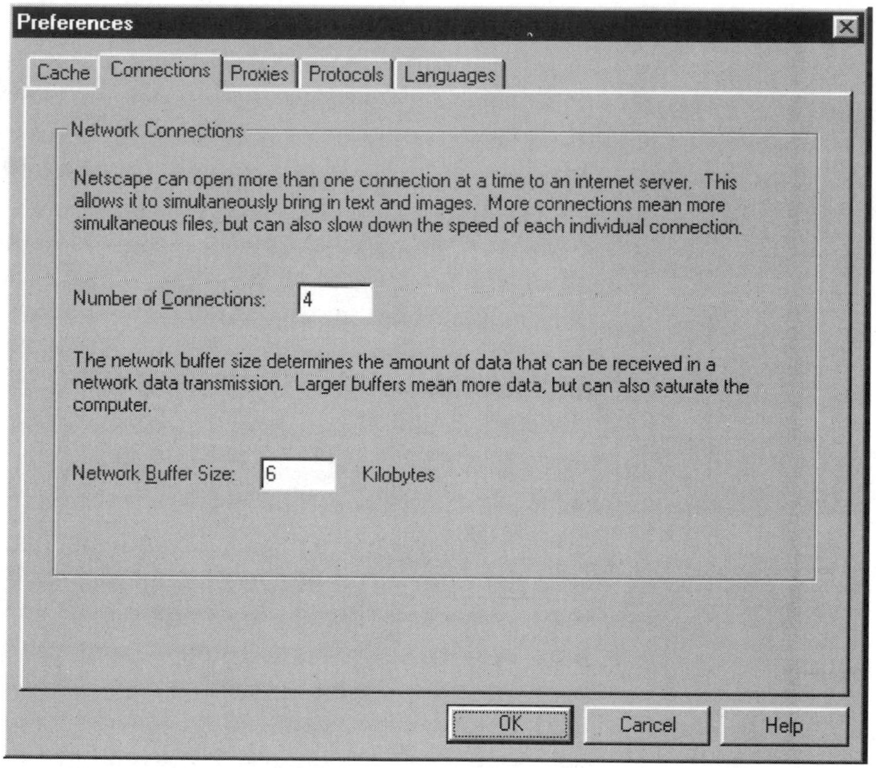

Figure 2-36: *The Connections tab.*

- The *Number of Connections* option has a default value of four. The value placed in this field specifies how many concurrent streams of data will be requested from and downloaded simultaneously from a single server. What this means is that as a page is downloaded, four (if you use the default setting) data files can be handled at one time. For example, the text in an HTML file and three graphic files can download at once. When they finish, if there are more graphics or other objects to be fetched, they too, will come in four at a time until all components of the page have been downloaded.

  You may, however, perceive a decrease in performance rather than an increase if you connect to the Internet with a 14.4 or 28.8K modem. This is because the number of connections generally increases the number of different data streams coming in, but doesn't increase the amount of data *in total* that can be transferred. Each additional stream you add reduces the amount of "space" available on your phone line for each of the other streams. If you have an older computer and a slow connection, you might find it more satisfactory if you reduce the number from 4 to 2 or 3.

- *Network Buffer Size* is by default set to 6K in the Connections tab. This value sets the maximum size of each chunk of information sent to you by the server. Navigator warns you that increasing this number may bring in more data at one time; this may can substantially increase performance, but too much may swamp the computer. *Swamping* means that you are asking the computer to take in and process more information than it is capable of doing in a single "gulp." When the computer swamps, incoming data is lost because it can't be processed fast enough, and everything starts acting flaky or you may cause a system halt. If you'd like to experiment with this number, and it is worth experimenting with, close all other running applications, so if your system hangs, your data won't be lost. Then put a significantly higher value in this entry box—32K on a 486 DX266 worked well for me—and click OK. Close and restart Navigator. Surf around for a while and see if you notice any improvements in speed or discover any problems, and then adjust the Network Buffer Size accordingly. Edge it up if all is OK, and work it down if you experience difficulty.

THE PROXY TAB

Proxy servers and firewalls are used to create a safe, regulated environment that separates an organization's internal private LAN or Intranet from the Internet. The proxy server acts as a trusted intermediary between the two, preventing unauthorized intrusion from the Internet into the organization's system. Users inside a firewall don't interact directly with the Internet. Instead, they connect to the proxy server which then makes the necessary connections to retrieve the information or resource that was requested.

If you have a direct connection to the Internet, or make your connection directly through a dial-up PPP or SLIP account with your ISP, you do not need to configure a proxy. The default setting for this tab is No Proxies. However, if you access the Internet from a private network that has a firewall between it and the Internet, you will need to configure for Proxies and will need information or assistance from your network administrator.

The Proxies tab offers three choices: No Proxies, manual Proxy Configuration, and Automatic Proxy Configuration.

- *No Proxies* is the proper choice if you have a direct connection to the Internet, or make your connection directly through a dial-up PPP or SLIP account with an ISP.

- Use *Manual Proxy Configuration* if your network administrator has not made a proxy configuration file available. Click on the Manual Proxy Configuration radio button, then click on the View button to display the set of proxy configuration entry boxes, as seen in Figure 2-37. You will need to enter the IP address or host name and the port number it uses for each Internet service offered by your proxy server. You need to get this information from your network administrator.

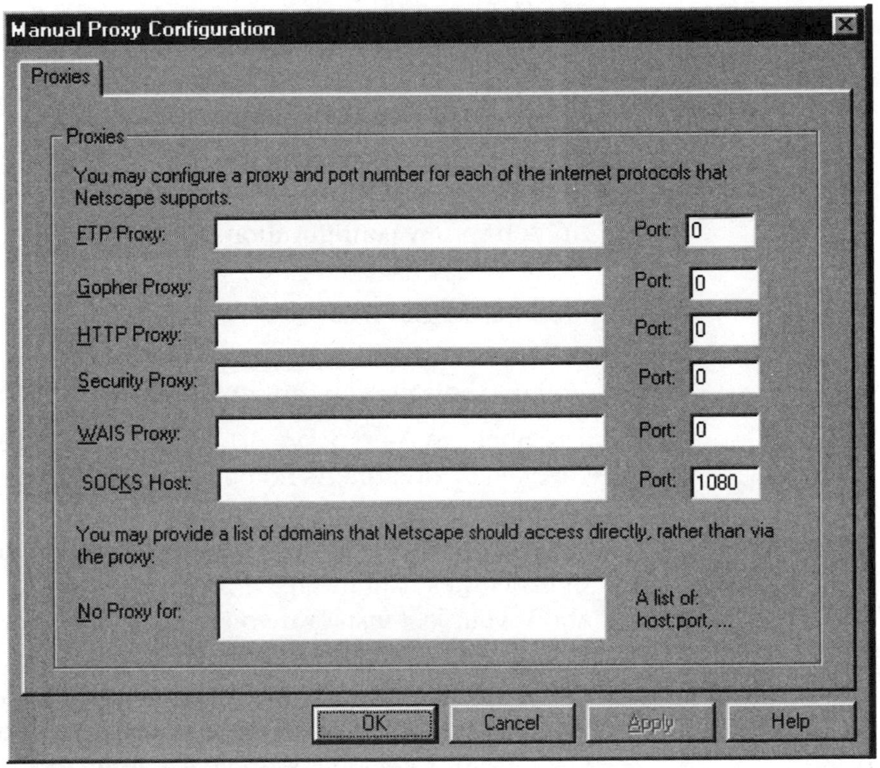

Figure 2-37: *Consult with your network administrator to find out the addresses and port numbers you require to direct Navigator to the proper proxy services.*

Depending on how your organization's network is set up, you may also have to list the domain name or local host name of your organization's internal servers in the No Proxy for entry field. Again, consult your network administrator for advice.

■ The *Automatic Proxy Configuration* and *Configuration Location (URL)* options are used when your network administrator has created and made available a proxy configuration file for Navigator. Ask your network administrator if one is available, and if so, where it is stored. Enter the URL of the configuration file in the entry box, and Navigator uses it to set up your proxy configuration.

THE PROTOCOLS TAB

The Protocols Tab as seen in Figure 2-38 offers three security or privacy-related options you can set. They are . . .

■ The Show an Alert *Before Accepting a Cookie* check box is unchecked by default. As noted earlier in the chapter in the section, "How Private Is Your Personal Workspace?" cookies are text files that an Internet server stores on your computer. Internet sites usually create cookies to store information about your last visit or if you have a particular plug-in installed. The next time you log on to that site, the server retrieves the cookie and uses the information stored in the cookie. Netscape uses a cookie to store the information you write in your Personal Workspace notepad. Other sites, for example, may use cookies to store the date of your last visit, or answers to a questionnaire you filled out on what areas of interest you have. With this information stored and retrieved from your hard disk, the site might build special pages used to greet you or point you to areas of the site that match your interests. Because the information stored in a cookie file does contain personal information, Netscape has engineered the use of cookies so that only the server that placed the cookie on your hard disk can read that cookie.

If you check this box and a server attempts to write cookie information to your hard disk, an alert similar to the one seen in Figure 2-39 will appear onscreen. If you don't want the cookie information to be written to disk, click on the Cancel button in the alert box. You can't totally disable the use of cookies, but you can refuse them one by one if you turn on the alert.

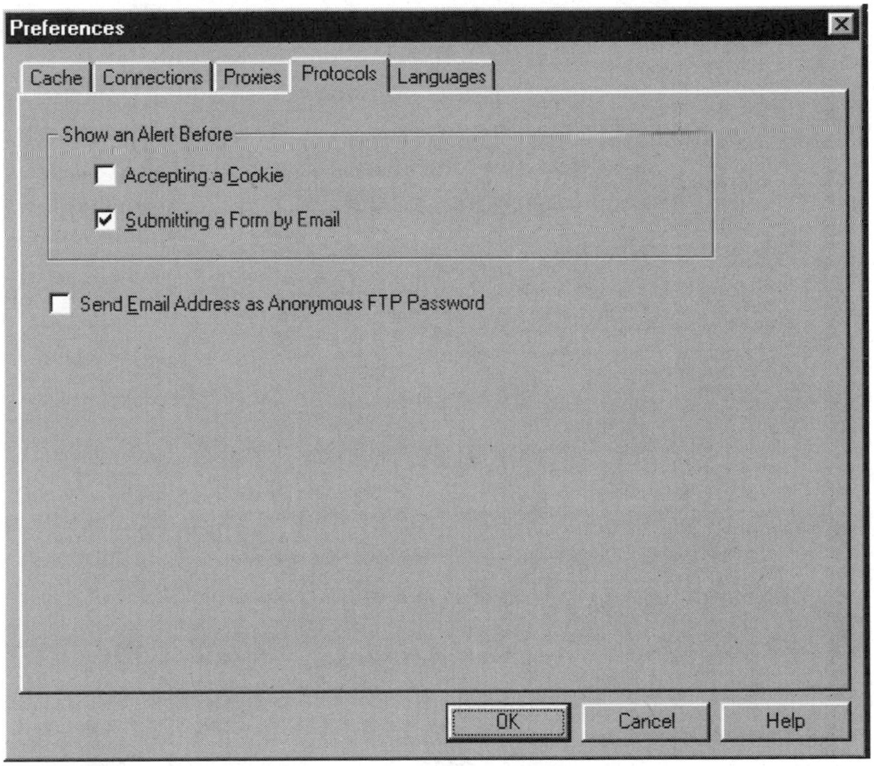

Figure 2-38: *The Protocols tab offers three security- or privacy-related options you can set.*

■ By default the Show an Alert *Submitting a Form by Email* checkbox is checked. If you leave this box checked you will be notified whenever you transmit a form using the e-mail protocol. Some pages on the Web use the mail protocol to send form information. The mail protocol is not a secure protocol at present, so caution should be used when sending information of a personal nature by e-mail. We recommend you leave this checkbox checked.

■ If you check the *Send Email Address as Anonymous FTP Password* checkbox your full e-mail address will be sent as the anonymous FTP password. For example, if your e-mail address is janed@mycompany.com, that is what will be sent as the password. On the other hand if you leave it unchecked Navigator will substitute mozilla for janed and send the following as the password: mozilla@mycompany.com. Some FTP sites won't accept mozilla as the password and will refuse the connection. If you don't mind FTP servers having your full e-mail address, uncheck this box. If this is only an occasional problem for you see Chapter 5, "Power Search & Retrieval," for information on another way to send a password to an FTP site. From a privacy standpoint, we recommend that you leave this box unchecked.

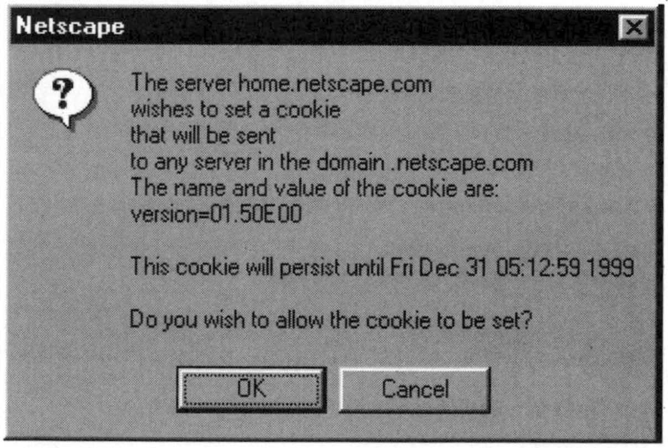

Figure 2-39: *You'll receive a warning like this if you ask Navigator to warn you when cookies are being written to your disk.*

THE LANGUAGES TAB

The Languages Tab of Network Preferences sports only two check-boxes—*Enable Java* and *Enable JavaScript*.

■ By default, these are checked, which means that you are giving permission for Java applets and JavaScripts to download and run on your computer. Opinion varies widely on how these options should be set. Many are enthusiastic about the use of Java applets and JavaScript, and an increasing number of Internet sites use Java and JavaScript. Netscape's Personal Workspace and the framed version of Netscape's home page both require that JavaScript is enabled if they are to work. Others feel that even though Java and JavaScript are designed as secure applications and security issues brought to Netscape's and Sun's attention have been promptly addressed, the technology is still too new to be trusted.

The choice, however, is up to you; refer to Chapter 7, "Maintaining Your Privacy on the Internet," for more information on the security issues surrounding Java and JavaScript. If you decide to disable either Java or JavaScript, uncheck these checkboxes.

THE SECURITY PREFERENCES

The last set of preferences on the Options menu is Security Options. Chapter 7, "Maintaining Your Privacy on the Internet," covers these preference settings and issues surrounding security and privacy in detail.

THE EDITOR PREFERENCES

If you are working with a copy of Navigator Gold, you might have noticed that you have an additional set of options—those for the Netscape Editor. Editor preferences are grouped into three tabs, General, Appearance, and Publish.

THE GENERAL TAB

The Editor Preferences General tab, shown in Figure 2-40, is broken into three areas: one for identifying you, one for specifying helper applications you may want to use, and one to locate the template file that you want to use.

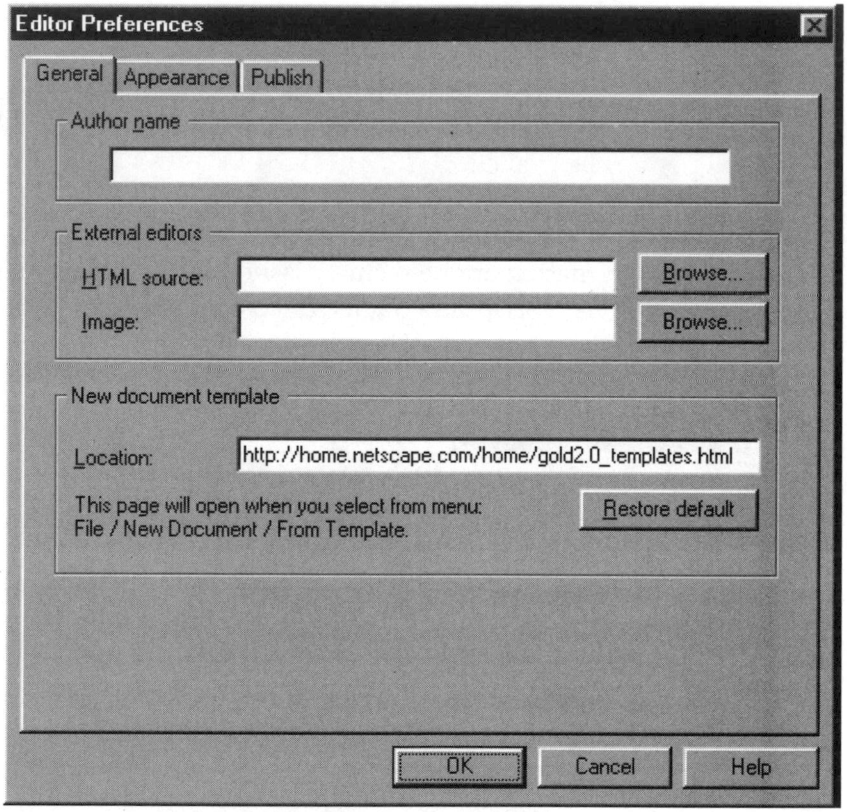

Figure 2-40: *Navigator Gold's Editor makes it easy and WYSIWYG to create HTML documents that are graphical and content-rich.*

■ In the *Author name* entry box, put your name, or your company's name. The information placed in this field will automatically be placed in a META tag at the top of every document you create in the Editor. It is not displayed as HTML code to those viewing your site, but it is visible in the source code, and to the various indexing and search engines that catalog Web pages. If you wish to change the Author name on a case-by-case basis, you can edit the automatically made entry by choosing Document from the Editor's Properties menu, and editing the Author name for a specific document.

■ The *External Editors* field has two entry fields; *HTML source* and *Image*. The application entered in the *HTML source* field is called into action after you choose Edit Document Source from the Editor's View menu. You should specify your favorite text editor or HTML editing utility in this field. If you don't make an entry in this field, you will be prompted for the information when you choose Edit Document Source from within the Editor.

The *Image* field is where you can specify a bitmap editing application you have on your system. When you right-click on an image you've placed in a document and choose Edit Image from the shortcut menu, the program specified here launches and loads the image. If no entry is made in this field, the Edit Image command is not offered on the shortcut menu. Choose a paint type program (not a vector drawing program) such as Paint Shop Pro (found on the Companion CD-ROM) or Adobe Photoshop. Unfortunately, because Web graphics are in the JPEG or GIF file format, the Windows Paint program can't be used as an Image Editor.

■ The *Location* field in the *New document template* section is where you set the location of the HTML file, which is opened from the File menu when you choose New Document and then choose From Template. By default, the address in this field is the page on Netscape's site that leads to a wide variety of HTML documents they've designed for your use. If you prefer to use one of your own documents as a template, put the URL in this field. When it loads, it will appear in a new browser window. To bring the document into the Netscape Editor, click on the Edit button on the toolbar, or choose Edit Document from the File menu.

If you use your own locally available document, it is not a true template like one you may have used in your word processor or desktop publishing program. It is *not a copy* of the HTML file you pointed to, but the original HTML document, so be sure to use Save As instead of Save and give it another name or you will have changed your "template" file through your edits. When you use an HTML file from the Internet, it is downloaded to your computer and is not saved back to the Internet using the Save or Save As command. To save to your hard disk, use Save. To post it to your server site use Save, and then the Publish command.

If you have entered an URL in the Location field *other* than Netscape's, and now would like to change it back to Netscape's template page, click on the Restore default button.

THE APPEARANCE TAB

The Editor Preferences' Appearance tab is used to specify which colors are used in all new documents you create in the Netscape Editor. You have a choice to use the default Browser colors (the default setting), or to define a custom set of color specifications. The capability to set a default color scheme for all new documents is a great time saver when you are creating a number of pages that need to become a set of visually consistent documents. Any specifications you make in this tab can be overridden in a local document from within the Editor; you'd chose Preferences from the Editor's menu, then choose Document and then choose the Appearance tab. You can also change the scheme specified in these options at any time. The changes will affect only new documents, and not the current document or documents you've already created.

■ By default, the *Use Browser's colors* radio button is selected. The colors referred to here are the link colors, background color, and/or background image you specified for documents viewed in the Browser, Mail, and News windows in the Options menu's General Preferences Appearance tab. To use a different color scheme or one of the predefined document color schemes that Navigator provides, you must choose the *Use custom colors* radio button instead of the default Use Browser's colors radio button. When you do, the rest of the options in this tab and a preview of what the colors scheme looks like become available, as seen in Figure 2-41.

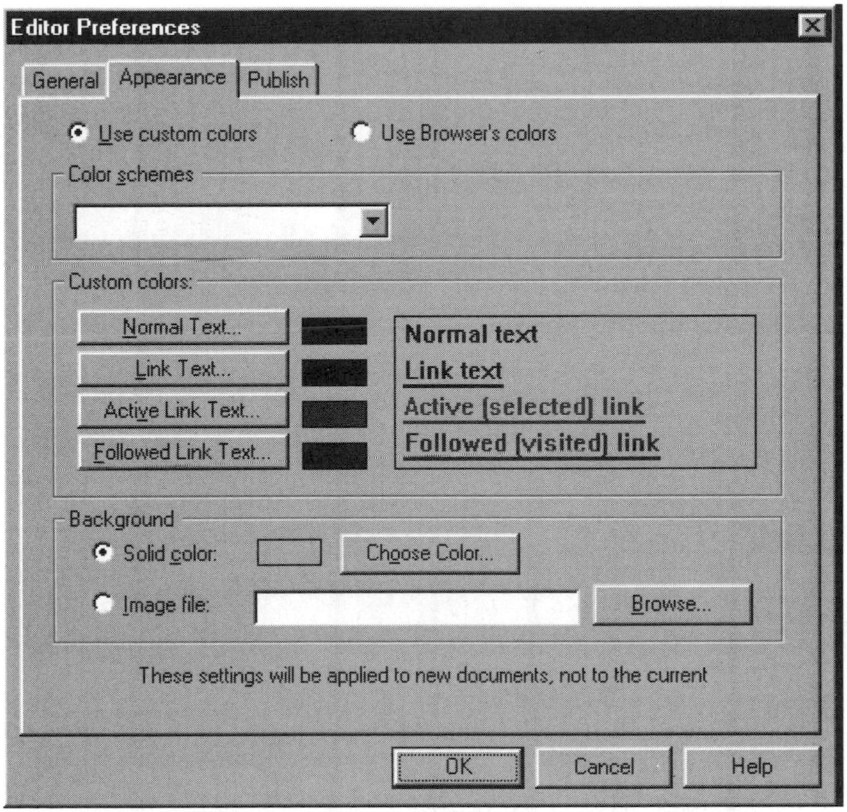

Figure 2-41: *To choose a color scheme, or one you've invented yourself, take a trip to the General Preferences Appearance tab.*

■   The rest of the dialog box is extremely similar to the Options menu's General Preferences Appearance tab discussed earlier in the chapter. In this case, the order of the link and text colors is a little different, and you must click the buttons to bring up the color picker. The buttons are clearly labeled with the name of the element for which you are selecting a color. What is significantly different about this tab is that it offers predefined color schemes. Be sure to choose the *Color schemes* drop-down list. Choose Netscape Default Colors and the list will retract. With Netscape Default Colors highlighted, press the Down arrow key to move through the choices. The entries and the preview in the Custom colors section below change to show you what each scheme looks like. If you see one you like, leave it selected and then edit any one of the colors to fine-tune the scheme to your liking, or add a tiling background image. Don't be alarmed that the scheme name disappears from the closed drop-down list as soon as you click any of the other options, or if you close the Editor Preferences dialog box by clicking OK. The scheme may not appear in the closed drop-down, but the colors specified by the scheme remain in place.

THE PUBLISH TAB

The Publish tab (see Figure 2-42), is where default preferences are set for how links are maintained in documents you create. It is also where Netscape's One Button Publishing feature looks for default server location and connection information.

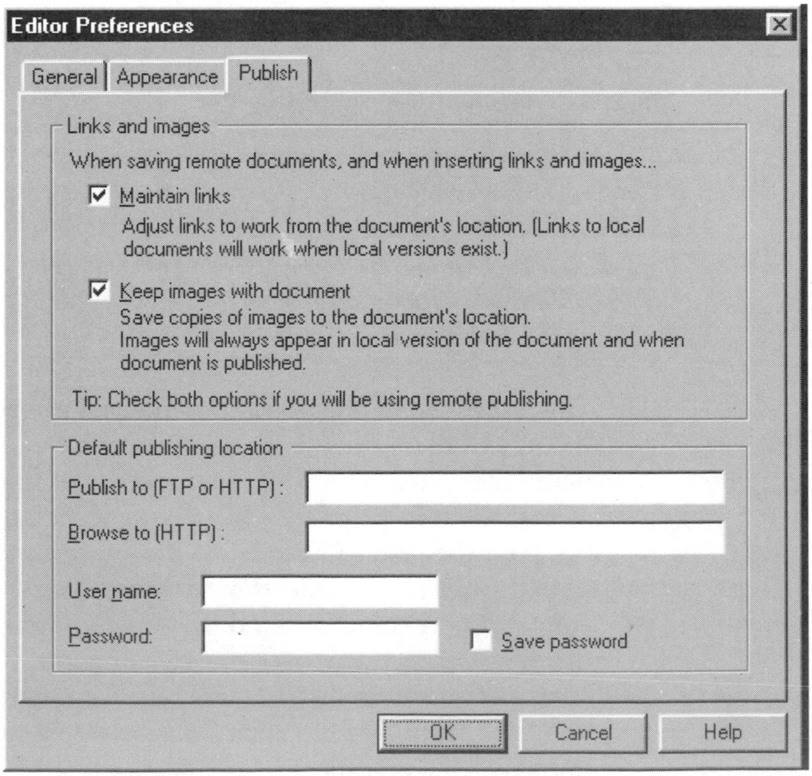

Figure 2-42: *One of Navigator Gold's most powerful features is to Publish a document; it automatically fixes hyperlink references to the path on your ISP's commercial server.*

One Button Publishing is a Navigator Gold feature that makes home page publishing a breeze because it can collect the necessary files and then automatically upload the files to the server that hosts your home page. It also handles another problem.

When you create pages on your PC, the path specified in the local links between the HTML page and inline and embedded objects, such as graphics and multimedia elements, point to *your* computer and not the location on the server where they ultimately go. If you create a page and all of the elements linked to that page in a single folder on your hard disk, and then upload them all to a directory on the server, Navigator will automatically adjust the links so that they remain relative to each other and will continue to work, no matter how different the path on the server is from the path on your hard disk. (See Chapter 5, "Power Search & Retrieval," for more information about links and One Button Publishing")

■ The Links and images section of the Publish tab offers two options, *Maintain links* and *Keep images with document*. Both are checked by default, and Navigator recommends that you accept these defaults if you're creating documents that will be published remotely (as opposed to your e-mail). We agree with the Editor's advice, if you have a relatively uncomplicated site that makes putting everything in one directory feasible. If you have a very large site or absolutely must put different kinds of elements in different directories, you should uncheck these option boxes. When they are unchecked, you'll have to edit the links by hand, so the elements can be found when they are uploaded to the server. This makes your job much harder, and it becomes much more likely that an element will fail to load on the server either because the path to the element was entered incorrectly or because a file isn't in the correct location. Navigator Gold is superb at handling the sites typical of an individual user, small business or department workgroup, but as your needs grow and your site management needs become more complex, you may find that you need more powerful site management tools. If your pages are on your own Netscape-based server, you should look into Netscape Livewire Pro, which can easily handle the management of multiple folders and other issues that arise when working with large sites.

The *Default publishing location* on the Publish tab asks for information about where you normally upload your pages and how you make that connection. This information will be used whenever you choose File, Publish from the Editor's menu unless you change it for the current transfer in the Publish Files dialog box that appears.

- In the Publish to (FTP or HTTP) field, enter the URL of the server directory where your pages are located. Most Internet hosting services allow you to post directly to the directory where the files are supposed to go, but some ask you to submit your pages to them, and then they post them. Ask your provider for the URL where your pages should go and how you should access them—by FTP or by HTTP file transfer. A typical entry here would be ftp://ftp.myprovider.com/user/myname/index.html or http://myprovider.com/user/myname/index.html.

- Browse to (HTTP) is a thoughtful feature. The URL you enter here is the address that the Navigator Gold browser will automatically go to when you choose Default Publish Location from the browser's Go menu (or press Alt+G+D). Usually, the URL that is entered in this field is the URL of the home page you are currently building or editing, but you can add any URL on the Internet or any local file URL you like here, and you can change it at any time as your projects or needs change. Some find it handy to put the URL of their bookmark list or of a reference source here.

- The *User name* and *Password* entry fields are where you should put the username and password your Internet hosting service gave you for accessing the password-protected FTP or HTTP upload directory on their server. This is not necessarily the same username and password you use for e-mail or to logon. If you want Navigator to remember your password and automatically send it to the server when you logon, check the *Save password* checkbox. Although it is convenient to have Navigator handle the entire logon and upload of files to the server without stopping to prompt you for a password, this does pose a security risk. When Navigator remembers your password, anyone who has physical access to your computer will be able to logon as you and post files to your site's directory.

When you have made all of your entries in the various Editor Preferences tab, click OK to close the dialog box and have your changes take effect. Choose Cancel if you wish to discard the changes you've made, and use the settings that were in effect before you entered the dialog.

HELPER APPLICATIONS & MIME TYPES

Navigator by itself is a great program, but what makes it an awesome program is its *extensibility*. If Navigator doesn't natively support a file type or a graphic format, no problem: add a plug-in or a helper application to handle the job. Plug-ins, such as Shockwave, VDOLive, and Live 3D, are programs that are specifically designed to work inside Navigator. In Chapter 9, "Taking a Look at Plug-ins," you'll see numerous examples of plug-ins and helper applications that are currently available for use with Navigator. More and more plug-ins are written and released daily. But plug-ins haven't been written yet to handle *all* of the possible kinds of files that can be created and posted on the Web. That's where Helper Applications come in. If you have an application that can open or play a specific file type, you can tell Navigator to call that program whenever you encounter that kind of file. For example, if you want to view Windows Metafiles or TIF images online, in e-mail, or in the alt.binaries newsgroups, you need to install a Helper Application.

The Internet is full of all different kinds of data in different formats—text formats, graphic, video, sound—and more. MIME (Multipurpose Internet Mail Extensions) is a standard that among other things enables servers and client software (Web browsers, mail readers, and other Internet software) to identify and specify different data types. When you are connected to the Internet and connect to a page, click a link to a object, download a file, and so on, data that is sent from the Internet server to Navigator is preceded by the MIME type for the data. To decide how to handle the data, Navigator doesn't look in the file's header or look at the file extension, it just proceeds on the basis of the MIME type information the server sent.

Navigator checks its plug-in directory to see if there is a plug-in present that can handle the MIME type. It also checks the information in the Helpers tab of General Preferences (see Figure 2-43) to see if the type is listed, and if so, what direction has been given for handling that MIME type. If the MIME type sent by the server is not found in the Helper tab listing, and no plug-in claims the type, Navigator asks you what to do with the file.

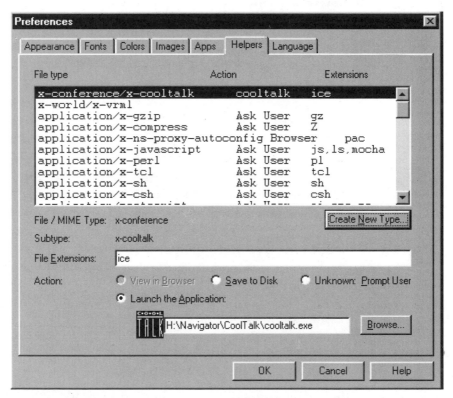

Figure 2-43: *The Helpers tab lists the MIME type associated with a file format. You can assign a third-party program to each MIME type.*

However, when you access files locally instead of from an Internet server, your computer doesn't know anything about sending MIME types information to programs. So another scheme is employed. For local files, Navigator looks at the file extension and then matches the file extension with a MIME type that is associated with that extension.

If no extension is present, Navigator assumes the file is text and tries to display it as text. If the wrong extension is on the file (a TIF file with a GIF extension, for example), Navigator assumes it is a GIF and handles it as such. When it can't open it because it is using the wrong method, a missing graphic icon appears.

When MIME was developed, the authors knew that data types other than those common at the time would need to be assigned. MIME was left open-ended, so that when new data formats demand a description, the sponsors of that format can register a universally recognized MIME type for the data. But even this was not enough because registration takes time and needs change. So MIME's authors wrote a format that "experimental" or non-registered MIME types should take, and made recommendations about how it should be used. Experimental MIME types have x- somewhere in their name. As tenuous as this may sound, what it does is enable someone to say about a new or previously undefined data type—"I'm giving it the image/x-something MIME type." If the server that dispenses the file calls it image/x-something, and you've installed a helper or plug-in that is capable of handling the file type, and it's been assigned the duty of handling files with the image/x-something MIME format, Navigator will automatically hand the file over to the helper or plug-in.

REMOVING OR EDITING A MIME TYPE

The method for removing an entry from the Helpers list that you no longer need or that was entered incorrectly depends on whether you are using the 16-bit or 32-bit version of Navigator. The 16-bit version stores all of its configuration information in the NETSCAPE.INI file, which is usually in the Navigator directory. Check the [Netscape] section of the WIN.INI file to confirm the location of the NETSCAPE.INI file. The 32-bit version of Navigator doesn't use a NETSCAPE.INI file, but instead writes all configuration settings to the Windows 95 Registry.

With the 16-bit version, open NETSCAPE.INI in a text editor such as NOTEPAD.EXE or TEXTPAD.EXE (found on the Companion CD-ROM). Navigator writes MIME and Helper application information in the [Viewers] section, and information about file extensions in the [Suffixes] section. Scroll down until you find the [Viewers] section.

Let's take a look at the [Viewers] section first. For this example, we added two new MIME types to Navigator, image/wmf and image/tga. When we did this in the Helpers tab, Navigator appended the following lines to the [Viewers] section:

```
image/wmf=
TYPE0=image/wmf
image/tga=D:\windows\psp\psp.exe
TYPE1=image/tga
```

Notice that two lines were added for each new MIME type and that one of the lines, the TYPE= line, is sequentially numbered. In this example, if you removed the two image/wmf entries, you would also need to edit the TYPE1=image/tga line to renumber it so that it reads TYPE0=image/tga. If you are correcting a spelling mistake or editing the format of the MIME type—for example, changing the image/wmf to image/x-wmf—make your edits wherever necessary, but you don't have to renumber anything. When you're done, scroll down to the [Suffixes] section. In the example we're using here, where new MIME types for wmf and tga were added, the following lines were appended to the [Suffixes] entry:

```
image/wmf=wmf
image/tga=tga
```

Remove or edit the entry as necessary. Save the file, and you're done.

Windows 95 users don't have it quite so easy. To delete a MIME type, it is necessary to use the Windows 95 Registry Editor. The Registry holds all of the hardware configuration information about your computer, how Windows is set up, and configuration information on almost all of the programs you have installed. Do *not* edit this file unless you have made a backup of the registry file first and know how to restore the file if necessary. If the Registry is damaged by an error you make, a disk error due to a power blackout, or for any other reason, your computer may not boot properly and you might have to reinstall Windows 95 and all of your software. Also keep in mind that when you make a change in the Registry, it is immediately saved to the Registry file and there is no undo feature of any kind, nor is there an option to close the Registry without saving changes.

TIP

Microsoft has issued a utility in the Windows 95 Resource Kit that backs up and restores the system Registry. The software comes on disk with the printed copy of the Resource Kit or you can download the software that comes with the Resource Kit from Microsoft's Internet site. You'll find all of the Windows 95 Resource Kit software at: http://www.microsoft.com/windows/software/reskit.htm.

Cautions having been given, it really isn't hard to use the Registry Editor safely. Before opening the Registry Editor, you should close all running programs, including Navigator and any virus detection software you might use. To launch the Registry Editor, click the Start button then choose Run. In the Run dialog box, enter REGEDIT.EXE, then press Enter. REGEDIT.EXE is usually found in your Windows folder.

When the Registry Editor opens, choose Edit, then Find. In the text entry box, enter the MIME type you are looking for. In this example, we are looking for the image/wmf MIME entry we made earlier in Navigator. The search will take a few moments, but as seen in Figure 2-44, you should end up in the following key entry: My Computer\HKEY_CURRENT_USER\Software\Netscape\ Netscape Navigator\Suffixes.

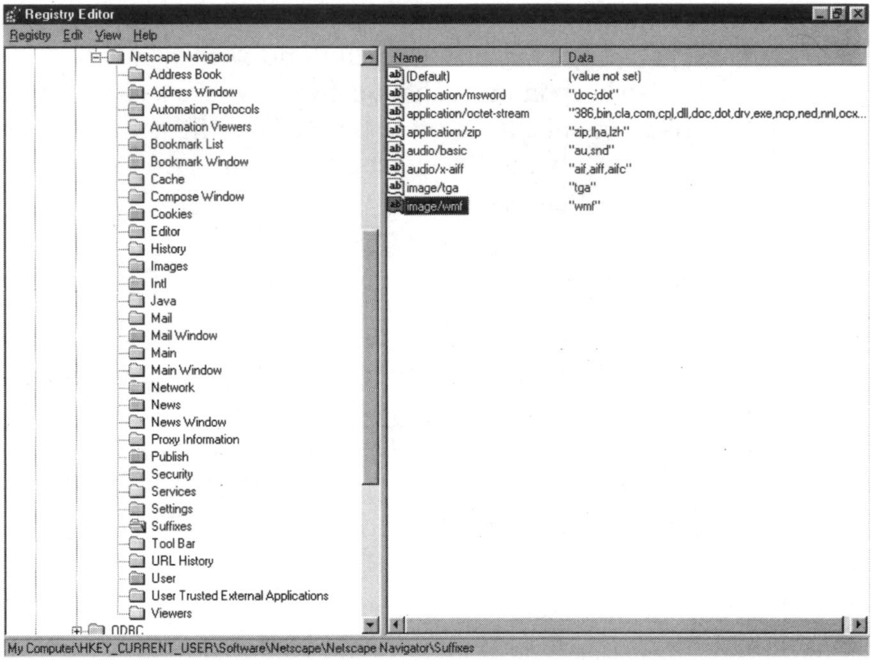

Figure 2-44: *Editing the Windows 95 Registry is not a novice's sport, but it is sometimes the only thing to do to correct or remove a MIME type.*

Right-click (in the Name column) on the name of the MIME type you want to delete, then choose Delete from the shortcut menu. Click Yes in the confirmation box that appears. The shortcut menu also offers Modify and Rename as options on the shortcut. Even if these are the actions you ultimately want to take, don't choose them. Because this is not the only place in the Registry that changes need to be made, you are less likely to make mistakes if you delete the faulty MIME entry and then make a correct entry later in Navigator.

After you've deleted the entry, press F3 or choose Edit, Find Again from the menu. The search should take you to the following section of the Editor:
My Computer\HKEY_CURRENT_USER\Software\Netscape\ Netscape Navigator\Viewers.

Here you will see two listings: image/wmf and Type 1 "image/ wmf." You need to delete both. Click on the entry in the Name column, then press the Delete key or choose Delete from the shortcut menu, then click on Yes in the confirmation box. Changes made here also cause the change to be made in the section: My Computer\HKEY_USERS\Default\Software\Netscape\ Netscape Navigator\Viewers and Suffixes.

From the Registry menu choose Exit. The Registry Editor closes, and you're done.

The steps that you just read through apply to MIME types that you enter. If for some reason you want to delete or modify one of the pre-established MIME types that Navigator or a Navigator plug-in established, the search may have taken you to My Computer\HKEY_CLASSES_ROOT\MIME\Database\Content Type section. If so, make your deletions or modifications here.

TROUBLESHOOTING

INTERNET SHORTCUTS & FILE ASSOCIATIONS

Have you ever clicked an Internet shortcut or on a file and expected Navigator to open up and handle the file—only to see another Web browser or Internet software program pop up? If so, it's because the other program has impolitely assumed that you want it to handle Internet files for you and has changed your file associations to call it, instead of Navigator. Programs are getting more polite, but it is not uncommon for the last installed browser to claim all of the Internet file extensions. The quickest way to fix this is to close the other program and open Navigator. When Navigator begins to load, it stops and displays the question box shown in Figure 2-45, asking you if you want to make Navigator your default browser. Click Yes, and Navigator will take care of reassociating the file types. You also manually edit URL file associations in Windows 95 Explorer's View/Options menu.

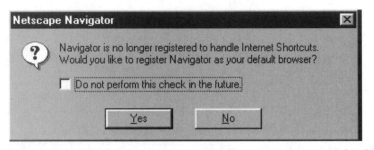

Figure 2-45: *The last program you install on your system might claim a file type you don't want it to. Let Navigator handle Web media types.*

The following file types are normally associated with Netscape Navigator:

URL: File Transfer Protocol
URL: Gopher Protocol
URL: HyperText Transfer Protocol
URL: MailTo Protocol
URL: News Protocol
URL: Secure News Protocol

The URLs to follow should be set to operate with Windows 95 system handlers or the application of your choice. When you double-click Open in the Actions field for these URLs, an abbreviated Editing action for type dialog box appears. (See the following steps.) To allow the system to handle these URLs in the Application used to perform action field, enter the line in the list below:

For URL: File Protocol use:

rundll32.exe url.dll,FileProtocolHandler

For URL: TN3270 Telnet Protocol use:

rundll32.exe url.dll,TelnetProtocolHandler

For URL: Telnet Protocol use:

rundll32.exeurl.dll,TelnetProtocolHandler %l

To manually edit File Associations:

1. From My Computer, open any hard disk window. From the View menu choose Options. From the Options dialog box, choose the File Types tab. Scroll down in the Registered Types scroll box until you come to listings that begin with URL:. Double-click the first one you want to change. This opens the Edit File Type window shown in Figure 2-46.

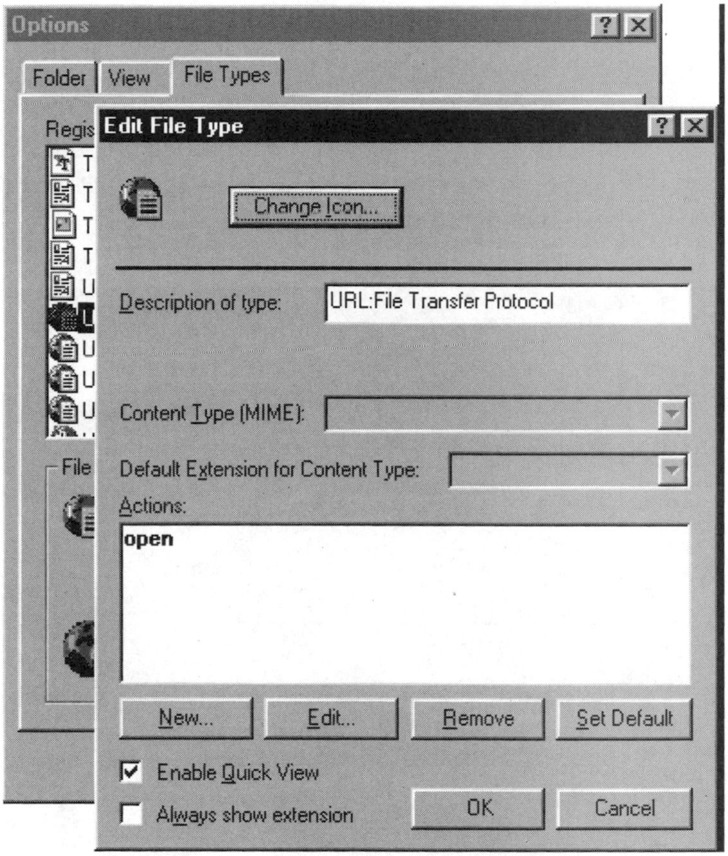

Figure 2-46: *You can manually edit a mistyped file association through Windows 95's Options menu under My Computer.*

2. In the Actions field, double-click on the word Open. The Editing action for type: dialog box appears. In the Application used to perform action entry field, enter the complete path to your copy of NETSCAPE.EXE; after the path, press the spacebar, and then enter -h. Alternatively, you can use the Browse button to enter the location of NETSCAPE.EXE. If you use Browse, be sure to append the -h parameter to the end of the path.

3. Make sure that the DDE checkbox is checked, and that %1 is in the DDE message entry field.

4. In the Application field, replace any entry there with the word Netscape.

5. The DDE Application Not Running field should be empty.

6. The Topic field should read WWW_OpenURL. The dialog box should look like Figure 2-47, except that it will contain the path to your copy of Navigator.

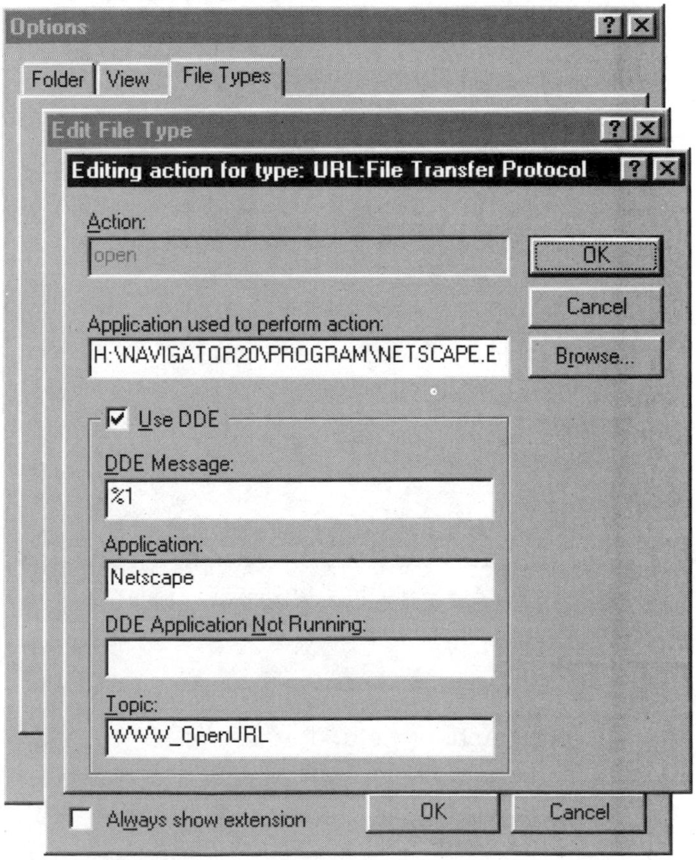

Figure 2-47: *The Editing action for type should look like this when you've finished editing the fields.*

7. Click OK to close the window, then click Close to close the Edit File Type window. In the Options File Types, double-click the next URL: file type you wish to change and repeat the above steps. When you've finished, click Close to exit the Options dialog box.

MOVING ON

Now that you have your system, as well as Navigator, optimized, and your hardware and software performing at their best, it's time to take your ship into high seas and deep waters. "Power Navigation" is the title of Chapter 3, and in it, you'll learn about the speed, handling, and lifesaving maneuvers that will make your outings on the Web more rewarding. And a little more adventurous!

Tapping Into the Power of Navigator

3

Power
Navigation

Even a 28.8K modem and an ISDN connection won't stop the bottleneck that occurs due to the mechanics of getting where you want to go on the Net. And if you should find something worthy of bringing home, that should happen as quickly as possible, too. You might not be able to change your connection speed or surf during off-peak hours, but what you can change is how fast and efficiently things happen on your end. This boils down to how effectively you tap into the power of Navigator's tools.

It's one of life's paradoxes that you need to invest some front-end time to learn new tools, new shortcuts, and to customize your environment, in order to achieve your goal of accomplishing more in less time. The initial time spent with learning the power of Navigator is worth it, because it pays you back every day you log on—both in time and in connection charges. With some of the tips and techniques you'll find in this chapter, you may even have enough time to surf the Net *and* get outdoors every once in a while!

ELEMENTS OF THE WEB BROWSER WINDOW

Before attempting to break any speed records, let's check out the make and model of the vehicle, and what controls are available—what they're called and what they do. Significant changes have been made in Navigator 3.0 that you'll want to become familiar with.

THE INTERFACE

When you learn what all the elements of the Navigator interface do, and the visual clues they provide, you can work a lot faster. Navigator 3.0 and Navigator Gold share almost identical interfaces, so if you learn one, you've essentially learned them both. This makes it easy for you if you use different versions at home and work. The difference between the two in terms of interface design is that Navigator Gold has an Edit button on the toolbar.

Figure 3-1 shows the elements of Navigator's browser window and Figure 3-2 shows the Navigator Gold interface. The numbers next to each element in Figure 3-1 correspond to the list that follows, which describes what each element does. Taking time now to become acquainted with the interface will save you time later as well as answer the common question, "Why is that envelope in the corner of the window?" (Hint: See number 11 in the list.)

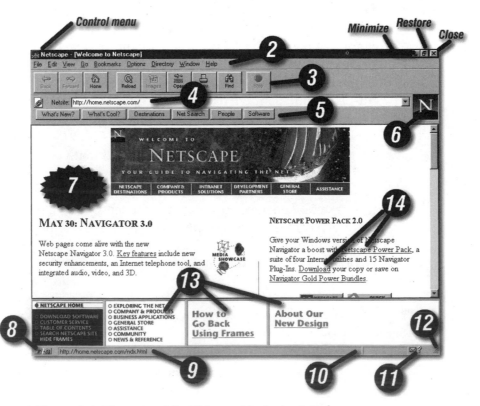

Figure 3-1: *Elements of the Netscape Navigator interface.*

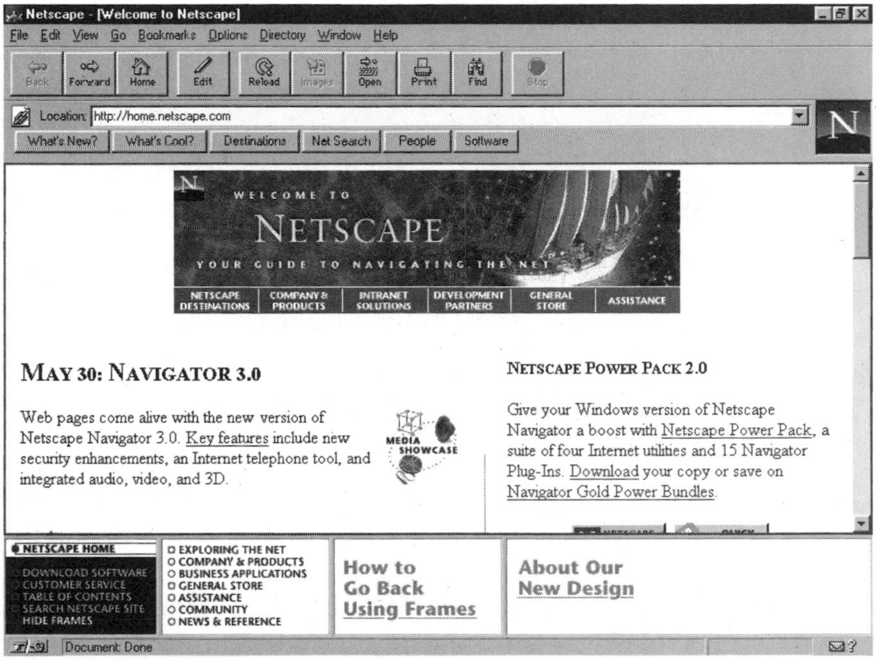

Figure 3-2: *Netscape Navigator Gold's interface.*

1. *The Title Bar.* The title bar displays across the top of the window. The name the author gave the page is displayed within brackets on the title bar. If you are looking at a graphic, multimedia file, or a file opened from your hard disk, the title bar will display the name of the file and, in the case of graphics, the size of the image.

2. *The Menu Bar.* The menu bar holds nine (ten for Navigator Gold) drop-down lists from which you can issue commands or set options. New to the menu bar in this version is the Window menu. Many, but not all of the commands available on the menus can also be accessed through keyboard shortcuts, the right mouse shortcut menu, or from the toolbar or Directory buttons.

3. *The Toolbar.* Below the menu bar is the toolbar. The toolbar in Netscape Navigator contains nine frequently used commands. Netscape Navigator Gold sports an additional button that launches the Netscape Editor. The toolbar is onscreen by default, but you can toggle it on and off whenever you like by pressing Alt+O+T or choosing Show Toolbar from the Options menu on the menu bar.

4. *The Location Field/Go to: field.* The Location/Go to: field displays the Uniform Resource Locator (URL)—the address of the document that is currently loaded in the browser's content or page window. The Location field changes its name from Location to Go to: whenever you type something in the field. The display of the Location/Go to: field can be toggled on and off by pressing Alt+O+L or by choosing Show Location from the Options menu on the menu bar. In this chapter, we'll refer to the Location/Go to: field frequently; there's a lot you can do with this little sliver of screen real estate. We recommend that you always choose to display the Location/Go to: field.

   The *Link icon,* as seen in Figure 3-2, is positioned to the left of the Location/Go to: field. This interface element, which looks like a link in a chain, works with the information in the Location/Go to: field. Double-click on the Link icon, and the URL displayed in the Location/Go to: field is copied to the Windows Clipboard. Click and drag the Link icon into the Bookmarks window to create a bookmark for the URL in the Location/Go to: field; dragging the Link icon into Gold's Editor window creates a hypertext link in an HTML document that references the URL in the Location/Go to: field.

5. *The Directory Buttons.* The Directory buttons are single mouse-click shortcuts to a vast array of Internet search engines, directories, sites, and Netscape Navigator information. The Directory buttons are displayed by default, but like the toolbar they can be toggled on and off at will. To do this, press Alt+O+D or choose Show Directory Buttons from the Options menu on the menu bar. Note that in Navigator

3, the Handbook button has been replaced by the Destinations button and that the Net Directory button has been replaced by a People button. Access to Handbook information has moved to the Help menu.

6. *The Logo Button.* The famous animated Netscape logo to the right of the Location field serves two purposes. Most users know that when the shooting stars are active, a document you've requested is loading, but it also has another function. Clicking on the logo will always take you to Netscape Communications' home page.

7. *The Page Display* or *Content Window.* The Content window is the area within a Netscape Navigator window that displays the document or file you are viewing. With all navigational assistants turned on, it's located between the Directory buttons and the Status line. In Netscape Navigator 3.0, the content window may display a single page, or a page that is composed of several documents displayed within frames.

8. *The Security Indicator.* This is the key icon found in the bottom left corner of the window. You can tell at a glance if the document you are viewing is an insecure document (a broken key on a gray background) or a secure document (an unbroken key on a solid blue background). It is not recommended that you send personal or financial information, such as your credit card information, if the Security indicator is a broken key. See Chapter 7, "Maintaining Your Privacy on the Internet," for more information on document and site security and for variations on this icon.

9. *Status Line* or *Status Message Area.* The long gray, recessed area to the right of the Security indicator displays a wide variety of messages about URLs, connection status, or elements your cursor is currently hovering over. This area can also display information about what the various buttons on the Netscape Navigator interface do, as well as the URL of a link your cursor is hovering over. Java applets and JavaScripts may also write information to the Status message area. Check the Status line whenever you are in doubt about what is currently happening in Navigator's browser window.

10. *The Progress Bar.* When you load a document or file into the content window, the Progress bar (to the right of the Status line) progressively fills with color to graphically indicate the progress being made. When the document has fully loaded, the Progress bar loses its color and returns to its original "empty" state.

11. *The Mail Icon.* The envelope in the lower right-hand corner of the window is the Mail icon. Clicking this icon is by far the fastest way to open the Netscape Mail window. If you have enabled automail checking and have logged into your mail server in the current Navigator session, the icon will display an exclamation point next to the envelope if you have new or unread mail. If there is no new mail, then the envelope alone will display. If you have not logged into your mail server in the session, a question mark appears next to the envelope. See Chapter 6, "Person to Person With Navigator Mail & Netscape News," for more information on Netscape Mail.

12. *Windows Interface Controls.* You'll also notice that the Navigator window has the usual Windows interface controls, such as the control menu icon in the upper left corner of the window. In Windows 95, the Minimize, Restore, and Close buttons are in the upper right corner of the window, and the new, window-resizing decorative "tread marks" are in the lower right-hand corner when Navigator's window isn't maximized in Windows 95.

13. *Frames.* Introduced in version 2 of Navigator, frames provide site authors with the ability to break the content window into one or more windows called *frames*. Figure 3-1 shows the Netscape home page displayed in five frames. Each frame has content that is separate from that of the other frames, and is referenced by its own URL. Frames are sort of like a split-screen TV display, where you watch different channels on the same screen; with frames, you are viewing different Web pages all within one window.

14. *Hypertext Link.* Links in Web pages take you to a new page, start a file download, play a sound or video, and so on

when you click on them. When text in a document also serves as a link, it is displayed as colored, underlined text by default. A graphic that also is a link may or may not have a colored border around it; a visible border around a graphic link is the decision of the author who created the site. A graphic that has had a special kind of attribute, called an *image map*, applied to it is divided into invisible regions that have links associated with each region. The areas of the graphic that contain links and the graphic itself don't display colored borders to indicate where the links are located or even that they are present. In Figure 3-1, the colored, underlined words (key features, Netscape Power Pack, and so on) as well as the Media Showcase graphic are links that are associated with different pages you can visit. The Welcome to Netscape graphic at the top of the page (seen in Figure 3-1) is an image mapped graphic. If you put your cursor over the Welcome to Netscape text, you will find that your cursor changes into the pointing-hand cursor that appears whenever you hover over a link.

When you've already visited a location referenced by a link, the color of the underlined text or the graphic border changes to a different color. The colors used to signify links are specified by the author of the page, but you can choose to display different colors if you wish. To change the colors used to signify links, see Chapter 2, "Installing & Customizing Navigator."

CUSTOM CURSORS TELL A STORY

In Netscape Navigator, your cursor changes shape when you do different things (see Figure 3-3). Many of the cursors are the familiar, standard Windows cursors, such as the Normal Select (the Arrow pointer), the Busy cursor (the Hourglass), the Text Select (the I-Beam), and the Unavailable (the International "no") resize cursors. Netscape Navigator has a few additional cursors in its collection that are worth familiarizing yourself with. In the following sections, we'll show you how you can save time and avoid frustration by taking a cue from the cursor.

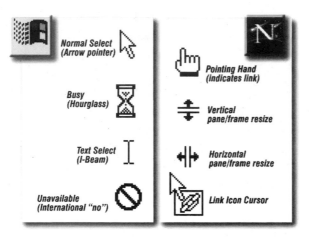

Figure 3-3: *Windows/Netscape Navigator cursors.*

FINDING "INVISIBLE LINKS" WITH THE POINTING HAND CURSOR

One of the most frequent shapes the cursor takes is that of the pointing hand. The pointing hand cursor is displayed whenever your cursor is hovering over a link. The Status line becomes active, and it displays the URL or address of the link you are pointing to—which helps you identify the link.

You can put this twosome to work for you even when you're staring at a seemingly blank, slow-loading page. Netscape Navigator often receives information about link location within a document and can act on the information *before* the text and the graphics are downloaded and displayed. The next time you find yourself tapping your fingers with impatience, move your cursor over the page and see if Netscape can display the pointing hand cursor. The pointing hand cursor just might find the link to the support page or to the software download area you seek; if it does, click the cursor on the "invisible" link. You'll scoot off of the slow page and on to your destination.

Even after a page has fully loaded, you may still need to use the cursor to find invisible links. Some Web page authors expect you to click on graphics to jump to other pages, but neglect to give you a visual hint (such as a link-colored border around the graphic) or provide a text label that describes the purpose of the graphic. The next time you are presented with a page that is graphically rich but doesn't appear to give you a way to navigate to other pages, move your cursor over the graphics. If your cursor changes into the pointing hand cursor, you've found an invisible link. Glance at the Status line; if it reports a URL that looks appealing to you, click on the graphic, and you're on your way to a new page.

TIP

All links are displayed in Netscape Navigator as colored, underlined text by default. If none of the colored links on the pages you view are underlined, it's because underlining has been turned off in Link Styles. See Chapter 2, "Installing & Customizing Navigator," for more information on configuring General Preferences Options.

THE LINK ARROW CURSOR

Hypertext links can be dragged from Web pages, e-mail messages, or newsgroup articles and dropped into other documents. This is a convenient, quick, and typo-proof way to copy the URL or address into another document. How do you know if a document can accept the drag and drop link? Look at the cursor—when the link is over inhospitable ground, the cursor becomes the Windows unavailable cursor—which looks like the international "no" symbol. But when you move the link over a document window that *can* accept the link, the cursor changes from the unavailable cursor into the link arrow cursor. You'll see the link arrow cursor when dragging links (or the link icon) into the Bookmarks window, or Gold's Editor window, and over other OLE-aware applications (see Figure 3-4) such as Adobe PageMaker, CorelDRAW!, TextPad, MS Office applications, MS Exchange, and WordPad to name but a few.

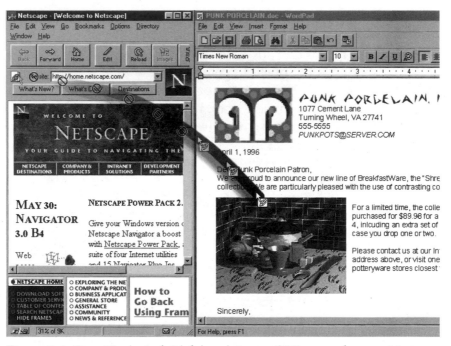

Figure 3-4: *Drag Navigator's Link icon into any OLE-aware document to copy the URL of the Web current page.*

THE TEXT SELECT CURSOR

In text-entry fields such as the Mail and New Message Composition windows and in HTML forms, where you can enter text, Navigator uses Windows' text-select (I-beam) cursor to establish the starting point of a selection, or to place an insertion point (a blinking bar) in the window to mark the place where new text can be entered.

However, in the text area (*not* form fields) of an HTML document, the text-select cursor acts a little differently: it appears only when your cursor is hovering over *selectable* text. This is because the text displayed in the content window, in the Document Source and Document Info windows, and in e-mail messages and newsgroup articles you've received is read-only—you can't add text.

Some HTML documents may contain fancy text or tables that appear to be selectable text, but they are actually graphics. You can easily tell the difference by looking at which cursor is displayed when you hover over the element. If the cursor becomes the I-Beam, it is text and can be saved to the clipboard by dragging the cursor over it and pressing Ctrl+C, or by saving the entire text of the page (press Ctrl+S or choose File and then Save as from the menu). However, if your cursor doesn't change into the I-Beam and remains an arrow pointer as you hover over the item, that's a tip-off that the element is a graphic. And graphics are saved not by highlighting, but by right-clicking on the graphic and choosing Save Image as from the shortcut menu.

THE RESIZE CURSORS

Navigator uses the standard Windows resizing cursors for resizing entire Navigator windows. For resizing frame windows in documents or the panes in the Mail or News windows, Navigator uses cursors that are similar in operation and in appearance to the pane-resizing cursor used by Windows Explorer and File Manager. The tip here is that the frames in Navigator frameset documents can be resized only if the author of the document specified that they can be resized. If you want a better view of a frame in a frameset document, hover your cursor over the frame's border. If the frame can be resized, the cursor changes into the frame/pane resize cursor. If the cursor *doesn't* change to the frame/pane resize cursor, all the click-dragging in the world won't change the frame's dimensions. In this case, the author probably used the NoResize attribute in the HTML document.

THE SHORTCUT MENU

If you use Windows 95, you probably use the context-sensitive shortcut menus to speed up copying, pasting, and performing other hard-disk housekeeping. If you are a Windows 3.1 user, then you're in for a treat, because you can use Navigator's shortcut menus too. Shortcut menus are small menus that pop up just off the point of your cursor whenever you right-mouse click over an area or object that supports shortcut menus. On the menu is a set of commands for the things you would most likely want to do with the object or text you clicked over.

You can right-mouse click your way to a shortcut menu if you click over almost any area of a document—empty space, text, links, graphics, and embedded objects are just a few of the object types that can support a shortcut menu. The number one rule when working in any of Netscape Navigator's modules is to right-mouse click over anything and everything. You'll be surprised to find that the command you're looking for will probably be on the shortcut menu.

In this chapter and throughout the book, we'll remind you of the options that are available with a single click of the right mouse button so you won't waste time hunting through menus and toolbars. Figure 3-5 is a guide to many of the places in Netscape Navigator where right-clicking will bring up a shortcut menu.

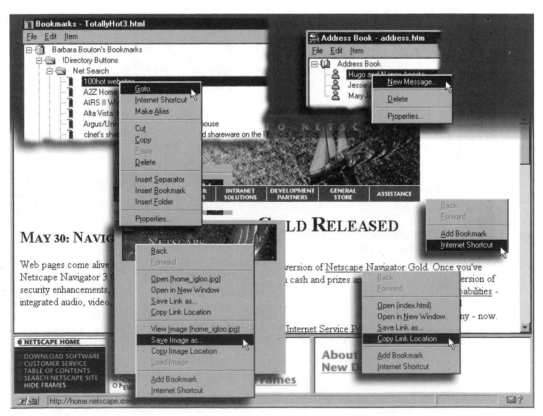

Figure 3-5: *Right-click almost anywhere to display context-sensitive shortcut menus.*

Now that we've taken a quick jaunt around Navigator's window to get some bearings and know how to "read" the cursors and invisible links and where to find shortcut menus, it's time to put this new knowledge into action. In the following section, you'll find some tricks that will get you to the Web page you want in record time.

GETTING TO KNOW URL A LITTLE BETTER

There are over ten different ways to notify Navigator that you want to visit an Internet address; you've probably found and used many of the available methods already. But you might not use some of the quickest methods, because they are not well documented or exceptionally obvious. In this section, we'll examine the methods that give the quickest, most reliable results and tell you when it's the best time to use them.

THE ANATOMY OF A URL

Netscape Navigator has the ability under certain circumstances to make connections using *partial* URLs for URLs that use the HTTP, FTP, and Gopher Internet protocols. In sections to follow, you'll see how working with partial URLs can save you time, especially when connecting to sites whose names are too long to memorize or type accurately. But to make the quickest, most direct connection to a site, it's important to understand how a basic URL is constructed so that you can take advantage of entering partial URLs. Let's take a look at the basic structure of the most common types of URLs.

In general, the URL can be one of three different types, and these types share some common URL elements. Figure 3-6 shows an annotation of the Location/Go To: field in Navigator, with callouts indicating the names of the various parts of a URL.

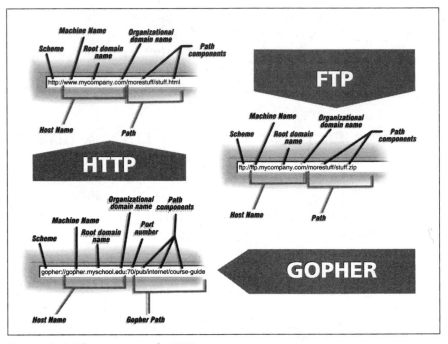

Figure 3-6: *The anatomy of a URL.*

THE SCHEME

The first part of a URL is the *scheme*. Schemes refer to the Internet protocol used to interact with the object or site the URL refers to. The most common schemes you will encounter on the Web are HTTP, FTP, and Gopher. The scheme name for the HyperText Transfer Protocol is http; for the File Transfer Protocol, ftp; and for the Gopher protocol, gopher. The scheme of these three URLs is followed by a colon and two forward slashes (://), which indicates that what follows :// is scheme-specific, and that it conforms to Internet syntax rules for the scheme.

THE HOST NAME

The second part of an HTTP, FTP, or Gopher URL is the fully qualified domain (host name) or *IP address*. A fully qualified address may consist of only the root level domain name, such as *mygroup.org* or *mycompany.com*; or it may also include the machine name of a computer located in the host's domain. WWW is by far the most common machine name in a domain and is written in syntax as *www.mycompany.com*. A machine name, if used, precedes the root level host domain name. Machine names may contain more than one word, with each word separated by a period. In the following example, www.justforfun.offhours is the machine name of a server in the myschool.edu domain:

```
www.justforfun.offhours.myschool.edu
```

Occasionally, you'll also see a colon and a number directly after the domain organizational extension, such as:

```
www.justforfun.offhours.myschool.edu:8080
```

This indicates that the site you are trying to reach is not at the standard port used by the scheme. When no port number is given, the default port number for the scheme is assumed.

DOMAIN VS. MACHINE NAMES

In a URL, the domain name is the primary name of the site. This is the name that the owner of the site registered with the InterNIC, the organization that assigns IP addresses. The machine name is the specific name that the owner of the domain gave to the machine (computer) that is being accessed. It may be helpful to think of the domain name as a family name or surname, while a machine name is similar to a first name. Just like people, machines may have compound (more than one) first names—like Jo Ann or Billy Bob. Sometimes machine names appear to be scheme names; for example, when the machine name is ftp or gopher, but they are not. It just looks like it because the owner of the domain decided to name the machine after the service it provides.

THE PATH

The third part of a URL is the *path* or *pathname*. The pathname is separated from the hostname by a forward slash and may itself contain forward slashes that denote the hierarchy that is followed to find the requested object. When no pathname is given, the server you are connecting to usually will display the top-level document or directory. A pathname is the path the scheme uses to find the resource you request—which, coincidentally, sometimes corresponds to the actual disk drive path on the server.

The scheme, host name, and path are the basic components of the HTTP, FTP, or Gopher URLs you are likely to see or are required to enter to access a site. Each scheme has optional parameters that may be required, such as search strings, local anchor tags, or references to form fields. FTP URLs also require that your user name and password precede the host name as part of the URL; but you almost never have to bother with this detail, because Netscape Navigator automatically adds that information for you when accessing most anonymous FTP sites.

TIP

If you are accessing a private site that does not use anonymous FTP login you can edit the URL to automatically enter the username and password you were given by the site's administrator for use at this particular site. The syntax for entering both your username and password is as follows:

ftp://username:password@ftp.somesite.com

If you don't want to enter your password in the URL for security or other reasons, you can just enter your username and the FTP server will query you for your password. To do so, use a URL that follows this format:

ftp://username@ftp.somesite.com

Other protocols such as Mailto, NEWS, Telnet, WAIS, and File are also valid Internet schemes, but they are not schemes that Netscape Navigator can shortcut with a partial URL.

SPEED UP YOUR TRAVEL WITH PARTIAL URLs

The Location/Go to: field is your gateway to the Internet. The usual way to enter a new URL in the Location/Go to: field is to click once to highlight the current entry, and then type in the full URL of where you want to go. Although it's a perfectly standard thing to do, it's not the fastest or the least error-prone way. The fastest way to get somewhere is to enter only *part* of the URL in the Location field, and let Navigator do the rest. In most applications nothing less than a full URL will work; but Netscape Navigator is a smart application, and when it "sees" a partial URL, it makes some pretty logical assumptions and fills in the rest of the URL for you. As long as you understand what these assumptions are, you'll make your connection with a lot less typing and without making typographical errors. Here's how you can put assumptions into action . . . .

One of the most common addresses on the Web is an address that refers to a Web site on a machine called www that belongs to the com domain. For example, http://www.sgi.com, or http://www.corel.com are the URLs of two prominent companies, Silicon Graphics, Inc. and Corel Corporation.

Notice that in these two examples there is one and only one machine name, www, before the site name. When you want to go to an address that follows this format, all you have to do is enter the site name in the Location box—sgi or corel in these examples—and press the Enter key. When Netscape Navigator sees only one word in the Location/Go to: field, Navigator assumes that you want to access a Web page that is on a machine called www in the com domain. Navigator then helpfully puts the http://www. before the word you entered, tacks a .com on the end, and sends your request for the page.

TIP

Don't be alarmed when using partial URLs if the Status *line first reports that the partial URL can't be found. This is normal behavior, because Netscape Navigator hasn't translated the partial URL into a full URL yet. It will automatically translate the URL after it reports the failure to find the URL, and you're soon on your way.*

However, if an attention box displays that says that the server is not responding or that a DNS entry can't be found, click on OK to dismiss the box, click in the Location/Go to: field, and then press the Enter key. This sends out the request again, and you should make your connection. Sometimes servers don't respond right away because of heavy network traffic. Try again by resending the request. In heavy network traffic, the second or third try often works. But if the site you want to reach or the DNS server you use is not up and receiving requests, you'll have to try again later.

You may also get the error message if you have a wrong address. Check your spelling of the address or do a search using one of the search sites discussed in Chapter 5, "Power Search & Retrieval."

Let's suppose that from a previous trip to the Adobe Systems' site (http://www.adobe.com), you learned that the URL path for information about Adobe Acrobat was /Acrobat. How would you use this information to go directly to the Acrobat section of Adobe's site using a partial URL?

If you enter *adobe* into the Location/Go to: field, you get Adobe Systems' top level: its home page. But if you enter *adobe/Acrobat* in the Location/Go to: field, the Acrobat page will display. This neat trick works only if you know the *exact* domain name and path, including any usage of upper- and lowercase letters. Domain names are usually lowercase, but both upper- and lowercase characters are commonly used in the path. Proper usage of *capitalization is a must;* if you type *adobe/acrobat* (all lowercase), you'll get a notice that the requested object doesn't exist on the server. The server sees /Acrobat as being entirely different than /acrobat.

This additional trick can save you time if the path is simple, if it's easy to remember, and if the Webmaster hasn't changed the location of what you're looking for. Otherwise, it's usually faster to either go to the top-level page and drill down, or to use a bookmark you saved earlier.

When com addresses don't follow the www.business.com format discussed earlier, there are still some shortcuts you can use. For example, if the com address uses only the domain name as in *bigbusiness.com*, enter *bigbusiness.com* as the shortcut. When the com address includes a machine name other than www—as in *sales.bigbusiness.com*, enter *sales.bigbusiness.com* as the shortcut and you'll reach your destination. Table 3-1 summarizes all the shortcuts you can use to reach HTTP URLs in the com domain, and Table 3-2 summarizes the available shortcuts for the other top-level domains.

Full URL example	Partial URL
http://www.company.com	company
http://www.company.com/morestuff/stuff.html	company/morestuff/stuff.html
http://company.com	company.com
http://more.than.one.machine.company.com.	more.than.one.machine.company.com.

Table 3-1: *Partial URLs for Web sites in the com domain.*

This partial URL magic also works for other kinds of addresses in any of the other top-level domains, such as gov, edu, net, org, or mil. For these domains, type the entire host name—for example, unix2.nysed.gov or mit.edu or eff.org—and off you go. Table 3-2 shows the shortcuts that are available.

Full URL example	Partial URL
http://myschool.edu	myschool.edu
http://more.than.one.machine.myschool.edu	more.than.one.machine.myschool.edu
http://federal.gov	federal.gov
http://more.than.one.machine.federal.gov	more.than.one.machine.federal.gov
http://charity.org	charity.org
http://more.than.one.machine.charity.org	more.than.one.machine.charity.org
http://army.mil	army.mil
http://more.than.one.machine.army.mil	more.than.one.machine.army.mil
http://free.net	free.net
http://more.than.one.machine.free.net	more.than.one.machine.free.net

Table 3-2: *Partial URLs for Web sites in top-level domains other than com.*

DIFFERENT SHORTCUTS FOR DIFFERENT SCHEMES

What about addresses that don't begin with http://? Partial URLs can work here too, provided that the machine name is the same as the scheme. For example, if the full URL is ftp://ftp.somecompany.com, you can skip the ftp:// and the .com. But if the address is ftp://ftp2.somecompany.com, you'll need to enter the entire URL because the machine name is ftp2 and not simply ftp. The same rules apply to gopher addresses: gopher.someplace.org will work, but gopherplace.someplace.org will not. Table 3-3 is a summary of partial URLs you can use to reach ftp and gopher sites. These partial URLs work the same in all of the top-level domains—com, edu, mil, net, and org.

Full URL example	Partial URL
ftp://ftp.company.com	ftp.company
ftp://ftp2.company.com/	no partial URL
ftp://ftp2.company.com/ morestuff/stuff.zip	no partial URL
ftp://more.than.one. machine.company.com	no partial URL
gopher://gopher. company.com	gopher.company.com
gopher://gopher2. company.com/	no partial URL
gopher://gopher2.company. com/pub/course-guide	no partial URL
gopher://more.than.one. machine.company.com	no partial URL
The partial URL methods work with all of the other organizational domains—.com, .edu, .mil, .net, and .org.	

Table 3-3: *Partial URLs for FTP and Gopher sites.*

If all of the preceding methods for quickly entering a URL were foolproof techniques, we could wind up our power navigation discussions right here. But the Internet is no more a utopia than the real world, and you'll frequently encounter a *snag* in the Net—or at least in your approach to accessing it—that requires workarounds and an understanding of some special Navigator features. Let's take a look now at a little troubleshooting you can perform, and documentation techniques for your travels to ensure smooth sailing. . . .

THE POWER USER'S TRAVEL TIPS

The reason why most folks pack travel provisions in a car—a tire inflater, a sewing kit, a box of band-aids, and so on—is to buy some sort of insurance so that when a mishap occurs, the voyage doesn't grind to a halt. Similarly, there are a number of things you can take with you—most of them mental notes—to ensure that the moment you log on to the Net, you have all the things you need to workaround unexpected potholes in cyberspace.

TAKING THE "NOT FOUND" OUT OF THE NOT FOUND ERROR MESSAGE

The Not Found or 404 Object Not Found error message (see Figure 3-7) can be the rock in the road to speedy Internet travel. These messages are received when you've asked for a page or object from a server and the server either can't find it or is not authorized to provide it. The most common reasons why you don't get what you ask for include a typographical mistake in the URL you used, the object has moved to a new location on the site, or the object has been removed from the site.

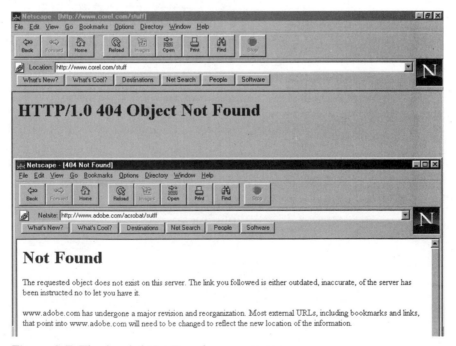

Figure 3-7: *The dreaded Not Found error message.*

Although the error message might seem like a brick wall, careful editing of the URL in the location field will often enable you to find what you're looking for.

First, carefully look at the URL and make sure everything is spelled correctly. Common errors are com spelled as con, spaces in the address (remove them), and uppercase letters that should be lower and vice versa. Capitalization is a hard one to puzzle out, because there is no rule on when, if ever, capitalized characters in a URL appear. But URLs are case-sensitive, and you must type in the correct case.

Try looking for the object in different places on the server. This is most efficiently accomplished by "backtracking" your way through the URL. For example, when the URL you're trying to reach is http://one.two.three.com/more/stillmore/sales/widget.html, place your cursor at the end of the URL in the Location field, and click once. This highlights the entire URL. Click once more to unhighlight the entire URL and get the blinking insertion cursor. Then click and drag the text-select or I-Beam cursor to the left and select all of the text up to the first forward slash you find; in this example, widget.html would be selected. Now, press the Delete key.

The address now reads as http://one.two.three.com/more/stillmore/sales/. Press Enter to request the new URL. If you get an error message or the page that displays doesn't have a link that looks like it will go to what you're looking for, repeat the process of backing up one more level. In this example, the edited URL would now be http://one.two.three.com/more/stillmore/.

Keep backing your way through the URL until you find what you're looking for or until you reach the host name. In this example, that would be after you tried the still more and then the more paths and were left with http://one.two.three.com/. If you still don't find what you were looking for, use the site's search feature if it provides one, or use one of the Internet search engines.

BOOKMARKS

Bookmarks are the bread crumbs you leave behind so you can re-
trace your path later. Any time you find a site you think you want
to revisit, make a bookmark immediately. When you've
bookmarked a site, the address is conveniently stored in your personal bookmarks list. Bookmarks are easy to make; most of the
time a Ctrl+D or a right-mouse click and picking Add Bookmark
will do it. Bookmarks are easy to use: Pick one from the Bookmarks
menu or from the Bookmarks window (Ctrl+B). When you use
bookmarks, you don't have to remember how you found your way
to the site, what the address is, or type (or *mis*type!) long, strange
URLs into the Location/Go to: field. The smart use of bookmarks
will save you enormous amounts of time and make visiting sites
that are not linked a lot easier. Bookmarks are so essential and so
versatile that Chapter 4, "Retracing Your Steps," is dedicated
almost exclusively to the use of them.

HISTORY LIST

The History list is great for tracing where you've been in a single
Navigator session. If you've been someplace and you want to go
back, look in the History list. Clicking on any entry in the History
list will take you to the site. But the entries in the History list are
not keepers from session to session; they can only be accessed as
long as the Navigator window they are associated with is open.
Each Navigator window has its own History list; if you close the
browser window, the History list that tracked where you went in
that window goes with it (see Figure 3-8). If you want to return to a
site you've been to in the current session, but don't find the entry
you're looking for in the History list, it may be in a different
browser window's History list. And if this other window is still
open, *save* the location to your Bookmarks before closing it. To
make a bookmark from a History list entry, open the History list by
pressing Ctrl+H or Alt+W+H or by choosing Window from the
menu bar, and then History. Select the entry you want to bookmark
and then click the Create Bookmark button. Done!

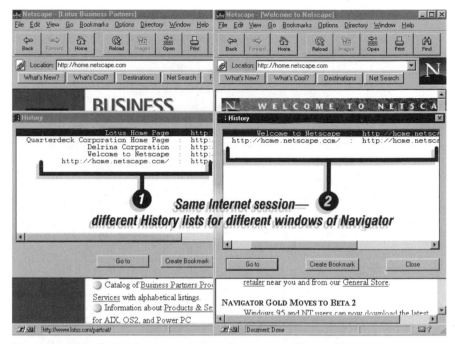

Figure 3-8: *Each Web browser window has its own History list.*

It is a good practice to go review the History list just before you close the browser window. Navigator Gold users should always check their History lists before clicking on the Edit button on the toolbar, because part of what the Edit command does is close the browser window, which in turn clears the History list associated with that window.

Even if you faithfully check all your History lists before you close the browser windows, you may not find some entries you expected to find in the lists. "Missing" entries usually turn out to be sites that were viewed in a frame. This is due to the nature of frames and framesets. The History list will accurately track frameset URLs, but it ignores the URLs that correspond to the individual frames that make up a frameset page.

A frameset is a "master" page that has its own URL, and each frame in the frameset also has its own URL. When you view a frameset page, only the URL for the frameset is displayed in the Location/Go to: field and is tracked in the History list. If you click a link, one of the frame windows, and that frame or one of the other frames in the frameset displays the page you jumped to; the URL listed in the Location field doesn't change. You have, as far as Navigator is concerned, made a trip to a new page without leaving the page (the frameset) you started from. An example of this travel without movement can be seen in Figure 3-9, where Macromedia's home page is displayed within the framed version of Netscape's home page. The jump to Macromedia was made from the framed version of Inline Plugin's What's New page. The Macromedia page will *not* be logged in the History list, because you never actually left the What's New page. Try *that* in real life!

Figure 3-9: *Macromedia's home page displays within a frame in Netscape's home page.*

So the History list wasn't exactly in error reporting the "non-jump" to Macromedia's site, but the History list in this instance is of no use if you were planning on using your History list to backtrack through the sites you visited while "framed." A change in tactics is therefore in order here: Use the Back button on the toolbar or right-click in the frame and choose Back from shortcut menu to "page" back through the pages that have been displayed in that frame. Alternatively you can create a bookmark for the site that is displayed in the frame by right-clicking in the frame and choosing Add Bookmark from the shortcut menu. Don't use the Add Bookmark command from the Bookmarks menu—that makes a bookmark to the frameset, which in this case is at Netscape and not Macromedia!

THE LOCATION/GO TO: FIELD DROP-DOWN

The Location/Go to: field drop-down list (click the down arrow at the end of the field) stores all the addresses that you actually type into the field during a session. It doesn't store the addresses of links you take or bookmarks used in a session, however. When you close Navigator, the drop-down list stores only the *last ten places* that were entered in the list. When you next start Netscape Navigator, the last ten entries from your previous session are listed, and any new URLs you type into the field are added to the list. Because the list is persistent from session to session, it can be a life saver if you forgot to make a bookmark for a site. It's always worth a quick look here before retyping addresses or redoing a search for a previously visited site.

REMOVING AN ENTRY FROM THE LOCATION DROP-DOWN LIST

If you've visited games.games.games.com on a company machine (by accident, of course!) and you don't want your boss to see it listed in the Location drop-down list, you can remove the URL from the list. The safest way is to quickly visit ten (or fewer) new places to bump the offending entry off the list. Just remember that you must type each URL into the Location field, and that you must close and restart Navigator to "purge" the list.

There is another way to edit this list, but it's not for the faint-of-heart. The entries in the list are stored in the Netscape.ini file if you are using the 16-bit, Windows 3.1 version of Netscape Navigator, and are saved to the Windows 95 Registry if you are using the 32-bit, Windows 95 version. If you've never successfully edited a Windows 3.1 ini file or the Windows 95 Registry, stick to the first method. But if you can hack system files with confidence, the following steps show you where to find the entries and edit them. Be sure you've backed up the files before you edit them, and that you know how to restore them if you make a mistake. A misplaced hack in a Navigator.ini file might make Navigator crash in future sessions. But if you make a mistake editing the Windows 95 Registry, *Windows 95* may not run at all.

To edit the Netscape.ini file:

1. Make sure Navigator is not running.

2. Open Navigator.ini in a text editor such as notepad.exe. The Netscape.ini file is usually found in either the Windows directory or in the directory where Navigator is installed.

3. Scroll down through the file until you find a section that looks something like this, but probably has ten entries:

   ```
   [URL History]
   URL_1=http://www.games.games.games.com
   URL_2=http://home.netscape.com
   ```

4. Find the line containing the URL you want to remove.

5. Select all the text to the right of the = (equals sign) and replace it with a more appropriate URL.

6. Save the file (Ctrl+S or File, Save), open Navigator, and admire your handiwork.

To edit the Windows 95 Registry:

1. Close all running applications, including Netscape Navigator.

2. From the Start Menu, choose Run, enter regedit.exe in the Run dialog box, and press the Enter key.

3. When the Registry Editor opens, you want to go to HKEY_CURRENT_USER\Software\Netscape\Netscape Navigator\URL History. Drill down through the tree structure until you get to the URL History folder, then open it.

4. In the left pane is the tree you worked your way through, and in the right pane is a list of URLs. Look in the Data column to find the URL you want to edit, then double-click on the corresponding URL entry in the Name column. This opens the Edit String dialog box as seen in Figure 3-10.

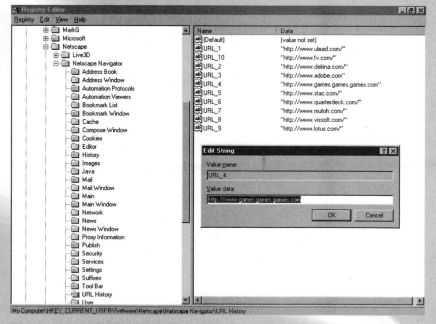

Figure 3-10: *Edit the Windows 95 Registry to remove an entry from the Location field drop-down list.*

5. Replace the http://www.games.games.games.com entry in the Value data field with a more appropriate entry. http://home.netscape.com is a good choice.

6. Click on the OK button to close the Edit String dialog box. The change you made should be evident in the right pane. If so, choose Exit from the Registry menu to close the Registry Editor. The Registry Editor automatically saves all changes you make when you close the program.

7. Open Navigator and view your handiwork from the Location drop-down list.

GETTING MORE IN ONE GULP ONCE YOU'VE ARRIVED

Speeding up your travel isn't limited to getting to a site; it also involves getting things done faster once you *get* there. Two inter-related strategies for packing more into each online session are 1) increase the size of the content window, and 2) use keyboard and right-mouse click shortcuts. The following sections show you how to use keyboard shortcuts and other easy-to-use strategies to navigate quickly, devoting a lot of screen real estate to navigational aides.

USE KEYBOARD SHORTCUTS

In this era of graphical, point-and-click operating systems and applications, it might seem odd to recommend that you take the time to learn keyboard shortcuts—but keystroking can shave time off navigation in a way that mousing can't. Many times the trusty keyboard can get something done faster than hunting through menus or even hitting the right icon. Speed should be reason enough to recommend the use of keyboard shortcuts.

Once you have mastered the keyboard shortcuts, you won't need the toolbar and the Directory buttons, and you can turn off their display. When you turn off the display of such interface elements, there's more space for the content window. The larger the content window, the quicker and easier it is for you to discern what is available on a page you're visiting, because less of the page's content is scrolled offscreen. Figure 3-11 shows how much screen real estate you can gain when you turn off the display of the toolbar and the Directory buttons.

Figure 3-11: *Turning off the toolbar and the Directory buttons lets you see more on each page.*

Many of the shortcuts that Netscape Navigator uses are common ones that you may already know, such as Ctrl+P to print or Esc to stop an action. Other keyboard shortcuts are specific to Navigator, but most are well thought-out and, with a little practice, can become as second nature as Alt+F4 (Quit application). Appendix C contains a complete list of keyboard shortcuts that you can use to speed up your work. You've probably already noticed that keyboard shortcuts are sprinkled liberally through this and other chapters; the intention is that frequent reference to them will help you become familiar with them. Keyboard shortcuts are true Power User techniques that you alone can decide to make work for you.

THE DIRECTORY BUTTONS

These buttons put all kinds of useful places just one click away—search engines and directories, the Destinations jumplists, What's Cool? and What's New? lists, and information on Netscape software. At a glance, the Directory buttons would seem like power navigation tools, but in practice they are definitely not. On a day-to-day basis, you'll save more time if the space the Directory buttons occupy onscreen is lent to the content window. If you turn the Directory buttons display off, you gain more screen real estate; and you still can get to the cool stuff on the Directory buttons in just two clicks or a few keystrokes. The list that follows provides tips on how to maintain easy access to the information of the Directory buttons when you have turned off their display:

- All of the sites accessible from the Directory buttons bar plus a few more sites are also available from either the Directory menu or the Help menu.

- If you don't like to use menus and would rather use the Directory buttons, toggle them on only when you want to use them. As mentioned earlier in the chapter, the Directory buttons can easily be toggled on and off, by pressing Alt+O+D or by choosing Show Directory Buttons from the Options menu.

- An even bigger time-saver in the long run is to visit each place the buttons take you to and then bookmark the addresses. Or just look in the Totally Hot bookmarks list on the Companion CD, we've bookmarked them for you along with other related sites. For the Net Search and People sites that are not hosted on Netscape's site, you'll save time and help cut down network traffic when you use bookmarks instead of the Directory buttons, because you'll go directly to the search or directory site without an intermediate stop on Netscape's busy home page. To make these bookmarks easy to get to, place all the bookmarks for directory button items in a bookmarks folder called !Directory Buttons. The exclamation point in front of the folder name forces the folder to appear at the top of the Directory menu's bookmark list. See Chapter 4, "Retracing Your Steps," for more information on creating and managing bookmarks and bookmark folders.

THE TOOLBAR

The toolbar contains many useful commands; but like the Directory buttons, the toolbar takes up a lot of screen real estate. All of the commands it sports can be given either through a keystroke or two, or by picking its equivalent from one of the menus. You also have the option to toggle the toolbar on or off (Alt+D+T) so it only takes up space when you want to use it. Appendix C describes different keyboard, menu, and shortcut menu commands you can use if you choose to maximize screen real estate and not to display the toolbar.

GETTING A SECOND "HOME"

The Home button on the toolbar by default goes to the Netscape home page. And guess what? Clicking on the Netscape logo button *always* takes you to Netscape's home page, too. Why settle for two buttons that go to one place when they can go to different places? You can redefine the Home button (see Chapter 2, "Installing & Customizing Navigator") so that it goes to any location. Choose a location that you like to keep in frequent contact with, and make your "home" your company's home page, a headline news page, your favorite search engine, or to a file on your hard disk.

Use the Home button or press Alt+G+H whenever you want to quickly go to your personal "home" site, and click on the Logo button when you want to check for Netscape news and update information. Now there's no wasted screen space, no extra typing, and you can still get to Netscape's home with one click.

DIGGING YOUR WAY OUT OF A SLOW CONNECTION

Sometimes it seems like pages take forever to load, and some pages will *never* load due to a server error. When you find yourself confronted with one of these slugs, you have several options.

Click on the Stop button or press the Esc key to stop the loading of the page. If you think that the page is loading slowly because it contains too many large graphic or multimedia files, turn off Auto Load Images from the Options menu (if this feature is on), then reload the page. If you turn off AutoLoad Images before you reach a site, you can selectively open any images you want to see by right-mouse clicking the image. Choose Load This Image, and Navigator will download and display the image (see Figure 3-12).

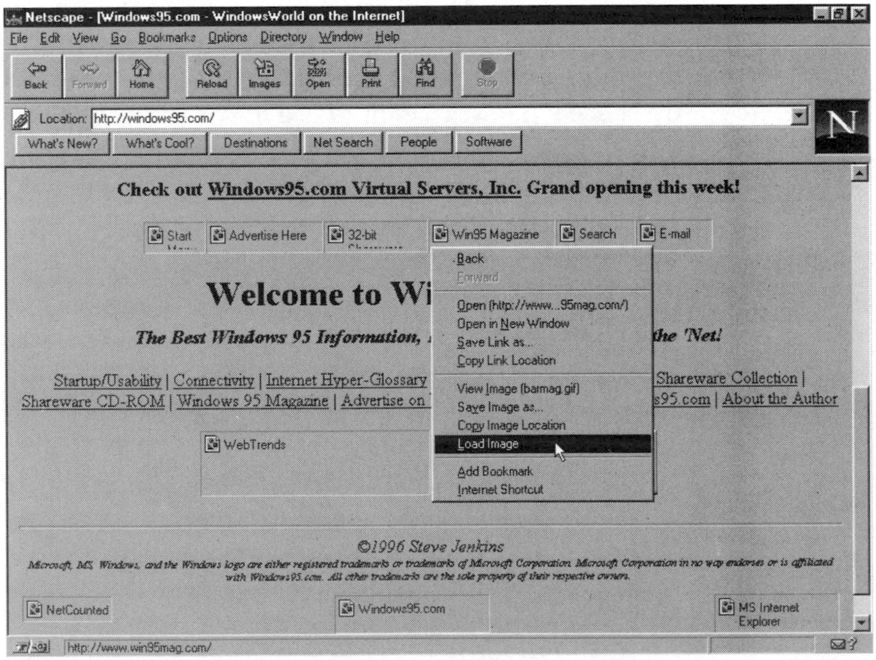

Figure 3-12: *Load a single image by right-clicking on the missing graphic icon.*

TIP

If you already reached a site, some of the large graphics on the page in question may have already been stored in your cache and will load again, even if AutoLoad Images is turned off. To prevent them from loading and continuing to slow you down, you will have to flush the cache. To do this, choose Options, Network Preferences, then the Cache tab. On the Cache tab, click Clear Memory Cache Now, then click on Clear Disk Cache Now. Click OK each time you are asked to confirm the cache clearance. Chapter 2, "Installing & Customizing Navigator," discusses these and other preference options in detail.

If you think the page is not loading or is taking too long to load because of network traffic, click on the Stop button or press the Esc key to stop the loading of the page. Then reload the page by pressing Ctrl+R or by clicking in the Location field and then pressing the Enter key. Each connection request you make is separate and may travel through the Internet by a different route. Just like the nation's highways, some Internet routes may be faster than others at any given time.

The Stop button or the Esc key is also used to stop the animation of animated GIF files (see Chapter 6, "Person to Person With Navigator Mail & Netscape News," for information on animated GIFs) and other multimedia files.

ADVANCED NAVIGATION

In your quest to use Navigator to its fullest, learning how to move efficiently between Navigator's new framed windows and how to manage the use of multiple Navigator windows is paramount. In this section you'll learn the in's and out's of frame navigation and how to use multiple Navigator windows to increase your online productivity through multitasking.

FRAME NAVIGATION

Navigator 3.0's introduction of frameset documents offers new possibilities for Web site designers, but may be a bit puzzling for users. As mentioned earlier, a frameset is a collection of frames (windows) that are displayed within a single Web browser window. Each frame in a frameset contains a document or object that has its own URL and can act independently of all the other frames in the frameset. The content displayed in each frame may physically be located on the same server, or might reside on a server halfway around the world. It's all up to the designer of the page as to where the visual content of your display comes from, and what happens when you access a link in a document that is in a frame. Sometimes a new window opens to display the site you linked to, but many times the content of the place you linked to *replaces* the content in one of the frames in the current frameset. Though being in several places at once is a wonderful way to present data, it created navigational problems for users of Navigator 2. In version 2 of Navigator, clicking on the Back button on the toolbar took users to the last *site* visited, *not* the last page that was in the frame. Netscape heard its users' pleas for an easier way to navigate.

In Navigator 3, to move forward or backward in a frame, right-click in the frame and choose Back or Forward from the shortcut menu *or* click the Back or Forward button on the toolbar.

USING MULTIPLE WINDOWS

You can have as many Navigator browser windows open as you like, each connected to a different site, as long as you have enough system resources and bandwidth on your Internet connection to support them all.

One of the best times to open another Web browser window is when a site is taking a long time to load. While the document loads, you can open a new browser window and surf to another site, another page on the first site (if you know the URL), or load a page you've saved to your hard disk. Think of this action as personal multitasking; why wait for a document to load to put Navigator to use? You can also read and send mail, read newsgroups, manage your bookmarks list, or download files while you have several browser windows open.

Another great time to put multiple windows to use is when you're visiting a site with a lot of appealing links. You can jump to as many links as you want by opening each new link in its own window without losing the window that holds the original page. When you want to return to the original page to continue reading it, or to access the links it provides, it's ready and waiting for you in its own window. When you use multiple windows in a situation like this, you never waste your time or add to Internet traffic by reloading the original page.

Here's an example of how to open a link in a new window:

1. From Navigator's browser window, click the What's Cool? Directory button or choose What's Cool? from the Directory menu. A long list of notable sites appears.

   Checking the What's New! and What's Cool? pages is a great way to find many interesting sites you might have otherwise overlooked.

2. Scroll down the list until you find a link that interests you. Right-mouse click the link to display the shortcut menu.

3. From the shortcut menu, choose New Window with this Link (see Figure 3-13). Navigator loads the page you've selected in a new window, without closing the What's Cool? window.

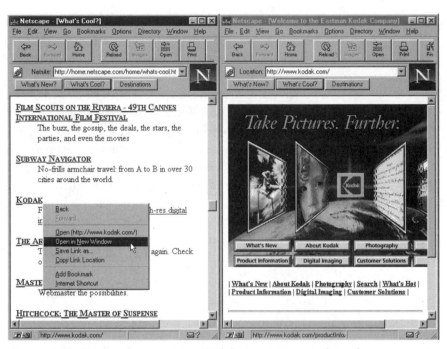

Figure 3-13: *Open a document in a Web browser new window when you want to keep the original window open.*

4. To switch back to the What's Cool? window or any open window(s) (except the Bookmarks window), repeatedly press Ctrl+Tab until the window you want comes to the front. Or select the desired window from the list at the bottom of Navigator's Window menu.

TIP

You can have only one copy of Navigator open at a time, but you can open up to four independent browser windows by choosing New Web Browser from the File menu. If four browser windows aren't enough, you can open additional windows by right-clicking a link and choosing Open in New Window from the shortcut menu.

MANAGING BANDWIDTH

Keep in mind that although you can have Navigator doing many different things at once, Navigator can do nothing to increase the amount of information that can be transmitted through the connection you have to the Internet. If you are downloading files and linking to different sites, all of the information has to come through the same connection, and this connection can only hold so much information. Netscape Navigator will dutifully keep track of the separate download threads, for example, but the more processes you have going, the slower each thread will be.

There are several occasions upon which opening multiple browser windows can save you time, and often without delaying a single online transaction (see Figure 3-14). But there are other actions you take that eat into the bandwidth of that skinny telephone wire connected to your modem.

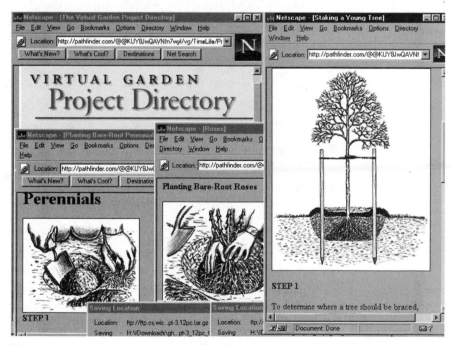

Figure 3-14: *You can download and read mail and Web pages without a slowdown if you plan ahead.*

Use the following list as a guide to help you establish an online balance between the activities that use up bandwidth and those that don't. When you have too many bandwidth-consuming activities going, postpone the launching of another until some of the processes finish. Or choose one of the bandwidth-free activities in the list while you wait, and you'll be well on your way to using your online time more efficiently:

■ The content of pages that have already loaded in Navigator windows is stored in your memory or disk cache. Leaving these windows open so you can read them doesn't require any additional bandwidth.

■ Save pages to a folder on your hard drive and then read the documents when you're offline—or when you're online and waiting for Web pages to load or files to download. It's easy to forget that Navigator is not simply an online tool, but a *local system browser* as well. Loading graphics and pages from a local drive doesn't take up any bandwidth, because the information comes from a disk—not through the modem. See the next section, "Power Saving," for more information on saving Web pages.

■ Reading e-mail that's already been received and writing e-mail don't take up bandwidth.

■ Sending or receiving e-mail does take up bandwidth.

■ Writing an article for a newsgroup doesn't use up bandwidth or cause an online delay.

■ Sending a newsgroup article you've written does take up bandwidth.

■ Opening the Bookmarks window or managing bookmarks doesn't take up bandwidth.

■ Refreshing a page (View, Refresh) won't slow other windows down, because the information will come from your disk cache and not from the Internet.

■ Loading a *new* page from the Internet *does* require significant additional bandwidth.

■ Downloading files takes up *a lot* of bandwidth.

- Reading newsgroups does take up bandwidth, because each new message has to be transferred to you.

- Using a bookmark to make a connection takes up bandwidth.

- Reloading pages takes up bandwidth, because a new connection must be made to the server where the page resides.

POWER SAVING

Sites appear and disappear on the Web on a daily basis, and the content of familiar sites changes with equal regularity. When you see something on the Web that you want to keep for reference or share with a friend, you need to act immediately! First, save a bookmark for the page so you can find the page again. Then decide if you want to save the page. You have several options for saving the content of Web pages; choose the one that works best for you:

- You can save the text of the page as unformatted ASCII text to your hard disk.

- You can save the text within the structure of its HTML formatting along with the other elements of the page.

- If you're in a crunch for free hard-disk space, you can print the page to save it.

- You can e-mail the page to yourself or to a friend, so it's located in your mail folder and not saved to a location on a hard disk you might not find again! This is particularly useful if you have different e-mail accounts at home and at work. Watch out for copyright issues, though; if in doubt, e-mail the URL and not the page.

Whatever your decision is, it's best to save that document when you *first see the page.* If you wait, you may never have the opportunity again.

Because a Web site can often be composed of different object types—text, graphics, executable files you can download, and so on—Navigator needs your input as to how elements of a Web site should be saved. The following sections describe the best ways to retrieve and catalog the gems you've discovered online.

SAVING DIFFERENT TYPES OF WEB ELEMENTS

If you want to save something to your hard drive so you can view or use it when you're not connected to the Internet, you have to explicitly save the item—either by downloading it, choosing File, Save As from the menu, or right-clicking over the object and by choosing Save (Link, Image, etc.) as from the shortcut menu. When you save a page or frame, only the text is saved; any graphics or objects referenced by the document need to be individually saved.

SAVING TEXT FROM HTML PAGES

The textual content of single HTML pages or HTML pages in frames can be easily saved by pressing Ctrl+S, or choosing File, then Save As. When saving an HTML page, you have an important decision to make: Do you want to preserve the page's HTML formatting, or will you be happy with plain text with none of the original formatting or the HTML tags or links? Which option you choose depends on how you intend to use the document.

If you plan to import textual content of the saved page into another application, you probably want to save the page as unformatted text. When Navigator saves a page as text, it automatically performs the tedious task of stripping out the HTML tags, because the tags make documents hard to read. For example, if you are saving recipe pages and plan to import them into your cookbook database, you don't want or need the HTML tags that surround the text. The HTML tags make the recipes attractive and easy to read in the Web browser, but you won't find them an enhancement when they're displayed in your database program.

To save the page as an ASCII text file with all of the HTML tags removed, choose Plain Text (*.txt) in the Save as type drop-down box (see Figure 3-15).

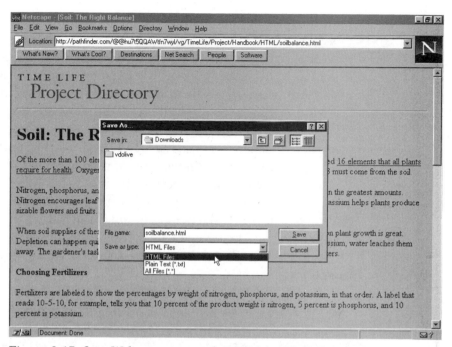

Figure 3-15: *Save Web pages to your hard disk in either Plain Text or Source format.*

When you save the page as a Source file by choosing HTML Files (*.htm, *.html) in the Save as type drop-down box, all of the HTML tags are preserved in the document. This is the option you should choose if you want to learn how to write HTML pages by studying examples, or if you intend to view the document in Netscape Navigator later. Pages saved as HTML files load from your hard disk and display in Navigator with all of their functionality intact—colored text, bolding, and so on, as well as any hypertext links in the document.

SAVING PAGES AS E-MAIL

Pages can be saved by e-mailing them to yourself or to a friend who might be interested in the information you've found. When you e-mail a page from the Web browser window, the page is sent as an attachment to the mail message. The attachment consists of the HTML document but not the graphics and other linked or embedded objects that are referenced in the HTML document.

If the recipient of the e-mailed page is not using Navigator or Navigator Gold to read the e-mail, he or she will receive the raw HTML source document (see Figure 3-16). The recipient can open the page in his or her Web browser, if a text editor is used to strip out the mail reader's header information and to save the remaining HTML portion of the message in a file that has an htm file extension. When the recipient uses Navigator or Navigator Gold to read e-mail, he or she won't see the HTML code—what will appear is the page in his or her message window as it appeared on the Web. If the recipient is offline when reading the e-mail, the graphics and other non-text objects will display as broken icons. But when the e-mail is read while the person is still connected to the Internet, Navigator will fetch the graphics and other objects and display them in the e-mailed document, as seen in Figure 3-17. How's that for service?

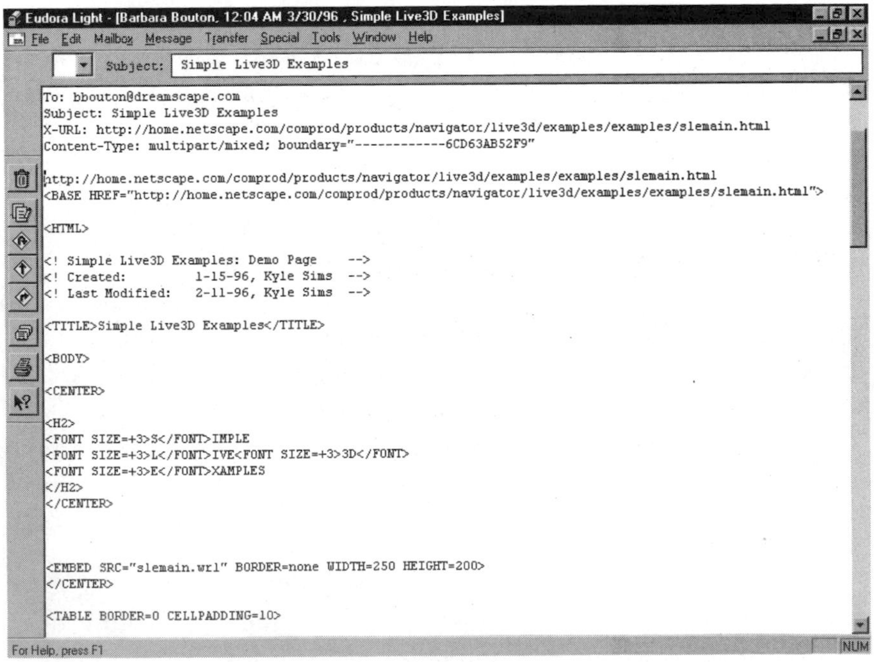

Figure 3-16: *How a page you've e-mailed looks when the recipient doesn't use Netscape Mail.*

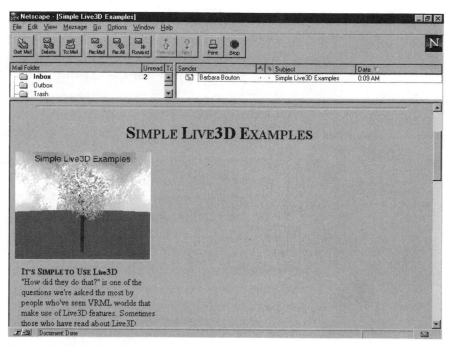

Figure 3-17: *How a page you've e-mailed looks when the recipient uses Netscape Mail.*

To mail the current page or frame in the browser window, choose File, then Mail Frame, which brings up the mail message composition window with the frame or page already listed as an attachment. All you have to do is address the mail and send it. See Chapter 6, "Person to Person With Navigator Mail & Netscape News," for more information.

SAVING GRAPHICS OR MULTIMEDIA OBJECTS

If the contents of the page or frame you are saving is not an HTML document but instead is a graphic, VRML, or other multimedia object, choose File, Save As from the menu, or right-click the object. The Save As dialog box that appears will suggest the appropriate file format for the object. You can change the name of the file and the location where it will be stored, but *don't change* the file name extension or the type of file that the Save as type drop-down suggests.

Saving the Document by Printing It   To print a page from a Navigator window, choose File, Print from the menu, or press Ctrl+P. The standard Windows print dialog box appears; select the number of copies you want, and print.

TIP

Text entered into forms doesn't print, and neither does JavaScript nor Java-generated content. If you want to create a record of a form you filled out or Java-generated text on a page, press the Print Screen button on your keyboard. Pressing Print Screen sends a copy of the page to the clipboard. Then open a paint program such as MS Paint or Paint Shop Pro, and press Ctrl+V to paste the image into the paint program. From there, you can print the page as a graphic or save the file to a disk in the bitmap file type of your application's choice.

Saving to the Clipboard   You save the text in a document by selecting it and copying it to the Windows Clipboard. Once it is on the Windows Clipboard, it can be pasted into any application that accepts text input.

The text is copied as plain ASCII text and will not retain any of the font or paragraph attributes such as bold, italic, or the large size associated with headings. Also, the URL information that is associated with a link and any graphics or embedded objects will not be copied to the Clipboard. To save this kind of information, you must right-click the link or object and choose the appropriate save option from the shortcut menu.

TIP

To avoid keeping a memory-hungry text editor or word processor open, while running Navigator, save text you've copied to the clipboard in the clipboard's native file format, .CLP. Text that has been copied to the clipboard is saved by choosing File, Save As from the Clipboard Viewer menu. When your Navigator session is finished, load the CLP files back onto the clipboard by choosing File, Open from the Clipboard Viewer menu, then paste the contents of the clipboard into any application that accepts text. Windows 3.1 users will find the Clipboard viewer in the Accessories group. Windows 95 users will find the Clipboard viewer in the Start menu's Programs, Accessories folder or can use Add/Remove Programs to install it if it was not installed.

OFFLINE SURFING

You've seen throughout this chapter that there are many ways to make your online time more productive. But it is possible that some of your most productive online time may actually take place when you're *not* connected to the Internet. When you're online and constrained by time and patience, there is a tendency to skim through pages and avoid graphics and other large objects that could potentially change your opinion of the site's content, or conversely enhance your understanding of a site. But what if Web pages could be transferred to your hard disk, with all the links and graphics intact? You could then "surf in haste, and peruse at leisure"!

SAVING A PAGE WITH GOLD'S EDITOR   Netscape Navigator Gold's Editor makes offline surfing a reality. With Gold's Editor you can, with only a few clicks, save any single HTML page (but not frameset documents) to a hard disk along with related graphics and links. Navigator Gold will automatically download all of the text and graphical elements that make up the page and change the link references in the document so all elements function properly when viewed from their new location. Let's take a look at how it works:

1. Establish a connection to the Internet, then open Navigator Gold.

2. Use the browser to go to any site or any single page of a site you'd like to capture. Don't choose a page that is displayed in frames; the Gold Editor only works with single pages. For the purposes of this example, we'll visit the page where the VRML version 1 specifications are kept: http://www.hyperreal.com/~mpesce/vrml/vrml.tech/vrml10-3.html.

3. When the page you've chosen to go to has completely loaded—the comets in the Netscape logo have stopped streaking, the wait cursor has been replaced by the arrow pointer, and the progress bar has cleared—click the Edit button on the toolbar or press Alt+F+E. Navigator Gold closes the Web browser window and loads the page into the Editor window. The Save Remote Document dialog box appears as seen in Figure 3-18.

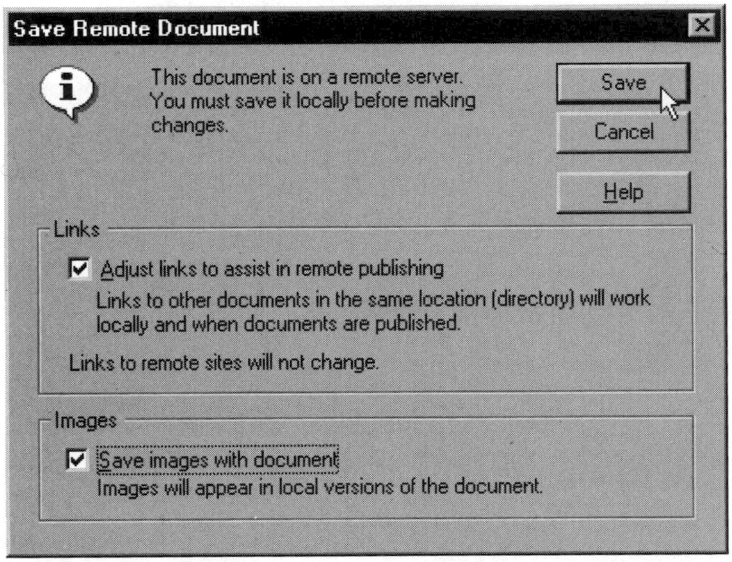

Save Remote Document

ⓘ This document is on a remote server. You must save it locally before making changes.

Save

Cancel

Help

Links

☑ Adjust links to assist in remote publishing

Links to other documents in the same location (directory) will work locally and when documents are published.

Links to remote sites will not change.

Images

☑ Save images with document

Images will appear in local versions of the document.

Figure 3-18: *Navigator Gold's Save Remote Document dialog.*

4. Make sure the Links checkbox and the Images checkbox are checked. You want the Editor to adjust the links so they will play properly on your hard disk; if you don't download the images, they won't be available when you are offline. Click Save. Heed the advice given in the Netscape Editor Hint attention box about getting permission for use of copyrighted images or documents. Click OK.

5. In the Save As dialog box that appears, choose a place on your hard disk to store the page and its graphics. I'd recommended that you create a folder for the file instead of mixing the site in with other files. A single folder will be easier to delete later, and you'll avoid the risk of overwriting any files that might have the same name in a particular location on the hard disk. In the Filename entry field, accept the name that the Editor placed in the field. It is the name of the document you are saving. Then, click the Save button.

6. The Saving Document dialog box appears and continuously reports on the progress that is being made in saving the files to your hard disk, as seen in Figure 3-19. If you want to stop the saving process, press the Cancel button. When the download is complete, the Saving Document dialog closes, and the process is complete.

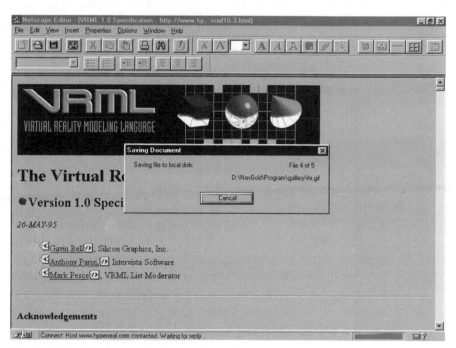

Figure 3-19: *Navigator Gold saves a Web page and its related graphics to your hard disk.*

7. To see how successful the transfer was, close your connection to the Internet, but don't close Navigator Gold. From the Editor's File menu, choose New Web Browser. When the Web Browser window opens, press Ctrl+O or choose File, Open to open the file you saved to your hard disk. It will appear in all its graphical glory, as seen in Figure 3-20.

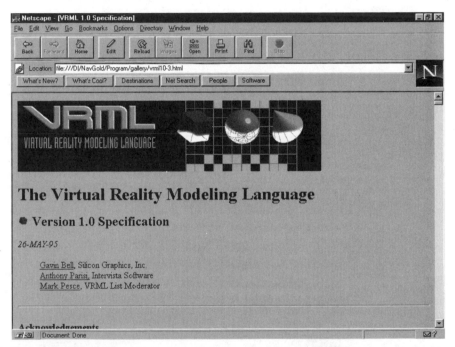

Figure 3-20: *A Web page, automatically captured from the Internet, loads from your hard disk for offline reading.*

Notice that the location box points to a location on your hard disk. If you move around in the document, you will see that mailto: address links are functional as are all internal links to parts of the page. Links to other pages and resources out on the Web are also intact and will work if you establish an Internet connection.

USING THIRD-PARTY SITE SAVERS As you saw in the preceding example, Navigator Gold did a great job capturing a single page, and many times that's all you'll need or want. But if you need to capture an entire site or parts of large sites—or if you need the embedded and linked objects, such as sounds and video—you'll need a dedicated, third-party site saving program.

CD-ROM

Site saving programs like WebEx (found on the Companion CD) and GrabNet (both are shareware) will go to any page on the Internet you specify and then proceed to transfer as many pages from the site as you require. Once the site has been transferred to your hard disk and you've logged off, you can use the site saver program along with Navigator to view the pages. Because these programs replicate the structure of the site, and have collected all the necessary graphics and other elements, you can interact with the site on your hard disk exactly as you would the online site. If you run into a link to a page that was not part of the site you asked the site saver to collect, or if you excluded certain kinds of elements (such as all the files in an FTP site) from the saving process, you can always go online and make the jump from the local file to the online file.

The specific operational details vary with each site saver program; but many come with companion programs that are used to automatically log on to your account, run the site saver, and then log off. With these utilities, you can save even more time by scheduling the site saver to perform its download magic when you're away from your desk, or when you're busy doing something else like sleeping or eating!

For all the apparently wonderful things a site saver can perform, there is a downside or two to site savers. For one thing, you can easily fill your hard disk if you save lots of sites—so save only those sites you're serious about examining later. Site saving utilities usually compress the files they download, but even compressed files can easily overrun the capacity of your hard disk. Another possible snag in the automated routine of saving sites is that if the site saving program encounters a problem connecting to a site and hangs, or if your system malfunctions, it is possible that the site saver will not be able to close your connection to the Internet. To avoid unexpected connection charges, be sure that you've configured your Internet system settings to timeout, and end the connections after a reasonable period of inactivity is detected. See Chapter 2, "Installing & Customizing Navigator," for information on how to configure your system's timeout settings.

COPYRIGHT ALERT!

Because of the way the WWW is constructed, you can download and save any HTML page on your computer—and most, if not all, of the components of the page: graphics, sound, movies, the works. But simply because you can use this power doesn't always mean you *should*. Once a Web element has been copied to your machine, the act of copying it *doesn't* make it your property.

The authors and artists who create the content of every page and site you visit hold the copyright on the contents of their pages. Unless something is explicitly marked as being public domain, the copyright still belongs to the author of the work, even if there are no copyright notices anywhere to be seen. Even if the content of a Web site bears the message, "Hi, I made this list and made this picture, and everyone is free to use it," the author still retains the copyright. You can't claim it as your own or use it without permission.

Which brings us to this question: Is it legal to save a site or part of a site to my hard disk? The answer, unfortunately, is ambiguous. If a site saved to your hard disk, or other media storage attached to your system, is for your *personal* use, and you plan to simply read the site's content offline and eventually delete it, and there is no clear indication in the saved site's text that offline reading or site saving is prohibited—the answer is probably yes. But if you make any commercial or organizational use of the site you saved, or distribute parts of the site, then the answer is probably no.

Whenever you're in doubt about whether it's OK to "snatch" a site or to use something you've found on the Internet, contact the author or the Webmaster and ask.

MOVING ON

We've briefly discussed the purposefulness of bookmarks and History lists in this chapter as a means for documenting locations of future interest on the Net. But these tools you find in Navigator's workspace are like those household widgets you see advertised on late-night television: They're multipurpose, amazing, do-it-quicker utilities. In Chapter 4, "Retracing Your Steps," you'll see how Internet Shortcuts, bookmarks, and History lists can be used in a wealth of navigation situations to become true *power* tools.

4

Retracing Your Steps

With Bookmarks, Internet Shortcuts & History Lists

One of the great joys of surfing and searching the World Wide Web is the feeling of adventure. You never really know where your journey will end, what path it will take, or exactly where you'll find that one piece of information that made the whole trip a success. That's because no matter how specific your goal may be, you are bound to run into a link along the way that looks too good to pass up. And when you follow that link, it often exposes yet another alluring link. Before you know it, you are far away from where you started. Even when you have lots of time to surf, you'll probably run out of time before you fully explore all the places you've been or tried all the links that looked inviting.

Finding places you really want to visit on the Web is one thing; getting back to them quickly and without distractions is another. When you find a cool place on the Web, you need to remember its Universal Resource Locator (URL) or address if you want to go directly there without retracing your original steps. You could write the address down on a piece of paper or develop a really good mnemonic for remembering the address, but the easiest and quickest thing to do is to make a Netscape Navigator *bookmark*. Netscape Navigator's bookmarks store the URL of the site you've marked so that you can jump directly to that site whenever you want.

Using bookmarks is a bit like taking the interstate instead of the scenic route. This chapter explores the power of bookmarks—how to make them, use them, organize them, share them, and even have them tell you when a bookmarked site has changed and may merit a new visit.

INTO THE FAST LANE WITH BOOKMARKS

Like all good computer programs, Netscape Navigator provides commands and management tools to accomplish a number of tasks faster and more accurately than you could on your own. Navigator's bookmarks are the electronic equivalents of the traditional paper or plastic bookmarks you tuck between pages in a book.

Navigator can store the address of every Web site that interests you, so that you don't have to remember the address or hunt for that scrap of paper you scribbled it on. And Navigator can read those long, complex URL addresses directly, saving you the time spent in typing (or *mis*typing) them into Navigator's Location box. Electronic bookmarks are also easily (and accurately) shared with friends and co-workers via e-mail, in newsgroup postings, over a network, or to a floppy disk. Additionally, if you have a WWW home page and want to post a list of links to your favorite sites on the Net, your bookmarks list is a great place to look for URLs.

In this chapter we will show you the smartest, quickest ways to create, manage, and use bookmarks, and we'll make recommendations on which methods are the most efficient in different situations.

TOURING THE BOOKMARKS WINDOW

To really put bookmarks to effective use, you'll need to visit the Bookmarks window frequently. The Bookmarks window is the command center where you not only can see all of the bookmarks you've made, but you can also tap into a wide variety of organizing, editing, and management features as well. And the Bookmarks window is your jumping-off spot for a powerful new time-saving feature called What's New?

In the course of this chapter we will be constantly referring to the Bookmarks window and its features, so before we get into making and using bookmarks, let's get our bearings and take a quick look at the window where much of the activity takes place. To access the Bookmarks window:

From any Netscape Navigator module—the Web browser, Netscape Mail, Netscape News—or from Netscape Navigator Gold's Editor module, press Ctrl+B or choose Window, then choose Bookmarks from the menu bar. The Bookmarks window opens.

The Bookmarks window, shown in Figure 4-1, displays a list that has a number of bookmarks entered into it. Some of the bookmarks stored in this bookmarks list have been moved into folders, to make finding them easier. Your bookmark list will look different, depending on how many bookmarks you've already made and whether you've done any organizing of the bookmarks tree on your own.

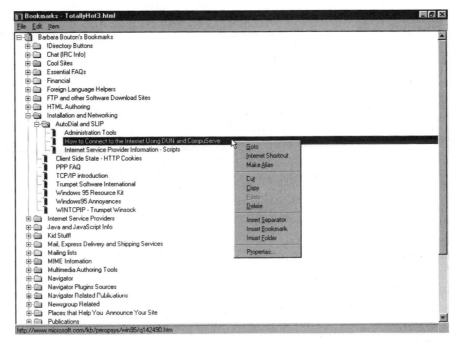

Figure 4-1: *The Bookmarks window can be called from any Navigator module.*

As you see onscreen (or in Figure 4-1), the Bookmarks window contains all the usual Windows elements—title bar, menu bar, scroll bar, status bar, and the control menu, minimize, restore, and close buttons. Within the content window, all of the bookmarks that are stored in the current bookmark file are arranged in a hierarchical tree display, similar in concept to the one used by Windows's Explorer or File Manager to display drives, files, and folders (subdirectories).

Like the files and folders in Explorer, bookmarks and bookmark folders can be rearranged by dragging and dropping them into a new location within the tree structure. Similarly, if you right-click on a bookmark or folder, a context-sensitive shortcut menu appears that lists things you can do with the item in addition to bringing up its Properties window.

Netscape Navigator uses different kinds of bookmark icons and folder icons to indicate special properties or the status of the entry. When you know what the various icons mean, you can tell at a glance what's going on in your list.

FOLDER ICONS

Netscape Navigator uses icons within the bookmark window to signify various types of folders and the connection status of bookmarks. Figure 4-2 shows the different kinds of folder icons. The folder names have been edited in the figure to describe the related icon.

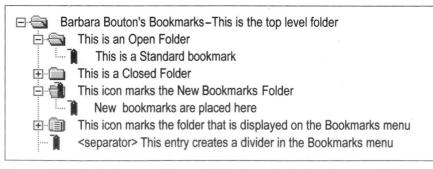

Figure 4-2: *Navigator uses different folder icons to display the current status of the folder.*

Top Level Folder. The first folder in the tree is the top level folder. By default, this folder bears the name you entered into the Identity tab of Navigator's Mail and News Preferences configuration window. If your bookmark file starts out with —'s Bookmarks, then review Chapter 2, "Installing & Customizing Navigator," on how to configure Netscape Navigator. All bookmarks and folders you add to your bookmark list branch off from the top level folder.

Open Folder Icon. The second folder icon in the bookmark tree shown in Figure 4-2 is the Open Folder icon. A folder is open when you can see the names of the bookmarks and subfolders that are contained within the folder. Notice that the bookmarks and subfolders branch from and are indented one level from the folder that contains them. To close an open folder, click the box with the minus sign (located to the left of the folder).

Closed Folder Icon. The third folder in the tree in Figure 4-2 is the Closed Folder icon. The bookmarks and subfolders contained within this folder have been hidden from view. To view the contents of a closed folder, click the box with the plus sign (to the left of the folder).

New Bookmarks Folder. When an Open or Closed folder icon has a maroon ribbon placed on top of the icon, like the fifth icon in Figure 4-2's tree, that folder takes on a new attribute. It becomes the New Bookmarks folder. All new bookmarks made from any of Navigator's other windows will be placed in this folder. Unless you've picked a different folder, as was done in this example, by default the top level folder is the New Bookmarks folder, and it will be the icon with the ribbon on it.

Bookmarks Menu Folder. The last folder in Figure 4-2's tree is the Bookmarks Menu folder. Navigator indicates which folder is currently the Bookmarks Menu folder by placing a drawing of a list on top of the folder icon. Only the bookmarks and subfolders that are stored in this folder will display on the Navigator Web browser's Bookmarks menu. To use bookmarks that are not stored in the Bookmarks Menu folder you need to open the Bookmarks Window. Unless you've chosen a different folder to be the Bookmarks Menu folder, as was done in this example, the top level folder is also the Bookmarks Menu folder. When the top level folder is the Bookmarks Menu folder, all of the bookmarks and bookmark folders appear as entries in the Bookmarks menu in Navigator's window, *if* there is room for all of them to display in the menu.

Separator Icon. The last icon in Figure 4-2 isn't really a bookmark or a folder. It's a Standard bookmark icon with the word *<separator>* after it, but we are mentioning it here because it is related to the Bookmarks Menu folder. Wherever this separator icon appears within the Bookmarks Menu folder's tree in the Bookmarks window, the Navigator Web browser places a gray separator bar in the browser's Bookmarks menu. Separators are placed in the Bookmarks window to create sections of bookmarks and bookmark folders within the Web browser's Bookmarks menu.

BOOKMARK ICONS

Netscape Navigator uses three different bookmark icons—the Standard icon, the Question Mark icon, and the Excited icon—to signify the connection status of the bookmark. Figure 4-3 contains a close-up look at these icons.

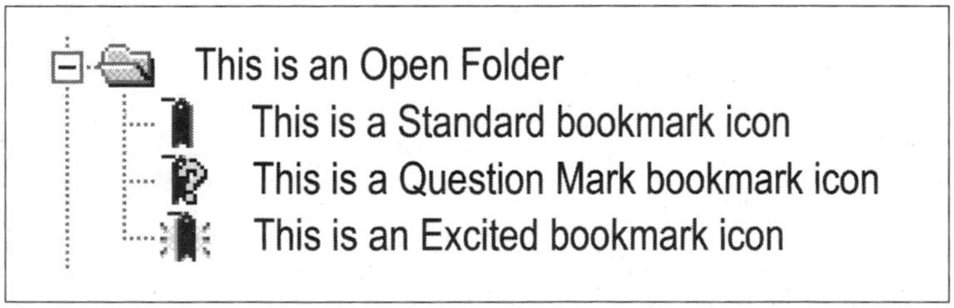

This is an Open Folder
This is a Standard bookmark icon
This is a Question Mark bookmark icon
This is an Excited bookmark icon

Figure 4-3: *The bookmark icons indicate the last connection status of a bookmark.*

Standard Icon. The Standard bookmark icon looks like a plain maroon ribbon (see the first icon in Figure 4-3). When the Standard icon is displayed next to a bookmark, it means that the last time you used the bookmark, Netscape Navigator was able to make the connection for you. Most of your bookmarks will be marked with the Standard icon.

Question Mark Icon. Navigator's Question Mark icon is a maroon ribbon with a big yellow question mark on it (see the second icon in Figure 4-3). This icon is used to indicate that Navigator is uncertain whether or not the bookmark successfully connects to the site or resource it marks. Netscape Navigator flags bookmarks with the Question Mark icon under the following circumstances:

- When you've created a bookmark but have not yet used the bookmark in Netscape Navigator to go to the site.

- When you've created a bookmark but the last time you tried to use the bookmark you were not able to connect to the site.

- When you've used the What's New? bookmark-checking feature (described later in the chapter), and Navigator had trouble connecting to the site. Navigator may have had problems connecting because the bookmark contains a typographic error; or network traffic was too heavy to make the connection in a reasonable amount of time; or Navigator connected but was unable to determine if the site had changed.

Excited Icon. The Excited ribbon icon (see the third icon in Figure 4-3), has three small yellow and red lines radiating out from each side of the maroon ribbon. The Excited icon tells you that the What's New? search feature has determined that the site *has* changed since you last visited using the bookmark. The Excited bookmark icon is a visual reminder that the site has changed and that it may merit another visit from you.

Now that you've become familiar with the Bookmarks window, let's see how to put its features to use. Throughout the rest of the chapter, you'll be returning to this familiar ground as you learn how to create, manage, and optimize your bookmarks, bookmark folders, and bookmark lists. But before you can manage bookmarks, you have to create some. The next section shows you the smartest method of making a bookmark under a variety of conditions.

CREATING BOOKMARKS . . .

Netscape Navigator provides a variety of ways to create a bookmark, each of which has its own unique twist. Be sure to keep the following methods in mind when you embark on your next online cybertrip. Bookmark creation doesn't require any input from you other than a few keystrokes or mouse clicks. The techniques described are ideal for quickly grabbing the address (URL) of a site or resource without interrupting your journey with housekeeping tasks—you just keep on moving.

Save the method shown in "Using the Bookmarks Window" for when you're offline and the meter isn't running on your connect time. Unlike the other ways to create bookmarks, making a bookmark from the Bookmark window's Bookmark Properties window requires your active involvement in entering information. But it also provides an opportunity to add meaningful names and searchable descriptions to a bookmark entry.

. . . FOR THE CURRENT PAGE OR FILE

Whenever you land on a page that you'd like to bookmark, press Ctrl+D and a bookmark for the page is made. If you prefer to use the menus, you can make the bookmark by choosing Add Bookmark from the Bookmarks menu as seen in Figure 4-4. Whichever method you choose, Navigator will create a bookmark for you that bears the name of the page as it appears on Navigator's title bar.

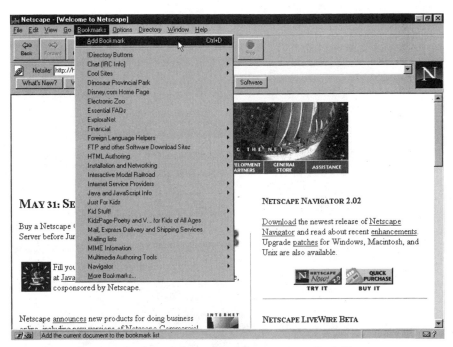

Figure 4-4: *Create a bookmark from this menu, or press Ctrl+D.*

Bookmarks can be made for any page at a site, not just the site's top level or home page. With large sites or sites that have many distinct areas, it's a great time saver to mark the subpages that interest you. For example, if you visit the site of a software manufacturer, you might want to bookmark the home page so you can always find the site, and then bookmark the main technical support page, the FTP software update page, and so on.

. . . FOR A FRAME

Creating a bookmark for the contents of a single frame in a frameset document, rather than for the entire frameset, requires a slightly different approach. Instead of making the bookmark from the Bookmarks menu or by using the keyboard shortcut Ctrl+D, the bookmark for a single frame is most easily made from the right-click shortcut menu.

1. Open a framed page in Navigator's content window. Anatomy of an Eye, shown in Figure 4-5, is a good example of a frameset page. At the time this book went to press, Anatomy of an Eye could be found at http://home.netscape.com/comprod/products/navigator/version_2.0/frames/eye/index.html.

We'll use this page as the example page in the following steps. If you are following along, you can use this page or any other frames document whose page design contains traditionally created content. Single frames whose content is generated on the fly by a Java applet or by JavaScript can't be bookmarked.

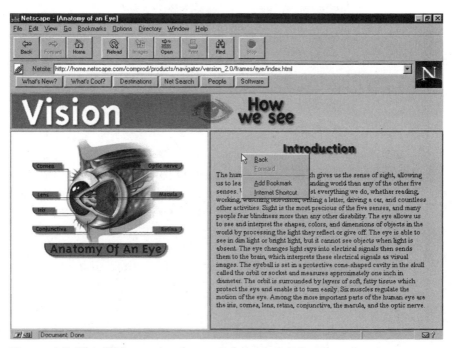

Figure 4-5: *This Web page is a frameset document; it has three frames.*

2. Right click in the Introduction frame or any frame that contains HTML (HyperText Markup Language) text, and choose Add Bookmark from the shortcut menu. A bookmark is created that refers to the HTML document in the frame. In this example, the bookmark made refers to the page, intro.html.

If this page had contained hypertext links (colored, underlined text) or graphic that is a hypertext link, right-clicking it and choosing Add Bookmark would have made a bookmark to the page to which the link refers.

However, right-clicking a graphic that is *not* a link or one that is an image map (a graphic that contains multiple "hot spots" that when clicked act as a link to another page or resource), makes a bookmark to the page the graphic is currently displayed in and not to the graphic itself or any of the links in the image mapped graphic. Making bookmarks to these kinds of elements requires a trip to a different, but related window—the Frame Info window. The Frame Info window displays the URLs of the component parts that make up the frame. It is similar to the Document Info window, which shows all of the components in an entire frameset document. Once you've spotted the URL of the element you want to bookmark in the Frame (or Document) Info window, you're only a few mouse clicks away from successfully creating the bookmark you want. Let's see how it is done by taking another look at the Anatomy of an Eye frameset.

In the Anatomy of an Eye frameset, the lower left frame contains an HTML document called eye_diagram.html. The only thing "in" this HTML document is an image mapped graphic, eyesmall.gif. To make a bookmark to the graphic, you would need to perform the following steps:

1. Click an empty part of the frame (in this example, the one with the eyeball), to make that frame the active frame.

2. Choose View and then Frame Info from Navigator's menu bar. The Document Info window opens.

   As you can see in Figure 4-6, the document is split into two panes. The upper pane lists all of the elements of the frame document, and the bottom pane lists additional information about the frame's base document.

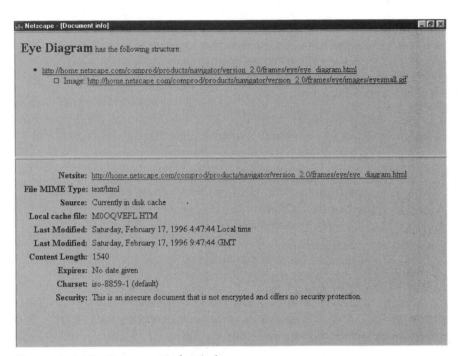

Figure 4-6: *The Document Info window.*

3. Click the http://home.netscape.com/comprod/products/
   navigator/version_2.0/frames/eye/images/eyesmall.gif,
   link. This URL corresponds to the graphic of the eyeball.
   When you click the link, the bottom pane changes to display information about the graphic. You can click and drag
   the pane separator up to increase the size of the bottom
   pane, so you can see more of the pane's contents.

4. In the bottom pane, right-click the link, and choose Add
   Bookmark from the shortcut menu. You can also scroll
   down and right-click the graphic to make the bookmark as
   seen in Figure 4-7.

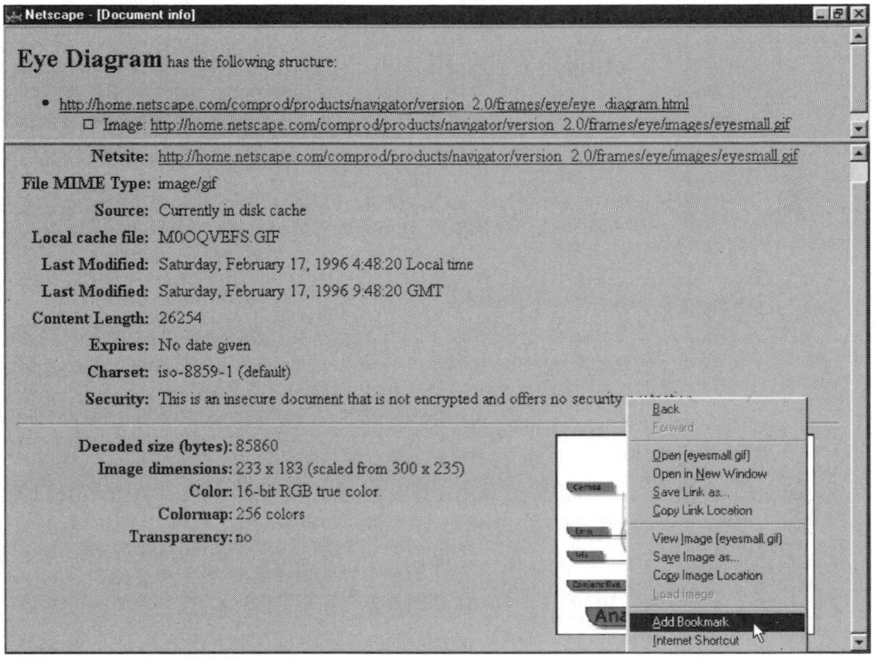

Figure 4-7: *Use the shortcut menu to make bookmarks from the Document Info window.*

5. Close the Document Info window by pressing Alt+F4, or click the Close button in the upper right corner of the window.

   To verify that the bookmark has been made to the eyesmall.gif image and not the whole frameset, press Ctrl+B to open the Bookmarks window. Double-click the following bookmark: http://home.netscape.com/ comprod/products/navigator/version_2.0/frames/eye/ images/eyesmall.gif. The graphic loads into a new Navigator's window as graphic. If you choose Document Source from the View menu, you'll actually see the binary code of the graphic instead of the HTML source code that is seen when viewing a page or a frameset.

But what if you wanted to make bookmarks to one or more of the links in the image map of the eye? That's one of those things you can't do from here. Because the image map is in a framed document, you need to click each link you want to bookmark, and when the page loads, make the bookmark from the displayed page, just as you did to make the bookmark to the Information page earlier.

... FROM A LINK

Virtually every Web page you encounter is peppered with links that can take you to a new page or new site, start the download of a file, or load an object that can be "played" by a plug-in such as a VRML world or a video. Many times you will see a link that looks like it leads to something interesting, but you don't have the time or inclination to go there now. Perhaps another link on the page is more immediately compelling. Instead of just moving on past the link, linger a moment and bookmark it. Then you can quickly come back to the link when it's more convenient for you, and take the path the link provides to a cool site, great video, or vital (or maybe just fun) piece of software.

Making a bookmark for the link is simple and it won't slow you down at all. Whenever you see a link—in a Web page, or in the Document Info or Frame Info window—you can make a bookmark by following the two simple steps you saw earlier—right-click the link. When the shortcut menu appears, choose Add Bookmark.

You'll find the new bookmark in the Bookmarks window, in the folder that is currently set as the New Bookmarks folder. This works for any kind of link, such as a link to another HTML page or frameset, a file, a graphic, a mailto address, or an embedded object such as a sound or movie.

Note, however, that whenever you create a bookmark from the shortcut menu, only the URL address of the link is copied. The identifying text or graphic that you right-clicked is not copied and doesn't become the name of the bookmark.

To keep the bookmark from going nameless, Navigator gives it the same name as the URL it's copied from. While this scheme keeps you from having hundreds of bookmarks named "Click Here," URLs aren't very evocative as bookmark names. The name of a bookmark can be changed to something more meaningful by editing the bookmark's properties in the Bookmarks window. You'll see how to do this later in the chapter.

Web pages aren't the only place you find links—Netscape Mail and News messages also may contain links that you might want to bookmark. The shortcut menu is not the answer this time, but rather, Navigator's drag-and-drop ability. To make bookmarks from links that appear in the body of mail messages and newsgroup articles, follow these steps:

1. Open Netscape Mail by clicking the envelope icon in the lower right corner of the browser window or choose Netscape Mail from the Window menu. If Navigator prompts you for a mail password, either enter it or click cancel. We won't be sending any mail, so being properly connected to the mail server is not important.

2. Press Ctrl+B or choose Bookmarks from the Mail (or browser) menu. Resize and arrange the Mail window and the Bookmarks window so that they are side by side.

3. Click the Mail window to make it active. If you haven't deleted it, there should be a Welcome! message from Mozilla in the inbox. This message was "installed" when you installed Navigator. To open the message from Mozilla, click the message in the list of message titles in the upper right pane of the Mail window. The mail message will now load into the content window.

4. Use the scroll bars in the Message Content pane to scroll down to the bottom of the message. Click and drag the link from the Mail Message Content pane into the Bookmarks window and drop the link on top of the folder you want to store the link in (see Figure 4-8). If you want it in the root of the Bookmarks tree, drop it on the top level folder that bears your name. Just as you saw in Chapter 3, "Power Navigation," in the section on the Link icon, your cursor takes on the Unavailable shape when over the Mail window, but changes into the arrow with the chain link when over the Bookmarks window.

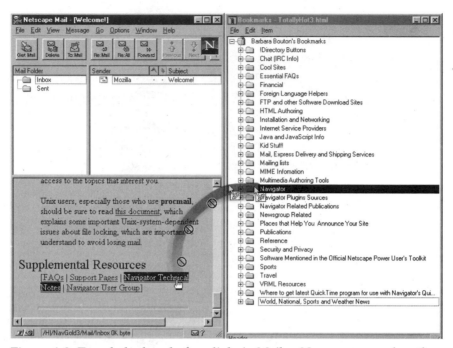

Figure 4-8: *To make bookmarks from links in Mail or News messages, drag the link into the Bookmarks window.*

. . . FROM THE HISTORY LIST

What do you do when you've been to a place on the Internet and you later (in the same Netscape Navigator session) decide you should have bookmarked the entry? You could find your way back to the site and then bookmark it, but a much quicker way is to open the History List. The History List window displays a list of all the URLs you've visited since you launched Netscape Navigator, and it provides a handy Make Bookmark button.

To create a bookmark from an entry in the History List:

1. Press Ctrl+H, or choose History List from the Window menu. The History List window opens.

2. Select the entry in the History List entry you want to book-mark by clicking it once with the left mouse button. The entry clicked becomes highlighted.

3. Click the Create Bookmark button at the bottom of the History window, as seen in Figure 4-9. Netscape Navigator creates a bookmark for the entry.

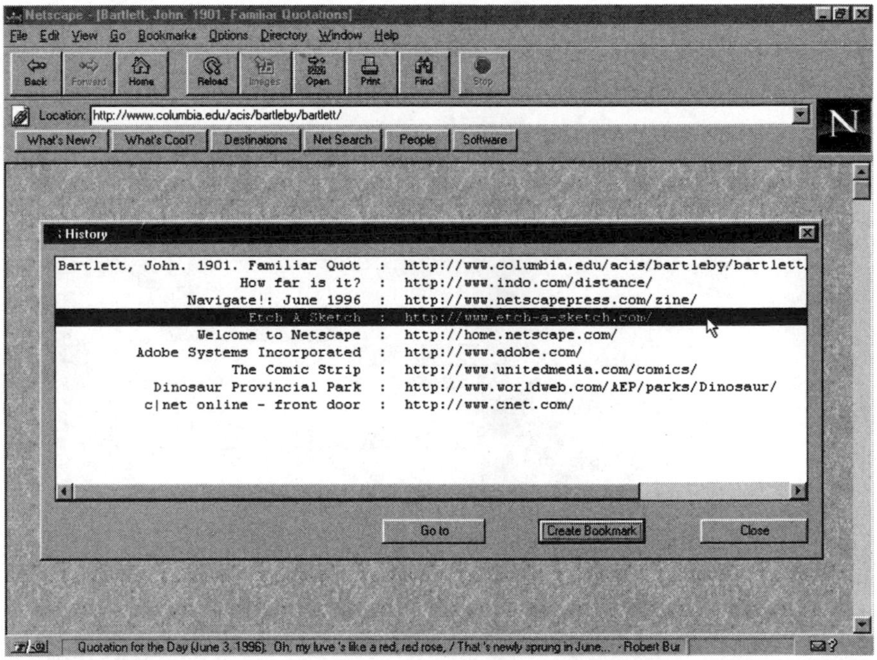

Figure 4-9: *Create a bookmark from the History window.*

. . . FROM THE BOOKMARKS WINDOW

How do you make a bookmark for a URL you've found in a maga-zine or for a site a co-worker told you about? You make it from the Bookmarks window! The Bookmarks window is the place to go not only when you want to see all your bookmarks or make changes to bookmarks and bookmark lists, but also when you want to create a bookmark for a URL that isn't already in an electronic format.

To create a bookmark in the Bookmarks window:

1. Open the Bookmarks window by pressing Ctrl+B or by choosing Go to Bookmarks from the Bookmarks menu. The Bookmarks window opens, or comes to the front if it was already open.

2. Right-click the folder in which you want to store the bookmark. Then, from the shortcut menu choose Insert Bookmark. You can also choose Insert Bookmark from the Bookmarks window's Item menu. In either case, the General tab of the Bookmark Properties window appears, as seen in Figure 4-10.

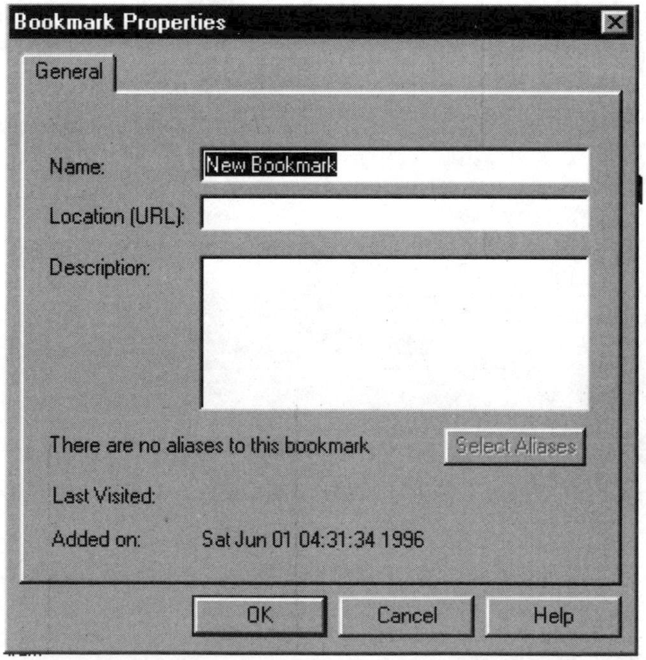

Figure 4-10: *Use the Bookmark Properties window to create a new bookmark.*

3. The cursor is automatically inserted into the Name field and New Bookmark is highlighted. Enter a descriptive word or phrase to replace the default text. Text entered in the Name field will appear in the Bookmarks window and in the Bookmarks menu.

4. Insert your cursor into the Location (URL) field and type in the URL for the Bookmark. Be sure to enter a complete URL including the necessary protocol prefix; for example, http://www.adobe.com is the full URL of Adobe Systems' home page, and ftp://ftp2.netscape.com is the full URL for one of Netscape's many File Transfer Protocol (FTP) servers.

TIP

You can also paste a URL that is stored on the Windows clipboard into the Location (URL) field by right-clicking in the Location (URL) field and then choosing Paste from the shortcut menu.

This method works well if you have a plain text file that contains URLs from which you can copy. A URL can also be copied to the clipboard from a link on a Web page, by clicking over the link with the right mouse button and then choosing Copy Link Location. Once the URL has been copied to the clipboard it can be pasted into any document or program that accepts text.

5. Insert your cursor into the Description field of the Bookmark Properties window. Enter anything you like—or nothing at all. Text entered here is visible only in the Bookmark Properties window and in the bookmark list file when it is saved. Entering keywords and/or a description is recommended for the reasons described following these steps.

6. When you have finished making your entries for the new bookmark, click the OK button on the bottom of the Bookmark Properties window and the new bookmark will be added to your list.

It's a good idea to add descriptions for bookmarks, for several reasons. The description you write is included in the HTML or text file that is created when you save a bookmark file. If you write a good description of the site, you will have a much better idea of why you thought the link was important.

> **TIP**
>
> *If you e-mail a bookmark list, post it as a newsgroup article, or open it in a browser window, the bookmark description is visible. So make sure that whatever you write is something you wouldn't mind others seeing!*

Another reason to maintain good descriptions of your bookmarks is that Netscape Navigator's Find feature locates bookmarks based on their descriptions. Find can be used to search for any text string in the Name, Location (URL), or Description field.

For example, if the site you are bookmarking is named Welcome to XYZ (not a very descriptive site name), it will be hard to remember that this company is a hot stock prospect because it makes the best widgets and thing-a-ma-bobs on earth. But if you take the time to enter keywords and phrases—such as "hot stock prices"; "widgets"; "thing-a-ma-bobs"—along with any other details about the site, you'll be able to locate this bookmark and other similar sites with Navigator's Find feature. Using Find is covered later in this chapter.

THE DANGER OF USING PARTIAL URLS

In Chapter 3, "Power Navigation," you saw that it is possible, under some circumstances, to enter a partial URL in the Location field of the Web browser and still make a successful connection. Although you can use these same partial URLs when entering information in the Location (URL) entry box in the Bookmark Properties box, it is *not* recommended that you do so. Full URLs should be used in bookmarks for the following reasons:

First, it takes a little longer for Navigator to look up and connect to a site when a partial URL has been entered. You save time when typing a short URL into the Location field but lose a little bit of time when you use that bookmark. If you use the bookmark frequently, you will eventually lose more time on the lookup than you saved by not typing in the full URL in the first place.

➡

Second, you may want to publish, post, or mail your bookmark list; or you may want to share it or one of your bookmarked addresses with someone who is *not* using Netscape Navigator. Without a full URL they will not be able to use the information you've given them unless they type in the missing address elements. It is much more polite and professional to use a full URL when sharing addresses.

Be kind to yourself and others; use full URLs when creating bookmarks.

EDITING BOOKMARK PROPERTIES

Sometimes you'll need to edit an existing bookmark to make its name more meaningful, or to add a description to the bookmark. Web pages move to new locations frequently, and you may need to enter a change of address for the page. Editing an existing bookmark is almost the same as creating a bookmark in the Bookmarks window. The steps that follow can also be used to change the name of a folder.

To edit an existing bookmark or folder entry:

1. Right-click the bookmark in the Bookmarks window. Choose Properties from the shortcut menu. The familiar Bookmark Properties window for the bookmark opens.

2. Insert your cursor into the field that needs editing and make your changes or additions.

3. Click OK. The Bookmark Properties window closes and the changes you've made are saved.

. . . TO A FILE ON YOUR HARD DISK

Bookmarks aren't limited to documents or resources on the Internet. You can also make bookmarks to HTML documents, images, sounds, movies, and other inline and embeddable objects that are stored on your local or network drives. These can be files and resources you've created yourself or ones that you've saved to disk from the Internet. Making links to HTML documents and other kinds of files such as graphics, sounds, and movies on your hard disk is particularly useful if you're not using Netscape Navigator Gold to create HTML pages and want to see how the document looks before you e-mail or post it.

TIP

You might also want to make a bookmark to a bookmark list file. When a bookmark list file is loaded in the browser window, all of the links are active and can be used to connect. This is a good way to have simultaneous access to more than one bookmark list at a time—load a bookmark list in the browser window while your default bookmark list is accessed from the Bookmarks window. See Figure 4-11.

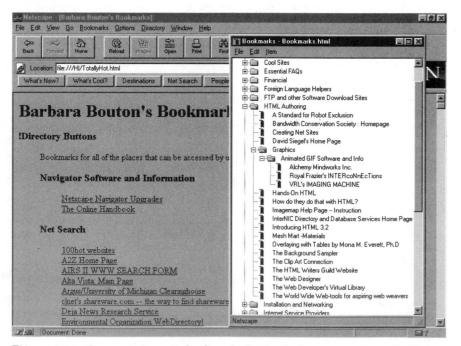

Figure 4-11: *Open an alternate bookmarks list in the browser and use the links in the list to go to your favorite places or use your regular Bookmarks list.*

With storage capacity far greater than what you have on your own hard disk, many businesses and organizations create internal networks (their own *Intranets*) where HTML documents are used companywide to share information and improve communication among employees. If your organization has an Intranet, you'll want to make extensive use of bookmarks to local documents. See Chapter 8, "The Intranet," for more information on the value of the Intranet and the role Netscape Navigator plays.

The following steps describe the easiest and most foolproof method for creating a bookmark to a locally stored HTML document or other viewable or playable object.

1. Open a Netscape Navigator Web browser window and resize it so that it takes up only a small part of the screen. Then open Windows Explorer or File Manager. Resize and arrange the Explorer or File Manager window so that you can see both it and the Netscape Navigator window.

2. Find the file you want to bookmark and then click and drag the file from the Explorer or File Manager window and drop it in Netscape Navigator's browser window.

   Figure 4-12 shows a photograph, saved in the Joint Photographic Experts Group (JPEG) file format, that was dragged into the content window from an Explorer window. The file was displayed when it was dropped into the content window. Notice that the browser's Location/Go to: field now displays a URL that describes the location of the file on your hard disk. Unlike URLs that refer to Internet resources, this URL starts with *file:///*. The rest of the URL after the *file:///* is the regular DOS path to the file, except that the colon that follows the drive letter in the DOS path has been replaced with a | (pipe character).

Figure 4-12: *The Location/Go to: field displays the URL for a locally stored file.*

Now that the file or document is loaded in the content window and Navigator has entered the URL to your local or local network drive in the Location field, you can make the bookmark.

3. Press Ctrl+D, or choose Bookmarks, Add Bookmark from the browser's menu bar to make the bookmark.

TIP

If the file you dragged from your hard drive into the content window is an HTML document and it contains valid local or Internet links, you can bookmark these links now. To do so, right-click the links and choose Add Bookmark from the shortcut menu.

If you prefer to open files rather than dragging and dropping them into Navigator's content window, press Ctrl+O or choose File then Open file from Navigator's menu bar. Use the Open dialog box to find the file. If you are opening a file that is not an HTML file, such as a graphic, choose the appropriate file type, or choose All files (*.*) from the Files of Type drop-down list so that you can see the file in the file and folder field. When you find the file you want, double-click it to open it in the content window of the browser. After the document loads, make your bookmarks as described above.

ON YOUR WAY WITH BOOKMARKS

Using bookmarks is even easier than making them. There really is only one way to use a bookmark—by clicking it—and only two places where bookmarks are found—in the Bookmarks menu and the Bookmarks window.

THE BOOKMARKS MENU

If you have only a few bookmarks, or you have organized your bookmarks into a small number of folders, the quickest way to get to them is from the Web browser's Bookmarks menu. Netscape Navigator lists as many of your bookmarks and bookmark folders as it can fit at the bottom of the menu.

To use a bookmark that is listed on the Bookmarks menu, perform the following steps:

1. Click the Bookmarks menu once to drop down the menu. Then move your cursor down the list, stopping when you find the bookmark or the folder that contains the bookmark you want to use.

   If you stop over the name of a folder, the menu will fly out a submenu containing a list of bookmarks that can be selected from that folder (see Figure 4-13).

Notice that the status line at the bottom of the browser window changes to display the URL of the bookmark where your cursor is currently located. Reading the URL from the status line sometimes makes it easier to confirm that the bookmark is the one you want to use.

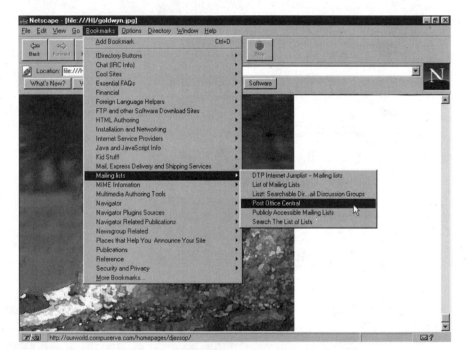

Figure 4-13: *Bookmarks in a folder display on a flyout menu.*

2. When you've found the bookmark you want, left-click the bookmark's name once. Netscape Navigator reads the URL that is stored in the bookmark and takes you to that site as fast as the Internet and your modem can carry you.

If you have more bookmarks than will fit at the bottom of the Bookmarks menu, the last entry on the list will read "More Bookmarks." Choosing More Bookmarks opens the Bookmarks window where you can find the bookmark you are looking for.

> **TIP**
>
> *When there's not enough room for all your bookmarks to fit on the Bookmarks menu, you might want to consider moving individual bookmarks into folders. You also might make a new folder that covers a broad category and then move related folders into that folder. For example, make a folder called Fun and then move folders that you already have, or create new ones that relate to things such as sports, movies, and recreation into the subfolders in the Fun folder. You can also limit the display on the Bookmarks menu by choosing a different folder to be the Bookmark Menu folder. Changing which folder is the Bookmark Menu folder is covered later in the chapter.*
>
> *If you must have access to all your bookmarks, just forget about the Bookmarks menu and go straight to the Bookmarks window by pressing Crtl+B when you want to use a bookmark.*

LAUNCHING A BOOKMARK FROM THE BOOKMARKS WINDOW

When you have too many bookmarks to display on the Bookmarks menu—or you need to search for a bookmark—use the Bookmarks window to launch the bookmark you want.

1. Open the Bookmarks window by pressing Crtl+B, or choose Window then Bookmarks. Scroll through the bookmark list, opening folders where necessary.

2. When you find the bookmark you think you want to use, click it once to display its URL on the status line of the Bookmarks window. Or right-click the bookmark and check the bookmark's properties. When you are satisfied that you've found the right bookmark, launch it by double-clicking on the bookmark's name in the content window. Netscape Navigator then takes you to the site.

Activating a bookmark to get someplace on the Internet never gets any harder or more complicated than executing one or two clicks on the bookmark's name.

ORGANIZING BOOKMARKS

Managing and *finding* the bookmark you want to use out of the hundreds of bookmarks you'll make is another matter. Fortunately, Netscape Navigator has robust features that make the organization of bookmarks easy. In the following sections, we'll show you how to build your own organization strategy and how to make the Bookmark feature more effective.

Finding the bookmark you want could become more time consuming than finding the site all over again by doing an Internet search or retracing your steps. So before you get into this predicament, you need to map out a plan for creating a *number* of folders that correspond to the kinds of sites you bookmark, then store your bookmarks in the appropriate folders.

This is one task you should not put off; it's much easier to organize your bookmarks while you still have relatively few. Also, make it a practice at the end of each online session to file new bookmarks you've made. When you do, the sites are still fresh in your mind, and adding good descriptions or editing the bookmark's name is easier.

PLANNING AHEAD

Before you create folders in which to store your bookmarks, think about the *kinds* of bookmarks you save and how you work: would it be easier to save bookmarks based on the project they relate to or on their similarity to each other? For example, does it make more sense to you to store all bookmarks relating to a single company in a single folder? Or would it be better to create a folder called, for example, Investor Information, where you store bookmarks that link to *any* company you've found that offers investor information.

Can your interests be divided into broad categories, such as work-related, hobby-related, education-related, entertainment-related, and so on? If so, then these or any others you come up with would make good first-level folders on your bookmark tree.

While you think about the structure of the bookmark tree you want to create, keep in mind that you can make as many folders as you want any time you want, and that folders can be nested within each other by placing a folder within a folder to create a new branch on the folder tree. You can also make copies or aliases of bookmarks, so the same bookmark can be stored in two different places if that assists your planning. For example, you could create a hierarchy like the organizational plan shown in Figure 4-14.

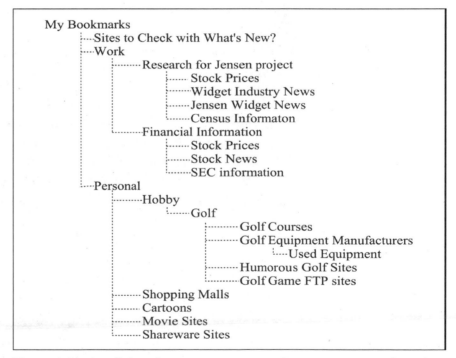

Figure 4-14: *A well thought out tree structure makes management tasks easier.*

A structure such as that shown in Figure 4-14 could contain hundreds of bookmarks and folders, but it would collapse down to only three entries when only the second-level folders are open: Sites to Check with What's New?; Work; and Personal. This kind of organizational structure is much easier to navigate than scrolling through a long list of bookmarks that relate to different topics in the root of the bookmarks folder. It also makes it easier to share only your business- or hobby-related bookmarks with co-workers or friends, because you can copy only the branch of the bookmark tree that is appropriate.

CREATING FOLDERS

Once you know which folders you want to create and where in the tree they should be, the hard part is over. Follow these steps to create a folder.

1. Open the Bookmarks window (Ctrl+B). To create a folder that branches directly off from the top level folder, right-click the top level folder once or in any part of the root of the tree that is not within a subfolder, and choose Insert Folder from the shortcut menu. To create a subfolder for a folder you've already made, right-click the folder it should branch from or within the subfolder tree and as before, choose Insert Folder from the shortcut menu.

2. In either case, the familiar Bookmark Properties window appears with the Location (URL) field dimmed. Enter a name for the folder in the Name field. Enter keywords or a description in the Description field.

3. Click OK when you are done entering information and the new folder is created.

If the new folder didn't appear where you expected it to, drag the folder's icon on top of the desired destination folder. This trick also works if you decide later that the folder should go in a different place in the tree.

MOVING & COPYING FOLDERS & BOOKMARKS

To move bookmarks from one folder to another, select the folder or bookmarks you want to move and drag them into the new folder.

To make a copy of a folder and its contents or an individual bookmark, click the folder or bookmark's name, then press Crtl+C (or choose Copy from the right-click shortcut menu). To paste the copy of the folder into the tree, click the folder you want the folder copied to, then press Ctrl I V (or choose Paste from the shortcut menu). You can also Cut and Delete folders using the shortcut menu or by pressing Ctrl+X for Cut and by pressing the Delete key for Delete.

Note that when you move, copy, cut, or delete a folder, all of the bookmarks and folders contained within the folder also move.

SELECTING BOOKMARKS & FOLDERS

Netscape Navigator uses most of the selection techniques you have become familiar with from your experience with working with files in Windows Explorer or File Manager. Select groups of entries when you want to perform the same action on all of them: copying, moving, deleting, sorting, or checking them using What's New? Use these techniques to select entries in the bookmark tree:

- Individual entries in the bookmark tree are selected by left-clicking the entry's title once.

- Multiple entries that directly follow one another in the bookmark tree can be selected by clicking the first one in the group you want, then holding down the Shift key while clicking the last one in the group you want to select. The first and last items plus all of the items in between will be selected.

- To select multiple entries that are not sequential in the list, left-click each bookmark or folder while holding down the Ctrl key.

- For all operations except What's New? and making aliases for bookmarks, selecting a folder by clicking its title once selects all of the contents of the folder, even though the individual entries in the folder are not highlighted.

Sorting Bookmarks

When bookmarks and folders are created, they fall into place in the list depending on which folder is currently the New Bookmarks folder or on which folder was highlighted at the time you made the entry. If you'd like to organize all your folders and the bookmarks within each folder in alphabetical order rather than the semi-chronological order in which they were made, use the Sort feature.

Sorting your bookmarks takes only these few steps:

1. Open the Bookmarks window (Ctrl+B). Click any folder in the list to select it. Selecting a folder makes the Sort Bookmarks menu item available.

2. From the Bookmarks menu, choose Item, then choose Sort Bookmarks. Navigator sorts the entire list by alphabetical order. Sort always works on the entire list and not a selected portion of the list.

Tip

You can force a frequently used bookmark or folder to the top of the alphabetical list by placing any non-alphabetical keyboard character, punctuation mark (except the hyphen and the single quote mark), or number in front of the name.

For example, I have a folder I frequently use that contains bookmarks to the day's new stories. Normally a folder called News would be in the middle of the bookmark tree (in its appropriate alphabetical order). But because I have a large number of folders defined, News never makes it onto the Bookmarks menu. To make the News folder appear at the top of the list, I changed the folder's name from News *to* !News. *Now I can find and use my news-related bookmarks very quickly.*

Any of the following keyboard characters or punctuation marks can be used. They are listed here in the order in which they would appear in the sort.

   *! " # % & ( ) * , . / : ; ? @ [ ] ^ _ ` { \ } ~ + < = >*

Titles that start with numbers appear in the sort after those that start with the special keyboard characters and before those that start with letters of the alphabet.

FINDING BOOKMARKS

Netscape Navigator has a built-in full text-search engine. Not only can you search for text that is on a Web page, in the Mail window, or in the News window, but you can also search for text stored in the bookmarks list. No matter which module of Navigator you are using, Find can always be called into action by pressing Ctrl+F or by choosing Find from the Edit menu. Pressing F3 always makes Find repeat the search, looking for the next item that matches your request. Once you've used Find in one module, you basically know how to use it in any other module.

To use Find, perform the following steps:

1. From the Bookmarks window, press Ctrl+F. The Search Headers dialog box appears as seen in Figure 4-15. The title of this dialog box is somewhat misleading. Find searches the Name, Location (URL), and the Description fields of all folders and bookmarks.

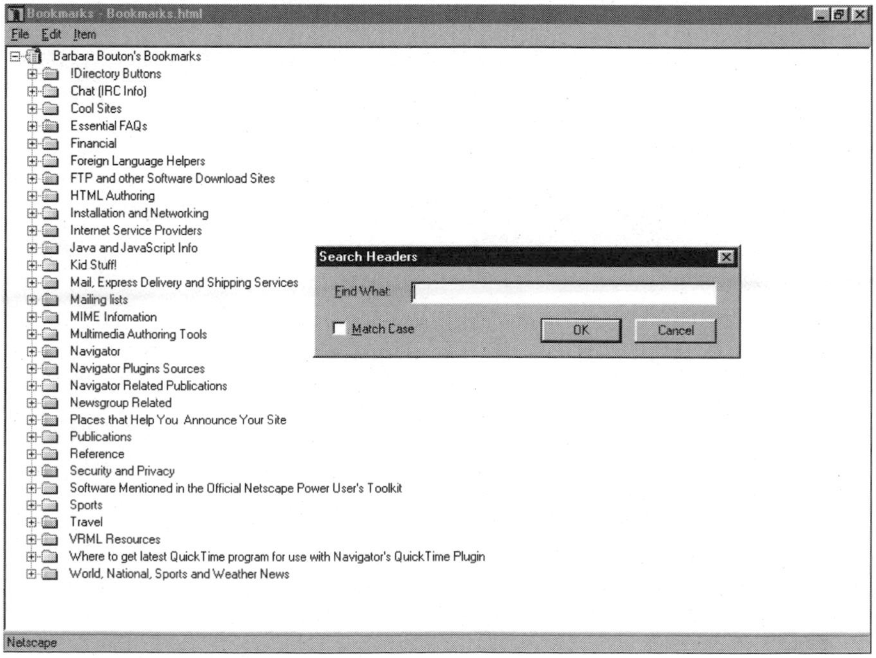

Figure 4-15: *Use Find to search for text contained in a bookmark's URL, name, or description.*

2. In the Find What field, enter the exact word or phrase you wish to search for. If you want to do a case-sensitive search, (that is, find only the instances that exactly match the text you typed into the Find What field), check the Match Case check box. The case-sensitive search differentiates between capital and lowercase letters. If your search is not case-sensitive, be sure the Match Case check box is unchecked.

3. Click OK to start the search. If the search is successful, Find highlights the first entry it finds that contains the specified text. If Find can't locate any text to match your request, it displays a Not Found attention box.

4. If the search is successful but the entry found is not the one you had in mind, press F3 or choose Find Again from the Edit menu. Find then looks for another entry that matches your requirements. Continue with this process until you find what you're looking for or until no more matches are found.

You can greatly improve your chances of finding an elusive entry if you've entered a description or a keyword for the entry in the Bookmark Properties field of the bookmark. For example, if you are interested in antiques in general but specifically interested in antique hand tools, add the keyword *antique* to all of your bookmarks that relate in any way to antiques. To the sites you've bookmarked as having information about antique hand tools, add the phrase *hand tools* somewhere in your description of the site. Later, when you want to find all your antique sites, search using the word *antique*, but when you only want the sites relating to antique hand tools, search on the phrase *hand tools* instead.

SPECIFYING A DEFAULT FOLDER FOR BOOKMARKS

By default, Navigator inserts new bookmarks made from the browser window at the end of the bookmark list, at the same hierarchical level as subfolders. To designate a folder you've created as the new default folder for newly added bookmarks, right-click the name of the folder you want to designate as the new default folder

and choose Use For New Bookmarks (see Figure 4-16) or from the
Item menu choose Set to New Bookmarks. The folder you selected
becomes the default storage folder for all new bookmarks and will
remain so until you designate another folder as the default.

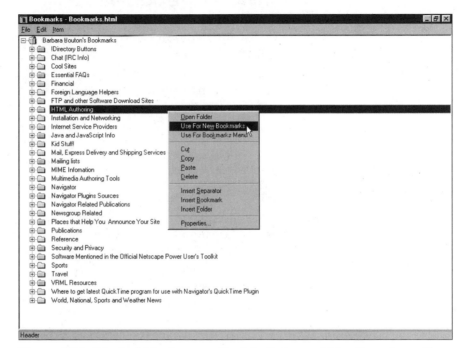

Figure 4-16: *Select a folder to use as the default storage folder, then choose Use
For New Bookmarks.*

TIP

*If you know that many of the bookmarks you'll make in the current
session belong to a single category—for example, companies that
make pepper grinders or sites that contain poetry—make a folder in the
Bookmarks window for that category or choose an existing folder if it is
relevant before you start saving bookmarks. Then specify the new or
relevant folder as the New Bookmarks folder. Now all the bookmarks
you make will automatically be deposited in the proper folder.*

If you should encounter a site that has numerous links that interest you but do not relate to the current default folder's topic, temporarily designate a new default folder for those links.

STREAMLINING THE BOOKMARKS MENU DISPLAY

When you don't want all of your bookmarks and bookmark folders to display on the Bookmarks menu, use the shortcut menu's Use For Bookmarks Menu command or the Item menu's Set to Bookmark Menu Folder command to change the default from the top-level folder to any other folder you choose. Then only the folder you've designated and the bookmarks and subfolders it contains will display.

This feature really comes in handy when you know you will be going only to specific kinds of sites. For example, if you've divided your bookmarks into main categories such as Work and Personal, as suggested earlier, you could use the Set to Bookmark Menu Folder command to designate the Work folder and thereby restrict the display on the Bookmarks menu to only work-related bookmarks. When lunch time comes along and you want to surf, switch the default to the Personal folder and off you go with nary a work-related bookmark in sight on the Bookmarks menu.

To use this command to change the Bookmarks menu's display, follow these steps:

1. Open the Bookmarks window (Ctrl+B). Right-click on the folder you wish to designate as the new Bookmarks menu folder. Choose Use For Bookmarks Menu.

2. Alternatively, click the folder and then from the Item menu, choose Set to Bookmark Menu Folder. The icon of the chosen folder changes to one that has a small picture of a list on it and the Bookmarks menu will now display only bookmarks that are in this folder or in its subfolders. To see what this icon looks like, see the fourth, second level folder icon in Figure 4-2 at the beginning of this chapter.

WHAT'S NEW? AUTO-CHECKING FOR CHANGES

There are probably sites you visit regularly just to see if any changes have been made since your last visit. Checking pages for updates can eat up a lot of your online time, because you must wait for the connection to be made, wait for the page to download, then hunt around the page to see if anything looks different. Even though many Webmasters update their pages regularly, you never know *when* they might have made a change. Consequently, you *can* spend unnecessary time visiting a site that hasn't changed.

Why "unnecessary?" Because Netscape Navigator's appropriately named What's New? feature is designed to help you quickly spot bookmarked sites that have changed since you last used the bookmark. So you can spend your time on what's *really* new, not *what you've already seen*! To use What's New? follow these steps:

1. Open the Bookmarks window (Ctrl+B) or choose Window and then Bookmarks from the Web browser, the Mail window, or the News window. Choose one or more bookmarks. (Use Shift+click to select contiguous bookmarks, or use Ctrl+click to select noncontiguous bookmarks.) When all the desired sites are selected and highlighted, choose File, What's New?

2. In the What's New? dialog box, click the Selected Bookmarks radio button, then click the Start Checking button. The Checking For Changed Bookmarks attention box appears, as seen in Figure 4-17.

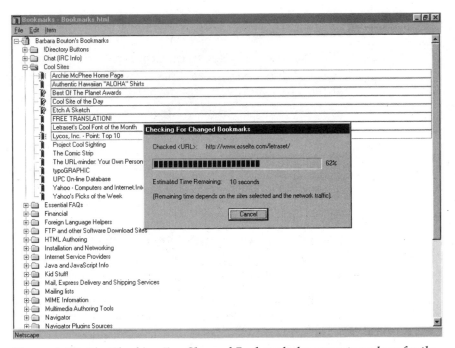

Figure 4-17: *The Checking For Changed Bookmarks box reports on how far the check has proceeded.*

The Checking for Changed Bookmarks attention box gives information on which URL is currently being checked. A progress bar shows what percentage of the bookmarks you specified have been checked, and how much longer Navigator expects the process to take.

When the check has been completed, the attention box shown in Figure 4-18 appears and reports on how many of the URLs were checked, how many of those sites it could reach, and how may of them it determined had changed and therefore marked as changed.

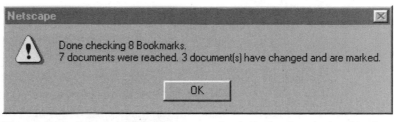

Figure 4-18: *What's New? reports on what it finds when it searches for sites that have changed.*

TRAP

Avoid checking your entire bookmark list unless it is very small. It takes around five minutes to check 100 bookmarks, and bookmark lists with 800 entries are not uncommon. What's New? can check sites much quicker than you can; but, even so, the amount of time required is significant. Additionally, while you are checking you're using a lot of Internet resources, so only check the links you are most interested in.

If by accident you ask What's New? to check all your bookmarks, click the Cancel button in the Checking For Changed Bookmarks box.

3. When you've finished reading the report, click OK to dismiss the attention box. It is important that you close this box, because Navigator won't respond to any other commands you give it while this box is open.

TIP

If, at any time, the keyboard shortcuts do not work, (pressing them does not produce the required results), or other parts of Navigator appear not to respond to your requests, it may be that you have an open Netscape Navigator dialog box hiding behind the current window.

To find the hidden dialog box, click the Minimize button in the upper right corner of each window you have open until you find the open dialog box. Or press Alt+Tab to display the icons of currently running applications. If you see one that looks like a Microsoft Windows flag, continue to hold the Alt key and press and release the Tab key until the flag icon is selected. Then let go of the Tab and Alt keys to bring that application to the front. If it is an open dialog box, such as the Open Bookmarks or Save As dialog, either make a selection or press Cancel.

File download boxes are titled Saving Location; they always display a progress bar. If you are using the Norton AntiVirus Scanner plug-in, the file download box will be called Viewing Location. Do not close these boxes—closing a Saving Location or Viewing Location dialog box before a file has been fully transferred to you will leave you with a partial, nonworking file, and you'll have to start the download all over again to retrieve the file.

When you look at the bookmarks that you asked What's New? to search, you'll usually find that some of the icons next to the bookmarks have changed to Excited and Question Mark bookmarks as a result of the search. (See the section "Bookmark Icons" earlier in this chapter to review what the different icons mean.)

WHAT'S NEW? TELLS YOU IF A SITE HAS CHANGED

When Netscape Navigator conducts a What's New? search for changed bookmarks, it goes to each site and queries the server. Instead of asking the server to provide the page or the resource, as it normally does when you use a bookmark, it asks the server to provide the date and time the page or resource was last updated. Navigator takes the date supplied by the server and compares it to the date and time information Navigator stores in your bookmark file.

When that date is older than the date in your bookmark file, Navigator displays the Standard icon next to the bookmark; when it is newer than the date in your bookmark file, Navigator places the Excited icon next to the bookmark. If the server won't or can't give Navigator the information requested, Navigator flags the bookmark with the Question Mark icon.

USING BOOKMARK ALIASES

The quickest way to automate the What's New? feature is to make a single folder to hold all the bookmarks of all the sites you want to check regularly. Selecting files from one folder is much quicker than hunting all through the tree to find the bookmarks you want to check. This may sound like it flies in the face of the previous advice that you should sort your bookmarks by topic, but it doesn't have to.

Whenever you make a bookmark, store it in the appropriate place but also make a bookmark alias and put the alias in a folder that contains only aliases to sites you want to check regularly. This folder could be called something like "What's New?" or "Sites to

Check." A bookmark alias is a live, linked duplicate of the original bookmark. Anything you can do with the original, you can do with the alias. If you edit the name, URL, or description properties of the original bookmark, all of the aliases change to reflect the edit. And if you edit the properties of the alias, all the aliases *and* the original are updated.

Using an alias is preferable to using a copy of a bookmark because copies of bookmarks are independent of each other and therefore changes made to one are not reflected in the other copies. When you use bookmark copies, keeping your bookmark list becomes more difficult.

To create an alias for a bookmark:

1. From the Bookmarks window, right-click the bookmark you want to alias and then choose Make Alias from the shortcut menu. You can also select the bookmark by clicking it once, and then choose Make Alias from the Item menu.

    The alias appears directly under the original. Click and drag the alias into any folder you like.

You can tell if a bookmark is an alias just by looking at how its name is displayed in the Bookmarks tree. Original bookmarks are displayed in a normal typeface, and aliases are displayed in an italic typeface. The Bookmark Properties General tab for any bookmark identifies if the bookmark is an alias and how many, if any, aliases have been created for the bookmark.

If you want to find all of the aliases to a bookmark, right-click either the original bookmark or one of the aliases and then choose Properties. In the General tab, click the Select Aliases button (see Figure 4-19). Then click either the OK or Cancel button to close the Bookmark Properties window. When you look in the Bookmark tree you will see that Navigator found and selected all of the aliases for you. This is a very handy feature if you want to remove a bookmark and all of its aliases from your list of bookmarks. Just one press of the delete key will delete all of the selected aliases. If you used Select Aliases from the original bookmark's Bookmark Properties window, the original bookmark will also be selected and deleted along with its aliases.

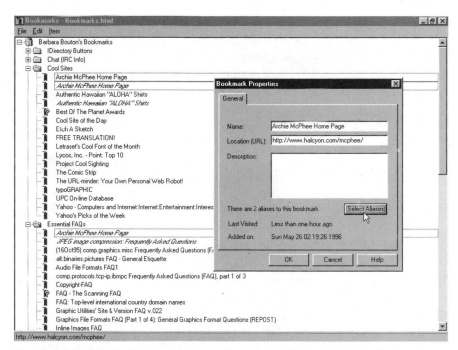

Figure 4-19: *Use the Bookmark Properties Select Aliases button to find and select all of the aliases for a particular bookmark.*

BOOKMARK LISTS

Netscape Navigator displays only one bookmark list file at a time, but you can have as many bookmark lists as you like. Depending on how you like to work, you may prefer to keep separate bookmark lists for different projects instead of keeping all your projects in one big bookmark list. And if you regularly share or receive bookmark lists from others it may be more convenient to keep multiple bookmark lists. Creating new bookmark lists and managing them is easy to do if you follow the steps outlined in this section.

A Netscape Navigator bookmark list file is a specially formatted HTML file that is generated and maintained by Navigator. Figure 4-20 shows the beginning of a bookmark list file. If you look at the source text of your bookmark list file, it will look similar to Figure 4-20 but will contain your name, and the folders and links will refer to ones you've made. To view your bookmark list, open it in a text editor or open the file in a Web browser window, then choose View and then Document Source from the menu bar. The default name for the bookmark list is bookmark.html and is found in the Navigator20 folder.

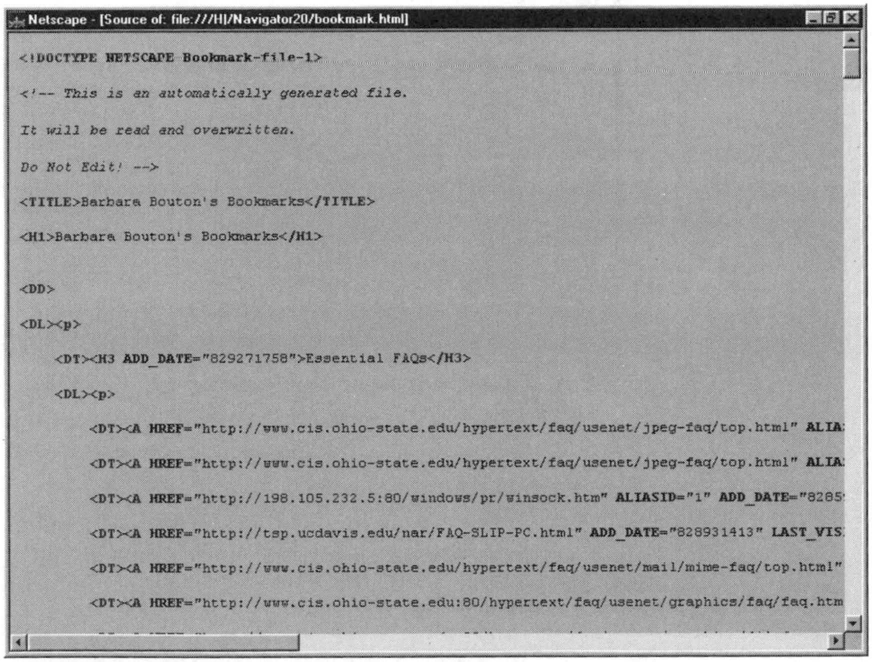


```
<!DOCTYPE NETSCAPE Bookmark-file-1>
<!-- This is an automatically generated file.
It will be read and overwritten.
Do Not Edit! -->
<TITLE>Barbara Bouton's Bookmarks</TITLE>
<H1>Barbara Bouton's Bookmarks</H1>
<DD>
<DL><p>
    <DT><H3 ADD_DATE="829271758">Essential FAQs</H3>
    <DL><p>
        <DT><A HREF="http://www.cis.ohio-state.edu/hypertext/faq/usenet/jpeg-faq/top.html" ALIA
        <DT><A HREF="http://www.cis.ohio-state.edu/hypertext/faq/usenet/jpeg-faq/top.html" ALIA
        <DT><A HREF="http://198.105.232.5:80/windows/pr/winsock.htm" ALIASID="1" ADD_DATE="8285
        <DT><A HREF="http://tsp.ucdavis.edu/nar/FAQ-SLIP-PC.html" ADD_DATE="828931413" LAST_VIS
        <DT><A HREF="http://www.cis.ohio-state.edu/hypertext/faq/usenet/mail/mime-faq/top.html"
        <DT><A HREF="http://www.cis.ohio-state.edu:80/hypertext/faq/usenet/graphics/faq/faq.htm
```

Figure 4-20: *The source code header of a bookmark file.*

TRAP

Heed the warning found at the top of the bookmark list file and don't edit this file yourself. Your efforts will be wasted, because Netscape Navigator will overwrite any changes you've made the next time it opens the file. This warning also suggests that to create a new bookmark file you should let Netscape Navigator do it. But Netscape Navigator doesn't have a "create new bookmark list" command, so you'll have to do the next best thing—give it a file it can overwrite, thereby turning it into a legitimate Netscape Navigator bookmark file.

CREATING A NEW BOOKMARK LIST

To create a new bookmark list, you can make a copy of your current bookmark list and rename the copy to something appropriate, such as "mymarks.html" or "stockmkt.html." But it is often simpler and safer to create an empty text file instead.

To create an empty text file, open up a text editor such as Windows Notepad or WordPad. Press the spacebar to insert a single space within the document. Save the file (File, Save). Exit WordPad or Notepad (File, Exit).

When saving the file, name the file something other than "bookmark.htm" or "bookmark.html" (this keeps you from accidentally overwriting your current bookmark list). If you use WordPad, save the document as text and be sure that the filename carries the extension .htm or .html. In this and the following examples, we'll assume that you created a file called stocks.htm.

You can save the file to any location on your hard disk, but you'll save time in the long run if you save your bookmark files all in one place. Navigator's Program folder is a good place, because this is the folder that Navigator's File Open points to the first time you use it in each session.

OPENING A NEW BOOKMARK FILE

As opposed to *appending* an HTML file that contains bookmarks onto an existing bookmark file, opening *any* file using the File, Open command will *destroy* the contents of the file you are opening *if the file has not previously been used as a Netscape Navigator bookmark file.* So if a friend gives you an HTML file that contains a list of links, or you've created such a file, *don't Open* the file, *use Import instead* to add it to your current bookmark list.

On the other hand, if your friend gives you a copy of their Netscape Navigator 1.0 or later bookmarks file, or you don't care if the contents of the file are overwritten, you can use the Open command.

In the following example steps, an empty file that was created for the express purpose of creating a new bookmark file is opened.

In this situation, we want Netscape Navigator to overwrite the space we entered in the file and thereby convert a plain text file to a new bookmark file to which entries can be added.

1. Open up the Bookmarks Window (Ctrl+B, or choose Window then Bookmarks from the menu bar).

2. From the File menu of the Bookmarks window, choose File then Open. Use the Open bookmark file to find the Stocks.htm file you created in the previous section. When you've found the file on your hard disk, double-click on the entry to Open the file, or click it once to select the file, then press the Open button.

Netscape Navigator now overwrites anything that was in the file—in this case, a space—to create a bookmark file whose main entry is called Main Bookmarks. The next time you open this file, Navigator retitles the top level folder from Main Bookmarks to Your Name's Bookmarks. Note that the title bar of the Bookmarks window shows the filename of the bookmark file, "stocks.htm." Check the title bar when you are in doubt as to which bookmark list you currently have open.

IMPORTING A BOOKMARK LIST

If you have URLs in an HTML file that you want to use as the foundation of a new bookmarks list, or you want to append these URLs to an existing bookmark list, you'll need a different approach. Use Netscape Navigator's Import command. The Import command appends the imported file's information to the current bookmark list. All it takes is the following steps:

1. Open the Bookmarks window. Make sure that the bookmark list that displays is the list to which you want to append the imported list. From the File menu of the Bookmarks window, choose Import.

2. Use the Import Bookmarks file dialog box to locate and select the HTML file you wish to append to the current bookmarks list. Click the Open button. The document will be appended to the list in the Bookmarks window.

Whenever you import a bookmark file, make sure that it is either a Netscape Navigator bookmark file or a plain HTML document that only contains links and no other HTML objects, text, graphics, or other elements such as a table. Importing HTML documents that contain elements other than links may produce unexpected results, nonfunctioning links, or other problems that could mess up your bookmark file. If the file you want to import contains such elements, open the file in Navigator Gold's Editor (or other HTML editor if you don't have Navigator Gold) and remove the non-link elements.

You don't have to do anything special to make a new list that displays the next time you open Navigator. Navigator always saves and displays the last bookmark list you used.

SHARING YOUR BOOKMARKS WITH OTHERS

Once you've scouted all over the Internet, bookmarked the very best sites, and organized them to your satisfaction, the natural inclination is to share them with friends or co-workers. Netscape Navigator makes it easy to share your bookmark lists. You can quickly save a copy of your entire bookmark file to a floppy, or you can attach it to an e-mail message. The ins and outs of e-mailing bookmarks and bookmark lists is covered in Chapter 6, "Person to Person With Navigator Mail & Netscape News."

SAVING BOOKMARK LISTS

By the way, you may have noticed that the File menu in the Bookmarks window doesn't have a Save command, only a Save As command. This is because each time you make a change in the Bookmarks window, Navigator automatically saves the bookmark list, so you don't have to remember to save the file after you've made changes. The purpose of the Save As command is to make a copy of the file for backup purposes or for sharing the file with others.

USING SAVE AS

Saving your entire bookmark list to file is as easy as choosing File, Save As from the Bookmarks window. Give the file a name other than "bookmarks.htm" or "bookmarks.html," to avoid accidentally overwriting your default bookmark list. Once the file is saved, you can give it to someone, open it in another application, or save it as a backup copy.

Note: Netscape Navigator stores information in the bookmark file indicating the date you made the bookmark, the date you last visited the site the mark refers to, the date you last modified the bookmark entry, and whether or not the bookmark is an alias of a bookmark. If you consider this information confidential, *do not* give anyone the file created by the Save As command unless you've edited out the personal information. You can do this with a text editor.

To remove the confidential information, open the file in a text editor such as Notepad or WordPad. Each bookmark entry is a long text string that looks something like this:

```
<DT><A HREF="http://winsite.com/hot/win95.html"
ADD_DATE="824536570" LAST_VISIT="824536573"
LAST_MODIFIED="824536573">http://winsite.com/hot/win95.html</
A>
<DD>Great site for Windows 95 software.
```

Each entry in your list will of course have a different URL, a different description, and the date code numbers, but the structure of the entry will be the same. Note that the line may break differently in your text editor than it does on this page.

The information you need to remove from the entry is the following:

```
ADD_DATE="824536570" LAST_VISIT="824536573"
LAST_MODIFIED="824536573"
```

For each entry, select and delete the personal information, taking care not to delete the " (quotation mark) that comes at the end of the URL or the > (greater than symbol) that comes at the end of the deleted section. The entry should look like this when you're finished. Note that there are no spaces anywhere in the text string that starts with the HREF and ends with </A>.

```
HREF="http://winsite.com/hot/win95.html">http://winsite.com/
hot/win95.html</A>
<DD>Great site for Windows 95 software.
```

Only bookmarks that have descriptions will have a line that begins with <DD>. You can edit or remove the descriptions if you like without harming the document. When you are done editing, be sure to save the file in a text format and give the filename an .htm or .html extension.

CRACKING THE DATE CODE

Navigator's date codes look quite mysterious, because they measure time counted in seconds. Navigator specifies dates in the Bookmarks list as number of seconds that passed since 00:00:00 GMT on January 1, 1970. January 1, 1996 would be 820472400.

INTERNET SHORTCUTS

An Internet Shortcut, (not available in Windows 3.1x) is similar to a bookmark in that double-clicking one will take you somewhere. But an Internet Shortcut is different and does serve another purpose.

An Internet Shortcut works like any other shortcut you can make in Windows 95 to a file that is not an application program. The differences between an Internet Shortcut and a Windows 95 shortcut are the following: the referenced resource needs to be displayed within a Web browser to work, and the resource typically is not stored locally on a hard disk but rather on a server out on the Internet somewhere.

Internet Shortcuts are created by Navigator, but once they are created, they "live" outside of Navigator. They are independent objects that are managed (copied, deleted, moved, sorted, and launched) by the Windows 95 file management system. Because they no longer belong to Netscape Navigator, they can't be tracked using the What's New? feature. However, they do come in handy: an Internet Shortcut can be made from items on Web pages that are not links—such as graphics, as well as pages and elements that are displayed in frames.

CREATING INTERNET SHORTCUTS

Creating an Internet Shortcut from any of Navigator's modules or from the Bookmarks window is never more complicated than a few mouse clicks or a quick click and drag. The method you choose depends on whether you can see the Windows desktop and the object in Navigator that you want to create the shortcut for.

■ If you a have a clear line of sight between a link or bookmark in one of Navigator's windows and the Windows 95 desktop (or any open Windows 95 Explorer window), you can just click and drag the bookmark or link to the desktop or the Explorer window. See Figure 4-21.

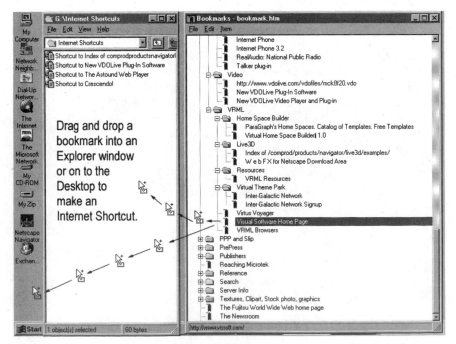

Figure 4-21: *Drag a bookmark onto the desktop or into an Explorer window to make an Internet Shortcut.*

- When the desktop or an Explorer window is not visible, you can right-click the link, object, or bookmark and choose Internet Shortcut from the shortcut menu. The shortcut will be placed on the Windows 95 desktop.

- To make an Internet Shortcut for a page, right-click an empty part of the page and choose Internet Shortcut from the shortcut menu. The Create Internet Shortcut dialog box appears. If you want, edit the Description of the shortcut and then click OK. The Internet Shortcut is placed on the desktop.

- To make an Internet Shortcut to a page element such as a graphic that is not a link on the page, choose Document Info or Frame Info from the View menu. The top pane of either Info window displays all of the elements of the page or frame as individual links. In the top pane, click the link to the element you are interested in. The bottom pane changes to display information about that item and displays the graphic if the link was to a graphic. When the Internet Shortcut you're making is to a document or frame, right-click its link in the bottom pane to bring up the shortcut menu. When the Internet Shortcut is to a graphic, right-click the graphic to bring up the shortcut menu. In both cases, choose Internet Shortcut from the shortcut menu, change the Description if necessary, and click OK.

LAUNCHING AN INTERNET SHORTCUT

To launch an Internet Shortcut, double-click the shortcut. The icon for an Internet Shortcut is shown in Figure 4-22. (See Chapter 1, "The Best Way to Explore the Web," for information on how to change this icon to a different one.) If you are already online and have Netscape Navigator open, Navigator will make the connection to the site without any additional effort on your part. If you are not online at the time you launch the shortcut, Navigator will open and try to make the connection. It will be successful only if your Windows configuration allows AutoDial connections. AutoDial is a feature, commonly acquired by installing a copy of the Windows Plus! pack, that automatically dials your Internet provider whenever you do something that requires an Internet connection. If you don't have the Windows Plus! pack installed, use your usual proce-dure for dialing in and logging onto your Internet connection. See Chapter 2, "Installing & Customizing Navigator," for more infor-mation on automating your Internet connections and how to install AutoDial capability without purchasing the Windows Plus! Pack.

Figure 4-22: *An Internet Shortcut.*

TIP

If you installed any Web browser software after you installed Netscape Navigator, that browser may be the one that is launched. To correct this situation, edit the file associations for URLs in Windows 95 Explorer's View/Options menu so that they refer to the version of Netscape Navi-gator you use. These topics, along with other customizing and optimiz-ing subjects, are covered in Chapter 2.

MOVING ON

While it's true that the World Wide Web is a happily cluttered combi-nation supermarket, public library, and toy store, bookmarks are only keys to online resources. Once you have the address, you need a strategy not only for bringing the goods home but also for making a *contribution* to the Internet's resources. Chapter 5, "Power Search & Retrieval," shows you how to find new sites and resources out on the Web and the most inventive and efficient means for managing file transfers (FTP) both *from* and *to* your own machine.

5

Power Search & Retrieval

Not that long ago, if you wanted to locate a physical book, you could conduct a search in a library using the Dewey decimal card system. Similarly, grocery aisles are stocked according to food or product category, and hardware stores carry inventory lists so that you can quickly locate the bin where a number 5 widget is located.

If you take physical offerings in stores and other resource centers and multiply the total number of goods by about a billion, then you get an idea of the diverse cyber-goods all awaiting you online in locations scattered around the globe. Let's suppose you need to write a term paper on thermodynamics or need to know if there's been a safety recall on your 1987 Pontiac station wagon. The information *is* indeed out there, but it immediately becomes apparent that you need a quick way to find the path to this information—quicker than hopping in the car and trying to locate it from remote physical resources.

In this chapter, we'll take you through the process of conducting the smartest, quickest search for people, information, files, and other goods you need from the Internet. After all, you want to optimize your time, so you can invest it in playing with the goods, not trying to *find* them!

Let's ponder the process and come up with a strategy through this chapter for finding, contributing, and managing information between the Internet and your hard disk. This chapter is divided into three parts:

- How to use search engines and directories on the Net to get the information you want.

- How to send and retrieve FTP information. E-mail is great, but document creation and file reception and transmission make your searches result in more tangible, useful information.

- How to organize and store the information you've found and downloaded. Unless you use a hard disk organization strategy, files can be as hard to find on your hard disk as they can be on the Web!

NAVIGATOR—THE GUIDE TO THE GUIDES

Sometimes it seems that the only thing that is growing faster than the Web is the number of sites devoted to helping you find what's on the Web. There are over 250 different Internet directory, search, and metasearch sites with more being added each day. The race is on between these sites to see who can index the most pages or provide the most comprehensive listings or the most relevant results. With so many search sites wanting to be the one you choose when you need Internet directions, what you really need is a guide to the guides. Navigator and this chapter are just that—the Guide to the Guides.

Netscape knows that one of the most important forms of assistance they can provide is to make it easy to find and visit the many search sites that are available. They also know that you don't always need to do a full-blown search of the Internet to find common information or some of the most popular or useful sites. So with a little more than a click or two on the Directory Buttons bar, or by tapping in a few words in a place that you may not have thought of, they have provided a pathway for searching that's always in reach.

TIP

If the buttons on the Directory Buttons bar have different labels on them and they lead to different places, it's because you are probably using a copy of Navigator that has been customized for use in your organization. The Netscape Administration Kit is a new tool that network administrators can use to customize the Directory Buttons, the menus, preference settings, and even the animated logo in the upper right corner of the screen. These custom configurations are stored in the NETSCAPE.LCK file.

USING THE LOCATION/GO TO FIELD

A quick and not quite obvious way to do a search is to type into the Location/Go to: field of Navigator's Browser window. As you saw in Chapter 3, "Power Navigation," in the section on using partial URLs, Navigator can intelligently handle information entered in this field even if it is not a complete URL. New to version 3 of Navigator is the ability to handle information that is not strictly URL related, but instead is search related.

You can now type two or more keywords into the Location/Go to: field and Navigator will automatically send the keywords to one of five Search services. For this new technique to work you must use more than one word and separate the words by a space; otherwise, Navigator will think you are looking for a URL. You can use Boolean search techniques (discussed later in the chapter), but they may or may not work. When you use the Location/Go to: field for entering search criteria, you don't know which service will process your request. Each search service uses different search syntax and it may not interpret your request as efficiently as if you went directly to the site and looked up the proper syntax for that site. That said, this new feature is very convenient and often produces acceptable results if what you're searching for is a fairly narrow topic, for example Marx brothers movies and not 20th-century entertainment. Let's see how it works:

With Navigator open and an Internet connection established, click in the Location/Go to: field and enter the words **Hawaiian shirt** and then press Enter. In a few moments a search site's page loads with the results of the search.

In Figure 5-1 you can see that Navigator passed along the keywords to Infoseek and Infoseek's page is loaded with the results of the search. Infoseek found 17,920 places on the Net that contain either the word Hawaiian or the word shirt, but it did correctly guess that we would value a site that prominently uses both—in this case Paradise On A Hanger, a Net site that specializes in selling Hawaiian shirts.

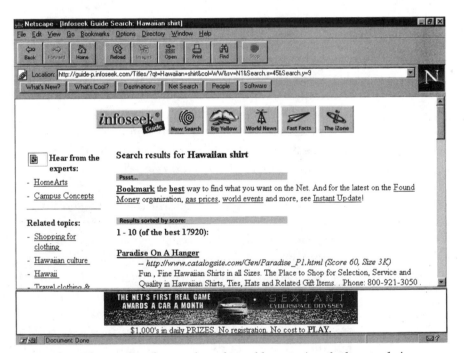

Figure 5-1: *The results of a search performed by entering the keywords in Navigator's Location/Go to: field.*

When you did this same search, you may have ended up with entirely different results because Navigator randomly sends the search to any one of the five services Netscape has deemed to be premium search services. My search just happened to go to Infoseek. I repeated the search from the Location/Go to: field several times to see what the results were. All five of the premium sites came up with useful results, with Infoseek and Lycos providing the most relevant results. Which service provides the best results varies depending on what you are looking for. You should always try several search services or try changing the words you use to search if the first doesn't yield what you are looking for. Later in the chapter you'll see how to use advanced search techniques to quickly narrow down the field when a search produces too many results. But as you saw here, sometimes you can get lucky and get good results with almost no effort.

THE DIRECTORY BUTTONS BAR

If you look on the Directory Buttons bar (see Figure 5-2) you'll see an entire toolbar devoted to speeding your way to information. The What's New? and What's Cool? buttons lead to long lists (see Figure 5-3) of new sites that you may find useful, thought provoking, or just plain fun.

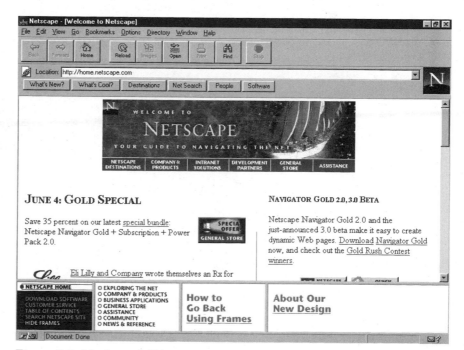

Figure 5-2: *Navigator's Directory Buttons bar can speed your way to search sites as well as an ample selection of cool and new sites.*

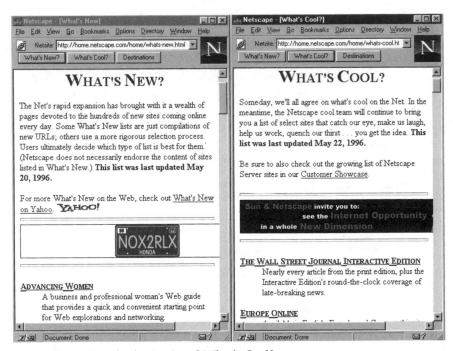

Figure 5-3: *The What's New? and What's Cool? pages.*

The Destinations button, new to version 3, leads to a page on Netscape's site (see Figure 5-4) that contains links to outstanding sites specializing in such various categories as Entertainment, Finance, General News, Hardware and Software, Marketplace, Sports, Technology, News, and Travel. The Software button takes you to a page where you can register and purchase Navigator software, download the latest version of Navigator, find and download Navigator plug-ins, or sign up for a personal digital security certificate.

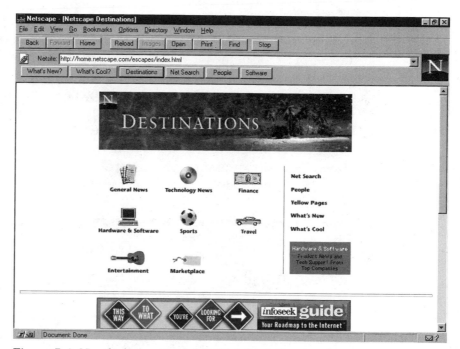

Figure 5-4: *Use the links provided by Netscape's Destinations to visit outstanding sites.*

NET SEARCH

The next two buttons on the Directory Buttons bar are labeled Net Search and People. These buttons replace the Net Directory and Net Search buttons found in previous versions of Navigator. The Net Search button leads you to search and directory sites that are useful when looking for information or sites that deal with specific topics. The People button is the one to click when you want to find a person or a business.

Click Net Search, and you are whisked away to a page chock-full of links to the top Internet search and directory sites as seen in Figure 5-5. The top of the page features a section where you can quickly enter a keyword or phrase and use any one of five different search sites—Infoseek, Excite, Lycos, Magellan, or Yahoo!—to find the information you are looking for. If you prefer to use a different search site, or if you want to do a complex search, you can click one of the many links to search sites on this page and go directly to that site. Using the search sites on the Net Search page and performing complex searches are discussed later in this chapter.

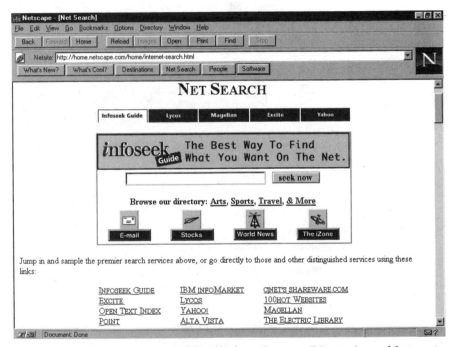

Figure 5-5: *Net Search Page is full of links to Internet Directories and Internet Search sites.*

PEOPLE (& BUSINESSES)

The page that is displayed when you click the People button looks similar to the Net Search page. On the People page, however, all of the listed sites specialize in finding the address (e-mail, home page, and physical), phone numbers, and other information relating to individuals or companies.

These directory services are making it easier all the time to find an individual's e-mail address. If you're looking for someone's address, start your search here on the People page. However, the very best way on Earth to find out someone's e-mail address is to ask them. The search engines are good and getting better, but there are hundreds of thousands of addresses you won't find because they are company-issued accounts or because the user is a member of one of the online services. The People directories find e-mail addresses in one of three ways—from the person registering with the service, from a posting to a public mailing list or newsgroup, or they bought it from a site that solicited the address from its owner. If the person you're looking for is new to the Net or just uses it to surf Web pages, you are unlikely to find the address in a directory. If you want to ask someone for their e-mail address and you don't know their phone number, use the People directories—they are full of physical addresses and phone numbers. This information is fairly easy for them to come by; they look it up in the telephone book for you!

Finding the e-mail addresses and other information about businesses is another matter altogether. Businesses usually actively promote their address. For example, if you choose to use the WhoWhere? Search service (found in the People list of search sites), you can search for e-mail addresses, phone numbers, and street addresses; find companies on the Net; and check out the Yellow Pages. These aren't ordinary Yellow Pages. You not only can look up a business' address and phone number, but you can also do a preliminary credit check or look at a street map to see exactly where the business is located.

Let's see what the Web has to say about Microsoft:

1. With Navigator open and an Internet connection established, click the People button on the Directory Button bar. When the People page loads, scroll down if necessary and click the WhoWhere? Link.

2. When the WhoWhere? page loads, click the Yellow Pages link. Click the With Credit Rating button. After the screen reloads, enter the name Microsoft in the *Search by Company Name* field. In the *City* field, enter Redmond and from the Selected State drop-down list choose Washington. Your screen should look like the one in Figure 5-6.

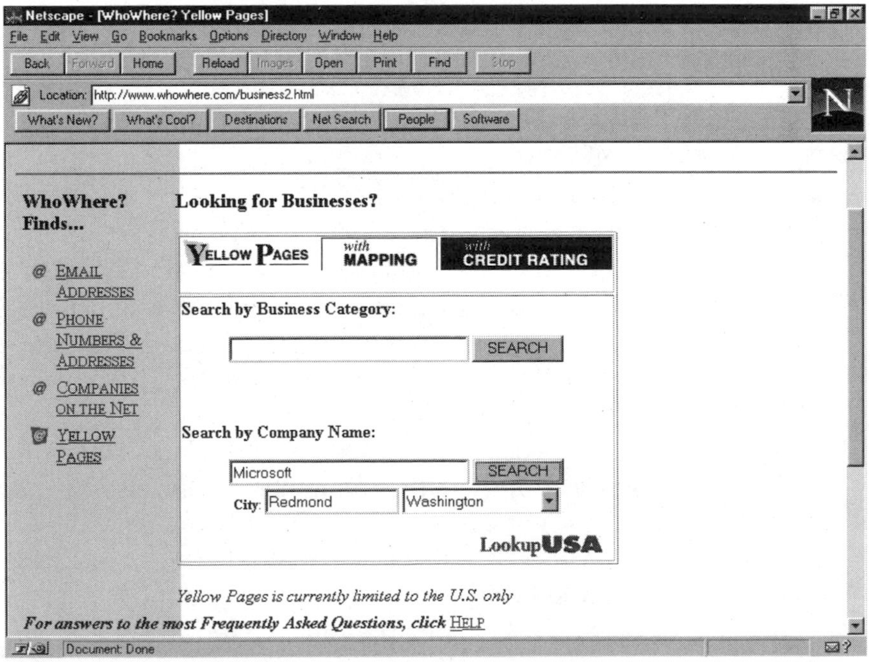

Figure 5-6: *Do a preliminary credit check on a company from the WhoWhere? Yellow Pages.*

3. Click the Search button. If the company you entered is in the database, a page from American Directory Assistance will appear onscreen with the address and phone number. In Figure 5-7 you can see the information for Microsoft.

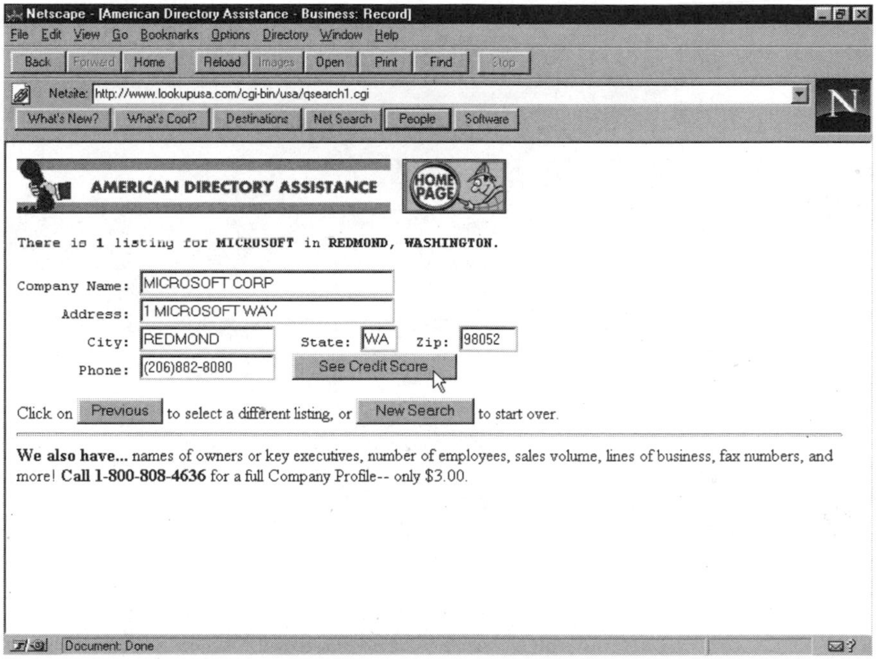

Figure 5-7: *The Search results for Microsoft—you're only one click away from their "credit rating."*

If you look in Navigator's Location field you'll see that you are no longer at WhoWhere? but have been automatically transferred to the site for American Business Information, Inc., lookupusa.com. American Business Information is providing the credit information, not WhoWhere? You can also reach this site directly by making a bookmark now (press Ctrl+D), or you can use the bookmark we've provided for this site in the Totally Hot Bookmarks list on the Companion CD-ROM.

4. Press the See Credit Score button to reveal American Business Information's rating of Microsoft, as shown in Figure 5-8. If you intend to use this information as a basis of deciding credit reliability, be sure to read the entire Credit Score page where American Business Information describes how they arrived at their rating.

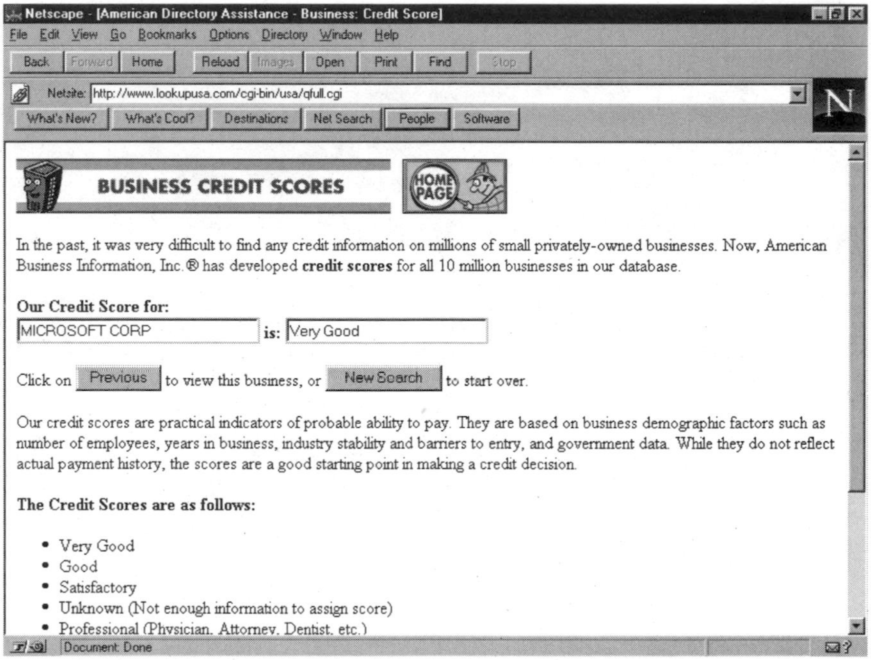

Figure 5-8: *Microsoft's "credit rating."*

5. To see where Microsoft in Redmond Microsoft is located, click Back on the toolbar twice to return to the WhoWhere? Yellow Pages page. Click the With Mapping button, next to the With Credit Rating button. When the screen reloads, enter Microsoft in the *What Business Name* field and enter Redmond and WA in the appropriate *Where?* fields. Then click the Look It Up button.

This time WhoWhere? passed you along to BigBook's site. BigBook is a very useful site that you'll want to explore later. We've bookmarked it for you in the Totally Hot Bookmarks list, or you can bookmark it now, by scrolling down to the bottom of the page and right-clicking the Home link. Choose Add Bookmark from the shortcut menu.

6. BigBook was able to find a listing for Microsoft in its database, and reports its findings on the Search Results. Take a moment to read the Search Results page. Then scroll down

to the bottom of the page. If you are a registered user of BigBook, you can save this search on Microsoft to your private address book or vote on how well you like the company. All users can click the company name to go to the company's home page or click the Map button to view a map that shows where the company is located. Click the Map button.

7. The company information for Microsoft is displayed at the top of the page and a map showing the part of Redmond where Microsoft is located is displayed at the bottom of the page. Click the Zoom In button to "move in" closer and see a smaller, more detailed section of the map. In Figure 5-9 we've zoomed all the way in by clicking the Zoom In button twice. As you can see, Microsoft Way is just off of Leary WY NE, on the south side of the railroad tracks. Conversely, if you keep clicking the Zoom Out button, you'll find that Redmond is north and east of Seattle, near Routes 520 and 202.

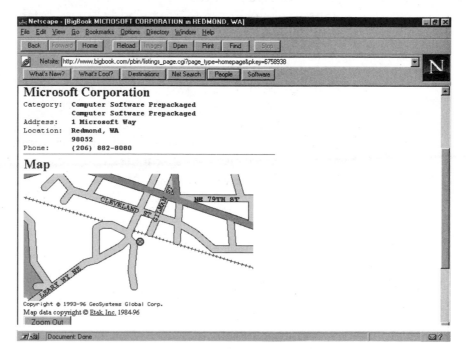

Figure 5-9: *You can zoom in to get street-level detail.*

TIP

In the preceding steps we accessed one search service, WhoWhere? but automatically obtained information from two additional search sites. Many of the search sites on the Web "move" you around like this to give you wider access to information than they alone can provide. It always pays to keep an eye on the Location field to see where you are. If the search service you started out with has transferred you to a new site to get specialized information, bookmark the site so you can go back there directly and more quickly the next time you need that kind of information.

Many of these search services base their listings on telephone yellow and white page listings. These services typically find e-mail addresses by searching Web sites, newsgroups, and mailing lists. Most offer a quick and easy way for you to add or correct your e-mail information listing in each site's database (so friends can find you) or to remove it if you do not want to be listed. Just remember that any information you add to these databases, such as your birth date or your kids' names, will be available for the whole world to see, use, and sometimes abuse. Don't feel you need to answer any question just because it appears on a form, and don't hesitate to ask the operators of a site to remove information about you that you don't want posted.

Let's begin with an examination of the way information is catalogued on the Internet and take a look at the different types of facilities—Directories, Search Engines, and Metasearch Engines—that you can access to find the information you need.

INTERNET DIRECTORIES

An Internet directory service can be thought of as a huge, very well organized bookmarks list that contains a short comment about each bookmark. Yahoo!, probably the best known Internet directory service, started out as just that—the personal bookmark list of two college students. It's grown a bit since then, and many other directory services have joined Yahoo! on the Web.

The common feature of Internet directories is that they categorize *other* Web sites based upon the *general* topic that each site covers. Directory-based sites don't index every word or create an inventory of contents of a page or site; rather, they base their site listing on a short description of the site as a whole. Typically a site becomes listed in a directory because the authors of the site have explicitly asked to be listed by the directory service and have submitted a short description of what their site contains.

The directory of a large service such as Yahoo! is much too large to view in its entirety, so its users are provided with a list of major categories and sub-categories that can be used as the starting point of a search. Searching for something by browsing through the categories is not necessarily the fastest way to find what you're looking for, but you often find related things along the way that interest you. It is also a good method of searching if you're not quite sure what it is you're looking for or if you are looking for general information.

If browsing your way through a directory site isn't your style, most services also provide a way to do a keyword search of the entire directory or a portion of the directory. For example, if you are looking for sites on Ancient Egypt, you could browse in the Archaeology section (see Figure 5-10) of the directory, or the section on the Middle East, or you could search the index using various keywords and phrases, such as Egypt (which would lead you to a listing of sites that have something to do with modern or ancient Egypt), or on the phrase, "Ancient Egypt," which would narrow your search down considerably.

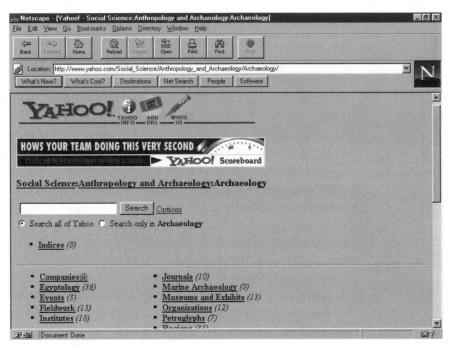

Figure 5-10: *Browsing through Yahoo!'s Archaeology listings can take you to a section on Egyptology or to one on Marine Archaeology, depending on your interest.*

Once you've performed a search, Yahoo! returns the results—the URLs of sites that match your request. If there is not enough information for you to choose from, or when looking at the results you don't see anything that looks promising, you can use other popular search engines to perform the same search without the need to re-enter the search criteria. Yahoo! and other search sites thoughtfully provide links to other services and pass along the keyword you used.

Although Yahoo! may be the most popular directory that encompasses all types of Web sites within its database, there *are* others to choose from. There are also directories that specialize in certain *types* of sites, such as business directories, employment directories, and many more.

SEARCH ENGINES

Search engines are a different type of Internet service from directories; search engines are Web sites that actively seek out information on the Web and automatically index it. The results of all this indexing are stored in a large database that you can query. The index built by a search engine is different from that of the directory services in that they concentrate on the words on a page instead of what the focus of interest is at a particular site as described by its author. Many of the search sites index every word on every page they come across while others may look only at the first 250 to 500 words on a page. When you use a search engine, you get many more "hits" than with a directory service, which is indexing sites and not individual words. This doesn't always mean that you get better results, however. For example, if you were looking for information on the construction industry, you could search a directory service for the word "construction" and get pretty good results. Perform the same search on a search engine site, and you would get thousands of hits, but many of them would refer to pages that contained the infamous words "This page is under construction!"

Search engines are extremely useful; you just may have to work at narrowing down your search by using multiple keywords and Boolean search techniques (discussed later in this chapter). As with many other things today, the differences between directory services and search engines are blurring as technologies and ideas converge. Many of the search engine sites have combined the power of directory searching with that of the huge indexed database. For example if you look at Infoseek's opening page (shown in Figure 5-11) you'll see an entry field where you can enter the keywords you want to use to search the database, or you can click one of the links to areas of popular interest on the right side of the page. We clicked Business & Finance and were presented with the page you see in Figure 5-12. This page offers 13 links to relevant sites, more links to areas of interest, just like a directory, and still offers the opportunity to search the entire database or only that part of the database that Infoseek has determined to relate to Business & Finance.

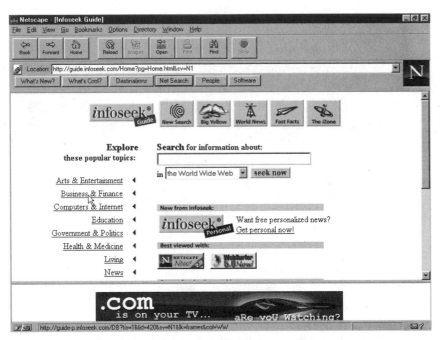

Figure 5-11: *Infoseek's opening page offers many options.*

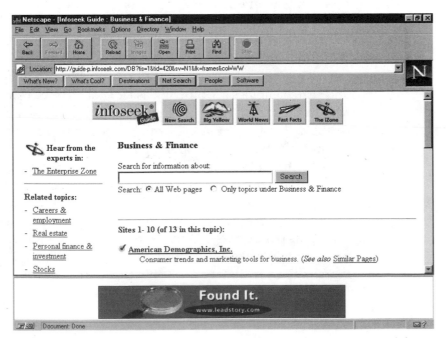

Figure 5-12: *You can browse through a specific area of interest or search by keyword.*

METASEARCH ENGINES

A Metasearch Engine is a Web search engine that searches the search engines! Instead of indexing or listing submitted sites or sending out search robots to index the Internet, a metasearch site will format your query into the proper format for each target search site and then submit the query. Some present the results in a unified list while others report separate results from each site.

One of the most effective metasearch engines is MetaCrawler (see Figure 5-13—http://metacrawler.cs.washington.edu:8080/index.html) because it not only performs the search, but it also throws out all the duplicate entries and evaluates which results may be most useful to you. The downside to all this power and convenience is that it sometimes takes several minutes to return results; five minutes is not unusual, and there is no status report while you wait. To speed up the process, MetaCrawler offers you the opportunity to limit your search to sites in a specific continent, your country, or your domain. You can further restrict the search to specific Internet domains, for example com or edu domains. And you can set a time limit on the search or ask it to do either a fast or a normal (comprehensive) search.

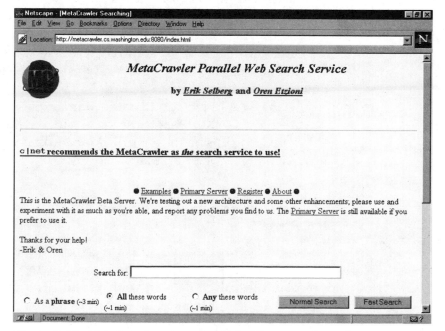

Figure 5-13: *MetaCrawler winnows out duplicate search results.*

SavvySearch (http://savvy.cs.colostate.edu:2000/) is another extremely useful and fairly quick metasearch site, particularly if your native language is not English. You can view the SavvySearch page and conduct your search in 20 different languages. Based on the number of relevant results SavvySeach finds with searches similar to yours, SavvySearch's metasearch engine intelligently picks the best four sites (out of 25 available sites) for conducting your search. If your search is unfruitful, you can ask SavvySearch to extend the search to more sites. Similar to MetaCrawler, SavvySearch can combine duplicate results into a single "hit," making it easier for you to find what you're looking for. To enable this feature, be sure to check the Integrate results check box on the SavvySearch search page.

The metasearch sites do take a little longer to get results, but they often save you time because they are able to bring results in from many different sources. When using metasearch sites, always check out their examples or help section to make sure that you are using the proper syntax for your search. If you goof and use the wrong syntax, the search will take longer and you probably won't get the results you want. For example, MetaCrawler allows you to use the Boolean operator NOT. When using MetaCrawler, you can put a – (minus sign) before any word or phrase to exclude pages that contain the word or phrase being included in the search results. SavvySearch doesn't currently support this kind of limit in a search and would interpret the word you were trying to exclude as one that should be included. For example, if you searched for Marx +brothers –Karl as your keywords with MetaCrawler, you would get results that would include all of the Marx brothers but wouldn't include references to Karl Marx. The same search with SavvySearch would produce results on the comedic Marx brothers *and* on the communist philosopher, Karl Marx.

PLANNING YOUR SEARCH

When you've decided that you need to go online and perform a search, the next question is where do I start? There are many great sites from which you could start your search. To perform a productive search, you should first pinpoint and define exactly what you're looking for.

After you've decided what the topic is, try and come up with a list of all the words relating to the information you want to find, as well as ones that should be excluded. Next, think of the conditions that would help or hinder your search—would the information be most likely found on the Web or in a newsgroup, or could the sites' location affect the search? For example, my father-in-law asked me to do some genealogy research on the family name Bouton. Bouton also means button in French and is the last name of the famous baseball pitcher, Jim Bouton. By using a search site (I used MetaCrawler) that allowed me to search only in the United States and allowed me to exclude words such as sports and baseball, I was able to come up with a much tighter and effective search.

Which search service you use, once you've established what it is you need to find, depends entirely on that need. Use the following tips to help you decide which is the right kind of search site to use and how to make the search more productive:

- If your topic is narrow, try doing a simple two- or three-keyword search from the Location/Go to: field. You must use more than one word or Navigator will interpret the single word as a request for a URL.

- If you're not sure what exactly you are looking for or if your topic is very broad, start your search with a directory service such as Yahoo!

- When using any search or metasearch engine, be sure to look for the Help or Search tips or Syntax page to minimize waiting time. There's usually a link somewhere on the opening page of the service that will lead you to directions that are specific to that particular search site.

- Narrow the scope of your search when possible. Many search sites allow you to search only the Web, or only newsgroups, or only a specific geographic area.

  If you are fairly certain that the information you're looking for can be found in a newsgroup archive or if you're looking for an article you read in a newsgroup, but can't remember exactly which one or when you read it, use the Deja News Research Service (http://www.dejanews.com/).

Pick the Power Search option. From there pick the Create a Query filter. Follow the onscreen directions and conduct your search. You'll find the article you're looking for in no time flat.

If you are looking for any WWW site that contains specific kinds of content such as Java or JavaScript; or multimedia files, such as AVI files or QuickTime movies, use Hotbot (http://www.hotbot.com). It is the only one (now at least) that makes searching for this kind of information easy.

- If your search returns too many results to be useful and you can't easily narrow the search, use a metasearch engine like MetaCrawler (http://metacrawler.cs.washington.edu:8080/index.html).

- If you're looking for shareware or freeware, use a search site such as Jumbo (http://www.jumbo.com) or c|net's shareware.com (http://www.shareware.com).

- Use specialized directories or search engines if you can. For example, The World Wide Web Virtual Library: Sport section has links to almost everything on the Internet that has to do with sports (http://www.atm.ch.cam.ac.uk/sports/sports.html). The Government Information INFOMINE (http://lib-www.ucr.edu/govinfo.html) is a great place to find anything to do with the United States. Some state governments are also covered here. The MonsterBoard has over 55,000 job listings (http://199.94.216.77:80/), and c|net provides one of the best ways to find and use specialized directory and search engines (http://www.search.com/).

PERFORMING THE SEARCH— USING BOOLEAN OPERATORS

Once you've defined your search criteria and found the most appropriate search engine to search from, the next thing you need to know is how to effectively enter your search criteria. Many of the search sites allow the use of Boolean operators. Boolean operators provide a way to include and exclude words or concepts and to control the way your keywords are interpreted by the search engine.

Although each search engine site provides tips on the use of their engine and on the proper syntax for entering Boolean operators in searches, the following information pertains to most of them and will aid in obtaining the best information from your search.

Using Boolean operators is not difficult, but it does require you to think about how you want to conduct your search. The basic Boolean operators used by most search sites are AND, OR, and NOT. The AND operator is sometimes entered as +, or &, or a space. The NOT operator is sometimes entered as – (minus sign). It is not usually necessary to type the Boolean operators in uppercase letters when conducting searches, but it does help visually separate the operators from the keywords.

AND

The AND operator is used when you need to find information that contains more than one keyword. For example, when looking for sites pertaining to employment opportunities, you would type the search criteria as *employment* AND *opportunities*. The search engine would return only the sites within its database that contained both words: employment and opportunities. Therefore, the AND operator is used to help refine and limit your search results.

There are times, depending on the search engine you are using, when you can use Boolean symbols in place of the AND operator, such as + or &. Some search sites use commas or spaces between words to indicate a Boolean AND.

OR

The OR operator works opposite to the way the AND operator works. When using the OR operator, the search engine will find sites within its database that contain either one of the keywords, but not necessarily both. For example, if you wanted information on either *football* or *basketball* sports, the criteria would be typed as *football* OR *basketball*.

The OR operator usually returns a wide range of results and is often not effective in refining the search.

NOT

The NOT operator is similar to the AND operator in that it also allows you to refine your search results. Use NOT to exclude pages from the results that contain specified words or phrases. For example, if you wanted information on trees, but not on maple trees, you would enter *trees* NOT *maple* in the search criteria. This entry would tell the engine to return all sites containing the word *tree*, but not the ones that also contained the word *maple*, therefore eliminating sites pertaining to maple trees.

As with the AND operator, the NOT operator also has a symbol (–) that some sites will recognize as the NOT operator.

PARENTHESES OR QUOTATION MARKS

Another common search technique is using parentheses or quotation marks to combine keywords. By using these symbols, you are telling the search engine that you wish to find sites within its database that contain the keywords as a string. For example, if you wanted to find information on picture frames but not eyeglass frames, you could type *picture frame* as the phrase to be searched for. If the words are enclosed in quote marks or parentheses, most search engines will treat this as a phrase and not two different keywords.

Notice that picture frame is all lowercase. Many search engines will return more results if the keywords are all lower case. If you entered Picture Frame, some engines would only return pages that had the phrase with the mixed upper- and lowercase. This sensitivity to case is sometimes useful because it helps when you are searching for proper nouns, such as people's names or geographic names.

WILDCARD SYMBOL

The asterisk (*) can be used as a kind of wildcard. The * symbol allows the search of plurals or of similar words. For example, if you type **ball* in the search criteria, you may find results returned for football, basketball, or even racquetball! Not all search sites support this symbol.

THE ORDER OF OPERATION

When combining Boolean operators, you need to follow some general rules of thumb. Similar to the order in which math equations are evaluated, there are also orders in which these operators are performed. The AND and NOT commands are usually done prior to the OR command. When searching for information on either the language of Germany or Italy, the search criteria should be typed as *(German OR Italian) AND language*. By putting German OR Italian within parentheses, you force the search engine to first find all sites that contain the words German or Italian and then to look through that list for all sites that contain the word language. This search would return information on the German language and the Italian language.

If you didn't use any parentheses, the search engine would look for all sites that contained the words Italian and language and then look for sites that contain the word German. This would produce Italian language-related sites but it also would include any site that contained the word German even if the page didn't include the word language.

Once you've learned these Boolean tricks, you will be able to perform many advanced searches for information.

THE WEB AUTHORS' "TALENT AGENT" TIPS

Although most of this chapter is devoted to an understanding of search and directory capabilities that Navigator offers, many advanced users are paying special attention to the authoring of Web content, the words on each page, which will be read by a search engine, as well as the abstract submitted separately to a directory search service. In corporate Intranets or out on the cyber-highway, it's important to know how to leverage search engines and HTML properties to get your *own* message recognized!

Let's suppose that you need to put a Web page on an Internet server; this example begins with the presumption that your ISP has provided you with a domain name. The easiest way to go about creating content for the Web is through Navigator Gold's Editor. As you'll see throughout this book, Navigator Gold's Editor offers a WYSIWYG interface that is no more challenging to use than a word processor.

In Figure 5-14, you can see a simple home page for a future site devoted to the history of 3D. The page was created using one or two graphics programs that can export to GIF89a format, and the text is courtesy of Navigator Gold's Editor. If you'd like to check out this page's construction, you can find it in the CHAP05/3D folder on the Companion CD-ROM.

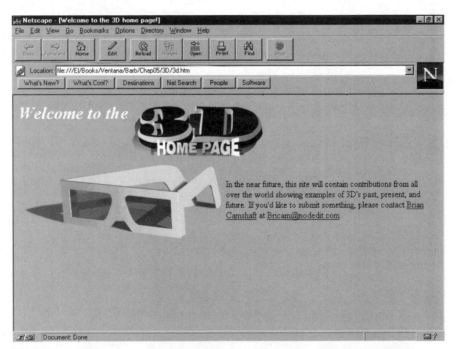

Figure 5-14: *If you can create it, you can publish it . . . to the world, using Navigator Gold's Editor, an Internet site, and Navigator Gold's one-button publishing system.*

Let's also presume that you know the domain name that your Internet Service Provider obtained for you on their server. It's not really that hard to get the Web page to the ISP; you simply open a connection and send the files that make up the site. What is a little hard, however, is getting your Web site immediately recognized by as many surfers as possible. This can be accomplished by registering your site with a directory service, or more immediately—and a little less effectively—by taking advantage of HTML's Meta tag.

THE META TAGS

Although a thorough discourse on HTML code is not possible in this book, there is an area in Navigator Gold's Editor where you can add a Meta tag to an HTML document as easily as typing a description into a field—Navigator Gold's Editor insulates the creative user from much of the underlying source code of the HyperText Markup Language.

Meta tags are found in the Head section of an HTML document. They contain information that Web browsers and other Internet agents such as the robots or Web crawlers that search engines send out on the Web to find, identify, and index pages. The content of Meta tags is quite flexible. One use of a Meta tag is to include keywords that the search robots look for to help them index or evaluate your page.

Some Web crawlers ignore the information in Meta tags and look at only the first 250 words in an HTML document, while others rely on the Meta information. To ensure that your site is categorized correctly, it's usually a good idea to begin your page on Canadian Geese, for example, with a clear statement about geese, and not with an except from the Gettysburg Address. You'd be surprised at how many Web authors digress from the site's topic at the beginning of a document—and are largely ignored or misrepresented on a search engine as a result.

Here's where the Meta tag information comes into play. If you own Navigator Gold, load the 3D.HTM document on the Companion CD-ROM into the Editor, then choose Properties, Document. Under the General tab, you'll see that in the Description field, the phrases "3D graphics," "really cool 3-D animations," and so on have been entered. The description information entered here is actually placed within a Meta tag. Meta tags are always put at the top of the document between the Head tags; you can have multiple Meta tags that serve different purposes. Some search engines will use this information as part of their description of your page. In Figure 5-15, you can see the General tab in Navigator Gold's Editor. Each of the fields in the General tab corresponds to a Meta tag that Navigator Gold will generate if you enter anything in the field.

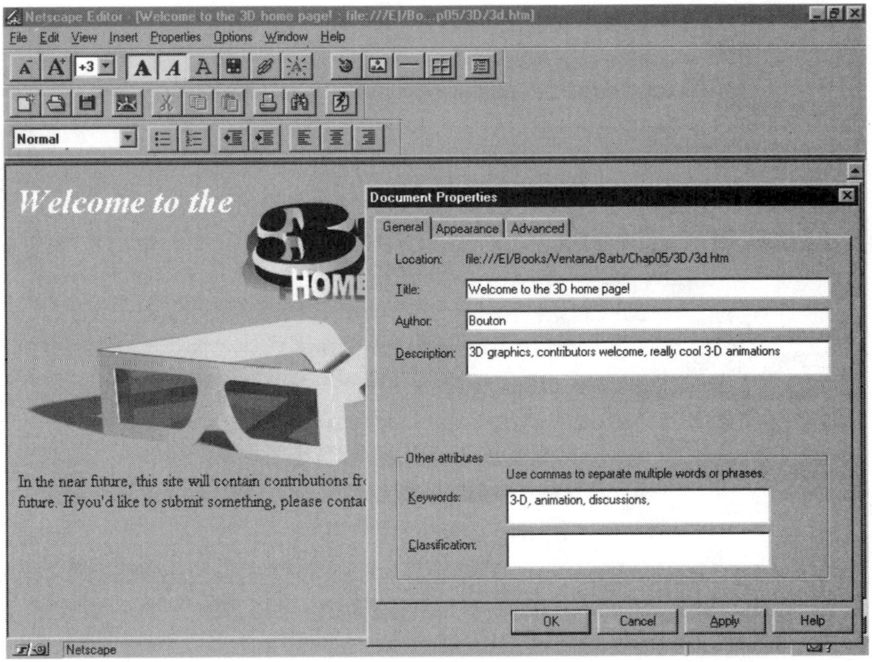

Figure 5-15: *The contents of the Description field in a document edited in Navigator Gold contains information that is placed in a Meta tag in the Head section of the HTML document. This information is used by Web crawlers and robots.*

Meta tag information is not used to construct the page display and therefore is not seen by casual surfers unless they take a peek at the source code of the document. Again, Meta tags contain information for Internet agents such as browsers and robots. They do not loudly advertise the information to the world, but they do allow an author to supplement what search engine robots and other agents will find within the document.

The Generator Meta tag is automatically inserted by Navigator Gold and is not edited by the user. This Meta tag tells all interested agents that the document was prepared using Navigator Gold. However, you do get the opportunity to claim your work, by entering your name in the Author field in the General tab. Navigator Gold will generate a Meta tag to hold this information. Navigator

Gold gets this information from user information on your machine, so if you share a computer at work, make certain that the Author field contains your own name. If it doesn't, edit the information in the Document Properties General tab.

Additionally, you can provide keywords that will go in another Meta tag to allow a Web crawler to more accurately index your site. Be careful if you're contemplating using misleading keywords in this field, however! A few disreputable businesses on the Web have discovered that if you put sexually oriented keywords into a Meta tag, you get a lot of hits on your site. Unfortunately, this trick also destroys the efficiency of the search engines, and there goes the self-governing quality of the Web. You could additionally attract the attention of the FBI if you get too creative with your Meta tag attractions. Huxley's "Big Brother" never arrived as 1984 came and went, but Uncle Sam can still give you a very hard time if you suggest you're doing something other than legitimate business on the Web.

REGISTERING WITH SEARCH SITES

If you've been using Navigator Gold to create a Web site, you'll want everyone to be able to use the Internet search tools to find your pages, just as you use the search tools to find pages of interest. Putting Meta tags in an HTML document (because this is free advertising), will help whenever a Web-crawling-robot-indexer happens across your page. But you don't have to wait anxiously for a Web robot to find you; you can register the site with the search engines and hasten their visit. And if you want to be listed in directory services that don't search for sites, registering is the only way to get listed.

Every search site has a link somewhere on it that will lead you to guidelines and/or a submittal form for entering your site in their database. Every site has different forms and criteria for registration. You can go around the Web and register your site with as many different search sites as you have the time and patience for. Or you can help speed up the process a bit and use one of the Internet services that are set up to do some of the legwork for you.

Submit It! and PostMaster are the two most frequently used sites for submitting your pages to multiple search sites. Submit It! (see Figure 5-16) is a totally free service. By filling out one form (which includes room for an author abstract or page description) on their page (http://www.submit-it.com/), your site will be registered with 15 of the most popular search services. PostMaster (http://www.netcreations.com/postmaster/registration/try.html) is a commercial service that will post your listing to over 250 sites for $500. PostMaster does have a limited free service that will post your listing to approximately two dozen sites.

Figure 5-16: *Use Submit It! to register your Web site with 15 major search sites.*

FTP

We've presumed in this chapter that for the most part, your own searches will be conducted for information usually found on Web sites in the form of HTML documents. However, the Web is also heavily populated with software and other binary (non-text) files— software, plug-ins, images, sounds, and other multimedia objects. You'll find large collections of shareware, freeware, and demos at sites whose primary purpose is file distribution. You'll also find software and other offerings scattered about the Web on various companies' and individuals' home pages and FTP sites. FTP stands for File Transfer Protocol and not surprisingly this Internet protocol is designed for the efficient transfer of binary files. Files can also be transferred using HTTP protocol. Navigator is capable of handling both FTP and HTTP file transfers. Which one you'll use to retrieve files depends on what kind of server the file resides on. Web servers use the HTTP protocol to transfer files and FTP servers use the FTP protocol. Sometimes content providers will offer the same file through both kinds of services. It is usually more convenient to download from within a Web page because you don't have to leave the page to get the file, but files sometimes download quicker if you go to an FTP site to get them.

Let's take a look at how FTP works and the smartest way to browse and search for a specific file you need.

SEARCHING FOR SOFTWARE

If you know the name or part of the name of a program you want to find on the Internet, you can use the general search engines such as Alta Vista or Infoseek. Yahoo! is particularly good at finding sites that contain jumplists or lists of links to a number of different downloadable software that falls into a specific category. Desktop publishing files and helpful links can be found on a list like the

DTP Internet Jumplist (http://www.teleport.com/~eidos/dtpij/dtpij.html) while a wide assortment of Internet-related software can be found at Tucows (http://www.tucows.com). Finding a good jumplist for your area of interest is particularly valuable because the authors of the pages tend to list only the most recent versions of really cool or useful software. Many jumplist authors also include helpful descriptions or reviews of the software. When you find a good jumplist, be sure to bookmark it; you'll want to go back frequently.

But when you don't have a good jumplist handy or you are looking for a specific file, try one of the software specific search sites. Jumbo, shareware.com, and the search facilities at the major software FTP sites (Internet sites devoted to storing files so you can download them) are among your best bets. All these sites can be used to search for a specific file or to browse through or search for general categories of software, such as desktop utilities. Most of these sites break their listings or databases into areas that pertain to operating system (Win 3.1, Win 95, NT, Macintosh, UNIX) and then break these sections into categories of software—word processing, graphics utilities, system utilities, and so on.

The Totally Hot Bookmarks file on the Companion CD-ROM has a number of entries for search sites, major FTP sites, and jumplists.

Let's see how one of these sites works by visiting c | net's shareware.com. At shareware.com you can either browse through categories of software or you can search for software, based on the software's name or keywords that might be in the software's name or description. None of the software in shareware.com's database is actually on c | net's servers; rather, the database points to a number of different FTP sites from which you can download the software. In the following example search, we'll look for a small, quick-loading graphics viewer that isn't bogged down with editing tools. A program like this can be used as a Navigator helper application or for times when you don't have Navigator open.

1. With Navigator open and an Internet connection established, click the Net Search button on Navigator's Directory Buttons bar. Scroll down if necessary, and then click the link for c | net's shareware.com. The shareware.com site loads after a few moments. See Figure 5-17.

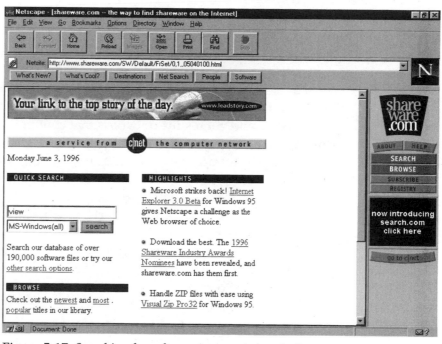

Figure 5-17: *Searching for software is easy at c | net's shareware.com.*

The opening page offers a Quick Search option and links to pages that offer more advanced search options. All of the different levels of search options on shareware.com allow you to restrict a search to programs that run on a specific operating system or relate to either games or programming. Whenever a search site offers a way to restrict a search based on platform, date, or other useful criteria, use it. It will weed out a lot of files you aren't interested in. In this example you can limit your search to only those programs that run under the following operating systems or that fit two specific categories of software: MS Windows All (includes Windows 3.1, Windows 95, and Windows NT), Windows 3.1, Windows 95, Windows NT, Macintosh, DOS, OS/2, UNIX, Netware, Amigia, Atari, PC Games, Source-Code, and All of the categories.

Once you've narrowed the search some by choosing the appropriate operating system or area of interest, it's time to think about the search words you'll use. Shareware.com treats its entries a little differently than other sites in that it doesn't use the words you've entered as keywords; rather, it uses them as "raw" words. For example, a keyword-based search uses the entire word and only reports back with results that match that word. A raw word search, such as shareware.com, takes the word you entered and looks at it as a sequence of letters. Whenever it finds a similar sequence, it considers it a match. For example, if you entered *gra* as the search word, you would get results on words that contained those three letters in that order: **gra**phite, **gra**phic, **gra**phics, **gra**phically, and **gra**pe would be found as well, as un**gra**cious. You can use this to your advantage to narrow or broaden searches. For example, if you entered the word *zip* you would get many more "hits" than if you entered *zipping* or *WinZip*, and similarly, entering *art* would yield many more hits than would *clipart*.

When using shareware.com's Quick Search, you can only enter one word for the search. If you are looking for a specific file and know its name or part of its name, such as WinZip or GoldWave (a sound editor), entering that name in the entry field usually offers good results. If you don't know the name of the software you want, only the category, for example, spreadsheet, graphics, communications, and so on, you can enter it here as well, but you'll probably get hundreds of responses that you'll have to wade through. In that case you'll get much better results if you skip the Quick Search and use the more advanced search options to narrow your search. Just for fun, I entered the word *viewer* as the Quick Search word and chose the default of MS Windows (all). I gave up counting how many hits were returned after paging through 250 responses. Using Quick Search to quickly find the graphics viewer program isn't going to work, so we'll need to move on to the more advanced searches where the search can be narrowed down a bit and made more useful.

2. Click the text link *other search options* in the paragraph below the Quick Search form or click the Search button in the left frame. If you have the no frames version of the page displayed on your screen, click the word *Search* in the graphic at the top of the page.

3. On the page that follows, seen in Figure 5-18, you are given an opportunity to do a more advanced Quick Search or to move to the Power Search page. The advanced Quick Search offers more options—the ability to specify a second word and the option to limit the files displayed. The wording here is misleading. The value you choose from the drop-down list isn't the limit of how many "hits" you'll get in total, but rather how many are displayed on each page. The higher the number, the longer the page. The smaller the number, the more times you'll have to advance the page to see more listings.

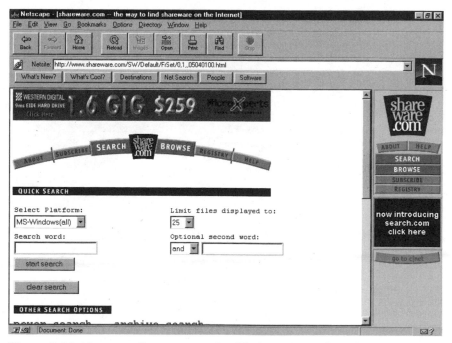

Figure 5-18: *You can refine your search with the options offered by the advanced Quick Search.*

The advanced Quick Search may do the trick for you because you can specify the relationship between the two search words using the Boolean AND or the OR. In short, using a Boolean AND means that both words must be found; the OR means either word must be found to produce a result. Using AND usually produces fewer, more appropriate results, and using OR produces a much wider range of results, but can be a useful alternative to an even broader search. For example, if you wanted baseball- or football-related files it would be better to use baseball OR football rather than a single search on the word sports.

But there will be times, like in our example search, when you need even more control than the advanced Quick Search can provide, so let's move on to the Power Search which also allows the use of the Boolean NOT and other search criteria.

4. Click the text link, Power Search, under the Other Search Options graphic. See Figure 5-19.

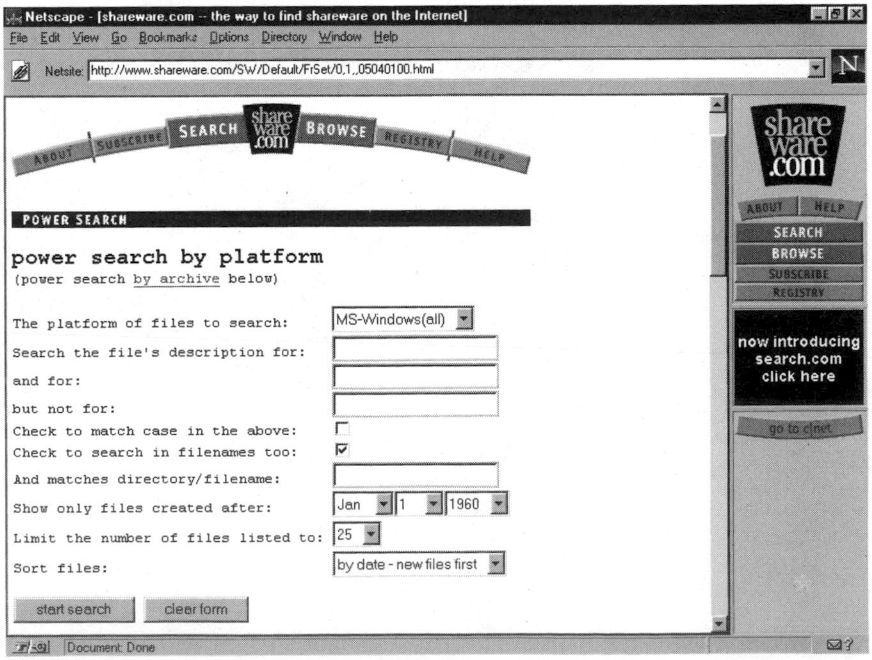

Figure 5-19: *The most powerful searches are performed using the Power Search options.*

5. For this example, leave *The platform of files to search* drop-down list set to the default of MS Windows (all). In your own searches you may want to limit the search to a particular version of the Windows operating system. Shareware.com detects the version of the browser you are using to determine what this default should be. If you used the Macintosh or UNIX version of Navigator, the default would change to Macintosh or UNIX.

6. In the *Search the file's description for:* entry field, enter the word **graphic**. In the entry field below (*and for:*) enter the word **view**. In the *but not for:* entry field enter the word **edit**. This means that we are looking for a file description that contains words that contain all or part of the word graphic and view (for example, the words graphics and viewer would match), and does not contain the word edit in any form (this would exclude edit, editor, editing, edits, editorial, and so on).

7. The two check boxes offer further control over the search. Checking the first restricts the search to a case-sensitive one (Graphic wouldn't match graphic). Checking the second check box makes the search look for the search words in the filename as well as the file description. For this exercise, accept the default settings, where the first is not checked and the second one is checked.

8. The *And matches directory/filename field:* is a rather obtuse and difficult to use limiting factor. What they are allowing you to enter here is the path or filename that you presume would be used on the site that stores the file. If you knew that information, you probably wouldn't need to do a search at all! This could possibly come in handy if you were looking for something that could be in two different places and you guess it would be in one rather than the other. For example, when doing searches on graphics programs, the default directory for graphics would usually be a directory called graphics. But some sites separate CAD-related graphics from general graphics. If you were looking

for something CAD-specific, you might try entering CAD into this field. It just might work to your advantage if any of the sites indexed by shareware.com have a directory called CAD. However, most of the time and in this example search, you will leave this field blank.

9. The next set of controls relates to limiting the search by date. These controls can be very useful if you have a rough idea of when a program was released or if you want to search for files that are very recent. For this example, we'll look for files that are less than one year old. Use the drop-down lists to set the date Aug 1 1995 or any date you want to use.

10. You can leave the *Limit the number of files listed to:* set to 25 for this example. I like longer page displays and usually set this to 50, but it is a matter of personal preference. The longer the page, the longer the page takes to load, but then there are fewer pages that have to be loaded to see all of the results.

11. The last option has to do with how the results are sorted when they are displayed. The default is by date—new files first. The alternative is by path/directory, which is often not very useful because if you've defined your search, most results will come from the same directory anyway. Besides, you don't have to know the path and directory to the file because when you want to download the file, you'll click a link that loads the entire path to the file for you. Leave this setting at the default *of by date—new files* first.

Your screen should look like the one in Figure 5-20. If it does, click the start search button. If you want to edit one of the entries, click in the field or on the drop-down and change it now. Don't click the Clear Form button unless you want to start over from scratch.

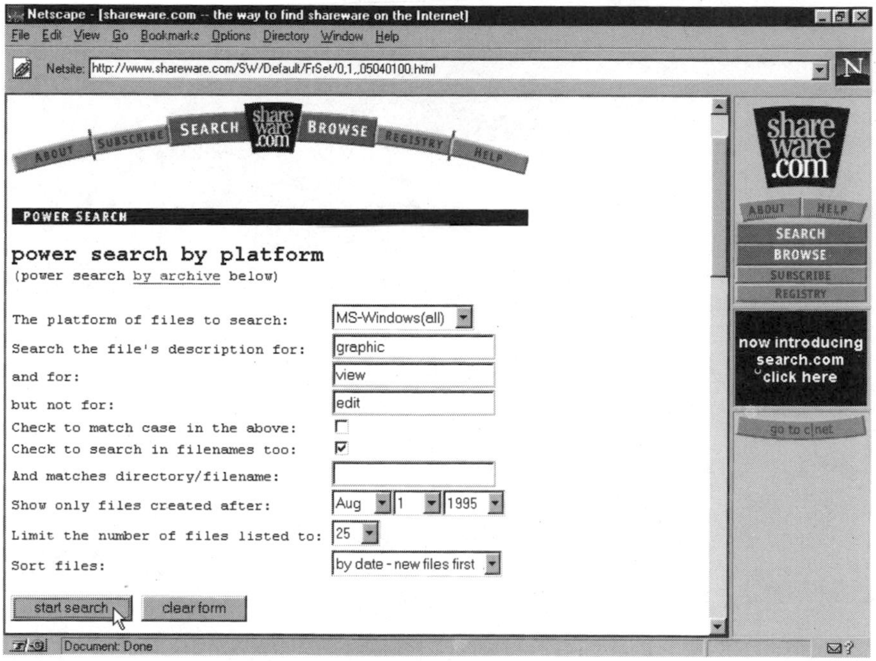

Figure 5-20: *A completed Power Search form.*

After you've clicked Start Search, your request will be sent to shareware.com. It will take a few moments to send, process, and receive the results. When the results page loads, it will look something like that shown in Figure 5-21. It will not be identical because you are doing the search on a different day than I did, and new software will have been added to the archives. Scroll down the list. You will see that the same file may be listed more than once. That may be because the FTP sites have several different versions of the file, some older than others. The other reason for repeats is that shareware.com has searched many different sites, and the program may be found on more than one site. New files added to a particular site are marked with a little graphic that says *new*. Scroll down to the bottom of the page to where it says search summary. The search summary tells you how long the search took, how many files are displayed on the current page, and that there are more files for you to view if you choose.

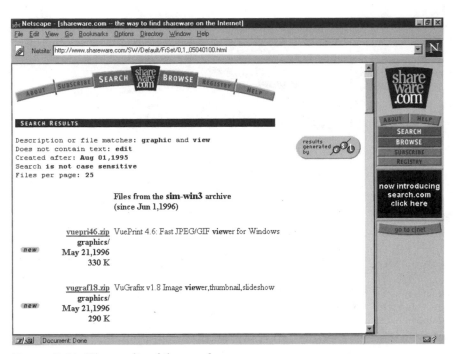

Figure 5-21: *The results of the search.*

12. Click the Next 25 link. A new page with 25 additional files will load. When I did the search, 72 files were found and displayed on three different pages. To move forward and back between the pages that have displayed, use the Previous 25 or the Next 25 links or use the Back or Forward button on Navigator's toolbar or the Back command on the shortcut menu.

Now that you've seen what's available, it's time to bring the file home. In the next section, you'll see how.

YOU'VE FOUND IT, NOW DOWNLOAD IT

In the search I did, both tp201.zip, a PhotoCD viewer, and polyv220.zip, an image viewer for Windows 95, look interesting. I only planned on downloading one file, but it looks like I'll have to download them both and see which one suits my needs the best.

That happens a lot when searching for files because the file descriptions are often very short or because you find a file that offers some feature you could use, but weren't looking for at the moment. Click the link to the file (the first file) you want to download. I've clicked tp201.zip link. Shareware.com loads a new page that lists places all over the world where the file can be downloaded. (See Figure 5-22.) This file is coming from the Simtel archive that has mirror (duplicate) sites all over. If the file were coming from a company or individual's site, there may not be as many choices of where to download from as when downloading from one of the big FTP sites like Simtel or Winsite. If you scroll down the page, you'll find estimated download times for the file, what the green square rating system rates (it rates how easy it is to connect to the download site) and advice on being persistent and patient. Popular FTP sites are often very busy, and you may not be able to connect if you are downloading during peak hours. The best time to download is around 3 AM EST and, and the worst time is usually between 1 PM and 3 PM EST.

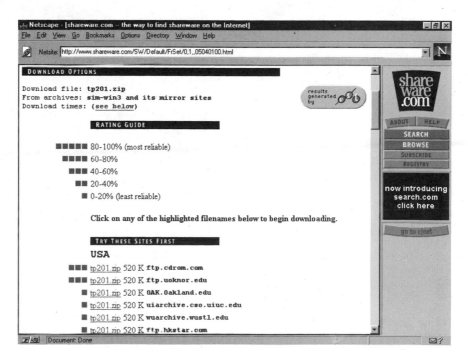

Figure 5-22: *This file can be downloaded from sites all over the world.*

Shareware.com requests that you use the site that is geographically closest to you, and that is a request that a good Internet citizen honors. The sites you download from and many of the sites that have to handle the data as it makes its way from them to you donate their time, money, and equipment to offer the service. When you make the trip short from the download site to your computer, you reduce Internet traffic and everybody's costs, making the Net a faster, cheaper place to be. If you absolutely must get a file, and the only way you can get it is from overseas, pick a part of the world that is asleep, somewhere where it is between midnight and 6 AM. Don't download from overseas sites during *their* prime time; the connection will be slow, and you will most likely be bumping a local user. The Earthtime plug-in for Netscape Navigator (see Chapter 9, "Taking a Look at Plug-ins") is handy to have around when you need to figure out what time it is in different parts of the world.

To download from one of the FTP sites requires no more than a few mouse clicks. Pick the site you want to download from and click the link.

What happens next depends on whether the site is busy or not. If the site is too busy to handle another connection, it will send a notice to you that explains that it is too busy and requests that you try again later. At this point you can try another site or wait a bit and try again. To clear the notice and go back to the download page, click the Back button on the toolbar or use the Back command on the right-click shortcut menu.

TIP

If you need to postpone the download for an indefinite period of time, right-click the link and choose Add Bookmark. With a bookmark to the file, you can go directly to the download site anytime in the future, without having to redo the search.

If the site isn't too busy, Navigator will log you into the server and start the downloading process. It displays the standard Windows Save As dialog box. Pick the place on your hard disk where you want the file to be stored and then click Save.

If you don't have a helper application or a plug-in defined for the kind of file you are downloading (EXE, ZIP, MOV, AVI, and so on), Navigator will display the Unknown File Type dialog box before displaying the Save As dialog box. The Unknown File Type dialog, shown in Figure 5-23, is always displayed when you try to save or display a file that isn't natively supported or for which you don't have a helper application or plug-in installed that knows how to handle the file. The files you download from FTP sites are usually file archives in the self-extracting EXE format or in the ZIP format that you want to save to disk. To save the file to your hard disk, click Save File on the Unknown File Type dialog box.

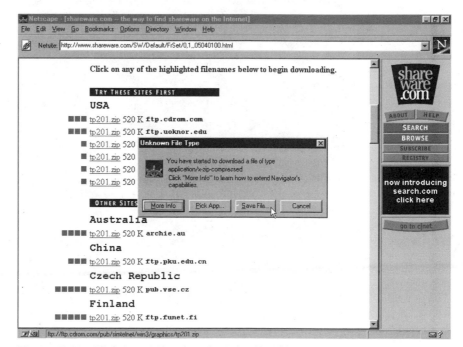

Figure 5-23: *Click Save File when downloading files.*

It is possible to set up WinZip or StuffIt Expander for Windows as a helper application to automatically handle EXE and ZIP files, but I don't recommend it. If you set up one of these as a helper for the archived files that you download, the archives will automatically be expanded when they have finished downloading. This takes up extra disk space, uses system resources, and interrupts your session. I find that it is much more convenient to expand, evaluate, and virus check downloaded software when I'm offline.

I do, however, highly recommend that you install the Norton Virus Scanner plug-in that comes in the Netscape Power Pack 2.0. When this plug-in is installed, you won't get the Unknown File Type dialog box because Norton steps in and handles the file download. When the file has downloaded, it scans the file for possible virus infection, notifies you of its findings, and asks you where to put the file archive. It is quite non-intrusive, and it automatically scans files for viruses, so I don't have to remember to do it.

You're done. If you want to go back and get a second file from the same search results page(s) as the first file that you downloaded, click the Back button and repeat the download process.

TIP

C | net's shareware.com offers its users a handy way to keep on top of new shareware/freeware/demo software as it becomes available. Every week they send out an e-mail edition of Shareware Dispatch, *a publication tailored to your software interests. Click the Subscribe button on shareware.com's image map at the top of the page and just fill out the forms. You'll find a weekly update in your e-mail inbox.*

Retrieving files from a search site is not the only way to receive files. If you know the address for an FTP site, you can enter the URL for the FTP site in Navigator's Location/Go to: field. As shown in Figure 5-24, what you usually see onscreen when the page for the FTP site loads are a few paragraphs telling you where you are, what the house rules are, and sometimes tips for using the site. This introductory information is followed by a list of links to various directories on the system. Click the links to make your way through the file structure of the server until you find the file you want. Many times, if you scroll down the page, you'll find a readme or index file that describes what the files and folders on that page are. These files are almost always text files that will display in Navigator's window if you click their link.

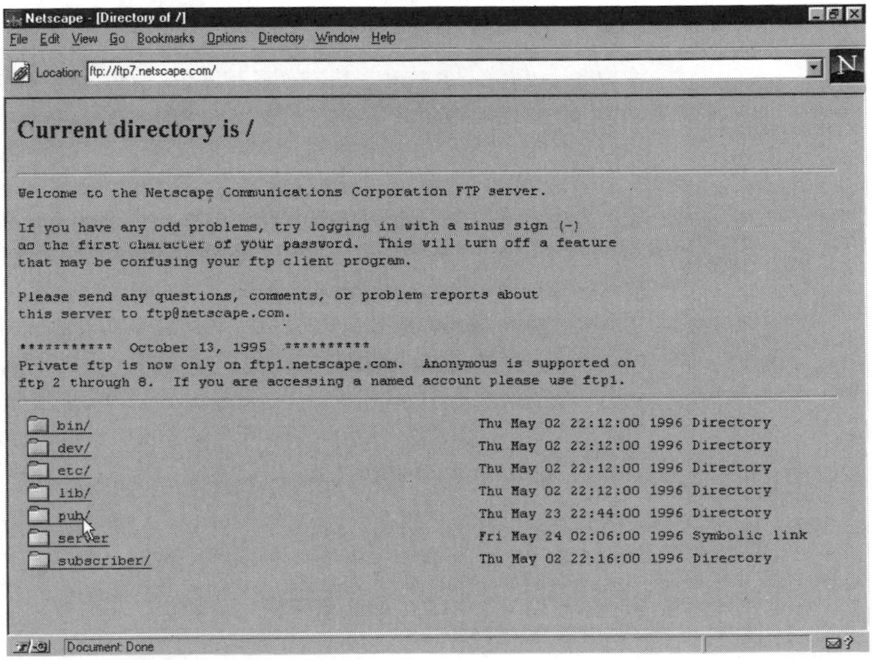

Figure 5-24: *Netscape's FTP site.*

TIP

When you enter an FTP site, it may not be obvious where you should start. In Figure 5-24, Netscape offers a number of directories, but no readme or index text to guide you as to where you are most likely to find files to download. On most public access servers, the files that are available to you all branch off from the /pub directory. So when in doubt, look for a pub directory.

When you find the file you want, click the link just as you did at c | net's shareware.com. The process of downloading is the same from this point on.

TIP

With all of the Navigator plug-ins that are available for viewing or playing diverse media, such as Acrobat or Envoy portable documents, sounds, graphics, business presentations, and movies, Web authors are packing more and more into their pages for your online viewing pleasure. But you may not always want to view these elements while online. You may, instead, want to download them for future reference or just to play them when you're not online and racking up connect charges. Navigator makes downloading these files easy if you know how—Shift+click the link or right-click the link and choose Save link as. *With either method the Save As dialog box will appear. Accept the filename suggested or rename the file, pick a location where the file should be saved, and click Save.*

LOGGING ONTO AN FTP SITE

Usually when you access a public FTP site, you use a URL that looks similar to this one: ftp://ftp.somesite.com/.

When you access a site using a standard URL such as this, it is said that you are logging on anonymously. Actually it is semi-anonymous, and Navigator handles the entire login process. The FTP site expects you to log in with a username of anonymous and to use your full e-mail address as your password. Navigator by default protects your privacy and uses only the part of your e-mail address that follows the @ sign and substitutes mozilla for the name part of your address when sending the password. For example, if your e-mail address is janed@isp.com, Navigator tells FTP sites that your address is mozilla@isp.com. However, if you *want* Navigator to use your full e-mail address as the password, go to the Options menu and choose Network Preferences. Click the Protocols tab and then check the Send E-Mail Address as Anonymous FTP Password check box.

Navigator's automatic login process works great when logging into anonymous FTP sites, but private FTP sites, such as an Intranet, usually issue you a username and a password that you must use to gain access. Under these circumstances, you need to supply the information. Some sites will query you for each when you access the page while others require you to add your username and password to the URL itself. The syntax for an FTP URL that contains both a username and a password is: ftp://username: password@ftp.someprivateftpsite.com/.

Some sites will allow you the option of putting only the username in the URL and then send a dialog box asking for the password. The URL in this case would be: ftp:// username@ftp.someprivateftpsite.com/.

WHAT DO I DO WITH THIS FILE NOW?

Unlike common file formats such as HTML, GIF images, and VRML virtual worlds on the Web, there are also many resources on the Internet whose file formats are proprietary or that have been encoded for transport across the Internet using a proprietary compression scheme. For example, many Windows graphics designers use CorelDRAW in its different versions (Corel Corporation currently sells and supports versions 3, 4, 5, and 6). Until Corel Corporation releases CorelDRAW for the Macintosh this year, the CDR extension will be meaningless to Macintosh users who surf the Net and even to Windows users who don't have DRAW or do have the program, but not the same version as that was used by the artist who posted the file on the Net.

Also, folks like to post large, proprietary user files on the Net and frequently rationalize that it's okay because they used an archiving software to compress the file to a fraction of its opened size. Macintosh, DOS/Windows, and UNIX users, however, all use different sorts of compression schemes for archiving files. The Mac uses either StuffIt or CompactPro, and Windows and DOS users usually use an implementation of PKZip (such as WinZip) but also use ARC, ARJ, and LZH compression utilities. UNIX users tend to use the Free Software Foundation's g-zip compression technology employed in a number of utilities today for UNIX systems when a file needs to be posted.

It's logical, then, that if you're going to search through the relics in the greatest pyramid in the universe, you're going to encounter some sealed passages, and a knowledge of different file formats and what can be used to decompress these files are your keys that unlock the doors.

Before we get into compression, let's take a look at common file types you might encounter on the Web besides HTML, GIF, and JPEG types that Navigator can decode and display with no outside assistance. In the following section, you'll learn about file formats created on other systems. Surprisingly, you might already own a utility that will let you play foreign media. If you've stumbled across a Macintosh site, for example, that seems to have really cool images and sounds for downloading, don't be put off because you think that the media is proprietary. The Macintosh OS doesn't use file extensions, but most Web servers *insist* upon file extensions. Understanding and using file extensions is new to Mac users and even many Windows users are bound to learn what kind(s) of applications are associated with some of the more unusual file types. Let's explore your options in this and other examples of how you can get the most from Web content that was created and posted using a machine other than Windows.

AU, AIF & WAV

AU is the file extension given to a sound file typically created on a Sun workstation but is also the native sound file format for other UNIX-based workstations. The AU format is the most common of sound file formats on the Web, and Navigator's LiveAudio feature will automatically play these files if you have a sound card installed on your system; no decoding software is needed when you hit this type of file on a Web page.

AIF is short for the Macintosh term aiff, a type of sound file native to the Macintosh operating system. As mentioned earlier in this chapter, the Macintosh does not use file extensions, so a file named, for example, WOWEE.AIF means that the individual that posted it has edited the filename to make it easy for Windows 3.1 users to use the file. There is limited support in Windows 3.1x and

Windows 95 for playing a native Macintosh sound file. Navigator's LiveAudio will play the sound, but your best bet for saving such a file to a format that can be played in different Windows applications is to convert the sound to Windows WAV format with a utility such as Chris Craig's GoldWave (found on the Companion CD-ROM).

It should be noted here that WAV files are supported through Navigator, and you can send or post a WAV file through the Web, but UNIX Navigator users won't be able to decode and play the sound without a third-party helper application. LiveAudio is currently available only in the Windows and Macintosh versions of Navigator. Additionally, if you don't have a sound card installed, LiveAudio will not play any type of sound in Navigator. In other words, your system may be sound-capable due to the use of PC Speaker for Windows, an utility that shipped with programs such as Icon HearIt for Windows 3.1x, but this software sound driver will not play sounds on the Web. Windows 95 and Navigator use a different compression for sounds than Windows 3.1x used, and software-only drivers are not a solution for the playback of Web sounds of any format.

DOC FILES

Generally, but not always, the *.DOC extension at the end of a file signifies that the file content was authored in a version of MS Word. However, although unusual in 1996, the DOC extension was sometimes used by DOS program creators and others to signify that the file is a text file—plain ASCII text—and WinWord has nothing to do with the file. An example of this might be README.DOC. If such a file looks funny when opened in Word, this file contains plain, unformatted text, and you'd be best off renaming the file README.TXT.

If you plan to post a WinWord document, you might want to also support alternative versions of the document, such as a plain text file or even an Adobe Acrobat PDF file for non-Word users. If you want to access a WinWord DOC file, but don't own Word, the free INSO WordViewer plug-in for Navigator will allow you to open the document, read it, and even copy sections out of it as unformatted text. The WordViewer plug-in is part of Netscape PowerPack or can be downloaded from Inso (http://www.inso.com/). Alternatively, WordPad, the mini-word processor that ships with Windows 95 can open a DOC file, and Windows 3.1x surfers can use Windows Write utility for viewing documents created in WinWord 95 and previous versions of Word.

COPING WITH "GARBAGE TEXT"

Windows word processors, such as Word and WordPerfect, as well as many of the common text and word editors on the Macintosh, use hidden formatting code to specify typesetter's quotes, for example, and other extended characters for a more polished looking document. Unfortunately, these hidden codes for tabs, indents, and other formatting introduce gibberish to legible text when a text editor, mail reader, and occasionally Navigator try to display the content of the message.

In Figure 5-25, you can see a story that was saved as a WinWord 95 document and what it looks like when Windows 3.1 Write utility tries to open it.

One workaround to removing the character "garbage" from a document saved using formatting codes is to perform a search and replace for the offending characters. In Figure 5-25, you can see that I've chosen to replace the Æ character with a single quote mark throughout the document. It's really not hard to guess what the misplaced character is, and the Windows Character Map utility can tell you what the correct code is for any character in a document.

Alternatively, utilities such as TextPad (found on the Companion CD-ROM) can strip garbage characters out of a document and can save files in a plain text format for DOS, Macintosh, or UNIX machines.

CD-ROM

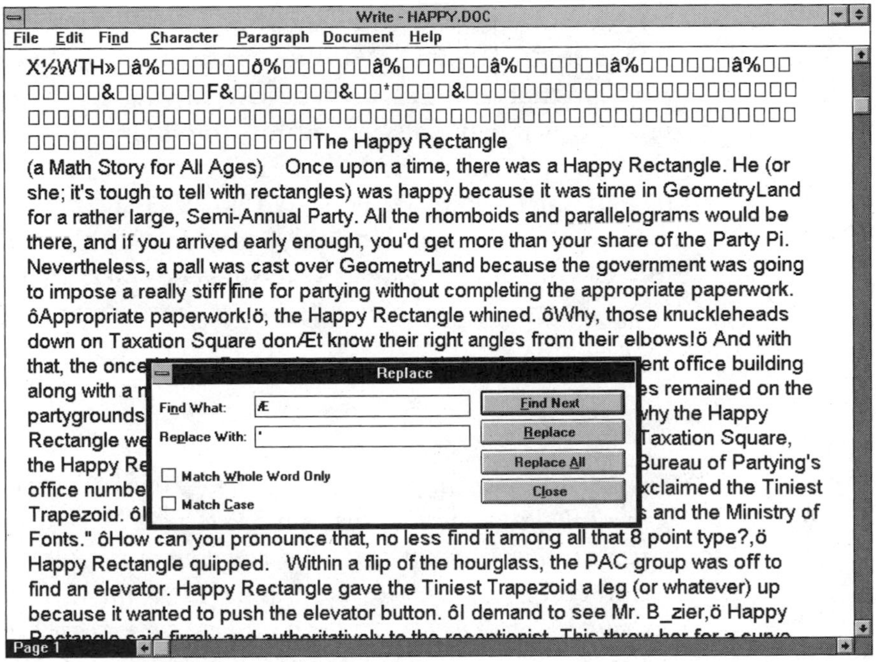

Figure 5-25: *Text that contains formatting codes can make it impossible to read in an ASCII text editor utility.*

EXE FILES

Software manufacturers, including Netscape, will bundle the setup routine as well as the component files to a program within a file which ends with EXE. If you're surfing the Net and find an EXE file, do *not* assume that this is simply a program's executable file that can be run directly from a location on your hard disk.

For example, the ASAP WordPower trial program is distributed as ASAPZIP.EXE. It would be a big mistake to simply double-click this file's icon after downloading, without making sure it was isolated in its own folder first. Why? Because when you double-click this file, it extracts 11 files that are placed in whatever directory the ASAPZIP.EXE happens to be in. If you extracted it in an already crowded directory it would be difficult to know which files belonged to WordPower. WordPower is not, by any means, the only program that does this, so to be safe, always treat files EXE file extensions as if they will decompress into many component files—put them into their own folder or directory. It's a good idea to create a folder on your hard disk (DOWNLOAD is a good name) and create a folder nested within the download folder for each EXE file you download. In this way, you can keep track of the component setup files and easily delete "leftover" components after you've run the EXE file.

TIP

If you are uploading or sending a archive of files as an e-mail attachment that contains files that can also be used by UNIX and Macintosh users (graphics, sounds, movies, common word-processing files, etc.), don't save the archive of files as a self-extracting EXE file. If you do, they won't be able to open the file. If you save it as a ZIP format file, they will be able to open the file because an EXE file actually contains a small DOS-based program that runs to extract the file, and this program won't run on their computers. When you send the file in a plain ZIP format file, a UNIX or Macintosh user can use a program written for their kind of computer that can open files that have been archived using ZIP.

MPEG

The Motion Picture Experts Group (MPEG) has designed a file format and a compression method that makes it possible to show large size, full motion videos, much larger and better in quality than Video for Windows (AVI) files on your computer.

Unfortunately, at the time of this writing, MPEG movies are extremely processor-intensive to playback; don't try to play the file on a 486 machine unless you have a video card that supports MPEG. Navigator does not natively support this media type, and you'll need a plug-in to play the file within Navigator Browser. The good news is that there are a number of third-party plug-ins available to play MPEG movies. Check out the Netscape Plug-ins section of the Totally Hot Bookmarks List for information and links to MPEG-capable Navigator Plug-ins on the Companion CD-ROM.

The best suggestion I can offer at present concerning MPEG files for most users is that if a site offers a variety of file formats for downloading a video, choose AVI over MPEG. This will enable Win3.1x, Windows 95, and Win NT to view such a file with native operating system support.

PS FILES

The PS extension to a file indicates that it's actually printer instructions intended to be sent to a PostScript printer. UNIX users, the first true "Netizens" needed a foolproof way to send formatted text long before Windows and Macintosh users got into surfing. Years ago, there was only one way to view the contents of a PostScript file: you could print the contents to a PostScript printer.

Today, if you encounter a PostScript file on the Web, it'll most likely be a research paper, and you can still print the file to a PostScript printer; however, there are two quicker options at your disposal. GhostScript is a freeware, cross-platform utility that "writes" the PostScript file to screen, thus eliminating the need to generate hard copy. The Totally Hot Bookmarks List on the Companion CD-ROM contains links to a site where you can download the latest copy of GhostScript and a Window's GhostScript viewer.

Adobe Acrobat Distiller can also parse the PostScript file to Acrobat PDF format which can be read online or printed. The Envoy Tumbleweed Publisher can convert PS files into a format that the Envoy reader plug-in (Windows or Macintosh) can use. Like Adobe's Acrobat, Envoy documents can be read on- or offline, and their contents can be printed. Either of these two options is a good choice because Acrobat and Envoy documents, like PostScript, are platform-independent, and a user on any computer platform can access the document with the proper plug-in or reader program. Additionally, you can print an Acrobat and Envoy document to either a PostScript or a non-PostScript printer.

PNG FILES

The Portable Network Graphic (PNG) format is picking up some momentum as a bitmap graphics format used on the Web. Created to circumvent legal issues around licensing CompuServe's GIF format, PNG is a royalty-free, cross-platform, bitmap format capable of storing 32 bits of information (soon, applications will be able to include masking information in PNG images) and containing a native compression scheme for quick downloads. At present, only a handful of graphics applications support the creation of a PNG graphic. Fortunately, Paint Shop Pro has this capability, and a copy of this program is on the Companion CD-ROM.

Navigator support of the PNG graphics format is *not* native however, and users must have the FIGleaf Inline plug-in installed in Navigator to view a PNG image or use Paint Shop Pro as a helper application. The image quality of PNG images is typically much better than GIFs and equal to that of Progressive JPEGs. Progressive JPEGs, however, are typically smaller in file size, and they are natively supported by Navigator (version 2 and later).

PDF FILES

As mentioned in the previous section, Adobe Acrobat documents (documents that bear the PDF extension) are platform-independent creations and only require that you have either the Acrobat Reader standalone program or the Acrobat plug-in for Navigator to view, print, and copy from if the document's author specified this privilege.

Many sites, including the U.S. government, are getting into "PDFing" documents; I submitted my 1040 form this year using an electronic, PDF form downloaded from the Internal Revenue Service's Web site (which is actually more light-hearted than you might imagine if you have a chance to surf there!).

The Acrobat plug-in is free to download from Adobe's Web site (http://www.adobe.com). You'll also find it on the Companion CD-ROM.

EVY FILES

The Envoy portable document format uses the file extension EVY. Envoy is a technology separate from Adobe Acrobat's document format—the Envoy Run-Time Player will not read Acrobat documents, and vice versa. Envoy documents can be created as standalone documents which require the browser utility to decode, or an Envoy document can also be encapsulated to include the browser within an EXE file. You can download the Envoy plug-in from http://www.twcorp.com or install it from the Companion CD-ROM.

TIFF FILES

The Tagged Image File Format (TIFF) is commonly used in desktop publishing for high-quality photographic images; its use by Macintosh designers has been popular for many years, and only recently have Windows applications supported this high-fidelity color image type.

Oddly, there is no native Windows support for TIFF images; PC Paintbrush accepts only BMP and Device Independent Bitmap (DIB) images. Generally, you will not find a TIFF image on a Web site in its uncompressed state—TIFF images are typically three times larger than an equivalent GIF image and more than ten times the size of an equivalent JPEG image.

If by chance you come across a TIFF image and would like to view it, the FIGleaf Inline plug-in and the TMS ViewDirector Imaging plug-in for Navigator (found on the Companion-CD-ROM) will display TIFF files. If you haven't installed either of these plug-ins, Word for Windows and Windows 95's WordPad will view the file if you insert it into a Word document. Paint Shop Pro, the paint program on the Companion CD-ROM will view the file, and you can edit it. Naturally, the high-end image editors such as Photoshop and Fractal Design Paint will view and allow you to modify an image whose file extension is TIF.

The preceding sections are intended to familiarize you with different, common file formats that users might post on the Web. This list is not definitive and complete because virtually any computer file that can be created in any application can be posted. However, it is not obvious to even many experienced surfers that archived files populate the Web in forms *other* than the familiar PKZip format.

ACCESSING DIFFERENT FILE COMPRESSION SCHEMES

The compression utility originally created by Phil Katz, PKZip (or *Zip* files), has been with the Intel-based computing community from the early days of DOS. Since the advent of Windows computing, Niko Mak's WinZip has all but replaced the need to go to a DOS command prompt to uncompress a zipped file you received from a colleague or from the Web.

However, different operating systems have come to need—and develop—compression schemes, and independent invention has given way to no fewer than eight different commonly used archiving formats for documents distributed across the Internet. In the following sections, we'll identify a compression type, suggest whether the contents of a compressed file are worth the effort to decode, and what utility would make it easiest to uncompress the file's information.

THE DIFFERENCE BETWEEN COMPRESSION & ARCHIVING

In our discussions in this chapter, we use the term "compression" almost synonymously with "archiving," but the processes and results can be different. For example, both the GIF and JPEG formats for bitmap images are compressed, but they are not archived.

COMPRESSION

Compression, as it relates to image files, usually means that the image information is in a highly efficient, economical format when stored on your hard disk. When a GIF or JPEG image is loaded into a browser or other application capable of reading either type of file, the image information is decompressed on the fly and loaded into system memory at sometimes a significantly larger size than is stored on disk. A JPEG image (an image with the JPG extension) can expand into memory at sizes up to 100 times the size of the stored file although this is a seldom used compression ratio, and JPEG images such as this are generally of low quality (you'd question the acsthetics and common sense of the file's creator).

Additionally, TIFF and Targa (TGA) images are sometimes compressed using the LZW format of on the fly compression. Depending upon the image content, LZW compression can reduce file size to about a third of the original when stored on hard disk or sent across the Net.

ARCHIVING

Archiving is an entirely different way to economically store any type of information: text files, spreadsheets . . . any type of computer data can be archived for downloading or copying purposes. Archives can contain one or more files. When a file is an archive, you generally have no way of knowing what the file contents of the archive are without extracting a copy of the information or browsing the archive in a utility such as WinZip. To make use of archived information, you need to "unpack" a copy of the file through the appropriate decompression utility. Files that are archived are usually also compressed, but you cannot access them on the fly as with compressed image or video files. Some archive formats such as Tape Archive Retrieval (TAR) do not offer file compression, rather they hold a collection of files that need to be distributed with each other.

DECOMPRESSING FOREIGN FILE FORMATS

Many of the formats for files described in the previous section are cross-platform; TIFF, PDF, and many other content-rich documents can be shared between Windows, UNIX, and Macintosh users. However, due to the reality that the smaller the file, the easier it is to be accessed on the Web, not one but many different archiving utilities have been created to serve different operating platforms. Windows and DOS users have adopted Phil Katz's Zip archiving method to the point where it has become nearly ubiquitous in the Intel-based world. But what happens when you encounter a file with a Z or GZ extension, or multiple file extensions such as SIT.HQX?

The following sections describe different file compression types used on the Macintosh and UNIX-based systems, what you do with such a file, and the best way to "pry the lid off the can."

HQX, BIN, SEA & SIT FILES

Unlike a straightforward archiving utility, a different number of processes need to be used on a Macintosh file to ensure that a file, or several contained within an archive, can travel intact from Macintosh user to Macintosh user. SEA and SIT are file extensions that refer to file archives that were created with the Macintosh file archiving program StuffIt. HQX is a file extension associated with BinHex encoding, and BIN is the file extension associated with MacBinary encoding. The BinHex process is commonly used in the Macintosh world as a special kind of ASCII-based "wrapper" that preserves the integrity of the Macintosh file. MacBinary is also an encoding scheme designed to protect Macintosh files, but it is less commonly used.

To back up a little, virtually every file that Macintosh users create and work with is a two-some: there's a content file—called a data fork, and a resource fork, which is a simple pointer file that indicates to the operating system which program was used in the file's creation and which application should be used to open the file. Resource forks that are not protected by the BinHex or MacBinary process become corrupted when transported via Internet protocols. Occasionally, you might find a folder named resource.frk on your system if you worked on a network in a mixed computing environment, and it's okay to delete these files because Windows only uses the information in the data fork of a file.

A BinHexed or MacBinary encoded Macintosh file is a single file that contains both the data and the resource forks. On the Internet, a BinHexed or MacBinary file usually contains an archived file in the SEA or SIT format, but a single file can be BinHexed or MacBinary encoded as well. Making these files useful requires a two-step process—decoding the BinHex or MacBinary and then uncompressing the file archive.

Therefore, in your Internet travels, if you come across a file that has the extension SEA, SIT, HQX, BIN, or a combination of these extensions, they were most probably posted by a Macintosh user. If you think the file contains information you can use—a graphic, sound, movie or other cross-platform file—go ahead and download the file. If you have a copy of StuffIt Expander for Windows (you do—it's on the Companion CD-ROM) you can extract the file on your Windows computer. If you'd like to see how you can use a Macintosh file, install StuffIt Expander for Windows and follow along with us through the following steps:

1. In the Chap05 folder of the Companion CD-ROM is a BinHexed, Stuffed file called Mac.sit.hqx. Inside the file is a JPEG graphics file called IMAGE.JPEG. Copy Mac.sit.hqx to a unique folder on your hard disk (DOWNLOAD is a good folder name) and then launch StuffIt Expander for Windows. Win 3.1x users cannot see the long filename of this file, but this is okay; StuffIt Expander doesn't look at file names. Instead, it looks inside the file to see how the contents have been compressed, so don't worry that the file-name on the Companion CD-ROM appears truncated. Alternatively in this example, you can use any BinHex file you've downloaded from the Net; we've provided you with a file here whose contents can be accessed by Navigator.

2. Launch StuffIt Expander, then drag and drop the Mac.sit.hqx folder onto the StuffIt workspace, as shown in Figure 5-26.

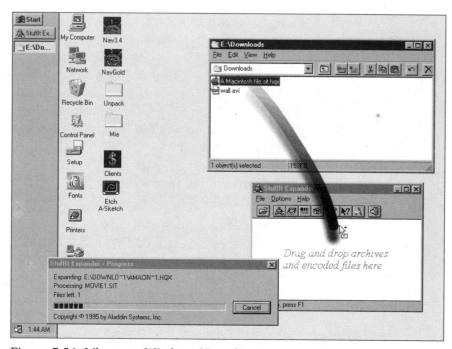

Figure 5-26: *Like many Windows 95 applications—and Macintosh applications—StuffIt Expander for Windows offers drag-and-drop support.*

3. Immediately, StuffIt Expander removes the HQX layer and then uncompresses the JPEG contents to produce IMAGE.JPG in the same location as the HQX file on your hard disk. If you'd like the HQX and SIT archives to be automatically deleted from your hard disk upon uncompression, you can choose this from the Options menu in StuffIt. This might not be such a good idea—if a file fails to uncompress, you've lost the compressed original.

4. Because the file is in the JPEG format, you can view this image by simply dragging the file into Navigator's Browser, as shown in Figure 5-27. In actuality, you might not find too many BinHexed and Stuffed JPEG files on the Web. The JPEG format contains intrinsic compression, but a Macintosh user might include a JPEG file in a collection of graphics files or if he or she wanted to make it easy for other Macintosh users to open the file.

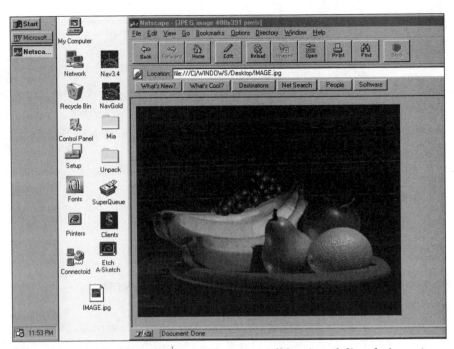

Figure 5-27: *GIF, and JPEG format images can all be viewed directly in Navigator's Browser.*

SIT & SEA FILES

As mentioned in the HQX section, the contents of a Macintosh archived file contains two layers; once you've peeled away the BinHex transportation scheme, there's still the act of decompressing the file to be performed. Generally, a Stuffed, BinHexed file will appear as something like MYFILE.SIT.HQX on a server, and fortunately, StuffIt Expander for Windows takes care of unpacking both layers.

A SIT extension indicates that Aladdin Systems technology was used for the archiving of one or more files, and so does the SEA extension. Usually, there will be nothing of interest to Windows users within a SEA (*self-extracting archive*) file—this self-extraction scheme is generally used to compress program files which cannot be run on a Windows or DOS machine. But once in a while you do run across a SEA file that does contain some kind of cross-platform file you can use. StuffIt Expander for Windows can open the SEA file for you.

STUFFIT EXPANDER FOR WINDOWS

Aladdin Systems is to be commended on many counts for bringing a binary-compatible version of their Macintosh compression technology to Windows users. StuffIt Expander for Windows will uncompress a BinHex encoded file and the SIT file beneath the HQX shell, in addition to unscrambling an SEA or self-extracting file.

Because Windows and the Macintosh use different end of line codes (Windows ASCII text uses a carriage return code in addition to an end of line code), you might run into a "garbage character" dilemma when trying to read Macintosh text messages compressed within an archive. This is not the archiving utility's fault, and StuffIt Expander will automatically remove "garbage characters" from text messages as it expands a Macintosh file if you specify this option on the Options tab.

In addition to Aladdin's own StuffIt compression, StuffIt Expander for Windows also handles two different types of UNIX encoding and the ARC and ZIP format commonly used for Windows compressed files.

UU & UUE FILES

The UNIX to UNIX encoding/compression file format allows files sent from UNIX machines to travel safely across the Internet, and occasionally you'll want to access such an encoded file for non-platform specific data. It is not uncommon for uuencoded files to be split into parts so that each part is short enough to be contained in one electronic mail message, in cases the recipient's mail reader places a limit on the maximum size of a mail message. StuffIt Expander for Windows can be used to "stitch" UU and UUE encoded files into the original file, but the freeware version of StuffIt for Windows will only uncompress the first file it finds in a multi-file UU file archive.

EssCode for Windows (see the Totally Hot Bookmarks List on the Companion CD-ROM) can uuencoded a file that has been split into multiple files. Additionally it can uuencode files and encode and decode single and multipart MIME files. This utility is invaluable for any Internet user, particularly if you want to access the multipart graphic files typically found in the alt.binary newsgroups.

GZIP, TAR & Z FILES

GZip (short for GNU zip) is a utility commonly used with UNIX systems to compress files. GZip files—files that end in .GZ— always contain a single file inside. GZip compression is based around the PKZip compression algorithm.

Files ending with a .Z extension have been compressed with a proprietary UNIX compression scheme. Like GZip files, they only contain one file.

TAR (Tape Archive Retrieval) files don't have to be stored on tape; this is an old format used on UNIX machines to group files into one file. Files that have been combined into a TAR archive have *not* been compressed because the format does not provide for compression. It is fairly common to find older files on the Web in this format.

StuffIt Expander for Windows can open but not create GZip files. WinZip can open GZip TAR and Z file formats along with several other GZip or Z based variants. It can't, however, create any of these kinds of files.

WinZip can open many kinds of file formats in addition to the UNIX formats discussed—ARC, ARJ, LZH, and files with the ZIP extension. In the next section, you'll see what you've been missing if you're still unzipping files using a DOS command line.

WinZip: The Graphical Way to Encode & Decode Files

File compression is not a straightforward concept; many users do not realize that archived files aren't touched when a copy of them is uncompressed, and this sometimes leads to an overly congested hard disk. If you've already unzipped (unarchived) a file, and whatever is inside works successfully, you can either move the archive to long-term storage media such as an Iomega Zip disk, a floppy disk, or a tape backup, or you can delete the archive file as it will serve no future purpose.

Nico Mak's WinZip is a most user-friendly implementation of the Zip algorithm originally marketed by PKWare. A copy of WinZip is on the Companion CD-ROM, and if you'd like to install it now, we'll review some procedures and a few of its features shortly. Part of the beauty of WinZip is that an absolute novice can unarchive anything with the ZIP, ARJ, or other archive formats that uses DOS/Windows compression schemes as well as several UNIX formats such as GZip and TAR.

New to version 6.1 of WinZip (Nico Mak updates his program frequently, so this version might already be behind!) is the WinZip Wizard, a familiar step-by-step series of dialog boxes that will assist any user who has installed this archiving utility in managing, compressing, and decompressing files. In Figure 5-28, I've already clicked the Wizard button in WinZip, and the menus take me through where WinZip has detected ZIP archived files on my hard disk. In addition to being able to track down a file after you've downloaded it, the WinZip Wizard can help alert more advanced users that there are Zipped files in places they never check—and delete them if they're not important.

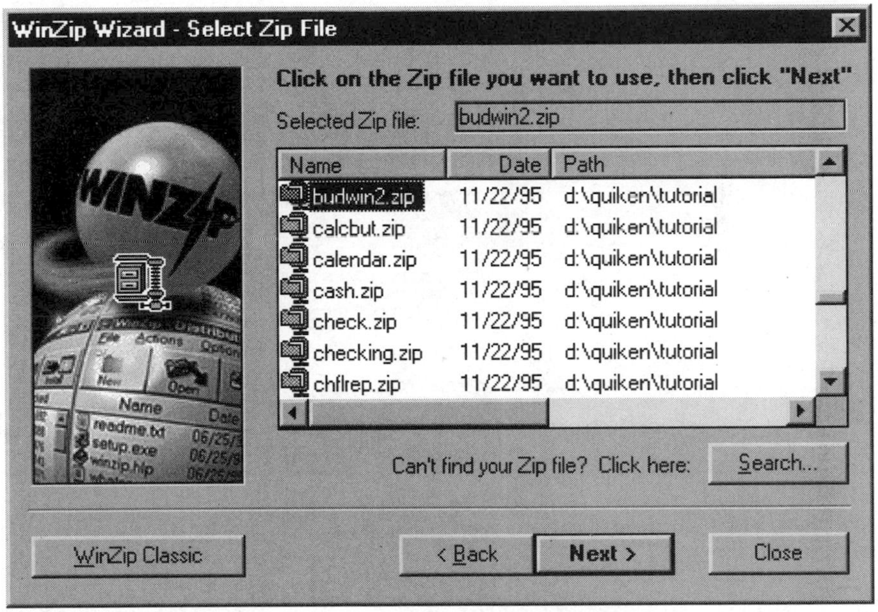

Figure 5-28: *The WinZip Wizard can guide you through locating and decompressing a Zipped file, even if you've never used the program before.*

Most users who have discovered WinZip leave the program in its "classic" configuration, which is the default, as shown in Figure 5-29. As you can see, archived Zip files can be examined without uncompressing, they can be scanned for viruses if you own a virus checking program from vendors such as McAfee Associates (http://www.mcafee.com) or Symantec (http://www.symantec.com), and you can uncompress one or all files in a Zip file to an existing folder (directory), or you can create a new folder on the fly through WinZip's interface.

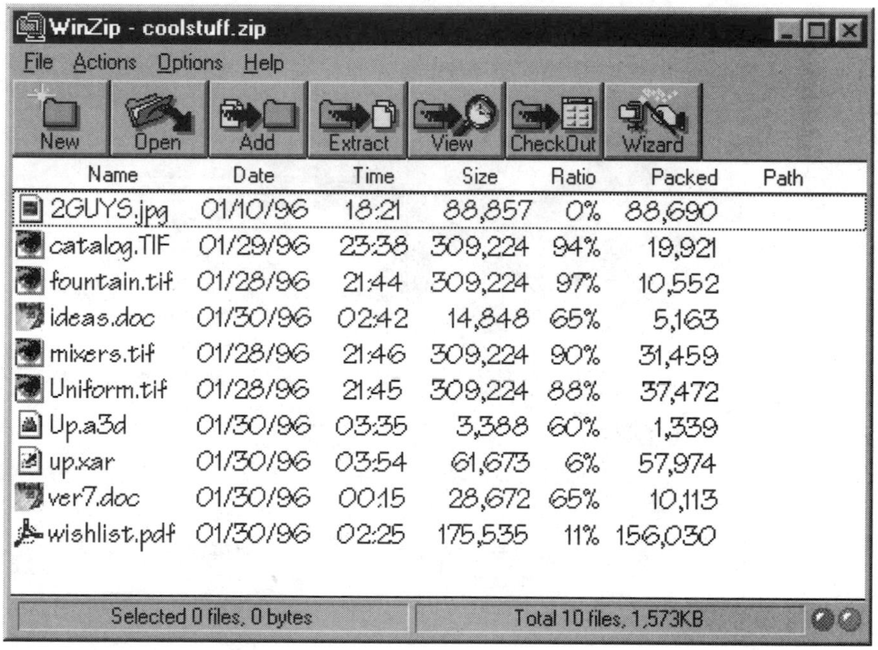

Name	Date	Time	Size	Ratio	Packed	Path
2GUYS.jpg	01/10/96	18:21	88,857	0%	88,690	
catalog.TIF	01/29/96	23:38	309,224	94%	19,921	
fountain.tif	01/28/96	21:44	309,224	97%	10,552	
ideas.doc	01/30/96	02:42	14,848	65%	5,163	
mixers.tif	01/28/96	21:46	309,224	90%	31,459	
Uniform.tif	01/28/96	21:45	309,224	88%	37,472	
Up.a3d	01/30/96	03:35	3,388	60%	1,339	
up.xar	01/30/96	03:54	61,673	6%	57,974	
ver7.doc	01/30/96	00:15	28,672	65%	10,113	
wishlist.pdf	01/30/96	02:25	175,535	11%	156,030	

WinZip - coolstuff.zip

File Actions Options Help

New Open Add Extract View CheckOut Wizard

Selected 0 files, 0 bytes   Total 10 files, 1,573KB

Figure 5-29: *Uncompressing and managing Zip files is no harder than organizing your own hard disk with WinZip.*

Users of Windows 95 will appreciate how tightly WinZip integrates with the operating system. By default, WinZip's setup will put an Add to Zip command on the shortcut menu when you're on Windows 95's desktop or in a folder window. You simply right-click one or more files, choose Add to Zip, and WinZip launches to offer you options for your file compressing session. You can also drag a file into a Zip icon on the desktop or into a folder window to add the file to an existing archive. This feature is handy when you want to gather together additional files to attach to Internet mail.

SENDING FILES BY FTP

Both the Netscape Navigator and the Navigator Gold programs also have the capability to *send* files to FTP sites. Navigator makes it as easy to send a file as it is to receive a file. The only catch is that you can only send a file by FTP if you have upload privileges to that site. Not all FTP sites are set up to accept uploads. If your organization has an Intranet, if you have a home page that needs maintaining, or if you need to submit a problem file to a tech support site, Navigator's ability to upload will come in handy.

> **TIP**
>
> *Most of the shareware FTP sites have a special FTP directory where files can be uploaded. But they usually also have a set of procedures and standards you must meet for them to accept your file. Before uploading to a public FTP site, look around or send e-mail to the maintainers of the site and ask them how and where they prefer to receive files.*

Navigator Gold's One Button Publishing is particularly useful for automating the process of sending the many files that make up a typical Web site. First, let's take a look at how Navigator Gold can make maintaining your Web site a breeze. If you don't have a Web site to maintain or don't have Navigator Gold, don't skip over these sections because much of the actual uploading process is the same when you use Navigator. We will cover Navigator's methods later in the chapter.

ONE BUTTON PUBLISHING

If you have a home page or contribute pages to your organization's Internet or Intranet site, Navigator Gold's Editor features an easy way to transfer your pages and their contents from your computer to the Internet/Intranet server. Navigator Gold can not only send your HTML and related files, but its One Button Publishing can automatically maintain the relative links you've established.

Some of the tricks to making Gold's One Button Publishing work for you is to create a directory or folder structure that mimics that found on the server and then always use relative links to describe where the files are located. When relative names are used, it won't matter if you are storing your files on D drive but on the server they are stored on a different physical drive than the second drive in the computer. When your files are transferred from your computer to the server, the links will work and not be broken because they refer to a path that doesn't exist on the server.

The very best way to ensure that links aren't broken is to store all files in the same folder. This makes creating the relative links easier and less prone to error, and it also makes transferring them easier when they are in one place. Gold has the capability of uploading all files or selected files that are in a single directory.

If your site works beautifully on your local system but doesn't work properly after being transferred to the server, check that the case of the filename and extension is the same for the file and in the document. If the actual file name is logo.GIF, for example, you cannot reference it as logo.gif. Unlike Windows, many servers will report an error because they are case sensitive and don't see logo.GIF and Logo.gif as being the same thing.

By default, Navigator Gold automatically creates relative links when you create links in Gold's editor if you've left the Links and Images check boxes checked in the Editor Preference's Publish tab. But sometimes you may have to edit an existing document that uses absolute links, or you may be entering HTML code using a text editor. In the sections that follow, you'll see how to write relative links and how to write absolute links. Note that forward slashes / are used in link paths and not the backslash \ that is used in DOS file paths.

SYNTAX FOR RELATIVE LINKS

A relative link is one whose path is described as being relative to the current directory of the document you're working on. In this example we'll assume that the document in which the links are made is on C drive in a folder called COMPANY. Its DOS path would be C:\MIDWEST\WEB\COMPANY\INDEX.HTML. A relative link to a file called sales.htm that is stored the same folder (COMPANY) would only contain the file name and would look like this:

```
<a href="sales.htm"></a>
```

A relative link to a file that is located in a subfolder (down the directory tree) of COMPANY (C:\COMPANY\GRAPHICS\LOGO\ BIGLOGO.GIF) would look like this:

```
<a href="graphics/logo/biglogl.gif"></a>
```

A relative link to a file whose DOS path is two folders up from COMPANY in the MIDWEST folder would be:

```
<a href="../../regions.htm"></a>
```

or

```
<a href="../MIDWEST/regions.htm"></a>
```

A relative link to C:\SUPPORT\PROGRAMS\RELEASENOTES\LEARN.HTML would be:

```
<a href="../support/programs/releasenotes/learn.html"></a>
```

SYNTAX FOR ABSOLUTE LINKS

Absolute links are best used to refer to documents that are located on a computer other than your own computer such as one on Netscape's site or a server on your organization's network. But an absolute link can be created to location on your hard disk. An absolute link gives the complete URL or, if referring to a file on your organization's network system, it gives the complete path including the drive letter. For example:

```
<a href="file:///F|/shareware.htm"></a>
```

and

```
<a href="http://home.netscape.com"></a>
```

are both absolute links. The first is absolute link to a document on a drive other than the drive where the document containing the link is stored. The second example is an absolute link to Netscape's home page which also is on a server other than the one on which the HTML document is located that contains the link.

USING ONE BUTTON PUBLISHING

Use Gold's One Button Publishing to send your Web pages to the server after you've finished composing and testing them. Gold can send all or some of the files in a single folder. If you've saved all your pages and their related files to a single folder, you can send a whole site all at once. If you have a more complicated site, one that uses multiple directories for example, you will have to send the contents of each folder separately. Gold's One Button Publishing requires that at least one HTML file is sent in each batch. If you have a folder of just graphics or multimedia objects that do not have an HTML document that goes in that folder, you could create a "dummy" HTML document in Gold's editor (one that contains only a single word or space), save it in the same folder as the graphics, and then use the dummy file to start up the One Button Publishing feature. Alternatively, you could use the regular, drag and drop FTP method discussed later in the chapter to send multiple files using either Navigator or Navigator Gold:

1. With the HTML document that you want to upload open in Navigator Gold's Editor and an Internet connection established, click the Publish button on the end of the toolbar. In Figure 5-30, it's the one with the lightning bolt going through a page.

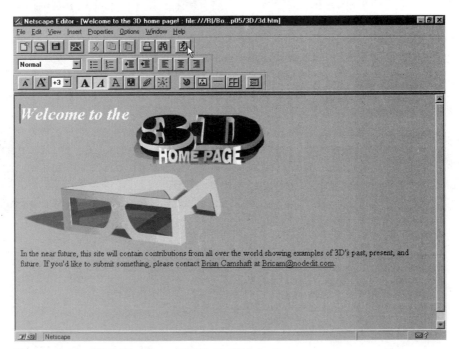

Figure 5-30: *Click Navigator Gold's Publish button.*

2. The Publish Files options box appears as shown in Figure 5-31. Choose any additional files you want to upload by clicking one of the Include files radio buttons. Click the *Images in the document* to send all graphic files referenced by the HTML document you are sending.

   Click on the *All files in document's folder* to activate the scrolling list below where you get a chance to *exclude* files that are in the directory. By default, all files in the folder where the current HTML document is saved are selected. Scroll through the list and click (to deselect) any files you don't want to upload. You can send *any* kind of file—HTML, text, graphic, multimedia, word processing document, and so on. The files you send don't have to be related to the page currently in the Editor's window; they just have to be going to the same place on the remote site.

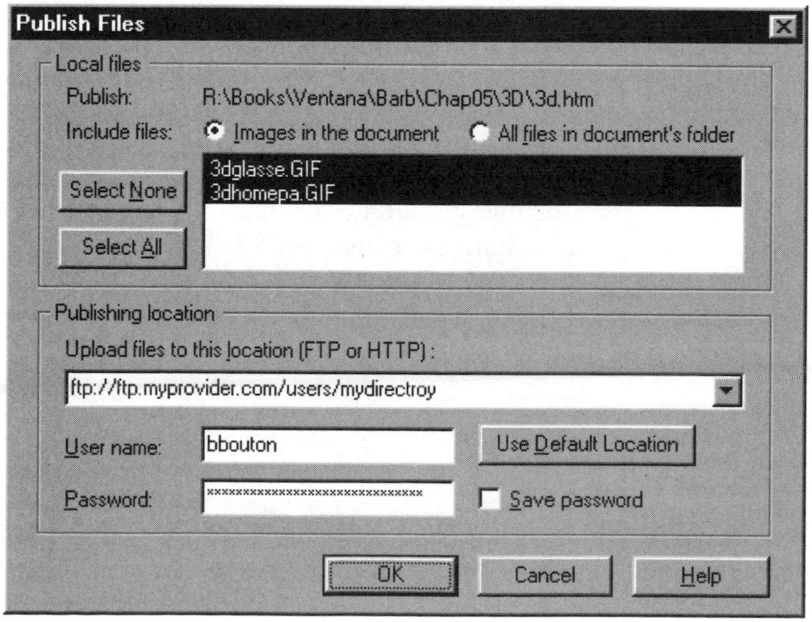

Figure 5-31: *Navigator Gold's Publish Files options.*

3. Check the Publishing Location section of the Publish dialog box. The information shown here is the site, name, and password you entered in the Publish tab of Editor Preferences for the default publishing location. If this is not where you want to send the files to be published, edit the fields as follows:

In the Publishing Location section, enter the full URL of the FTP or HTTP server where the files should be sent. Be sure to include the path to the directory on the server. For example: ftp://ftp.myprovider.com/users/mydirectory.

Enter your username and password (click the save password box so as not to retype your password every time).

If the settings displayed in the Publishing Location field are not the default settings and you would like to publish to the default location, click Use Default Location.

4. Click OK to begin sending the files. When uploading to a non-secure site, Navigator displays the Security Information box to remind you that you are about to perform a non-secure transfer of data.

5. Click on Continue in the Security Information dialog box. Navigator begins the upload and displays the Publishing Document dialog box (Figure 5-32) which shows information about the progress of the upload and which files are being uploaded at that time. It also displays the standard progress indicators: the progress percentage in the bottom left status bar and solid line progress bar in the bottom right corner of the window. You can stop the transfer at any time by clicking Cancel.

Figure 5-32: *You can see the progress of your upload in the Publishing Document dialog box.*

When the files have been uploaded, Navigator displays the Published Files box (Figure 5-33), which reports how many files were uploaded successfully and if there were any files that could not be uploaded. Click OK.

Figure 5-33: *Navigator's Publish Files message box announces that your upload was successful.*

6. If you have not specified a Default Publishing Location Information in Editor Preferences, Navigator Gold returns you to the Editor window; otherwise, Navigator asks if you want to browse to the default publishing location now. Click Yes to go to the HTTP site you specified in Editor Preferences to view the pages you uploaded, or click No to return to Gold's Editor.

7. If you choose to browse to the default publishing location, Navigator will go to the site specified in your settings (see above instructions) where you can view the work you've uploaded.

Navigator Gold provides a fast and effective means of transporting and uploading the documents that make up a Web site, *and* it helps you maintain the integrity of the links, so visitors to your Web site don't get the infamous 404 Not Found notice. But you sometimes need to send files other than Web pages, and you might not be using Netscape Gold. Both Navigator and Navigator Gold offer another way to send files. The next section shows you how.

Sending Files With Navigator

One Button Publishing isn't the only way to upload files from
Navigator or from Navigator Gold, but it is a way that you may
have overlooked because the menu item that is used in the process
only appears on the File menu when you are logged into an FTP
site. Let's take a look at the process; you never know when you'll
need to send a file, and with Navigator you already have the software needed to do it.

To upload a file, log on to an FTP site that you have access privileges to. As soon as you've logged on, a new item appears on the
File menu—Upload file. If you choose Upload File, a Upload File
dialog box opens that allows you to browse to the file on your hard
disk that you want to upload. Click the file you want to upload,
and then click Open. Navigator will begin the upload process by
asking you if you want to upload the file. Click Yes, and the file
upload process begins. From here on in it is identical to steps 4-7 in
the previous section.

The Upload File command from the File menu only handles the
upload of one file at a time, but if you don't mind doing a little
drag-and-drop from Windows Explorer or from Windows File
Manager, you can send as many files as you like in one step. To
send multiple files, resize and arrange the browser window so
you can see both the FTP listing in the browser window and the
Explorer or File Manager window that contains the files you want
to send. Select the files in the Explorer or File Manager window
and drag them into the browser window. Navigator will ask you if
you want to upload the files. Answer Yes and off they go.

With either the single or multiple file upload, if you try to upload
to a site that doesn't accept uploads, Navigator will display a dialog box informing you that it could not carry out the task because
the site denied permission.

MOVING ON

You've seen the ways to search for people, businesses, and all kinds of information kept in computers around the world. But what if you're searching for personal contact and not just things? If your next Internet quest is for conversation and correspondence, look no further than the following page. You will see how to make the best use of Navigator 3.0's tightly integrated News and Mail capabilities. Chapter 6, "Person to Person With Navigator Mail & Netscape News," shows you how convenient these facilities can make your life, and who knows—you may never want to lick another stamp or lug home all 25 pounds of the Sunday paper again!

Person to Person With Navigator Mail & Netscape News

As recently as two years ago, if you were asked to quickly list the top vehicles for communication, a natural response would have been, "Well, we have a telephone, a television, my aunt wrote me a letter today, we get the Sunday paper delivered . . . and the coffee shop down the street is where I talk to the neighbors and find out what's happening." And out of all these communications delivery systems, only one—the telephone—offers two-way feedback at your fingertips.

The Internet shouldn't be thought of as an *additional* vehicle for two-way communications; in a very real way, when Navigator is used, the Internet can serve as a *replacement* for mail and news. The Internet not only provides immediate communication, but the *content* of your communications can be expressed in a way that some stationery and a stamp simply cannot. You can, for example, e-mail a video clip of your new daughter to your family halfway across the Earth, and you can send the e-mail at any time, seven days a week. News is also being completely redefined as electronic content, and delivery methods change the speed and form of up-to-the-minute information.

This chapter examines the methods that Navigator provides by which you become an active, and *inter*active, participant in the online medium of today's communications.

MAIL VS. NEWS

Internet mail (e-mail) and news are two closely related forms of online communication, each with its unique differences. Mail, like physical mail or personal or conference telephone calls, is person-to-person. You direct your mail communication to a limited number of specific individuals, and your conversation is private.

Internet News is much more like the gang at the coffee shop or a public meeting. When you communicate using Navigator's News capabilities, you speak with everyone in the "room" who cares to listen. It is important to maintain the intellectual distinction between your audiences: one you pass a note to, for the other you take the microphone and announce your message.

Both mail and news are message-based communications on the Internet; Navigator recognizes mail and news' commonalties and presents you with interface features that are similar wherever their features or functions overlap. Navigator generally makes mail and news transport appear and work the same. For example, the Message Composition window is the same in both Navigator Mail and Navigator News: both share a three-pane layout, toolbars, shortcut menus, and so on. Once you've learned how one works, you'll have the other almost completely mastered. There *are* some differences, though, and we'll point out these differences as well as additional features in the section, "A Different Type of Mail: Navigator's News Window Services," found later in this chapter.

But before you can send any e-mail or participate in newsgroup communications, you need to provide Navigator with the information it needs to make the necessary connections to Mail and News services. In the next section, we'll make configuration recommendations for Navigator Mail and News Preferences. When you've finished, Mail and News will provide exactly the services you'd expect from them.

ESTABLISHING A "STREET ADDRESS" FOR MAIL & NEWS IN NAVIGATOR

Even though you might have used a mail reader and a newsgroup reader prior to purchasing Navigator, and you have your system connected to the Internet through a service provider, Navigator needs information from you to make connections and provide you with integrated Mail services. If you invest a little time right now to configure Navigator's Mail and News Preferences, you'll have your connections and preferences in place and ready to serve you the next time you hop online. Let's walk through the options you have for Mail and News Preferences, and see what the best options are for your work or leisure style of communications. The settings you make in Mail and News Preferences apply to both Netscape Mail and Netscape News unless otherwise noted.

APPEARANCE OPTIONS

In Figure 6-1, the Options, Mail and News Preferences command has been chosen, and you can see the first of five tabbed menus—Appearance—that you can configure to make reading, and accessing, Navigator Mail and News a lot easier.

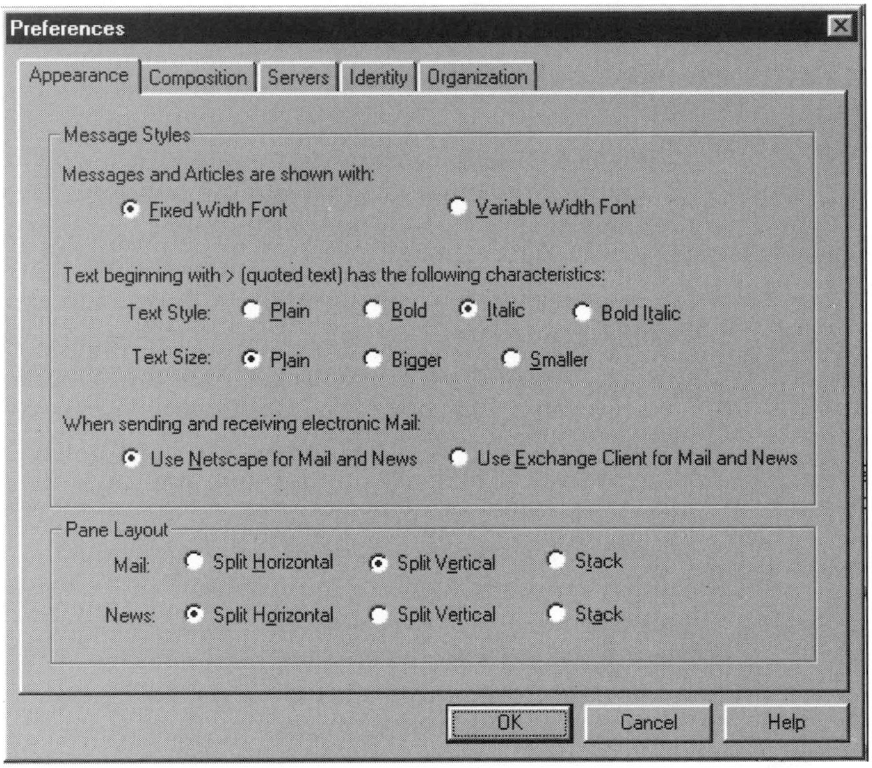

Figure 6-1: *The Appearance options allow you to specify font characteristics and other aspects that affect the way you see e-mail.*

■ Messages can be displayed in a fixed-width font (monospaced type, such as Courier) or with a variable-width font (a proportional font, such as Times New Roman). The appearance of Mail and News messages is a personal choice, but fixed-width type is usually quicker to read onscreen. Proportional fonts are great for typesetting articles on a printed page, but their appearance as bitmap fonts on a monitor can slow down your reading due to irregular character spacing and the illegibility of certain characters at different monitor display resolutions. Click the Fixed Width Font or the Variable Width Font radio button in the *Messages and Articles are shown with:* section to determine which kind of font is used for message display.

- Quote-backs—text that is posted within the body of correspondence as a contextual reminder of what the sender is replying to—are often hard to distinguish from *new* content. Many mail readers display quote-backs in the same text style as replies, or at best will bracket the quote-back in greater than/less than symbols. If you have trouble quickly finding the new content in a message that has quote-backs, you can choose a *Text Style* (*Plain, Bold, Italic,* or *Bold Italic*) and a *Text Size* (*Plain, Bigger* or *Smaller*) for the quote-back portion of your e-mail and news articles, by clicking the appropriate radio button(s). It should be mentioned here that Bigger and Smaller Text Size options are relative to the base font in which your the message appears; *global* changes to font size display in Navigator can be found in Chapter 2, "Installing & Customizing Navigator."

- When sending and receiving electronic mail and news, you have your choice to correspond directly through Netscape Navigator or to use Microsoft Exchange services. If you work at a large corporation that uses MS Exchange as a transport mechanism for groupware document preparation, or if you use OLE (Object Linking and Embedding) as a procedure for creating compound documents or for other corporate reasons, this option seems appealing. However, be aware that as of this writing, MS Exchange only supports mail and can't be used to access newsgroups. Also any e-mail you send or receive from Navigator when using MS Exchange as your Mail and News program can only contain plain ASCII text. RTF files, OLE objects, and such will *not* make it through intact, and you cannot send attachments to e-mail unless you have also entered text in the message window.

  If you chose to (or are required to) use MS Exchange instead of Netscape's Mail and News services, you will also need to go to the Windows 95 Mail/Fax Control Panel and add Netscape Internet Transport to your MS Exchange profile. Netscape Internet Transport becomes an option you can select if you install Navigator *after* you install MS Exchange. MS Exchange will guide you through the process with a wizard.

However, if you're a *private* user of Netscape, there's no logical reason for relegating your correspondence to MS Exchange because it does not support the graphically-rich Mail content as Netscape does. For example, Netscape can display an HTML document mailed to you with all the graphics, HTML formatting, and embedded, self-playing media objects intact. MS Exchange cannot provide these services and will strip your Mail of any enhanced content.

If your MIS director at work issues a "Thou shalt use MS Exchange as your only Mail program" dictum, then this choice in Appearance has been made for you. If not, leave this option set at Use Netscape Mail and News Services.

■ The last section of the Appearance tab deals with how the three different panes that make up a Mail or News window are positioned in the window. Three choices for page layout are offered: *Split Horizontal, Split Vertical* and *Stack*. You configure the Mail and News window separately, so you can use one layout style in the Mail window and another layout style in the News window. Figure 6-2 shows how Mail window looks in the different layouts. Split Horizontal is the default layout for both the Mail and News window, and the one you'll see throughout this chapter. You may want to try the Split Vertical, which affords more of a portrait view of your messages. You can change the layout at any time by coming to the Appearance options tab, but you must close and reopen the Mail or News window to see the new layout.

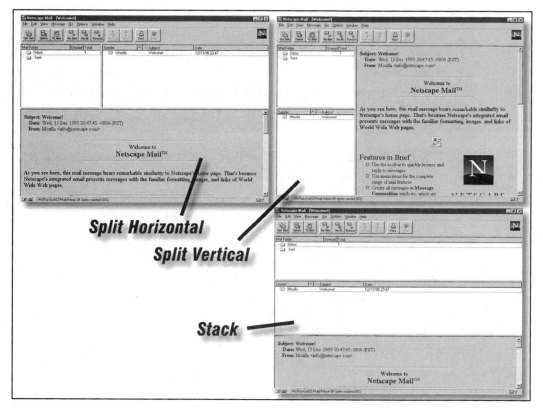

Figure 6-2: *Navigator Mail and News offer three different page layouts so you can choose the one that suits you best.*

MAIL COMPOSITION OPTIONS

The characteristics of e-mail and news messages sent and received over the Internet dictate that e-mail is encoded and decoded using non-platform-specific procedures, and the end result should simply be your e-mail—the transport and encoding should be transparent to the user. Navigator is fully MIME (Multipurpose Internet Mail Extensions)-capable, and uses MIME encoding to handle the many different types of files that are encountered within Web pages and e-mail. However, Navigator offers preferences as to how your correspondence is broadcast and received, and the Composition tab can often provide a means to ensure the legibility of your e-mail and can keep backup copies in the event that e-mail is not successfully sent.

In Figure 6-3, you can see the Composition tab, which is the second tab in the Mail and New Preferences options.

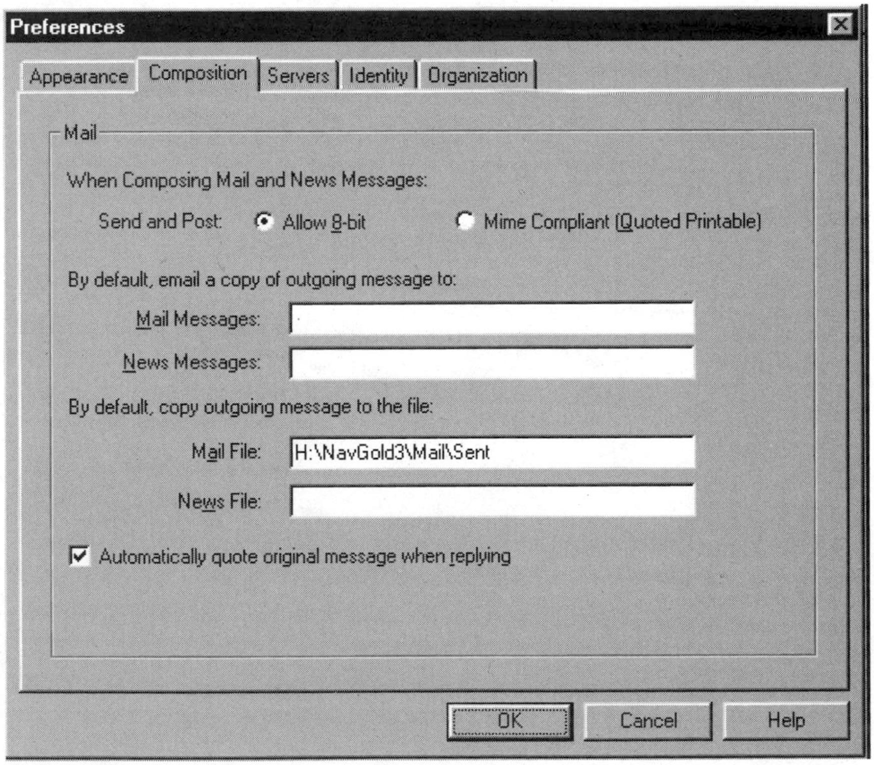

Figure 6-3: *Composition options can affect the way your messages are encoded, whether you keep backup copies on your hard disk, and whether quote-backs are automatically added to your e-mail.*

- You have a choice as to how your messages are encoded so that they can safely travel through the Internet e-mail system. Two radio button options are available in the *Send and Post* section: Allow 8-bit and Mime Compliant (Quoted

Printable).You should accept the default value of Allow 8-bit to ensure that your message will be compatible with the largest number of e-mail systems that handle your e-mail and postings. Mime Compliant (Quoted Printable) should *only* be selected if you are sending to someone who has trouble with your e-mail because their MIME e-mail reader misinterprets non-ASCII special characters. MIME capability is *always* present in all Navigator applications, however, and enabling or disabling this option simply changes the way certain hard-to-interpret characters are sent.

■ You can automatically e-mail a copy of *all* the e-mail you send by placing an address in the *By default, e-mail a copy of outgoing message to: Mail Messages:* field. Enter an address in the *News Messages:* field, and a copy of your newsgroup posts (messages) will be automatically e-mailed to that address. This feature can be useful if you have an Internet account at work in addition to one at home and want to have access to your correspondence no matter where you are. You simply mail your office correspondence to your home account.

There's a danger, however, if you put someone *else's* address (your boss, your spouse, your workgroup) in either of these boxes because you may not want them to have copies of *every* piece of correspondence. Unless you're on probation or you only put your *own* alternate e-mail address in these fields, it's best to leave these option fields blank.

■ You might find that regular correspondents eventually drop the quote-back routine and simply mail you a response to an opinion you've expressed. If you've forgotten the topic, however, this leaves you to reply without your original information to depend upon. The *By default, copy outgoing message to the file: Mail File:* field can be pathed to a location on your hard disk, which makes a copy of a sent piece of e-mail easy to retrieve at a moment's notice. This is also a good way to track when and what you've sent to whom. It's fine to leave the default path Navigator sets in this options field. Use the companion field *News File:* to automatically store copies of posts you make to newsgroups on your hard disk. If the hard disk that Navigator is installed on doesn't have a lot of free space on it and you have another drive that is less crowded you may want to create folders on that drive for your mail and news messages copies. If so, enter the path to these folders in this tab.

- The *Automatically quote original message when replying* checkbox is a handy feature, but it might require your manual intervention when you receive a large file with graphical or other Web elements embedded. If you leave this option checked, a copy of the entire message you are responding to is inserted in your reply message. When you quote back, you can be assured that the recipient can contextualize your response, but you might want to edit the quote-back in the message-composition window to keep the quote-back brief, to the point, and clear of enhanced elements originally contained in the message. It is considered bad Netiquette to quote back large amounts of text just to add a short message such as "Yes," "OK," or "I agree."

   It is also unnecessary to quote back what was quoted back to you in a message. The potential "Hall of Mirrors" endless quote-back has to stop with *someone*, and it might as well be with you!

SERVERS OPTIONS

The Servers options on the third tab of Navigator Preferences has fields that cannot be entirely completed without some information from your Internet Service Provider (ISP). In Figure 6-4, you can see the fields completed for Servers information regarding a fictitious person, Ms. Ima User. Your own Servers information will be different, of course, but the following is a checklist of the information you need. The checklist will also help you figure out whether you can provide the information by yourself without a call to your ISP.

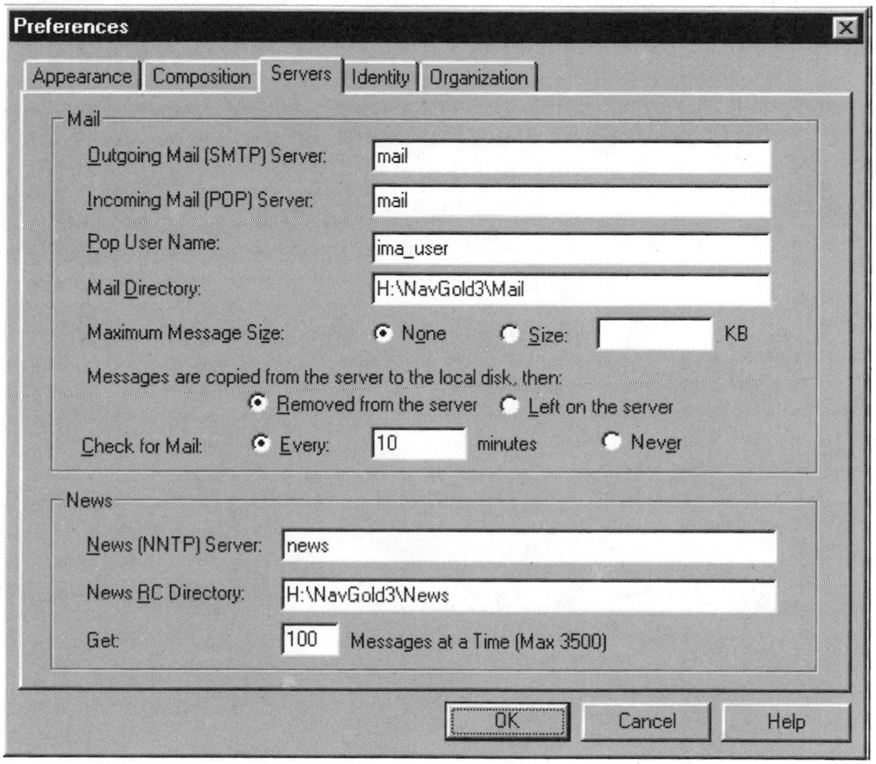

Figure 6-4: *The Servers options direct your e-mail to you, and it automatically manages information on e-mail disposal, e-mail size, and moving messages to your hard disk.*

■ The *Outgoing Mail SMTP Server:* field needs the name of the Send Mail Transport Protocol (SMTP) Server used by your ISP's Mail system. In many cases, the name is simply "mail." But you should check with your ISP if they didn't provide you with this information when you subscribed to them.

■ The *Incoming Mail (POP) Server:* field is where you should put the name of the server where your Point of Presence (POP) mail account is located. This is the server you access to receive mail. Your ISP should have provided you with a name for this server; but if they didn't, try "mail." Mail is the most common name for this server.

- The *POP User Name:* field is where you put the unique part of your Internet mail address. For example, if your address is ima_user@ducktail.com, the name you enter in this field is "ima_user" but without the quote marks. Be sure to enter the information here exactly (upper and/or lowercase, underscores included) as it appears in your Internet address. Your POP user name is usually, but not always the same name you use to sign in to your ISP's system.

- The *Mail Directory:* field is where you should enter the path to the folder in which you want Navigator to store your mailboxes and mail messages. Navigator usually fills this in for you, but if you'd like to store mail in another place or on another drive, you can. First use File Manager or MS Explorer to create the new mail folder (directory). Then enter the path to the folder in this field.

- The *Maximum Message Size:* option sets a maximum limit on the size of a single downloaded message. You can specify that there is no size limit by clicking the *None* radio button, or you can click the *Size* radio button and a enter value in kilobytes in the entry field to the right of the Size option.

    Any message sent to you that exceeds the limit you've specified will be shortened, and the overage will be left on the server. If you decide that you want to see the message in its entirety and you've enabled the option to leave messages on the mail server, you can set this option to None and then retrieve the entire message.

    The downside to specifying an upper limit to message sizes is that you might not be able to read mailing list digests you've subscribed to, such as the HTML Writer's Guild Digest, or receive files that have been uuencoded or BinHex-encoded. See "Receiving File Attachments" later in this chapter for information on different encoding schemes. Be sure to evaluate the size of e-mail that you typically get before setting any limits.

■ The *Messages are copied from the server to the local disk, then:* options determine what happens to messages after you fetch them from the mail server. Your options are 1) Removed from the server, and 2) Left on the server. Some ISPs won't let you leave messages on the server once they have been retrieved, because it requires too much hard disk space to archive your mail, so you might not have a choice here. Unless you have a reason to leave messages you've already received on the server, it is a friendly practice to remove them after you've retrieved them.

However, you might choose to leave messages on the server if you are traveling with your laptop computer and want to monitor your e-mail for urgent messages, but don't want to answer all of them until you get back to the office. Once you are back at the office, you could download to your desktop computer all of the messages that arrived while you were away.

■ By setting the *Check for Mail:* options you can have Navigator check the Mail for new messages periodically while you do other things. The frequency with which Navigator checks your e-mail depends upon your personal or business needs. For example, if your business is of an extremely timely nature, such as real estate or stocks and bonds, you might want Navigator to check your e-mail every few minutes. Navigator can only perform this function for you if you have an active Internet connection and you've opened the Mail window at least once and entered your Mail password. You don't have to be using Mail or have the Mail window open for the subsequent checking—you can read Web pages, send or receive files by FTP, or read headline news while Navigator checks for new e-mail. If new e-mail is found on the server, the envelope icon in the lower right hand corner of all Navigator windows will have an exclamation mark next to it. Navigator does *not* automatically download the new messages, but instead leaves the decision up to you as to when you want to get them. If you prefer to always check for e-mail manually, choose the *Never* radio button on this Preferences, Servers tab.

If you've set Navigator Mail to check for e-mail and you've configured your system to AutoDial when Internet services are required (see Chapter 2, "Installing & Customizing Navigator"), and Navigator is open but you are *not* online, you will be prompted to start an Internet connection when the time period you specified has elapsed. If you find this annoying, set your Check for Mail to Never.

■ The *News (NNTP) Server:* field of News options is where you should put the address of the primary news server you use to receive newsgroups. Usually, the news server address you'd enter here is the one that your Internet provider gave you. The format for these addresses is usually *news.ServiceProviderName.com*. You don't have to use the news server that your ISP provides if you can obtain access to another news server. You may want to use one of the public-access news servers if your ISP does not carry a newsgroup that you are interested in. Check the Totally Hot Bookmarks List on the Companion CD-ROM for links to sites that list the addresses of public servers.

CD-ROM

■ The *News RC directory* is where Navigator saves the subscription information files for each news server you use. Unless you have a compelling reason to change this setting, the default location in this field of the Preferences servers tab is fine. If you had a version of Navigator installed in a different directory and didn't uninstall the previous version, Navigator will use the previous News RC directory and the files in it. If you want to tidy up the organization of your hard disk, you can move your original RC files into a new folder in your current version, and then enter the new path in the News (NNTP) Server field.

■ The amount you specify in the *Get: # Messages at a Time (MAX 3500)* field determines the maximum number of newsgroup messages that will be downloaded. What value you set depends upon your own system resources, patience, and personal preferences. The more you choose to download, the longer the newsgroup will take to load. A default value of 100 will probably serve your average needs if you check newsgroups daily. If you find that you are "missing" some of the posts you would expect to find and frequently have to use the *Add from Newest Messages* and *Add from Oldest Messages* commands on the Netscape News Options menu, try setting this to a larger value.

IDENTITY OPTIONS

In the Identity tab, you can choose to where e-mail is automatically returned to, what name you choose for yourself online, and how you can automatically sign a message you mail. Figure 6-5 shows the Identity options for Mail and News Preferences.

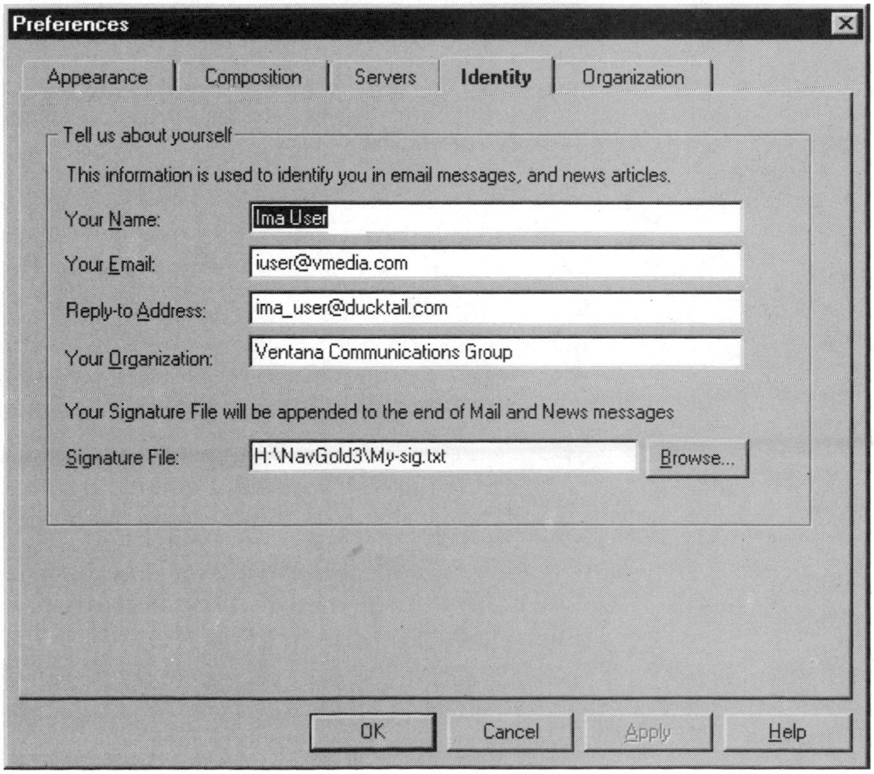

Figure 6-5: *Your Internet address and name you choose as a Mail recipient can be different; specify them in the Identity tab.*

■ The first field in the Identity tab, *Your Name:*, is not as straight-forward as it might seem. If you have a single Internet account, but you, your spouse, or other family member also uses the account, each of you can use your own name in your own copy of Navigator. The Your Name field does *not* have to be the person who pays the monthly ISP bills. The name you enter in this field, however, is the name that will be used in the From line of e-mail and newsgroup messages you send. You should enter your legal, birth certificate-type first and last name. If you decide to get creative and use a nickname or a screen name, remember that this is the name that will appear on e-mail to your boss, your mom, and your best customer. On the other hand, if you intend to post messages to an adult-content newsgroup, you may want to change your name here just before you send the post—*but be darned sure you change it back before you send e-mail anywhere else!*

("Smithers, do you know anything about this e-mail from 'HoneyCakes'?")

■ The *Your E mail:* field is where you fill in your full Internet e-mail address. Watch punctuation, spaces, and upper and lowercase, or your mail won't go through. The format for this address is usually the log on account name you estab-lished with—or were assigned by—your ISP followed by an @ ("at") sign, which is then followed by the domain name of your ISP: for example, ima_user@vmedia.com.

■ The *Reply-to Address:* field holds the address that will be used when people respond to your e-mail or respond privately to your News postings by choosing Reply. If no address is entered here, your e-mail address will be used. If you want your e-mail sent to a different address than the one you've sent the mail from, enter the address here. When you have more than one account and would like to try to funnel most of your incoming mail to the address you use most often, this feature is very handy. It is also useful if your outgoing company or organizational e-mail is forwarded through a number of different gateways, and you want to ensure that one of those addresses is not mistaken for your *direct* address. Specifying an address here solves a common problem that people might have with getting e-mail back to you.

■   The *Your Organization:* field is an optional field. Put the name of your company, your title, department, the organization you are affiliated with, or whatever your company or organizational policy requires. If none of these apply, you can put in a slogan, a favorite quote, or—better yet—provide a link to your home or your company's home page. If you enter a URL here, use the complete URL: for example, http://www.mycompany.com. For recipients of your e-mail who also use Netscape Navigator, this line will appear as a hypertext link, which will take them to your page when clicked.

■   The *Signature File:* field deserves a little in-depth explanation. Using this feature saves you the trouble of typing and possibly mistyping your return address or any other information you want distributed to everyone you write to. Let's take a look at what signature files are and how to create them.

CREATING A SIGNATURE FILE

If you've ever stapled your business card to a letter, you've performed the real-world equivalent of using an e-mail signature file. The advantage a signature file has over a business card is that it can "autodial." When your signature file contains a URL or mailto: address, readers of your e-mail can click the URL and immediately visit your home page, visit your favorite Internet site, or send e-mail directly to you.

A signature file is an ASCII text file that is automatically appended to the bottom of all the e-mail and newsgroup posts that you send. It establishes who you are, how to get in touch with you, and what affiliation you have (if any) with a company or organization. And like many business cards, your signature file may contain other information—what you do, product line, interests, or slogans.

Disclaimers stating that opinions expressed in your e-mail are your own and not your company's, school's, or organization's are also common elements in a signature file. Witty sayings and little pictures made out of ASCII text characters are also quite common in e-mail. GIFs, JPEG images, colored text, and other fancy formatting *cannot* be included in a signature file. Only ASCII text (created with only the keyboard keys—no extended characters such as cent signs or the Alt+0153 Trademark symbol) is supported. See Figure 6-6 for some samples of signature files.

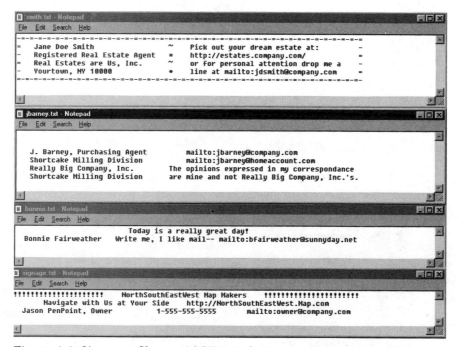

Figure 6-6: *Signature files are ASCII text closings to your messages. They can include a slogan, a text design, and your URL.*

TIP

Give the content and design of your signature file as much thought as you give to your business card. Keep the content of the file short and to the point. An overly elaborate or long signature file can overshadow the content of your message and may annoy frequent recipients of your e-mail. In fact, Navigator will flag you if your signature text file is longer than four lines, but it will accept a signature file of any length.

If you plan to participate in mailing lists or newsgroups, you'll get "flamed" (chastised on the newsgroup or through private e-mail) if the other participants think your signature file uses up too much of their hard disk space, increases their download time unnecessarily, and eats up Internet bandwidth. Keep signature files to a maximum of six lines.

To create a signature file:

1. Open a text editor such as NOTEPAD.EXE or TEXTPAD.EXE. Notepad comes with Windows, and TextPad is a great shareware text editor found on the Companion CD-ROM.

2. Choose a fixed-space (monospace) font such as Courier. If you are using Notepad, the default font is fine. Make sure you are at the top of the file, unless you want to include blank lines as part of the signature. This can be useful for creating white space, but it also increases the size of your signature file.

3. If you want a border or a separator line around your signature file, choose a character or pattern of characters, enter 80 of them, and then press Enter. For example, 80 asterisks, equals signs, or plus signs—or a mix of characters. Eighty characters is the most common line length for a signature that extends from screen edge to screen edge at a 640 by 480 resolution. You can make your signature file fewer than 80 characters wide, some older Mail readers use a 60 character line width. But don't use more than 80 characters in your signature, or the characters will word-wrap on most users' screens.

4. If you are creating a box around your signature file, enter the character or pattern at the beginning and at the end of each 80-character line. You'll have to fill the space between the first and last character in each line with spaces.

5. Press Insert on your keyboard to toggle from the insert to the overwrite method of entering text. This prevents your line from becoming longer than 80 characters as you enter your text. Use spaces to create white space between different elements of your design. If you include your e-mail address (you should), enter it as a mailto: URL. For example, mailto:me@myprovider.com.

   To enter an address for your home page or your company's, use a complete URL such as http://www.company.com/.

6. When you've finished designing your signature file, make sure that the cursor is at the end of the last line, and that no blank lines follow, or the blank lines will become part of the signature. Save the file as ASCII or plain text to your hard disk. Saving the file in Navigator's folder is a good place; it's easy to find and won't accidentally be deleted.

7. Open Navigator if it isn't already open, and go back to the Identity tab in Mail and News Preferences. In the Signature File text entry field, enter the full path to the signature file you created. If you're uncertain of the path, use the Browse button to find the file. Then click OK to close the dialog box.

You're done. To take your new signature file out for a test drive, open up the Navigator Mail window. Press Ctrl+M or click the To: Mail button on the toolbar to open up a new Message Composition window. Your new signature file is automatically inserted in the message field. See Figure 6-7.

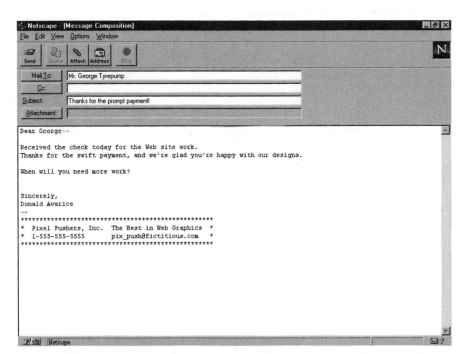

Figure 6-7: *Your signature file—your personal or corporate tag line—can be automatically appended to your e-mail.*

To see your signature file in action, send a message to yourself. Enter your e-mail address in the *Mail To:* field, enter a subject in the *Subject:* field, then tap out a message to yourself. The body of your e-mail message is entered above the two hyphens that precede the signature.

The signature is entered in the Message Composition window as editable text, so if you want to make a custom addition to the signature, insert your cursor where you want to make a change—then type away. If you decide at any time that you want to send a message *without* the signature file, highlight the signature text in the message field and press the Backspace key to delete it. When subscribing or unsubscribing to automated mailing lists, you should always remove your signature file. Signature files confuse automated mailservers and mailbots.

To change your signature on a *permanent* basis, edit the signature file itself with a text editor. You can also create a different signature file and then specify the new file in the Identity tab's Signature File field.

TIP

Want to use fancy letters in your signature file, but don't have the time to figure out how to create them using ASCII characters? Check out Ian Bagley's freeware SiggenPro 2D. You'll find it at http://www.netlink.co.uk/users/bagley/index.html. But use this program sparingly, or you'll end up with a huge signature file.

If you'd like to automate your signature file so that it contains a different tagline each time you send a message, try a shareware program called SigGen by Ken Kyler. You can find out more about SigGen and download the latest version from http://www.kyler.com/~ken/. SigGen for Windows 95 users can be found on the Companion CD-ROM.

For more information about creating and using ASCII characters for signatures or for artwork, check out the ASCII Art Reference FAQ at http://gagme.wwa.com/~boba/faq.html.

Bookmarks to all of these sites can be found in the Totally Hot Bookmarks List on the Companion CD-ROM.

ORGANIZATION OPTIONS

In the Organization tab of Mail and News Preferences, you choose if your e-mail password will be remembered, if Mail and News messages should be threaded, and how they should be sorted—by date, subject, or sender. Figure 6-8 shows the Organization options for Mail and News.

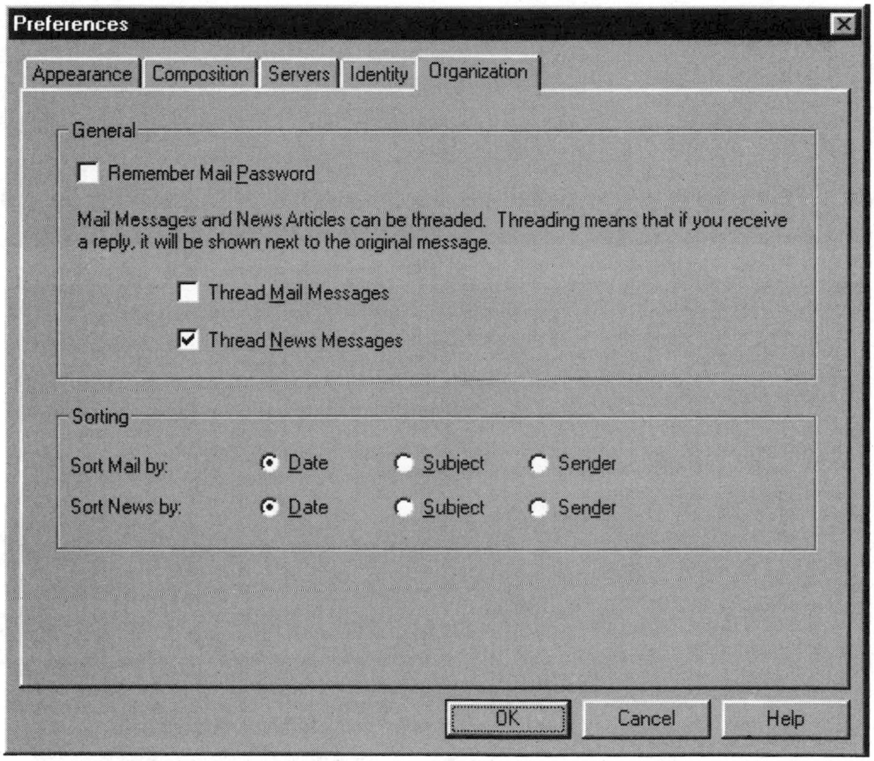

Figure 6-8: *Specify how often the password to your e-mail must be entered in the Organization tab.*

■ The Remember Mail Password checkbox in the Organization tab determines whether the password your ISP gave you for your Mail account is remembered from session to session of Navigator. When unchecked, Navigator Mail opens the Password Entry Dialog box shown in Figure 6-9. You must put in the password if you want Navigator Mail to check and retrieve e-mail from the mail server. If you dismiss this box without entering a password, you or anyone who has access to your computer *can* still read, send, manage, or delete mail.

The password protection offered in Navigator Mail only keeps others from retrieving and reading mail that is on the mail server. It *does not* keep those who have physical access to your machine and who don't know the mail password from reading mail you've already retrieved, deleting mail from your mailboxes, or even sending mail from your copy of Navigator, complete with your name and signature file on it.

As it stands in Navigator 3, this doesn't offer a lot of protection, so you might as well check the box, enter your password once, and never be bothered with having to enter your password again. Improvements to this feature to strengthen your security options are scheduled in up-coming releases of Navigator.

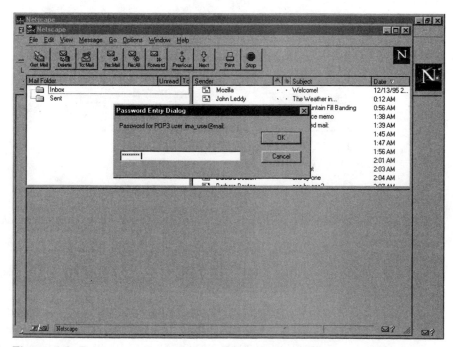

Figure 6-9: *Enter your password once in Navigator, so that it remembers the password from session to session.*

■   The *Thread Mail* and *Thread News Messages* checkboxes determine where new e-mail and messages will be positioned in
the Message Header pane when they are downloaded.
Check these checkboxes when you want Navigator to collect
all of the messages that pertain to a single subject in their
own sub-tree, so you can read them in the order in which
they were received. Threading messages also makes saving,
copying, and moving topic-related messages easier. New
messages received that belong to a thread will be added to
the bottom of thread sub-tree. When message threading is
enabled, the threads are displayed in the Message Header
tree along with messages that don't belong to a thread. The
messages are arranged according to the sort order that is
selected in the next set of options on the Organization tab.

■   The Sorting options on the Organization tab refer to how
Mail and News messages and message threads should be
ordered in the Message Header tree. Your options are *Date*,
Subject, and *Sender*. The default choice is to sort by Date, but
you should choose whatever best suits your needs. You are
never locked into the choices you've made for Sort order,
because you can change these options at any time. If you do
decide to change the default settings and you have the Mail
window open when you make the change, the change won't
take effect until you've closed and reopened the Mail window. You can also temporarily override the settings in the
Mail and News windows–see "Changing Mail & News Sort
& Display Options" later in the chapter.

GETTING IN FRONT OF YOUR NEW WRITING DESK

Now that you've customized, personalized, and organized
Navigator's Mail and News features to operate the way you want
in the background, it's time to explore some of Navigator's *foreground* personal communications features. We'll start with a trip to
Netscape Mail.

When you open the Navigator Mail window—by either choosing Netscape Mail from the Window menu of any open Navigator or Netscape Navigator Gold window, or by single-clicking the mail icon in the lower right of any window—you are presented with a three-paned window with a handy toolbar across the top (see Figures 6-10 and 6-11). As noted earlier in the section on Appearance Options and as seen in previously in Figure 6-2, there are three different ways the panes can be arranged on the page. No matter where onscreen a pane appears, it always contains the same content and works the same. In this chapter we'll assume that you are using the default layout, Split Horizontal.

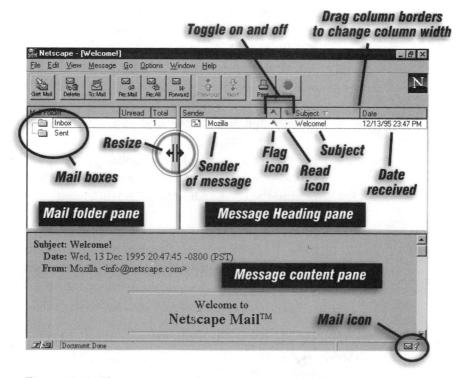

Figure 6-10: *The Netscape Mail window and its components.*

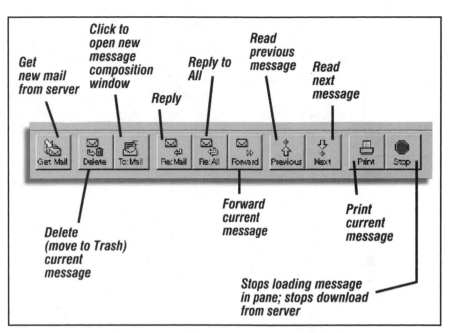

Figure 6-11: *The toolbar offers easy access to common commands.*

Each pane in the Mail (or News) window can be resized by dragging on the pane borders. The width of each column in the top two panes is changed by dragging the separators between the column titles, very much like you'd do in a spreadsheet program.

Columns and panes aren't the only things that drag and drop in Netscape Mail. Just as files in Windows Explorer can be dragged from folder to folder, e-mail messages can be dragged from one folder to another.

THE MAIL WINDOW: A THREE-PART CONCERTO

Navigator's Mail window brings the power and the diversity of content you've found on the Web to your own personal, interactive communications.

If you've used MS Exchange or other e-mail programs, you'll feel right at home in the Netscape Mail window. The window is divided into three panes: the Mail Folder, the Message Header, and the Message Content panes. These panes work together to help organize incoming e-mail, alert you when e-mail arrives, and provide you with a place to read your messages. Along with the Mail Composition window, they're sort of a combination in and out box affixed to your personal writing desk. There are additional features to your writing desk that we'll cover in this chapter, and you can also work in *other* applications' desktops to produce content that can be an element within your correspondence.

THE MAIL FOLDER & MESSAGE HEADER PANES

The Mail Folder pane, in the top-left of the Mail window, contains a tree-like structure of mailboxes. Mailboxes are the folders that are used to store and organize your correspondence. Messages can be dragged out of the Message Header pane and dropped into any folder. You can create as many mailboxes as you need.

It is often very useful to create a mailbox to hold correspondence that relates to a specific project or topic, or to hold e-mail that comes from a single person or organization. Mailboxes can also be used to separate your personal from your business correspondence, or to hold e-mail you haven't had a chance to go through yet. Navigator automatically creates the Inbox, Outbox, Sent, and Trash mailboxes. The Inbox and the Sent box are created when you install Navigator. The Outbox and the Trash mailboxes are automatically created when you've written a message that hasn't been sent yet (on the one hand) or consigned some writing to the dumpster by selecting it and pressing Delete (on the other hand). These four mailboxes that Navigator automatically creates, always appear at the top of the tree. All mailboxes that you create are arranged in alphabetical order under these four.

CREATING A MAILBOX

To create a new mailbox, choose New Folder from the File menu. Enter a name for the new Mail Folder in the Netscape User Prompt dialog, as seen in Figure 6-12. Mailbox names can't be edited, so type carefully. If you create a lot of e-mail folders, you may want some to appear higher in the tree than they normally would. To make a folder appear directly below the Trash folder, use an exclamation mark or a number as the first character of the folder name. For example, a folder named "!Hot" would appear right after the Trash folder. Figure 6-13 shows how the Mail Folder pane looks when you've added several mailboxes, and some mailbox names start with non-alphabetic characters.

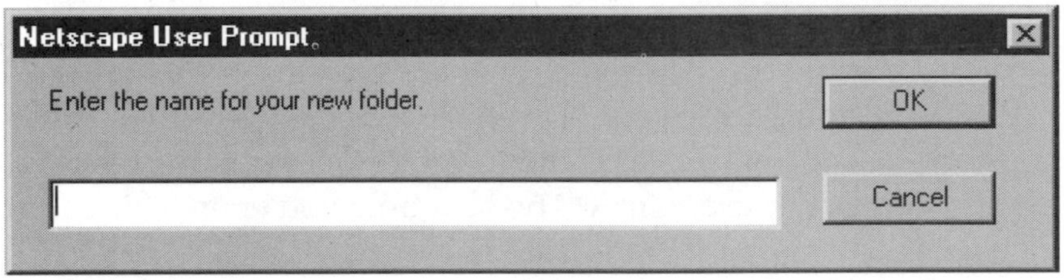

Figure 6-12: *Enter the name for a new mailbox folder in this dialog box. Type carefully, because names can't be edited once created.*

Figure 6-13: *Use non-alphabetic characters to force frequently used mailboxes to the top of the Mail Folder pane.*

NEW FOLDER VS. ADD FOLDER—AN IMPORTANT DIFFERENCE

When creating a new mailbox, be sure to choose New Folder and *not* Add Folder from the File menu. New Folder creates a brand-new folder that you get to name and puts the records for that folder in the same place your other mailbox information is stored.

Add Folder is used when you want temporary access to an existing Navigator Mail folder that is somewhere else on your drive or network. The folder is not moved to your e-mail storage area, but you and anyone else who has access to the folder has complete control over its contents—messages can be added, deleted, moved, or copied from it. The next time you open Navigator, the folder will *not* appear in the Mail Folder pane.

Adding folders is a good way to share a common message folder on your network, or to transfer the contents of your e-mail folders if you install a new copy of Navigator into a new directory. However, if you empty and delete this folder, it's gone forever for you and any other users.

TRAP

The ability to add folders does bring up the possibility that others—co-workers, for example—could be reading your message folders without your knowledge or consent, by adding them to their copy of Navigator Mail. If you don't want this to happen, be sure that only you have network rights to the folder where you store your messages. Discuss this with your network administrator. If you are using Windows for Workgroups or Windows 95, either put your Navigator Mail directories on a drive that is not shared, or unshare the entire drive and then share only the directories and folders that you don't mind being public information. Check your MS Windows documentation for how to share entire drives or only specified directories.

WASTED SPACE & COMPACTING MAILBOXES

After you've been using Navigator Mail for a while, you may notice that the status line reports the amount of wasted space in a mailbox. Mailboxes are actually database files; and like most databases, when you delete records (e-mail messages, in this case) the information is discarded, but the *space* the information occupied in the database is not. To take the "air" out of the mailbox file, so that the disk space the mailbox file occupies consists of only e-mail and not spaces where e-mail was, you compact the mailbox. To do this, select the mailbox and press Ctrl+K, or right-click the mailbox and choose Compress Folder from the shortcut menu.

You'll want to keep an eye on the amount of space that is wasted. No one ever has enough hard disk space, and large e-mail folders take longer to load or scroll through. But if you've let this chore slip off your to-do list, Navigator will remind you from time to time by displaying the question box seen in Figure 6-14.

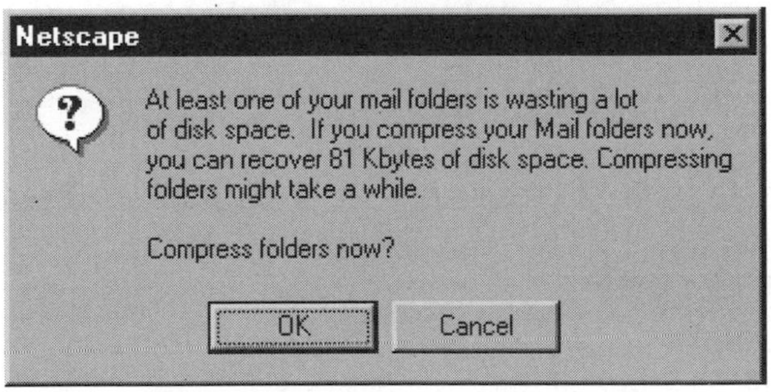

Figure 6-14: *Navigator keeps an eye on wasted space so you don't have to.*

TIP

If you made a mailbox you no longer need, empty the mailbox, then right-click on the unwanted folder, and choose Delete Folder. Navigator will only allow you to delete empty e-mail folders.

CHANGING MAIL & NEWS SORT & DISPLAY OPTIONS

A small gray triangle on the Sender, Subject, or Date column headings is the visual clue that Navigator uses to tell you what sort order is being used in the message headings pane in both the Mail and News windows. To temporarily change the sort order of messages and override the settings you made in Mail and News Preferences, click the column head that corresponds to how you would like the message headings sorted.

The Sort menu, which is a submenu of the View menu item on both the Mail and News window's menu bar offers a number of sorting options. News and Mail message threading can be toggled on and off temporarily, and messages can be sorted by Date, Subject, Sender, and by Message Number. News servers catalog messages by number, and sorting by number is useful if someone has told you to look at a specific message and they referenced the message number. The Sort menu also offers you the option of displaying the results of a sort in ascending or descending order. If you want ascending order, make sure the Ascending entry in the Sort menu has a check mark next to it. To change to a descending display, click the Ascending menu item to remove the check mark beside it.

THE BEST STRATEGY FOR SIFTING THROUGH YOUR MAIL

When the mail carrier brings physical mail, many people sift through it and sort it into categories:

- Open right away (checks, letters from Mom).

- Open when you've finished with the good stuff (bills and other official mail).

- Junk you may throw out without looking at it (circulars, sales notices, alumni solicitations, and so on).

Although checks haven't started to arrive via e-mail yet, some of your e-mail is much more important to you than the rest—and junk mail has found its way into e-mail. Virtually all of the tasks you'd do with actual, physical mail have Navigator equivalents: sorting, reading, filing, discarding, replying, forwarding, and passing a copy of a message to others.

One of the most efficient ways to wade through a lot of e-mail is to adopt the "handle it once" strategy. When you get your e-mail, decide what to do with it right away. Otherwise, you can easily become flooded with e-mail and miss that important memo from the boss, or a question from an important customer. Read and reply to the important stuff, immediately toss the junk, and then read (or file for later reading) the remainder of the e-mail. You probably already follow a similar procedure with your physical mail; with Navigator, you have the tools to quickly accomplish these tasks with your electronic mail. Let's take a look at how it's done:

1. Retrieve your e-mail by pressing the Get Mail button. New e-mail is automatically placed in the Inbox, and a list of received messages appears in the Message Heading pane.

2. Scroll to the top of the list. If the first message looks important enough to read *after* you've handled your priority mail, skip over the message. Skipping over a relatively important message may sound strange, but what we want to do here is to go through the list and make a quick determination of the importance of each e-mail message *without* taking the time to open each message. This process mimics the process you perform when you shuffle through and rough sort physical mail without opening each envelope.

3. If the message looks like junk e-mail and you don't want to read it at all, flag it by clicking the Flag column next to the Sender's name so that the little red flag appears. Flagging e-mail doesn't waste your time by opening the e-mail message; it simply marks it, so you can find it or perform operations such as delete, copy, move, or forward on the group of flagged messages.

On the other hand, if the first message looks like it is something you want to attend to right away, click the message title to display it in the Message Content pane. If the message needs a response, all the tools you need are right at the tip of your mouse. Right-click in the Message Content pane to display the shortcut menu. The shortcut menu contains the Reply, Reply to All, Forward, and Forward Quoted commands, as well as the Add to Address Book, Delete Message, and Unscramble (ROT-13) commands. Alternatively, right-clicking the message title in the Message Header pane brings up a similar shortcut menu, except that the Address Book and the Unscramble (ROT-13) commands are not available.

- The first four commands will bring up the Message Composition window with the appropriate addresses inserted and with a copy of the message you are responding to quoted back (if you enabled this option in Mail and News Preferences). If you didn't enable automatic quote-back, you can still quote the message back by clicking the Quote button on the Message Composition toolbar.

- The Address Book command opens the Address Book window with entries made for the correspondent. All you need to do is add a Nick Name and a description. This is the best way to build up your Address Book.

- The Delete Message command moves the message to the Trash mailbox.

- The last command (Unscramble ROT-13) is covered in the following section.

After you've read and responded (if necessary) to the message, you should move it out of the Inbox and into an appropriate mailbox or remove the message by deleting it. To file the message, click the message title in the Message Header pane (the message title is already highlighted) and drag-and-drop it into a mailbox folder. To delete the message, use the Delete command on the shortcut menu or click the message title in the Message Header pane and press Delete.

When you've worked your way through the list—responding to priority e-mail, skipping over good but not urgent e-mail, and flagging junk e-mail, click in the Message Heading pane and then choose Select Flagged Messages from the Edit menu. With the flagged messages selected, press Delete (or from the menu choose Message, Move), then choose the Trash mailbox from the Move submenu. Don't try to drag the flagged messages into the Trash; clicking them will deselect all of the messages except the one you clicked on.

With your priority e-mail answered and filed and the junk e-mail moved to the Trash, the only messages left in the e-mail message heading window are the ones you deferred for later reading. If you have time to go through them now, you can quickly step through your messages and decide what you want to do with them by clicking the Previous and Next buttons on the toolbar. These buttons move you from unread message to unread message.

When you've read a message, it no longer appears in bold type, and the green Read icon is not displayed in the header line to the left of the Subject. You can change an unread message into a read message or vice versa by clicking in the Read icon column next to the message header Subject. Or you can select some or all of the messages and mark them all read or unread by choosing Mark as Read or Mark as Unread from the Message menu. If you'd prefer to defer reading these messages, select them all by pressing Ctrl+A. Then, move them out of the Inbox into a folder you've created for unattended messages by choosing Move from the Message menu, then choosing the mailbox you want to move them to from the flyout menu. This will leave you with an empty Inbox, which will make sifting through the *next* batch of e-mail easier to cope with!

UNSCRAMBLING (ROT-13)

If you ever got a magic decoder ring from a box of cereal, you'll immediately appreciate ROT-13 encoding. ROT-13 is a simple encoding method that shifts each character in a message to the alphabetical right by 13 letters—A becomes N, B becomes O, and so on. ROT-13 encoding is used in e-mail and in newsgroups to "mask" parts of the text that the creator doesn't want you to read at first glance. The answer to a riddle, the plot ending to a movie or story, or something that they think you might find objectionable are acceptably masked through ROT-13 encoding.

To decode a ROT-13 scrambled message, right-click the ROT-13 scrambled text in the Message Content window, then choose Unscramble (ROT-13). The message will then display in its original unscrambled format.

Navigator at present doesn't have an option for *applying* ROT-13 scrambling to messages you want to send, but here's a workaround. Send the message that you want ROT-13 to encode as a normal e-mail message to yourself. Display it in the Message Content window, right-click the text, then choose Unscramble (ROT-13). Navigator can't tell the difference between text that has been shifted or not, so it takes your original message and "unscrambles" it into an ROT-13 message. The message itself hasn't changed—only the display of the text is changed—so select the now-scrambled text, copy it to the Clipboard, then paste it into a new e-mail or newsgroup message or a reply to a message. Figure 6-15 shows an original message that Jack e-mailed to himself and the encoded version he copied from the Message Content pane.

The reason why our little trick to produce ROT-13 encoding worked is because there are 26 letters in the alphabet and the encoding scheme shifts everything by 13, or half of the number of characters. This means that if you "add" 13 characters to A, you get N. It also means that if you "add" or "subtract" 13 characters to N you get A.

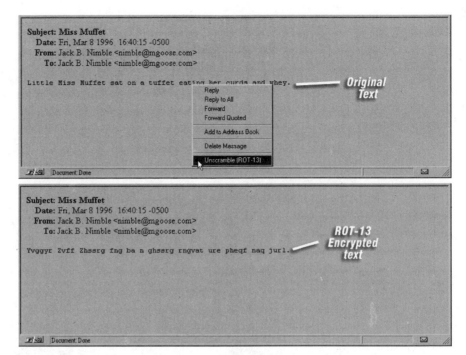

Figure 6-15: *ROT-13 encryption can be accomplished by allowing Navigator to filter the original message content.*

CREATING A SIMPLE E-MAIL MESSAGE

All you need is something to say, the address of the person you want to share it with, and Navigator to compose new e-mail. From any Navigator window, press Ctrl+M to open the Message Composition window seen in Figure 6-16. In the Mail To: field, type in the address of the person you're writing to. Better yet, if you've made an entry in your Address Book for a correspondent, enter his or her Nick Name in this field, or click the Mail To: button to pick his or her name from the Select Addresses dialog box. From the Select Addresses dialog box, you can choose whom the Mail To: addressee will be, as well as those who should receive copies (cc) and blind carbon copies (bcc) of the message. Enter a Subject for the message. The more informative your subject line, the greater your chances that your recipient will read your message. If you want to attach a document or file to the message, click the Attachment button. The fine points of attachments are discussed later in this chapter. Enter your message and click Send.

Figure 6-16: *The Message Composition window is used to write e-mail and News messages.*

SENDING DEFERRED MAIL

If the picture on the Send button has a small clock on the lower right corner of the envelope, the message will not be immediately sent; instead, it will be moved to your Outbox. Mail in the Outbox is not sent until you press Ctrl+H, or choose Send Mail in Outbox from the Navigator Mail menu. You decide when e-mail is sent by choosing Immediate Delivery or Deferred Delivery from the Message Composition window's Options menu. This choice stays in effect for all messages you send until you change it.

Sending e-mail immediately is the default option for sending e-mail, but changing the default to Deferred Delivery has its merits. Deferred delivery is useful when you are writing messages offline, but more importantly, some messages are written in haste—you might want to reconsider that colorful description of your boss, family member, or newsgroup member after you've chilled out for five minutes. When you delay delivery, it gives you a chance to edit (or delete) your message. Messages in the Outbox can be opened for editing (in the round-about way discussed next) or deleting anytime before you send them, but once they've been sent—they're delivered.

TIP

INSO CyberSpell for Netscape Mail (http://www.inso.com) is a must-have plug-in for all Navigator users. Nothing makes your correspondence look quite as uneducated as misspelled words and punctuation errors. CyberSpell inserts itself into the Message Composition window's menu, so it's always available to spell-check your message before you send it. If you purchased the Netscape Power Pack, you already have CyberSpell, but if you didn't, surf over to INSO and check out the trialware version.

EDITING A MESSAGE IN THE OUTBOX

Once a message has been sent to the Outbox it is no longer editable. You can delete or forward a copy of the message, but you can't edit the content of the message nor can you change or add attachments to the message. The Outbox works like the other mailboxes; clicking a message title in the Message Header window displays the message in the Message Content pane, not the Message Composition window. The Message Content pane, like the Navigator Browser window, is read-only. You can select text in the Message Content pane and copy it to the clipboard, but you can't insert or delete text in the Message Content pane.

So what happens when you discover a typo or want to make a change or an addition to a composed, but unsent message? You have to recreate it. Fortunately that's not as much work as it sounds because you can copy the contents of the flawed message to the clipboard. To do so . . .

With the outbound message you want to edit displayed in the Message Content pane, click and drag the cursor to select the text of the message. Then, with the text highlighted, press Ctrl+C or choose Edit and then Copy from the menu. Press Ctrl+M or click the To Mail: button on the toolbar to open a new Message Composition window. Insert your cursor in the message composition portion of the window and press Ctrl+P to paste the contents of clipboard. Make your corrections or changes as necessary. Be sure to fill in the Mail To: and Subject: fields and add any Attachments you want to send. When you're sure this message is correct, go to the Outbox and send the faulty message to the Trash. Then return to the Message Composition window and click Send on the toolbar. The fixed message will be sent to the Outbox.

NAVIGATOR'S LITTLE BEIGE BOOK: THE ADDRESS BOOK

Like the list of addresses for traditional mail that can be kept in MS Word 7 and other word processors, Navigator offers an online Address Book where you keep the addresses you use most frequently. If you've already taken a look at Chapter 4, "Retracing Your Steps," you'll notice a similarity between the Address Book and the Bookmarks window; and if you haven't, you'll still feel at home because the Address Book operates a lot like Windows Explorer. Each folder in the address tree stores the information associated with one person. The information about the person with whom you correspond contains her or his name, e-mail address, the nickname you give him or her, and an optional description where you can put other information about the person. Figure 6-17 shows the Address Book window and Address Book Properties for one of the entries in the list.

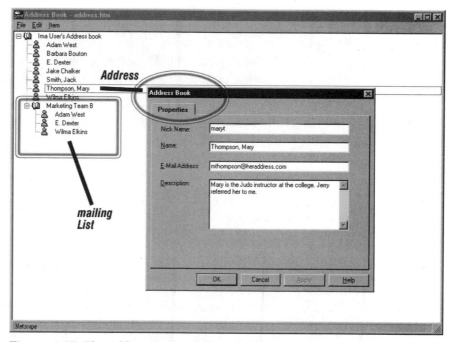

Figure 6-17: *The Address Book window, with the Properties tab open for one of the entries.*

ADDING AN ADDRESS

Addresses are added to the Address Book by opening the Address Book from any of Navigator's Window menus, choosing Item from the Address Book window's menu, then choosing Add User. Fill out the Properties box, and you're done. The most foolproof way to add an entry for someone in the Address Book is to capture the information from a message they've sent you. Display the message, right-click the Message Content pane, then choose Add to Address Book. Existing Address Books created by Navigator or Navigator Gold version 2 or later can be appended to your current Address Book by choosing File, then Import from the Address Book menu. Then use the Import address book file dialog box to open the list you want to add. Address Book files, like Bookmarks list files, are created and maintained by Navigator. They are automatically written HTML files and by default are called address.htm.

> **TIP**
>
> *It's easier to find entries in the Address Book if you enter the person's name in the Name field of the Properties tab in a "telephone directory" style, like: Smith, Jack; or Jones, Janice. The Address Book tree displays entries in alphabetical order, and this method keeps you from having to sort through 16 Jasons to find Jason White.*

NICKNAMES

Using nicknames to address e-mail is a great time-saver and helps ensure that the e-mail you send is addressed correctly. Nicknames can be entered into any field in the mail composition window that calls for an e-mail address. As soon as you click out of the Address entry field, Navigator reads the nickname and replaces it with the person's name and e-mail address as it was entered it in the Address Book Properties window. Nicknames must be lowercase and can only contain letters and numbers—no spaces, underscores, hyphens, or other characters. Nicknames are never seen by the recipient of the e-mail, but use a little discretion here anyway—it's probably not a career-enhancer if word gets around that your Navigator nickname for the department supervisor is "clown."

MAILING LISTS

When you regularly need to send the same message to many different people, the quickest way is to create a mailing list. When you send a message to the list, everyone on the list gets the e-mail. Mailing lists replace the need to send multiple messages, and you can't forget to add someone on the Cc: line—Navigator remembers for you. To create a mailing list, open the Address Book and choose Insert List from the Item menu. Fill in the fields to give the group a Nick Name, a (formal) Name (the recipients on the list will all see this name, so keep it kind), and a Description of when you want to use this list. Descriptions are reminders to yourself.

To add members to the list, click and drag their folders onto the List folder. List folders look like open books. Navigator will create an *alias* (a shortcut) for each person in the list. If you update their information in either the Properties tab associated with the original entry or the alias' Properties tab, the change will also be reflected in all of entries for that person in any of the lists you've added them to as well as the original entry.

To send e-mail and any attachments to the e-mail to the members of the list, select the list in the Address Book, then press Ctrl+M. Alternatively, click the Address or Cc: buttons in any Message Composition window and pick the list from the dialog box, or type in the nickname for the list in any Mail Composition field that will accept an e-mail address. You can then enter a subject, attach any attachments, write your message, and send it.

SAVING YOUR ADDRESS BOOK

If you want to share your Address Book with a co-worker, move it between home and work, or save it to a file for backup purposes, it's a snap. From the File menu of the Address Book window, choose Save As. The Save address book file dialog box appears. Give the file a name, choose a place on your hard disk to save it, then click Save. Just like bookmarks (but *unlike* documents in the Web browser window), the file is saved as an HTML document with the HTML tags intact if you pick either Source or Plain Text from the Save as Type drop-down box.

A DIFFERENT TYPE OF MAIL: NAVIGATOR'S NEWS WINDOW SERVICES

Not all of the correspondence you'll receive through the Internet comes with the same sort of prerequisite for response as Mail service does. Newsgroups are a popular phenomenon on the Net. If you've ever wanted a continuing, exhaustive, extensive collection of fact and fiction on Elvis, stamp collections, ketchup, or a thousand other topics, subscribing to a newsgroup is faster and more fun than a trip to the library on any day.

Navigator's News window (see Figure 6-18) looks very similar to the Mail window, and it works almost identically to the Mail window. The difference between the two lies not so much in what they do and how they work, but in the *nature* of the messages they work with. Mail messages are downloaded to your computer, and although the newsgroup messages headings are displayed, the messages themselves are never stored on your computer. Instead, they are sent upon request for you to read online. If you read a message you want to keep, you must explicitly save the message to your hard disk. Reading newsgroup messages is similar to walking over to a bulletin board and reading the posted notices.

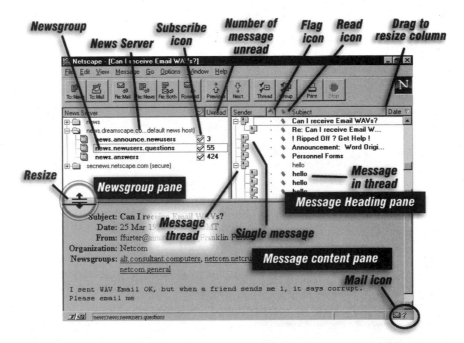

Figure 6-18: *The News Window.*

You use the newsgroup pane to choose which news server and which newsgroups hold the messages that you want to read. There are over 13,000 newsgroups to choose from, so until you select some of these, the only ones you see at first are the three default newsgroups seen in Figure 6-18. The Message Heading pane shows all of the currently available messages in the newsgroup. Unlike e-mail (which lasts forever because you've moved it to your hard disk), news articles expire and disappear from the news server.

How quickly this happens depends on the policies of the news server and how much traffic the group gets; the more traffic, the sooner the messages expire.

The toolbar shown in Figure 6-19 contains many of the commands you'll use most often when reading and writing in the News window. From left to right, the features are as follows:

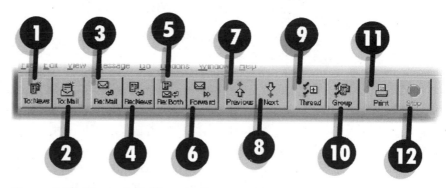

Figure 6-19: *Navigator's News toolbar.*

1. *To: News*—Opens up a Message Composition window with the currently selected newsgroup's address placed in the Newsgroup Address field. Use this button to send a new message to the newsgroup. If you want to send to a different newsgroup, replace the address with the address of the group you wish to send a message to.

2. *To: Mail*—Sends a new, private e-mail message to anyone.

3. *Re: Mail*—Lets you reply privately by e-mail to the person who wrote the newsgroup post that is currently displayed in the Message Content pane. That person's e-mail address is automatically entered in the Mail To: field, and a Subject is entered which repeats that of the newsgroup post. This function is also available on the right-click shortcut menu.

4. *Re: News*—Sends a reply to the newsgroup. Think twice before using this button (see "Points on What *Not* to Do in Newsgroups" later in this chapter). The Message Composition window opens with the newsgroup listed in the Newsgroups field, and the Subject line is filled in with the same topic as that of the current message in the Message Content window. This function is also available on the right-click shortcut menu.

5. *Re: Both*—Sends a reply to the newsgroup and an identical, but private, e-mail message to the person who wrote the post that is in the Message Content window. This function is also available on the right-click shortcut menu.

6. *Forward*—Forwards by e-mail the newsgroup message currently displayed in the Message Content window to the individual of your choice. Use this feature to e-mail posts to yourself that you want to save. This function is also available on the right-click shortcut menu.

7. *Previous*—Opens the next unread message that is closer to the top of the Message Header pane than the message you last read.

8. *Next*—Opens the next unread message that is closer to the bottom of the Message Header pane than the message you last read.

9. *Thread*—Marks as read all of the messages in the thread you are currently reading. Do this when you want to "hide" a thread from being displayed by the Previous and Next buttons. This feature is especially useful when there are threads you don't want to read in a group. Mark these threads as read one by one, then select Show Only Unread Messages from the Options menu. To see all the messages again, including the ones you marked as read, choose Show All Messages from the Options menu.

10. *Group*—Marks all of the messages in the group as read. By default, when you open a newsgroup, Navigator only shows you unread messages. If you click this button after each session, you'll only see brand-new messages in your

next session. This will save you a lot of load time and time spent wading through messages you don't care about. See the Tip in "Reading Newsgroup Messages" later in the chapter for another good use for this feature.

11. *Print*—Prints the post currently displayed in the Message Content window. See "Printing From Navigator" later in the chapter for information on how to print all the messages in a thread or a collection of unrelated messages.

12. *Stop*—Stops the transmission of information from the server. If a newsgroup takes too long to load, press Stop. To reduce the number of message headers that load, change the value in the Get # Messages at a Time option in the Servers tab of Mail and News Preferences.

FINDING THE NEWSGROUPS THAT ARE AVAILABLE

To find out what groups a news server carries, click the title of the news server in the Newsgroups pane. From the Options menu, choose Show All Newsgroups. Navigator will tell you that this will take a while—and it will. This list is *very* long. When it finally displays, scroll through the list, opening folders and subfolders until you find something interesting. You subscribe to the group by checking the Subscribe checkbox next to the newsgroup name. When you've fished out all the newsgroups you want, choose Show Subscribed Newsgroups, and the tree of servers and newsgroups will collapse to only those you selected. New newsgroups are added to the Internet daily, so from time to time it pays to check what's been added. To do this, you *don't* have to wade through the entire list again like you did when you chose Show All Newsgroups: Choose Show New Newsgroups from the Options menu, and only new groups that have become available on your news server will display.

Keep in mind that all news servers do not offer the same selection of newsgroups, so you'll have to go through the process described above to see what each news server offers.

ADDING ANOTHER NEWS SERVER

The news server that you entered in Mail and News Preferences is the default server, but you can read newsgroups from any number of servers as long as you have access to the server. One server that you have access to is Netscape's Secure Newsgroup server. This server carries only newsgroups that pertain to Netscape products. To take a look at what the Netscape server has to offer, choose Open News Host from the File menu. Type in the address of the server in the prompt dialog box that appears, in this case enter: snews://secnews.netscape.com.

Click OK, and in a few seconds a new server, secnews.netscape.com, appears in the Newsgroup window. The address for this server began with snews// and not the usual news:// because it is a secure newsgroup server. See Chapter 7, "Maintaining Your Privacy on the Internet," for more information on secure services. To see all the newsgroups available on this server, right-click the name and choose Show All Newsgroups.

DECODING MULTI-PART BINARY FILES

Navigator will display and/or decode *single-part* binary files if they're in a format that Navigator supports. Figure 6-20 shows a picture of a sheep from alt.binaries.clip-art. This image was automatically decoded and displayed in the Message Content pane because it was entirely contained within one message and because Navigator natively supports the display of GIF format image. Right-click the image when it displays, then choose Save Image As to save it to your hard disk. Many of the binary files you'll find in the binary archives are divided into several parts because they are very large. To assemble these, you'll need a program like ESS-Code.

(See the Totally Hot Bookmarks List on the Companion CD-ROM for links to download sites for the Windows 3.1 and the Windows 95 versions of Ess-Code.) To decode and reassemble a uuencoded, multi-part binary file, save each file as text by pressing Ctrl+S and choosing Plain Text (*.txt), and give each part a filename that includes the part number and an extension of .uue: for example, flower1.uue, flower2.uue, and so on for as many parts as the file is broken into. Open the first file in ESS-Code, choose UUdecode from the File menu, choose flower1.uue, and follow the prompts from there. ESS-Code will find the other parts of the file for you. If the file was MIME encoded, choose the MIME-De-Code file from ESS-Codes file menu instead and follow the prompts.

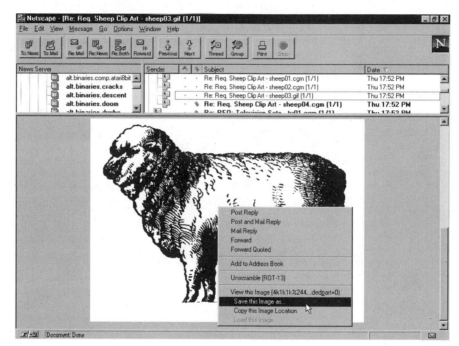

Figure 6-20: *Navigator automatically decodes single-part GIF format images like the one of this sheep.*

READING NEWSGROUP MESSAGES

Reading newsgroup messages is just like reading e-mail messages, but the "mailbox" is the newsgroup. Click a newsgroup, and the messages in that group display in the Message Heading pane. Click a message header, and the message displays in the Message Content window. The Navigator News window supports the right-click to bring up the shortcut menu; usc it to speed up your work.

TIP

Navigator is an online news reader—as soon as you choose another newsgroup or close the window, the messages are gone because they are not downloaded and stored on your computer. If you pay for your connect time by the hour or you want to defer reading newsgroup posts, there is a workaround for saving the messages. Flag all the messages you want to save by clicking in the Flag icon column next to each message. Click the Forward button (number 6 in Figure 6-19), and send the messages to your e-mail address. When you pick up your e-mail, all of the messages will be in one file, and you can read them at your leisure. The drawback to this method is that from the Navigator Mail window, you will not be able to post a response to the newsgroup. You will be limited to responding privately by e-mail to the person who wrote a post.

Which leads us to a workaround for the workaround. Before you close the News window (after you have forwarded the flagged messages), but with the messages you forwarded still flagged, click Group on the toolbar. The Group button marks all messages in the newsgroup as having been read. Then from the Edit menu, choose Select Flagged Messages. From the Message menu, choose Mark as Unread. Finally, close the News window. The next time you view this newsgroup, only the messages that you forwarded to yourself, plus any new messages, will display. If there was a post you wanted to respond to, it will be in the list if the post hasn't expired.

Points on What Not to Do in Newsgroups

Newsgroups are communities and as such have their own rules. If you break a rule, you will definitely get flamed (receive e-mail from countless people who hold your IQ in question). Before you post to *any* newsgroup, read the group for a while to learn what is acceptable in that group. What is acceptable in one group is often totally *unacceptable* in another. Find the FAQ (Frequently Asked Questions) for the group and read it before posting, so you don't ask an unnecessary question. See the Totally Hot Bookmarks List on the Companion CD-ROM for sites that carry the FAQs for many of the newsgroups.

- Never send attachments of any kind to a newsgroup unless it is a special kind of newsgroup with the word "binaries" in its name. Most newsgroups don't accept attachments; it will be removed, and you'll get flamed.

- Do not send enhanced e-mail (discussed later in this chapter) to a newsgroup. Newsgroups are not meant to handle this kind of correspondence.

- Never post a message or reply to a message unless you have something that will significantly add to the conversation. Newsgroups have a worldwide audience, and each post that is made adds to Internet congestion, adds to the time people spend online, and adds to the cost that your Internet provider pays for newsgroup access.

- Never send a commercial announcement or solicitation of any kind to any group except to a group that explicitly wants to receive such announcements.

- If someone has said something in a newsgroup you find offensive and you feel you must reply, *don't* post your reply to the group—send it as private e-mail. Otherwise, you fan the flames and clog up everyone's Inbox with non-constructive messages. (When responding to the message, click the Re: Mail button, *not* the Re: News button.)

- Never send the same message to more than one newsgroup unless you absolutely, positively *must*. If you do, don't send them as separate messages—send them as one message addressed to the various newsgroups. Separate the newsgroup names in the Newsgroup field with commas. For example: alt.test, misc.test.

- Do not send test messages to newsgroups. If you want to be sure your newsgroup messages are being sent and received, send a test message addressed to either *alt.test* or *misc.test*. Then go to these newsgroups and see if your message arrived. (Choose Add Newsgroup from the File menu, and type the address in the prompt box that appears.) These groups exist for the function of testing news. If you don't type the word "Ignore" in the Subject line of your test message, you will receive a number of automatically generated messages from servers around the world acknowledging receipt of your test message.

FILE ATTACHMENTS

If you send overnight letters using express couriers, you can now save a lot of money and get your document out within minutes by using Navigator Mail. Navigator Mail is adept at sending *file attachments* with e-mail; an attachment can be any kind of file—you're not limited to plain text or HTML files. For example, you can send: spreadsheets, word processing documents, CAD files, software programs, multimedia files or archived files. When you send a file attachment with your e-mail, it's a lot like tossing a floppy disk in an envelope. In fact, if the content you urgently need to send to someone can fit on a floppy diskette with room to spare, it's a good candidate for a file attachment.

When you send a file as an attachment to an e-mail message, Navigator encodes the file in the industry standard ASCII-based MIME format. When the file is received, the recipient's e-mail software decodes the file from the ASCII format back into its original 8-bit binary format. The encoding and decoding process is necessary because Internet e-mail service protocols were designed to only handle text and not binary data.

The encoding and decoding process happens quite quickly, but what may *not* happen as quickly is the time it takes to transfer the encoded file. When binary data is translated into ASCII, the resulting encoded file grows by more than a third in size, so a 320K DTP file becomes 442K when it is MIME encoded. If you or the recipient of the file has a slow Internet connection, you should try to limit the size of the files you send to about 100K.

TIP

One way to reduce the time it takes to send file attachments is to archive files using an archiving and compression utility like PKZip. The 320K DTP file becomes only 89K when zipped and 122K when translated into MIME format.

When the person you send an attachment to uses a MIME-compliant e-mail program like Navigator or Eudora, the decoding process occurs without the need for any user intervention. On the other hand, if the addressee's e-mail reader program doesn't understand MIME, they'll receive a single or series of sequential e-mail messages filled with the MIME encoded text that makes up the file you sent. There are many freeware and shareware programs that can take these MIME-filled e-mail messages and decode them back to the file's original state.

TIP

Ask if it's OK before you send a file attached to an e-mail message to someone who receives his or her Internet e-mail through an online service (the addresses of some of the most popular services have addresses that end in: @compuserve.com, @aol.com, @msn.com, or @prodigy.com). At the present time, subscribers of online services who receive e-mail from the Internet via their online service's e-mail system usually have to manually decode file attachments using a decoding utility, such as ESS-Code.

Each online service's e-mail system was engineered to serve its members' communications needs within the confines of that service. The online services are trying very hard to make the transfer of MIME e-mail attachments between the services' internal e-mail system and the Internet as easy as the transfer of ASCII-based e-mail, but have not yet arrived at a workable solution

BEFORE YOU ATTACH A FILE . . .

You can attach as many files as you like to an e-mail message but if you have a lot of files, or if each file you're sending is a large file, attach the files to different messages. If a network error occurs or some other problem develops in transit, *some* of your files might still get through, and you won't have to resend the sum total. This technique is called not putting all your eggs into one basket!

But before you click a button, you should decide if you want to send the file as-is or if you want to compress the file with a file compression program such as PKZip. If the files are small, there is an advantage to leaving them in their native state if your recipient is *also* using Navigator Mail. When Navigator is configured with a plug-in or helper application that can handle the kind of file you send, the recipient can view the attachment just by clicking the attachment link. If your correspondent hasn't configured an appropriate plug-in or helper application, she or he can save the file to disk by right-clicking the attachment. Figure 6-21 shows an Acrobat document of a federal tax form that was e-mailed as an attachment and viewed in the stand-alone version of Acrobat Reader.

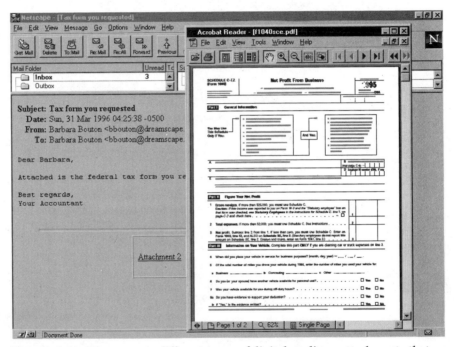

Figure 6-21: *You can pass different types of digital media as attachments that accompany a message.*

RECEIVING FILE ATTACHMENTS

Receiving file attachments that are sent to you is the other half of the file attachments story. Netscape Navigator also handles *incoming* attachments with grace. Attachments sent to you by a MIME-capable mailer are handled automatically. An attachment appears in the message pane either as a displayed inline object or as a link to the attachment (see Figure 6-22). *Inline* objects are attachments that Navigator automatically displays onscreen.

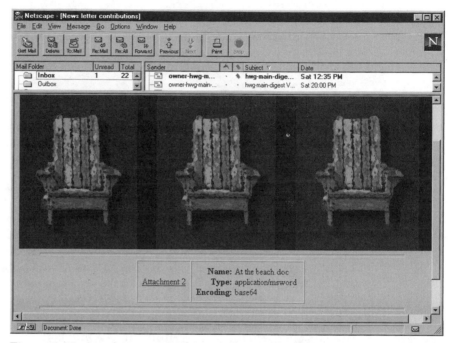

Figure 6-22: *Attachments can play as inline media if Navigator recognizes and supports the file type.*

Only files that are of a type that Navigator supports internally, such as ASCII text, HTML documents, or GIF or JPEG graphics, can be viewed inline. Any type of file, however, can be displayed as a link, which when clicked will either display the attachment, display it using a plug-in or helper application, or bring up the Unknown File Type dialog box seen in Figure 6-23. The Unknown File Type dialog box should be familiar to you because it is the same dialog box you saw in Chapter 5, "Power Search and Retrieval." This dialog box is displayed by Navigator whenever you ask it to handle a file type that is unknown to it—whether in e-mail, in newsgroups, or when downloading or saving files from HTML pages or FTP sites.

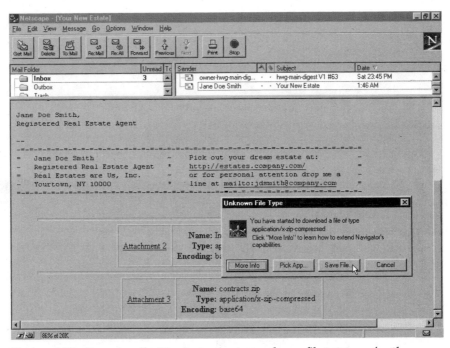

Figure 6-23: *Occasionally, Navigator is stumped on a file type; you're then provided with options for applications that will read the attachment.*

The choice to display as inline or as a link is made from the Mail window's View menu. You can change your method of viewing attachments at any time by choosing Attachments Inline or Attachments as Links from the Mail window's View menu.

TIP

Attachments are separated from the body of the message and from each other by a gray horizontal rule. If you've requested to view attachments in inline mode and you see a gray rule with nothing beneath it, switch the View to the Link mode. This happens sometimes when resources are low or if an animated GIF is running.

It is a fact of life that not everyone has upgraded to modern MIME-compliant mailing programs; many Internet citizens choose to use an older or platform-specific encoding scheme for e-mail attachments. One of these correspondents may send you a file attachment that is not in the MIME format. Most likely, the file will be encoded using either the BinHex (.HQX), MacBinary (.BIN), or uuencoded (.UUE) scheme. BinHex and MacBinary are common encoding schemes for Macintosh binary files, and UNIX users frequently use uuencoding. Uuencoding is also used by members of online services and by some corporate and university e-mail systems. Navigator will display attachments encoded with schemes other than MIME as links.

To decode these messages, you need to use a third-party decoder. ESS-Code (discussed earlier in the chapter) is an excellent uuencoder and decoder. StuffIt Expander for Windows (found on the Companion CD-ROM) will decode BinHex, MacBinary, or uuencoded files. Both of these programs can be configured as helper applications; see Chapter 2, "Installing & Customizing Navigator," for information on installing and using helper applications. Alternatively, you can save the links that need manual decoding as files to your hard disk and then run the decoding program outside of Netscape Navigator.

SAVING AN ATTACHMENT

Attachments you receive are stored in the e-mail message. As long as you keep the message that the file(s) is attached to in one of your mailboxes (other than the trash, of course), you can come back and view it at any time. This is a great way to keep multiple attachments together with the accompanying e-mail, so you always know where they came from and why. But if the attachment is a file that you need to install (a driver, a shareware program, a software patch), or is something that needs to be edited or placed into another program (such as a spreadsheet), or is a graphic bound for the company newsletter, you'll want to save it to your hard disk.

To save any attachment, right-click the link and choose Save Link as, as seen in Figure 6-24. Then give the file the same name as listed in the link box and save it to your hard disk.

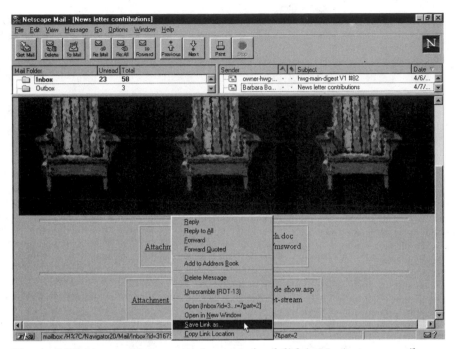

Figure 6-24: *You can save an attachment to hard disk in Navigator as easily as copying a file.*

PRINTING FROM NAVIGATOR

Printing from Navigator is one way to "save" an attachment or to share an e-mail message or newsgroup post with a colleague. The Navigator print engine is shared by all of the modules that make up Navigator, so the process of printing is always the same, no matter where you are or what you want to print. The Page Setup options set in the Page Setup dialog box (File, Page Setup) establish program-wide specifications for how a page will be printed (see Figure 6-25). These settings can be modified from any Navigator window that supports printing, and the changes will remain in effect until you change them from the same or a different Navigator window. If you haven't changed the defaults, Navigator will set each printed page with default margins of .5 inches, and will put information about the document and when it was printed in the header and footer of each printed page.

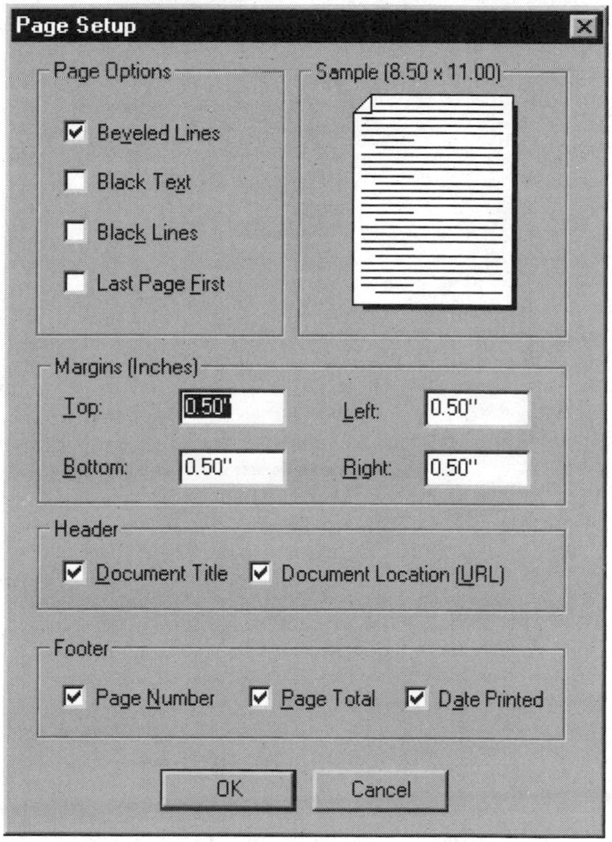

Figure 6-25: *Specify margin size and other print options in the Page Setup dialog box.*

Another program-wide printing feature is Print Preview, which is accessed by choosing Print Preview from the File menu. The Print Preview window, shown in Figure 6-26, shows how a document will look when printed with the current page setup.

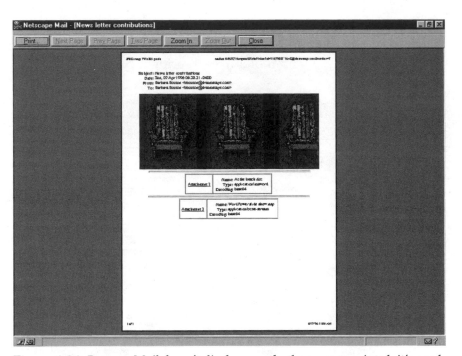

Figure 6-26: *Because Mail doesn't display exactly the same as printed, it's good to choose Preview before you print.*

To print an e-mail or newsgroup message, select the message in the Message Header window so that it becomes the current document and appears in the message pane. Click in the message pane, then press Ctrl+P (or choose File, then Print) to bring up a standard Windows print dialog box. Make any changes necessary to the settings in the print dialog, then click OK. Navigator sends whatever is displayed within the message pane to the printer, including what may not be visible but can be seen if you scroll through the message pane.

To print the attachments or objects that display as links, click the link to the attachment or object to open them one by one in the message pane, or right-click the images and choose Open in New Window to display them in a new Web browser window. Once they are opened in the message pane or a Web browser window, you can print them from Navigator. If you'd rather print them from a different program, save the files to disk.

TIP

If the Print button, the toolbar, or the Print Preview and Print menu commands are dimmed and therefore unavailable, it's because you have more than one message selected in the Message Header pane. Navigator 3 prints one message at a time and does not currently support batch printing of multiple messages.

There is a workaround for this current limitation. Select the messages you want to print, then click Forward on the toolbar. This will put all the messages you selected into one big e-mail message that contains all of the individual messages and their message headers. Address the e-mail to yourself. Click the Options menu in the Message Composition window and make sure that Deferred Delivery is selected. Then click Send. The message will be put into your Outbox. Open the Outbox, select the message, and print it.

As mentioned at the beginning of this section, e-mail attachments can be anything stored on a disk: a FAQ, a help file, or the spreadsheet that needs to be in Poughkeepsie by 5 PM. But if you've got an artistic flair, or share an office with a digital doodler, the possibilities for creating *enhanced* e-mail are just around the virtual corner, in the following section.

ADVANCED MAIL COMPOSITION

Second to the operating system on your PC, Navigator is perhaps the best collator, distributor, and interpreter of information that passes through your local and remote system connections. Web sites can become e-mail, e-mail can become a multimedia event, and the *creative* possibilities for your own e-mail are more limited by the appropriateness of the content than a challenge to your skills or Navigator's technology.

The following sections step outside of Netscape Navigator's Mail window for a while, as you see how other applications that you might own can be used in concert to make mail messages move, captivate, and impress the recipient with dimensions of correspondence that go beyond the written word.

THE EASIEST WAY TO CREATE HTML FOR MAIL

Hypertext Markup Language (HTML) belongs to the largest mail system on the Internet. It's called the World Wide Web. HTML documents, like the e-mail you write in the Mail window, are composed of ASCII text. However, there are special tags in this ASCII text-based markup language that do special things when interpreted by the right browser, which is almost universally Navigator's Browser. You can define links to other sites, make jumps within documents, display text in color or in frames . . . HTML is not your typical mail message!

However, HTML is a study in and of itself, and although you might not be fluent in HTML, there are still a number of ways that you can tap into some of HTML's power, and add graphical and other types of Web objects to your regular e-mail.

The easiest way to spruce up an attached file with HTML code is by using Navigator Gold's Editor. With Gold's Editor, you can create the page and then e-mail it from the Editor. If you don't have Navigator Gold, the alternatives are a text editor, a word processor, a DTP program such as Adobe PageMaker 6, or an HTML authoring tool.

In Figure 6-27, you can see some of the power of Navigator Gold's Editor window. The text appears exactly as you compose it in the Editor's window. It is sent as an attachment after you save the document locally. Choose File, Mail Message from the menu. Although this example looks as though it were composed in a DTP or word processor, there is complex underlying HTML code that Navigator Gold's Editor is generating, but neither you nor the recipient will see the ASCII text that Navigator interprets to display the layout unless you or the recipient chooses View, Document Source.

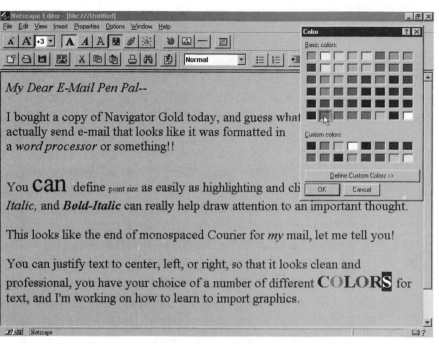

Figure 6-27: *Navigator Gold's Editor provides WYSIWYG features for composing an HTML document; HTML attachments can look more polished than text-only e-mail.*

The experience of working in Navigator Gold's Editor is not unlike the first time you received the "big box" of 164 crayons as a child; you're motivated to play with every drawing surface, or in this case, every message you intend to post. It should be noted, therefore, that HTML documents eat up a lot more Internet bandwidth than the same message sent as regular e-mail. Use the "toys" in the following sections with discretion and for the appropriate occasion; and yes, it's only human (and not *totally* irresponsible!) to give them a spin once or twice simply for the fun of it.

HOW DO YOU LEARN TO WRITE HTML?

As mentioned in the previous section, HTML is text-based code that the browser interprets to provide graphics, layout, and to call plug-ins for linked objects such as AVI files and other Web-designed elements. And as text-only, HTML is written by experienced individuals in any program that supports plain ASCII text. Navigator Gold makes it easy to generate code without learning it, but your interests in Web-wide communications might lead you to wanting to learn the inner workings of this language.

Full HTML documentation is beyond the scope of this book, but we recommend that you pick up a copy of *Official HTML Publishing for Netscape* (by Stuart Harris and Gayle Kidder) as a basis for your study. For learning how to create graphics, multimedia objects, animated GIFs, and other Web content to go into those HTML pages or into your Navigator e-mail, try *Multimedia Publishing for Netscape* by Gary David Bouton. Both are published by Netscape Press.

CD-ROM — To supplement your reading, check out the HTML Authoring (sites listed in the Totally Hot Bookmarks List on the Companion CD-ROM), as well as the HTML examples we've provided, to get you started. If you use Navigator Gold, check out the templates that are available from Netscape's site for inspiration and guidance. To get to the Netscape templates, choose New Document from the Browser or the Editor's File menu, then choose From Template from the submenu.

And when you see a page layout you like, take a look at the HTML source code by choosing Document Source from the View menu—or save the page to your hard disk as Source—and examine how the HTML tags make the document work.

WHICH OBJECTS CAN YOU ATTACH?

Through independent experimentation, you may have been delighted or disappointed that some programs and files go across the Internet with unexpected results on the receiving end. Almost anything that can be put on a Web page can be sent through e-mail as an attachment: graphics, sound, animation, and more. If what you've sent is natively supported by Navigator, objects will automatically display in your e-mail. If a plug-in or helper is required to play an object, it will appear in the e-mail as an attachment link.

The Internet is a constantly changing place, and it seems as though enhancements that didn't exist yesterday can be accomplished today. The following sections take you through the current "State of the Art" with respect to Web-bound data that can—and cannot—be sent as a self-playing object. Additionally, there are a few examples of enhancements you can add to your e-mail through the use of applications you might already own. If you have a drawing program or a modeling application, Web-authoring through e-mail can be easier than you think!

CREATING AN HTML "LETTERHEAD" MESSAGE

If you're familiar with HTML or you have Navigator Gold, it's not hard to make a *letterhead* mailing piece; the components of the mailed message can be a GIF image, which serves as the letterhead graphic, and an HTML document for the body of the letter. The HTML document can sport colored text and styles such as italic and bold sections but it shouldn't contain any inline objects and graphics because they don't transfer automatically and won't display in place in the HTML document. They can be sent as separate objects, though, and will appear as links in the recipient's mail in the order in which they're attached to the message.

> ### TIP
>
> *The way to e-mail an HTML document so that it displays with all the graphics and other elements neatly in place within the HTML page is to also place the HTML document and all of its component elements on an Internet, Intranet, or network server. The server must be accessible to the recipient when he or she reads your e-mail message for all of the elements to display properly. For example, when you read the Welcome! letter from Mozilla, the graphics display only if you are online when you read the document because they are downloaded from the Netscape site when you open the message.*

In Figure 6-28, you can see a mailing received from Billy Bland and his Polka Band (this is a fictitious message and sort of an obnoxious use of Internet e-mail, but you get the point). You can create your own electronic letterhead stationery by using a GIF or JPEG graphic as the letterhead part of the document. Use an existing graphic you have or, as shown in the following steps, create one for yourself.

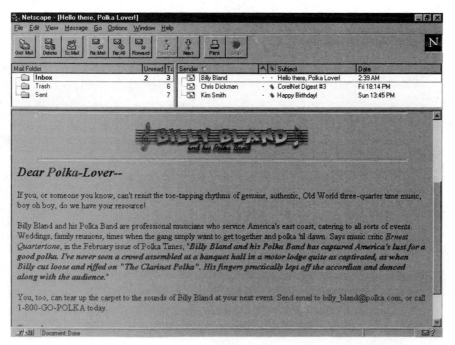

Figure 6-28: *An e-mail letterhead message can be sent if you know how to choreograph the elements.*

To create the letterhead GIF file, you'll need an application that can write to this format. Paint Shop Pro, a very capable shareware program, can be found on the Companion CD-ROM. To use this program to make a GIF 89a interlaced file (the most commonly used kind of graphic that Navigator supports natively), follow these steps:

1. After you've installed Paint Shop Pro, double-click the background swatch on the Select toolbox, then choose a background color for the letterhead image from Windows' color picker. Click OK when you've decided on a color.

2. Choose File, then New; then type 200 in the Width field, type 75 in the Height field, choose 16.7 million colors from the Image Type drop-down list, and click OK. GIF graphics need to be small in dimensions, and GIFs attached to e-mail look best when composed to a fairly squat, wide proportion. In Figure 6-28, you can see that Billy Bland's letterhead looks appropriate in a landscape-oriented composition within the Mail window.

3. Choose a foreground color from the Select toolbox that contrasts with the background color, then click the Text tool on the Paint toolbox, and click in the new image window. This action will display the Add Text dialog box. If you have more than 100 fonts installed on your PC, the box might take a moment or two to appear.

4. Choose a font, a font style, and a size for your text. Because of the small size of the GIF image, 36-point text should be the maximum size (see the following TIP). Type your name, slogan, or product in the Text field at the bottom of the dialog box, then click OK.

5. The text you typed will appear as a reverse video floating object in the image, held by a placement cursor. You are free to move the image until you get it placed where you want it. To fix it into place, click a part of the image background.

6. Choose Colors, Decrease Color Depth, then choose 256 colors (8-bit). Although it's good to design with a high number of colors, the GIF format is only capable of holding 256 unique colors; and Paint Shop Pro will flag you if you attempt to export a 16.7 million color image to this format.

7. Choose Palette: Optimized, then Color Reduction Method: Error Diffusion. Click OK.

8. Choose File, Save As, then pick a location on your hard disk to save to. Choose GIF-CompuServe from the List Files of Type drop-down list, choose Version 89a-Interlaced from the File Sub-Format, name the file (LETRHEAD.GIF). Click OK.

TIP

If you need to use text as a graphic when composing enhanced e-mail, a point—the measurement used in typography to specify font size—is approximately equal to monitor resolution (which is 72 pixels/inch). Therefore, if your paint application tells you that a font is 100 points tall, you will need an image at least 100 pixels in height to support the text. In case your paint program doesn't offer pixels as a unit of measurement, 72 points (or 72 pixels) equal an inch.

Admittedly, the preceding example was not a second-year college art course. But embellishments aside, those are the steps to take to make an image that can be attached, and will download speedily to the recipient. Here's how to arrange the letterhead message:

1. If you have an HTML document handy to use as the body of your letter, put the HTML file in the same folder as the graphic you created in the previous example. If you don't have Navigator Gold or HTML authoring experience, a plain ASCII text message created in Notepad.exe or TextPad.exe (found on the Companion CD-ROM) will work here.

2. In Navigator, double-click the Mail icon in the bottom right of the window, enter your password, then click the To: Mail button on the toolbar.

3. In the Message Composition window, fill in the address of the recipient, then click Attach.

4. Click the Attach File button in the Attachments dialog box, locate the GIF you saved earlier, click it to select it, then click OK.

CD-ROM

5. Repeat the last step with the HTML file (or the text file) you want to be received after the letterhead graphic. You don't want to enter your message in the Message Composition window because text entered in the window appears before any attachments—in this case, the letterhead graphic.

6. Change your signature file at this point if you'd like (this is your last chance before mailing), then click Send on the toolbar.

This basic procedure can be used to send different types of attachments, as you'll see in the next section.

MAILING A SELF-RUNNING ANIMATION

The difference between the GIF you saw how to create in Paint Shop Pro and an *animated* GIF—one of the hottest new Web elements—lies in the header information of the GIF file. Royal Frazier, a programmer, discovered a short time ago that the structure of the GIF format of computer graphics could be annotated, and that more than one image could be displayed in a sequence that looks like an animated AVI file. He also discovered that Navigator version 2.0 and later would "play" the GIF file when loaded into the browser window or referenced in an HTML document. The advantage to using animated GIFs in e-mail is that they can be fairly small, so they don't take long to transfer, and they don't require any special plug-in or helper applications to display within Navigator. On the Companion CD-ROM, you'll find a small collection of animated GIFs in the CHAP06 folder that are ready for you to use in your correspondence. If you'd like to *create* your own custom-animated GIF for your e-mail, read on.

As of this writing, only one Windows application—Steve Rimmer's GIF Construction Set, a shareware utility—allows non-programmers to write the same information into multiple GIF files to produce an animation. While GIF Construction Set is not a hard application to learn, you might need the resource images that make up an animated sequence. There are many animation packages available for Windows 95, and many of them are in the $200-$500 range. Also, if you're handy with a paint program, you might be able to correctly paint or draw several files that look like an animation when played in sequence.

If you purchased CorelDRAW 6, CorelMOTION 3D comes essentially free in the software bundle, and it can create a sequence of still images that can be imported into GIF Construction Set. Your other resources for images to make up an animated GIF could be a friend who is interested in modeling, digital video, animation, a clip art collection, or even a paint program, and has some time on the weekend. The important consideration here is that the sequence of still image files should be the same size (and that size should be no more than 100 pixels on a side) and the action that occurs in the images will produce the desired effect if the images are played one after the other. In Figure 6-29, you can see CorelMOTION 3D's workspace, with a 3D "Happy Birthday!" text object hovering in front of a bitmap background image.

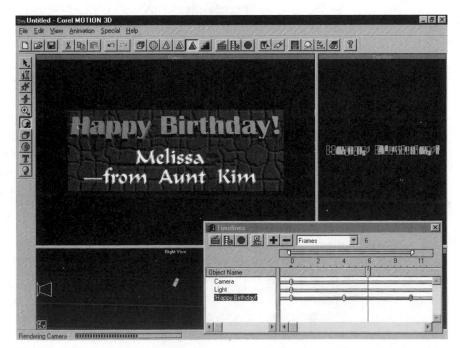

Figure 6-29: *Animation applications can create the resource images you need to design an animated GIF file.*

MOTION 3D was used to render 10 still images of the text object tilting and narrowing, then GIF Construction Set was used to create the animated GIF as shown in the steps to follow:

1. In GIF Construction Set, you begin an animated file by choosing File, New. This places a HEADER file at the top of the list in GIF Construction Set's onscreen list of animation ingredients. If you know how large, in pixel dimensions, your still images are, you can double-click the HEADER title now and specify these same dimensions. The HEADER has to carry the same pixel dimensions, or the animation will look funny when played in Navigator. But if you don't know the dimensions of your images, GIF Construction Set will tell you the information after you import one of the animation images; you can perform this step later in the process.

2. Click Insert, then click the LOOP button. This adds the LOOP information to the recipe; the animated GIF will play back and forth in Navigator, as though you created an endless loop of recorded sound or film.

3. Click Insert, then click the CONTROL button. This step places a CONTROL block of information in the animation that will tell Navigator to replace onscreen information with information to follow.

4. Click Insert, then Image. Choose the first image of the animation from your hard disk, and click OK to import a copy. At this point, GIF Construction Set will tell you that the color palette of the file to be imported does not match its own color palette. Without getting into the GIF Construction Set's documentation, your best option at this point is *Use it as it is (may introduce color shifts)*. Click this option, then click OK.

5. Every subsequent image file you import must have the CONTROL block placed before it; repeat steps 3 and 4 for as many images as you have that make up the animation. See Figure 6-30 for an idea of what GIF Construction Set's list should look like upon completing the work.

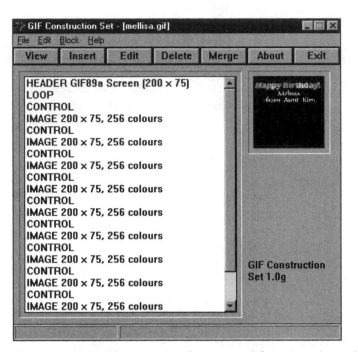

Figure 6-30: *GIF Construction Set is your ticket to creating animations you can attach to e-mail.*

6. Choose File, Save, then save the file in GIF format to your hard disk.

There are a number of animated GIFs in the CHAP06 folder of the Companion CD-ROM that were created using the same steps as those shown above.

In Figure 6-31, the same steps were used to attach the animated GIF as those used to create the letterhead attachment.

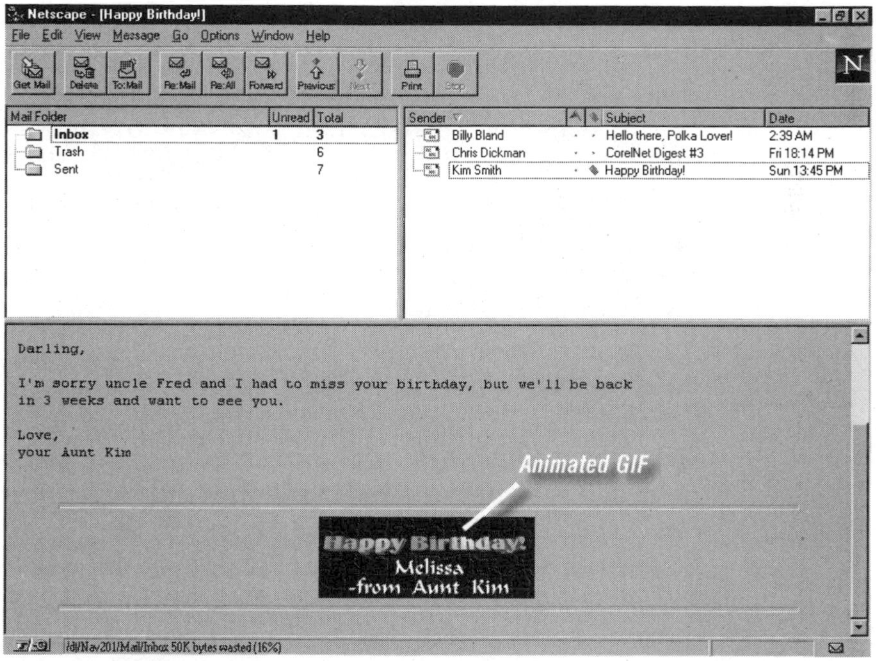

Figure 6-31: *Animated GIF images are attention-getting, small, and probably should be reserved for special mailings!*

The overuse of any Web element can become tiresome and even irritating if used without discretion. Already many sites are so densely peppered with animations that it's like surfing through mud on such a site. However, if your e-mail is to a friend, or to get positive attention from a potential customer, you now know the technique for animating an image—the *content* of the presentation is up to you.

YOU CAN SEND SIMPLE JAVASCRIPT APPLETS

If you're a whiz at programming, you can make simple JavaScript enhancements to your e-mail, such as a line of text that changes from Good Morning to Good Afternoon at 12 noon every day. JavaScript enhancements only work if your recipient is using Navigator 2 or later—other e-mail programs will show your script instead of performing the desired action. The JavaScript must be written into an HTML file that you send as your e-mail message.

(Click the Attach button on the Message Composition toolbar, choose Attach File, choose the HTML file you've written, and make sure the As Is radio button is chosen; then click OK.) Before you send JavaScript-enhanced e-mail, be sure to e-mail a copy to yourself to make sure it will work in the Message Content window, not all JavaScript features are supported in the Message Content window. To learn the ins and outs of JavaScript programming I recommend you take a look at *Official Netscape JavaScript Book* by Peter Kent, from Netscape Press.

MAILING A VIRTUAL WORLD—YOU'RE KIDDING, RIGHT?

Sending a VRML (Virtual Reality Modeling Language) file through e-mail is not an everyday sort of thing. However, if you need to help someone visualize something in 3D (like a floor plan, a manufacturing design, or a dinosaur), and if you have access to a DXF file (or the skill to create one) and a program that can write a Virtual World (*.WRL) file, you can e-mail someone a 3D file that they can walk or fly through onscreen.

There are one or two provisos to the following example, and bandwidth is one of them. Do *not*, under any circumstances, e-mail a VRML attachment to someone you're not good friends with, or who is not expecting the file. VRML files *begin* at about 40K for the simplest of "worlds" (a simple sphere and a cube qualify as a virtual world), and mailing a VRML file as a whim really cuts down on overall Internet throughput.

Also, you should alert the recipient, perhaps a day or two in advance, that you intend to e-mail a VRML file. This would give the recipient time to install the Netscape Live3D plug-in if it is not already installed. To view VRML worlds you need to have a plug-in that supports the display of VRML worlds. The Standard downloadable version of Navigator as well as the retail version of Navigator includes the Live3D plug-in and automatically installs it. The Minimum downloadable version of Navigator does not include the Live3D plug-in. The plug-in can be downloaded and installed separately from: http://home.netscape.com/comprod/mirror/navcomponents_download.html.

The specifications for the approved version 1 of VRML can be down-loaded from http://vrml.wired.com/vrml.tech/vrml10-3.html. In this specification document, you'll find sample code which, if you copy to a text editor, will produce simple VRML worlds you can play in Navigator's Browser or attach to e-mail. Also, check out the Aereal Inc. Web site (http://www.virtpark.com/theme/), where you can create 3D VRML text and download the file for your own use.

You have two options for the creation of a VRML file you want to e-mail: You can author the file in a text editor (it's actually possible if you read the VRML Specifications), or you can use a VRML authoring tool. Pioneer, by Caligari Software, is perhaps the most direct route to creating VRML files; it's about $100, and its graphical interface allows you to sculpt and bend and attach shapes without needing to know a line of VRML code. You do, however, need to spend some quality time with the documentation, and an artistic eye would serve you well if you decide that your e-mail should look every ounce as good as a commercial Web site. You can get a trial version of Pioneer at http://www.caligari.com. The following is an overview of how to use Pioneer to create a VRML file:

■   In Pioneer, you can create instant primitive 3D objects by clicking the icons on the Primitives panel. You then click and drag the primitives around in 3D space to align with other primitives to build more complex objects. In Figure 6-32, you can see that a clown figure has been constructed from spheres and a couple of cones. The VRML code that Pioneer generates so Navigator can reproduce what you see in Fountain's modeling space is beyond the capability of users without a degree in programming and math to write by hand.

Figure 6-32: *Soon this clown will be transformed into a VRML virtual world that Navigator's Live3D plug-in displays as a place that your e-mail recipient can fly or walk through onscreen.*

- Pioneer also allows you to import 3D object files from several other applications. The most common format for 3D models is the DXF format. Many manufacturers offer clip object collections in the DXF format of chairs, fighter jets, buildings, and other real-world shapes that you can simply pose in Pioneer and export.

- Pioneer saves and reads files in the virtual world WRL file type. When you have a scene composed, choose File, then Save Scene As. Find a location on your hard disk for the file, name it, and you have a file you can attach to e-mail as easily as a GIF or HTML document.

In Figure 6-33, you can see the attached WRL file playing in Netscape's Mail window. Upon receipt of this attachment, Navigator's Message Content pane will display the VRML file as an attachment link, with information identifying the type of file. Click it. If you have the Live3D plug-in installed correctly, the pane will display navigation controls, and the recipient of the virtual world can pan, tilt, and cruise through to get a complete view of your work.

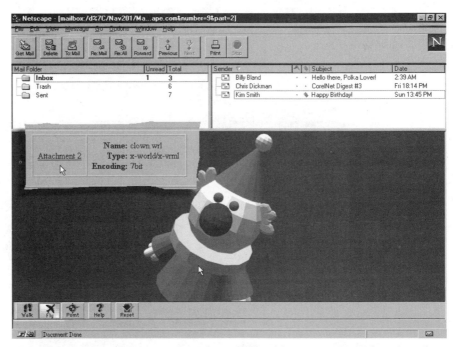

Figure 6-33: *Your online correspondent will be able to interact with a virtual world in the same way you can move graphics around in a page layout program—except a VRML world has three dimensions in which to navigate!*

In Figure 6-34, you can see perhaps a more commerce-oriented use for sending a VRML world as an attachment. If your office uses Navigator as an Intranet (in-office) communications tool, chances are that you can use one of your company's common access or Web servers to store your creations. When creating the HTML document you'd specify the location of all of the files, including the VRML file as being on the common access or Web server. Then just send the document from Engineering to Marketing announcing the latest innovation!

CD-ROM

If you'd like a first-hand look at this example, copy the AD-VANCE folder and its contents from the CHAP06 directory on the Companion CD-ROM. Then drag the ADVANCE. HTM document from the ADVANCE folder on your hard disk into Navigator's Browser window. Then have fun!

Note: If you used frames in your HTML document to keep the VRML world onscreen while allowing the memo to scroll, as we did in this example be sure to ask your recipients to open the link in a new browser window, because frameset documents can't be displayed within the Message Content window.

Figure 6-34: *Open links to frameset documents in a new browser window and then sit back and enjoy the view or fly around a VRML world.*

Attachments Can Be Wonderful . . . & Irritating

For all the splendid, thoughtful, and diverse gifts you can attach to your e-mail, use common sense when using all the new toys—don't send this stuff unsolicited or to mailing lists unless you *really* know that the recipient won't mind. Be kind to bandwidth and to the fact that all these attachments add to file sizes and increase download time. Many users pay by the hour.

Walking the Lines After a Storm: E-Mail Troubleshooting

Occasionally you will send an e-mail message that will be returned to you as having been rejected, refused, or undeliverable because the user was unknown or there was some kind of network difficulty. To get your e-mail back on track and in the right hands, follow these troubleshooting tips.

Use Header Information to Identify the Problem

From the Mail window's Options menu, choose Show All Headers or press Alt+O+L. This command toggles the full display of e-mail header information on and off. Normally you don't need to see all the routing and other information reported in the message header. But when troubleshooting undelivered e-mail, the cause of the problem is often listed in the Mail header.

Read the header of the message that you received carefully. Which server had the problem? Was it your ISP's mail server or the recipient's mail server that had difficulty? Does it say that there was a network error of some kind? Does it say that the host or the recipient is unknown?

IDENTITY ERRORS

When either the host or the recipient is unknown, the error is almost always caused either by a spelling mistake or because the recipient no longer has an account at that address. Check the address. If it's an addressing error, then resend the message with the corrected address. When resending the message, *don't use the Reply or the Forward commands, instead create a new message.* If you use Reply to send the message that bounced back to you, it will contain the address of the mail system that reported the error. If you use the Forward command, you'll end up with your message all in quote back and leave your recipient wondering.

Instead, go to the mailbox you've designated as the mailbox for messages you've sent, click on the message title to display it in the Message Content Pane, and then use the mouse to select the contents of your message. Copy the selected text to the Clipboard (Ctrl+C or Edit, Copy). Open a new Message Composition window (Ctrl+M or click the To: Mail button on the toolbar), and cut and paste the body of the message into the message pane. Fill in the address and Subject line, and attach any files that may need to be sent along with the new e-mail message. Click Send on the toolbar when you're done, and the next time you see the message it should be in the quote-back section of your recipient's reply.

FAULTY REPLY TO ADDRESSES

Sometimes you'll get e-mail back that *you* didn't address incorrectly, but rather was addressed to the wrong server. Some e-mail systems use one address for sending e-mail and another for receiving e-mail; so in such a case, when the message is replied to by clicking the Re: Mail or Re: All buttons on the toolbar or choosing Reply or Reply All from the shortcut menu, it often goes to the wrong place. When this is the problem, the tipoff is usually that the address is quite long and perhaps contains the word "gate" in it somewhere. Users whose e-mail systems work this way usually post their reply-to information in their signature file, so take a look there. If you don't find anything promising, try editing the address back so that it follows this format: username@something.com. Mail addresses are usually quite short.

TIP

If you correspond frequently with this person, create an Address Book entry for them that contains their correct address and then always use the Address Book to address your mail to them instead of the Reply commands. Don't make the Address Book entry from the Add to Address Book command on the shortcut menu, because this too takes its information from the From: field of the header when there is no entry in the Reply To: field of the message header and you'll get the wrong address again.

You'll also want to create an Address Book entry for private responses to those who post messages in Internet mailing lists. Unlike in the News window, there is no option to reply to the address in the From: line (which is the personal address of the author of the message) and to the address in the Reply To: line (which is the address of the mailing list software that forwards the messages to the members of the list). Using the toolbar buttons or the shortcut menu commands to respond to the message in this case will always send your response to the entire mailing list and not the individual.

If *your* e-mail system behaves this way, be sure to fill in the Reply-To-Address in the Identity tab of the Mail and News Preferences, so e-mail sent to you will reach you.

If your e-mail still comes back, call the person on the telephone and ask for the address. This way is really the quickest and most reliable. If you can't get a hold of him or her, try searching for the address in any of the Internet white pages services discussed in Chapter 5, "Power Search & Retrieval," or send e-mail to the postmaster at the address you're having difficulty reaching. The address for the postmaster usually looks like this: postmaster@wherever.com. Not all systems have a postmaster. And due to privacy concerns, not all postmasters will supply the information you seek, but it's worth a try. Postmasters are busy people, so save this option as your last resort.

NETWORK ERRORS

Mail sent via the Internet passes though many different computer systems and gateways, all of which fail at one time or another. The system was designed with great resiliency and redundancy, so most of the time your e-mail makes it through—no matter how far it has to travel or how circuitous the route. Occasionally your e-mail will hit a roadblock or a system error that it can't overcome in a reasonable amount of time. When this happens, the e-mail system makes every effort to return the e-mail you sent with an explanation of the difficulty. Usually your best course of action is to wait awhile and resend the e-mail.

Sometimes the message you get back tells you not to resend the message. This situation arises when the recipient's mail server is not responding. The Internet e-mail system patiently tries to contact the downed server. After four or five hours of no response, it notifies you of the situation and says it will continue to try for five days. If your e-mail is of a timely nature, you probably don't want to wait five days for the situation to resolve itself. Try resending the e-mail once more. If it still won't go through, consider using the phone, an express courier, or "snail mail" (the regular paper-based mail system).

MOVING ON

For all the communications innovations and new methods for personal expression the Internet has opened to users, the issue of Internet *security* still follows in the shadows of the new, remarkable technology. Netscape has provided several features in Navigator to make confidentiality in business transactions and correspondence closer to the interactions that happen every day in stores and closed boardrooms. Chapter 7, "Maintaining Your Privacy on the Internet," takes a closer look at the best ways you can ensure that your communications and other transactions are your *own* business, and that your e-mail is not subject to eavesdropping.

7

Maintaining Your Privacy on the Internet

Protecting the privacy of your correspondence and the data that you send and receive might not leap to the forefront of your priorities when you access the Net, but it's something that Netscape Communications has addressed through the investment of time and resources. Netscape products are built from the ground up with security in mind. In the same way that seat belts and airbags make riding in cars safer through automatic implementation, Netscape has built in a number of security features that automatically activate when you send or receive data, so you can concentrate on the *content* of your business or leisure activity. Even though the cyberspace equivalent of seat belts and airbags is designed into Navigator and other Netscape products, you still need to exercise your own good judgment and keep your eyes on the road to avoid potholes and bandits on the Information Superhighway.

This chapter examines the security and privacy issues of the Internet and what you and Navigator can do today—and in the future—to ensure your personal and corporate privacy.

THE SECURITY OF YOUR INTERNET ID

In the real world, when you need to prove your age, your legal right to drive, or your membership in a superstore discount club, you present your ID. In turn, when you want to verify that a merchant or customer is who they claim to be, you might ask for similar identification. A physical ID is then routinely inspected, and a photograph or signature is compared to that of the presenter. In the physical world identification process, you also examine the *quality* of the ID. You are much more likely to accept a passport or a driver's license with a picture on it than a business card or an ID card from a business or school you've never heard of. Proving your own identity or that of others on the Internet has historically been difficult because the only ID that Internet users have easy access to is an e-mail address.

Your e-mail address and the name you enter in the Identity field of the Options preferences in Navigator are used to identify you in your mail and newsgroup postings. In addition this information is usually requested when you download software or sign guest books on the Web. This is called an Internet identity and is seen whenever an e-mail message is sent, or an article is posted to a Usenet group. But e-mail addresses don't carry your photo, your signature, or your fingerprint, and they aren't issued or verified by an impartial authority like the Department of Motor Vehicles or the U.S. Immigration Authority. Nor does an e-mail address ensure that it is you sitting at your computer and not a co-worker, relative, or someone else with access to your PC.

In the same way that a physical ID can be forged, so can e-mail and server addresses. It is not common, but it's possible, for a skilled and determined user, sometimes referred to as a *hacker* or *cracker,* to "spoof" (trick) servers. Similarly, it is possible to intercept, divert, or eavesdrop on Internet traffic bound for a site on the Web, such as a bank transaction. The practitioners of spoofing and other malicious practices—when not referred to by their federal penitentiary numbers—are often called *crackers,* most likely from the term safecracker. The term *hacker* is usually, but not always, reserved for those who indulge in unauthorized online escapades for sport, not profit, or those who decompile computer code—

again, for thrills, not capital gain. With special software (*not* explained in this book for obvious reasons!), crackers or hackers can make a server think it's being accessed by someone other than the actual user. Internet ID forgers can also send e-mail from someone other than the named sender. However, you are much more likely to be impersonated by someone who has physical access to your computer—a malicious co-worker or a family member playing a prank—than a faceless Internet marauder.

As monetary transactions grow in number on the Web, it's important, then, to begin a pro-active campaign against cyber-theft, to ensure against personal loss, and to make certain that private communications are actually private. Therefore, when you're presented with an opportunity to download a file, for example, in exchange for a user ID or other personal information, it would be wise to consider a number of criteria and evaluate the quality of the merchandise first. If you use the Internet primarily to browse Web pages, proving your identity or being concerned about your identity being appropriated by others is probably not a concern that would give you a moment's pause. But there *are* situations when it is a vital concern. Verifying who you are dealing with and being able to positively identify yourself are extremely important when purchasing goods or services over the Internet, when accessing your organization's Intranet or other private site from the Internet, or when transmitting sensitive personal or business information.

As you will see in this chapter, Netscape Navigator 3.0 has put powerful new tools at your disposal to help you protect the privacy of your communications while they are in transit and a new, secure way to establish your identity to others and confirm the identity of people with whom you are communicating.

PRIVACY & SECURITY DEPEND ON COMMON SENSE

Before discussing the various methods that Netscape offers for secure transactions, Internet anonymity, and privacy issues, it's important to understand that the weakest link in any security system is often ourselves. Because cyberspace seems vast and free, even experienced users often forget to "take the keys out of the ignition" or to "return the family gems to the safe" whenever they go online.

The fact that we use passwords to protect our accounts does not ensure their safety, especially if you have a password that is easy to guess, taped to the front of your monitor, or slipped underneath your keyboard. To help maintain the secrecy and privacy of your passwords and IDs, it is imperative that you *never* share them with anyone.

If Samuel Clemens, better known as Mark Twain, were part of the Internet community these days, he might well revise his famous quote about secrecy: an *online* secret is something held by one, but *lost* by two. Privacy is best guarded by ourselves. We all need to think twice before sending e-mail to a co-worker about what a jerk the boss is or before announcing to a newsgroup that we won't be able to use our expensive new home computer next week because we're taking the family away on vacation. The need for exercising common sense is as much of a necessity online as it is in our everyday lives.

If you access the Internet or Intranet via your company's network, you should remember that the systems administrator almost always has access to your passwords and anything on your system. The law surrounding privacy in the workplace is evolving, but you will always be safer if you take the tack that your company may have the right to, and may actually be keeping tabs on, your online activity as well as your correspondence.

If you access the Internet though an Internet Access Provider, the systems administrator there also has access to the password you use to log on to their service. Their computers also typically track your usage of the system—when you logged on and off and what services you accessed—for billing purposes or as part of monitoring the performance of their system. This is not unlike the telephone company that maintains records on the long distance calls you make. The phone company is not in the business of breaching your privacy and neither is your ISP; both want satisfied customers.

Admittedly, all of this preceding discussion on potential security or violations of privacy may seem a bit intimidating. We've brought them to your attention so that you can make informed judgments about what you are comfortable doing or not doing on the Net. Many, if not all the issues, can be looked at as "worst-case scenarios." With the vast amount of information circling around the Net and an Intranet, the chances that your data will be intercepted for malicious use is quite low. Your common sense, coupled with the advanced security features Netscape and its partners have and continue to implement, make using the Internet safer and more worry-free every day.

CRYPTOGRAPHY: BEYOND PASSWORD SECURITY

Netscape bases many of the security features in the Navigator Browser and in its Internet servers on strong cryptography. Strong cryptography that was once available only to large corporations, financial institutions, and the government is now available to protect you in your Internet travels. It's important that you have a general understanding of what cryptography is all about and when and how it is used in order to appreciate the value of Netscape's security implementations. Cryptography is the art and science that underlies the process of changing messages and data into a form that can be read or used only by the intended recipient. Messages or data that are being sent are encrypted using special cryptographic techniques and are decrypted into usable form by the recipient using a complementary cryptographic technique.

Thousands of cryptographic techniques are available, from those provided by secret decoder rings found in cereal boxes to those used by governments to protect national secrets. Netscape has integrated a secure cryptographic method in its products that is based on the technique known as RSA public-key encryption. This form of encryption uses sets of "keys" to encrypt data. The longer the key used (measured in bits), the more secure the encryption. Navigator's public-key encryption methods are so secure that the government has classified some implementations of it as a munition, that can't be exported without a special, almost unattainable government permit. Consequentially, the kind of encryption used in Navigator varies according to where the product is delivered. The retail, boxed version of Navigator sold in the U.S. and Canada uses a long, secure 128-bit RSA key, as do Netscape server products. However, the export versions of Navigator and other Netscape products and any Netscape software that can be downloaded from Netscape's site uses a weaker 40-bit RSA key.

HOW WEAK IS WEAK?

A *single* message that was encrypted using the weaker, 40-bit key was decrypted by a French student, Damien Doligez, in 1995. It took 120 workstations and two parallel-processing supercomputers working for eight straight days to crack the message. If he wanted to open another message he would have to devote the same resources and time to the task. It is unlikely that anyone other than a government or someone with access to massive amounts of computational power (between 64 and 100 MPS per year) could open any message encrypted with the "weak" key.

The 128-bit RSA key that is approved for use in the U.S. and Canada is 1,000,000,000,000 (trillion) times harder to decrypt. It is not believed that even a government security agency could bring to bear enough computational power to crack open and read a single message that was encrypted using a 128-bit key.

PUBLIC-KEY VS. SECRET-KEY CRYPTOGRAPHY

Traditional cryptography known as *secret-key cryptography* is based on the sender and the receiver of material using the same secret key (essentially having the same secret decoder ring). The weakness to secret-key encryption is that the sender must find a safe way to provide the recipient with the key because anyone who intercepts a copy of the secret key or who can guess the secret key can unlock or decrypt the message.

RSA public-key cryptography, invented by Ronald Rivest, Adi Shamir, and Leonard Adelman, operates on a completely different principle. Every user of public-key encryption has two unique keys: a private key and a public key. These two keys are bound to each other in a relationship that cannot be discovered or guessed. And no one else in the world has the same set of public and private keys.

The public key in and of itself does nothing and offers no clue as to the nature or structure of the companion private key. Public keys are made public by distributing them widely. It is perfectly safe, even desirable to give it to anyone who asks for it or to deposit it with a public keyserver. A keyserver is a trusted third-party who accepts a copy of your public key from you and then gives an exact copy of the key to those who ask for a copy of your public key. When a person doesn't get a copy of your key directly from you, this process assures them that they have a true copy of your public key and not the key of someone who is impersonating you.

The private or secret key, on the other hand, is *never* distributed or revealed to anyone. The integrity of the system hinges on the secrecy of the private key.

When a message is sent using public-key encryption, the sender of the message uses his or her private key and the *recipient's* public key to encrypt the message. The combined use of these keys creates a uniquely encrypted message that can only be opened (decrypted) by using the recipient's private key and the sender's public key. It *always* takes two keys to encrypt and decrypt messages. But not any two keys. As soon as the sender uses the recipient's public key along with his or her own private key to lock the message, a mathematically unique relationship has been established. The only other keys on Earth that can understand the relationship and can unlock the message are the sender's public key and the recipient's private key. Even the sender can't unlock the message without the recipient's private key.

The biggest advantage of using public-key as opposed to secret-key cryptography is the increased security it offers because the private key never has to be transmitted or known to anyone except the owner of the key. It is used only by you in combination with the recipient's public key to create the encrypted message. The private key never leaves your computer. The private (secret key) is never published or included in correspondence, and unless you give someone your private key or they physically take it from you, it can't be guessed or used by an impostor.

For more information about public-key encryption and security issues, check the Totally Hot Bookmarks List's Security and Privacy section on the Companion CD-ROM for links to many sites and resources, such as RSA's home page (http://www.rsa.com/) and Netscape's own security-related pages.

Netscape servers and Netscape Navigator 3 both use public-key encryption as the basis of their security features. These features are invoked when you logon to a secure Web server or a secure news server. All transactions between you and the secure servers are automatically encrypted using RSA's public-key encryption. E-mail, however, travels by a different route and at the time of this writing is not protected by encryption. Be sure to see the sections on e-mail later in the chapter for information on how this will change with future versions of Navigator and what you can do in the interim to protect your e-mail.

NETSCAPE'S INTEGRATION OF PRODUCT SECURITY FEATURES

Netscape takes security issues very seriously. RSA public-key encryption is the foundation of many different Netscape server and browser security features. Navigator 3.0, for example, includes support for personal and site-based digital certificates and password protection for these certificates. These certificates use public-key encryption technology to assure positive identification of the senders and the receivers of messages. Netscape's SSL (Secure Sockets Layer) technology, a secure Internet transport protocol, has been upgraded to provide better certificate management, additional encryption mechanisms, and wider support for hardware devices. The Netscape security system provides seamless security because of all the components of the system: Navigator, the secure server, and the SSL transport mechanism all work together.

Let's take a closer look at some of these technologies.

SSL: THE PROTOCOL SECURITY LAYER

The Secure Sockets Layer is able to do its work because it is sandwiched between the transport TCP/IP protocol and the Internet application protocols such as HTTP and FTP. It is the SSL layer that negotiates the exchange of digital certificates used in the authentication exchange (a handshake of sorts) between the secure server and the browser, supervises the encryption of the data transported, and checks to see that the encrypted data stream is not altered in transit.

Few things in the world can't stand a little improving upon, and SSL is no exception. Version 3 of Navigator and the entire new line of Navigator servers are capable of using the newly released SSL 3, as well as SSL 2, the security protocol that was used in previous versions of Netscape products. SSL 3 builds on the already substantial security offered by SSL 2 by expanding the range of certificate types it can handle, by adding additional layers of checking, and by providing means to extend the capabilities of the protocol so it can easily be adapted to future needs. All of the actions that SSL takes are handled automatically without the need for you to intervene.

SSL was developed by Netscape, but it is an Open Systems standard. This means that other server and browser vendors can implement SSL technology into their products. This is a great advantage to users of the Internet because as each new secure server is added to the Internet, the entire Internet gets safer for all of us.

DIGITAL CERTIFICATES

Earlier in the chapter we talked about how RSA public encryption uses public and private keys to encrypt data. These same principles can also be used to check for identity—yours or a server's that you are communicating with—through the use of digital certificates. All certificates are digitally signed by an issuing authority. The purpose of a digital ID certificate is to make an irrevocable bond between a name (a person or a specific server) and a pair of public encryption keys generated for the certificate holder. These keys are used to sign a series of back and forth messages that are automatically exchanged between you and the secure server in the logon and verification process.

Each side sends a message that announces what their public key is. Because this message also contains the signature of the issuing authority, the messages containing the public keys can be verified. Each side then uses its own private key and the public key of the other to send a message. Each side uses its own private keys to verify the received messages. It is through this process of exchanging certificates with a server that a Navigator user can establish positive identity to the server, and the server can positively identify itself to the Navigator user. This exchange of ID is required to establish a truly secure connection.

All secure servers have to have a Site Certificate before they can operate in a secure fashion. They get their Site Certificate by applying for one from one of several Certificate Authorities. Certificate Authorities are trusted third parties who are in the business of taking applications, verifying that applicants are who they say they are and then giving them a certificate. Individuals obtain their personal digital certificate from VeriSign. VeriSign is a Certificate Authority that was "spun off" from RSA Data Security.

VeriSign & Digital ID

When you are issued a personal digital ID, you're getting the digital equivalent of a photo ID that also carries your fingerprint. Digital IDs are a lot like fingerprints, in that each one is unique and can't be forged by any known method. Because they are very new, there aren't many places on the Internet or even on most organizations' Intranets that require the use of digital ID certificates. But you can expect that in the future you will need one, just as you need a physical ID in the physical world. And also like the real world, you may accumulate a lot of them. General-purpose IDs, like the ones you can get from VeriSign, will be used like a driver's license. This proof of identity will most likely be used primarily for online shopping and for access to semi-private sites on the Web. Personal digital certificates will also be important for "signing" secure e-mail. With the digital ID, you have more than simple information encryption at your disposal—you have an electronic way of verifying your own identity as well as that of others.

Specific-purpose IDs will become much more common after the release of Netscape Certificate server (scheduled for fall 1996). Netscape Certificate servers will allow individual organizations the ability to issue certificates to personnel and other users who want or need to access that organization's Internet or Intranet site. The Certificate server will also make it easy to give different levels of access to the site based on security level of an individual's certificate. The Certificate server's built-in management features will make issuing, updating, and retiring a person's certificate easier for organizations to do than trying to track and manage passwords and PIN numbers. You'll use the digital certificates that are issued to you by various organizations in ways that are similar to the way you use your bank-issued ATM card to access your bank account or your employee ID card to get you past the plant gates.

DIGITAL ID CLASSES

VeriSign is a certificate-issuing authority that was set up by RSA Data Security to issue personal certificates. They have worked closely with Netscape to make obtaining and using digital certificates easy. When you installed Navigator, you had the option of going directly to VeriSign to obtain a personal certificate. VeriSign offers four different classes of certificates. What separates them from each other (other than cost) is the amount of proof you need to submit to VeriSign to prove that you are you and that you are the one who is applying for the certificate. As you can see from the chart below, the level of assurance each class offers ranges from you saying you are you (they take your word) to being investigated and submitting a number of different physical proofs of identity.

Unless you have a specific need (some sites you need to access require it), it is not necessary to get a certificate that goes above Class 1. This advice is based on the current (summer of 1996) situation. Possessing a Class 2 or 3 certificate will become more attractive and necessary for most users late in the year and in the years to come as more commerce and banking moves to the Internet and secure e-mail servers come online.

Certificate Class	Probable Use	Requirements for Obtaining the Certificate	Current Cost
Class 1	Web browsing and e-mail; will replace the use of user names and passwords on many semi-private sites.	Unique name and e-mail address.	$6.00 per year
Class 2	Used for secure e-mail, online transactions, and subscriptions. Currently available for residents in the United States and Canada only.	Third-party proof of name, address, and other personal information. For this class of digital ID, VeriSign checks the validity of the information you give against the information that Equifax (a large credit bureau and personal data vendor) has on file about you.	$12.00 per year
Class 3	Used for electronic banking, large-sum transactions, and membership-based online services. Currently available for residents in the United States and Canada only.	Personal presence before a Notary Public along with three physical proofs of identity or other registered credentials that are acceptable to VeriSign.	$24.00 per year for individuals
Class 4	Used for highly confidential transactions and communications. Currently available for residents in the United States and Canada only.	Thorough investigation with personal presence before an agent acceptable to VeriSign.	Individually priced

OBTAINING YOUR DIGITAL ID

When you first install Netscape Navigator version 3.0, you have
the option of registering the software at Netscape's site; this is what
happens if you answer Yes to Netscape's installation prompt that
asks you whether you'd like to continue setup with a trip to
Netscape's home page. The Netscape setup page also offers a link
to VeriSign where you can get a Digital ID or passport. If you by
chance declined to finish the Navigator setup, you can go to the
setup page by entering http://home.netscape.com/home/
setup.html in Navigator's location field. Take the link to VeriSign
from Netscape's setup page. It will take you to a special page for
Navigator users. Once you've obtained your Digital ID from
VeriSign (follow the onscreen prompts), there is no need to remember multiple passwords and usernames when accessing secure sites
that have been set up to offer access based upon the use of digital
certificates. Here's how to get your digital passport:

1. Go to the Netscape setup page at http://
   home.netscape.com/home/setup.html and click the Sign
   Up for a Digital Passport option, as shown in Figure 7-1. A
   new page displays. Click on the Free Digital ID button on
   the page.

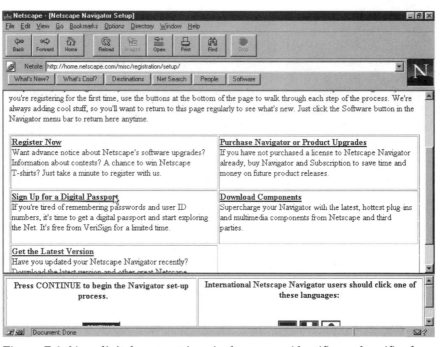

Figure 7-1: *Your digital passport is a single-resource identifier and verifier for a number of different resources on the Internet.*

2. Before connection to VeriSign's secure site, the standard Netscape Security alert is displayed: "You have requested a secure document. The document and any information you send back are encrypted for privacy while in transit. For more information on security choose Document Information from the View menu."
   Click Continue.

3. The VeriSign Digital ID Center page displays. Scroll down and follow the onscreen instructions to fill in the Identification Form. See Figure 7-2. When you've finished filling in the form and the Challenge information, click Continue.

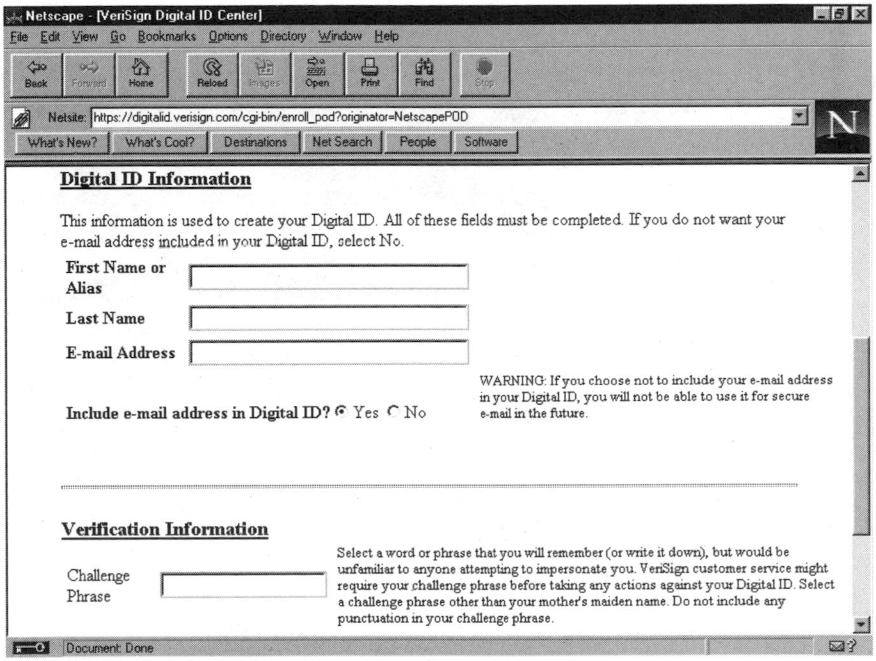

Figure 7-2: *VeriSign Identification Form page.*

4. The next screen asks you to verify the information you've just entered. If it is correct, scroll down and click Continue. If any of the information is incorrect or misspelled, click the Back button on the toolbar and correct and resubmit the information.

5. The page that appears contains the VeriSign Subscriber Agreement. Read the agreement and then choose to either Decline or Accept the agreement.

6. If you choose to accept the agreement, you move to the final stages of enrollment. Carefully read the Submit Request page as shown in Figure 7-3. Then click Submit. VeriSign will process your application. This may take a moment or two. Do not leave the page or close Navigator or you won't get your certificate.

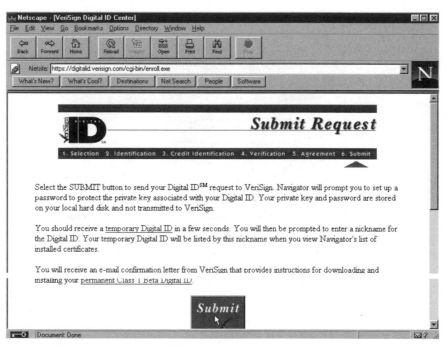

Figure 7-3: *VeriSign's Submit Request page.*

7. The next step is choosing a password for your Digital ID.
   Navigator gives you tips on how to select a password. See
   Figure 7-4.

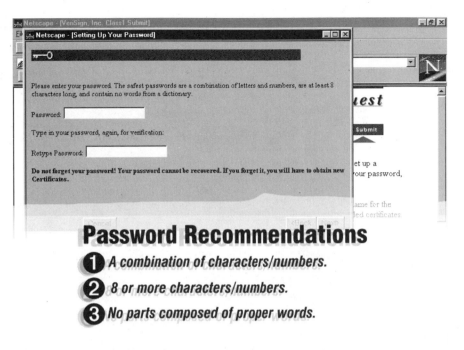

Figure 7-4: *You will be provided with suggestions for creating your Digital ID password during the process of obtaining the ID.*

Select a password, type it again to verify, and select next, where you will be asked how often you wish to be prompted to enter your password. Be sure to choose a password that you can remember, but that is not easily guessed. If you forget the password you selected for your Digital Certificate, you will need to obtain a new certificate.

8. You are now prompted to enter a nickname for your certificate. See Figure 7-5. This is the name that will display in Navigator's Certificate list in the Security Options tab. Enter a nickname. It can be the same name you entered earlier in the application process or it can be any other name you want. Click OK. The Digital ID Enrollment Complete page displays. Take a moment to read this page.

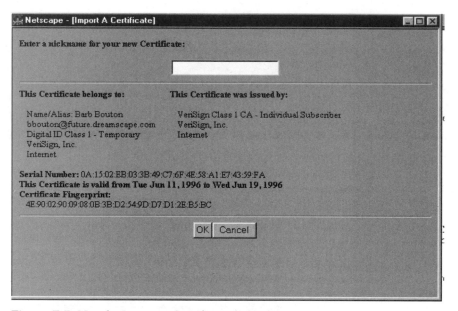

Figure 7-5: *Use the Import a Certificate dialog box to enter a nickname for your certificate.*

Now that you've completed the steps involved, you have obtained your very own temporary Digital ID! To turn the temporary ID into a permanent one, you will have to return to VeriSign's site after you've received an important piece of e-mail from them. VeriSign sends e-mail to the address you specified as an added security measure. Carefully follow the instructions in the e-mail message and you'll have completed the processes.

The conversion of the temporary ID to a permanent one works only if you have actually successfully acquired the temporary ID. To verify that the temporary Digital ID was installed successfully, you can perform the following steps:

1. From Navigator, select the Options and choose Security Preferences from the menu.

2. Select the Personal Certificates tab. If a certificate bearing the nickname you provided is in the list, the process was successful. If not, you'll have to start over. If you did not choose a nickname for your certificate, clicking the white space at the top of the box should highlight your certificate.

3. Select the certificate and then click More Info to view the information pertaining to your temporary digital certificate as seen in Figure 7-6. When you've finished looking at the information about your certificate, click OK. Then click OK on the Preferences dialog box to close it. You're finished for now.

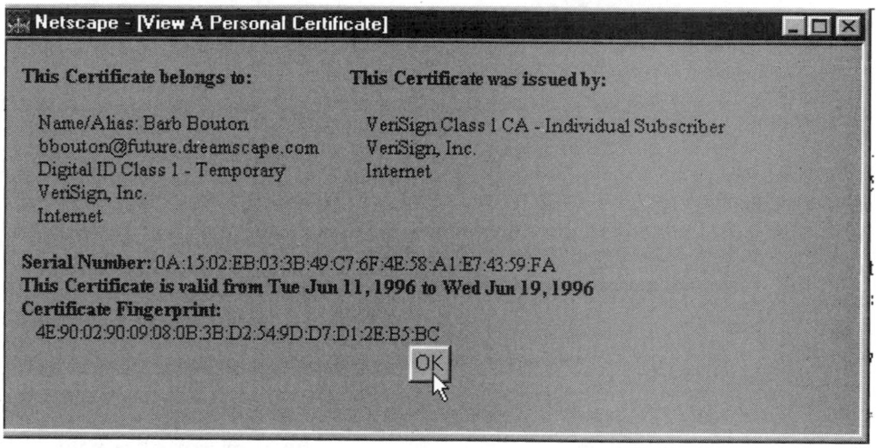

Netscape - [View A Personal Certificate]

This Certificate belongs to: This Certificate was issued by:

Name/Alias: Barb Bouton   VeriSign Class 1 CA - Individual Subscriber
bbouton@future.dreamscape.com   VeriSign, Inc.
Digital ID Class 1 - Temporary   Internet
VeriSign, Inc.
Internet

Serial Number: 0A:15:02:EB:03:3B:49:C7:6F:4E:58:A1:E7:43:59:FA
This Certificate is valid from Tue Jun 11, 1996 to Wed Jun 19, 1996
Certificate Fingerprint:
  4E:90:02:90:09:08:0B:3B:D2:54:9D:D7:D1:2E:B5:BC

OK

Figure 7-6: *Navigator displays detailed information about your personal Digital ID certificate.*

You will receive the e-mail message from VeriSign usually within a few minutes, but definitely within a 24-hour period. From the time VeriSign sent the message to you, you have 48 hours to come back and complete the process. If for some reason you are not able to complete the process within the 48 hours you will have to reapply.

USING DIGITAL IDs

The great thing about Digital IDs is that once you have one, you don't have to do anything special to use it. The certificate is stored within Navigator, and Navigator knows when it needs to be used (when you initiate a transaction of some kind with a secure server) and how to use it. Using the Digital ID is something that is completely transparent to you. You go about your business, and Navigator takes care of the security end of the deal.

WHO SUPPORTS DIGITAL IDS?

Client or *individual* Digital IDs are currently supported by Netscape Navigator 3.0. Microsoft has also announced that they will be supporting Digital IDs in their client applications as well. Server Digital IDs are being supported in products from IBM, Microsoft, Netscape, OpenMarket, Oracle, as well as many more. Also, Sun, CyberCash, Premenos, National Semiconductor, and Lotus have announced their intentions to implement VeriSign's Digital ID services.

SITE CERTIFICATES

Along with Digital IDs, Navigator also implements Site Certificates to ensure that the *site* you plan to connect to is in actuality the site you want to visit—that an unscrupulous profiteer is not masquerading as your trusted online banker, for example. When you attempt to connect to a site that bears a Site Certificate, the server presents the certificate during an SSL handshake—the security protocol layer that establishes a privacy of exchange between the sender and the receiver. Navigator then checks the certificate against the existing database of certificates that you've accepted. If the server's certificate is in the database, or if the server's certificate is signed by a Certificate Authority whose certificate is in the database, Navigator allows the connection to go through. You can view the list of certificates that have been accepted in the Security Options dialog box.

If the certificate presented by the site is *not* in your database or is not signed by an acceptable Certificate Authority, the connection will not continue. Navigator will not automatically accept site certificates that are signed by an unrecognized Certificate Authority. Instead, you will be prompted for a process of installing the new certificate if you so choose. Here are the steps you'd take to add a new certificate from an unknown site to your personal certificates list:

1. During the process of connecting to an unknown site certificate, the installation wizard first brings up a warning screen alerting you that Navigator has received an unrecognized certificate. The screen may be slightly different depending on whether it is a site certificate or a certificate for a new Certificate Authority.

2. The wizard then brings up information pertaining to the certificate, such as the organization that owns the certificate, the Certificate Authority that signed the certificate, and the type of encryption used.

   At this point, you can choose to see more information about the certificate by clicking the More Info button. Doing this will bring up details about the organization that owns the certificate, such as name, country, and other information, and the same details about the Certificate Authority involved. The More Info dialog box also offers details concerning the certificate serial number, time period in which the certificate is valid, and other information.

3. You now need to determine whether or not to trust the certificate. For site certificates, you can trust them for this session only, permanently, or not at all. For Certificate Authorities, the options are to trust them or not to trust them. It's your call.

4. The next prompt asks if you want to be warned each time before attempting to connect to this particular server.

5. For Certificate Authorities, the wizard will then ask you to enter a nickname to identify the Certificate Authority. The nickname will appear on the list under the Options | Security Preferences menu. Future releases of Navigator are expected to display the Certificate Authority's Common Name.

Although some setup time is required to identify certificates of sites that you and Navigator are unfamiliar with, you shouldn't think of this as user intervention or a costly investment of time. Electronic communications and transactions are unique in that you break new ground with every site you visit. Obtaining Site Certificate information doesn't ensure that the holders of the certificate are honorable, only that they are who they say they are and that you can conduct business with them that can't be tampered with enroute. Over time you may find that you trust each other, or you may decide that the organization is untrustworthy. But by accepting the certificate you enable the decision-making process to begin.

RECOGNIZING A SECURE SITE

A site can have secure, insecure, or mixed security states. Netscape Navigator tells you in a couple of ways that you have connected to a secure Internet site.

A security indicator in the bottom left corner of the Navigator screen has the image of a key. This icon will generally be a broken key on a neutral background to indicate that an insecure page is displayed. The key will become whole and the background will change to blue when you access a secure document. On secure sites, the key icon will change almost imperceptibly to represent different levels of encryption. Two teeth on the key represent high-grade encryption (uses a long key), and one tooth represents medium-grade encryption (uses a medium-sized key). When the user comes across a mixed security site containing *both* secure and insecure information, the icon is initially displayed as secure (whole key on blue), but when insecure information is accessed, the icon is replaced with a broken key on a neutral background.

Another way of knowing whether or not the site is secure is by looking at the URL in Navigator's Location field. If the current document is on a secure server, the URL begins with https:// instead of the usual http://. It is necessary to use the https:// for sites that implement SSL.

Unless the default is changed under the Options Security Preferences menu, Navigator will display a warning box whenever you are about to transfer information to an insecure site, giving you the opportunity to cancel the transaction if you don't feel it's a worthwhile gamble.

NAVIGATOR SECURITY PREFERENCE OPTIONS

We've already mentioned a few aspects pertaining to the Security Preference Options in Navigator. Let's continue and discuss the entire procedure for setting security options.

Open Navigator and choose Options, and then choose Security Preferences from the menu. As shown in Figure 7-7, the preferences then appear with four tab choices: General, Passwords, Personal Certificates, and Site Certificates.

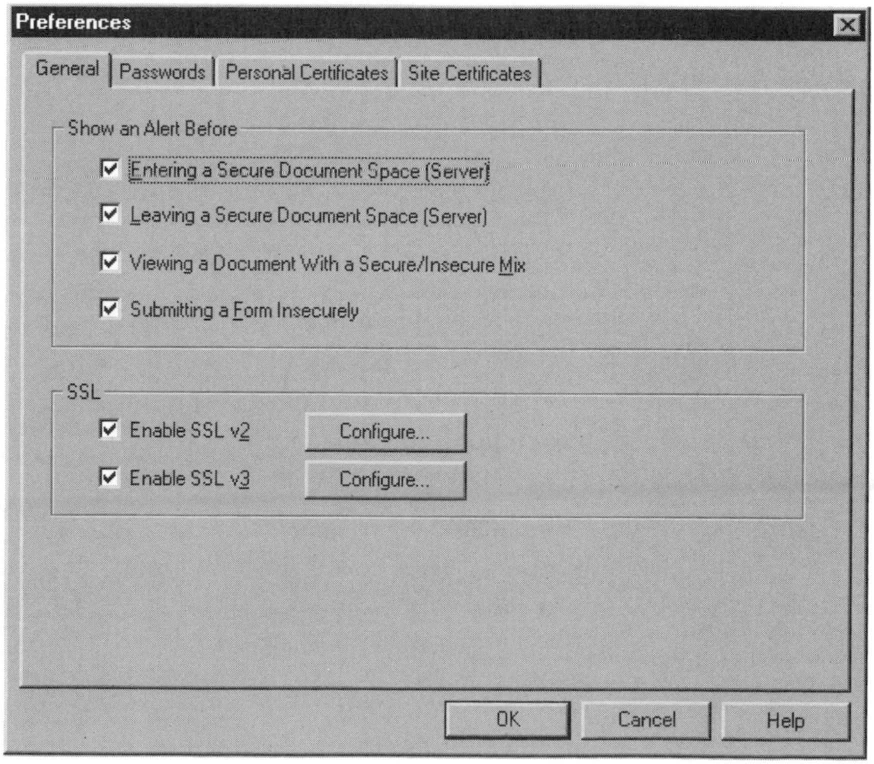

Figure 7-7: *The Navigator Security Preference dialog box.*

GENERAL SECURITY OPTIONS

Under the General tab, there are a few different options you can either enable or disable:

- *Show an alert before entering a secure document space (server)*—Navigator will show you an alert message before you enter a site that is secure or access a secure page on a site that offers both secure and insecure pages and resources. This option is a handy reminder that the business you conduct at this site while on secure pages is free from tampering while enroute to and from the server.

- *Show an alert before leaving a secure document space (server)*—Navigator will display a warning message when you are about to leave a secure section of the site to go into an insecure site or section of the site. If you surf to many different sites during an online session, this option, as well as the previous option, are good ones to leave on.

- *Show an alert before viewing a document with a secure/insecure mix*—With this option activated, Navigator will show you an alert message *before* you attempt to view a page (a frameset) that contains both secure and insecure information. This, too, is an important option to keep on, but it's up to you to decide when to volunteer confidential information to a site comprised of mixed security features.

- *Show an alert before submitting a form insecurely*—With this option enabled, Navigator will show you a warning message after you fill out an insecure form/information page, but before you actually *send* the information. This message warns you that the data you are about to send could be intercepted and allows you to change your mind at the last minute. It's *always* a good idea to leave this enabled.

- *Enable SSL v2 and Enable SSL v3*—The SSL options enable or disable the Secure Sockets Layer versions 2 and 3. Leaving these options selected allows you to securely access servers that support either or both of the protocols. If you have accessed a secure site and the transmission appears garbled, come to this section of the Security Preferences and make sure that both check boxes are checked. Also check the configuration for both protocols by clicking the Configure button next to each protocol. Both check box options should be checked for the SSL v2 configuration and only the first two check box options should be checked for the SSL v3 configuration.

The default settings under Security Preferences | General discussed up to this point are all enabled. It is the author's recommendation, and yes, it's a conservative one—to leave these options at their defaults.

SECURITY PASSWORD OPTIONS

The Passwords tab offers limited security measures through the creation of passwords and time-outs for the password(s) for computers which are accessible by others. Do *not* mistake these options for the sort of password that locks a keyboard or prevents the loading of an application! Password security only pertains to changes you or others can make to the Security Certificates you hold. However, this feature is valuable if you hold a certificate with, for example, your bank, or if your employer has given you unlimited access to the Internet, but the receptionist you sit next to has heavy restrictions on surfing using his or her computer.

You can choose to use or not to use a password, and you can specify the frequency with which Navigator asks for confirmation of your password. In Figure 7-8 you can see the Security Password options contained on this tab of the dialog box.

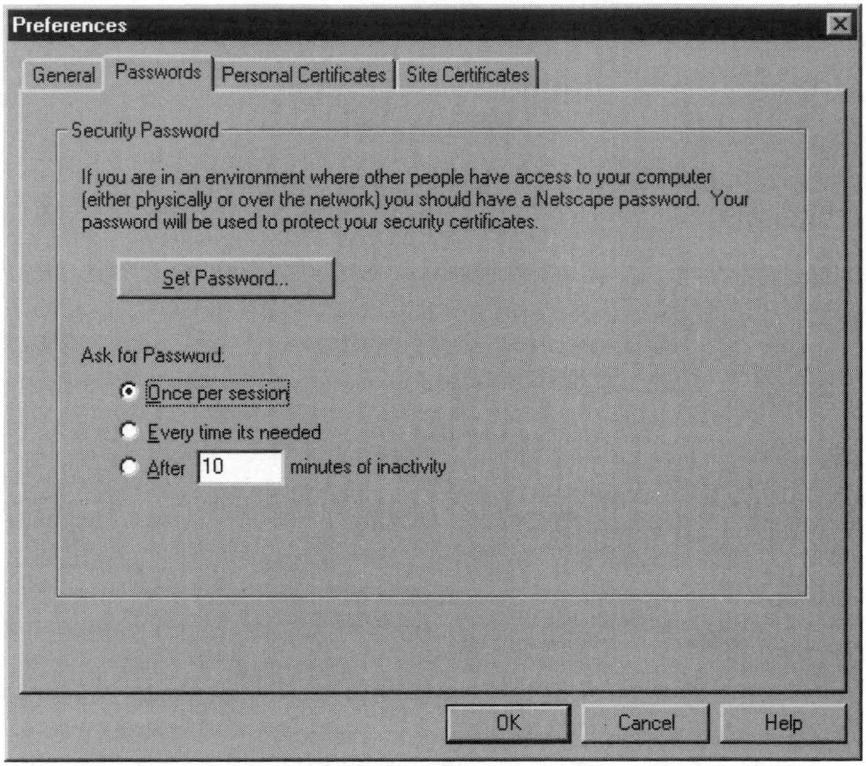

Figure 7-8: *Navigator Security Password options box.*

The default for the password options is to enable the password and ask for the user to enter it once per session. If you work in a large corporate environment, the Ask for Password Once per session will probably suffice, but if you're called away from your desk often, try specifying a minute value in the After X minutes of inactivity field. Private and home Navigator users will not likely need to specify a Password preference at all unless they reside with fellow surfers.

THE PERSONAL CERTIFICATES OPTIONS

This area of the Security Preferences menu is relevant only to users who have established Personal Certificates. This menu area contains the information pertaining to the personal certificates you hold. From time to time, you might want to check the information you present to a secure site through one or more Personal Certificate(s); you might have switched employers in the past year and might like to keep your personal bank Certificate information current. Information contained within Personal Certificates is obtained by clicking a Personal Certificate name, then clicking More Info.

The Delete Certificate and Obtain New Certificate options are sort of self-explanatory, and you also have the option in this tabbed menu to select a default certificate to present to sites. You might want to establish an "omnibus" Personal Certificate—one that contains only basic credit information, for example—to present for the bulk of your online transactions. In Figure 7-9, you can see the options on the Personal Certificates tab.

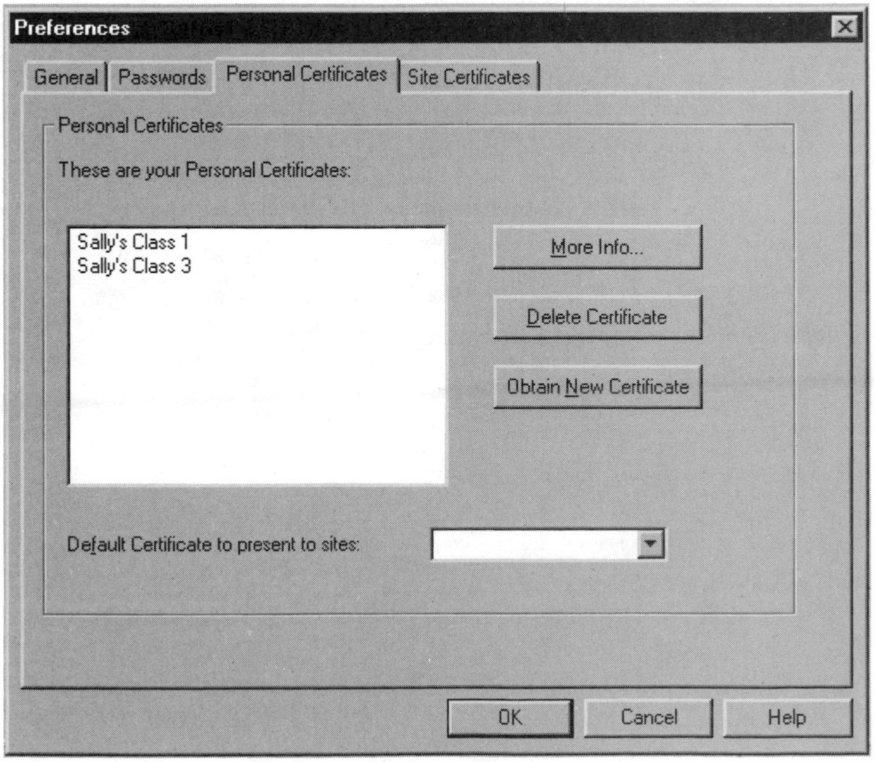

Figure 7-9: *Navigator Personal Certificates options box.*

As discussed earlier in the chapter, a Personal Certificate identifies you to others on the Internet. You can obtain more than one Personal Certificate for different reasons. Certain sites may require separate Personal Certificates to be used with their site, or you may wish to obtain different certificates for different transactions.

SITE CERTIFICATES OPTIONS

A Site Certificate confirms the identity of a site to you. When you ask to connect to a secure site, Navigator asks the site who they are and confirms the truthfulness of the answer by validating the certificate presented against the information in the certificate for that site as stored in your database. You can obtain many Site Certificates, each one representing a site or certificate authority. In Figure 7-10, you can see the Navigator options for Site Certificates.

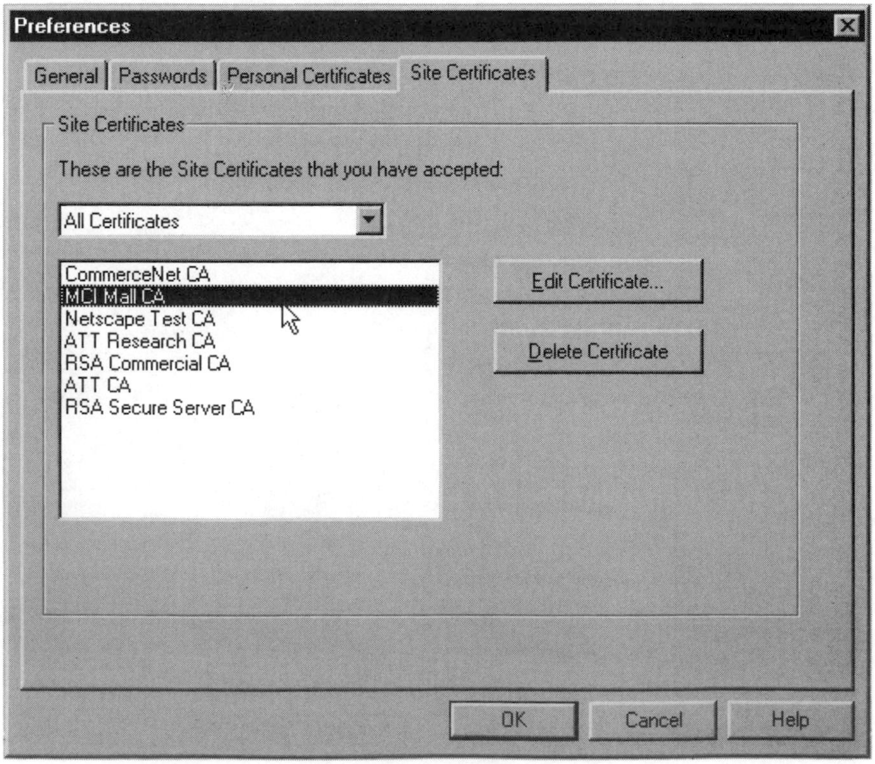

Figure 7-10: *Navigator Site Certificates options box.*

Under the Sites Certificates tab, you can quickly view both Site Certificates, Certificate Authorities, or all sites by choosing an option from the *These are the Site Certificates that you have accepted* drop-down list. Don't be alarmed if the list below the drop-down box is populated even though you installed Navigator only moments ago. Certificate Authorities such as CommerceNet and AT&T are Netscape business partners, and Netscape believes that these should be trusted sites of Navigator users. Eventually this list will also contain names of sites from which you've procured a Site Certificate.

The Edit Certificate button offers a display of the current information about a highlighted Certificate Authority or Site Certificate on the list. The term "edit" isn't quite straightforward here; you cannot *tamper* with information contained in a certificate or change the information it displays—this would circumvent the use of a certificate. Instead, you are provided with options regarding your willingness to accept connections to the site that bears the certificate or to sites that received their certificate from a specific Certificate Authority. To illustrate the Edit options a little more concretely, suppose that a Certificate Authority was discovered to be lax in the way it issued certificates. To remove the possibility of connecting to this Authority and the corresponding sites that it issued certificates to, you could click the *Do not allow connections to sites certified by this authority* radio button in the dialog box shown in Figure 7-11, and automatically, you'll make no future connections to one or several locations on the Net.

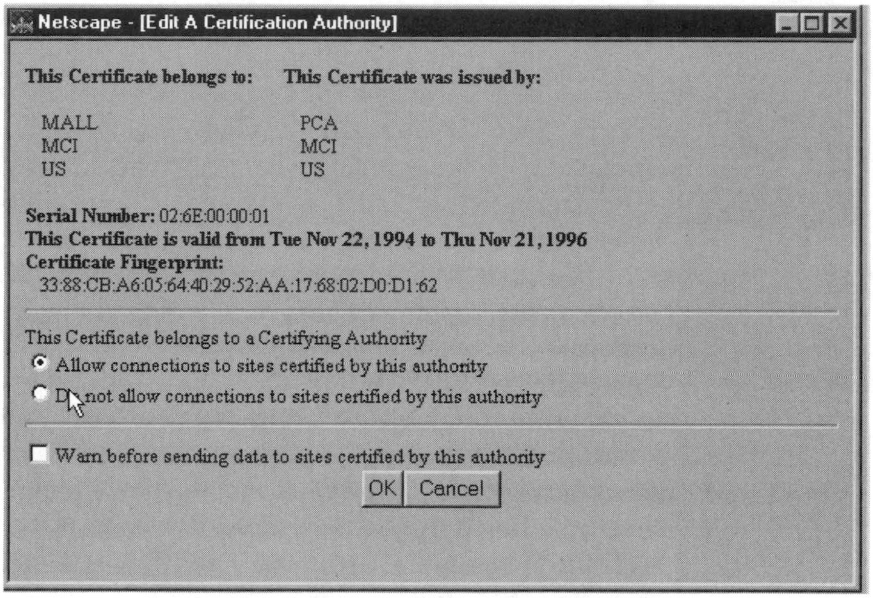

Figure 7-11: *You can choose to display an alert upon entering a site whose authority you decline, or you can refuse connection to an Authority or a Site Certificate holder through the Edit a Certification Authority dialog box.*

You can also decide to delete a certificate from a site or an authority by clicking the Delete Certificate button on this menu. Netscape will pop up a query box if you choose this option, so you're always forewarned that you might be making a decision you cannot reverse later.

For most users it's a good idea to accept all of the Site Certificates that Netscape has accepted on your behalf because these are the sites you are most likely to encounter in the near future.

JAVA & SECURITY

All current Netscape Browsers and Servers are Java capable. Java is an object-oriented programming language, modeled after C++ and developed by Sun Microsystems for general applications and for use on the World Wide Web. Many Web and Intranet developers are using Java to create applets or inserts to HTML documents to add interesting features and computational abilities to their sites that would otherwise be impossible or impractical. Applets written in Java are platform independent, meaning that a programmer can use Java to enhance an HTML document that can be downloaded and used by any kind of computer running a properly equipped browser, such as Navigator 2.0 or later. When the document is accessed by the browser and downloaded to the user's computer, the Java applet is run automatically as a seamless subset of the HTML code.

Because Java applets automatically download and run on your computer, Sun Microsystems and Netscape have worked closely to ensure that Java applets cannot be constructed in such a way that they can do potential harm to your computer, such as surreptitiously writing to your file system or activating links to another server. Java technology is new, and like all technology the possibility exists that it can be used in ways that its designers did not anticipate. There have been several reports by university researchers who have discovered potential weaknesses in the security of Java. In each case no known user was a victim of vandals exploiting the security weakness, and Sun and Netscape responded quickly with patches that removed the hazard.

JAVA APPLETS & JAVASCRIPT

A Java applet is simply an affectionate name for a small application that typically is limited in its feature set or in mainstream commercial appeal. It was created using the Java programming language developed by Sun Microsystems. Each application programmed in Java is compiled into an applet which is downloaded along with its associated HTML document. The document will contain <APPLET> tags and a relative link to each applet to be used in assembling the final display.

Another way to enhance page displays is to use JavaScript. JavaScript source code is placed directly into HTML documents within <SCRIPT> tags, eliminating the compile step required for Java applets. However, JavaScript is akin to Java programming language in name only. Originally, before the introduction of Java programming language, Netscape planned to call this Netscape scripting language LiveScript. Netscape and Sun are working together to make these two different approaches to programming interconnect with each other. All of Netscape's current browsers and server products are capable of running both JavaScripts and Java applications.

JavaScript is a *script*-based language that Netscape created to give developers, users, and Webmasters a way to automate or enhance the use of Netscape products. JavaScript requires programming skill beyond that required for HTML, but is much less demanding than Java programming. JavaScript accordingly offers more HTML authors greater flexibility for creating exciting pages without the need to call on the services of highly skilled programmers. Because the source script is included right in the HTML document, it allows the visitor to see more readily what the JavaScript does. For training purposes one can easily use the File and then Save as menu command in Navigator to capture a JavaScript enhanced page, make modifications, and reload with the file name in the Location field. Comparing Java programming language to JavaScript is analogous to comparing Visual Basic to a Word for Windows macro.

At this time there are no known security issues relating to using JavaScript because of the way in which it functions. Nevertheless, some misguided individual was able to make a macro for Word—the "template virus"—which was non-destructive but annoying, so Navigator 3.0 offers you the option of disabling the ability of the browser to run JavaScripts.

The newness of the Java and JavaScript technologies have made some users uncomfortable about the possible problems their use may pose to security and privacy. If you work in extremely secure areas such as research facilities and government locations, or if you—or your boss—decides that the security risk to view the Java and JavaScript-driven sites is too great, you do have the option to disable Navigator's ability to handle Java-based programs. This preference setting is not part of the Security Preferences tab, but rather resides on the Language tab in the Network Preferences window. By default, the use of Java and JavaScript is turned on. If you want to change either of these settings, see the following paragraph for instructions.

In Netscape Navigator 3.0, choose Options and then Network Preferences from the menu. Click the Languages tab. Here you will find two boxes, one to enable or disable Java and the other to enable or disable JavaScript (see Figure 7-12). Checking the Enable Java check box allows Navigator to download, process, and run Java applets. When the Enable JavaScript check box is checked, Navigator will read and execute any JavaScripts that are written into the HTML pages it encounters. If you believe that sites you visit aren't 100% friendly, you have the option to limit your view—and the accompanying security risks—of a Java- or JavaScript-enhanced site by disabling these functions.

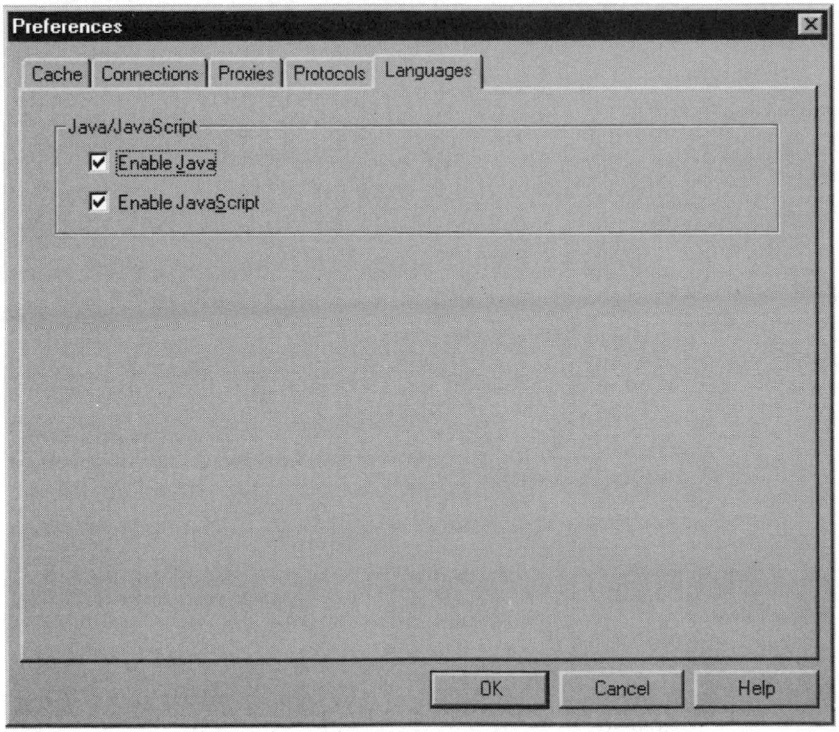

Figure 7-12: *To enable or disable Java or JavaScript, go to the Languages tab of the Preferences options.*

HOW PRIVATE IS E-MAIL?

At present, e-mail is not very secure because it is not being transferred in an encrypted state from one secure computer to another. The messages are usually sent as plain ASCII text, which is used and easily read by any kind of computer system. The Internet mail protocols, the current MIME specifications, and the installed base of mail reading programs do not intrinsically provide a way for automatically ensuring the privacy and security of e-mail and its attachments.

Progress is being made on these fronts, however. The specifications for S/MIME (a secure version of MIME) have been released. Netscape has announced a new version of its Mail Server, for release in the Fall of 1996, that will support S/MIME as well as SSL based security features, such as the ability to recognize and use Digital Security Certificates. These security enhancements are based on Open Systems specifications, and it is expected that other server vendors will follow suit and strengthen the security of their e-mail servers as well. Secure e-mail servers are only one-half of the picture, however. The client e-mail program needs the ability to generate and read secure e-mail messages as well. The next version, version 4, of Navigator is expected to be able to handle S/MIME and act as a secure e-mail program. Just as today the built-in security features of the Navigator browser and Netscape secure servers work hand in hand to make document transactions between them safe to conduct, e-mail will become a much more secure environment. When these new servers and browsers are released, Intranets can update their software and ensure the security of their internal e-mail services. However it would be wrong to think that every ISP and Internet user in the world will immediately and simultaneously adopt these new technologies. Plain, unsecured e-mail will continue to be exchanged for some time.

For then as well as for now, the answer for providing secure e-mail lies with the users of the system. If you have e-mail and e-mail attachments that you need to transmit securely, taking the time to encrypt it using public-key encryption is your only reliable answer; however, it is somewhat cumbersome to use, you must remember to use it, and both the sender and the receiver must have public-key software at their disposal and know how to use it.

Fortunately, PGP (Pretty Good Protection), a stand-alone, public-key encryption software program, is widely available and more than up to the task. PGP, originally written by Phil Zimmerman, is freely available around the world for both commercial and non-commercial use. To avoid breaking U.S. export laws, you just have to be careful where you download it from. In the U.S. it is free for non-commercial use and can be downloaded from MIT's Web site (http://web.mit.edu/network/pgp.html) by U.S. citizens living in the U.S. and by Canadian citizens living in Canada. For commercial use in the U.S., ViaCrypt's version of PGP is available. It is a serious violation of U.S. law to export (upload, send, or transfer) a copy of the PGP program to anyone outside of the U.S. or Canada because the public-key encryption it uses is so strong. But it is *not* against the law to send a PGP-encrypted message to a foreign recipient. International users, however, have easy access to many servers *outside* of the U.S. that distribute an international version of PGP that is compatible with the U.S. version. (See the International PGP home page at http://www.ifi.uio.no/~staalesc/PGP/.)

If you use a PGP shell program such as Private Idaho (http://www.eskimo.com/~joelm/pi.html) or WPGP (http://www.panix.com/~jgostl/wpgp/), it becomes quite easy to routinely use PGP to encrypt and decrypt your in- and outbound Netscape Navigator mail. By utilizing programs such as PGP for your e-mail, in combination with Netscape's security features for the Web, you'll be taking the steps necessary to obtain the Internet privacy you need and deserve.

But keep in mind that not all e-mail needs to be or should be encrypted. Only you can judge for yourself how necessary it is and how much risk you are willing to take. One way to put it into perspective is to compare e-mail to telephone conversations. It is widely known that it is very easy to listen in on cordless or cellular telephone conversations. All it takes is an inexpensive scanner and a desire to listen in, and many people do find it an amusing hobby to scan the phone frequencies. Yet, you'll find that many extremely private and sensitive business and personal conversations are conducted daily on these kinds of phones. The only difference in the levels of security provided between talking on a cordless phone or sending plain, unencrypted e-mail is that it is easier for anyone to listen to a phone conversation and much more likely.

SECURITY & MONEY

Because there are new methods constantly being developed to help ensure our security while online, the information, as well as the standards surrounding online security, seems to be in constant fluctuation. But one of the most relevant topics that is engendered in the word "security" is that of monetary transactions. Forget about the company's top secret product, and dismiss the co-worker's online affair—let's address how you pay for goods across the Internet.

HOW SAFE IS MY CREDIT CARD INFORMATION?

You can be assured that when entering and sending this type of information over a secure (HTTPS) Netscape Navigator form to a secure Netscape Commerce Server, FastTrack, or Enterprise Server, there will be little risk of an intruder stealing this information as it passes from your computer through the Internet and to the secure server. When you see a thin blue line across the top of Navigator's content window and the security indicator icon in the lower left corner takes the form of an unbroken key, you know that you have established a secure connection. All data you send is encrypted before it leaves your computer, and all incoming messages from the server are decrypted only after they have reached your computer.

Additionally, Netscape plans to introduce LivePayment server software in the third quarter of 1996 that will make it easier for online merchants to collect fees for large and small purchases. LivePayment will feature SSL encryption and support an open architecture so that SET (Secure Electronic Transactions) Internet protocol and emerging security layers can be adopted as an online merchant sees the need or preference for security options. LivePayment will present the user with a graphical interface, driven by an HTML form, that the merchant can customize to look like a cash register, or an automated transaction machine (ATM).

On the client side, Netscape Navigator 4 will provide users with an easy to use interface for keeping track of online transactions with areas for storing credit card numbers and other personal information. A receipt will also be issued upon conclusion of each online transaction, and Navigator 4 will enable users to export a collection of receipts to a personal finance program such as Quicken. Already many major companies and online banks, such as DigiCash and First Virtual, have announced plans to adopt LivePayment server software, and it will only be a matter of time before you can shop with even greater assurance of confidentiality on the Internet.

However, there is still the problem of trusting the security of the information *after* it has passed through the Internet, reached the secure server, and *then* enters the recipient's system. Is the business reputable? Are its employees trustworthy? What measures do they take to ensure that their hard disks or paper copies of your account information are secured against physical or electronic theft and misuse?

Of course, all these questions also apply to our everyday, face-to-face transactions. When you bought gas last week, did the attendant run your card through one or two times when you paid for the gas with your credit card? How many times have you presented your credit card as proof of identify and watched while the they copied down all the information on the card? How many times have you renewed a magazine subscription by sending back a post card with your credit card information written on the card? Have you ordered and paid for anything by phone or mail order?

The best insurance when conducting a credit card transaction in person, by phone, mail, or through the Internet is to *know who your vendor is.* If you had your choice, for example, of purchasing a T-shirt from Netscape's online General Store, or from a site called Bandit Bob's We Aim to Steal You Blind Emporium (I apologize if this is an actual site), user intuition should prevail, naturally, as it would if you were shopping in a physical mall.

TIP

Not all sites you may decide to do business with are hosted on secure servers. Many sites will encourage you to send in your order and credit card information via regular e-mail. Don't do it. Call them or fax them the information instead. Or ask them for their public PGP key and send the information as encrypted e-mail.

AN ALTERNATIVE—DIGITAL CASH

In the real world we don't always pay for services with a credit card; sometimes we actually use cash. In the world of cyberspace it is becoming increasingly apparent that there is a need for digitally based cash. Digital cash would be handy to have to pay for small purchases. And because the Internet is global, it would also be a great boon to Internet commerce if a universally accepted form of digital cash could be used to pay for goods and services when the buyer and the seller are in different countries. Cash also has another important property; it is anonymous. We sometimes pay for things with cash because we don't want a record of our purchase to be produced, or we don't want our identity to be revealed.

One way a system of virtual cash exchange could work across the Internet would be to use codes sent between users and banks (similar to today's checking system except entirely digital). Alternatively, you could arrange for a cash transfer from a participating online financial institution and in return receive "credits" that an online merchant would accept and redeem at the corresponding "online bank." The implementation might remind you of a science-fiction future on Earth where citizens exchange credits with a code or a card, thus eliminating bulky wallets.

Banks, financial institutions, and credit card companies are vitally interested in finding ways to make all kinds of financial transactions secure. Netscape is working closely with all of these groups to develop Open Systems security standards that will facilitate the growth of all forms of commerce and finance on the Internet, including that of digital cash.

The logistics of digital cash and its exchange are being worked out, but the political aspects are a thornier issue. Many governments are very concerned that their currency will be undermined by the use of WWW digital cash. They are also concerned about the anonymity that some forms of digital cash may provide. While they are not very concerned if you use digital cash to hide the cost of a surprise birthday gift for your spouse, they are concerned that it will be used by criminals to launder money or to pay for illicit goods. It's a given that the specifics of implementing digital cash must be agreeable to all concerned before it becomes an everyday transaction medium.

While the use and acceptance of digital cash is evolving, it is available today in various forms and with varying levels of anonymity. Companies such as First Virtual (http://www.fv.com/), CyberCash (http://www.cybercash.com/), and DigiCash (http://digicash.support.nl/) all have some form of digital cash available. If you need or want to use digital cash today, see what these companies have to offer.

MOVING ON

If you didn't listen carefully, you might think that someone mispronounced the word "Internet" in a conversation concerning your firm's in-office messaging system. The term "Intranet" is one of the fastest-growing buzzwords and is the topic of Chapter 8, "The Intranet." If you sit down to work on Monday, only to find the familiar Navigator Browser interface has replaced GroupWise or Lotus Notes, there's a reason. See how easy it is to connect co-workers to each other and to the world, through the Internet/Intranet connection described in the following chapter.

8

The Intranet

To say that online communications is an exploding field is an understatement on an order of magnitude with saying that the Atlantic Ocean is a big place. Corporations of every size around the world are polling so much information, it is becoming ungainly to store, hard to filter and organize, and it has become impossible to train employees to distill the information into the facts that drive a business' success.

Fortunately, businesses appear to be on the dawn of a different way of retrieving, organizing, and communicating information. It's called the *Intranet*, and the protocol, connectivity, and software is identical to the Internet, so your company, large or small, can work internally and externally with the same ease. This chapter doesn't contain example exercises because we're here to entertain and to explore the possibilities of establishing a business Intranet. We'll guide you, however, through some of the financial and capability issues of a Netscape Intranet, and in this chapter you'll see exactly how far Navigator and related Netscape products can extend your profession to the world's front door.

FROM NOS, TO NOTES, TO THE INTRANET

Ever since the first implementation of a computer in business—
what we refer to today as "Big Iron," "Mainframes," or "legacy
machines"—engineers have devoted a great deal of time investigat-
ing methods by which a series of local or offsite offices could share
connections to the computers.

THE NETWORK OPERATING SYSTEM

The network operating system (NOS) was conceived of as a
supplement to the local disk operating system (DOS). A NOS such
as Novell's NetWare or Banyon's VINES uses proprietary protocols
to enable computers to "talk" to one another, share resources, and
provide network security. Although the NOS is still a very important part of business networks today, many industry analysts believe that *Open Systems* (non-proprietary, protocol-based)
Intranetworking will replace proprietary, single-vendor NOSes in
the next two to five years.

One of the largest problems that businesses have to overcome
when using a traditional network operating system is one of a
mixed computing environment. Many companies have a variety of
computers—IBM and compatible PCs, Macintosh, UNIX, as well as
mainframe and mini-computers that need to work together. Because
each type of computer is fundamentally different and incompatible
with other types, elaborate gateways and special client software
must be patched together to make these disparate computer systems
work as a single unit. The resulting system is far from seamless and
can be quite expensive to set up and maintain.

Businesses today tend to make an evolutionary instead of a revolutionary change toward new connectivity solutions because of the
capital investment that companies *presently* have in hardware and
software. Because of the cost and because each kind of computer
has its special strength and use, no one is going to throw out all
their computers and standardize on a single type. Organizations
use different kinds of computers to make sense of and manage
information. NOSes enable connectivity among them and the information they contain, but do not in and of themselves make the
transfer of information easy; nor do they make communications

between the people who use the different computers effortless. In an effort to overcome this "friction" of communication and information, groupware was born.

ALONG COMES GROUPWARE

Groupware is a somewhat amorphous term that describes software whose purpose is to make it easier for people to work together and access, manage, and exchange information without having to know or care where or on what kind of computer the information is actually stored.

IBM's Lotus Notes was one of the first successful groupware products and the product that is often associated with the term *groupware*. Notes was not designed as a replacement for a network operating system such as NetWare, but instead rests on top of the NOS. Notes is a proprietary system based on a complex system of databases. The databases, the linkages between the databases, and the applications that view and manage the information must be set up and maintained by skilled Notes programmers. Notes users can create different views of data and work together on projects, but typically are constrained in their use of Notes by the features that the corporate Notes programmer has provided them.

Lotus Notes is a robust solution to the problem of making it easy to work together and access information. But it is also a very expensive, proprietary solution, with a steep user learning curve. It is also a "top-down" solution—users can manipulate and add data to the underlying databases, but it is difficult if not impossible for the average user to create a database or Notes-type application.

INTERNET—THE NEW GROUPWARE SOLUTION

Lotus Notes was a great idea that was conceived of before the rise of the Internet. In many ways, one might look at Lotus Notes as a proprietary mirror of the World Wide Web. Companies looking to improve the flow of information and communication within their organization once had little choice other than Notes. Today, however, companies have found that Intranets and new products such as Navigator 3 bring Internet-like capabilities inside the enterprise and that they offer a viable, graphically rich, low-cost, and easy-to-use alternative to Notes.

On average, establishing and maintaining a Notes-enhanced network costs ten times more than an equivalently loaded Intranet, and Notes requires expensive skilled labor for setup and maintenance. In comparison, an Intranet server such as Netscape's FastTrack can be set up and maintained by a novice Webmaster. Maintaining the Notes database infrastructure requires a skilled programmer. On the other hand, with easy-to-use Intranet HTML publishing tools like Navigator Gold or site management tools like LiveWire Pro, the individuals who generate the content can publish and update the information themselves.

Cost is an important concern to all organizations, but what is most important are the *results* you get from the investment. Intranet computing is fundamentally different than Notes in that it is document-centric, not database-centric. Everyday users understand, are comfortable using, and can easily generate documents, while very few are comfortable working with databases. Intranet computing brings a level of empowerment to users because it allows them to create, link, and publish information on their own.

Companies that have established Intranets find that these Intranets grow in unexpected, exciting, and productive ways because the Intranet users build it themselves to suit their needs. Groups that exist within organizations that have never worked together and may not have even known of each other's existence discover each other on the Intranet and many times end up working together to solve a problem that is common to both groups. Powerful, synergistic working relationships develop because Intranets—like the Internet—offer so many easy ways to share information, to exchange ideas, and to transfer data.

RETHINKING BUSINESS CONNECTIVITY

One of the downsides of technology invading the business office has traditionally been the lack of user empowerment. All over the world, if an employee has an office with a door, chances are good that there's a dartboard with a photo of the Information Services director tacked on a wall! To be fair, IS directors have been given a bad name due to their multiple responsibilities: maintaining and upgrading hardware and software, securing documents on servers, troubleshooting, educating the end user, and recently, governing the outside connections to branch offices across the world.

If we consider for a moment the services the Internet provides— mail, FTP, and search engines, to name but a few—it becomes clear that given the massive traffic of the Internet at any given hour, it is a superbly self-governed organism. And with the addition of the Navigator Browser as a graphical front end for users, the Internet can be accessed with little or no time spent educating a user on how Navigator's Browser works. A company Intranet restores the balance of power between the technologically advanced and the computer novice and allows professionals experienced in financial, human relations and services, and other departmental concerns to get about their business without the restrictions and limitations imposed by a retro-fitted network operating system. Already many Fortune 500 companies such as Hewlett-Packard, Levi Strauss, AT&T, and others are discovering that there is indeed a "back door" more easily accessed than the forward movement toward more complicated operating systems and layers of networking.

WHO NEEDS AN INTRANET CONNECTION?

If your business consists of fewer than five users, it's unlikely that you'd need to establish an office Intranet. But you *could*, almost as easily as configuring your system and Navigator to access the Internet. An office Intranet would be of the most use to employees who need to publish—and this doesn't necessarily mean a book or magazine publisher—and continually update a large number of documents. If you consider what the World Wide Web consists of— a large number of linked, structured documents, it makes perfect sense to adopt the convention and connectivity of the Internet for private commercial use.

Unlike groupware, whose organizational engine has been compared earlier in this chapter to a database, the Intranet, like the Internet, is document oriented. In fact, there is no functional difference between an in-house HTTP server and an Internet Service Provider's server that handles documents. The advantage of using an Intranet for corporate communications is several-fold, and the following sections describe some of the advantages that you might want to consider when better, more efficient corporation-wide communications are a priority.

PUSHING & PULLING DOCUMENTS

The distribution of electronic information can happen in two ways—it can be pushed or it can be pulled. When you view a Web page, you are *pulling* information that you want, when you want it, and when you need it. It's *just-in-time* information. When you receive e-mail or paper-based documents, the information is *pushed* to you; you get the information when it becomes available, which is not necessarily when you are interested in it. Both forms of serving information are of use to businesses, and both are extremely easy to use when you have an Intranet.

One of the problems that organizations have is providing easy-to-use information in a timely and accurate manner. Paper-based publications, expensive to produce, distribute, and update, have the advantage of being universally accessible—if you have a copy in your native language, you can read it almost anywhere that has a light source. Electronic documents have a decided advantage over paper-based documents in that they are easier to update, and if put into an easily accessible site can be downloaded at any time. With traditional networks however, it is not easy to publish documents from diverse sources that are usable across different operating system platforms and across applications. When information is made available on the Intranet, anyone within your organization with Navigator can read, save, and print the information. It doesn't matter if the person who created the document is a Windows user but the *user* of the document is a Macintosh or UNIX user.

The Intranet is ideally suited for both push and pull information services. When information is presented in the form of Web pages, it is easy to browse for the information you need. Additionally, the hypertext capability of HTML helps you find and make sense of related information. Traditional NOSes provide you with a common area for information, but you almost have to be clairvoyant to know what's available before you can request it. For example, is HR022.doc the bulletin on pension plan benefits or is it the announcement on the company picnic? It's hard to tell when it is one file in a list of files, but easy to decipher when it is presented as an HTML document.

As a user of the Internet, you've seen how easy it is to publish and retrieve information. HTML-based documents are easy to create and update, especially if you use a WYSIWYG authoring tool such as Navigator Gold's Editor.

COMPUTER PROTOCOL IS COMPUTER PROTOCOL

If you're running Windows 95 at an office, you're probably already aware that the built-in networking runs under a proprietary protocol called NETBUI. As described in Chapter 2, "Installing & Customizing Navigator," the Internet uses a *non*-proprietary protocol called TCP/IP that can be used to network computers of any type. A mixed computing environment is easily accomplished using the Internet protocol.

TCP/IP and the other common Internet/Intranet protocols: HTTP, FTP, Mail, News, and so on are also platform independent, open systems protocols. The importance of open systems software can't be overstated. Because the fundamental structure of open systems software is publicly known and available, any company can write software to meet a specific need. The worldwide adoption of the Internet ensures a healthy and steady stream of innovative software that can be used on any kind of computer.

An Intranet that uses Navigator as the common browser requires no special setup beyond the establishment of a TCP/IP connection, a server domain, and local connections that can easily run in tandem with workgroup or other local or proprietary protocols.

THE IMMEDIATE BENEFITS OF A CORPORATE INTRANET

Quietly, without ceremony, corporations are switching or adding Intranet communications almost overnight; an employee will walk in on a Monday morning and surprise—clicking on the familiar Navigator icon leads them to a new world to build and explore— their organization's Intranet.

At the same time that a corporate Intranet provides structured communications, it also is very creatively liberating, removing the intimidation of traditional corporate networks. Let's take a look at some key points that have played a deciding role in many firms swinging over to Intranet communications.

USERS' CONTROL OVER COMMUNICATIONS CONTENT

In a network operating system (NOS), the systems administrator is often responsible for posting documents, updating, and changing them. This "control issue" inevitably leads to workflow bottle-necks. Let's suppose that you are the keeper of the corporate tele-phone directory. In dynamic businesses, this list could very well change weekly. In a NOS environment, this means *finding* the sys-tems administrator on a regular basis, encouraging him or her to find time to distribute the revised document across all or selected parts of the network, and then going through the process again *next* week.

In an Intranet environment, *personal* publishing is the foundation of the connectivity. This employee directory can be located on the directory keeper's hard disk; modifications can be added as quickly as the keeper is informed of changes, and the directory in HTML format can be posted—by the keeper, not the systems ad-ministrator—on the Intranet server in minutes.

Quite simply, an Intranet puts the power to distribute informa-tion into the hands of those who have the information. Document accuracy, speed of updates, and efficient routing are the side ben-efits of an open communications system.

REDUCED TRAINING COSTS

It seems that every company that has become wired in the past decade has under-estimated the cost of office automation. One significant hidden expense is the cost of training or retraining employees to make use of new, advanced, proprietary communications features. Lotus Notes is a particularly complex groupware system to implement because it adds a layer of sophistication to an already existing network operating system—the typical user is forced to understand and leverage both layers to make communications work.

In contrast, any user on an Intranet with a copy of Navigator Gold and access to an Intranet server can both publish and receive documents. The learning curve for Navigator's Browser is extremely shallow in comparison to groupware. In fact, many companies are able to avoid formal training costs by adopting the scheme wherein an employee who learns to navigate the browser is required to train two other employees, and a snowball effect quickly gets the entire staff up and running in no time.

Users also *like* the Navigator Browser's interface—it's graphical and straightforward, and users who are new to computing will be encouraged to put the extra hours into mastering the features. When corporate communications are Netscape-based, "fun-time" surfing on the Intranet or the Web becomes an education in how the *company's* Intranet works!

THE PAPERLESS OFFICE

HTML communications might very well shrink the need for paper-based publishing to nearly nothing in the next decade. Electronic publishing has increased the volume of overall communications, but it can also pave the way to a paperless office environment.

Already, many Intranet offices are on an enterprise-wide campaign to convert existing documents in physical or proprietary electronic format to HTML. For example, let's look at a company that manufactures automobile parts. The catalog of parts must be compiled in an indexed format. When published, it most likely would be several inches thick, and contain errors that would require addendum sheets to be printed and inserted. Printing costs to distribute the manual to many thousands of recipients would be enormous. Additionally, the printing and distribution would take anywhere from days to weeks, and this estimate is *conservative* if the automobile company has overseas offices.

The physical catalog would eventually become outdated and at regular intervals would have to be recycled or repurposed as a doorstop. In addition, traveling corporate members would be adding several pounds of documentation to their travel gear as they prepared for their destinations.

The same automotive company could begin with composing the parts catalog as a hyperlink document using nothing more than a text editor, Navigator Gold, and FastTrack software (described later in this chapter) for the conversion of graphics to formats such as GIF, JPEG, or other formats supported by Navigator plug-ins. If the document was traditionally typeset with no electronic original, OCR software, a scanner, and a proofreader could quickly get the documentation into digital format. From here, Navigator Gold's Editor could make links, so the end user could quickly locate a section they need, and the document—the catalog—would be posted on the company's Intranet server.

Within the office, updates and corrections to the parts catalog can be made by the keeper of the document. Users can access the pages they need and print on demand to laser printers. Field workers can dial into the Intranet from a laptop computer and access the data they need. Alternatively, the entire catalog can be translated to CD format in case a field worker needs quick, complete access without having to dial in to the Intranet.

If any of the preceding sounds like science fiction, it isn't. Recently, when specifying the floor plans for a new office building, a technology company made no provisions for filing cabinets. The company had confidence that documents could be more quickly distributed, stored, and retrieved across an Intranet than by moseying down the hall and wasting time searching through physical folders for information. The University of Southern California is building a new campus that has no physical library. Resources are stored on the library's computers; every dormitory room has a data port, and students conduct research by logging into the network.

USC is confident that this will allow multi-user access to specific documents. Remember how the book you needed at finals time always seemed to be checked out? Additionally, vandalism of physical documents has all but been eliminated with the paperless, online resource center. With a good backup system in place, an electronic resource that is lost due to equipment or other failure can be easily replaced even if the document is "out of print."

FAST, CONTENT-RICH COMMUNICATIONS

The World Wide Web is the graphical part of the Internet, and surfers are entertained by multimedia presentations that appear and grow on the Web at an exponential rate. However, multimedia content *isn't* limited to the Web, and in fact, the only reason why multimedia can *exist* on the Web is because of the fact that Navigator's browser supports many different digital media types. With a Netscape-based Intranet, users in an office can benefit from multimedia presentations. Imagine a technician who needs to see how a part works or how to assemble something. The in-house graphics designer could create an animation in any number of applications such as Macromedia Extreme3D or Director, Fractal Design Painter, or even GIF Construction Set.

For ambitious, media-oriented firms such as advertising agencies, RealAudio and VDOLive documents can help users visualize a concept. The document content can then be created in-house or subcontracted and integrated with corporate HTML documents. It's important to note here that Intranet communications can be linked to the Internet, but this is not a necessity. One of the distinct advantages that multimedia content playback has within an Intranet is that media plays *very* fast. Intranet communications happen at the speed of EtherNet or other local area network technologies. In contrast, Internet communications travel at the speed of the weakest link—which is usually a POTS (plain old telephone service) line connecting at 28.8K at best. Because multimedia content, as well as any other content, is stored on a local server, bandwidth can be much greater in capacity and speed, thus allowing for communications content that was only a dream a few years ago.

WORKING WITH INTRANET CONTENT

The groupware idea of distributed document preparation already contains basic support for formatted text and graphics when Navigator is used as the front end for a corporate Intranet. In addition, different media types evolve on a daily basis. One of the largest persistent problems that a mixed computing environment faces is the different types of text-formatting applications used by Macintosh, UNIX, and DOS/Windows systems. Historically, text formatting could not be preserved when, for example, a word processing document was mailed to a Macintosh user from a Windows user. The workaround often adopted has been to equip all machines with binary-compatible word processing applications, amounting to a significant investment, both in acquisition and upgrading. Because the formatting of documents, the *lingua franca* (common language) of Internet communications is HTML, non-platform specific documents can be shared and edited without the loss of paragraph and text attributes. Granted, a document creator has less control over the specifics of document formatting: font selection and a few other specifics don't carry from computer to computer but are instead left to be interpreted by the host machine's browser.

However, plans are underway between Adobe, Microsoft, and Netscape to develop a new font technology (code name *OpenType*) that will give content creators control over the fonts that are displayed in Intranet and Internet documents. OpenType is a scalable, platform-independent digital typeface format. Future versions of Navigator will fully support OpenType, which will make Internet/Intranet documents easier to read and allow users and companies to present a consistent look to their documents.

The current state of graphics support for HTML-based documents is quite good; it qualitatively exceeds the standard for the graphics supported in Windows only four years ago. The GIF 89a graphics format can be created in more than a dozen applications for Windows (including Paint Shop Pro, Photoshop, CorelPhoto-Paint, Picture Publisher, Fractal Design Painter, and more), and the GIF89a format requires no special utility to be accessed and modified by Macintosh or UNIX users. Additionally, many paint programs have added support for the PNG bitmap file type, an alternative to GIF, which copyright issues still surround. The progressive JPEG format is also supported by Navigator 2 and higher, and this format for bitmap graphics offers streaming download capability in addition to 24 bit per pixel color fidelity for photographic quality images.

BEYOND HTML

For our discussions up to this point, it should be noted that Intranet and Internet users *aren't* limited to the restrictions of HTML-formatted documents. HTML documents can be used to call virtually any kind of document to the screen. As shown in Chapter 9, "Taking a Look at Plug-ins," there are a wide variety of Navigator plug-ins that can faithfully display or "play" a document that is in an application-specific format. Almost every software manufacturer either has, or is in the process of developing, a Netscape plug-in to make the documents, presentations, or graphics that their applications create easy to play inside of Navigator's browser window. Already, Adobe Acrobat, Web Presenter, and Novell's Envoy viewer offer document and presentation file formats that preserve the cosmetic appearance of a document. Plug-ins from Inso, Software Publishing Corporation, Macromedia, Autodesk, and many others make viewing word processing, business slide shows, multimedia presentations, and technical drawings a simple matter.

One of the great advantages of Netscape's extensible architecture is that media types that are not supported today *will* be supported tomorrow and at a reasonable (usually free) price. Software manufacturers are eager to create Netscape-compatible viewer plug-ins for their products—and get the plug-ins distributed far and wide—because when everyone can easily view the output of their programs, more will be inclined to buy the software that is the authoring tool for the documents.

For example, one of the graphics plug-ins that perhaps holds the most corporate fascination for interactive exchange and platform-independent document distribution is Corel Corp.'s CMX Viewer. At present, CorelDRAW, a vector drawing program, has an overwhelming share of the Windows graphics market and is scheduled to release a binary-compatible Macintosh version in July 1996. This means that an organization can use their existing CorelDRAW software to produce Intranet-ready graphics that can be viewed by any user on the Intranet or Internet who has installed the free CMX viewer plug-in in their copy of Navigator. If the user also has a copy of CorelDRAW installed, they can edit the Web graphic in addition to viewing it. Like a Navigator Intranet, the CMX (Corel Media eXchange) route to document preparation requires a minimum of retraining or user intervention. In essence, if you know how CorelDRAW's tools work, and how to use Navigator Gold's Editor, you can create and post enhanced documents and send Intranet e-mail.

In Figure 8-1, you can see version 5 of CorelDRAW being used to create a map. Because vector graphics are resolution-independent, they lose no design content when the graphic is zoomed in on or resized. Therefore, map-making, technical drawings . . . anything that requires precision and detail . . . are perfect targets for drawing applications. In contrast, GIF and JPEG images are of fixed resolution and would require a file of massive dimensions to display legible text or intricate diagrams.

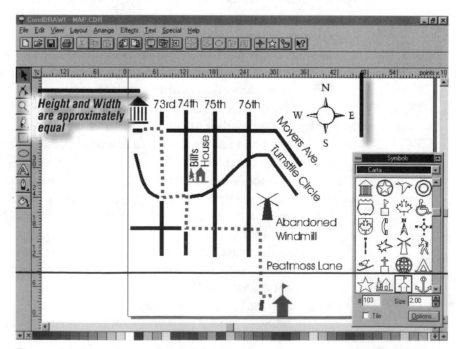

Figure 8-1: *If you have a detailed design, schematic, map, or other diagram you need to share, CorelDRAW can export to the CMX format that any Navigator user with the plug-in filter can access.*

To convert your CorelDRAW work to CMX format (at the time of this writing), you need to take a mental note of what the finished proportion of your graphic will be when embedded within an HTML document. In Figure 8-1, you'll notice that the rulers in CorelDRAW measure units in points. A typographic point is roughly equivalent to monitor resolution—that is, 72 points per inch, and a monitor has a resolution of 72 pixels/inch. Once you've decided on a final viewing size for the graphic, you select all the objects on the page, then stretch them, disproportionately, to fill the default 8 1/2" by 11" page in DRAW. You then choose File, Export, and choose the Corel Presentation Exchange, *.CMX format from the List Files of Type drop-down list. The graphic is now in a format that can be embedded in an HTML document as seen in Figure 8-2.

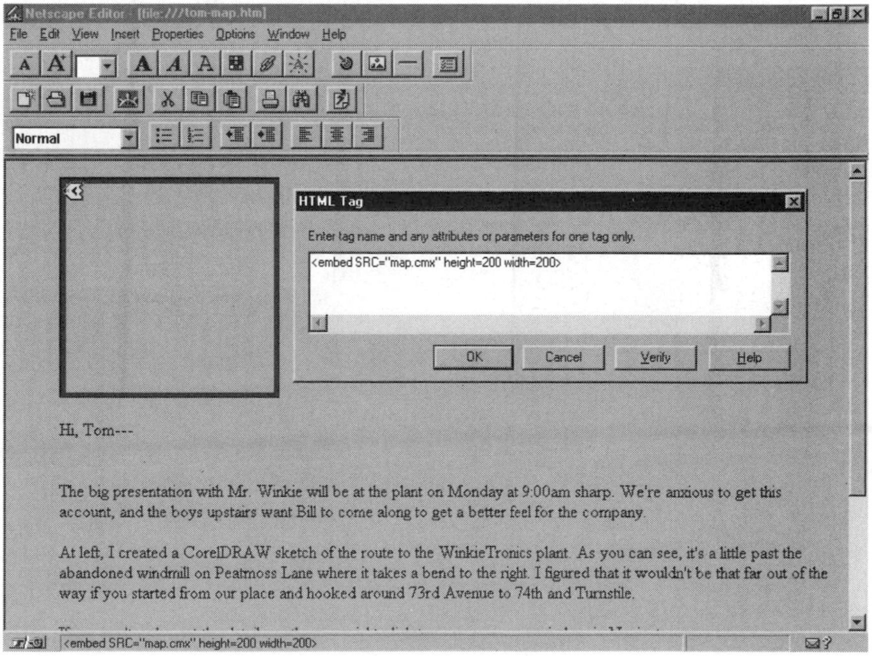

Figure 8-2: *Use Navigator Gold's Editor to embed scalable, vector-based drawings in an HTML document.*

Macromedia has released the Afterburner utility for Macintosh and Windows versions of FreeHand, and FreeHand can also be used to create and distribute scalable designs in a similar way to Corel Corp.'s offering. The disadvantage of Macromedia's implementation of Web-ready authoring tools is that a separate utility is required (the Afterburner utility) to compress the media into Shockwave for FreeHand format. And the user must have a Shockwave plug-in for Navigator for each type of media presented across an Intranet or the Internet; the Shockwave player for Director work is not the same as the Shockwave plug-in for FreeHand, and so on.

In Figure 8-3, you can see the document that Frank, our fictitious marketing person, has sent to Tom; Tom has right-clicked the graphic to display the PopUp menu command, and a duplicate of the map appears in a separate window that can be scaled to any size to be viewed more clearly.

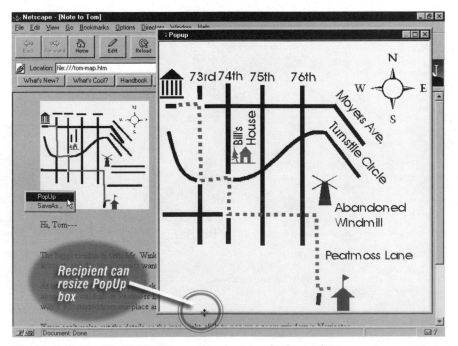

Figure 8-3: *Corel's CMX Viewer plug-in extends the media types you can use in an Intranet communication.*

This message and accompanying map could be delivered in a number of different ways across an Intranet. The most conventional way would be to attach it to an e-mail message, the same way that you'd attach a file to Internet mail. Alternatively, if Frank needed to send detailed instructions on a physical location to a *number* of co-workers, the HTML document could be posted to a specific site on the Intranet server. Navigator Gold features one-button publishing: simply choose File, Publish from Navigator Gold's Editor, and you'll be prompted to provide the location (the HTTP or FTP address) for the document, whether to include images within the document for posting, and whether to publish all the contents of the document's folder, or only the document itself.

Essentially, anything you can compose to the Web, you can compose to an Intranet location. There are possibilities yet undiscovered for educational and commerce purposes when your interoffice communications are open-ended in architecture; and as mentioned earlier, new media types are being added every day to Netscape's standard for document viewing and sharing.

COMMUNICATIONS WITH FEWER HUMAN LAYERS

One of the most compelling reasons to implement an office Intranet is that it reduces the *friction* of communications. Let's suppose that you have a terrific idea that you'd like your department manager to look at right away. Unfortunately, the manager is a busy person and only sets aside Friday afternoons for group discussions. Additionally, if you're new to this office, you might not be familiar with procedures for submitting new ideas and feel a little reluctant and intimidated to approach your manager face to face in the hall (if indeed, you ever *see* the manager in the hall!). With an Intranet, you simply post enhanced e-mail or send your manager a note with a link to a set of documents, videos, slide shows, or graphics that back up your proposal. Your manager reads and views your material at his or her leisure, and by the time Friday afternoon rolls around, there's been plenty of time to consider the merits of your proposal.

Companies have come to value the cross-pollination of ideas in an open environment. Mailing lists and newsgroups in large corporations are excellent ways of bringing together talents that might not know of one another. Consider this: your technical group's product at the XWare company has a wonderful concept for converting DXF files to VRML files automatically. However, the processing time for the conversion is too slow to make a feasible product. However, another technical group at XWare is working on a general-purpose data signal processor (DSP). Under ordinary corporate communications, or even under groupware, your group might never know of the other group's work. But, in an Intranet, you can easily share news of your work through a mailing list or a newsgroup, as can the DSP technical group. You simply subscribe to appropriate corporate newsgroups, and when you discover an opportunity for collaboration, the company at large benefits from a resource and synergy that would not have been discovered otherwise.

The author was once a consultant for a large firm whose in-house publishing department was completely unaware that the company also had a mail order division that stocked printer supplies. The publishing department was paying retail prices for laser toner cartridges when, with the benefit of an Intranet, they would have known of the mail order division and could have received immediate delivery and a better price for the goods. The point is that as firms grow larger, individual departments fall out of touch, and the best way to prevent this is with an open system of communications.

IMPLEMENTING AN INTRANET

There was a time in modern computing when setting up a local area network (LAN) presented a logistical nightmare, and the idea of an internal network that also freely hooked into communications around the world . . . well, that was a dream.

The exponential increase in commonly available processing power for personal computers has changed the way we look at network communications. Furthermore, Navigator has changed the way we can go about establishing a flexible network for a variety of services. The following sections discuss the components you might consider for establishing an office Intranet.

THE INTRANET SERVER

Depending upon the traffic—the number of clients as well as the typical size of the media distributed—your choice of server hardware could be anything from a 386, to a Pentium, to a workstation. The operating system for the hardware can be one of the many different versions of UNIX, or Windows NT. Along with the hardware and operating system software, the server needs to have Internet server software. Here's where a distinction needs to be made between a network operating system's server software, and the specific types of Internet protocol software—*also* called server software—Netscape can provide to make your enterprise servers into Internet and Intranet hosts.

Netscape's server software (described in more detail later) does not include a network operating system. Instead, Netscape server software makes a computer into an Intranet server by adding layers of different Internet protocols to the already existing operating system. For example, a computer that uses Windows NT server as its operating system can be used as an Intranet server with Netscape server software, but a computer using the less expensive Windows NT workstation as its operating system can also function as an Intranet server. Therefore, it is not of great concern which operating system is used on the Intranet server; the OS simply has to be one the Netscape server software supports. At present time, FastTrack, Netscape's entry-level general purpose server software, is available for Windows NT 3.51 running on a Pentium or DEC Alpha workstation, HP-UX 9.03 10.x, HP9000/700, SGI IRIX 5.3 6.2, and SUN Solaris 2.4 and 2.5. Additionally, an IBM RS-6000 can use FastTrack software.

THE CLIENT SYSTEM

To access an Intranet that is based on Netscape servers, or any other vendor's server software, requires a browser that was created for the operating system used by the person accessing the server (the client). The Netscape Navigator Browser is available in versions suitable for Windows 3.1x, Windows 95, Windows NT, the 68K and PowerPC operating systems on the Macintosh, and a wide variety of UNIX systems. It is also available in English, Brazilian Portuguese, Dutch, French, German, Italian, Korean, Japanese, Spanish, and Swedish language versions. The client system must have TCP/IP protocol enabled on their computer and a connection to at least one Intranet server.

Beyond the basic hardware configuration and Navigator Browser, the key element to establishing an Intranet is Netscape FastTrack server software, which happily is as easy to set up as Navigator Browser software. In the following sections, we'll take a look at what FastTrack does, how it's implemented in the Intranet, what your options are, and how the competition stacks up against what is quickly becoming the de facto networking product for small and large firms alike.

THE FASTTRACK SERVER

Earlier in this chapter, I mentioned that there are different types of server software. The basic, traditional purpose of a network server is to play host to the clients—computers that subscribe to server resources. This is the network operating system approach to inter-office communications. Intranet communications, however, use a set of network protocols that is different from those used by a traditional proprietary network operating system. It is the Intranet server software that provides these protocols and the management tools to configure and run the Internet server software. In this section, we'll discuss the Netscape FastTrack server. The FastTrack server is a very inexpensive (under $300), powerful, and secure Web server. Netscape has made the once complex task of setting up a Web server so simple that a computing novice should be able to set up the FastTrack server in less than an hour.

Netscape's FastTrack server can be used as an Internet or Intranet Web page server. It is ideal for small organizations or as a departmental Web server. Because FastTrack fully supports Secure Sockets Layers (SSL) and digital certificates (more about these later), it can be set up as either a secure or insecure server. With Netscape FastTrack as your Intranet server software, you can offer your co-workers the same kind of graphically based content they have come to expect when visiting sites on the World Wide Web.

Part of the beauty of Intranet communications is that many of the users of your Intranet already have acquired a familiarity with how Navigator works and how to navigate Web pages, download software, and fill in forms and the like because they have honed these skills by surfing the Internet.

NAVIGATOR GOLD AUTHORING

As mentioned throughout this book, Navigator Gold is an enhanced version of Navigator browser, which facilitates composition of HTML documents and the linking and embedding of different Web media types such as Video for Windows movies, Macromedia Director projects, and sounds. Navigator Gold is included with the FastTrack server software, making it a breeze to publish content-rich HTML documents to local servers or to remote servers that are part of the Intranet. FastTrack offers one-button publishing of HTML documents created in Navigator Gold, or any other HTTP-compatible authoring tool. In Chapter 6, "Person to Person With Navigator Mail & Netscape News," you saw how Navigator Gold's WYSIWYG document creation interface is used.

SCALABLE SERVICES

Depending on your needs and as your Intranet grows, you may want to add custom or additional services to your in-house communications. FastTrack is an entry-level Intranet Web server (a new version of Netscape Communications Server software) whose power is extended through other communications services. One of the most important improvements to FastTrack is that it includes native support for SSL. A corporation can migrate upwards to Netscape Enterprise Server from Netscape Commerce *or* Communications servers with a minimum of reconfiguration. Enterprise Server is the industrial strength server that Netscape is hoping all users of communications and transactions servers will eventually move to.

Netscape has a complete line of special servers to meet any need you may have. The cost of additional Netscape services such as Mail or News is $995. If the computer you use as a server has the horsepower, you might decide to include different Intranet services on the same machine. However, in the same way that the Internet is a collection of many different types of computer hardware running different operating systems, your Intranet might be composed of several different servers running on separate computers. You could easily configure, for example, a mail server on one machine, a Proxy server on another, and the whole array of enterprise computers—and services—could be administrated through a remote server, that is, any of the servers you use to provide specific services, or even a client machine.

It should be noted that Netscape FastTrack takes advantage of the many innovations that Netscape has developed that have been adopted as new Open Systems Interconnection standards by the Internet community. When you use Netscape Intranet servers, you benefit from the proven track record Netscape has for balancing innovation with reliable performance. FastTrack supports the Internet Application Framework, as well as Java and JavaScript. This means that any utility or application developed in these languages can be installed on the server and called by any client, regardless of the client's operating system. Additionally, the "grown up" version of FastTrack, Netscape Enterprise Server, includes support for Visual Basic and Microsoft Object Linking and Embedding (OLE). OLE and Visual Basic are currently supported only in MS Windows operating environments, but this can be seen as an advantage to systems administrators who are more experienced and more comfortable with familiar programming tools. In fact, WinCGI (Common Gateway Interface) scripts can be written in Visual Basic and can be called from the server to transfer databases from mainframe systems. The problem of transferring legacy data from proprietary records held on proprietary operating systems has historically required expensive, custom software, well-paid consultants, and time. With an Intranet, moving information to and from any node on the platform-independent network requires only a knowledge of how the database is stored and some scripting language skills.

Additionally, many third-party companies have developed programs that seamlessly integrate with Netscape servers to perform specialized data services such as conversion of information into HTML format, specialized search engines, or database connectivity options.

SYSTEM SECURITY

Security is perhaps the prime concern of firms that want to implement an Intranet. Security is also a double-edged sword. You want to keep workers "focused"—capable of accessing Intranet and Internet documents, but not, for example, privileged to surf to games or adult areas of the external Web. Moreover, you may need to be assured that employees don't bring material back from these sites, either because the subject matter is inappropriate for the work environment or because it may contain a virus. You might also want access restricted to some corporate documents on the local server, but most importantly, you want users to be able to leverage the Intranet to be productive for content-providing individuals.

The Netscape solution for Intranet security is two-pronged: The administrative tools that come with FastTrack and Enterprise server can control the flow of access to documents, directories, and applications to particular user names or passwords to groups or entire domains under an Intranet. With the introduction of Netscape Certificate server in the later part of 1996, organizations will also have the option of issuing personal, digital identify certificates to employees and other users of their Intranet. The digit certificates can be used by all of the various Netscape servers to control and validate access within the Intranet.

Additionally, the Secure Sockets Layer (SSL), Netscape's technology which encrypts packets of information for secure transmission and the use of secure digital certificates, is fully implemented to allow verification of credit transactions and confidential information that might pass from outside customers to within the Intranet. See Chapter 7, "Maintaining Your Privacy on the Internet," on Netscape security features.

THE PROXY SERVER

Proxy servers are used to isolate an Intranet from unwanted intrusion by outside communications or persons, while providing a secure gateway for customers or employees working from remote locations. Proxy servers in conjunction with firewall software regulate the flow of information in and out of the Intranet. Usually, a server is placed outside of a company firewall as a checkpoint for visitors who need access or information from within an Intranet. The server outside of the firewall receives requests, passes them to the appropriate server inside the enterprise, and with verification, the data request is then passed back from the Intranet to the visitor. A Proxy server can also be used without a connection to the Internet or *any* off-site connections. As an internal security device, a Proxy server can restrict access of local documents only to the individuals with specific security privileges.

Intranet communications do not have the unique advantage of internal/external communications, nor do they offer unique security features. Network operating systems have used proprietary gateways and security features as part of the networking options in the past. Traditionally, however, much user intervention has been required to successfully share secured information. A Netscape-based Intranet, through its use of site certificates, personal certificates, and the Secure Sockets Layer, makes providing high levels of security much more automatic and transparent to users. Netscape Proxy Server software seamlessly integrates with other Netscape server software, as well as software from other Open Systems manufacturers.

WHERE DO WE GROW FROM HERE?

The evolution of modern business depends upon the cyclic principle that up-front costs lead to a more productive environment, which in turn generates more revenue that is often re-invested for more productivity tools.

Scalability—the capability to upsize or downsize the features offered through the Intranet to meet the needs of a specific user and their equipment—is only one area where Netscape Communications offers a solution. Extensibility is another issue—how can I protect my initial investment when I need to upgrade the Intranet?

As business needs grow, the Intranet-enhanced work environment can add communications support to either FastTrack or Enterprise Server through additional server software. As mentioned earlier, a Netscape-based Intranet can include Netscape or other third-party services. Netscape is also aggressively pricing other server software in the form of the SuiteSpot bundle, which is essentially five different types of Intranet server software for the price of four. Building upon FastTrack or Enterprise Server is an attractive option for growing businesses in light of the fact that no additional client licenses need to be purchased as new servers or services are added—clients can continue to use their current version of Netscape Navigator regardless of future configurations of the Intranet.

THE INFORMATION AGE INTRANET

Companies who purchase Netscape Enterprise server, the transaction and information server, can take advantage of the built-in support the Enterprise server provides for connecting to a wide variety of industry standard database management systems (DBMS) without having to buy additional system software to accomplish the task. The following section describes the operational and feature advantages of running a growing business under the Netscape system.

Businesses that are service-oriented or product-oriented need to maintain an inventory list, a pricing list, a mailing list, and so on to track day-to-day transactions. Company databases typically store massive amounts of important business information and have been a driving force in some areas of office automation. As mentioned earlier in this chapter, an Intranet is document-centric instead of database-centric (as network groupware is), but many companies do need a way to integrate their database assets with their document-centered assets to provide a total Intranet business solution.

Both FastTrack and Enterprise server software include native support for querying Oracle, Sybase, or Informix database servers. Netscape Communications itself does not offer a database server; databases require optimized transaction hardware, and machines that act as servers for databases are frequently offered by the same manufacturers as the software, such as Oracle. These databases can easily be queried by users from the browser from a Web page's HTML-based form. If the user has an appropriate browser plug-in installed, queries can also be made from an embedded form created in applications such as Microsoft Excel.

The Enterprise server's ability to seamlessly integrate with external databases comes as a standard feature whereas other company's server products require expensive additional purchases to attain this functionality or you are locked into using a specific database product. Netscape builds its servers upon established, common protocols and features development tools that enable you to work with existing systems you have in place.

LiveWire

If you're into Web authoring—the creation of multimedia, multi-page, HTML sites—you'll immediately appreciate the need for site management. Even a modest Web creation can consist of a dozen individual HTML-linked pages and a score of embedded or linked media elements. In a way, managing an Intranet can be compared to hosting a Web site on a server, and LiveWire is the Netscape product that offers drag-and-drop site management tools in addition to tight integration with FastTrack server software.

In addition to tracking locations of pages that make up a site, LiveWire also can perform link verification. This feature is important for Intranet sites that contain content-critical linked objects and hypertext links to other sites because there is nothing more irritating and time-wasting in online communications than a "dead link" on a page. LiveWire can check to make certain all links lead to where they are supposed to, and Navigator Gold's Editor, the publishing edition of the Navigator Browser, can verify tagged items such as videos and sounds. LiveWire also offers graphics file format conversions, so a user of Navigator Gold can easily compose a graphically rich document from TIFF, PCX, Macintosh PICT, or other file formats not directly supported through Navigator's Browser. For text-based documents, Microsoft Word, Corel WordPerfect, FrameMaker, and RTF documents can also be filtered to HTML using LiveWire.

Netscape's solution to publishing Intranet content can therefore be thought of as a triumvirate: FastTrack provides easy, basic Intranet connectivity, LiveWire helps manage and maintain documents, and Navigator Gold is the WYSIWYG document creation program.

FROM INTERNET TO INTRANET . . . AND BACK AGAIN

In addition to CGI, WinCGI, and Visual Basic, a Netscape-based Intranet also includes support for ODBC (Open Database Connectivity) through JavaScript Application Programming Interface (API). Netscape is also betting heavily that software developers will use Java to write Web-ready applications and utilities. These applications' first target will be the consumer market, with desktop utilities and home shopping interfaces for the Net being some of the first implementations of Java programming to be rolled out. The home market might be seen by some as a "seed market," to introduce Java to users during their leisure computing time, and in the same way Navigator skills developed at home become useful at work, Java business implementations will migrate from the home to the office. The advantage that Java presents over OLE is its platform-independence. Microsoft has established proprietary standards for connectivity while Netscape standards are completely portable and open. In order for a successful Intranet to operate, the system upon which it is based has to encourage outside developers to make extensions, plug-ins, and improvements to the overall quality of interoffice communications.

Developers who want to design applications, front ends for data management, and utilities to enhance document content will find that the Netscape Intranet offers flexibility for both Internet and Intranet content development. Because Java, Visual Basic, OLE, CGI, and other programming and scripting languages can be used to write "Web applets," developers with experience in a specific language will find it easy to make contributions. Additionally, Netscape is again leading the way by looking at the "big picture" of global communications and commerce with the development of two new types of Open Systems based servers—the Netscape Directory Server and the Netscape Certificate Server.

NETSCAPE DIRECTORY SERVER

Netscape's Directory server is a result of understanding that there is a need to provide directory services that can not only dispense the names of servers like the present DNS (Domain Name Server), but can also serve location information about other Internet or Intranet resources. Additionally there is a need for organizations and users to be able to locate other users' addresses. The Netscape directory server uses the Lightweight Directory Access Protocol (LDAP) and is capable of hooking into UNIX databases to provide names and e-mail addresses. The Netscape directory also supports x.509 security keys (distributed by a Netscape Certificate server, explained next). Users will be able to log into a Directory server using Internet naming such as a Simple Mail Transfer Protocol (SMTP) mail address, and the repository can be customized to provide, for example, images of users. The initial implementation of the Directory server software will probably be for government, educational, and other institutional entities, but large corporations running an Intranet will also benefit from this high-traffic server software. Netscape, working with the University of Michigan on the adaptation of LDAP for Netscape products, estimates that an average UNIX server (a Sun SPARC 20 was used as a test server) will be able to support 200,000 entries and 100,000 hits per hour.

NETSCAPE CERTIFICATE SERVER

The Certificate server is intended to abstract the user from the problems associated with identifying oneself for Intranet or Internet access. Netscape is currently implementing the same version 3 (X.509) RSA public-key encryption standards used for Internet commerce in the Certificate server software; this will allow encrypted communications, message integrity through a digital signature, and authentication for companies where intraoffice security is an issue. From the Certificate server, business administrators will be able to easily manage a database of security certificates, defining levels of security for employees and revoke, renew, and issue new certificates.

The Certificate server will also take advantage of LDAP directory services, so the Directory server can be used in tandem with the Certificate server to distribute Certificates of authority on an enterprise level within an organization. Netscape plans to integrate the Certificate server with all future Netscape server products, thus eliminating multiple logins for users who want to access a variety of Intranet services. For more information on Netscape security, certificates, and public key encryption, see Chapter 7, "Maintaining Your Privacy on the Internet."

MOVING ON

The term *extensibility* is often used as assurance that a particular application is not destined toward obsolescence. Many manufacturers of commercial software such as Adobe Systems and Macromedia encourage third-party vendors to develop plug-ins that extend the functionality of a program. This extensibility concept allows a manufacturer to continue refining a flagship product and also invites fresh perspectives and innovations from the outside. Chapter 9, "Taking a Look at Plug-ins," examines the popular trend that has captured the attention and resources of practically every technology firm on the globe: how can we get our product to play in Navigator through a plug-in?

Chapter 9 provides an extensive report on the hottest, the coolest, and the most productive plug-ins you'll want to add to your own copy of Navigator.

Extending Navigator Through Plug-ins, Helper Applications & New Technology

Taking a Look at Plug-ins

Because Netscape anticipated that it would take a little while for manufacturers to understand and implement Navigator's plug-in architecture, Navigator 3.0 is capable of using two methods for bringing Web media objects to a visitor of a site. Navigator supports both plug-ins and helper applications. The difference between a plug-in and a helper application is that a plug-in needs Navigator in order to run, but a helper application can be run as a stand-alone program. Both plug-ins and helper applications accomplish something that Navigator does not natively support, such as playing a Shockwave Director movie or displaying an MS Word document. Navigator's openly published API (Application Programming Interface) gives third-party software developers the information they need to make their product work with, and *within* Navigator. This means that you can have an astonishing array of software at your disposal through the extensibility of Navigator's architecture.

In almost all events, plug-ins and helper applications are used by Navigator to display or play something, as opposed to creating something. Plug-ins and helper apps are designed to work with Web media that was created in one or more specific applications—commonly called *authoring tools* when used in the context of creating Web content. It seems that every software company has built—

or is in the process of building—a plug-in that displays work produced by that company's application. For example, there are plug-ins that display MS Office files, Macromedia product files, Corel product files, Autodesk AutoCAD files, and so on. Almost without exception, "player" plug-ins are free, because software companies realize that to sell the authoring programs, customers require the assurance that visitors to their Web sites can see the work, and get the player without having to spend money.

There are a few plug-ins that are actually complete programs in themselves—there is no other program that creates content that these plug-ins "play." Symantec's Norton AntiVirus plug-in, which checks files you download from the Internet for viruses, and Starfish Software's EarthTime plug-in, which displays the current time in various parts of the world, are examples of this type of "complete plug-in." Unlike the player type of plug-in, complete program-type plug-ins are usually available in limited trial versions . . . and if you want to continue to use them after the evaluation time limit (usually 30 days), you must buy them.

This chapter takes a look at some of the hottest plug-ins for downloading images and viewing interactive presentations. You'll also see some smart tools for browsing multimedia presentations and graphically rich business presentations. And you'll find out how to locate and install Netscape plug-ins and helper applications that will make your system capable of playing back sound in real-time.

New plug-ins are created and distributed daily, and currently plug-ins are updated regularly. There were over a hundred Navigator plug-ins available at the time of this writing, and although a complete documentation of this field of software would break this book's binding, this chapter highlights some of the most exciting and valuable ones.

Before we move into the plug-in showcase, an overview of plug-ins and helper applications software and the ways they impact your system is important. The following section tells you where you can find plug-ins and helper applications, how to work with them, and the problems you may encounter if you add *too many* plug-ins to your system and Navigator.

PLUG-INS VS. HELPER APPLICATIONS

Plug-ins typically play a file from within a Navigator window. Some plug-ins are able to play a file *within* a document, while other times they open a new Navigator window to display Web content. The type of file you wish to view or hear determines whether the event is played as an inline object, or from within a new document window. When a helper application is called to handle a file type not supported by Navigator or a plug-in, the file is loaded into the helper application's program window. When you've moved on to another Web page or closed Navigator, a helper application *doesn't* close automatically. It stays open and continues to use system resources. Helper applications close only when you close them manually, by using the helper application's menu bar or window close box. Netscape *plug-ins*, on the other hand, stay running and use system resources only as long as they are needed. As soon as you close the Navigator window a plug-in is running in, or move on to a different page or a different site within the plug-in's window, the plug-in application closes down and releases whatever system resources it was using.

Any application you have on your system could be used as a helper application, but only software that was specifically designed to be a Navigator plug-in can be added to Navigator's file folders. Because plug-ins are usually designed to be used within a specific version of Navigator, they do not always work as anticipated if you use them with a brand new version of Navigator. Whenever you update Navigator (which appears to happen weekly with public beta releases!), you may find that you need to also update the plug-ins you've installed. Conversely, helper applications are designed as stand-alone pieces of software, and are not usually sensitive to version to version changes in Navigator's API.

HOW DOES NAVIGATOR KNOW WHEN TO USE A PLUG-IN OR HELPER APPLICATION?

After you request a Web page from a server, the server then begins to send all of the elements of the page that the author specified. Before sending each component (text, graphic, multimedia file, and so on) the server sends a message informing Navigator of the MIME (Multipurpose Internet Mail Extension) type attributed to the file. Based on the MIME information, Navigator checks to see if you own a plug-in or helper application specified for handling the MIME type, or if other instructions such as Launch in Browser, Save to Disk, or Unknown: Prompt User, have been specified in your copy of Navigator's Helpers tab of General Preferences.

If Navigator finds a match between an available browsing assistant on your system and the MIME type for the incoming file, Navigator launches the plug-in or helper application and passes the file to the other program. If the file is passed to a plug-in, Navigator will automatically close the plug-in and free up the memory it used after you're done browsing the file. When Navigator passes a file to a helper application, Navigator hands over all responsibility—including closing the application—to the helper application.

When Navigator is unable to find a suitable plug-in or helper application, or you've set that file type to Unknown: Prompt User, you will see the familiar Unknown File Type dialog box when you encounter a Web page with media not supported through your current collection of plug-ins and helper apps. See Chapter 2, "Installing & Customizing Navigator," for more information on MIME types and helper applications.

PLUG-INS VS. HELPER APPLICATIONS: UNIQUE ADVANTAGES

Plug-ins have an advantage over helper applications in that they display content *inline*; Web page media can be played as embedded sights and sounds from an area of an HTML document itself, not in a separate document window. For example, a page you visit might contain standard HTML text, a movie, sound, a VRML world, and a spreadsheet all on the same HTML page. To see, hear, or interact with any of these elements, you never have to leave the page—all the elements play in place. If you used helper applications to browse each of these elements instead of plug-ins, the HTML page would almost surely be obscured by a plethora of application windows: one for sound, one for the video, one for the VRML world, and yet another for the spreadsheet. The act of merely jockeying the windows around and making sure that you closed them when you'd finished would be a job in and of itself!

However, there *are* a few advantages to using a helper application instead of a plug-in. Because a helper application is a stand-alone program, you're likely to have a wider variety of tools with which to work with Web objects, the most important of them being *editing tools*. For example, if you use a helper application to view a graphic file or a word processing document, once it has loaded into the helper application, you are free to not only view the file, but also to edit the file using any of the tools the helper application provides.

It is also easier to switch helper applications on the fly. Changing the application that is associated with a helper application is easier than respecifying a Navigator plug-in to browse Web page content, because all you do is select the file type you want to change, and then use the Browse button to pick a different application. You don't have to close Navigator and restart to do this, as you do with respecifying or adding plug-ins.

COLLECTING PLUG-INS

Acquiring and installing a collection of plug-ins balanced between business and leisure in orientation can greatly enhance your online experience. With a wide range of plug-ins installed, there will be fewer times you are stopped from viewing or participating in what a site has to offer, because you have to leave a site and download an appropriate plug-in. Some carefully chosen plug-ins also makes receiving enhanced e-mail (and e-mail attachments) much easier if you already have the tools you need waiting in the wings to play or display the Web page elements.

However, every plug-in you install takes up *some* hard disk space. Some plug-ins take up as much as 4 or 5MB, while others are very small. The point is that hard disk space is not infinite—nor is your free time—and you might not be able to spare *either* commodity to find and download every plug-in on earth.

To make it easier for you to evaluate some of the most useful plug-ins without filling your hard disk with the file archives, and to save you download time, we've included 20 "Author's Picks" Navigator plug-ins on the Companion CD-ROM. Many of the plug-ins from the Companion CD are documented in this chapter; you'll also find plug-ins discussed that are *not* on the Companion CD. They're fascinating and useful, but manufacturer or time restrictions prohibited us from bringing them to you on the CD. Many of the plug-ins mentioned but not offered directly can be found in either downloadable evaluation versions or the registered CD version of the Netscape Power Pack, or they can be obtained from the respective company's home page. In any case, you'll want to read through this chapter to see which plug-ins appeal to you, and you'll definitely want to check out the offerings on the Companion CD-ROM.

AS THE POWER USER'S TOOLKIT GOES TO PRESS . . .

Although every attempt was made to procure the most current versions of plug-ins for the Companion CD-ROM, by the time you read this, some will no longer be the most current version. Navigator plug-ins, like Navigator itself, update frequently. It's the sad reality that content can be posted on the Web faster than ink dries on the printed pages from a commercial press, but we've anticipated your needs for the most recent plug-ins, so read on.

In most cases the plug-ins on the Companion CD-ROM should work with your current copy of Navigator, but simply won't be the most recent version of a specific plug-in. If you find one that doesn't work, or if you find one that you can't live without, you'll want to visit the maker's site and get the latest version. To make this easy for you, the Web addresses of each plug-in manufacturer in this chapter are listed in the overview area of the documentation. Additionally, the Navigator Plug-ins Sources folder of the *Totally Hot Bookmarks List* on the Companion CD-ROM contains bookmarks to all the sites where the plug-ins are available. This folder also contains links to many *additional* plug-ins that are available for Navigator.

As new plug-ins become available, you'll want to keep an eye on Iworld's Plug-In Plaza (http://www.browserwatch.com/) and Netscape's own plug-in pages (http://home.netscape.com/comprod/mirror/navcomponents_download.html). These two sites specialize in identifying and providing links to currently available plug-ins.

INSTALLING PLUG-INS

Plug-ins are installed the same way as any other program. Some plug-ins come with setup programs that lead you through the setup process; many feature an install wizard that requires minimal user intervention. Others are so simple in design that they are comprised of a Navigator plug-in DLL file and a README or two. In this case, the plug-in might not have a setup program; instead it requires you to read the instructions to find out exactly where the file(s) should be placed.

Regardless of how many—or how few—files are needed to make a plug-in run, there will always be one file that needs to be placed in Navigator's PROGRAM/PLUGINS folder. If you've had previous copies of Navigator on your drive, or if you currently have more than one copy of Navigator installed (such as Navigator Gold in addition to Navigator), the plug-in's setup program may put the plug-in file in the wrong place. Make sure that the setup program *assumes* that the copy of Navigator into which the plug-in is to be installed is correct. If the installation program doesn't ask, and you don't find the plug-in in the PROGRAM/PLUGINS folder, you'll need to find the file after the installation is over and move it to the proper location.

If you have more than one copy of Navigator on your computer, you must install the plug-in into *each* copy of Navigator. Usually this means running the plug-in installation once for each copy of Navigator. However, with simple plug-ins that don't come with many support files, you may be able to simply place a copy of the plug-in into each PROGRAM/PLUGINS folder of Navigator you have on your system.

As with all software, it is strongly recommended that you close *all* running applications before installing plug-ins. This includes screen savers, anti-virus software, let background printing finish before you begin installation, close modem connections—think twice about stuff you've taken for commonplace PC activity. Finally, and of most significance, you must *not* have Navigator running when you install a Navigator plug-in. At the very least, you'll halt the installation, or may cause Navigator or your system to crash.

Once a plug-in has been successfully installed, your involvement in the process of displaying or playing online media is practically nil. To have a Navigator plug-in decipher Web page content usually requires no user input. With a few exceptions, notably EarthTime, Navigator will know when to launch the plug-in.

THE PROBLEM OF COMPETING PLUG-INS

Many of the third-party plug-ins and helper applications available perform overlapping duties in that they can handle the same type of file. Some plug-ins and helper applications also handle file formats such as AVI, QuickTime movies, and VRML worlds which are directly supported by Navigator 3's *built-in* plug-ins. This poses a problem—which plug-in or helper application "wins" when two different ones both want to handle a specific file? The contest winner in this event depends on several factors. First, is it two plug-ins that are contending for the job, or is it a plug-in and a helper application?

When two plug-ins are vying for the honor of displaying Web content, the winner is the one whose DLL file (Dynamic Link Library) appears first in ascending alphabetical order in Navigator's plug-in folder. For example, the file name for Silicon Graphics' VRML plug-in *Cosmo* is NPCOSMOP.DLL. The Netscape Live3D plug-in is named NPL3D32.DLL. In this case, the Cosmo plug-in is first alphabetically and will be the one that displays the file.

To find out the DLL file name for a plug-in before you install it, consult the documentation for the plug-in. After the plug-in has been installed, you can choose About Plug-ins from Navigator's Help menu for a list of installed plug-ins and the file types they handle, as shown in Figure 9-1.

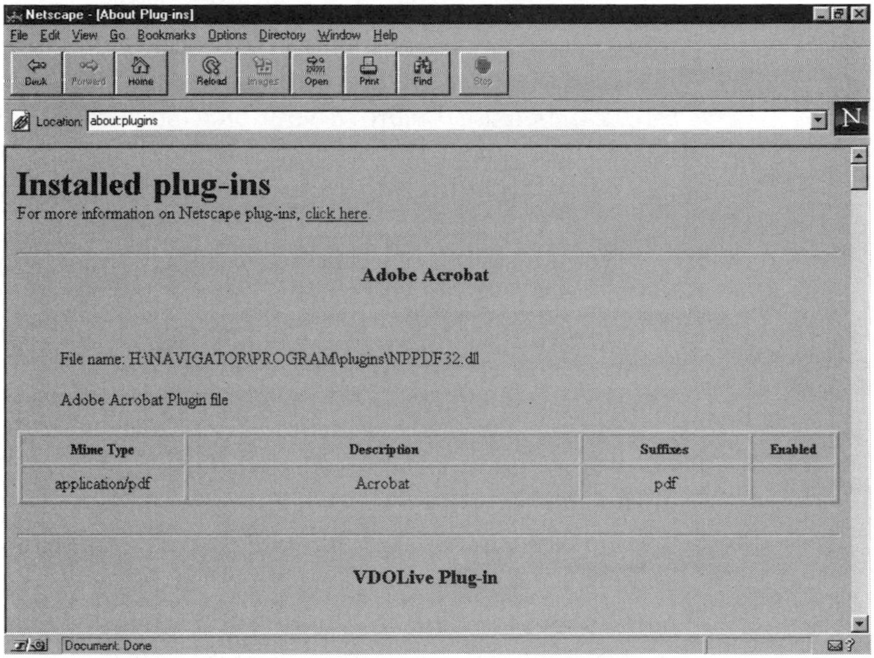

Figure 9-1: *Find out which plug-ins are installed from the About Plug-ins page.*

There is currently no way to have Navigator ask you to choose between applications, so you will have to find the plug-in application you like best and then make sure that its DLL file either comes first alphabetically in the list of files in the plug-in folder, or you'll have to remove from the plug-ins folder the DLL that conflicts with your chosen plug-in. If you're trying out a lot of plug-ins, you may want to create a folder in Navigator's PROGRAM folder to hold disabled plug-ins. Make sure you always install and remove Navigator plug-ins from the PLUGINS folder when Navigator is *not* running. Moving plug-ins while Navigator is running is akin to stepping out of a car or train before it's halted, and your reward for "hot swapping" a plug-in might be a system crash.

When a conflict is between a helper application and a plug-in that was created to handle a specific MIME type, the plug-in always wins. This is because every time you start Navigator, it scans the PROGRAM/PLUGINS folder and allows a plug-in to claim the file type it was designed to handle. You can temporarily override this within a single session by going to the Helpers tab of General Preferences, and clicking on the Launch the Application radio button; you then use the Browse button to specify the path to the helper application. The next time you launch Navigator, you will have to perform the same steps if you don't want the plug-in to handle the file type.

Beyond installation and possible conflicts among plug-ins, installation is not difficult, and in most cases, a plug-in can be installed with less effort and time than a system application that has modest features. In the following section, we move from installation to recommendation, as we peruse 20 of the best plug-ins to enhance your surfing experience.

THE NAVIGATOR PLUG-IN SHOWCASE

In the pages to follow, you'll see a wide range of plug-in software that can extend your Internet or Intranet horizons. In each section, we've provided information on what the plug-in does, where you can get it, and any special system requirements there are to use the plug-in. Some of the plug-ins will run on all versions of Windows, while some run only on specific versions such as Windows 3.1 or Windows 95. We've also noted if the plug-in is available for platforms *other* than Windows.

If you create content for a home page or for your organization's Intranet, you will also find information about which authoring program (or programs) can create files viewed by the plug-in, as well as any other special requirements there might be for authoring or distributing the files.

Enough said. Let's take a walk through the Plug-in Showcase, and start at the top of the alphabet with . . .

ACROBAT READER 3 BY ADOBE SYSTEMS

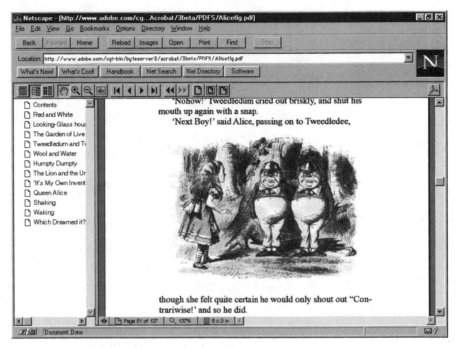

Figure 9-2: *Adobe Acrobat Reader in action.*

Acrobat documents are platform- and software-independent, electronic, portable documents. An Acrobat document (PDF file) can be viewed and printed from any kind of computer, even when the application software and the fonts used to create the document are not present on the viewer's system. Acrobat documents can be created from any kind of finished document, such as word processing, desktop publishing, spreadsheet, graphics, or database files. Acrobat documents preserve the look and layout of the original document, complete with scalable fonts and graphics. Because PDF files are electronic and Web ready, they can also contain elements that are not possible in printed documents such as embedded sounds, movies, and hypertext links to different sections of the

CD-ROM

document, to other Acrobat documents and to URLs on the Web. Several documents on the Companion CD-ROM are in Acrobat format, including *The Argyle Pages*, a hyperlink compendium of resources for Web and traditional authoring tools.

Acrobat Reader 3, the current version as of this writing, can display both *optimized* and *non-optimized* Acrobat files. When downloaded from a properly configured server, each page in an optimized Acrobat file can be read as soon as it arrives on your computer—the Acrobat document is a streaming file in this sense. Non-optimized Acrobat files must be downloaded completely before any page in the document can be viewed. Optimized files are created using Acrobat Exchange 3 and must be sent from a server, such as a Netscape server, that is capable of sending *byte-ranges*. Byte-range capable servers can "reach into" a file and send only the parts of a file that are requested.

The Adobe Acrobat 3 plug-in is particularly useful on both the Internet and the Intranet. For more information see Adobe Systems, Inc.'s home page at http://www.adobe.com.

Authoring software required: *Adobe Acrobat Exchange,* which includes the Acrobat PDF Writer or *Adobe Acrobat Pro,* which includes Acrobat PDF Writer and Acrobat Distiller. The Acrobat suite of tools is for the conversion of an existing document and has no document creation tools, per se. The Acrobat *creation* program can be any application on your system that you can print from. To create optimized PDF files, you need version 3 or later of these programs.

Good places to find Acrobat documents: For Internet optimized files in the Acrobat format, see http://www.adobe.com/Acrobat/ 3beta/amexamp.html. To view Acrobat files, some of which may have been enhanced for Internet viewing, see http:// www.adobe.com/Acrobat/PDFsites.html.

CD-ROM

Where you can get the plug-in:
The Companion CD-ROM
Netscape Power Pack
Adobe Systems at http://www.adobe.com/Acrobat/

Platform availability: Windows3.1, Windows 95, Windows NT, Macintosh, and OS/2. A UNIX version is expected.

System requirements: Minimum system requirements for Windows 3.1 (or 3.11),Windows for Workgroups, Windows 95, or Microsoft Windows NT are: a 386-based personal computer (486 or Pentium recommended); 4MB application RAM; 3MB of free hard-disk space; plus 2MB temporary space available during installation.

ASAP WEBSHOW
BY SOFTWARE PUBLISHING CORPORATION

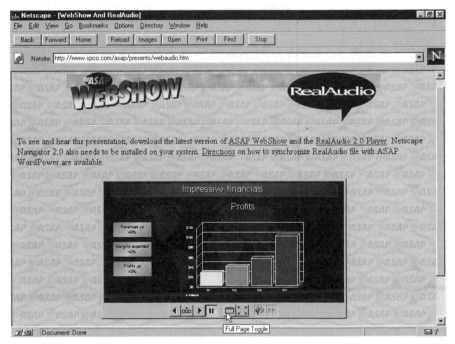

Figure 9-3: *Self-running slide shows with sound can be played inside Navigator with ASAP WebShow and RealAudio plug-ins.*

The ASAP WebShow plug-in allows you to view business presentations that were created in ASAP WordPower. When used with the RealAudio plug-in, sound that has been attached to the ASAP WordPower presentation plays synchronously with each slide in the presentation. Because the presentations are vector-based drawings, you can choose to display the show at full page, full screen or partial screen size without any loss of image detail. ASAP WebShow offers a number of user controls from a VCR-like control strip as well as from the right-click shortcut menu. Options available to someone browsing an ASAP presentation include the ability to go to a specific slide, enable or disable auto advance, pause the show, print or save the show, edit the show (if you have ASAP WordPower installed on your computer), and view the show at different preset sizes.

ASAP WebShow files are very small, making them ideal as e-mail attachments, as embedded objects in Web pages, or locally run Intranet presentations. The presentation shown in Figure 9-3 contains 11 slides plus synchronous RealAudio sound, but is only 41K. When sound is not used, 20 graphically rich slides can take up only 37K; you could carry almost 40 presentations around with you on a floppy diskette. For more information, visit Software Publishing Corporation at http://www.spco.com.

Authoring software required: ASAP WordPower is the application in which ASAP WebShow viewable presentations are created. It is an extremely easy to use, template-driven slide show creation program from which even novices can get results quickly. The Windows 95 version of ASAP WordPower can also import PowerPoint 7.0 files and convert them into the ASAP WordPower format. ASAP WordPower is available on a 30-day trial basis and can be downloaded from Software Publishing Corp.'s Web site.

Where you can get the plug-in:
Netscape Power Pack
Software Publishing Corporation at http://www.spco.com/

Platform availability: Windows 3.1, Windows 95, and Windows NT

System requirements: A 486 or better with 1MB of memory available after all other programs in use are running. Windows 3.1, Windows 95, or Windows NT operating systems; DOS 5.0 or higher; approximately 1MB of hard disk space; a mouse; and a 16-color VGA or higher display. A sound card and the RealAudio plug-in is necessary to hear the audio portion of any presentation.

ASTOUND WEB PLAYER
BY ASTOUND, INC.

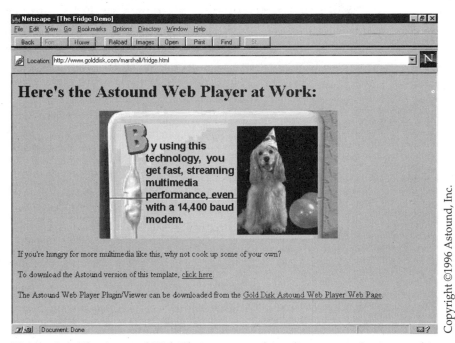

Figure 9-4: *The Astound Web Player runs multimedia presentations created in Astound or Studio M.*

The Astound Web Player plays Astound, Inc.'s (formerly GoldDisk, Inc.) Astound and Studio M multimedia projects inside of a Navigator window. The animations, sounds, and graphics in the presentation begin to play before the entire file downloads, which makes viewing complex or large files a much more pleasant and immediate experience.

Authoring software required: The authoring programs used to create presentations played by the Astound Web Player are Astound, Inc.'s Astound or Studio M. Astound is a full-featured, interactive, multimedia authoring tool. Charts, slide shows, animations, and sounds can be created in Astound. QuickTime and AVI movies can be included in Astound presentations. Studio M is a low-cost electronic greeting card, personal multimedia creation program.

Although Astound offers perhaps the most flexible tools and options for creating presentations with impact almost on par with Macromedia Director! interactive movies, it should be noted that the Astound authoring tool has a steep learning curve. Do *not* expect to author an Astound file without a background in graphics, a little animation, or some experience with a presentation package such as MS PowerPoint.

The free Astound Web Installer is used to prepare Astound or Studio M presentation files for Web distribution. The Web Installer breaks up the presentation into small sections that download quickly and begin playing as soon as they arrive. Thirty-day trial versions of Astound and Studio M and the free Astound Web Installer can be downloaded from Astound Inc.'s Web site.

Where you can get the plug-in:
The Companion CD-ROM
Netscape Power Pack
Astound, Inc. at http://www.golddisk.com/

Platform availability: Windows 3.1, Windows 95, and Macintosh

System requirements: A 386 or better with at least 4MB of RAM. Windows 3.1, Windows 95 operating systems; approximately 2MB of hard disk space; 16-color VGA or higher display. A sound card is necessary to hear the audio portion of any presentation.

CARBONCOPY/NET
BY MICROCOM, INC.

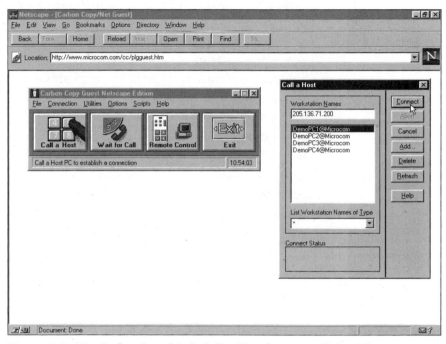

Figure 9-5: *Use CarbonCopy/Net's Call a Host feature to dial another computer on the Internet or Intranet.*

Netscape's CoolTalk (see Chapter 10, "CoolTalk") is great for one-on-one conferencing, but when you need to actually *control* a computer at the other end of the line, you need remote control software. Microcom has created a Navigator plug-in version of CarbonCopy, its widely respected remote control software. When you have the CarbonCopy/Net plug-in installed, you can connect to and remotely control another PC on the Internet or the Intranet. The PC you "call" must also be using CarbonCopy/Net.

CarbonCopy/Net puts the computer you're calling under your direct control—you can run programs and use printers that are accessible to the remote computer all within Navigator's Browser window. The screens you see are actually the screens that are displaying on the remote computer, so it really is like you were operating the computer locally instead of from buildings or miles away. Because of bandwidth limitations over the Internet, don't expect equal performance from an application that is being run remotely; nevertheless, CarbonCopy/Net is a remarkable technology. If you work in a SOHO (Small Office Home Office), telecommute, or support clients on an Intranet, this can be an invaluable utility to have.

Where you can get the plug-in:
Netscape Power Pack
Microcom, Inc. at http://www.microcom.com/

Platform availability: Windows 3.1, Windows 95, and DOS

System requirements: The same basic requirements as Navigator, 8MB of hard disk space and a direct connection to the Internet. CarbonCopy/Net will not currently work with Internet connections that are made via online services such as CompuServe or America Online.

CyberSpell for Netscape Mail
by Inso Corporation

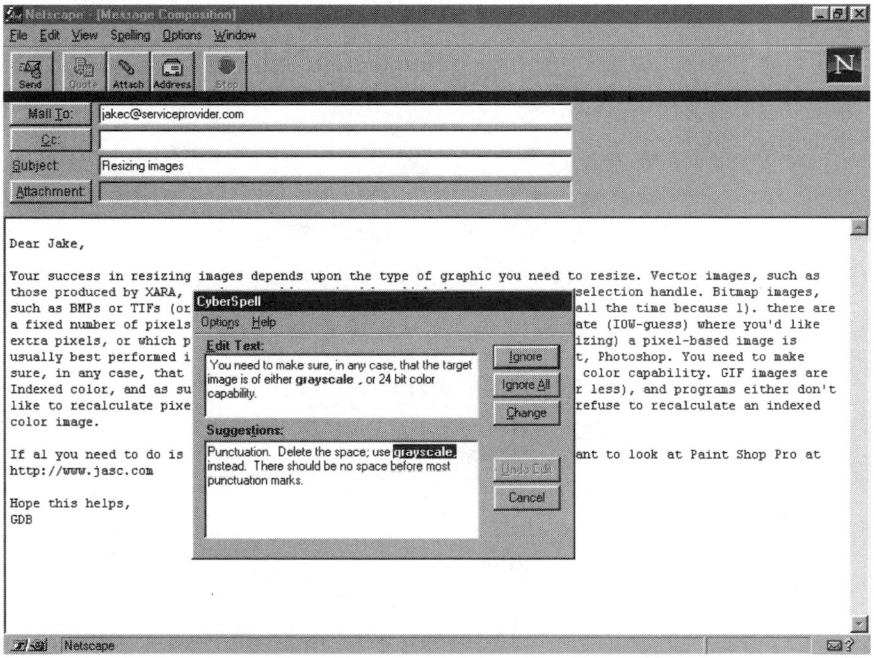

Figure 9-6: *CyberSpell checks the spelling, punctuation, and grammar of your Netscape Mail.*

CyberSpell is a must-have plug-in for Netscape users. Nothing is as embarrassing and makes your communication lack professionalism more than misspelled words, missing or faulty punctuation, and bad grammar. CyberSpell can check your e-mail for all of these problems and can offer suggestions to correct them.

CyberSpell is convenient to use because it installs an additional menu item, Spelling, onto the Message Composition window's menu bar in Navigator. You have your choice of performing a Quick Spell, which provides spell checking and limited punctuation and grammar checking, or Power Spell, which performs a more robust analysis of your grammar and runs punctuation checking. You can add your own words to a custom dictionary and CyberSpell will automatically use any MS Word custom dictionaries it finds on your computer.

One of the nicest features of CyberSpell is that it is Internet savvy—it won't flag most Internet addresses, and it also ignores emoticons such as ;-) or :-o.

Where you can get the plug-in:
Netscape Power Pack
Inso Corporation at http://www.inso.com/

Platform availability: Windows 3.1, Windows 95, and Windows NT

System requirements: The same system requirements as for Navigator and approximately 2MB of hard disk space.

DocuMagix HotPage
by DocuMagix, Inc.

Figure 9-7: *Capture Web pages and store them in a convenient file cabinet for later use.*

If you've ever wished you could organize and store Web pages you've download into an easy-to-use virtual file cabinet, then you'll definitely want to try DocuMagix HotPage. This Navigator helper application is designed to capture Web pages and save them to your hard disk for offline viewing. Where and how it saves them is what makes this application special. HotPage inserts an additional menu item on Navigator's menu bar. When you want to HotSave or HotPrint a Web page, just pick HotSave or HotPrint from the menu bar. HotPage will save the page to a "filing cabinet." You can create as many cabinets as you like and each cabinet can have as many file drawers in it as you need to organize your collection of pages. Web pages can be stored in their original HTML format, including graphics (HotSave), or they can be saved as a single fax-like graphic (HotPrint).

HotSaved pages are "live" when loaded from your hard disk into Navigator's Browser window—all the links work. If you have an Internet connection open you can easily return to the original site or you can click any of the links and go to wherever they lead. HotPrinted documents are no longer HTML documents; instead they are highly compressed black and white graphics that can be marked up using HotPages "sticky note" and WebLink URL-embedding tools. Click a WebLink, and HotPage will have Navigator take you to the URL if you have an Internet connection open. HotPrinted documents are also easily faxed or appended to other documents such as word processing documents.

HotPage has a robust search engine for those times when you've forgotten which "drawer" you filed a document in, or if you want to find all documents that you've saved that are on the same topic. HotPage can also be set up to automatically receive incoming faxes (if you have a fax modem and fax software) and automatically file them in your file cabinet. If you have one of those nifty personal page scanners, you may already be familiar with how HotPage works, because HotPage is made by the same folks who make the popular paper management software PaperMaster that comes with many personal page scanners. If you have PaperMaster, HotPage will integrate with it so that all of your saved Web pages, faxes, and scanned documents can be stored in the same file cabinet.

HotPage is a commercial program (around $50). A trial version (fully functional except for the faxing features) can be downloaded from DocuMagix's home page.

Where you can get the plug-in:
DocuMagix Inc. at http://www.documagix.com/

Platform availability: Windows 3.1, Windows 95

System requirements: 486 or better; 8MB RAM (and 4MB permanent swap file for Windows 3.1); 7MB of hard disk space; VGA or better graphics; and a fax modem and fax software if you want to access the fax features.

EARTHTIME/LITE
BY STARFISH SOFTWARE, INC.

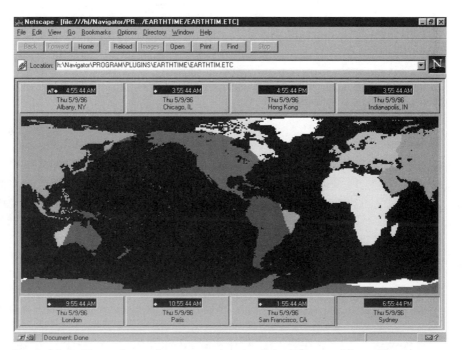

Figure 9-8: *Keep tabs on the current time in eight different cities with EarthTime.*

When you need to know what time it is anywhere in the world, the EarthTime plug-in has the answer. Launch the EarthTime plug-in from the Start menu and EarthTime automatically opens a new, separate copy of Navigator. Inside the browser window, EarthTime displays a large map of the world, and the current time for eight cities of your choice. EarthTime can not only tell you what time it is in over 400 cities, but it also provides information on population, latitude and longitude, current moon phase, time of sun rise and set, and the city and country area code for each city.

Also included is a utility that converts common measurements: weight, volume, and distance as well as some not so common ones such as torque, magnetic flux, specific heat, angular velocity, and more. Windows 95 users can use EarthTime to precisely and accurately set their computer's system clock. EarthTime accomplishes this by checking in with an Internet Time Server found on the Internet and then resetting the system clock on your computer.

EarthTime is a handy utility to have around when you are trying to schedule CoolTalk calls with far-away friends at a mutually agreeable time, or when trying to determine when off-peak hours are for a server located in a foreign country.

TIP

Because EarthTime is actually a program that runs in Navigator, you launch EarthTime from the Start menu or by double-clicking the EarthTime plug-in icon that is placed on your desktop by the setup program.

Starfish Software has made EarthTime/Trial version available to Navigator users on a 30-day trial basis.

Where you can get the plug-in:
Netscape Power Pack
Starfish Software, Inc. at http://www.starfishsoftware.com

Platform availability: Windows 95, Windows NT

System requirements: The same system requirements as for Navigator and approximately 1MB of hard disk space.

FIGleaf Inline
by Carberry Technology

Figure 9-9: *You can zoom in for a magnified view of a graphic with FIGleaf Inline.*

FIGleaf Inline allows you to view and zoom into a wide variety of embedded bitmap and vector graphics. This versatile plug-in can handle the following image formats: Computer Graphics Metafile (CGM), CCITT Group 4 Type I (G4), CCITT Group 4 Type II (TG4), Encapsulated PostScript (EPSI/EPSF), Graphics Interchange Format (GIF), Joint Photographic Experts Group (JPEG), Microsoft Windows Bitmap (BMP), Microsoft Windows Metafile (MWF), Portable Bitmap (PBM), Portable Greymap (PGM), Portable Network Graphics (PNG), Portable Pixmap (PPM), Sun Raster files (SUN), Tagged Image File Format (TIFF), Silicon Graphics RGB (RGB).

With FIGleaf you can flip or rotate images and zoom in to get a better view of the image. This is particularly useful when viewing small graphics, or if you have a vision impairment. Vector images, like the frog in Figure 9-9, will retain their clarity because vector images are resolution-independent. Bitmap images are resolution-dependent and will get blocky if you zoom in very close. FIGleaf works only with images that are placed in an HTML document as an embedded graphic. When you click the link to the embedded graphic, the graphic opens up on a new "page" of its own, replacing the current page. To return to the page you were viewing, click Back on the toolbar or choose the Back command on the right-click shortcut menu.

This highly recommended $19.95 plug-in will handle the bulk of your online and offline graphic viewing needs. A downloadable, trial version is available from Carberry Technology.

Where you can get the plug-in:
Netscape Power Pack
Carberry Technology at http://www.ct.ebt.com/

Platform availability: Windows 95, Windows NT. Windows 3.1 and Macintosh versions are planned.

System requirements: The same system requirements as for Navigator and approximately 1MB of hard disk space.

FutureSplash
by FutureWave Software, Inc.

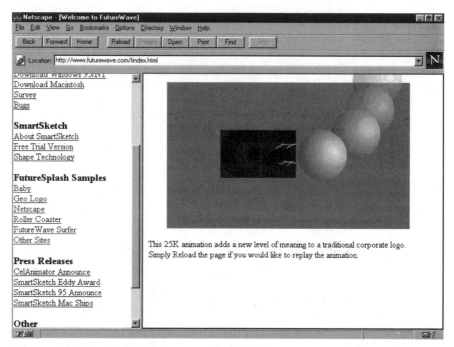

Figure 9-10: *In this 25K animation, the ball zooms in and hits the rectangle, shattering it to reveal the logotype. The rest of the company name streams in and pushes the broken pieces out of the way.*

FutureSplash is a plug-in for viewing vector-based animation created in FutureWave's Cel Animator. These animations download very quickly and run smoothly even over slow connections. One of the reasons for the speed is that the animations stream to your computer and begin playing as soon as the first part of the file arrives. The FutureSplash plug-in supports Netscape's LiveConnect technology that allows Java and JavaScript to interact with plug-ins.

FutureSplash animations are just plain fun to watch and they are a welcome enhancement to any Web or Intranet page. I'm sure you'll be seeing FutureSplash animations cropping up all over the

Web, so load the plug-in and go to FutureWave's site and get a sneak preview of Web things to come.

Authoring software required: FutureWave's Cel Animator

Where you can get the plug-in:
FutureWave Software Inc. at http://www.futurewave.com

Platform availability: Windows 3.1, Windows 95, Windows NT, and Macintosh

System requirements: The system requirements are the same as for Navigator. The plug-in requires less than 150K of hard disk space.

LIGHTNING STRIKE
BY INFINOP

Figure 9-11: *Large graphics display with blinding speed when they've been compressed with the Lightning Strike Compression Engine.*

The Lightning Strike plug-in is used to display *wavelet* compressed images that were compressed with the Lightning Strike Compression Engine. These files are extremely small and display very quickly. Lightning Strike's wavelet compression is routinely able to produce compression ratios of over 100:1. The original image shown in Figure 9-11 was over 1.1MB, but when compressed it weighs in at only 20K. Like JPEG, this is a form of *lossy* compression. Lossy compression discards a small amount of original file information in return for compression ratios that far surpass other methods for compressing and restoring a file in real-time.

Lightning Strike's implementation of wavelet compression is a powerful scheme that makes providing large, full-color bitmaps possible over even the slowest of connections. Unfortunately, the technology is very new and has not been widely adopted for Internet use. It is gaining acceptance, however, in the Intranet with organizations with large collections of photos. With the amazing compression ratios Lightning Strike offers, employees can quickly "flip through" full-size images without spending a lot of time or bogging down the network with the transfer of large images. If your organization has such a need, you definitely want to take a look at this technology and at this plug-in. But even if you don't have an immediate need, you still might want to load the plug-in and go to the InfinOp's site and take a look at the pictures there. You'll be amazed by how good they look and how quickly they load.

Authoring software required: To create files in the Lightning Strikes format, you need to compress them using Lightning Strike Compression Engine. The compression program is currently available free of charge to private individuals, non-profit, and educational organizations.

Where you can get the plug-in:
The Companion CD-ROM
Netscape Power Pack
InfinOp at http://www.infinop.com/

Platform availability: Windows 3.1, Windows 95, Windows NT, Macintosh, Solaris 2.4, and Digital UNIX 3.2

System requirements: The same system requirements as for Navigator, and less than 1/2MB of hard disk space.

Norton AntiVirus Internet Scanner by Symantec, Inc.

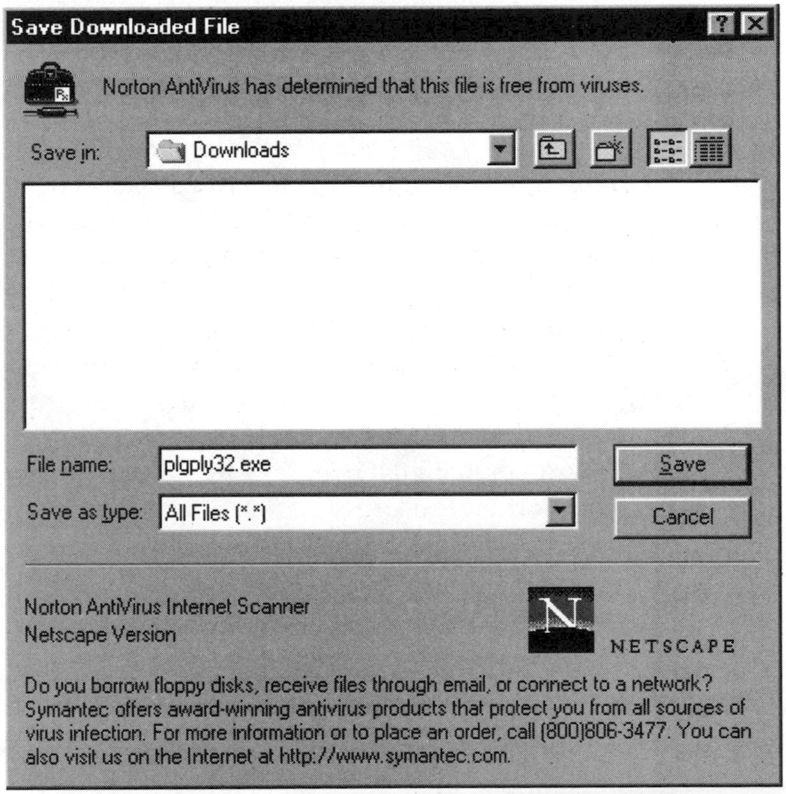

Save Downloaded File

Norton AntiVirus has determined that this file is free from viruses.

Save in: Downloads

File name: plgply32.exe   Save

Save as type: All Files (*.*)   Cancel

Norton AntiVirus Internet Scanner
Netscape Version

NETSCAPE

Do you borrow floppy disks, receive files through email, or connect to a network? Symantec offers award-winning antivirus products that protect you from all sources of virus infection. For more information or to place an order, call (800)806-3477. You can also visit us on the Internet at http://www.symantec.com.

Figure 9-12: *The Norton AntiVirus Internet Scanner plug-in automatically checks files you download for viruses.*

A computer virus cannot enter your system if you're only browsing HTML pages, but the moment you decide to download an archived file, your system could become infected, and your precious files could become trash. At the time of this writing, a virus entitled "PKZip version 3" and the MS Word "Concept" virus are finding their way to user machines through dishonestly labeled files that can be downloaded through the Net. Note: There is no PKZip version 3, and PKWare, the makers of PKZip, have publicly stated that there will be no version 3 due to the assumed name of the virus.

Netscape has licensed the Norton AntiVirus Internet Scanner plug-in from Symantec Corporation. Available only as part of the Netscape Power Pack, this plug-in takes the worry out of surfing for files and from opening up e-mail attachments.

The Norton AntiVirus Internet Scanner is very easy to use. When installed, it scans every file you download for over 7,200 known virus signatures including the MS Word "Concept" virus—in actuality not a virus, but a complicated Word macro that turns every document into a template. If Norton AntiVirus finds a problem, it won't write the file to disk, and it promptly alerts you to the problem. If it finds that the file is virus-free, it tells you this, then asks where on your system you would like to store the downloaded file.

But even if you already use a virus-detection program, unless you update it regularly, you might as well not use it; new computer viruses crop up with the irritating regularity of mail-order catalogs! Users of Norton AntiVirus Internet Scanner can get frequent updates from Symantec's AntiVirus Research Center at http://www.symantec.com/avcenter/index.html.

Where you can get the plug-in:
Netscape Power Pack

Platform availability: Windows 3.1, Windows 95, Windows NT

System requirements: The same system requirements as for Navigator and approximately 4MB of hard disk space.

OpenScape
by Business@Web

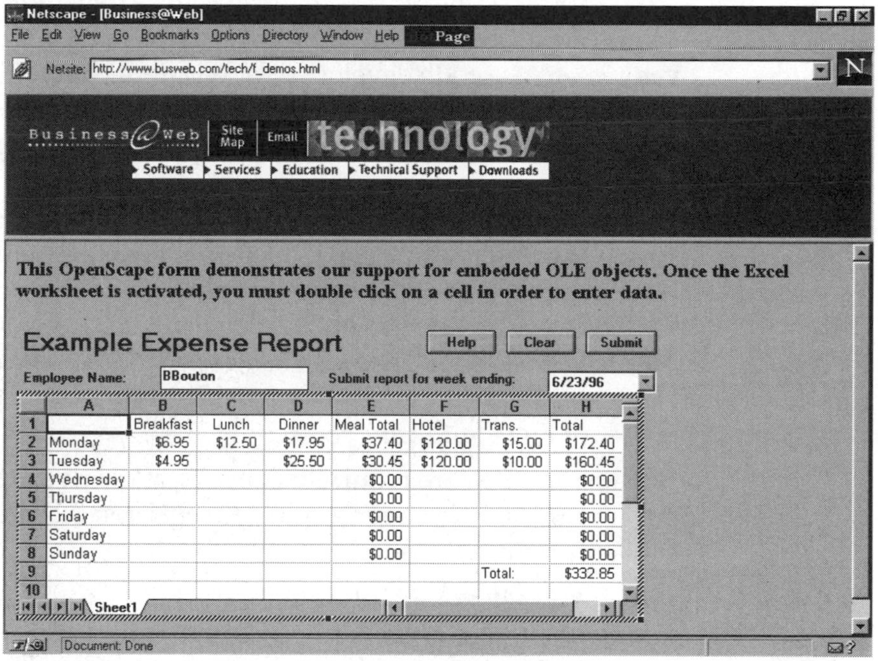

Figure 9-13: *Run OpenScape applications like this OLE-enabled spreadsheet.*

The OpenScape plug-in is a little different from most of the plug-ins we've discussed. It is a runtime player that allows you to run programs that were created using Business@Web's Visual Basic-compatible programming tools. These tools are designed to enable programmers to quickly build Web-aware and capable applications that seamlessly integrate with an enterprise's legacy software and client/server applications and databases. OpenScape can interact and tap into the resources of such high-powered enterprise applications as SAP R/3, Baan IV, PeopleSoft, Open Environment's Entera.

The OpenScape plug-in allows Intranet users and remote users who access the Intranet to use Navigator as a convenient and easy-to-use front end for accessing these powerful existing enterprise applications and back-end services.

The applications built with OpenScape's development tools have a building block-like structure that makes it easy for software developers to use code developed for one application in another. While OpenScape's development tools are primarily designed for very large enterprise use, they can also be used to create simple applications that can enhance the value of almost any Web site. The development tools come in five different versions, each one more powerful than the next. Business@Web has made both the Navigator plug-in and the very capable, authoring program, OpenScape Internet version, available for free download. Business@Web's Web site also has a number of useful tutorials and pre-built sample applications available to give you a peek at the power of these authoring tools.

Authoring software required: Any one of the five OpenScape programming applications. A free OpenScape Internet edition is available for download.

Where you can get the plug-in:
The Companion CD-ROM
Business@Web at http://www.busweb.com

Platform availability: Windows 3.1x, Windows 95, and Windows NT. A Macintosh version is in development.

System requirements: The same system requirements as for Navigator and approximately 2MB of hard disk space. Windows 3.1 users must have OLE 2.02 installed.

THE POINTCAST NETWORK
BY THE POINTCAST, INC.

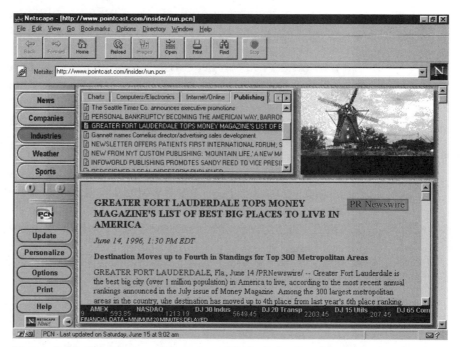

Figure 9-14: *Keep on top of the news with the PointCast Network plug-in.*

If up-to-date world, national, business, and political news, as well as weather, sports, investments, lifestyle, or other topical information is important to you, be sure to check out the PointCast Network plug-in. This Navigator plug-in is designed to find and bring you the news that interests you—news from *Time, People,* and *Money* magazines, as well as other publications. You can track the stock prices (at least a 20-minute delay) and automatically receive press releases and other company information related to up to 25 different companies. PointCast is sort of a clipping service for people interested in specific news who don't have the time to troll for a particular topic of interest from the ever-increasing mass of available information, both traditional and electronic. It's broadcasting on an intimate level (the opposite of "broadcast" would be "pointcast").

You can configure PointCast to bring you only the kinds of news you are interested in, and you can specify how often PointCast updates its information. If you have a direct, continuous connection to the Internet, you can get constant updates if you prefer.

One of the features of PointCast that you will either love or hate is that it installs itself as your system's screen saver. When the screen saver launches after a user-defined period of inactivity, PointCast's SmartScreen will scroll the latest news stories and stock prices across your screen so you can keep on top of the news while doing non–computer-related business. If you don't care for this feature, or perhaps you don't want casual passersby at the office to know which stocks you're interested in, you can disable PointCast's screen saver function by going to Windows Control Panel and choosing a different screen saver.

The PointCast Network plug-in and the broadcast services it provides are free for individual, non-commercial use. Be sure to read the license agreement carefully. For more information on PointCast visit them at http://www.pointcast.com.

TIP

The PointCast Network can be run as a stand-alone application or as a Navigator plug-in. PointCast operates a little differently from most plug-ins. To launch PointCast as a Navigator plug-in, you have to access the following URL on PointCast's site: http://www.pointcast.com/insider/run.pcn.

Where you can get the plug-in:
PointCast, Inc. at http://www.pointcast.com/

Platform availability: Windows 3.1 and Windows 95. Windows NT, Macintosh OS, and Unix versions are currently under development.

System requirements: 486/33 or better with 8MB of RAM; 10MB free disk space; Windows 3.1, Windows for Workgroups, or Windows 95; 256 video color mode or higher.

REALAUDIO
BY PROGRESSIVE NETWORKS, INC.

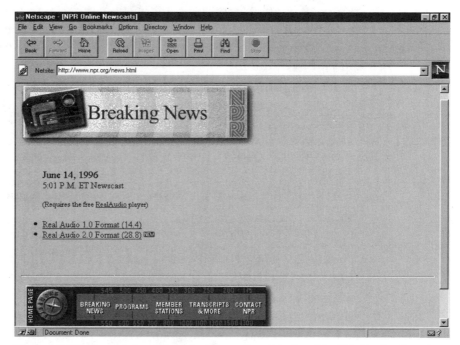

Figure 9-15: *You can hear the latest news from National Public Radio if you've installed the RealAudio plug-in.*

RealAudio is a full-featured, real-time streaming audio plug-in for Navigator. Listen to live events, speeches, or latest news from National Public Radio with RealAudio. RealAudio can also be used to distribute recordings of speeches and other events and works with ASAP WebShow to bring sound to multimedia productions. With a 28.8K modem, you can expect to hear near FM-quality sound, and even with a 14.4K modem, you'll receive high-quality AM sound.

Progressive Network's Timecast RealAudio Guide (http://www.timecast.com/) provides daily schedules of RealAudio broadcasts as well as a listing of sites that contain RealAudio content. There are hundreds of sites that offer a wide range of content from sports, education, entertainment, news, politics, and of course, music. If you want content more diverse than your current collection of audio CDs, you'll find RealAudio to be a must-have plug-in.

Authoring software required: If you'd like to offer RealAudio broadcasts or audio on demand, you can convert a variety of sound files to RealAudio format with the RealAudio Encoder. RealAudio also accepts live sound sources that are passed to the encoder through your sound card. To broadcast RealAudio sound, you'll need a copy of RealAudio Personal Server, or the RealAudio server. For more information visit http://www.realaudio.com/.

Where you can get the plug-in:
Netscape Power Pack
Progressive Networks, Inc. at http://www.realaudio.com/

Platform availability: Windows 3.1, Windows 95, Windows NT, and Macintosh. A Unix version is currently under development.

System requirements: For 14.4K operation, 486/33 SX or better with 4MB of RAM and 2MB of hard disk space. For 28.8K connection, a 486/66 DX 8MB of RAM; 2MB free disk space. Both require a 16-bit sound card.

SHOCKWAVE FOR DIRECTOR
BY MACROMEDIA, INC

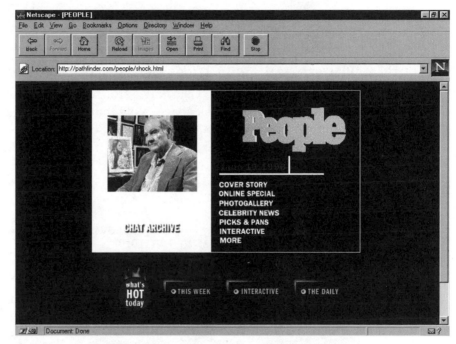

Figure 9-16: *Visit Shockwave-enhanced sites like People Online.*

Shockwave is the title Macromedia has given to compressed, streaming versions of files generated by Macromedia Director!, an interactive authoring tool used commercially for years to create interactive kiosks, tutorial diskettes, interactive games, and now Web presentations. A "shocked" Director movie can be as small as a reported 6K (Macromedia has a contest going to see who can create the smallest Shockwave file), and the Shockwave plug-in for Navigator can bring you presentations with animation, sound, and interactivity.

Authoring software required: Macromedia Director version 4 or later. Users of Director can compress a project using the Afterburner utility to create a Shockwave copy of the work, or they may choose to publish the same work as a platform-dependent executable file. Shockwave titles, however, are platform-independent—a Macintosh user of Director can shock a title so that it may be played by Windows users, and vice versa.

Where you can get the plug-in:
Netscape Power Pack
Macromedia, Inc. at http://www.macromedia.com

Platform availability: Windows 3.1, Windows 95, Macintosh

System requirements: Basic Navigator requirements, plus approximately 2MB of hard disk space. Note that your Navigator disk cache needs to be set to at least 10MB. (See Chapter 2, "Installing & Customizing Navigator," for information on setting the disk cache size.) Windows 3.1 users need to have at least 460K of free conventional memory before launching Windows.

VDOLIVE
BY VDONET CORPORATION

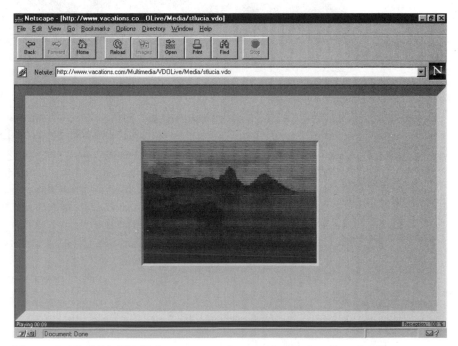

Figure 9-17: *With VDOLive you can view movies as they download.*

VDOLive offers real-time streaming video over the Internet. With VDOLive's special video format, as soon as the first frames of a video arrive at your computer, they start playing. This is a great advantage over movie files that can be downloaded, because video files that are more than a few seconds are huge and take a long time to receive. Additionally, VDOLive won't clog up your hard disk with large files, because VDOLive transmissions are never written to your hard disk, or to your hard disk cache. Like Navigator's LiveVideo, VDOLive movies play inside the Web page, but because VDO uses a proprietary video format, you won't have to choose between LiveVideo and VDOLive. Both can be installed without conflicting with each other.

With the VDOLive plug-in installed, you can watch CBS News' live coverage of the presidential conventions (http://www. cbsnews.com/), audition talent for a play at Talentworks (http:// www.talentworks.com/), or see what that vacation hideaway really looks like at Preview Vacations (http://www.vacations.com/ Multimedia/VDOLive/). While you can indeed view VDOLive movies on the Internet, this program really shines on the Intranet where connection speeds are much greater. Typical Intranet use of VDOLive is for training materials, corporate news, and information.

Authoring software required: For broadcast of VDOLive, you'll need a copy of either VDOLive Personal Server or VDOLive Video Server. Both of these come with the software necessary to compress an AVI video file into VDOLive's file format. To capture video for broadcast later as a VDOLive movie, you'll need a video capture board. For more information, visit VDOnet Corporation at http:// www.vdo.net.

Where you can get the plug-in:
The Companion CD-ROM
Netscape Power Pack
VDOnet Corporation at http://www.vdo.net

Platform availability: Windows 3.1, Windows 95. A Macintosh version is under development.

System requirements: A 486 or better; 8MB of RAM; at least a 14.4K modem. A sound card is required to hear the audio content of VDOLive movies. Windows 3.1 users must have Microsoft Video for Windows installed, and if you're using Trumpet Winsock it must be version 2.1F or later.

WHIP!
BY AUTODESK, INC.

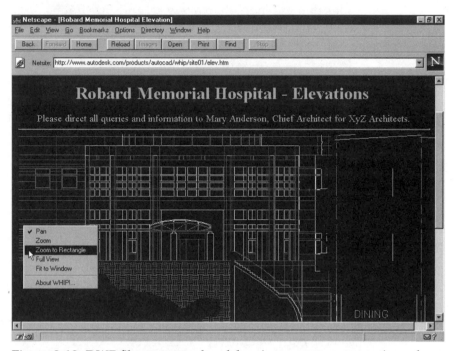

Figure 9-18: *DWF files are vector-based drawings, so you can zoom in as close as you like without losing detail or focus.*

Autodesk's AutoCAD has been the bread and butter graphics program of architects, industrial designers, and engineers for years. Now Autodesk has created a wonderful new tool for the technical community with its release of the Whip! plug-in. Whip! not only allows AutoCAD drawings to be viewed within Navigator, but you can also pan around and zoom into and out of the drawing without the limitations found in bitmap-based design work, where pixels tend to become distorted when zoomed in on too closely. Users can also click embedded URLs to go to another part of a Whip! Drawing, or out to a different page where supporting information is installed. The Whip! plug-in reads files in the Autodesk's DWF (Drawing Web Format) files.

Whip! presentations can be seen as offering VRML-like capabilities to technical illustrators and CAD designers who are unfamiliar with the tag-style format of VRML. Additionally, Whip! supports the concept of open and secure data, which means that if you want your recipient to be able to edit the file, they can; but if you want to protect the data from revision you can do that too.

For more information on this plug-in, be sure to visit Autodesk's Web site at http://www.autodesk.com/.

Authoring software required: AutoCAD 13 with a forthcoming Whip! driver update expected to be released in late summer of 1996. Autodesk has also announced a utility for release in the fall of 1996 that will convert AutoCAD 12, DWG, and DXF files to the DWF file format.

Where you can get the plug-in:
Autodesk Inc. at http://www.autodesk.com

Platform availability: Windows 95, Windows NT

System requirements: The system requirements are the same as for Navigator. For best results, use a 256 color video display and have approximately 1.5MB of open disk space.

WORD VIEWER
BY INSO CORPORATION

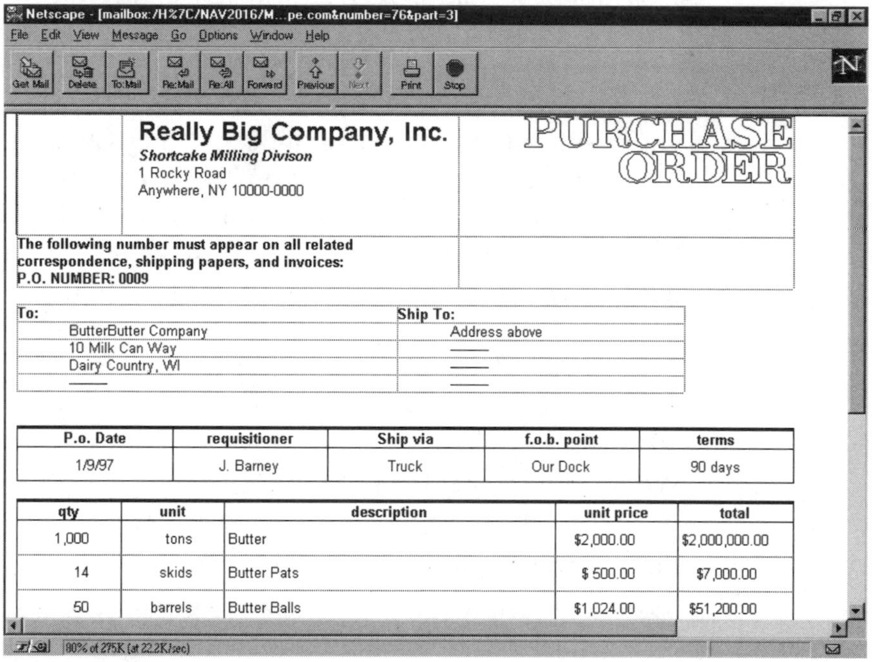

Figure 9-19: *View MS Word documents like this purchase order within Navigator's Message Content pane.*

Perhaps the most common kind of document file exchanged in business, through e-mail, and even on the Web is the Microsoft Word document. Before the advent of portable document formats such as Adobe Acrobat and Tumbleweed Software's Envoy, one of the best ways for DOS, Windows, and Macintosh users to exchange files without losing formatting and maintain the document in an editable form—was to exchange Word documents. It still is a good way, and even though many people own a copy of this popular word processing program, firing up Word every time a Word document is received as an e-mail attachment or is downloaded from the Net is perhaps *not* a good idea. Word is a full-featured application that takes a substantial amount of resources to run—resources that are better spent on maintaining a sound connection to the Internet. Another disadvantage to using Word as an online document browser is that Word is not a plug-in application. Being able to view Word document attachments within the Message Content window would be a speedy, preferred way to handle DOC files on the Net, and Inso Corporation has met the challenge.

The Word Viewer plug-in is free of charge to the Netscape community. The Word Viewer plug-in will display any Word 6 or 7 document that comes your way, and display it in the Browser, Mail, or News panes of Navigator. Not only can you view a Word document, even if you don't own a copy of MS Word, but you can also copy some or all of it to the Windows clipboard or print the document. You can't edit the document with Word Viewer, but once the document is on the clipboard it can be pasted into many different applications and the Navigator Mail's Message Composition window.

Because Inso's Word Viewer is a plug-in, it loads quickly and it gets the job done. The Word Viewer plug-in offers only one of the over 200 file formats that Inso's commercial product Quick View Plus can display. As a side note, QuickView Plus can also load and display an HTML document with some but not all formatting preserved, in lightning time, for those occasions when you want to browse HTML text.

Authoring software required: Microsoft Word will of course create MS Word documents, but so will Windows 95's WordPad. Many applications such as PageMaker, Quark Xpress, and almost every commercial word processor can export or import Word documents.

Where you can get the plug-in:
Netscape Power Pack
INSO Corporation at http://www.inso.com/

Platform availability: Windows 3.1, Windows 95, and Windows NT. A Macintosh version is in development.

System requirements: The system requirements are the same as for Navigator.

Moving On

It's apparent that Navigator brings us closer to a content creator's original idea through the extended uses for HTML, and that plug-ins and helper applications are re-shaping our idea of online communications to the point where it's unclear where our operating system ends and our extensions to real-time interactivity begin.

One method of communication that has historically meant instant idea exchange has been through language, another through the drawn picture. If you put both these vehicles together, put them in electronic format, and put your conduit to communications through a Navigator plug-in, what would you call it? Netscape calls it CoolTalk, coincidentally the title of our next and final chapter, and you'll learn in our closing chapter how to access CoolTalk, and how our concept of "talking" might be on the verge of redefinition through the use of the Internet.

CoolTalk

"**C**ool" has to be the vaguest and most overused adjective in the English language. It can mean anything from "not too bad" to "simply *mah*velous!" But on my personal cool-scale that goes from a blasé one to an ecstatic ten, CoolTalk comes in at a healthy 8.5, above classic Mustang convertibles but below Gertrude Stein and sunsets.

Here are some of the things you can do with this great new Netscape add-on:

■ Talk to friends or business associates without ever paying a phone bill.

■ Examine complete information on a caller before "picking up the phone."

■ Type real-time messages back and forth with an individual halfway around the world.

■ Place graphical information on a virtual whiteboard that both you and a remote Internet or Intranet user can mark up and edit as you talk.

■ Set up an answering machine that not only plays a greeting when people try to reach you with CoolTalk, but actually records their messages.

■ And best of all, you can access all these features from right within Netscape Navigator 3.0.

WHAT IS COOLTALK

CoolTalk is a program that sends and receives voice and other data *in real-time* over the Net or over an Intranet. If you're not familiar with the term real-time, here's what it means: when you talk, another user hears your voice right away, just as if you were using a telephone. There is no need to play a sound file. CoolTalk also sends and receives text and graphical information in real-time. In other words you can call your mother and not only tell her what's going on in your life, you can send her pictures of the kids as you speak. You can even draw circles and captions to make sure she knows which kid is which. And in return she can send you the text of some favorite recipes as she tells you about them. Perhaps the best way to think about CoolTalk is as a multimedia phone service.

Most of the services you've learned about in this book—bookmarks, plug-ins, the Web itself—are client-server based. You use a client program such as Netscape Navigator 3.0 to access information that's stored on a server. But CoolTalk is different. It's a *peer-to-peer* service. You communicate directly with other individuals, not with servers storing the information they've created. You are immediately in touch with millions of geeks, nerds, and even some regular people all around the world.

Pretty amazing, isn't it? And remember, this is all done using the Internet or an Intranet. That means no phone bills. Go ahead, call that high school buddy who's hooking into the Net from his mountain-top hut in Ladakh. (You can let me know by e-mail if there are no mountains in Ladakh.)

There is one slight catch, though: anyone you communicate with using CoolTalk has to be running CoolTalk as well. That's because the program uses special proprietary protocols to send and receive multimedia data as efficiently as possible. But since CoolTalk is part of Netscape Navigator 3.0, this exciting new technology is rapidly becoming commonplace. Not too long from now you might hear some self-satisfied young businessman say, "Have your avatar e-mail my droid, we'll do CoolTalk."

And that's when *I* move to Ladakh.

HARDWARE REQUIREMENTS

In addition to the requirements for running the rest of Netscape Navigator 3.0, CoolTalk has a few specific requirements of its own. Of course you can use Navigator 3.0 without it, but here's what you need to run CoolTalk:

- A 486 or better machine running at a speed of at least 50 MHz.
- At least 8MB of RAM.
- For SLIP and PPP connections, a modem with a speed of *at least* 14,400; I highly recommend a faster modem for this feature.
- If you plan to use the voice features (in addition to the Chat and White Board features), a Windows-compatible sound card with speakers and microphone.

TIP

For full duplex audio conferencing (letting both parties speak at the same time), you need a full duplex sound card.

OK, let's get busy and actually run CoolTalk.

RUNNING COOLTALK THE FIRST TIME

There are two ways to run CoolTalk:

- You can run it by itself.
- You can utilize its feature from within Netscape Navigator 3.0.

Later in this chapter, in the section called "Working With CoolTalk in Navigator 3.0," you'll learn about this second way of accessing CoolTalk. But for now let's run it in standalone mode.

In the Navigator folder or program group, double-click the CoolTalk icon. The CoolTalk Setup Wizard appears, as shown in Figure 10-1.

If you are using Windows 95's Dial-Up Networking and have configured it so that AutoDial is active, your system may try to connect to your Internet access provider as soon as you double click the CoolTalk icon. Simply click Cancel in the Connect To dialog box and continue with CoolTalk setup.

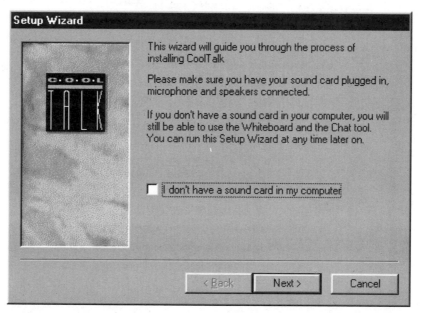

Figure 10-1: *The Setup Wizard.*

This dialog box lets you choose to run CoolTalk without a sound card, using only its Chat and White Board features. If you check the box indicating you don't have a sound card, you will not be presented with some of the dialog boxes shown in the next few steps, since CoolTalk doesn't need to test your card. You can skip ahead to the section "Testing Your Computer's Performance."

TESTING YOUR SOUND CARD

1. After reading the text in the first Setup Wizard dialog box, click Next. A new dialog box appears asking you for your modem speed, as shown in Figure 10-2.

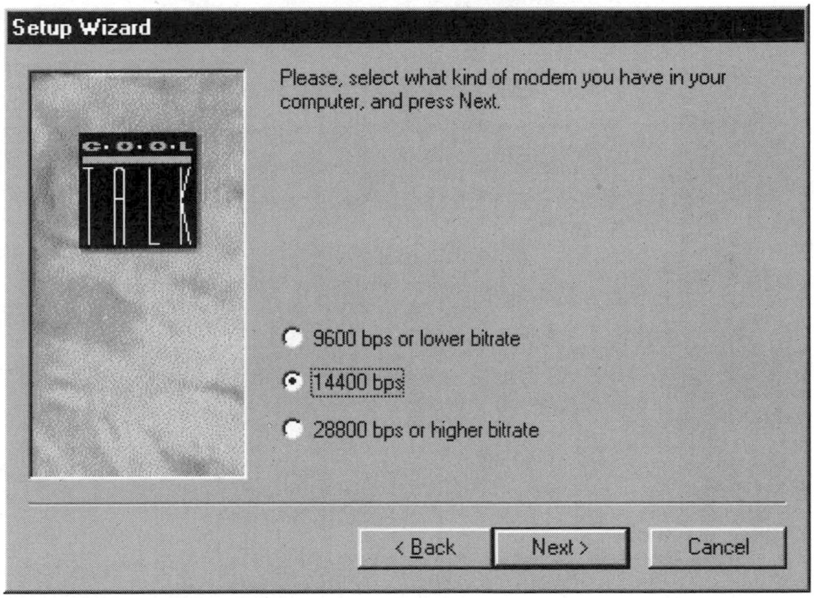

Setup Wizard

Please, select what kind of modem you have in your computer, and press Next.

C · O · O · L
TALK

○ 9600 bps or lower bitrate

◉ 14400 bps

○ 28800 bps or higher bitrate

[< Back] [Next >] [Cancel]

Figure 10-2: *The modem speed dialog box.*

TIP

If you have a hard-wired link rather than a modem connection to the Net, select the 28800 option button.

2. Select the correct modem speed and then click Next. A dialog box pops up telling you that Setup will now detect what audio devices are installed on your system. Make sure no programs that use audio are currently running, and then press Next to continue. After a few seconds a dialog box appears with the results of CoolTalk's tests, as shown in Figure 10-3.

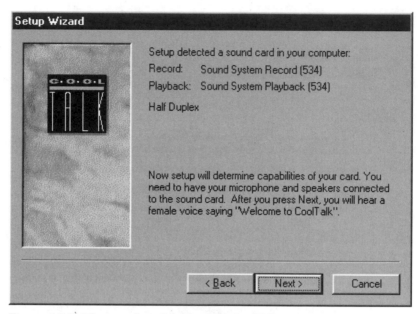

Figure 10-3: *The sound card detected by CoolTalk.*

TIP

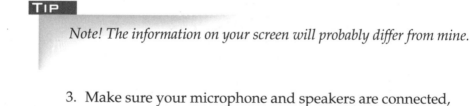

Note! The information on your screen will probably differ from mine.

3. Make sure your microphone and speakers are connected, and then click Next. If everything is working right, you'll hear a voice say "Welcome to CoolTalk." You will also see a new dialog box like the one below in Figure 10-4.

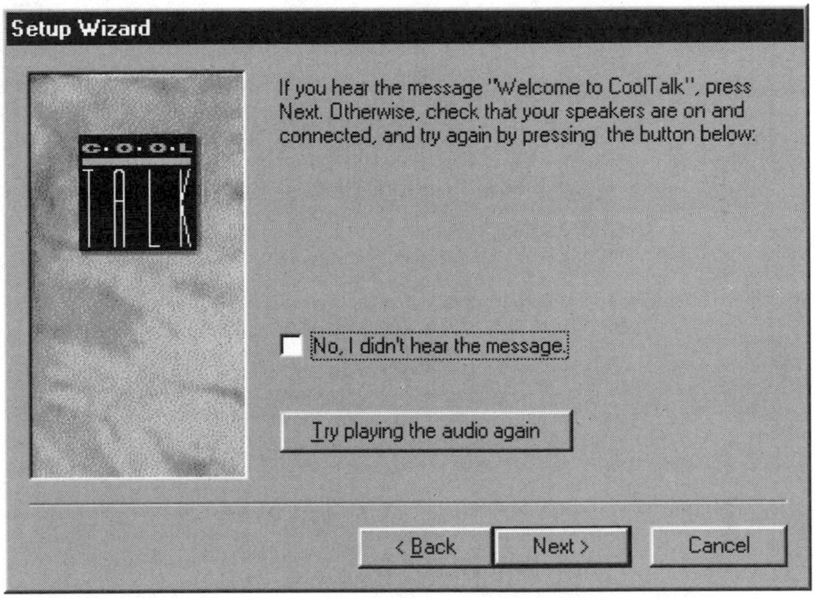

Figure 10-4: *Dialog box asking if you heard the "Welcome to CoolTalk" message.*

■ If you don't hear the message, make sure that your speakers are on and properly connected to your computer. You can click the "Try playing the audio again" button if you want. If you still don't hear the message, check the "No, I didn't hear the message" box. If you select this option, some of the dialog boxes shown in the next few steps will not appear.

4. Assuming you hear the message, simply click Next. A new dialog box appears informing you that Setup will now test playback at the 8 kHz sampling rate, as shown in Figure 10-5.

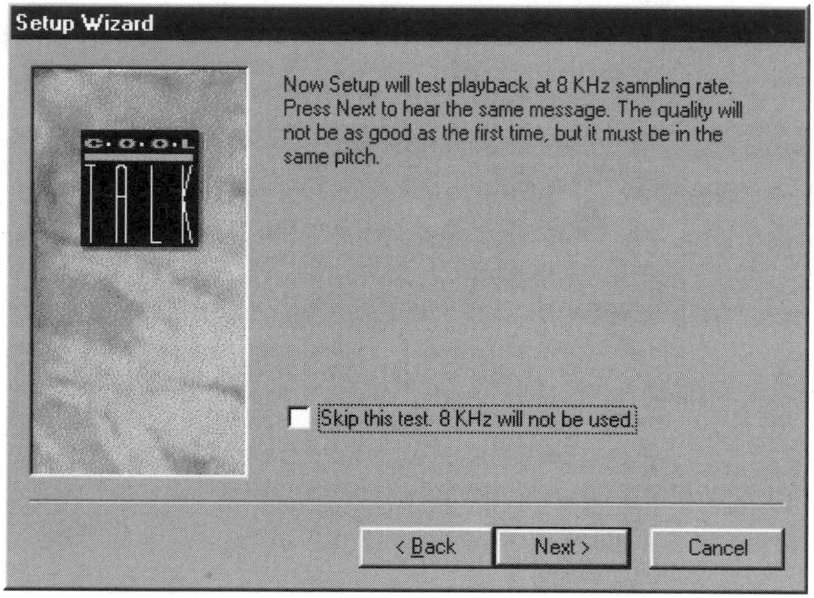

Figure 10-5: *Starting the 8 kHz test.*

SAMPLING RATES

The *sampling rate* is simply the rate at which analog sound (such as your voice) is turned into digital information that can be stored or played back on a computer or other digital device. Sampling is the process by which a piece of hardware "listens to" an analog sound at regular intervals. The information collected at these points in time may then be reassembled for playback. The higher the sampling rate, the more times per second your voice is sampled, and the higher the sampling rate the better you'll sound.

5. You should go ahead with this test, so simply click Next. Now you'll hear the same "Welcome to CoolTalk" message, but with slightly rougher sound. In addition, a new dialog box appears, as shown in Figure 10-6.

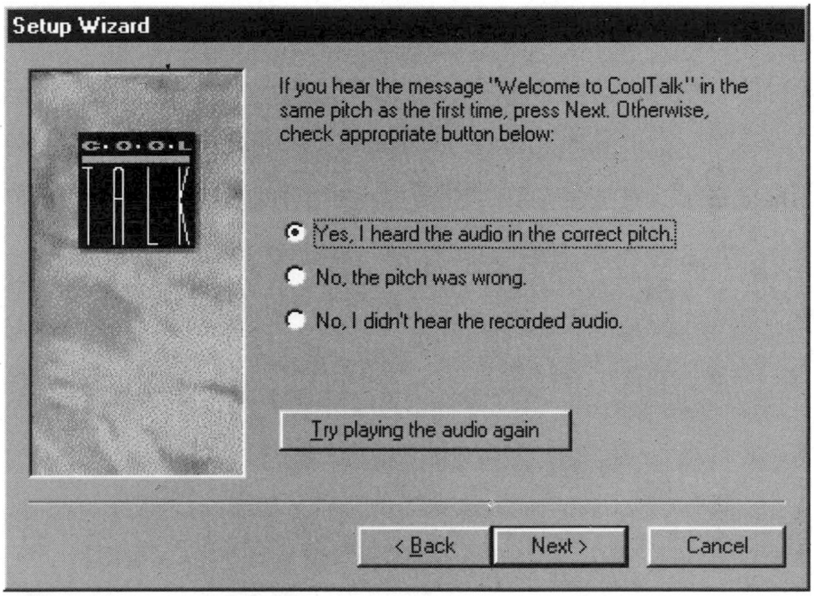

Figure 10-6: *The 8 kHz playback test.*

■ Click the appropriate option button. If everything is working right, you should be able to select "Yes, I heard the audio in the correct pitch." If you choose one of the other options, CoolTalk Setup will test your card at a lower sampling rate, and the dialog boxes that appear may not follow the steps outlined below. Don't worry about it, simply read each dialog box carefully and follow the instructions.

TIP

Even if you select "Yes, I heard the audio in the correct pitch," CoolTalk may go ahead and test your card at lower sampling rates. No problem, simply follow the instructions and catch up with us at step 6.

6. Click Next. A new dialog box pops up telling you that Setup will now test *recording* at the 8 kHz sampling rate.

7. Click Next for this test. The recording test dialog box appears, as shown in Figure 10-7.

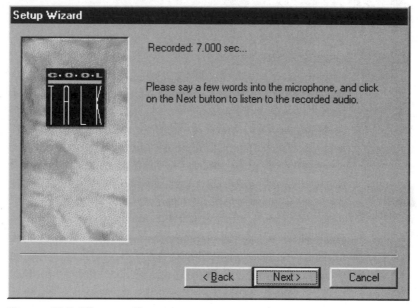

Figure 10-7: *The recording test.*

8. Say a few words such as "I *love* this book" into your microphone, then click Next when you are done. The recording test results dialog box appears, as shown in Figure 10-8.

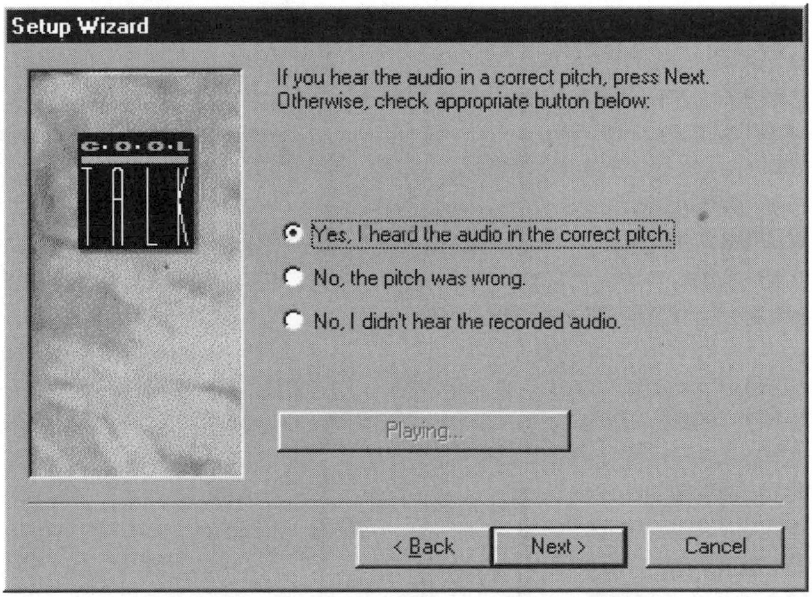

Figure 10-8: *The recording test results dialog box.*

■   Once again, click the appropriate option button. If everything is working right, you should be able to select "Yes, I heard the audio in the correct pitch." If you choose one of the other options, CoolTalk Setup will test your card at a lower sampling rate, and the dialog boxes that appear may not follow the steps outlined below. If that's the case, just read each dialog box carefully and follow the instructions.

TIP

Again, even if you select "Yes, I heard the audio in the correct pitch," CoolTalk may go ahead and test your card at lower sampling rates. No problem, simply follow the instructions and catch up with us at step 9.

9. Click Next to move on to the computer performance test, as shown below in Figure 10-9.

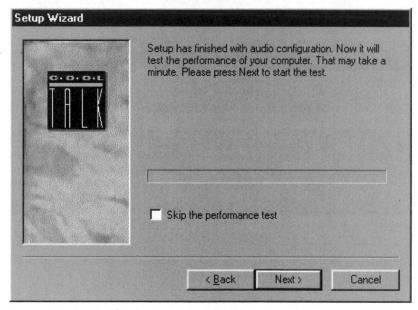

Figure 10-9: *The performance test dialog box.*

TESTING YOUR COMPUTER'S PERFORMANCE

Now it's time to find out if your machine has enough computing power to run CoolTalk. In the performance test dialog box shown above in Figure 10-9, click Next. The performance results dialog box appears, as shown in Figure 10-10.

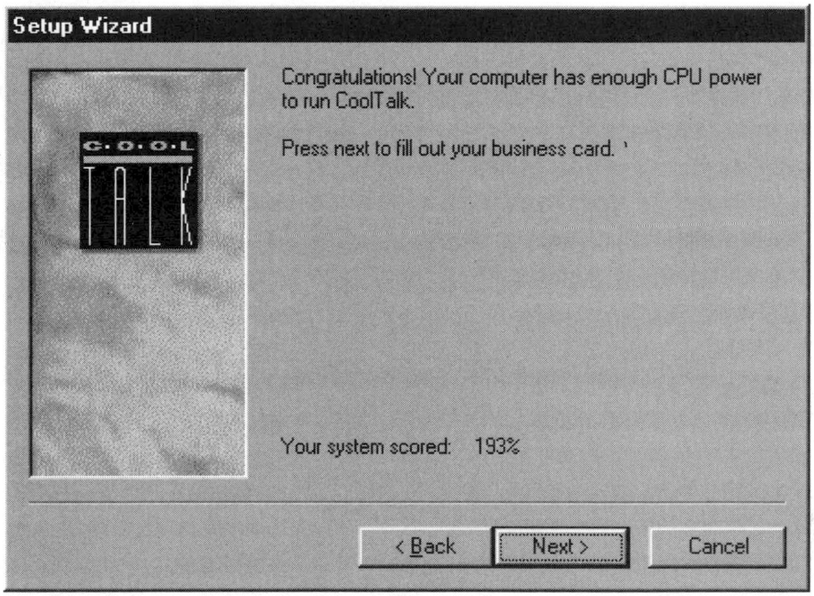

Figure 10-10: *The performance test results.*

Assuming your results were something like mine, click Next to fill out your CoolTalk business card.

WHAT'S A COOLTALK BUSINESS CARD?

I'm glad you asked.

As I'm sure you know, caller ID is rapidly becoming one of the most important features of the regular old telephone system. With a simple device you can find out the phone number of anyone who calls you—as long as they haven't blocked the caller ID information. That's great, but CoolTalk takes it a few steps further. Not only can you find out the phone number of somebody who calls you, you can find out their name, title, company name, address, fax number, and e-mail. Of course that's assuming they *want* you to know all this information. When a CoolTalk call comes into your machine, you might even see a picture of the person calling you. Now you can eliminate some of the anxiety of blind dating. ➡

How is all of this information made available? Every CoolTalk user can fill out a special electronic business card. When somebody calls you, you simply press a button in the CoolTalk conference window (see Figure 10-16 below) to access this information. And if the user has chosen to include a picture as part of the business card, this picture is displayed right on the information button itself.

How cool can you get?

FILLING OUT YOUR BUSINESS CARD

Want other users to know something about you when you call them? That's easy with CoolTalk. It's time to set up CoolTalk's business card feature, which is kind of like caller ID on steroids. If you've been following the steps in this chapter, you should now see the business card data form on your screen, as shown in Figure 10-11.

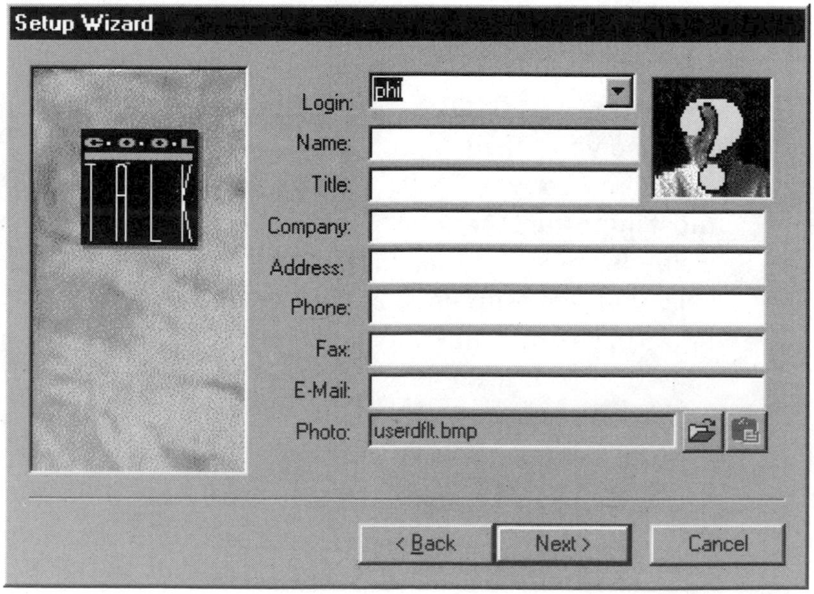

Figure 10-11: *The business card data form.*

How many times have you filled out a form like this? You can probably figure out what to do here. When you've completed the form, it should look something like Figure 10-12.

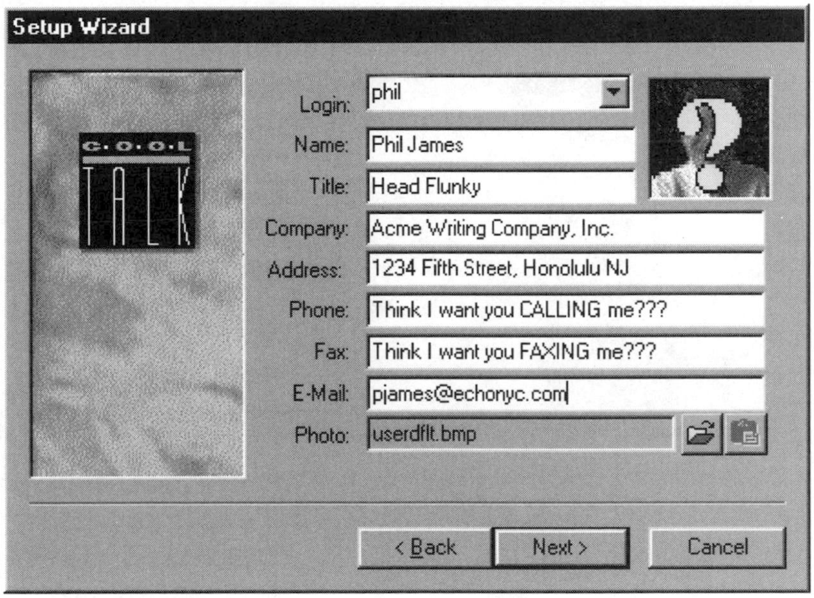

Figure 10-12: *A completed business card.*

But wait, there's more! Don't you want the world to know what you look like? Yes, you can actually add a picture to your business card. Here's how:

■ To add a picture from a file, click the button just to the right of the Photo field. A standard file selection dialog box appears, letting you choose a picture from anywhere on your system.

■ To add a picture that's already saved in the clipboard, click the button to the far right of the Photo field. The picture will be pasted in immediately.

In either case, your picture is plugged into your business card immediately, and your completed form should now look something like Figure 10-13.

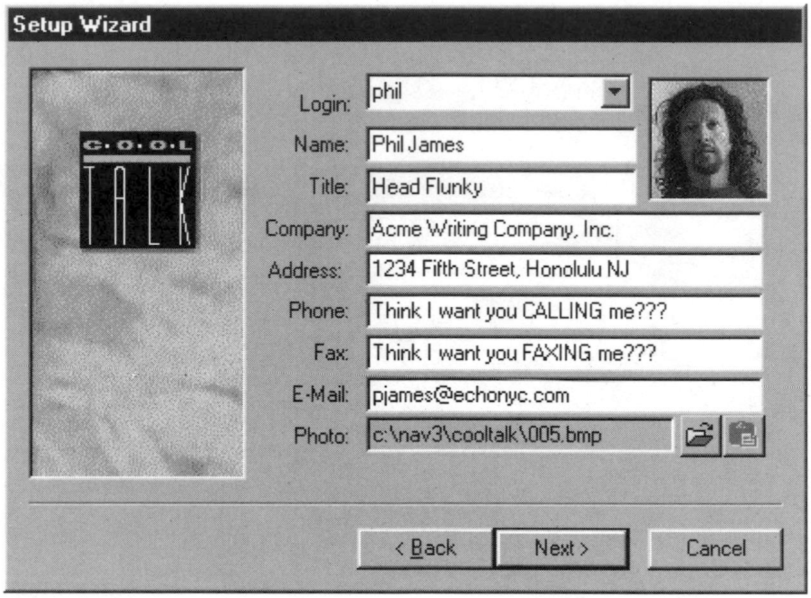

Figure 10-13: *A business card with picture.*

TIP

You probably already thought of this: it doesn't have to be a picture of you. It could be your company logo or even a favorite painting or cartoon. (Make sure you're not violating any copyrights, though.) And you've probably already thought of this too: if you locate some public domain photos, you can look just like Antonio Banderas or Michelle Pfeiffer for the day. This is an ideal feature for people with delusions of grandeur, multiple personality disorder, or problems finding a date.

OK, you've completed your business card. Click Next and a typical "the setup process is complete" dialog box appears. Now just hit Finish and you're ready to start communicating with other CoolTalk users. First you'll learn how to do this with the standalone program, then how to access these features from right within Netscape Navigator 3.0.

THE SYSTEM INFO PROGRAM

The CoolTalk Setup Wizard tested and configured the software to work optimally with your hardware. But suppose you have problems later. Do you need to reinstall the program just to diagnose a problem with your sound card?

Fortunately, no. CoolTalk includes a special System Info utility just for examining your computer's installed hardware. System Info is not exactly a geeks-only zone, but if you're intimidated by technobabble feel free to skip this sidebar until you really need it.

To get to System Info simply select it from the CoolTalk Help menu. The System Info window appears, as shown in Figure 10-14.

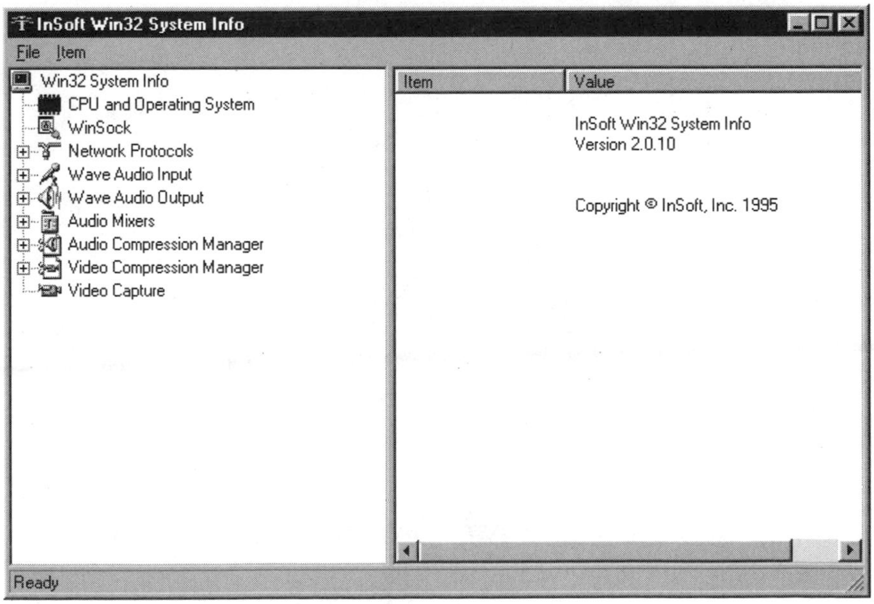

Figure 10-14: *The System Info window.*

Notice that the right pane of the window looks kind of empty. That's because you haven't selected an item to examine yet.

Expand one of the items on the left by clicking a plus (+) icon. For instance, I'll select Wave Audio Input. It expands into two items, SB16 Wave In and Microsoft Sound Mapper.

Chances are that your list will be completely different from mine. But as long as you've got a Wave Input device, you're in good shape. Now go ahead and select one of the items. Information about your hardware driver appears in the right pane, as shown in Figure 10-15.

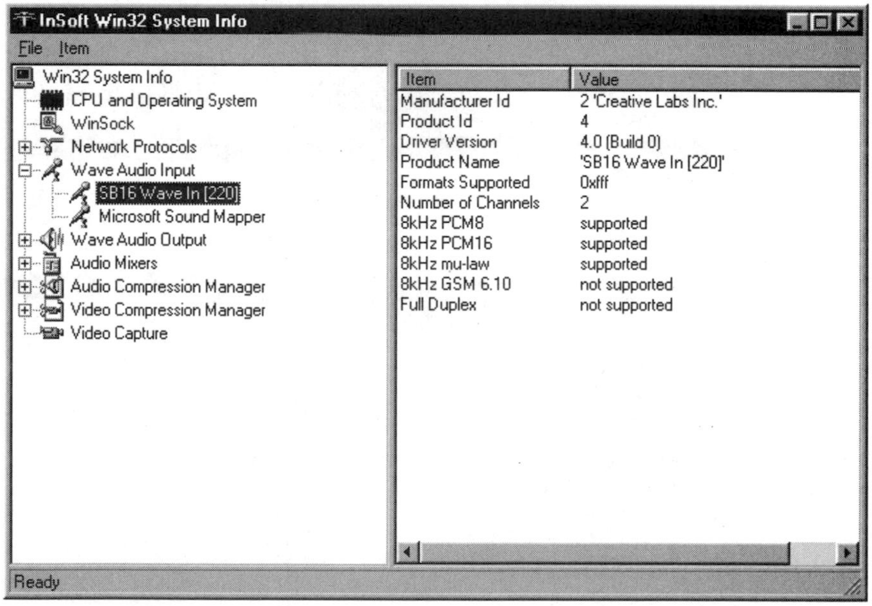

Figure 10-15: *System Info window, showing information on a Wave Input device.*

Notice that my sound card supports 8 kHz 16-bit stereo sound (8 kHz PCM16, 2 channels). You don't have to know what that means, but it's pretty good. When I speak into the mike the person at the other end of the CoolTalk connection won't think their computer is just making random noises. But you'll also notice that my input device does not support full duplex. That means we'll have to take turns talking if we want to have an intelligible conversation.

THE COOLTALK CONFERENCE WINDOW

If you just quit the Setup Wizard, the CoolTalk conference window is sitting on your desktop, as shown below in Figure 10-16.

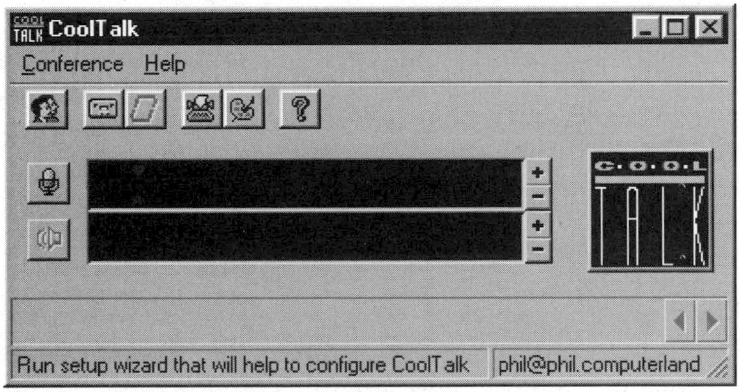

Figure 10-16: *The CoolTalk conference window.*

Let's take a quick look around and get familiar with this new communications tool before we actually initiate a call.

First, press the big square CoolTalk button at the right side of the window. Something like this pops up:

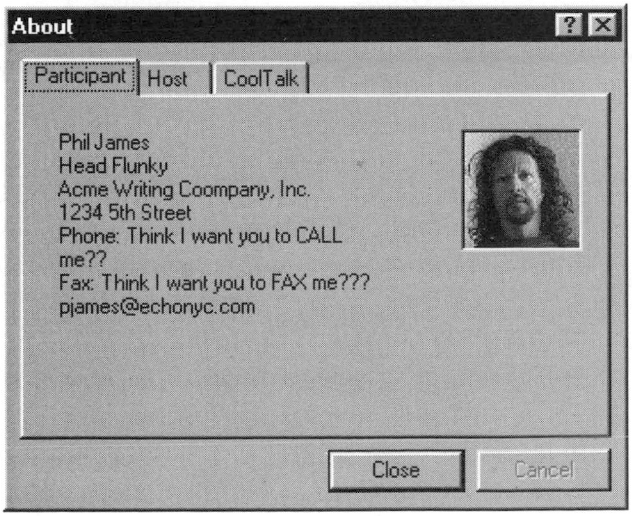

Figure 10-17: *CoolTalk user properties.*

Right now, the first two tabs show you information about yourself, including the data you entered into your electronic business card. When you actually establish a connection with somebody else, you will see information about the remote user as well.

Go ahead and close the About window for now. Back in the CoolTalk conference window, notice the large black area at the center, divided into two horizontal panels. This is where you'll see the volume level for your own voice and of the voice of the person you're talking to. Your voice is depicted in the top panel, the person you're talking to is in the lower one. You can adjust the mike sensitivity for your own voice by clicking the plus and minus buttons just to the right of the upper panel, and you can adjust the volume of the "incoming" voice by clicking the buttons to the right of the bottom panel.

The red arrows in the top panel need some explanation. They are used to adjust what is called the *silence level*. Your home may be full of ambient noise, and certainly your microphone could pick up at least the sound of your typing and your computer's fan. But you don't want CoolTalk to send every sound it hears, just the sound of your voice. The red arrows let you set the level of sound at which CoolTalk assumes you are speaking; everything less than that level is ignored as silence. To set the level higher, in other words to make CoolTalk ignore more ambient noise, use your mouse to drag the arrows to the right.

Let's give this a try.

1. Click the small microphone button to the left of the upper panel. This lets you check sound levels without actually being connected.

2. Try talking into the mike. You'll see green bars move to right across the panel. The dark green indicates sound that is really too soft for a clear conversation; the bright green indicates the ideal volume for talking; and if you see red bars you should get a job in a rock band. You can play with the mike sensitivity by using the up and down arrows.

3. If no green at all is showing when you're not talking, you can leave the red silence level arrows exactly where they are. But if there is some green in the window, indicating

significant ambient noise, you should drag the arrows to the right until they are just above that level, as shown below in Figure 10-18. That way CoolTalk starts to send audio immediately when you begin speaking.

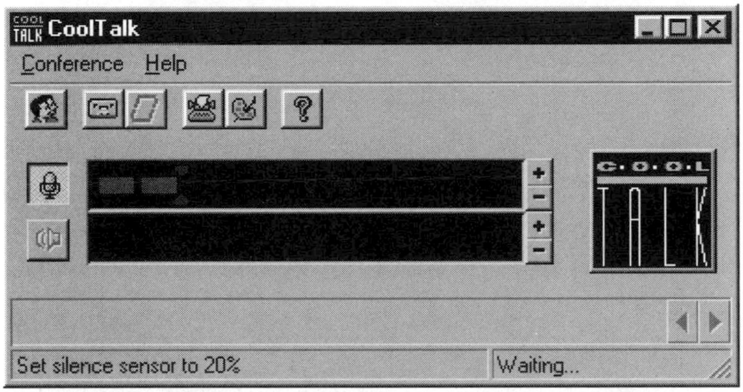

Figure 10-18: *A new silence level.*

Now you can click the microphone button again to return CoolTalk to its idle state.

As long as CoolTalk is running, it waits patiently for calls to come in. But just in case your computer isn't ringing off its virtual hook, let's start exploring by initiating a call.

INITIATING CALLS

You're not going to believe how easy this is. Before getting started make sure that you are connected to the Net or to your office Intranet, and then:

1. Click the Start Conference button at the top left of the CoolTalk conference window. The Open Conference dialog box appears, with the Address Book tab selected as shown in Figure 10-19.

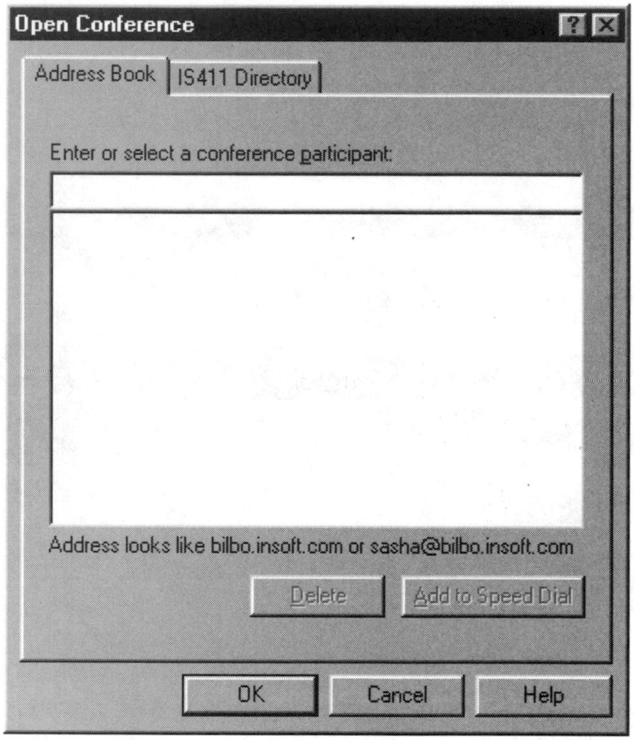

Figure 10-19: *The Open Conference dialog box.*

2. In the entry field at the top, type in the Internet or Intranet
   address for another CoolTalk user. You can use any of several address formats:

   ■ The user@domain format, as in jane@mycompany.com.

   ■ A domain name, as in jdoe.com (this translates to *any-
      one* at jdoe.com).

   ■ A numeric IP address.

   For this example, I'll type in a numeric IP address, as shown
   below in Figure 10-20.

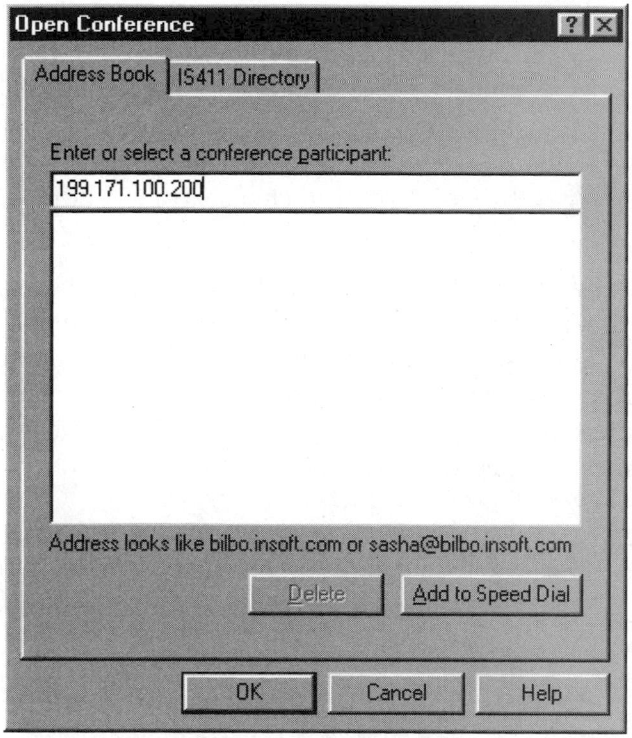

Figure 10-20: *The Address Book with a numeric IP address entered.*

TRAP

Don't enter the sample IP address in this book. It won't work. In order to establish a connection, you must enter the address of an actual CoolTalk user who is currently connected to the Net or to your Intranet.

3. Click OK. The Address Book disappears, and you are returned to the CoolTalk conference window, as shown above in Figure 10-16.

   ■ Notice that CoolTalk plays a ring sound to indicate that it is attempting to establish a connection.

■ Notice also that the status line at the bottom of the window indicates the progress of CoolTalk's attempt to
connect. Once it has established a connection, it indicates it is "inviting" the remote user to join the conference—in other words the remote phone is ringing. At
this point you can choose to cancel the call by hitting
the Escape key.

It's helpful to know what's going on at the other end of the connection. By default, the remote CoolTalk not only plays a ring when
you call, it also pops up an invitation on the remote user's screen. If
the remote user decides to blow you off, you are simply returned to
an idle state, ready to place another call. But if the remote user
wants to talk, here's what you see:

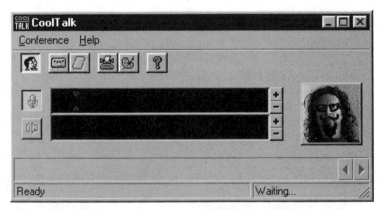

Figure 10-21: *Connected!*

Here's a puzzle like the ones you read in *Children's Highlights*
magazine as you waited for a measles shot: What is different about
the CoolTalk conference window?

There are several indications that you're connected to another
CoolTalk user:

■ The microphone button is depressed, indicating that you can
talk whenever you want.

- The status line at the bottom right of the window reads Waiting . . . , indicating that at this moment you are neither talking nor receiving audio from the other end. When the remote CoolTalker says something, the status message changes to Receiving, and when you say something it changes to Talking.

- Obviously, that's not a picture of you in the large square button.

And speaking of the large square button, put your mouse cursor directly over it. A tool tip indicates the identity of the person you've reached. But that's not all. Press the button now and the remote user's business card information pops up, as shown in Figure 10-22.

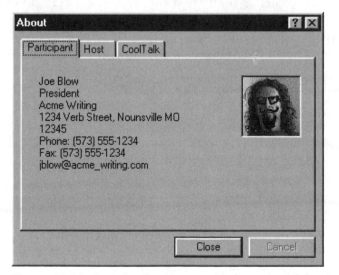

Figure 10-22: *Complete business card information of the remote CoolTalker.*

TIP

If you select the Host or CoolTalk tab, you can even get information about the remote user's system.

OK, all these user interface niceties are pretty nice niceties, but let's get busy doing what CoolTalk was made for: talking. Follow these steps carefully:

1. Talk.

2. Listen.

3. Repeat steps 1 and 2 until you're tired of the conversation.

Pretty technical stuff, huh? As you talk, watch the green level indicators for a while. If either voice is too loud or too soft, you can adjust the microphone sensitivity and audio volume while you're conversing. And if somebody fires up the vacuum cleaner you can tweak the silence level as well.

All good things must end. So what about hanging up? Either participant can do it. All you do is click the Leave Conference button (which is really just the depressed version of the Start Conference button). A dialog box pops up asking you if you really want to leave, as shown in Figure 10-23.

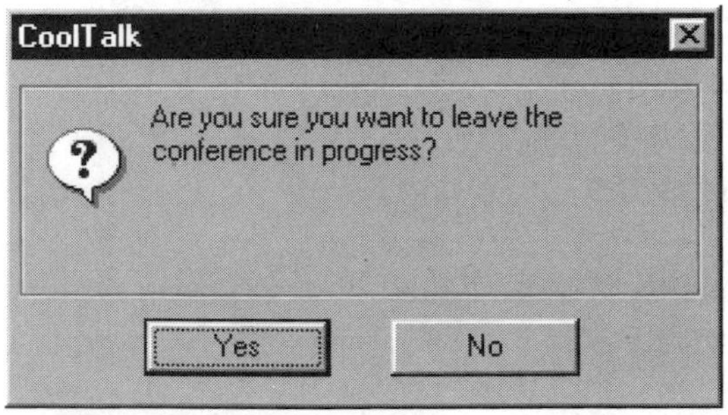

Figure 10-23: *The hang-up confirmation dialog box.*

If you answer yes, you are returned to the CoolTalk conference window in its idle state.

SPEED-DIAL BUTTONS

There are probably a few CoolTalk users you'll call over and over again. Wouldn't it be great if you could add each of them to a speed-dial button the way you can with your old-fashioned non-virtual phone?

Well you can. Follow along as I add our new pal to a speed-dial button.

1. From the CoolTalk conference window, click the Start Conference button. The Address Book appears again, as shown in Figure 10-19.

   Notice that the address we just called has been added to the address list. CoolTalk automatically adds new addresses to the list so that you can call them again.

2. Select the address we just called, <anyone>@199.171.100.200.

3. Click the Add to Speed-Dial button. The New Button Properties dialog box pops up, as shown in Figure 10-24.

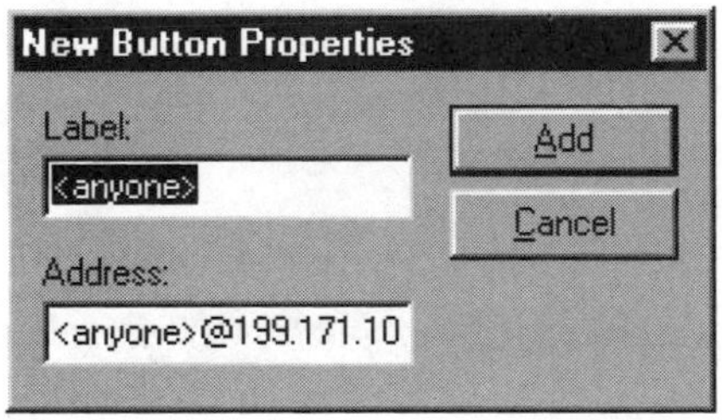

Figure 10-24: *The New Button Properties dialog box.*

4. If you want, enter a new label. This is the text that will appear on the speed-dial button, and it can be anything. For this example, I'll enter **Joe**.

5. Click the Add button. You are returned to the Address Book, but at this point you can click OK to return to the conference window.

Check it out: there's a brand new speed-dial button for Joe, as shown in Figure 10-25.

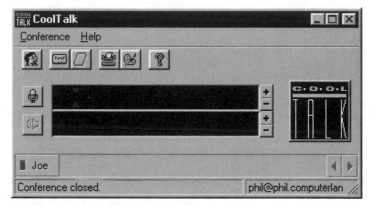

Figure 10-25: *The CoolTalk conference window showing a new speed-dial button.*

Now to call Joe you don't even have to access the Address Book. Instead, you simply click the button.

TIP

> *The green rectangle in the speed-dial button turns yellow when you establish a connection.*

DELETING SPEED-DIAL BUTTONS

Is your relationship with Joe getting strained? No problem. Just delete his speed-dial button—and make sure to send him e-mail telling him you did!

Here's how to delete a speed-dial button:

1. Right-click the speed-dial button. A context menu appears.

2. Click Delete.

That's all there is to it. No more button. Now just delete Joe from the Address Book and you're well on your way to having him out of your life.

TIP

You can even delete all your speed-dial buttons at once using the context menu, and you can change the label or address by selecting Properties.

IS411 SERVICE

OK, you've been CoolTalking with your friends for a couple of months, and now you're ready to look for other CoolTalk users. That's where IS411 service comes in.

IS411 service is really nothing more than a centralized address book that can be accessed from CoolTalk or from Navigator 3.0's browser window (more about that in the section on "Working with CoolTalk in Navigator 3.0"). There are many IS411 servers out on the Net, each with a list of CoolTalk users and their addresses. Calling these users with CoolTalk is as simple as using the Address Book, and many of them let you add your own address so that other CoolTalkers can find you. And if you get the right software, you can even set up local IS411 service on your own Intranet.

In a moment we'll access an IS411 server and see how this all works, but first you need to make sure we've got CoolTalk configured so that its IS411 feature works the way you want.

1. Select Options from CoolTalk's Conference menu. The Options dialog box appears, as shown in Figure 10-26.

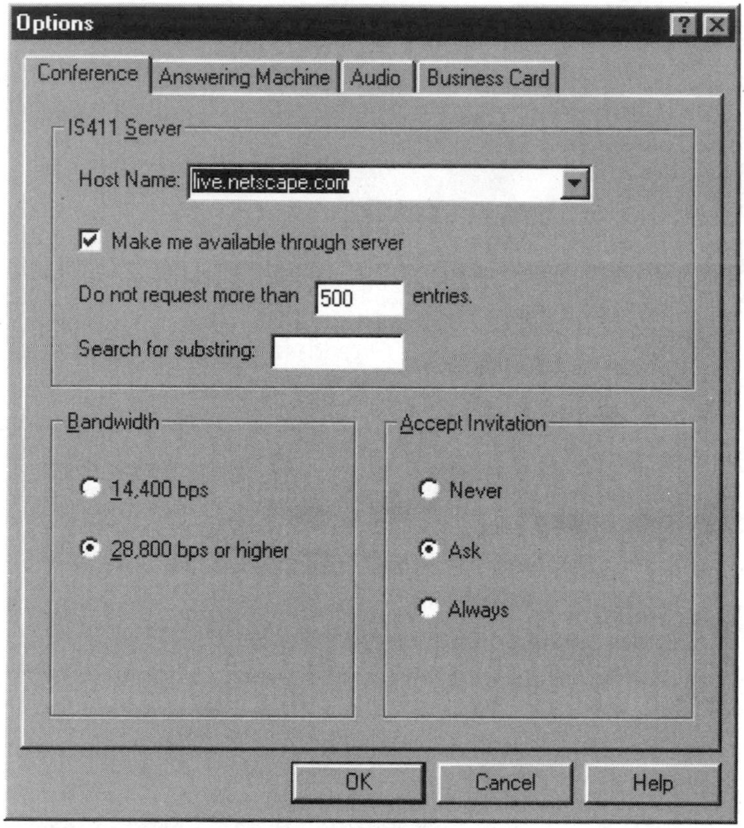

Figure 10-26: *The Options dialog box.*

■ If the Conference tab is not currently selected, select it now.

2. If you're currently connected to the Internet and don't know of a different IS411 server you want to access, leave the Host Name field alone.

  ■ If you're *not* connected to the Internet, you need to specify the address of an IS411 server on your Intranet. You will not be able to access this feature without access to a valid IS411 server.

3. If you do not wish your address to appear in this IS411 directory, in other words if you do not want other CoolTalk users to contact you, uncheck the "Make me available through server" checkbox.

TRAP

If you make yourself available on the default Netscape IS411 server, you may start receiving calls immediately from all kinds of propeller-heads and not-so-propeller-heads experimenting with their new software. This can be fun, but it also can turn into a major annoyance very quickly. I had to go back and uncheck this box right away to keep the phone from ringing constantly. Alternatively, you can select the Never option button in the Accept invitation area of this tab. That way your address will be advertised, but nobody will be able to reach you right now.

4. In the field where you can specify the number of entries you want to see, change the figure to 1000 for now. That way you'll be sure to grab the entire list of CoolTalk users registered at this server.

TRAP

If you specify a lower number than the total currently registered on the server, or the total that meet your search criterion, CoolTalk may not display any addresses at all!

5. Leave the Search for Substring field blank for now, since we want to see the complete list of CoolTalkers advertised on this server.
6. Click OK to return to the conference window.

Once you've completed this initial setup, getting a list of CoolTalk users via IS411 is just as easy as accessing the regular Address Book:

1. In the CoolTalk conference window, click the Start Conference button. The Address Book tab appears, as shown in Figure 10-23.

2. Switch to the IS411 Directory tab. It looks pretty much like the regular local Address Book, but as you can see in Figure 10-27 it's full of CoolTalk addresses.

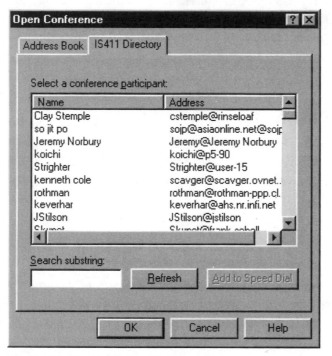

Figure 10-27: *The IS411 Directory tab.*

■ If you don't see any names and addresses in the IS411 tab, click the Refresh button to download a new list.

Now to call a CoolTalk user, simply double-click his or her name. You can also add a speed-dial button for any IS410-advertised user by selecting the name and clicking the Add to Speed-Dial button.

You now know all you need to know to start placing calls, either over the Net or an office Intranet. There are some other interesting things you can do with CoolTalk besides talk, but before learning about these let's take a quick look at how to answer incoming calls.

ANSWERING CALLS

As you might guess, this is *really* easy. Remember, though, that to answer calls you have to have CoolTalk running (it can be minimized, of course). Here's what it looks like when somebody calls you via CoolTalk:

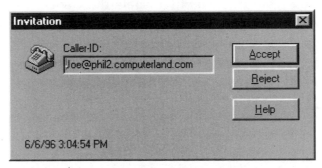

Figure 10-28: *The CoolTalk Invitation dialog box.*

Notice that the Invitation dialog box specifies the Caller-ID (a.k.a. CoolTalk address) of the person calling you, and separate buttons let you Accept or Reject the call. If you reject it, you're back in the idle state. If you accept the call, your window will look just like it did when you initiated a call, as shown in Figure 10-21.

THE COOLTALK WATCHDOG

Suppose you have a permanent connection to the Internet but you don't want to keep CoolTalk loaded all the time just to wait for incoming calls. Well, there's a much smaller and less resource-hungry utility that can handle this task for you: the CoolTalk Watchdog. When a call comes in, the Watchdog wakes up and launches CoolTalk itself.

When you first installed Netscape Navigator 3.0, you were asked if you wanted to install the CoolTalk Watchdog. If you said yes, a shortcut to the program was placed in your Startup folder, and you now have a little blue Watchdog icon in the Status Tray of your

Windows 95 TaskBar. This icon, which may look like a watchdog to people with better eyesight or wilder imagination than mine, indicates that the Watchdog is ready to launch CoolTalk at any time. If you want to temporarily disable this feature, simply double-click the icon. A red stop sign will cover it, indicating that the Watchdog is not currently active. Double-click again to reactivate it.

You can also permanently disable the CoolTalk Watchdog by deleting its shortcut from the Startup folder. And if you want to re-enable it, simply add it back to the Startup folder. The program name is WDOG.EXE, and it is located in the CoolTalk folder under your Netscape Navigator 3.0 main directory.

Suppose you're the gregarious type and want to answer all incoming calls without even clicking the Accept button. That's easy to set up:

1. Select Option from the Conferences menu. The Options dialog box pops up, as shown earlier in Figure 10-26.

2. Select the Conference tab if it's not already selected.

3. In the area labeled "Accept Invitation" click the Always option button. Now all calls will come through to you automatically.

Notice that you can also refuse all incoming calls by selecting the Never option button. This is equivalent to unplugging your regular telephone. But coolest of all, CoolTalk even includes its own answering machine for those rare times you are away from your computer or those even rarer times when you are trying to use your computer for some real work.

THE ANSWERING MACHINE

Turning your CoolTalk answering machine on and off is as simple as pressing a button. Specifically, the Answering Machine button, as shown below in Figure 10-29.

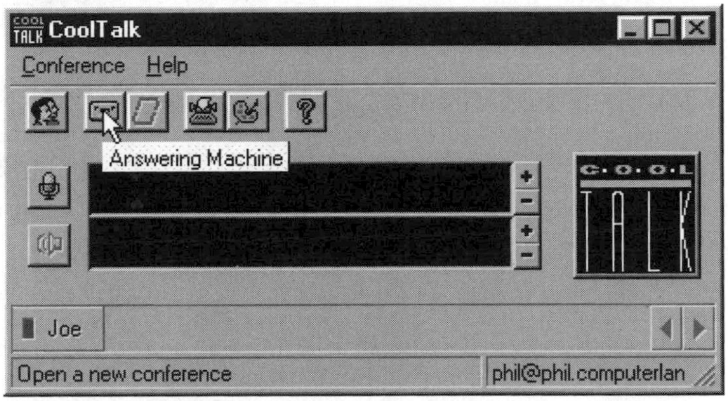

Figure 10-29: *The Answering Machine button.*

Click the button once to turn the answering machine on, click it again to turn it off. But before actually using the answering machine feature, let's make sure it's operating the way you want it to. Select Options from the Conference menu. When the Options dialog box appears, select the Answering Machine tab, as shown in Figure 10-30.

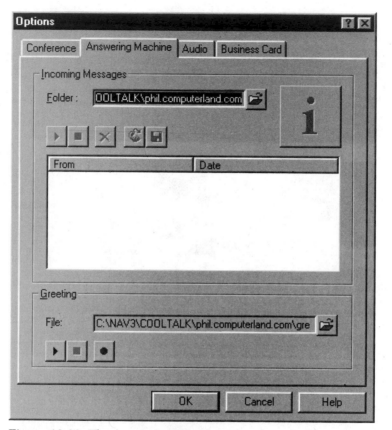

Figure 10-30: *The Answering Machine tab.*

There are only a few settings in this dialog box that you have to deal with right now: the folder in which you store messages you receive, and your outgoing greeting message. The first one of these is a no-brainer. If you want to change the folder for storing your messages, click the Browse button to the right of the folder field and select a new location. As for changing your greeting, that works pretty much the same way as your old plastic answering machine.

CHANGING YOUR GREETING

To hear CoolTalk's default greeting, click the Play Greeting button near the bottom of the Answering Machine tab (it looks like the play button on a CD or tape player). You should hear a generic

greeting that's perfectly fine to use but pretty bland and imper-
sonal. But you can say whatever you want to CoolTalkers who try
to reach you:

1. Click the red Record button. The Answering Machine tab
   will change appearance as shown below to indicate that
   you're recording a new greeting.

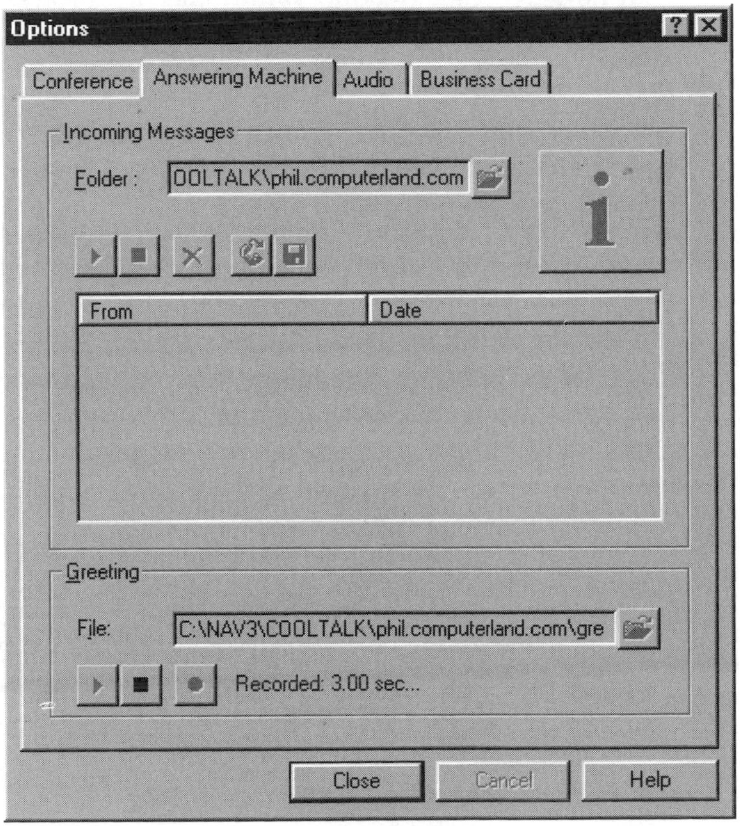

Figure 10-31: *Recording a new greeting.*

2. Speak your new greeting slowly and clearly into the
   microphone. When you have finished, click the middle
   Stop button.

3. To hear your new greeting message, click the Play button.

If you're anything like me, you'll need to record your greeting about a dozen times before you're halfway satisfied, and even then you won't quite sound like James Earl Jones.

By the way, you don't have to record your greeting in CoolTalk. You can go to a recording studio, hire a string section and backup singers, and create a Grammy-winning CoolTalk greeting if you want. Just make sure to save it as a .WAV file. Then to select it as your new CoolTalk greeting, simply click the Browse button to the right of the File field.

Click Close when you're done making changes in the Answering Machine tab.

LISTENING TO MESSAGES

Now the fun part.

1. Back in the conference window, turn your CoolTalk answering machine on by clicking the Answering Machine button shown above in Figure 10-29.

   ■ The button will look grayed or depressed when the answering machine is on.

2. To try this out, get another CoolTalk user to give you a call. When the call comes in, you have two opportunities to override the answering machine feature and pick the call up. First you get the usual Invitation dialog box, including the Caller-ID. If you do not answer the call at this time, a second dialog box pops up (Figure 10-32 below) allowing you to take the call instead of letting the answering machine get it.

Figure 10-32: *The Answering Machine dialog box.*

Yes, you can use CoolTalk's answering machine to screen your calls. If you want to talk to a caller, simply press the Pick Up button in the dialog box shown above.

3. For the purposes of this exercise, do not pick up the call. Just sit back and let the answering machine get it. You will hear your caller leave a message. After it's completed, your CoolTalk conference window should look like the one in Figure 10-33 below.

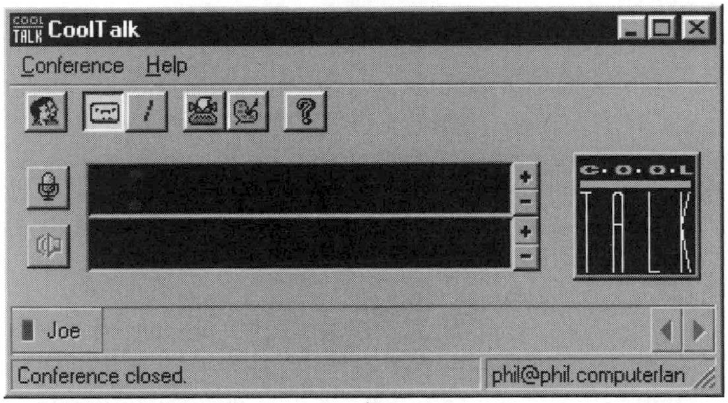

Figure 10-33: *The conference window after the answering machine has taken a call.*

4. Notice that the Read Messages button just to the right of the Answering Machine button now shows a bright red "1," indicating that you've received one new message. Click the button now to display your new message in the Answering Machine tab, as shown in Figure 10-34.

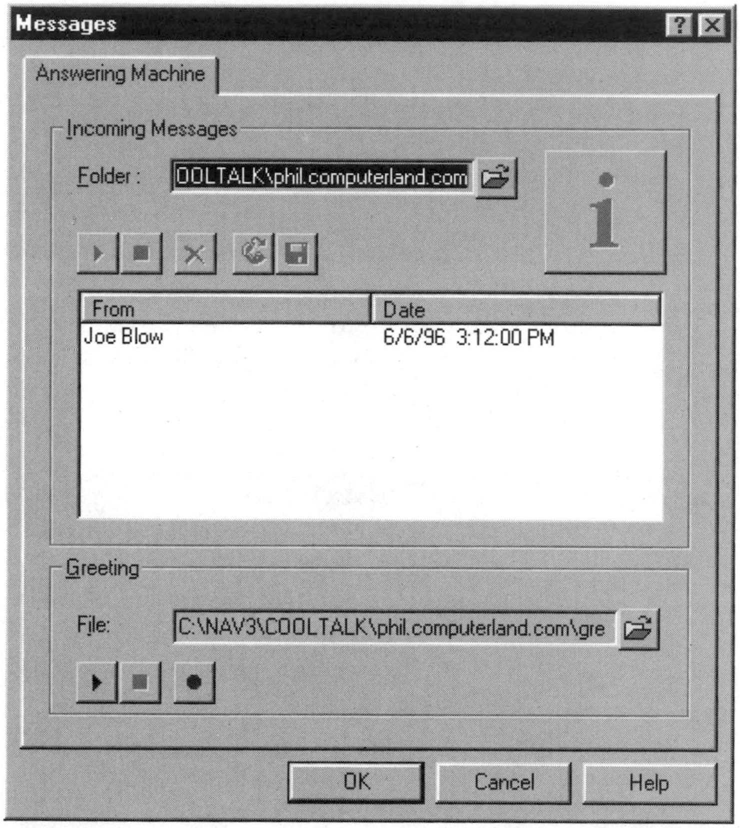

Figure 10-34: *The Answering Machine tab with one new message.*

5. Select the caller's name in the From field. The big square Information button now displays Joe Blow's picture, and pressing the button will show you his business card. In addition, the buttons above the message list are now activated, as shown in Figure 10-35.

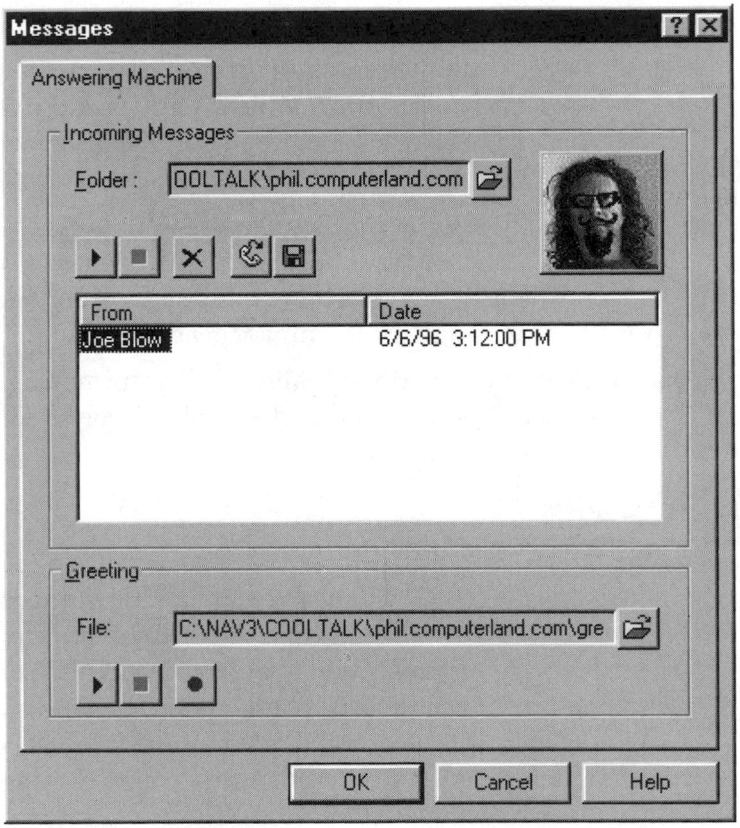

Figure 10-35: *The Answering Machine tab with message selected.*

6. You now have a variety of options:

   ■ To play the selected message, click the Play button above the message list.

TIP

You can also play a message simply by double-clicking it.

- To delete the message, click the Delete button.

- To call the sender of the message immediately, click the Call Back button, which is the second one from the right. (This is a feature your plastic answering machine probably doesn't even have!)

- To save the message to a .WAV file on your hard drive, click the rightmost Save WAVE File button. This is a great way to archive messages without growing your message list to unmanageable size.

7. When you're done dealing with your messages, click the OK button to return to the CoolTalk conference window.

CHAT

In geek-speak, chatting doesn't mean talking. It means typing messages back and forth in real-time. America Online, for instance, has specialized chat rooms where you can have typed conversations with people of like interests. (And if you can't find a chat room for your specific interests on AOL, your interests are very strange indeed.) Chatting is very different from leaving messages on a newsgroup or some online service. The "real-timeness" of chatting gives it a quality of immediacy and vibrancy much like voice conversation. And obviously it's a great means of communication for people with hearing or speech disabilities.

The CoolTalk Chat feature even lets you send entire text files. You can be CoolTalking with somebody about a particular legal document and send the text itself as you speak!

TIP

Even if you don't have a sound card, you can communicate with other CoolTalk users by using its Chat and White Board features.

Let's give it a try.

1. Connect with a CoolTalk user following the step-by-step instructions in the section "Initiating Calls" above. Once you are connected the CoolTalk conference window should look something like Figure 10-21.

2. Click the Chat Tool button, which seems to depict a typewriter. (I've really *got* to get glasses one of these days.) The Chat Tool window appears, as shown below in Figure 10-36.

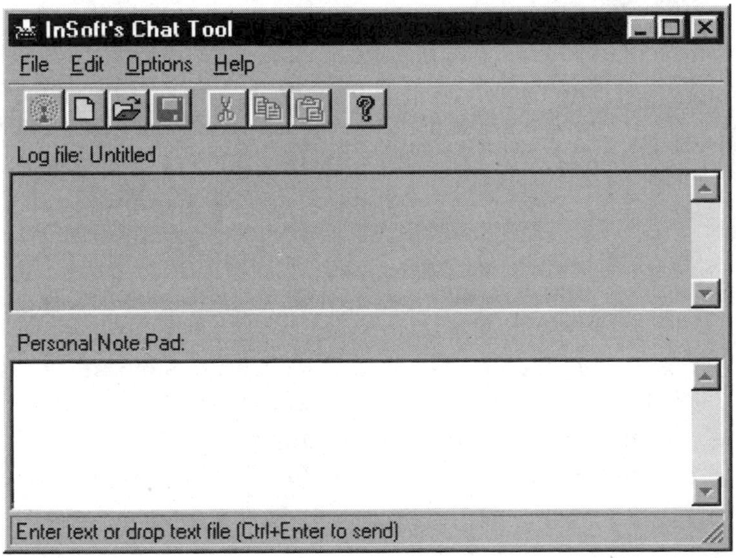

Figure 10-36: *The Chat Tool window.*

TIP

By default, CoolTalk is configured so that the Chat Tool window pops up as soon as the CoolTalker at the other end tries to chat with you. If you do not like this behavior, in other words if you don't want to feel "pushed" into a chat without explicitly requesting it yourself or agreeing to it by voice, select Options from the Chat Tool menu and uncheck Pop Up On Receive.

3. Type a word or sentence in the white Personal Note Pad pane. When you've completed it, send it by hitting Ctrl+Enter or clicking the Send button at the far left in the toolbar.

   Notice that as soon as you send your text, it appears in the upper Log panel. The Log panel keeps a running record of your entire Chat, including what you type and what the other CoolTalker types.

TIP

The CoolTalker at the other end of the connection doesn't see anything you type until you hit Ctrl+Enter or click the Send button. That gives you time to think about what you're saying. That's good, since both parties can keep a log of the entire chat!

The two of you can keep chatting indefinitely, and you can keep *talking* at the same time. You can facilitate communications by cutting, copying, and pasting text in the Personal Note Pad, and you can even copy text from the Log and paste it into the Note Pad. What a great way to remind somebody of what they said a few minutes ago! All of these editing tools are available via the usual editing buttons at the top of the Chat Tool window.

INCLUDING FILES

This Chat feature gets its own section because it's one of my favorites. It's really very simple: you can paste entire text files into the Personal Note Pad by clicking the Include button (the third from the left) and selecting the file you want to include. Figure 10-37 below shows you the result.

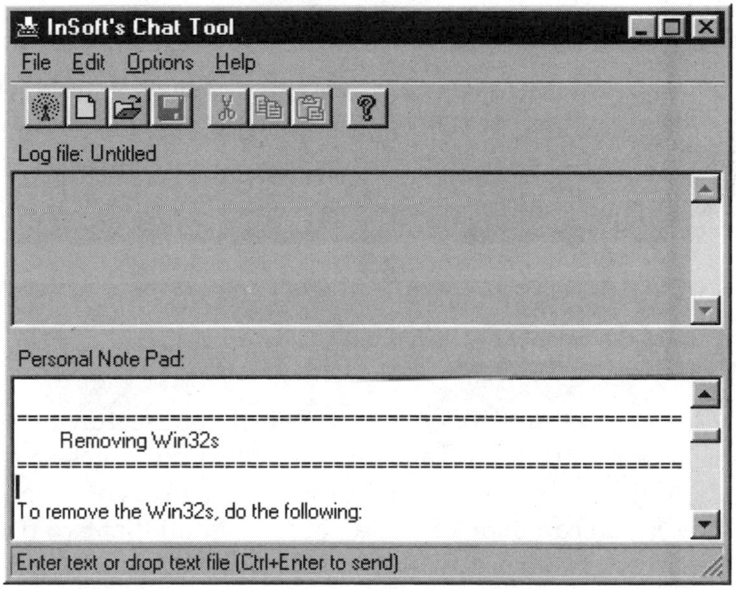

Figure 10-37: *The Personal Note Pad with an included file.*

There is no special procedure for sending included files: Ctrl+Enter will do the trick.

LOG FILES

At any point while the Chat Tool window is displayed, you can save the contents of the Log to a file by clicking the Save button. You might want to name your log file with the date of the chat session and the name of the other chatter, as in **4-1Joe**. You can also start an entire new log file by clicking the New button.

TRAP

Unless you save your current log file, the information in the Log panel will be lost when you select a new file.

LEAVING CHAT

When you're finished chatting with your fellow CoolTalker, simply close the Chat Tool window. This does not break your connection; you can keep talking as long as you want, and you can start chatting again simply by clicking the Chat Tool button in the CoolTalk conference window.

THE WHITE BOARD

You can think of CoolTalk's White Board feature as a Chat Tool on steroids. It lets you share not only text messages, but also graphics and even screen captures of whatever's on your monitor right now. Or you can think of it as a paint program that two people work in at once, collaboratively creating rich colorful content even though they might be thousands of miles apart.

If you've ever used any paint program, such as Microsoft Paint (which comes with Windows), you'll have no trouble figuring out the White Board. It's beyond the scope of this book to cover every detail of its operation. I'll just hit the important points as well as some interesting features that aren't immediately obvious. After that I think you'll find it's the kind of feature that's a lot more fun to learn by using.

STARTING THE WHITE BOARD

1. Connect with a CoolTalk user following the step-by-step instructions in the section "Initiating Calls" above. Once you are connected the conference window should look something like Figure 10-21.

2. Click the White Board button, which looks like an artist's palette. The White Board window appears, as shown below in Figure 10-38.

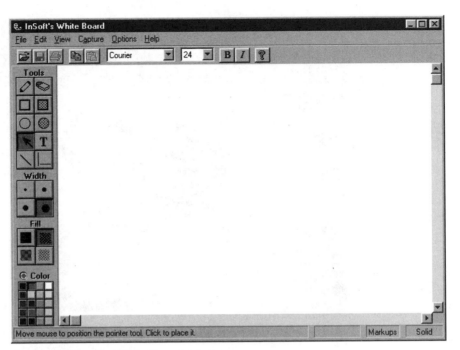

Figure 10-38: *The White Board window.*

By default, your White Board also pops up as soon as the CoolTalker you're connected with starts working with his or her White Board. If you don't like this behavior, uncheck the Pop Up On Receive option from the White Board's Options menu.

Now you can start adding elements to your White Board using the various tools and the width, fill, and color options at the left side of the window. You can also add text by selecting the text tool (the button with a big T on it) and choosing your font size and style at the top of the window. For example, Figure 10-39 shows my White Board with a few simple geometric shapes and some text.

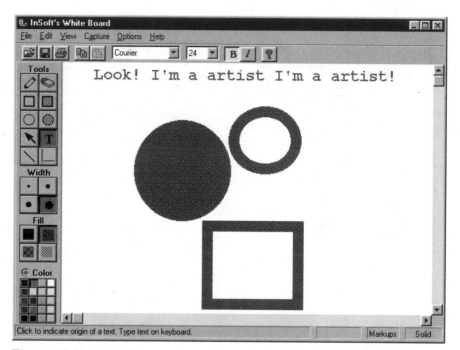

Figure 10-39: *My White Board with some important stuff on it.*

Notice the White Board's scroll bars. You are not limited to what you can fit within the window. This virtual White Board is less like the kind of white board you buy at an office supply store than it is like an endless roll of drawing paper.

You might be wondering what's going on at the other end of the CoolTalk connection. Here's the scoop:

- Everything you draw or paint appears on the remote White Board exactly as it appears on yours. Not only that, it gets there right away. If your CoolTalking friend starts unleashing his or her artistic talents, you'll see that right away too.

■   *Text* that's added to the White Board using the Text tool, on
    the other hand, is sent as soon as you hit Enter. This allows
    for a combination of collaboration and effective written con-
    versation. The White Board is a truly collaborative feature
    that adds a new dimension to the phrase "it's almost like
    being there."

And of course the two of you can keep yakking away into your
microphones as you create your collaborative masterpiece. Kids
could entertain themselves for hours with this. So could I.

TIP

*Don't like what's on your White Board? Of course you can delete parts
of the window using the Erase tool, but you might want to get rid of the
whole thing. Simply select Clear White Board from the Edit menu.
Remember, though, that you're erasing it for your fellow CoolTalker as
well!*

   *And what about if you're convinced your collaborative master-
piece will someday sell for millions at Sotheby's? Just click the File
Save button.*

PASTING IMAGES ONTO THE WHITE BOARD

One of the most interesting uses of the White Board is to share
graphical material that's already been created. Imagine talking to
somebody a thousand miles away and suddenly saying "Here, let
me show you a picture of my kids!" Or your cats or your
motherboard.

To paste an image onto the White Board:

1. Click the File Open button at the top left of the White Board
    window.

2. Using the standard Open dialog box that appears, select a
    file from your hard drive or a network drive.

    Notice that you can choose files from among seven differ-
    ent graphics formats.

3. Click the Open button. The dialog box disappears, and you are returned to the White Board window.

4. Your White Board cursor is now a cross-hairs, and an outline shows the size of the graphics you selected. Move the outline to the location on the White Board where you want to place it.

5. Once you have decided the location for your graphic, click the left mouse button. The new image is pasted onto the White Board, both locally and remotely.

TIP

You can also drag and drop graphics files directly onto the White Board. Simply select a file from anywhere on your hard drive and hold down your left mouse button while dragging it into the White Board window. When you let go of the mouse button, the cross-hairs cursor and outline appear as in step 4 above.

SCREEN CAPTURE

The White Board also includes a screen capture facility. You can capture a snapshot of a window, your entire desktop, or any region of your screen and then paste it onto the White Board. Think of how useful this can be in technical support settings. Instead of trying to describe how that brand new game is spewing unrecognizable garbage all over your screen, why not *show* it to the technical specialist who keeps insisting it's an RTFM problem?

Here's how to place a screen capture onto the White Board:

1. Select one of the options from the Capture menu.

Selecting Window lets you choose any window currently on your desktop; selecting Desktop captures your entire desktop; and selecting Region lets you choose a screen region to capture.

For this example go ahead and select Window. As soon as you do, the White Board is temporarily minimized, and a cross-hairs cursor lets you choose any window currently on your desktop.

2. Position the cross-hairs cursor over the CoolTalk conference window and click. The White Board pops back up. Your cursor now includes a moveable outline indicating the size of the captured image.

3. Move the outline to the location on the White Board where you want to place it, then simply click. An image of the conference window now appears exactly where you indicated, as you can see in Figure 10-40.

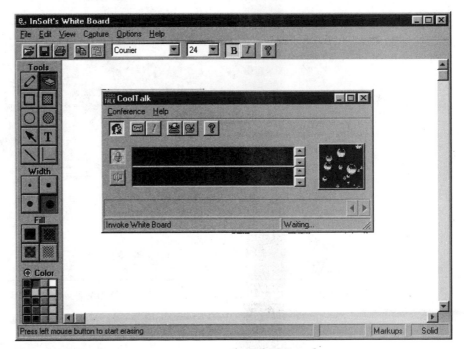

Figure 10-40: *A new screen capture on the White Board.*

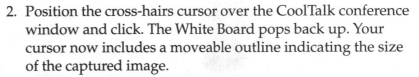

MARKUP & THE POINTER TOOL

As a convenience for collaborative work, the White Board distinguishes between static material in what's called the *image layer* (screen captures and images loaded from disk) and *markup* (anything you add to the White Board using the various drawing tools).

If these terms are unfamiliar to you, here's an example. Let's say you place a new image on the White Board in order to get your friend's feedback. Using the drawing tools, he puts a bunch of circles and arrows all over your picture, creating something like Figure 10-41.

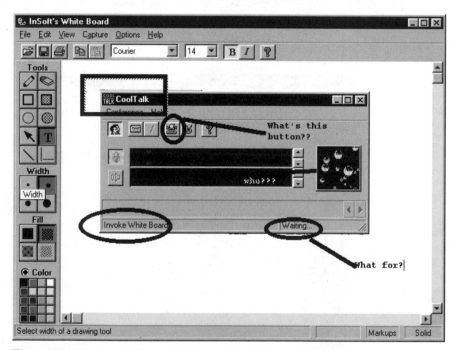

Figure 10-41: *A marked-up graphic on the White Board.*

And now let's say you think his comments are completely bogus. Wouldn't it be nice to get rid of what your pal added without getting rid of the original picture?

Well, you can! Just select Clear Markups from the Edit menu and you're back to ground zero, a nice clean screen capture just like the one in Figure 10-42. You can also erase portions of the markup using the Eraser tool, without deleting any of the underlying graphic. Needless to say, you can clear your own markups just as easily.

CoolTalk's White Board offers another feature that's especially useful for collaborative work: The Pointer tool. You select the Pointer tool by clicking the arrow button in the left hand tool bar. It then lets you place an arrow pointer anywhere on the White Board. But this highly visible arrow is not fixed in place like the other graphics tools such as lines and circles. If you still have the Pointer tool selected and you click your cursor somewhere else, the arrow moves to the new location. Thus as you discuss the various elements on your White Board with another CoolTalk user, you can point to them. You can think of the Pointer tool as your virtual index finger.

TIP

If you suspect that you and the person you're CoolTalking with are not seeing the same stuff on your White Board, you can make sure by selecting Synchronize Page from the Edit menu.

OTHER WHITE BOARD FEATURES

There's a lot more I could say about the White Board, but you'll have more fun exploring on your own. Let's move on now and take a look at how CoolTalk fits into Netscape Navigator 3.0.

WORKING WITH COOLTALK IN NAVIGATOR 3.0

It may seem to some of you that this book has taken a sharp turn into left field, covering a program that at first glance has nothing to do with Netscape Navigator 3.0. Well let's see if we can get things back on track. Let's start by loading up Navigator 3.0 itself.

TIP

We're going to be accessing an IS411 server on the Internet, so you need to make sure you're connected to the Net itself and not just your office Intranet. If you do not have an Internet connection, just follow along to get the general idea. You can apply what you learn here to your Intranet later if you get your own IS411 server.

1. Make sure you're connected to the Internet.

2. Double-click the Netscape Navigator 3.0 icon on your desktop or in its folder or program group.

3. In the Netsite box, type the URL http://live.netscape.com. After a few seconds the CoolTalk Phonebook page appears, as shown in Figure 10-42.

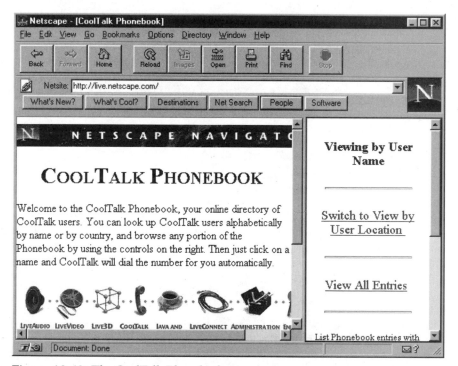

Figure 10-42: *The CoolTalk Phonebook page.*

As you can see, the frame on the left provides some introductory information about the Phonebook, while the right frame lets you actually look through the list of users. And how did these particular CoolTalk users get into the directory? On the Conference tab shown way up above in Figure 10-28, they checked the "Make me available through server" checkbox—or maybe they forgot to *uncheck* it. In fact, if you're currently running CoolTalk you're probably listed here too!

You can look for available CoolTalkers in several ways. To view all current users, click the View All Entries link in the right frame. A new page appears to the left, as shown in Figure 10-43.

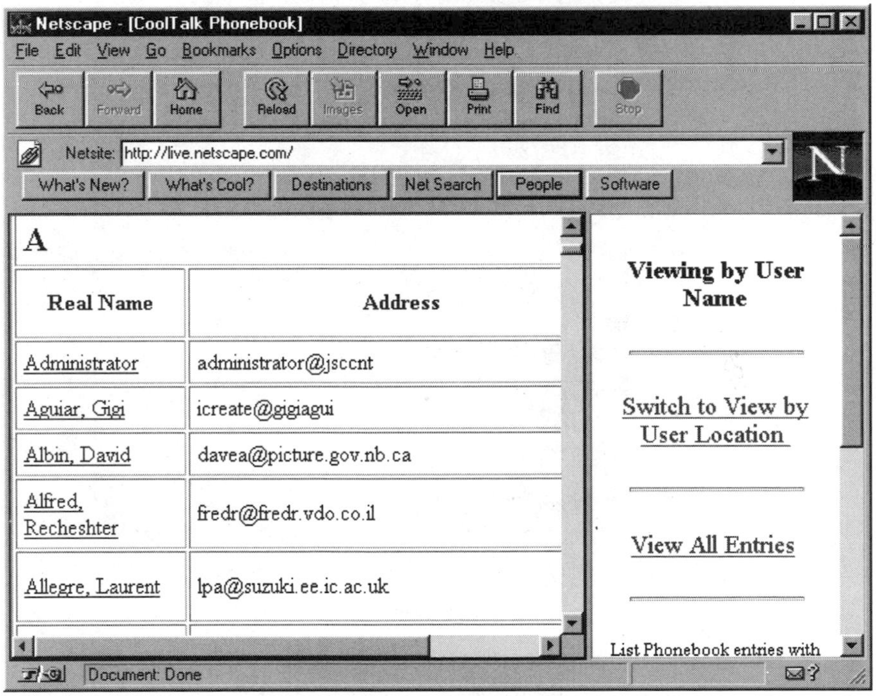

Figure 10-43: *List of CoolTalk users in the Phonebook.*

Notice that the users are sorted alphabetically by name.

Now click Switch to View by User Location in the right frame and then click View All Entries again. You should see something like Figure 10-44. All the same CoolTalkers are listed, but now they are organized by geographic area.

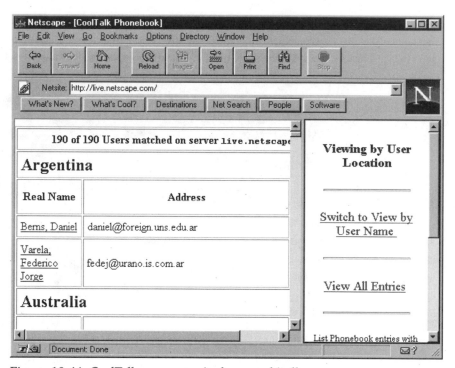

Figure 10-44: *CoolTalk users organized geographically.*

It is also very simple to find a particular user by scrolling down the right frame until you get to the alphabetic links. Just click one of the links to view all users whose names begin with that letter. Or if you're currently set to View by User Location, clicking a letter will view *locations* that begin with that letter.

Now the cool part: you can initiate a CoolTalk session simply by clicking a name in the left frame. If you don't have CoolTalk currently loaded, that doesn't matter a bit. Netscape Navigator 3.0 will automatically launch it with a command to call the individual you've selected. In a matter of moments you'll be talking, chatting, or whiteboarding.

Of course if you want to be old fashioned and use e-mail instead, the Phonebook also provides an e-mail address for each CoolTalk user. You can select and copy an address and then paste it right into the To field of the Navigator's message composition window.

Not too long from now there may be lots of different IS411 servers accessible via Web pages like this, some of them public and some of them private. You may even want to set up your own IS411 server on your office Intranet. You can get more information about IS411 servers as well as other new technologies at http://www.insoft.com.

CONCLUSION

Like the Internet itself, you've been to many places in the *Power User's Toolkit*—from system setup, to Service Providers, to extenders of Navigator's browsing capability, and points beyond.

Because Navigator and Navigator Gold have made it possible, even effortless for the most part, to conduct business on the Internet, a strange "commodity exchange" has blossomed. Remember the adage "Time is Money"? Time is actually becoming a *more important* commodity—you can always make more money, but you can never make more time!

We hope that by reading the *Power User's Toolkit*, you'll save on connect time by conducting searches more efficiently, save on download time by finding the fastest or least trafficked mirror FTP site, and save hours configuring Windows protocol connections perfectly the first time. Whether it's for business, education, or leisure, your best time spent is *participating* in Web activity, not finding directions and trying to *get* to the cyber-party!

When an author first sits down to write a book, it's usually a good idea to adopt the professional actor's tool of envisioning one's audience; "Who are you playing to?" With the *Power User's Toolkit*, I chose a very ambitious friend of mine who wanted to get up and running with Navigator and Internet communications, but wanted to know all the "cool stuff" from the beginning. My friend wanted to be the best surfer on Earth and really put Navigator through its paces. If this description reminds you of yourself, then I wrote this book for you, too.

Education is a funny thing, in that the truly curious mind finds that as you learn more, you find there is more *yet to* learn. With respect to Navigator, the personal power tool, and the Internet, one area you might want to pursue after you've closed the cover of this book, are other books on Internet content *creation*. Netscape Press has some superb ones, and there are also many papers and FAQs on the Net on creating VRML worlds, digital video and animation, HTML authoring, and more. The Totally Hot Bookmarks List contains numerous references to these topics and I'm sure you'll find many more as you travel the Web.

I guarantee that it won't be long before your quest for more from the Web provokes you to become an active participant and contributor to the world's largest resource center. Communication, whatever form it takes, is always a two-way street.

Appendices

Appendix A

About netscapepress.com

Netscapepress.com is where you will find the most up-to-date information about Netscape Press. Please visit the site at http://www.netscapepress.com/. Netscapepress.com features a catalog of other Netscape Press titles, technical support information, and updates to the book as needed.

Netscapepress.com is the home of *Navigate!*, the official electronic publication of Netscape Press. *Navigate!* is a monthly online publication that offers a wide range of articles and reviews aimed at Netscape users. *Navigate!* features interviews with industry icons and experts, as well as articles excerpted from upcoming Netscape Press titles. Learn how to improve your Web site or to use the best search engines online. Stay abreast of the latest technological innovations and impress your friends with your intimate knowledge of the world's most popular Internet browser.

Netscape Press is a joint effort between Ventana and Netscape Communications Corp., and serves as the publishing arm of Netscape.

Appendix B

About the Companion CD-ROM

The CD-ROM included with your copy of *Official Netscape Power User's Toolkit* contains valuable software programs and example files from the appropriate chapters.

To view the CD-ROM:

- **Windows 3.1/Windows 95/Windows NT:** Double-click on the LAUNCHME.EXE file from your Windows Explorer or File Manager.

You'll see a menu screen offering several choices. See "Navigating the CD-ROM" below for your option choices.

NAVIGATING THE CD-ROM

Your choices for navigating the CD-ROM appear on the opening screen. You can quit the CD, view the software, learn more about Netscape Press, browse the Hot Picks, or learn more about Ventana.

The software section lists all of the software programs, chapter examples, fonts, and textures on the CD. You can install the items one at a time to your hard drive. A complete listing of the programs follows in Table B-1.

If the Ventana Viewer does not run properly on your machine, you can access the material on the CD directly through File Manager (Windows 3.1x) or Windows Explorer (Windows 95).

PROGRAMS ON THE COMPANION CD-ROM

Program	Description
Argyle	An Acrobat document, ARGYLE.PDF, that contains resources for desktop publishing, Web authoring, and other content provider tools.
Fonts	A collection of charityware True Type and Type 1 fonts created by the Boutons that you can add to your system. For more information about charityware and licensing the fonts, please refer to the PUT-FONT.PDF file. The Type 1 fonts require Adobe Type Manager 3.0 or later to use in Windows applications.
Textures	A collection of seamless tiling TIFF images you can convert to GIF format and use for a Web page background, or use as is in other graphics programs. For instructions on using the texture files contained in the TEXTURES folder and the License Agreement governing their use, refer to the PUT-TEX.PDF file. The files in the ALPHAS subfolder are greyscale TIFF images that can be used with the corresponding file in the TEXTURES folder in modeling and other graphics programs. Read the PUT-TEX.PDF file for more details.
Totally Hot	A massive collection of useful and cool Web sites.
Chapter 1 Examples	The examples for Chapter 1.
Chapter 5 Examples	The examples for Chapter 5.
Chapter 6 Examples	The examples for Chapter 6.
Chapter 8 Examples	The examples for Chapter 8.
Envoy Plug-in	A Netscape Navigator plug-in that enables viewing of Envoy Documents.

Program	Description
Lightning Strike Plug-in	The Lightning Strike plug-in allows Web surfers to view Lightning Strike-compressed graphics through Netscape Navigator.
OpenScape	OpenScape is a tool for moving existing programs and software components across an Intranet or the Internet.
TrueSpeech	The TrueSpeech Player lets you play any TrueSpeech encoded sound files (.WAV) in real-time as you download them from the World Wide Web.
VDOLive Plug-in	A Netscape plug-in that allows surfers to view VDO-format video files directly within Web pages.
Acrobat Reader 3.0	This pre-release version of Acrobat 3.0 (previously code-named "Amber") allows you to view Adobe Acrobat portable document format files inside Netscape.
VRScout Plug-in	VRScout is a VRML browser Netscape plug-in that provides the user with an "aircraft cockpit"-type control panel for navigation.
Pueblo	Pueblo is a multimedia Internet client meant to allow users to easily navigate rich multi-user environments.
PowerMedia	Visual multimedia authoring software for the Web and the Netscape plug-in that allows you to view PowerMedia presentations.
The Black Box Filter Demo	A working demo of the Cutout filter, one of ten filters in Alien Skin's Black Box filter set.
CoolFusion	The CoolFusion plug-in plays real-time Video for Windows AVI files over the Web.
StuffIT Expander	A utility for expanding compressed files.
GoldWave	A great audio processing tool.
Instant Button Controls and Web Tools	Artbeat's Webtools contains an extensive library of decorative elements, including icons, buttons, bars, sounds, and tiles.
MapEdit	A utility for creating image maps.

Program	Description
Paint Shop Pro Demo	A shareware product with a wide variety of useful features for manipulating images.
SigGen32	SigGen32 is a 32-bit program for creating e-mail or newsgroup signature files. It works with any program that uses ASCII files for a signature, such as Netscape or Eudora.
GrabNet	GrabNet,™ ForeFront's dynamic browser companion tool, lets you intuitively collect and organize the information you gather from the World Wide Web. Grab snips of information—including images, text, and URLs—which will help you reuse, navigate, and organize Web sites within a customized collection of folders on your desktop.
WebEx	WebEx provides offline Web browsing by downloading important news and financial reports from the Internet or corporate Intranets for reading later on the commute home, during a plane trip, or in your favorite easy chair, wherever and whenever you want.
TextPad	Provides the power and functionality to satisfy your most demanding text editing requirements.
WinZip	An excellent, graphical compression and decompression utility.
Formula One/NET	With Formula One/NET, you can interact with embedded, live spreadsheets and charts through your Web browser.
Fractal Viewer	Fractal Viewer™ enables the use of in-line fractal images on the Web. This plug-in allows users to not only view such images, but also to zoom, stretch, flip, and rotate images, as well as set preferences that specify how much image detail is received by default.
Quickserver Software Developer's Kit (ver 1.0)	QuickServer offers an API that works with leading development tools like Visual Basic, Powerbuilder, C++, Delphi, and Java to allow developers to move high-performance client/ server applications to the Internet or private Intranets.

Program	Description
Worldgroup	A freely distributable Netscape plug-in that will launch a complete suite of applications hot-linked to your Web site.
Astound Web Player	The Astound Web Player plug-in plays both Astound and Studio M multimedia projects directly from a Web page.
Crescendo	With this plug-in, Web surfers can enjoy background music as they explore a Web page.
Internet Video Express Viewer	Video Express Viewer allows users to watch the endless volumes of video clips from the Internet, online services, and CD-ROMs in a sizable window. Smooth, natural motion, and synchronized sound provide outstanding viewing quality, even at full screen size.
Plugin Table of Contents	A plug-in that organizes all of the directories and files of a Web site into an easy-to-understand "tree" of related directories and files for easy navigation.
Sizzler	With the Sizzler plug-in, Web pages come alive with interactive animation.
V-Realm Browser	V-Realm is a virtual reality viewer that is compatible with most VRML worlds and is fully VRML 1.0 compliant. With V-Realm, you can browse and interact with full-motion virtual worlds that incorporate advanced images, video, audio, animation, and virtual reality technologies.
View Director	TMSSequoia ViewDirector enables you to view and manipulate TIFF images, CALS Type 1, JPEG, PCX/DCX, Microsoft Bitmap (BMP), and other image file formats, within the Navigator window.

Technical Support

Technical support is available for installation-related problems only. The technical support office is open from 8:00 A.M. to 6:00 P.M. Monday through Friday and can be reached via the following methods:

- Phone: (919) 544-9404 extension 81
- Faxback Answer System: (919) 544-9404 extension 85
- E-mail: help@vmedia.com
- FAX: (919) 544-9472
- World Wide Web: **http://www.vmedia.com/support**
- America Online: keyword *Ventana*

Limits of Liability & Disclaimer of Warranty

The authors and publisher of this book have used their best efforts in preparing the CD-ROM and the programs contained in it. These efforts include the development, research, and testing of the theories and programs to determine their effectiveness. The authors and publisher make no warranty of any kind expressed or implied, with regard to these programs or the documentation contained in this book.

The authors and publisher shall not be liable in the event of incidental or consequential damages in connection with, or arising out of, the furnishing, performance, or use of the programs, associated instructions, and/or claims of productivity gains.

Some of the software on this CD-ROM is shareware; there may be additional charges (owed to the software authors/makers) incurred for their registration and continued use. See individual program's README or VREADME.TXT files for more information.

Appendix C

Keyboard Shortcuts

Action	Keyboard Shortcut	Shortcut is Available in:				Common Windows Shortcut
		Browser	Mail	News	Editor	
Add Bookmark	Ctrl+D	Y	N	N	N	
Back	Alt+Right Arrow key	Y	N	N	N	
Bold	Ctrl+B	N	N	N	Y	Y
Bookmarks	Ctrl+B	Y	Y	Y	N	
Close	Ctrl+W	Y	Y	Y	Y	Y
Close Window	Alt+F4	Y	Y	Y	Y	Y
Compress This Folder	Ctrl+K	N	Y	N	N	
Copy	Ctrl+C	Y	Y	Y	Y	Y
Cut	Ctrl+X	Y	Y	Y	Y	Y
Delete	Del (Delete key)	Y	Y	Y	Y	
Delete Message	Del (Delete key)	N	Y	N	N	Y
Display the Bookmark Properties of a Selected Bookmark	Alt+Enter	Used in the Bookmarks Window				Y
Display the Start Menu and Taskbar	Ctrl+Esc	Y	Y	Y	Y	Y
Find	Ctrl+F	Y	Y	Y	Y	Y

Action	Keyboard Shortcut	Shortcut is Available in:				Common Windows Shortcut
		Browser	Mail	News	Editor	
Find Again	F3	Y	Y	Y	N	
Find Again	Ctrl+G	N	N	N	Y	
Fixed Width (Characters)	Ctrl+T	N	N	N	Y	
Forward (Mail or Post)	Ctrl+L	N	Y	Y	N	
Forward (One Page)	Alt+Left Arrow key	Y	N	N	N	
Get New Mail	Ctrl+T	N	Y	N	N	
Go to Bookmarks	Ctrl+B	Y	Y	Y	N	
Go to the End of a Document Window	Ctrl+End (FIX)	Y	Y	Y	Y	
Go to the Top of a Document Window	Ctrl+Home	Y	Y	Y	Y	Y
History	Ctrl+H	Y	N	N	Y	
Indent One Level (Paragraph Text)	Tab	N	N	N	Y	
Italic	Ctrl+I	N	N	N	Y	Y
Load Images	Ctrl+I	Y	N	N	N	
Mail Reply	Ctrl+R	N	N	Y	N	
Move Down a Document One Screen at a Time	PageDown	Y	Y	Y	Y	Y
Move Up a Document One Screen at a Time	PageUp	Y	Y	Y	Y	Y
New Document	Ctrl+N	N	N	N	Y	
New Line Break	Shift+Enter	N	N	N	Y	Y
New Mail Message	Ctrl+M	Y	Y	Y	N	Y
New Web Browser	Ctrl+N	Y	Y	Y	N	Y
Open File	Ctrl+O	Y	N	N	Y	Y
Open Location	Ctrl+L	Y	N	N	Y	
Paste	Ctrl+V	Y	Y	Y	Y	Y
Print Message(s)	Ctrl+P	N	Y	Y	N	Y
Redo	Ctrl+E	N	Y		N	

Action	Keyboard Shortcut	Shortcut is Available in:				Common Windows Shortcut
		Browser	Mail	News	Editor	
Reload	Ctrl+R	Y	N	N	Y	
Reload (Document)	Ctrl+R	Y	N	N	Y	
Remove One Indent Level (Paragraph Text)	Shift+Tab	N	N	N	Y	
Reply (Via Mail)	Ctrl+R	N	Y	Y	N	
Reply to All	Ctrl+Shift+R	N	Y	N	N	
Save	Ctrl+S	N	N	N	Y	
Save Frame As or Save As	Ctrl+S	Y	Y		N	Y
Select All	Ctrl+A	Y	N	N	Y	Y
Select All Messages	Ctrl+A	N	Y	Y	N	Y
Select Thread	Ctrl+Shift+A	N	Y	Y	N	
Send Mail in Outbox	Ctrl+H	N	Y	N	N	
Stop Loading	Esc	Y	Y	Y	?	Y
Toggle to Task Manager	Ctrl+Tab	Y	Y	Y	Y	Y
Undo	Ctrl+Z	Y	Y	Y	Y	Y

Index

MACROMEDIA

End-User License Agreement

PLEASE READ THIS DOCUMENT CAREFULLY BEFORE BREAKING THE SEAL ON THE MEDIA PACK-AGE. THIS AGREEMENT LICENSES THE ENCLOSED SOFTWARE TO YOU AND CONTAINS WARRANTY AND LIABILITY DISCLAIMERS. BY BREAKING THE SEAL ON THE MEDIA ENVELOPE, YOU ARE CON-FIRMING YOUR ACCEPTANCE OF THE SOFTWARE AND AGREEING TO BECOME BOUND BY THE TERMS OF THIS AGREEMENT. IF YOU DO NOT WISH TO DO SO, DO NOT BREAK THE SEAL. INSTEAD, PROMPTLY RETURN THE ENTIRE PACKAGE, INCLUDING THE UNOPENED MEDIA PACKAGE, TO THE PLACE WHERE YOU OBTAINED IT, FOR A FULL REFUND.

1. Definitions

(a) "Macromedia« Software" means the software program included in the enclosed package, and all related updates supplied by Macromedia.

(b) "Macromedia Product" means the Macromedia Software and the related
documentation and models and multimedia content (such as animation, sound, and graphics), and all related updates supplied by Macromedia.

2. License. This Agreement allows you to:
(a) Use the Macromedia Software on a single computer.

(b) Make one copy of the Macromedia Software in machine-readable form solely for backup purposes. You must reproduce on any such copy all copyright
notices and any other proprietary legends on the original copy of the Macromedia Software.

(c) Certain Macromedia Software is licensed with additional rights as set forth in the Supplementary Rights Addendum that may be included in the package for this Macromedia Product.

3. Supplementary Licenses
Certain rights are not granted under this Agreement, but may be available under a separate agreement. If you would like to enter into a Site or Network License, please contact Macromedia.

4. Restrictions

You may not make or distribute copies of the Macromedia Product, or electronically transfer the Macromedia Software from one computer to another or over a network. You may not decompile, reverse engineer, disassemble, or otherwise reduce the Macromedia Software to a human-perceivable form. Youmay not modify, rent, resell for profit, distribute, or create derivativeworks based upon the Macromedia Software or any part thereof. You will notexport or reexport, directly or indirectly, the Macromedia Product into any country prohibited by the United States Export Administration Act and the regulations thereunder.

5. Ownership

The foregoing license gives you limited rights to use the Macromedia Software. Although you own the disk on which the Macromedia Software is recorded, you do not become the owner of, and Macromedia retains title to, the Macromedia Product, and all copies thereof. All rights not specifically granted in this Agreement, includin Federal and International Copyrights, are reserved by Macromedia.

6. Limited Warranties

(a) Macromedia warrants that, for a period of ninety (90) days from the date of delivery (as evidenced by a copy of your receipt): (i) when used with a recommended hardware configuration, the Macromedia Software will perform in substantial conformance with the documentation supplied as part of the Macromedia Product; and (ii) that the media on which the Macromedia Software is furnished will be free from defects in materials and workmanship under normal use. EXCEPT AS SET FORTH IN THE FOREGOING LIMITED WARRANTY, MACROMEDIA DISCLAIMS ALL OTHER WARRANTIES, EITHER EXPRESS OR IMPLIED, INCLUDING THE WARRANTIES OF MERCHANTABILITY, FITNESS FOR A PARTICULAR PURPOSE, AND NON-IN-FRINGEMENT. IF APPLICABLE LAW IMPLIES ANY WARRANTIES WITH RESPECT TO THE MACROMEDIA PRODUCT, ALL SUCH WARRANTIES ARE LIMITED IN DURATION TO NINETY (90)

DAYS FROM THE DATE OF DELIVERY. No oral or written information or advice given by Macromedia, its dealers, distributors, agents, or employees shall create a warranty or in any way increase the scope of this warranty.

(b) SOME STATES DO NOT ALLOW THE EXCLUSION OF IMPLIED WARRANTIES, SO THE ABOVE EXCLUSION MAY NOT APPLY TO YOU. THIS WARRANTY GIVES YOU SPECIFIC LEGAL RIGHTS AND YOU MAY ALSO HAVE OTHER LEGAL RIGHTS WHICH VARY FROM STATE TO STATE.

7. Exclusive Remedy Your exclusive remedy under Section 6 is to return the Macromedia Software to the place you acquired it, with a copy of your receipt and a description of the problem. Macromedia will use reasonable commercial efforts to supply you with a replacement copy of the Macromedia Software that substantially conforms to the documentation, provide a replacement for the defective media, or refund to you your purchase price for the Macromedia Software, at its option. Macromedia shall have no responsibility with respect to Macromedia Software that has been altered in any way, if the media has been damaged by accident, abuse, or misapplication, or if the non conformance arises out of use of the Macromedia Software in conjunction with software not supplied by Macromedia.

8. Limitations of Damages

(a) MACROMEDIA SHALL NOT BE LIABLE FOR ANY INDIRECT, SPECIAL, INCIDENTAL OR CONSEQUENTIAL DAMAGES (INCLUDING DAMAGES FOR LOSS OF BUSINESS, LOSS OF PROFITS, OR THE LIKE), WHETHER BASED ON BREACH OF CONTRACT, TORT (INCLUDING NEGLIGENCE), PRODUCT LIABILITY, OR OTHERWISE, EVEN IF MACROMEDIA OR ITS REPRESENTATIVES HAVE BEEN ADVISED OF THE POSSIBILITY OF SUCH DAMAGES AND EVEN IF A REMEDY SET FORTH HEREIN IS FOUND TO HAVE FAILED OF ITS ESSENTIAL PURPOSE.

(b) Macromedia's total liability to you for actual damages for any cause whatsoever will be limited to the greater of $500 or the amount paid by you for the Macromedia Software that caused such damages.

(c) SOME STATES DO NOT ALLOW THE LIMITATION OR EXCLUSION OF LIABILITY FOR INCIDENTAL OR CONSEQUENTIAL DAMAGES, SO THE ABOVE LIMITATION OR EXCLUSION MAY NOT APPLY TO YOU.

9. Basis of Bargain

The limited warranty, exclusive remedies, and limited liability set forth above are fundamental elements of the basis of the bargain between Macromedia and you. Macromedia would not be able to provide the MacromediaSoftware on an economic basis without such limitations.

10. Government End Users

The Macromedia Product is "Restricted Computer Software." RESTRICTED RIGHTS LEGEND Use, duplication, or disclosure by the Government is subject to restrictions as set forth in subparagraph (c)(1)(ii) of the Rights in Technical Data and Computer Software clause at DFARS 252.227-7013. Manufacturer: Macromedia, Inc., 600 Townsend, San Francisco, CA 94103

11. General

This Agreement shall be governed by the internal laws of the State of California. This Agreement contains the complete agreement between the parties with respect to the subject matter hereof, and supersedes all prior or contemporaneous agreements or understandings, whether oral or written. All questions concerning this Agreement shall be directed to: Macromedia, Inc., 600 Townsend, San Francisco, CA 94103, Attention: Chief Financial Officer.

Macromedia is a registered trademark of Macromedia, Inc.
Suzanne Porta
Publisher Programs Associate
Macromedia, Inc.
600 Townsend Street, Suite 310
San Francisco, CA, 94103 USA
e-mail: sporta@macromedia.com

Navigate!
the online magazine for Netscape users

Empower
yourself with up-to-date tools for navigating the Net—in-depth reviews, where to find them and how to use them.

Enhance
your online experience—get to know the latest plug-ins that let you experience animation, video, virtual reality and sound...live, over the Internet.

Enliven
your Web pages—tips from experienced Web designers help you create pages with punch, spiced with multimedia and organized for easy navigation.

Enchant
your Web site visitors—learn to create interactive pages with JavaScript applets, program your own Internet applications and build added functionality into your site.

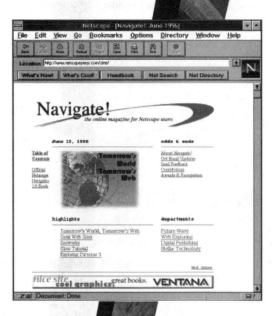

http:www.netscapepress.com/zine

Explore the Internet

Internet Business 500 🌐

$29.95, 488 pages, illustrated, part #: 287-9

This authoritative list of the most useful, most valuable online resources for business is also the most current list, linked to a regularly updated *Online Companion* on the Internet. The companion CD-ROM features a hypertext version of the entire book, linked to updates on Ventana Online.

Walking the World Wide Web, Second Edition 🌐

$39.95, 800 pages, illustrated, part #: 298-4

More than 30% new, this book now features 500 listings and an extensive index of servers, expanded and arranged by subject. This groundbreaking bestseller includes a CD-ROM enhanced with Ventana's exclusive PerpetuWAVE technology; updated online components that make it the richest resource available for Web travelers; Netscape Navigator; and a hypertext version of the book.

Quicken 5 on the Internet 🌐

$24.95, 472 pages, illustrated, part #: 448-0

Get your finances under control with *Quicken 5 on the Internet*. Quicken 5 helps make banker's hours a thing of the past—by incorporating Internet access and linking you directly to institutions that see a future in 24-hour services. *Quicken 5 on the Internet* provides complete guidelines to Quicken to aid your offline mastery and help you take advantage of online opportunities.

HTML Publishing on the Internet for Windows
HTML Publishing on the Internet for Macintosh

$49.95, 512 pages, illustrated
Windows part #: 229-1, Macintosh part #: 228-3

Successful publishing for the Internet requires an understanding of "nonlinear" presentation as well as specialized software. Both are here. Learn how HTML builds the hot links that let readers choose their own paths—and how to use effective design to drive your message for them. The enclosed CD-ROM includes Netscape Navigator, HoTMetaL LITE, graphic viewer, templates conversion software and more!

The Web Server Book

$49.95, 680 pages, illustrated, part #: 234-8

The cornerstone of Internet publishing is a set of UNIX tools, which transform a computer into a "server" that can be accessed by networked "clients." This step-by-step in-depth guide to the tools also features a look at key issues—including content development, services and security. The companion CD-ROM contains Linux™, Netscape Navigator™, ready-to-run server software and more.

The Windows NT Web Server Book

$49.95, 680 pages, illustrated, part #: 342-5

A complete toolkit for providing services on the Internet using the Windows NT operating system. This how-to guide includes adding the necessary World Wide Web server software, comparison of the major Windows NT server packages for the Web, becoming a global product provider and more! The CD-ROM features Alibaba™ Lite (a fully licensed Web server), support programs, scripts, forms, utilities and demos.

Books marked with this logo include a free Internet *Online Companion*™, featuring archives of free utilities plus a software archive and links to other Internet resources.

Web Pages Enhanced

Shockwave!

$49.95, 400 pages, illustrated, part #: 441-3

Breathe new life into your Web pages with Macromedia Shockwave. Ventana's *Shockwave!* teaches you how to enliven and animate your Web sites with online movies. Beginning with step-by-step exercises and examples, and ending with in-depth excursions into the use of Shockwave Lingo extensions, *Shockwave!* is a must-buy for both novices and experienced Director developers. Plus, tap into current Macromedia resources on the Internet with Ventana's *Online Companion.* The companion CD-ROM includes the Shockwave player plug-in, sample Director movies and tutorials, and much more!

Java Programming for the Internet

$49.95, 800 pages, illustrated, part #: 355-7

Create dynamic, interactive Internet applications with Java Programming for the Internet. Expand the scope of your online development with this comprehensive, step-by-step guide to creating Java applets. Includes four real-world, start-to-finish tutorials. The CD-ROM has all the programs, samples and applets from the book, plus shareware. Continual updates on Ventana's *Online Companion* will keep this information on the cutting edge.

Exploring Moving Worlds

$24.99, 288 pages, illustrated, part #: 467-7

Moving Worlds—a newly accepted standard that uses Java and JavaScript for animating objects in three dimensions—is billed as the next-generation implementation of VRML. *Exploring Moving Worlds* includes an overview of the Moving Worlds standard, detailed specifications on design and architecture, and software examples to help advanced Web developers create live content, animation and full motion on the Web.

Macromedia Director 5 Power Toolkit

$49.95, 552 pages, illustrated, part #: 289-5

Macromedia Director 5 Power Toolkit views the industry's hottest multimedia authoring environment from the inside out. Features tools, tips and professional tricks for producing power-packed projects for CD-ROM and Internet distribution. Dozens of exercises detail the principles behind successful multimedia presentations and the steps to achieve professional results. The companion CD-ROM includes utilities, sample presentations, animations, scripts and files.

Internet Power Toolkit

$49.95, 800 pages, illustrated, part #: 329-8

Plunge deeper into cyberspace with *Internet Power Toolkit*, the advanced guide to Internet tools, techniques and possibilities. Channel its array of Internet utilities and advice into increased productivity and profitability on the Internet. The CD-ROM features a wide variety of tools and utilities, including Netscape plug-ins, e-mail, searching, file managment, multimedia, online monitoring and more.

The 10 Secrets for Web Success

$19.95, 384 pages, illustrated, part #: 370-0

Create a winning Web site—by discovering what the visionaries behind some of the hottest sites on the Web know instinctively. Meet the people behind Yahoo, IUMA, Word and more, and learn the 10 key principles that set their sites apart from the masses. Discover a whole new way of thinking that will inspire and enhance your own efforts as a Web publisher.

Books marked with this logo include a free Internet *Online Companion*™, featuring archives of free utilities plus a software archive and links to other Internet resources.

TO ORDER ANY VENTANA TITLE, COMPLETE THIS ORDER FORM AND MAIL OR FAX IT TO US, WITH PAYMENT, FOR QUICK SHIPMENT.

TITLE	PART #	QTY	PRICE	TOTAL

SHIPPING

For all standard orders, please ADD $4.50/first book, $1.35/each additional.
For software kit orders, ADD $6.50/first kit, $2.00/each additional.
For "two-day air," ADD $8.25/first book, $2.25/each additional.
For "two-day air" on the kits, ADD $10.50/first kit, $4.00/each additional.
For orders to Canada, ADD $6.50/book.
For orders sent C.O.D., ADD $4.50 to your shipping rate.
North Carolina residents must ADD 6% sales tax.
International orders require additional shipping charges.

SUBTOTAL = $ _____
SHIPPING = $ _____
TAX   = $ _____
TOTAL   = $ _____

Or, save 15%–order online.
http://www.vmedia.com

Mail to: Ventana • PO Box 13964 • Research Triangle Park, NC 27709-3964 ☎ 800/743-5369 • Fax 919/544-9472

Name _____

E-mail _____ Daytime phone _____

Company _____

Address (No PO Box) _____

City _____ State _____ Zip _____

Payment enclosed ____VISA ____MC ____ Acc't # _____ Exp. date _____

Signature _____ Exact name on card _____

Check your local bookstore or software retailer for these and other bestselling titles, or call toll free:

800/743-5369

All technical support for this product is available from Ventana.
The technical support office is open from 8:00 A.M. to 6:00 P.M. (EST) Monday through Friday and can be reached via the following methods:

World Wide Web: http://www.netscapepress.com/support

E–mail: help@vmedia.com

Phone: (919) 544-9404 extension 81

FAX: (919) 544-9472

America Online: keyword **Ventana**